A *Backwoods Home* Anthology:

The Fourth Year

Published by
Backwoods Home Magazine
P. O. Box 712
Gold Beach, OR 97444

ISBN: 978-0-9846222-6-9

Editor: *Dave Duffy*

Art Director: *Don Childers*

Contributors:

Russ Davis, Robert L. Williams, Martin Harris, Karen McGeorge Sanders, Charles A. Sanders, Don Fallick, Christopher Maxwell, Bruce Allison, Grover Brinkman, Dianne L. Beetler, Lorne S. Inglehart, Michelle J. Richards, Jennifer Stein Barker, Richard Blunt, Lucy Shober, Windy Dankoff, Shelby Taylor, Robert Colby, Rev. J.D. Hooker, James E. Robertson, Dynah Geissal, Jim Watters, Jj, Bill McLean, Richard Lee Rose, Martin P. Waterman, Mark and Helen Hegener, Benjamin Wright, Jo Mason, Carl Watner, June Knight, Gene Townsend, John Earl Silveira, Walt Foster, Marjorie Burris, Roger DeGroot, Barbara Landi, Linda Cordle, Gary Hutchins, Julie Pfeiffer Watner, Therese Reid, Robert Callahan, Bruce Bair, Fran Jablway, Larry Elliott, Anita Evangelista, Darlene Campbell, Jan Palmer, Robert L. Williams III, Ron and Carol Oliver, Margaret Wright, Marlene Parkin, Ralph LaPlant, Ken Lefsaker, Jim Talbot, Lon Gillas, Dr. Stephenie Slahor, Jeff Butterfield, Susan Betz, Gene Check, Julia Leiterman, P.J. O'Rourke, Vern Modeland, Vernon Hopkins, Donald Koehler, Anne Westbrook Dominick, Petr Beckmann, Carla Emery, John R. Horton, Larry D. Weber, Sandy McPherson Carrubba, Mick Sagrillo, Craig Russell, Bill Palmroth.

Introduction

Not along ago I was demonstrating this magazine at the Dallas Convention Center during one of several Preparedness Expos I attend. John Silveira, *Backwoods Home Magazine's* senior editor, and I had layed out several issues on our display tables so that curious passers-bye could flip through the pages to see what the magazine was about.

These preparedness expos attract all kinds of people, from the Mormon-type who think it's prudent to have a year or so worth of food and supplies on hand to withstand any emergency that comes along to the doom and gloom-type who think it's prudent to keep a bazooka under your pillow, a gas mask in the closet, and a bomb shelter under the garden.

During a slow period in the Dallas Expo, Charlie Skeets, who demonstrates a very practical flint and magnesium firemaking tool you can carry in your pocket, walked across the aisle to *BHM's* booth and said to me: "Hey Dave, the guy who just left my booth said the earth's poles are going to switch in about 11 years and everybody on earth is going to freeze to death."

"Don't worry Charlie," I said. "Before that happens the ozone is going to melt and we're all going to roast to death."

"Don't sweat that either," Silveira interrupted. "Take a look at that chart on the wall next to your booth Charlie. It says the oceans will rise in five years and half the people in the United States are going to drown."

I turned to Silveira with a big grin and said, "And if we survive that the New World Order is going to enslave us anyway so we might as well be dead."

We all had a good laugh because the preparedness shows are loaded with booths selling products and books that are centered around incredible disasters of one sort or another. Most are predicated on pseudoscience, crackpot theories, or political conspiracies, and all of them have volumes of "documentation" to back up their claims.

But there are also booths like ours that are based on reality, that is, that it is simply prudent, not to mention fun, to be as self reliant as you can when it comes to things like taking care of yourself and your family. Never mind the imagined plagues, we say; let's deal with real problems, such as how to move to the country and house your family, grow good food, generate electricity and other energy that makes daily life more comfortable, and how to become educated about the mistakes and successes of the generations that have preceded us so that we don't make similar mistakes.

Where much of the rest of the show is the Disneyland of the preparedness world, we are the horse and buggy ride. While they soar into the stratosphere of imagined calamity, we dwell on the ground trying to figure out how to keep the rain out of the house, keep the woodstove fire efficient, and keep the generator humming smoothly. We are boring by comparison.

I bring all this up because I don't want you to be disappointed if you buy this book, or if you decide to subscribe to *Backwoods Home Magazine* and read our future issues. We are a very unsensational magazine, based on fact and science.

If you would like a pleasant read that gives you many practical ways to solve everyday problems associated with rural living, this book is a good place to start. The articles are based on real situations, written by knowledgeable people, and they have been scrutinized for accuracy. You may very well place the book in your bookshelf for further reference. Hopefully you'll do as 15,000 or so others have done and subscribe to *BHM* so you can acquire future issues without waiting for them to be compiled in a book.

— Dave Duffy

This anthology is dedicated
to the memory of my good friend
Tony Lamb
a creative genius
who would have appreciated its contents.

Profiles

Contents —

Special Supplement

Issue Number 19

Issue Number 20

Issue Number 21

Issue Number 22

Issue Number 23

Issue Number 24

Special supplement for *The Fourth Year*

Farm animals can help you achieve self sufficiency

By Dynah Geissal

Animals are a very important part of a self sufficient farm. They also require a tremendous amount of commitment. Little faces will be watching eagerly every morning and every evening for you to come to care for them. The thought of these faces is what gets me out of bed before dawn and what causes me to cut short a visit to town in late afternoon. In very hot or very cold weather it's impossible to leave at all because of the necessity of providing water three or four times a day. Last year I had to miss a favorite foot race in a town 60 miles away because of the 20-below weather. My running friends didn't understand the impossibility of leaving livestock in such weather. Twenty below is the danger point for livestock, and if there is wind too it can be deadly. I check on everyone at least every two hours during those times.

I have been lucky enough to always have had one or two friends with whom I could trade chores on occasion. And I remember the relief as the children became older and were able to take over some of the chores. A child of seven is capable of doing most anything that doesn't require heavy lifting. Children are enormously perceptive and will often notice something before an adult will. I always paid close attention to any observations they made about the animals. Nevertheless, even in the best of circumstances, livestock really ties you down. I want to emphasize that as strongly as possible.

A good rule of thumb is to never add more than one new kind of animal per year. Spend the year learning everything you can about them. Time spent watching your livestock is never wasted. That's one way you learn. A good farmer trusts her feelings and has a sense of each animal. That's very important and may be why children seem so perceptive. Their thoughts don't get in the way of their instincts. It is not a good goal to get through chores as quickly as possible. Spend time with your charges.

A few words about bedding and feed and then we'll move on into individual types of animals. *Deep bedding* is a term that I will use later on. It means that you only clean out the barn or chicken house or whatever once or twice a year and keep adding fresh bedding over the old. It should never be wet or smelly or packed down on top. Bedding is as important as feed for healthy animals, so don't skimp on it.

Many people, even those who should know better, try to get by on inadequate feed. Let me assure you that it never pays off. When money is short and the animals aren't yet paying for themselves, it's easy to think you can save money by feeding less quantity or a poorer quality; but what you get in return is more disease, less production, and livestock that is not content. The animals become frantic for food and spend more calories in their agitation than they would when they know that food is always available. Properly fed animals will eat the proper amount, unlike ones that are so concerned about getting enough that they eat voraciously and fight over what is there. In order to get the best production, you want the best nutrition and contented beasts.

There are some circumstances where free choice feed is inadvisable—as with rabbits not in production or penned horses—but we'll discuss that later.

Chickens

Chickens are a good choice for your first livestock. You could start with two hens and a rooster or even a dozen hens and a rooster. Your best bet is to buy *started pullets.* Those are young hens just about old enough to lay eggs. They are expensive compared to baby chicks, but they're also less likely to die.

Buying older birds from a farm is possible, but you can run into some problems. Many years ago I answered an ad for hens, one year old, a dollar apiece. The birds were very light weight but the person told me that they were not taken care of very well because of a divorce, and that they should be fine with good care. They didn't appear to be sick, but the lack of weight should have alerted me. Most of them never gained much weight, but worse, they introduced a disease that caused emaciation and death. I lost half my flock.

If you have neighbors who have had livestock for a long time, they can probably help you either by selling you what you need or by telling you who will. That's better than answering an ad, especially if you're new to livestock.

Get your chicken house in order before you bring home your birds. A building 10' x 7' is right for about 25 chickens. It's a good idea to have south-facing windows and a method of ventilation. Put in a chicken-size door so they can come and go. Each bird needs about 9" of roosting space. The roosts should be 3½ to 4 feet high and about 2 inches in diameter. Bedding can be sawdust, shavings, or straw. One nest box is necessary for every four hens.

You can buy feed from a feed store, but a better idea is to buy whole grain in bulk from a nearby farmer. You will pay only half as much as for whole grain from the feed store and much less than you would by buying laying mash.

Ideally, chickens should be fed three grains free choice. Wheat, barley, and cracked corn are best. Feed corn isn't grown where I live, so in my area the third grain is oats. When I can't get oats, I feed just wheat and barley. Oats have too much fiber to be the sole grain, and birds get too fat on just wheat.

In addition to whole grains, the birds need a protein supplement. Grains are only about 11% protein, and chickens need about 20% for top production. I use Hog Chow 40 and feed it free choice.

Another necessary addition is oyster shell, which I also feed free choice in a feeder high enough from the ground that the bedding isn't scratched into it, but not so high that the birds need to jump onto it. The height of an adult bird's back is about right. Oyster shell provides calcium, which is what makes the egg shell. Without it the birds will lay eggs with soft shells which will break easily, leading to egg eating.

In summer, when the chickens run in the field, they scratch up lots of tasty things and catch bugs and an occasional vole or garter snake. In that way they are able to supplement their diets. In winter I give them good quality alfalfa and now and then a shovelful of dirt. The feed store sells grit if you prefer.

Chickens need 14 hours of daylight for optimal egg laying. Decreasing hours of light causes a slowdown in production and triggers molting. Turning on and off a light in their house works only if you are consistent. Otherwise, it's worse than no light. You may want to buy a timer. I leave the light on all the time during the part of the year that we have less than 14 hours of daylight and they do fine. Use a low watt bulb; 60 is good. Put a shield between the light and the roosts. They want enough light so that they will eat and drink and move around, but they don't like a glare when they're roosting.

An egg is 90% water, so adequate consumption of water is essential. A store-bought waterer is nice. You'll have to put it on a platform so bedding isn't scratched into it. Buckets work fine too, as long as they're not so big that a chicken can drown in them. Keep the buckets filled, so the birds don't have to work to reach the water. Warm water in winter and cool in summer encourages more consumption.

The size and color of the egg is determined primarily by breed, but also by the age of the bird. The first eggs are small, called *pullet eggs*, and gradually increase in size. An older bird lays fewer but larger eggs. Most brown egg layers have yellow legs when they're young (some have green or black) and lay fairly dark colored eggs. After they've been laying for a while, the legs and the eggshells become paler.

A hen that is laying has a very red and relatively large comb. A non-layer has a pale-skinned comb. The pubic bones are on each side of the vent. If you can fit three fingers between them the bird is a layer. With a non-layer, you will only be able to fit one or two. All of this is relative to the breed, of course. My Rhode Islands have much bigger combs than my Buff Orpingtons, for example.

Generally speaking, the best layers will be the birds who are the first ones out in the morning and the last ones in at night. They're also (usually, but not always) the ones most chased by the rooster. I've had a few very aggressive hens who were excellent layers but didn't often put up with the rooster's attentions. Speaking of roosters, never have more than one for every ten hens, or the females will be run ragged and have no energy left for laying.

If you have dual purpose birds (meat and eggs) such as Rhode Islands or Barred Rocks, they will "go broody" now and then. If you want the hen to hatch chicks, be sure she is free of parasites and has plenty of nesting material. Mark each egg (they can be taken from other hens too if you want) with a grease pencil or a non-toxic marking pen. That way, if another hen lays in the nest, you'll know which to take. Don't let her set on an extremely small or extremely large egg.

The broody hen will get off the nest once or twice a day to eat and drink and maybe to take a dust bath. The chicks will start hatching around the 28th day and will finish by the 30th day. The chicks should peck out of their shells by themselves. If you help, there is a good chance they will bleed to death from the navel. If the membrane from the egg has dried, the chick may be trapped, so you really have nothing to lose by helping a bit. Try to open just enough for the beak, but if the chick still isn't hatched after a while open a little more. If the membrane gets really dry, it will stick to the chick so much that it will be impossible for it to emerge. You'll have to use judgment here, but in general the less you do, the better.

If you want eggs instead of chicks, there are things you can do to try to break a hen's broodiness. Moving her to another pen sometimes works. Getting her wet is said to work, but it never has for me. The traditional method is to hang a cage so that it swings from the ceiling and put her in it.

Chickens have a tendency to pile up in a corner when they're young, cold, or in an unfamiliar environment. Leaving a light on will usually prevent this. Overcrowding is another serious problem. Except for inadequate diet, it is the biggest threat to chickens.

In young birds, the most serious consequence is coccidiosis. Coccidiosis is something that's always around but only attacks when circumstances allow it. The most obvious sign is bloody stool. Herbal treatment with garlic, cayenne, and milk works very well, but the main thing is to correct the cause.

The number of birds per foot does not always indicate overcrowding because there are so many variables. Odor may be your best clue. You don't have to keep your chicken house spotless. Clean it once or twice a year, use deep bedding, and spread ashes around now and then. If the house smells offensive or of ammonia, you have overcrowding.

When I first raised large numbers of chickens, I read that the temperature should be reduced 5° per week. My birds were eight weeks old. The temperature was supposed to be 55°. Being thrifty, I accomplished that by keeping the brooder house vent closed rather than using a heat lamp. I began to see a lot of blood. At first, I thought they were pecking at each other, another overcrowding problem. In this case, there was too much respiration in the enclosed area. Chickens have a very fast rate of respiration and emit an amazing amount of moisture. Let me assure you that, except with chicks that are not yet feathered, ventilation is way more important than the ideal temperature (within reason, of course).

Other respiratory problems can be caused by improper ventilation, but if you use odor as your guide, you'll do all right. As I mentioned above, chickens can become cannibalistic if they don't have enough space. They begin by pecking each other's feathers. Once they draw blood, they're hooked.

Keeping birds busy when they have to be confined for long periods of time, such as winter, will help prevent cannibalism. Give them deep bedding to scratch in, alfalfa to peck at, and vegetable scraps to add interest. You can sprinkle some grain on the bedding or hang unharvested garden plants so that they have to reach for them.

Preventing boredom and providing proper ventilation will solve most problems. Of course, if you have 200 birds in a space meant for 100, nothing will make it all right.

In most cases, the only chicken disease that you want to treat is coccidiosis. Either treat it herbally or buy an antibiotic specifically for that purpose. Be sure to correct the cause. With any other disease, you're probably better off just to kill any unthrifty looking bird. (This does not include birds going through a normal molt).

Healthy chickens do not benefit from antibiotics given routinely, and besides, one reason to raise our own food is to get away from chemicals and additives. Also, disease organisms quickly become immune to medication. You want your birds to become immune, not the virus or bacteria. Actually, viruses are not usually susceptible to antibiotics anyway.

Parasites are another potential problem, especially if you get your birds "second hand" or if your chicken house has been used before. Chickens can get roundworms and should be wormed regularly for these. I use Piperazine in the drinking water three times a year. When you butcher a chicken, cut open the intestine. If roundworms are present, they will be readily visible. In a live bird the signs are poor production, pale comb, pale face, and a generally unthrifty appearance. If they are badly infected, you may see worms in the stool. The bird will be emaciated. If it gets to that point, it's best to kill the bird, worm the rest of the flock, and then treat with antibiotics. Severe worm infection depletes the immune system and makes the birds very susceptible to all sorts of diseases.

Lice are external parasites common to chickens and other birds. They are easily seen if you part the feathers under the bird, especially near the vent and under the wings. They suck blood, itch, and generally cause the bird distress. Provide a dust bath and you probably won't have the problem. I use ashes, and the box is almost always in use during the cold months when the chickens can't roll in the dirt outside.

Try to keep wild birds out of the chicken house, because they will introduce all sorts of parasites. If you reach under a hen to get an egg and lice crawl onto your hand, you have a serious problem. Chicken lice won't live on people, so you don't have to worry about that. You will have to resort to something more than ashes. Buy a dusting powder that is suitable for lactating dairy animals, poultry, and pets. These are the safest and they work just fine. You can try pouring some into the ashes in the dust bath, but if you still have lice after a couple of weeks you'll have to dust by hand. Not all birds will be equally infected. Some may not be at all.

Wear a mask to prevent breathing in the dust. Turn the chicken upside down and dust the vent area. Rub it in and toss the bird outside so you know which ones you've dusted. It's easiest to do this at night. Turn off the light and use a flashlight. It helps to have a partner. Obviously, don't put birds out in extreme weather. Additional measures are to change all nesting material and add ashes and poultry dust to each nest. Keep the dust bath filled with ashes and poultry dust for a couple of weeks at least.

Mites are another parasite that attack chickens. They live in the cracks of the building and the roosts during the day and crawl onto the birds at night to feed. They are very small and hard to see. They're red. Go out at night with the light off and take a flashlight. Put your hand under a bird. If mites are really bad they will be crawling on your hand. If that doesn't happen, pick up the bird and look under the feathers on the abdomen, especially near the vent. Mites move quickly, and you have to be fast to see them before they move away from the light. Some poultry dusts work for mites but not all. Check the label. Besides dusting, you will also have to treat the mite's hiding place. Used motor oil is what old timers used to paint the roosts and boards. Creosote is also used. These are not harmless products to have around your birds, but they are cheap. I've used motor oil and it works very well. You can also buy roost paint made especially for the purpose.

Scaly leg mites are another parasite. They mostly infect older birds. They get under the scales on the legs, giving them a rough ugly appearance. Once again, used motor oil is an effective remedy. You take each bird and dip its feet and legs all the way to the feathers. The oil suffocates the mites. I know used (or new) motor oil has all kinds of ugly things in it. You may prefer to buy a product especially to treat scaly leg mites. Still, I keep a bucket for the treatment of both kinds of mites, and it does work.

Pine tar is a good thing to have on hand. If a bird has a wound, put pine tar on it. It will keep the other birds from pecking at the wounded one. It works wonders. Chicken wounds heal very readily, even really nasty ones if they aren't aggravated.

With any antibiotics or other medication including poultry dust, be sure to check the withdrawal time before you sell any product from a treated animal. It is very important to maintain our credibility as conscientious farmers producing wholesome food.

Ducks

Ducks are easy keepers if they have free range and access to water. Most of the year they will forage for a lot of their feed, but still you should offer grain free choice. They don't need shelter except in the most extreme weather. When mine go into the chicken house for the night I know we're in for a really cold night and maybe a blizzard.

When ducks are confined they make a terrific mess with their water. They need to dip their beaks all the way under water when they've eaten, so a chicken waterer doesn't work well for them.

I've never seen a sick duck, and they should never be given medication unless you are absolutely certain it is safe for ducks.

In the spring, a duck can lay at least twice as many eggs as she can hatch, so you can take most of the first clutch. Leave one egg so she doesn't decide to move her nest to somewhere you can't find. Then you can take 10 or 12 for yourself. After that let her keep some for hatching. Ducks are good setters but poor mothers. They really have no way to protect their ducklings, especially if they hatch before there is much cover. For that reason I confine some ducklings with a mother in order to insure that I have some ducklings for the freezer. You can buy duck and goose food or make your own. If you use chick food, be sure it isn't medicated. Bread soaked in milk is good feed for babies. Be sure to provide whole grains for mom and plenty of water. They will all appreciate some greens too. Ducks need grit, as do all birds, so if they are confined, throw some dirt in for their gizzards. Don't let them swim until they are fully feathered if they are not with mother to take them under her wing.

Geese

Geese are said to be the most economical of fowl. They grow rapidly on range and don't need much supplementation until fall. They are much happier with access to water for swimming, although they can be raised without it.

Geese mate for life in most cases, and some ganders will accept two females to·form a trio. It's important to know this when you obtain your geese so that you can make the appropriate arrangements. Since geese live for about 20 years, it is advantageous to try for a trio. Besides giving you greater production, it gives you some insurance in case one goose dies. With a pair, the remaining one is likely to succumb also if its mate dies. In the case of a trio, the other two will not pine away if one dies.

Geese are excellent parents and hardly ever lose a gosling. There is a problem with fertility, however, especially before the age of three. When the goose is laying, take 10 to 12 eggs from the nest. Always leave at least one egg or she may hide her nest from you. When some are removed, she is encouraged to lay two clutches, thereby doubling her production.

If the nest is vulnerable to robber birds (magpies, ravens, etc.), construct a roof.

If you purchase goslings instead of older geese, raise them as you would ducklings (described above). They will need supplemental heat for about four weeks.

Geese are intelligent and are good "watch" animals. They're also very noisy, especially the Africans.

In late summer and early fall the geese will start eating large quantities of grain. They do that in order to store fat for the winter. They seem gluttonous at this season but it is a necessary preparation for winter.

For plucking geese and ducks, I heat the water to 170° and submerge them for three minutes, whereas for chickens, it's only for two minutes at 160°. Prior to dunking, we dry pluck the goose down and a heavenly pillow is created out of six to seven geese.

Rabbits

Rabbits are a good choice when you are ready to move beyond fowl. They are inexpensive and easy to care for. Although a person could easily obtain a trio from another backyard breeder, I strongly recommend purchasing quality breeding stock. They will cost around $10 instead of $5, but are well worth the extra money. They will have been bred for such traits as good mothering ability, rapid growth rate, and good meat type conformation.

You will need one cage for each rabbit and an additional one in which to put a doe when her litter is weaned. Wire cages are the most practical. A wood and wire hutch can be esthetically pleasing, but every bit of wood must be covered with hardware cloth (wire mesh) to prevent destruction by rabbit teeth. Another strike against wooden cages is that they are more likely to harbor disease because they cannot be kept as clean. Suspend the cages at a convenient height to allow the droppings to fall through. Provide each cage with a feeder, a waterer, and a chewing stick.

Rabbits can stand a lot of cold but should be protected from wind and precipitation. My cages are against the east wall of the barn where they are protected from the prevailing westerly winds. We have slatted fences that are easily raised or lowered to protect them from the occasional east winds. Even so, when the wind blows and the temperature drops to 10 below, each rabbit needs a nest box in order to stay warm and to protect the bottoms of the feet from frostbite.

Rabbits can live on a makeshift diet, but because they are confined and therefore unable to make up for any lack, they do best on pelletted feed. It can be supplemented with top quality alfalfa, vegetable scraps, and edible weeds. Don't feed too much fresh stuff at one time, though. Rabbits need fresh water at all times. In very hot or very cold weather that may mean watering three or four times a day.

Growing rabbits, and does in constant production, should be fed free choice unless a doe begins to get overly fat, in which case you'll have to cut down her ration. Check their condition every day by feeling the back bone and pelvic bone. They should be readily felt but not protruding.

A maintenance diet is 6 ounces of pellets daily and is usually fed to bucks and does that are not in production. This is not set in stone, of course, and there are some circumstances where you will need to feed more. Extreme cold is an example. If the rabbits were fed in the morning, there should still be feed in the evening. Each rabbit should be eager for food in the morning but not frantic when they are on limited rations. Bucks should be lean but not skinny.

Rabbits are inherently shy. They need to become accustomed to sounds, movement, and handling. Speak to them as you approach and while you're working with them. Handle them every day.

You can try breeding when the doe is five months and the buck is six months. Put the doe into the buck's cage. A doe is possessive of her territory and may hurt the buck if he is put into her cage. If there is a successful breeding, the buck will fall over. Gestation is about thirty days. Place a nest box stuffed with straw into the doe's cage three to five days before her due date. She will burrow into the straw to make her nest. Shortly before giving birth, she will line the nest with fur. If there are no kits on the 35th day, return her to the buck.

After the doe gives birth, she will clean and feed the babies and eat the afterbirth. Don't disturb her during this time. After she leaves the nest, check for any dead kits and be sure the live ones are well covered with fur and are in the back of the box. A doe usually only feeds the babies once a day for a few minutes.

By 10 days the babies can readily stand temperatures of 10 below if there is no wind. At 14 days remove the nest box unless it is extremely cold, in which case you can leave it in for another week. If so, the box will have to be cleaned frequently to prevent eye infection. If eye infection does occur, treat with diluted lemon juice.

Remove the doe at 28 to 35 days and rebreed on the 35th day unless she is in poor condition. Always take the doe from the cage instead of the kits to minimize stress. A good doe will produce 8 to 10 kits and stay in good condition on a 35 day breed-back schedule. There are exceptions such as a very young doe or extreme cold, and I wouldn't cull a doe under those circumstances. Give her a second chance or even a third, but no more. Fryers are ready at about 10 weeks and will dress out at 2¾ to 3¾ lbs.

Turkeys

Turkeys are easy to raise if you get *started poults.* These are two- to three-week old birds and are available at your feed store in May and June. Keep them warm until they're fully feathered or about six weeks old.

Feed young turkeys turkey starter and be sure they have fresh water available at all times. If you have skim milk, give them that too. Switch to turkey grower at around 10 weeks and begin to offer whole grains in a separate feeder. Turkeys, like other game birds, require a very high protein diet, so don't stint. If possible, let them out to range during the day where they can forage for insects and other goodies. Close them up at night to protect them from predators. Be sure to give them an adequate place to roost.

At around 16 weeks, switch to turkey finisher and continue offering whole grains. If your birds are not running loose at least part of each day, you will have to provide grit if they are getting whole grains. Turkeys are ready to butcher at around five months of age.

It's not worth keeping turkeys to breed unless you just want to try it for fun. Males usually aren't fertile for three years and even then the hatching rate is poor. Better to buy the poults in the spring.

Contrary to popular belief, turkeys are not stupid. They are different than other fowl. They are curious and companionable and these traits can sometimes get them into trouble. And, no, they do not drown by looking up at the rain. Mine run loose as much as possible after they're past the constant warmth stage and they do quite well for themselves.

Goats

Goats are an important addition to your farm. They provide both meat and milk, are hardy and relatively easy to care for, and are inexpensive compared to a cow. Brush goats, scrub goats, and so-called meat goats do not make good milkers. As with other livestock, it's a good idea to buy your first goats from an experienced breeder. Avoid the auction.

An honest breeder will help you select animals that are right for your needs. You may be able to purchase an older doe who is past her prime but still an excellent milker. If she is also a good mother with a superior genetic makeup, you will have the basis of a strong herd.

Buying a young kid as your first goat is an option, but the risk of something going wrong is much greater. An experienced milker will know what to do even if you don't. A rule of thumb is to have one doe for each member of the family if you intend to make all your own dairy products. Starting with two, however, will enable you to learn the ropes without being overwhelmed.

Many people who have only a few does do not want to be bothered keeping a buck. In that case, they must rent the services of someone else's buck in the fall. A buck is an important member of the herd, though, so if you have room for him you may want to keep your own. A buck should be gentle and easy to handle. Bucks are strong, and during rutting season, very aggressive. If he has not been routinely handled, he can be dangerous.

I let my buck run with the herd except in the fall if there are does that I don't want bred. There is no problem with his smell getting into the milk unless they are closely confined. Be sure to give the buck the excellent care that you give the does, with high quality feed and plenty of bedding if he is housed separately.

One acre of land can support four goats. Don't overcrowd them, and provide plenty of dairy quality alfalfa, and they will improve the land. Goats are browsers like deer, not grazers. They move from plant to plant, picking a bite here and a bite there. They will keep thistles, knapweed, and leafy spurge out of their pasture. If you keep more than four to the acre, they must be confined or the land will be overgrazed, just as with other livestock.

Goats require shelter from the elements. The barn or shed should be draft-free but not heated. One open door will not create a draft and will allow the goats to come and go as they wish. They know best about this. Cover the floor with straw, sawdust, or shavings. Deep bedding works very well, but don't let it become wet or packed on top.

Provide a hay feeder for your goats. They are very fastidious and will not eat soiled food. Another necessary piece of equipment is a milking stanchion. I have a large barn that once housed dairy cattle, so I have a stanchion (modified) for each milker. This is very convenient, but you can make do with just one.

In addition to the best alfalfa, each milker gets one pound of 3-way with molasses for each half gallon of milk she gives. Feed this when you milk.

Attach a mineral feed box to the wall inside the barn high enough that it is not easily soiled. Keep it filled with a dairy mineral mix. It should be mixed half and half with salt unless it is packaged that way when you buy it. If your area is deficient in selenium, it is very important to provide that either in the mix or in a block or some other way. Your neighbors or your feed dealer will know. Also provide a mineral salt block and a white salt block. That way the goats can choose what they need.

Sleeping platforms are the final piece of equipment for your barn. They are about 2' x 4' and about 3' off the floor. Not all goats use them, but the ones that do really appreciate them.

Unlike cows and horses, goats cannot tolerate getting wet, so be sure they always have access to shelter. Leave the door open except in extreme weather, like 20 below, when you will want to close the door to preserve heat.

Goats mate in the fall ordinarily, although there is some variation in certain breeds. Stagger the breedings so that the does are not all bred at once. That way you can have milk all year. If you don't have your own buck, be alert to each goat's cycle, which is approximately 21 days between the end of September and the end of January. Some will come into heat sooner, but if the weather is hot, the buck may not be fertile or interested.

Prepare for the goat's season by keeping in a jar a rag that has been rubbed over a fragrant buck. Present it frequently to the does, and when they are in heat you will know. Otherwise, if you have your own buck, your does will let you know when they are ready to visit him.

When a doe is in heat, leave her with the buck for at least three days. Watch her so that you will know if she comes in heat again, in which case you will have to rebreed. An easier way is to leave her with the buck for four weeks. In either case, pay attention to signs of heat later on.

I once sold a beautiful purebred buck to a man who claimed to know all about goats. The buck was a proven sire, so I was very surprised when the man returned in the spring demanding a replacement buck. The one I had sold him, he said, was no good. None of his does had kidded. I agreed to replace the buck on condition that he return the first one.

"Can't," he said, "we ate him."

"No deal," I said, "but maybe we can figure out what went wrong. When did you try to breed?"

"Early September," he said.

"How long did you leave him with the does?"

"About two weeks," he said.

"Are you sure they were all in heat during that time?"

"No," he said.

"Did you check whether they came in heat after that time?"

"No."

So my beautiful buck was eaten because of ignorance, and the family had a herd of dry does until the following fall.

A doe's due date is five months minus one day from breeding. Actually, it can be three to five days before or after. Give her a quiet place by herself, but in a familiar area. A part of the barn that can be closed off is ideal. Provide her with fresh water, alfalfa, and plenty of bedding. Place the water in a smallish bucket in a spot where she is not likely to drop a kid into it.

Most does have no trouble delivering on their own. If the labor has gone on a very long time though, and the doe is in great pain or is becoming exhausted, you will have to help. If the head and front feet are out, pull downward during the contraction. That's probably all the help that is needed.

There may be a head showing but no feet. In that case, reach in and try to bring the feet forward and out. Likewise when the front feet are showing but not the head, reach in and bring it forward and out.

A rear presentation poses no problem if the feet come first. Just help by pulling downward during a contraction as above. If the rump is coming out but not the feet, they will probably have to be brought out before the birth can proceed. If that cannot be managed, push the kid in and then arrange the legs. The main concern with a rear presentation is that a prolonged stay in the birth canal can compress the umbilical cord, thus depriving the kid of oxygen. In a forward presentation, all you need to do is to clean out the mouth and nose when the head emerges and it will be able to breathe.

Twins are the rule with goats, and this usually poses no problem. The second one ordinarily follows easily. Sometimes though, both kids will be coming at once. For that reason, whenever you need to help with a birth, be sure both feet are from one kid. If not, push one back and find both feet of the presenting kid before pulling.

All this can be scary at first. Don't do it unless it's really necessary. Err on the side of caution, but a doe who has been in heavy labor for over an hour probably needs help.

The mother will usually clean and dry her kid, but if she doesn't, you will have to. Dip the cord in iodine. Don't dab it on, really soak it. The kids should be up and nursing within 15 minutes, but if they're not, help them. It is important that they get colostrum as soon as possible. After the birthing, give Mom a pound of 3-way. That will be the only grain she gets until you begin to milk her—probably at three days. Too much grain will cause her milk to come in too quickly. Keep Mom and kids separate from the others for three to five days, or until they all seem healthy and strong.

The doe's milk will increase for about two months after kidding, at which time she should be giving at least a gallon a day unless she is a first freshener, in which case it may be slightly less. During these first two months I leave the kids with the mother and take the extra. After that, I separate the kids at night so that I get the morning milk. The kids are then freed to run with the herd during the day. There is some wailing during the first few nights of this routine, but it doesn't take them long to adjust.

The kids are butchered between six and nine months of age. I do it when the hay season starts, and by then it's usually cold enough to hang the meat for a couple of weeks, which greatly improves the product. I keep hay in the feeder at all times, even when there is abundant pasture. They won't eat much, but they like to have it available. When it begins to disappear quickly, I know the pasture is no longer of much use.

Male kids should be castrated at one month of age. An elastrator is easy and safe if you do it at the right time. If you wait too long, it will cause great pain and may bring complications.

Goats should be wormed three times a year. One of these times should be six to eight weeks before kidding. One worming should include the whole herd at one time. I use TBZ because it is the only wormer that is safe for both pregnant and lactating goats. Theoretically, wormers should vary, but I have had no parasite problems. When goats are not overcrowded, worm problems are minimal.

Give your goats an annual shot six to eight weeks before kidding also. The buck gets his at the end of March or a couple of months before pasture season begins. I give 8-way because I live in an area where animals are susceptible to red water disease. If that disease is not a problem in your area, give 7-way. Your neighbors can tell you if they vaccinate their cattle for red water. If they do, you should too.

Goats were mountain animals originally, so their hoofs were constantly worn down by rocks. These days, we have to trim the hoofs. It should be done every month so that there is minimal cutting, only a bit of trimming. Look at a new-born kid to see how the hoofs should look, or better yet, have someone show you how to trim.

One other seasonal chore is dusting for lice. I do that at the end of March. Use a dust that is safe for lactating dairy animals and do the dusting outside on a windless day. It's best to do it right after the morning milking so that it's mostly gone by the evening milking. If there are kids under eight weeks of age, don't use dust on them. Use ashes instead. I have found a yearly dusting to be all that is necessary, but this may vary in another climate.

Pigs

I love pigs. They are hardy, intelligent, and friendly. Buy weaners in the spring around the first of May. (Raising your own is a real production and not something to get into casually.) They need to be butcher size when it's cold enough to cure the hams and bacon. If you get them too early or keep them too long, they will be too fat by butcher weather.

Pigs need a three-sided shelter with plenty of bedding. Weaners can get really cold in wet, springy weather and need to be able to burrow into their litter. Try not to keep one pig alone. They need another for warmth as well as companionship. A single pig will not thrive unless it is allowed to run with the other barnyard creatures.

Pigs can be a good addition to your other animals except that they root—really root. If you're set up in a way that that is acceptable, confine them only until they know where home is and then let them out. I have done it and it's really fun to have old Porker follow me around. She'll choose a favorite spot in the barn for sleeping and adjust the straw to suit her. She will be a peaceful member of the livestock community.

Let's assume that you need to confine your pigs. You'll need about 12' x 12' of yard for four pigs plus the shelter, which should be about 6' x 4'. Install two troughs in the yard, one for feed and one for water. A water heater core cut in half works admirably.

Barley is the usual pig grain, although soft wheat is good too. Soft wheat can be fed as is, which is a real advantage. Ground or rolled barley can be fed as is also, but is too expensive unless a farmer can be found to grind it for you (rolled is best). Feeding pigs with grain from the feed store makes the whole thing a non-viable operation, so try to buy whole barley from a farmer instead, where it will only cost half as much. The whole barley (or hard wheat) will have to be soaked for three days to be digestible. Cooking it is a faster alternative, but that gets old really fast. Feed grain free choice.

Provide fresh water at least once a day, but be sure there is water in the trough at all times. In the summer, pigs love a mudbath. They also delight in running under the hose if you'll hold it for them. They squeal and chase each other like children. That and the mudbath will deter them somewhat from climbing into their water trough, which they will then refuse to drink.

A good butcher weight is 225 pounds. You will learn to recognize it with experience. The pigs will be starting to look really jowly, and you will be certain that it is no longer economical to keep them.

Calves

Raising a calf is relatively easy if you follow a few guidelines. Do get experience with other less expensive animals first, though. Where I live, a beef calf costs $175 to $250 if it is two weeks of age or less. A dairy-beef cross can be $100 less. Dairy farmers often breed their cows to beef bulls except when they want replacement heifers. These dairy cross calves can be a good deal for a family.

I have always gotten my calves from the livestock auction, but you need to be careful about what you buy. Go early and look over the calves. Write down the numbers of the ones that look promising. Choose only ones that look perky and alert. Don't even consider a calf that is hunched up and looks miserable, no matter what the price. If a calf is under five days of age, its chances of survival are poor. If you can't determine the age, ask someone who appears more familiar with cattle. Look at the rear ends and discount any that have scours.

The first couple of times I went to the auction, I didn't have a clue about how to buy a calf. One of the people who worked at the auction appeared knowledgeable and friendly, so I took a seat near him and he explained what I needed. He helped me choose and I was very pleased with what I got.

Another hint is to wait until late in the sale. Be sure you know how many calves there are so you don't wait too long. As you wait you will be getting an idea of what calves are going for that day. More importantly though, some nice calves may go much cheaper if other people have already bought what they want. I have gotten some real beauties because other people bid early.

Once I bought a calf for a very low price because she had no ears or tail. We had had a severe cold spell three weeks earlier, and I felt certain that she had been born then and had been frostbitten. She was healed, husky, and healthy, but since she looked so strange, no one wanted her. She was older and heavier than any of the other calves, and I got her for half the price.

If you have goats, you can raise a calf really cheaply. One goat can support one calf. If you don't have goats, you'll have to buy milk replacer. Lamb milk replacer is much superior to calf milk replacer and is well worth the extra expense. If you feed replacer, follow the directions on the bag.

If you're feeding goat milk, start with a pint every three hours. After a few days, if the calf is not scouring and seems hungry, gradually increase the amount to one quart every four hours. After a couple of weeks, increase the amount to one half gallon three times a day, once again, only if the calf seems hungry and is not scouring and also, once again, changing the amount gradually. If scours develop, back off on the amount you feed. After a month you can drop the middle feeding and give one half gallon morning and evening.

It's best to continue bottle feeding for six months, but if you have to buy milk replacer, I'd only feed for four months. They will do all right with that. From four months on, you can feed skim milk. When bottle feeding, hold the bottle fairly low to mimic the position of the udder. That ensures that the milk goes into the proper stomach. Be sure to warm the milk, especially with a very young calf, but even an older calf will feel better if the milk is at least lukewarm. There is no advantage in continuing to feed milk past six months of age.

When bottle feeding a calf (or any other animal for that matter), err on the side of leaving the animal a little hungry. Overfeeding can cause scouring. Backing off on the amount fed will usually stop the scouring, but if not, add a bit of ginger to the milk. If that doesn't correct the problems, use Kaopectate according to the directions on the bottle.

Calves begin to nibble alfalfa at about one week of age but don't consume much for the first month. Even so, make it available to them and when they begin eating it, provide fresh water also.

The calf will put on weight more quickly if you feed 3-way and Calf Manna. Start feeding when the calf begins eating hay and gradually increase up to seven pounds a day. This is not necessary, however, if the calf has access to plenty of top quality alfalfa and excellent pasture.

The calf needs shelter that is draft free but not heated. If the calf is confined when it is young, introduce it to pasture very gradually and always feed it first. If the pasture is already lush, give the calf a shot of 8-way (or 7-way if there is no red water in your area) a couple of weeks before it is turned out. If the calf is under two months of age, it will need a second shot at that age. If the calf always has access to pasture, there's no problem. Give the shot at two months in that case. Worm the calf in the fall and again in the spring. I use TBZ.

Butcher at about 800 pounds or in the fall after the calf is a year old.

Bees

Bees can be purchased by mail or you may be able to buy them locally. Buying locally is an advantage because not only is there less stress on the bees, but also you will be able to get advice from the beekeeper.

Bees are sold in two-, three-, four-, and sometimes five-pound packages. Buy one of the larger packages if possible, because it will be three weeks before any new workers are produced, and the original bees will be doing all the work of tending the queen, raising the young, cleaning the hive, gathering nectar and pollen, and producing honey. The best idea would be to start with two three- or four-pound packages with queens. If something happens to one hive, you won't have to start all over.

Order your bees so that they will arrive a couple of weeks before the fruit trees bloom. That way the hive will be strong when the main flow begins.

Each hive initially consists of a bottom board, a brood chamber (deep super), an entrance reducer, a telescope cover which is protected by metal, and ten frames with foundation. The frames are where the honey is stored. The bees can make the combs without foundation, but it takes a tremendous amount of time and energy, and extraction is difficult. The hive body should be painted.

Set up the hives where they are sheltered from the prevailing winds. In the north choose a sunny location and in the south a shady one. The entrance should face south. When the sun warms the front of the hive, the bees are encouraged to leave the hive earlier in the day.

Place the hives where they will not be knocked over by animals or raided by skunks. I have mine on a table in a fenced area. If you use a table, be sure that it is very strong, because a hive full of brood and honey is quite heavy. Also consider how tall a hive with four or five supers will be.

When the bees arrive, the queen will be housed in a separate cage with a few workers to attend her. Wait until evening to install the bees so that they won't be flying about before they know where home is. Before installing, feed the bees as much sugar syrup as they will take. That will be about ½ pint per cage. To make the syrup, heat five pounds of sugar and two quarts of water until the sugar is dissolved. Don't let it boil. Cool to lukewarm. Spread the syrup over the cage with a brush.

Place five frames in the brood chamber and push them close together. Remove the cork from the queen cage and poke a hole in the candy beneath the cork. Hang the queen cage between two frames with the candy on top. The bees will eat the candy and by the time it is consumed the workers will have become accustomed to the queen.

Remove the syrup can that comes with the cage of bees. Invert the cage over the frames and shake out as many bees as possible around the queen cage. Leave the cage on the frames with the opening facing down. Cover with a super if you have one. Otherwise a box will do. Replace the cover and top that with a stone.

In the morning, open the hive and remove the cage. If all the bees have not left the cage, place the cage near the entrance where they will find their way into the hive.

Fill a bee feeder with syrup. You can make a feeder from a quart jar with holes punched in the lid. Invert it over the frames and replace the super, lid and stone. Check the feeder every two or three days, but otherwise don't disturb the hive for five days. At that time check to see if the queen has been released. If she has not been, remove the candy.

In a week, look to see if the queen is laying. If she is not, or if she is dead or missing, replace her immediately. Continue feeding syrup until the comb is drawn out on six frames, or until the bees are covering ten frames, or until they no longer consume it. That will be about six weeks.

While feeding syrup, you will have to open the hive every two or three days unless you have purchased a Boardman feeder that is installed outside the entrance. The advantage of the Boardman feeder is that you don't have to open the hive to fill it. The disadvantage is that it encourages robbing, which can be a problem, especially before the hive is well established. Opening the hive to fill the feeder should not disturb the bees too much since you won't be getting into the frames. In any case, while feeding syrup use the smallest entrance and don't be in a hurry to stop feeding. Cool or rainy weather may prolong the need.

Bees require a source of water, so if there is no natural one, provide it. Make it shallow enough that the bees won't drown, or place rocks in a pan so that they can crawl out.

Check your bees weekly—no more—to see how much of the frames are filled. Always keep two frames ahead of what the bees have filled. Put the new frames outside the others, not in the middle, or the brood will not be kept warm by the cluster. If the bees don't have extra room for future building, they will be likely to swarm. If there are too many extra frames, the bees will feel overwhelmed and discouraged and may swarm because of that.

When the bees cover eight frames, put on a second super and add frames as before. The bottom super is called the brood chamber. The one on top of the brood chamber is the food chamber. Additional supers are for you, unless you want to leave the bees a second food chamber. If your winters are very long you may want to do that, at least until you determine how much is needed. Then you can take the extra when the next honey flow begins.

Spend time watching the bees come and go and you will learn how they're feeling. One bee doesn't tell you much, but the bees as a whole are somewhat like a single organism. The actions of the whole will tell you a lot. When the bees are busily going about their business and you can see pollen packed into the pockets on their rear legs, everything is probably good.

Before I had much experience with bees, I noticed that the air around the hive was awash with bees. I said to my husband, "You should see the bees. They're swarming all over the place." I didn't realize what I was saying, But they were indeed swarming and I lost my entire hive. Another lesson is that I had caused them great distress by looking for the queen every day. I was told that I had to be sure that my queen was alive and well or I would lose my hive, and in my concern I drove them away.

When you notice bees waiting to get into the hive, it's time to increase the size of the entrance. Later on the bees will be crowding around the enlarged entrance, and it will be time to remove the entrance reducer entirely. At that time, stuff grass or some such into half the entrance. After awhile you can remove that if the bees haven't already.

Use the same routine of enlarging the entrance if the bees are getting too hot. You will know this because the bees will be fanning the opening, trying to cool off the hive. If you see large numbers of bees clustered on the front of the hive and you already have the entire entrance open, lift the cover so that the front lip rests on the front of the super. The next step is to move the top back about half an inch. The idea is to cool off the hive without making the bees too vulnerable. Bees that are overheated may swarm, but bees that have too large an opening to protect will be intimidated and may also swarm or be robbed by other bees. Another option for cooling the hive, but one I've never had to use, is to shift the upper super a bit so that it's not set squarely on the one below, thereby letting in more air. Try not to make a space larger than ½ inch.

Most beekeepers remove the honey in late summer, leaving the brood chamber and the food chamber for the bees. Any honey made in the fall is also left. You can do that or wait till the honey flow in the spring and take what is left. I think that's a good idea until you really get to know how much the bees need. I don't know anyone else who does that, but it works for me. If you do that, remove the super, add a new super, and put the old one on top. Wait a month and then take the super and extract the honey. That way, any brood or bees in the combs will be gone.

In the fall when the honey flow is over, put the entrance reducer back in. Once the hive is established, it will probably not be necessary to use the smallest entrance again. The three inch one will be fine. The top super should have another entrance hole which should be left open all winter. That helps eliminate moisture from the hive. If your super doesn't have one, drill a three inch hole near the top of the super.

Don't open your hive in the winter or any time the temperature is less than 40°. At that temperature it's OK to lift the lid to see how many frames the bees are covering or to add frames. At 60° you can make a quick inspection to determine if the bees have enough honey. At 70°, in spring

(about the time the dandelions bloom), make a thorough inspection to find the queen and see if there is brood.

Some people wrap their hives for the winter. I did that once, but found mildew in the top super when I opened the hive in the spring. I knew that wasn't healthy, so I've never wrapped a hive since. Even in our severe weather the bees have been fine.

When working with bees, it is a good idea to have protective clothing. Even more important though is to be aware of the mood of the bees and to leave them alone when they are grouchy. Most of the time I wear no protective clothing if I'm only checking to see how many frames are being covered or to add frames. I just move slowly and calmly. If I open the hive and bees charge out aggressively, I close the hive and wait for another day. Usually they go about their business. If you're doing an inspection though, and have to manipulate frames you'll at least want to put on the bee hat and veil. In the beginning, long canvas bee gloves will give you more confidence. They're hard to work in though, so later on you'll probably do most of your work without them.

If you have to work when the bees are feeling unpleasant or if you just want to feel more secure, wear the hat and veil, coveralls, gloves, and boots. Turn up the collar on your coveralls and tie the veil securely. Put the gloves over your sleeves and secure the pant legs so that bees cannot fly up them. My coveralls have velcro at the ankles and wrists. Never stand in front of the entrance when you're working in the hive. It's best if the bees can move in and out normally.

Most people use a bee smoker to calm the bees, but although I have one, I've never used it. A hive tool is handy to have. There are lots of other goodies in the catalog, but I would advise against buying any until you know what you really need or want.

You can feed Terramycin in the fall if you are worried about disease. Place a board above the frames and sprinkle the powder on that. The bees will take what they need. Don't use the fall honey for human consumption, though.

Horses

Most people want a horse or two as part of their homestead. All horses can work as well as being used for pleasure, but they are herd animals, so if at all possible get more than one.

Unless you know horses or have a trusted friend who does, don't buy a horse at the auction. Too much money is involved and too many problems can be temporarily concealed. Likewise, avoid answering an ad in the paper. Find a reputable, knowledgeable horse person and ask her to help you.

Horses are very destructive if they do not have sufficient space. Their urine will burn the pasture, and they will eat the plants to the roots. They will strip the trees, and when rain comes, they will stomp everything into a morass. For these reasons horses with less than ideal pasture should be fenced most of the time that they are idle.

A horse that is corralled (or worse, stabled) will need exercise every day to stay in shape physically as well as mentally. In its natural state, a horse moves over large areas every day and will become quite neurotic when penned for long periods of time. Sheer boredom will result in a host of nasty habits such as cribbing, tail rubbing, and harassment of other nearby barnyard animals.

A horse needs to be able to get out of the wind, but even a tree can be enough shelter from rain or snow if they have a windblock. Access to a barn is appreciated, of course, but not really necessary.

If the horse is not working, feed a larger quantity of grass hay rather than a smaller quantity of alfalfa. They like to nibble most of the day and that will help them feel more content. It more closely mimics nature. One third to one half bale per head per day is about right, but pay attention to their condition. You should not be able to feel their ribs, but also don't let them get too fat. Provide fresh water at all times. A mineral salt block and a horse block will provide everything a non-working horse needs.

When a horse is working, feed it one pound of oats or 3-way for each hour of work. You may want to feed a better quality of hay so that it doesn't have to spend as much time eating. You'll want it to get plenty of rest if it's working all day.

If a horse has been saddled, brush it out before you turn it loose. The reason is that the saddle has flattened the hair and thereby eliminated the airspace that provides insulation. Allow the horse to cool down before feeding or watering. Half an hour is about right.

Any horse not on free range should be groomed daily. That means brushing and picking out the hoofs. Hoofs that crack should be treated with hoof dressing or pine tar. To prevent cracking, flood the area around the water trough to keep the hoof from drying.

Worm your horses three times a year and vary the type of wormer you use. Give a four-way shot in the spring. A properly cared for horse that has a rough coat should be suspected of having lice. Use a product meant especially for horses to eliminate the problem.

Get professional hoof care several times a year until you learn to do it yourself. Obtain a farrier with a good reputation because a dishonest one can cost you lots of money for questionable procedures. Example: corrective shoeing for a horse over six years old.

A final tip: horses can usually distinguish palatable plants from those that are poisonous or otherwise unsuitable. However, on a pasture that is overgrazed, a horse may eat something it normally wouldn't, resulting in colic or death. It's a very common mistake to believe that a horse has plenty of pasture when actually the plants available are unsuitable Feeding plenty of hay will eliminate the problem.

Basic treatments

Lemon juice: Full strength for ringworm; diluted for pink eye or other eye infections in goats, cows, rabbits.

Apple cider vinegar (pure—not flavored): Feed two tablespoons per day in grain to each goat to prevent mastitis. Feed to other livestock in water as a general tonic and for parasite and fly control.

Pine tar: As a hoof dressing and a wound dressing—especially to prevent cannibalism in chickens or turkeys and to deter flies on any animal wound.

Piperazine: Gentle but effective wormer that leaves the system within 24 hours.

Terramycin: Antibiotic, injectable or in powder; effective; short withdrawal period.

When I first had livestock, one of my biggest problems was sorting through the tremendous amount of information, much of it contradictory. In this article, I have attempted to tell you what you will need to know to get started in livestock. I found that too much data was confusing and overwhelming. In the beginning all I wanted was basic facts, and it was mind-boggling to wade through so much advice in an attempt to find out what was important. I hope I have succeeded in giving you what you need now without embellishment. There is much more to know, and as you become more involved you will probably want to delve more deeply into the subject.

As you grow more familiar with your animals, you will develop your own ways of doing things. Don't be afraid to experiment. Whatever works for you is the right way, as long as you always take into consideration the welfare of the animals in your care. Remember to trust your instincts. Δ

Special supplement for *The Fourth Year*

Gardening for self-sufficiency

By Martin P. Waterman

Self-sufficiency gardening differs from ordinary gardening, inasmuch as your objective is to create a safe and reliable year-round food supply for you and your family. How much food you want to grow and preserve will depend on how many people you intend to feed and for how long. Self-sufficiency gardening can be practiced at any level. You can even grow feed for livestock and fuel for your wood stove and fireplace. You can even grow lumber for construction and grains for alcohol. There are so many ways that gardening can bring about a greater self-sufficiency and independence, and these factors become apparent the more you participate and, of course, read material such as this.

The site

Site selection is very important. You want to have a site that will have good air circulation and sunlight. Even the poorest soils can be improved, but it is often best starting with soil that can support your garden. Plants such as beans will grow well in poor soils. However, plants such as melons, squash, and cucumbers need a soil that is rich in nutrients and organic matter. You may also want a site that is large enough so that you can expand your garden as needed.

Non-traditional garden spaces can also be used to produce food. Edible landscaping is the practice of substituting food-bearing plants for traditional landscape plants. For every landscape plant you may grow, be it a single specimen, shade tree, hedge, or perennial bed, there are edible alternatives. In this manner your property can produce an abundance of fruit and vegetables even without a formal garden.

Another method to supplement your garden is container gardening. Because urban lots are continually shrinking, seed breeders and plant developers have created versions of your favorite varieties that are dwarfed or come in a bush habit that make them ideal for growing in containers and small areas. In many cases, the yields from these compact plants can be as large or larger than conventional varieties. Some popular varieties include patio tomatoes, cucumbers, and peppers. You may be surprised how much food you can grow in containers.

Another advantage of container growing is that you can extend your season. If you are threatened by a late spring or early autumn frost, simply cover the containers with garbage bags or move them into the garage or a sheltered area overnight.

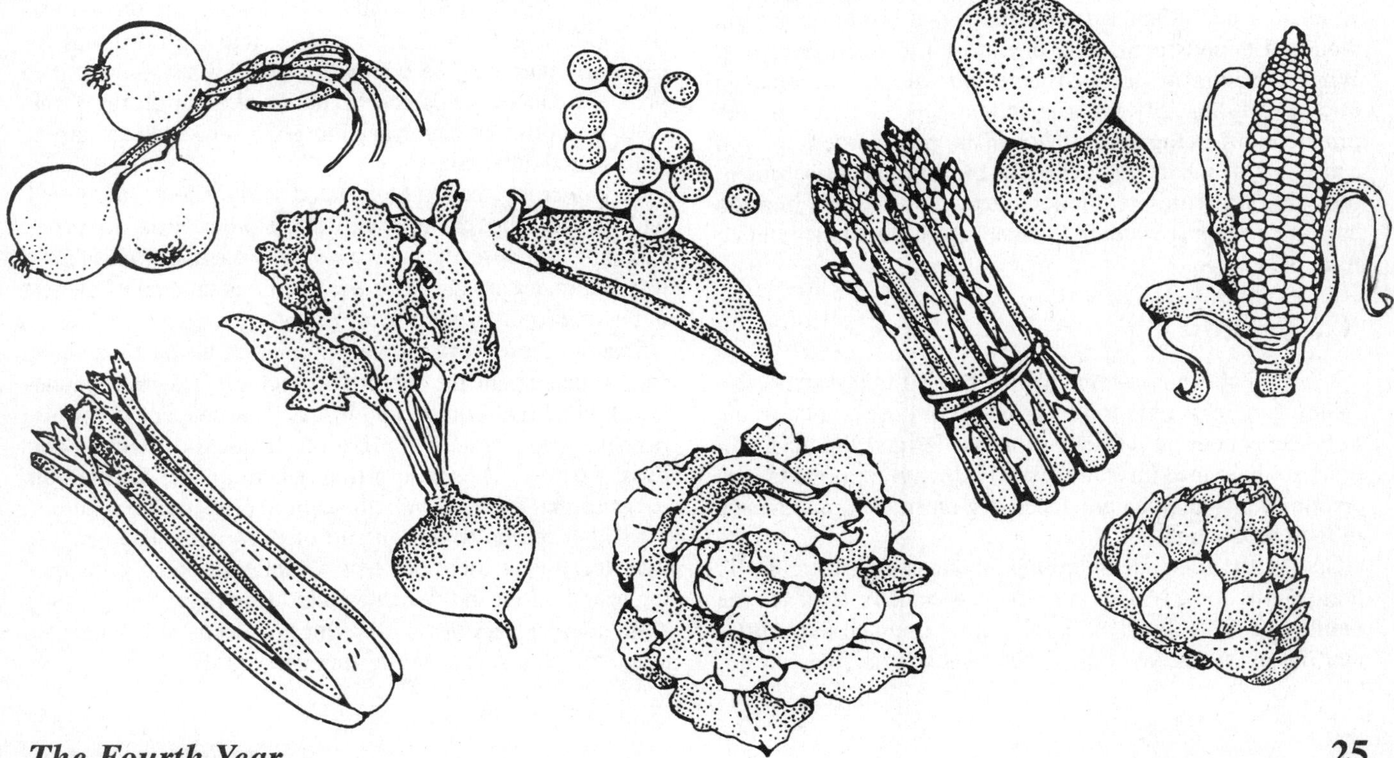

Growing with your garden

When some people realize that they can grow several thousand dollars worth of food in a relatively small space, they see it is a very desirable situation. Wanting more of a good thing, this becomes one of the motivators that get some people so excited about moving to rural surroundings or expanding their existing plantings. My first garden was a small patch; subsequently, I got the gardening bug. Actually, I got spoiled by eating fresh and delicious food, plus the money savings were substantial.

Some years I have grown as much as four acres of garden. That is a lot of garden, especially if you have to tend it yourself. I had a half acre of squash that produced several thousand pounds consisting of a dozen different varieties. What a feeling of pride to have the back of the pick-up truck overfilling. My point is simple. Once you master the principles of being self sufficient in your gardening, you can grow to whatever level you like. Many nurserymen, farmers, and rural residents started with small humble beginnings of just wanting to be able to have a fresh tomato from the garden.

Go organic

It is probably not a coincidence that so many self-sufficiency gardeners tend to be organic. For one, no one wants to be dependent on pesticides, herbicides and fungicides in order to guarantee their harvests. Furthermore, organic gardening means that you are dependent on safer natural means of food production.

One of the misunderstandings about using pesticides is that people don't realize that you can actually *increase* the number of pests. First of all, you also eliminate the beneficial insects when you spray, since most pesticides do not discriminate: they kill everything. When the population of the harmful insects rebounds, there may be no predators to help control them, so you may actually have to spray more and more. To make matters worse, many harmful insects quickly adapt and become resistant to certain pesticides. Unfortunately, many gardeners do not follow directions and think that by applying stronger mixtures they will come out ahead. In truth, they are usually costing themselves a great deal of money and wasted time, and in the end may still have to deal with a loss due to harmful insects. For every chemical cure there are usually several alternative organic methods available. You may have to be content not growing a certain vegetable or fruit if gentle methods cannot be found. In any case, there is such a wide selection of fruits and vegetables that you should always have bountiful harvests.

Seed saving

If you purchase a quarter of an ounce of seeds for a couple of dollars, you may think you are getting a good deal. However, you are paying $128 per pound. With these types of economics, you could easily spend a couple of hundred of dollars for seeds just to plant a small patch. Granted, you should be rewarded with several *thousand* dollars worth of food, but wouldn't you like to be able to keep most of that money for other things?

You can if you save your own seeds. There are many excellent books on seed saving and plant propagation, and this is one of the pillars of being self sufficient in your gardening needs.

It was common practice among settlers to have three gardens. The first was for immediate harvests, the second was for food to be put away for winter, and the third was for seeds to guarantee the continuity of harvests from year to year. Of course, seeds can be obtained from all three gardens, except some plants need to go to seed such as carrots, lettuce, and other crops.

Certain crops need to be isolated so they don't interbreed, and hybrid crops usually will not produce true offspring. Learning which seeds to save and how to save them is not a difficult undertaking. There has been a great deal of interest in historic (or *heirloom*) seeds.

Many of these varieties were popular in the past and many (while lacking in the picture-perfect supermarket appearance) will excel in taste and disease resistance. This is true because many predate the era of chemical-dependent gardens and were chosen in a time where people selected the varieties that could survive the natural pressures of nature.

Another reason to be self sufficient in your seed needs is that every year there are new varieties to keep gardeners interested. Your old favorites may disappear, and growing your favorite varieties and saving the seeds will guarantee you a constant supply of the varieties you like.

Composting and soil care

Good gardeners and farmers have an appreciation for soil similar to that of a violinist for his Stradivarius or an aircraft pilot for his jet fighter. If you take good care of your soil, it will always take good care of you.

One of the most popular ways to take care of your soil and to improve it is through composting. Composting adds organic material to the soil and benefits the garden in several ways. The most important advantage of using compost is that your soil structure will become more porous with better aeration. Therefore, it will be better able to retain moisture. The nutrient level of the soil is also improved, and less fertilizer is needed. A rich, spongy soil produces healthier plants and vegetables by encouraging strong, healthy root systems and makes weeding and weed pulling easier. A rich soil also promotes earthworms which are very beneficial for your garden.

A sure way to tell if your soil is lacking in organic matter is if it tends to become very hard and compacted during dry weather. The decomposition of what remains of your previous year's garden is the basis of the organic material in your garden. However, this material rarely provides enough organic matter to maintain and improve your soil each year. Therefore, you should practice composting.

Most self-sufficiency gardeners make their own compost. In order to make compost, you need a compost bin or a compost area. Compost bins are available and can be purchased from seed catalogs and garden centers. These bins are used to hold the collected material to be composted, such as grass clippings, food scraps, and other organic material. With all the concern today about society producing too much garbage, this is a partial solution that not only will reduce your garbage and take pressure off the land fills, but also improve your garden as well. It is surprising how many egg shells, fruit and vegetable peelings, and other scraps we will throw out over the course of a year. It is also a good way to recycle all those garden weeds that you have removed. Some enterprising gardeners purchase leaves from landscapers or sawdust from mills and woodworkers. Some gardeners have found that seaweed works well, while others will venture into swamps to gather mosses and other swampy things.

When material is put into a compost pile or bin, it ideally should start heating up, which will start decomposing the material rapidly. Temperatures can reach 140-160°F, and this high temperature is needed to kill weed seeds, bacteria, and plant diseases, as well as to break down the material so that it is useful in the garden. You can purchase compost thermometers and tools that help to turn and aerate the pile in order to keep the decomposing process going. It is often necessary to add a "starter" to activate or speed up the process. This is usually something with both nitrogen and protein, such as manure. Good rich garden soil or bone meal will also work well. It is also advisable to make sure the pile is always moist but never too wet or too dry. The pile should be turned every week or so.

Adding compost to the garden is relatively easy. It is just a matter of spreading it throughout the garden and tilling it under. The most common ways are to obtain peat moss or manure and add it to the garden. It is best to use composted manure. If you use fresh manure that has not been allowed to heat up and ferment, the weed seeds will not be killed, and you run the risk of having many weeds to contend with. In addition, fresh manure can burn the roots of certain plants.

If you do not want to purchase a compost bin, one can be quite easily and inexpensively assembled. Many designs have been used, ranging from building large wooden boxes to using turkey or chicken fencing in the shape of a square or circular pen.

If you can't compete, don't compete

It may not pay you to grow certain types of vegetables and fruits. This is more likely to depend on your geography than anything else. For instance, I live in potato country. I can purchase a 50 pound bag of #2 potatoes for under $3. That is six cents a pound. I cannot compete with potato growers, because they are subsidized by the government. Therefore, it is a waste of my energy to labor over two rows of potatoes to produce a couple hundred pounds when I can purchase them for $12. Instead, two more rows of tomatoes will produce at least 200 pounds of tomatoes. Tomatoes rarely sell for under 60 cents a pound, even in season. Therefore, I can produce $120 worth of tomatoes instead of

$12 worth of potatoes in the same space with about the same effort. In the winter, the same bag of potatoes is about $6. However, fresh tomatoes can now sell for as much as $2 per pound or more. Canned tomatoes work out to about the same. Therefore, the tomatoes that I froze or canned are worth double what they were in the summer, or about $240. In other words, the tomatoes now save me over twice as much money on my food bill.

There are exceptions to every rule. For instance, I will often grow a half row of gourmet potatoes. There are hundreds of varieties of potatoes, and you would be surprised how much flavor a garden-grown potato can pack over the bland selection at your local grocer. I choose very early varieties and end up with fresh potatoes early in the season when new potatoes are scarce and can cost as much as $6 for a five-pound bag shipped in from a warmer climate. That is $1.20 per pound, which makes them worthwhile to grow, especially because I love the taste of new potatoes. Other vegetables that I do not grow are turnips and corn, since I can purchase or trade produce for these cheaper than I can grow them.

Planning and planting

Investing in your garden is very much like investing in the stock market. Let me explain. There are high-risk and low-risk investments, and there are short-term and long-term investments. You do not want to grow too many risky crops. For instance, you should limit your production of the fruits and vegetables that are marginal in your area. This will save you the grief of having a total crop failure during some years. The majority of what you grow should be well suited to your area and growing conditions. It takes time and energy to grow, weed, water, and care for plants. Some plants will give you food in months, others in years. Therefore, you will have to strike a balance. If you plant a pear orchard, you could be waiting seven years for a decent harvest to begin. On the other hand, lettuce, radishes, and greens can be ready in less than 30 days.

Like all investments, it is wise never to put all your eggs in one basket. This means grow a wide variety of produce and keep trying and evaluating new varieties to see which ones do the best for you and are consistent with your tastes and objectives.

Best vegetables and fruit

The best self-sufficiency vegetables are those that bring the best return for the least effort and lend themselves to the storage and preparation methods that you like. That means that what is the best for one person may not be the best for another. For instance, I like fresh fried zucchini lightly spiced with Parmesan cheese. A half dozen plants (3 green and 3 yellow) will provide me with all I need throughout the season. I have never found an adequate way to preserve them . . . that is, until I discovered zucchini bread. Now I freeze about two to three dozen mini loaves. They are great at Christmas, and I usually use the last ones about the time the new zucchini is starting to flower.

If you grow the foods you like, you will automatically become more self-sufficient, since these are likely the foods you are most likely to purchase.

Small scale grain farming

Many gardeners are discovering that it is to their advantage to grow a little grain patch. This can be wheat, barley, or even corn. They can then mill their own organic grains to be made into breads or pastry. Many seed companies are starting to sell small quantities of grains. Grains have the ability to be stored for long periods of time and this for many self-sufficiency gardeners is just like having money in the bank. Just remember, it may be cheaper to purchase some grains wholesale or direct from another grower than it is to grow your own.

Medicinal herbs & spices

Have you ever stopped to look at the label of some of the processed foods that you eat? Some people find the amount of preservatives in foods frightening, especially since they do not understand why there have to be so many chemicals in their food. Different chemicals do different things. Some have nothing to do with keeping the food fresh: they make the food look fresh after sitting in a supermarket or warehouse for long periods of time. Diet is the first step towards minimizing the risk of disease. However, some gardeners look towards medicinal foods, so that in addition to preven-

tive maintenance of their health, they can have their own natural source of medicine.

Many plants have a proven track record of medicinal qualities, and there are many books on the subject. Native American plants were used by the Indians of North America, and this form of medicine predates European medicine. While many mock some of the medicinal cures that have been used for thousands of years, remember that many pharmaceutical products use extracts of those same plants.

One of the major criticisms of modern day medicine (besides the cost and inaccessibility for most) is that it treats the symptoms instead of the problem itself. Self-sufficiency gardening allows the practitioner to create natural preventive medicine through proper diet.

Storing your harvest

Storing your harvest should be considered even before you plant your garden. One reason for this is that you do not want all your produce to ripen at once. If you stagger your planting and plan it correctly, you can have food to eat and to store throughout the growing season. This way you are not overwhelmed by having to harvest and store the majority of your garden all at once.

Another reason you should study the ways of preserving your harvest is that it will definitely influence the fruit and vegetable varieties that you grow. Perusing cook books and books on preserving food may entice you to try growing different types of fruits and vegetables that you may have never considered. For instance, if you find a recipe you like for hot and spicy ketchup or barbecue sauce, you could find yourself growing more paste tomatoes and hot peppers. At the start of each season, I always try to figure out how much food I want to preserve and what delicacies I want to make. This is the time of year to do so, since the root cellar and the pantry will be running low. It is also fresh in my memory what the best foods were. Incidentally, these are usually the ones that I run out of first, such as hot pepper jam, strawberry rhubarb jam, pickled beets, and pickled beans. I find that salsa goes particularly fast, especially since it can also be used to season soups, stews, noodles, and pasta and goes great in a marinade for steak or chicken.

Storing your harvest is an art form. How much you want to get involved in food preservation will dictate what you are growing.

Freezing

Freezing is great so long as you don't lose electricity. Fortunately, we seem to have all our power failures in the dead of winter, and since the deep freeze is out on the back porch, we never have to worry about losing any food. If your supply of energy could be interrupted, you may need to look at other energy alternatives or forego freezing.

I like freezing because it is so easy, especially with certain foods such as strawberries, raspberries, peas, and string beans. I also use my freezer as a holding bin. For instance, since I am so busy in the autumn, I will freeze most of my small fruit and berries. In the depths of winter, when I have more time, I will make jams and jellies to remind me of my harvests and focus me on the coming season. There are many excellent books on freezing and actually some whole cookbooks on how to cook and freeze main courses and deserts. If you have a shortage of cookbooks, check out your local library.

Drying

I love dried fruit leathers such as apples and plums. Drying is a great way to preserve food and is an age-old method of keeping your harvest. Food dryers can be home made or you can purchase elaborate models. If you live in a warm climate, you can use the great outdoors and the desert sun to do your work for you. Even in the north, the sun can be used to cure squashes and onions or to bring your dried beans to perfection before storing for the winter.

Canning

Canning can be a lot of work, but it can also be a lot of fun. I find that mason or glass canning jars can be purchased very inexpensively at yard and garage sales. This is how I build my inventory, in addition to watching department store sales. When you can food, you have to be careful of food poisoning, so it is very important to follow directions, particularly when it comes to cleanliness and cooking temperatures. If you follow directions, you should never have any reason to worry.

The root cellar or cold room

It could pay you to have your own root cellar or cold room to store your harvests over the winter. There are hundreds of designs and some excellent books on the topic. One of the most interesting designs is to take an old van and park it nose first next to an embankment or hill. You then bury the van so that only the rear doors protrude. Of course, you should remove the interior and any chemicals or valuable parts before you plant the vehicle. A simple well ventilated cold room may also be what you need to hold your harvests. It can also be used to store food that you purchase from the supermarket or from other growers.

Other considerations

Gardeners are not limited to just growing fruits, nuts, and vegetables. Many gardeners grow their own craft items for making baskets and other art material.

In this area, many small growers sell jams and jellies and breads that they make from the crops that they harvest. You can actually compete against the local supermarkets and make money if you take the time to do your homework and research your market.

You can also sell your excess harvest. Local restaurants and farmers' markets are good avenues to investigate. With a few customers, it may pay you to purchase a greenhouse or look into hydroponic and other high-tech systems. Remember, you can also trade your harvest with others for food or even other services.

Your garden can also support bee hives, which will give you better pollination and a source of honey. As you find fruit and other varieties that are suited to your area, you can propagate more plants for your own use or to sell to others.

Being self-sufficient in your own food production is probably even more important today than in the past. There are fewer people producing food, with the bulk of production switching to larger farms and agribusiness. And the only way you can guarantee the quality and integrity of the food that you eat is to produce it yourself. Δ

WIN A FREE VITA-MIX ! ! ! (see page 6)

Backwoods Home magazine

... a practical journal of self reliance!

January/February 1993
No. 19
$3.50 U.S.
$4.50 Canada

RETURN OF THE CHESTNUT TREES

- SURVIVAL KITS
- RAISING EARTHWORMS
- LLAMAS GUARDING SHEEP
- USING & STORING WHEAT
- COUNTRY AUCTIONS
- THE FULLY-INFORMED JURY

Note from the publisher

The Vita-Mix contest

Ask self-sufficient people what their most useful kitchen item is and many of them will respond "a Vita-Mix." The Vita-Mix ad on the back cover of this issue will give you a good idea why they are so useful.

So we thought we'd give a Vita-Mix away in a contest that should also help us boost subscriptions. The Vita-Mix retails for about $500.

To be eligible for the contest, you must be a current subscriber. All subscribers will be automatically included in the computerized drawing that will take place March 1, 1993, so you do not need to send in a contest form. New **subscribers must get their paid subscriptions to us by the last day of February** so Lenie has time to input them into our database for the drawing.

Unlike other drawings where you are competing against hundreds of thousands of contest entrants, you will be competing against well under 10,000 people here. Although we print 65,000 magazines, our current subscriber list numbers about 6,000, because most of our magazines are sold as single-issue sales to non-subscribers at the newsstand. This contest, of course, is an attempt to convince those newsstand buyers to subscribe.

Printing and mail screw-ups

About 40 people have told us they did not get their Issue No. 17. We don't know what happened, but we are blaming the labeling machine of our Wisconsin printer who mails each issue from their in-plant post office. If you did not get Issue No. 17, or if you ever fail to get an issue, please notify us and we'll send you another.

Issue No. 18 also had a problem. Many subscribers had the wrong "expiration date" printed on their labels. This time we're sure the culprit was the printer's labeling machine. It mis-cut many labels so that instead of the "expiration date" being printed at the top of the label, it took the next subscriber's "expiration date" and printed it at the bottom of the previous subscriber's mailing label.

It doesn't end there. Several subscribers have complained to us that their magazine covers are torn beyond recognition when they get them in the mail. The photo on this page was sent to us by an irate subscriber who canceled his subscription. Please don't get angry; ask us for another copy of the issue. To guard against this in the future, we're considering putting a "plain wrap" paper cover on the outside of issues mailed to subscribers.

Mailed him a brick

To top off the mail problems, the other day I got a "postage due" notice in the magazine's mail box. So I trotted down to the post office, waited in a long line, and paid 27 cents for the "postage due" letter which was sent by a guy from Winnabow, North Carolina.

It was a form letter that began:

"Dear Friend:

"Check the envelope this letter came in. Notice the postage . . . IT'S ONLY 2 CENTS. That's right!! This letter was mailed to you by **FIRST CLASS** mail for only $0.02 postage! But that's not the best part . . .

"NOW YOU TOO CAN SEND ALL YOUR LETTERS VIA FIRST CLASS MAIL FOR ONLY 2 CENTS EACH!!"

He goes on to ask me to send him $15 so I can learn how.

I, of course, was not amused. When I got back to the office I mailed the guy a brick with a 2 cent stamp on it.

Independence 2000

There's a new show coming up for self-reliant people. It's called "Independence 2000" and will be held February 19, 20, and 21 at the Eugene Convention Center in Eugene, Oregon. We will be there and recommend you attend also. The show has an ad on page 17 of this issue, and it contains a $2 discount pass. It's the first time the show will be held, but I predict it won't be the last.

Show promoters in other parts of the country should take a good look at all the preparedness and self sufficiency shows that are taking place in the West. There is an independence movement going on in this country that is not being talked about in the mass media. Many people are fed up with the erosion of their personal independence and want to return to a more self reliant, less Government-regulated lifestyle. I think it's time we had a self reliance show somewhere other than the West.

Fully-informed jury article

While we're on the topic of independence, I'd like to bring your attention to the "Fully-informed jury" article on page 30 and the "Guilty by default" article on page 61. Both have strong themes that have to do with the erosion of our personal independence over the past several decades. They are "eye openers." Δ

COMMENTARY

My View

Taking care of yourself

With a new Democratic administration taking over in Washington, D.C., I'm just sitting here at my desk waiting for the nation's economy to come apart at the seams. I probably won't have to wait long.

Not that the Republicans were doing such a bad job of pouring the nation's wealth down the toilet with one hand while they marched us into the "New World Order" with the other. I just figure the Democrats will accelerate the downward fall because they promised the moon to just about everyone and now have a free-spending Democratic Congress to back up a free-spending President. Not to mention a Vice-President who has some billion dollar ideas about how to fix what he sees as major environmental problems.

But what the heck. Things could be worse. I could be old and sick and never having done what I dreamed of doing, or I could be young and dying of cancer and never have the chance to live my dreams. Or I could be starving in Somalia or hooked on crack in a New York City ghetto. Or I could even lose my appetite for Guinness Stout, which is every Irishman's living dream. Yes, things could be much worse.

"You worry too much," MacDougal tells me. "That's why you've got those bumps."

Those bumps are the red blotches that appear on my calves, sides, and upper arms with increasing frequency as this magazine grows. "Stress bumps," the doctors say and prescribe steroids, mild tranquilizers, exercise, and Transcendental Meditation. One of my neighbors has disowned me as a devil-worshipper because I have agreed to try Transcendental Meditation.

MacDougal's right. There's nothing to worry about. Whether it's Democrats or Republicans, Commies or Fascists, the country's heading into a deeper Recession and nothing will stop it; it's worldwide. So why should I worry? The Republicans were lucky Bush was defeated; now the Democrats will take the blame for the looming Depression, and maybe someone with rational ideas—like the Libertarians—will win next time around.

So what to do as we wait out the economic desolation that is just around the corner?

"Don't worry about it," MacDougal says. "Take care of yourself. If everyone did that there'd be no Recession to worry about. At least not for those individuals."

He's right, of course. Recessions and Depressions visit people who are dependent on Government for their well being. They are much less harsh on people who are self reliant, such as many of the readers of this magazine.

Government is not the answer to our problems, no matter who is in the White House or in our state capitols. At its best, Government can protect us from foreign enemies and domestic crime. At its worst Government is a large

Dave Duffy

bureaucracy that meddles into every little aspect of our lives, controlling prices, implementing regulations that hamper job-creating businesses, meddling in the private affairs of the citizen under the pretense of doing something good for society or for the environment.

Government does not generate wealth or any type of products that would benefit anyone. While private individuals try to create products and provide needed services to their fellow man, Government taxes everything it can think of to feed its unproductive bureaucracy and pay for unwise domestic schemes like price supports and unwise foreign schemes such as armed interventions.

Government wants you to become dependent upon it because that is their power base. Without the poor, the oppressed minorities, the floudering educational system, the drug problem, and the economic downturn, the Government would have little to do. Government likes all these problems, they help create them with misguided policies, and they give politicians seeking election something they can promise to fix. But, of course, Government will never fix anything. It never has and never will. It doesn't know how.

The only time anything ever gets fixed in this country is when people do it themselves. The only time the poor get out of poverty is when the individual does it himself; the Government, in fact, is in the "poor" business and needs the poor to remain that way so the bureaucrats who administer to the poor can keep their jobs.

And the only way the people in this country are going to survive this looming Depression, then crawl our way out of it, is if they do it themselves. The Clinton Government has already planned new taxes for businesses and the rich. Those taxes will simply put a lot of small businesses out of business and dry up the investment capital the rich normally invest in start-up businesses.

So depend upon Government to do about as much for you in the future as they have done for you in the past—nothing! Depend on yourself, not Government. You'll have much less to worry about, and you'll help the country as a whole because you won't be one of the voices calling for more Government control to solve problems Government never has and never will solve. Δ

SELF SUFFICIENCY

How to make your own "grab-and-go" survival kits

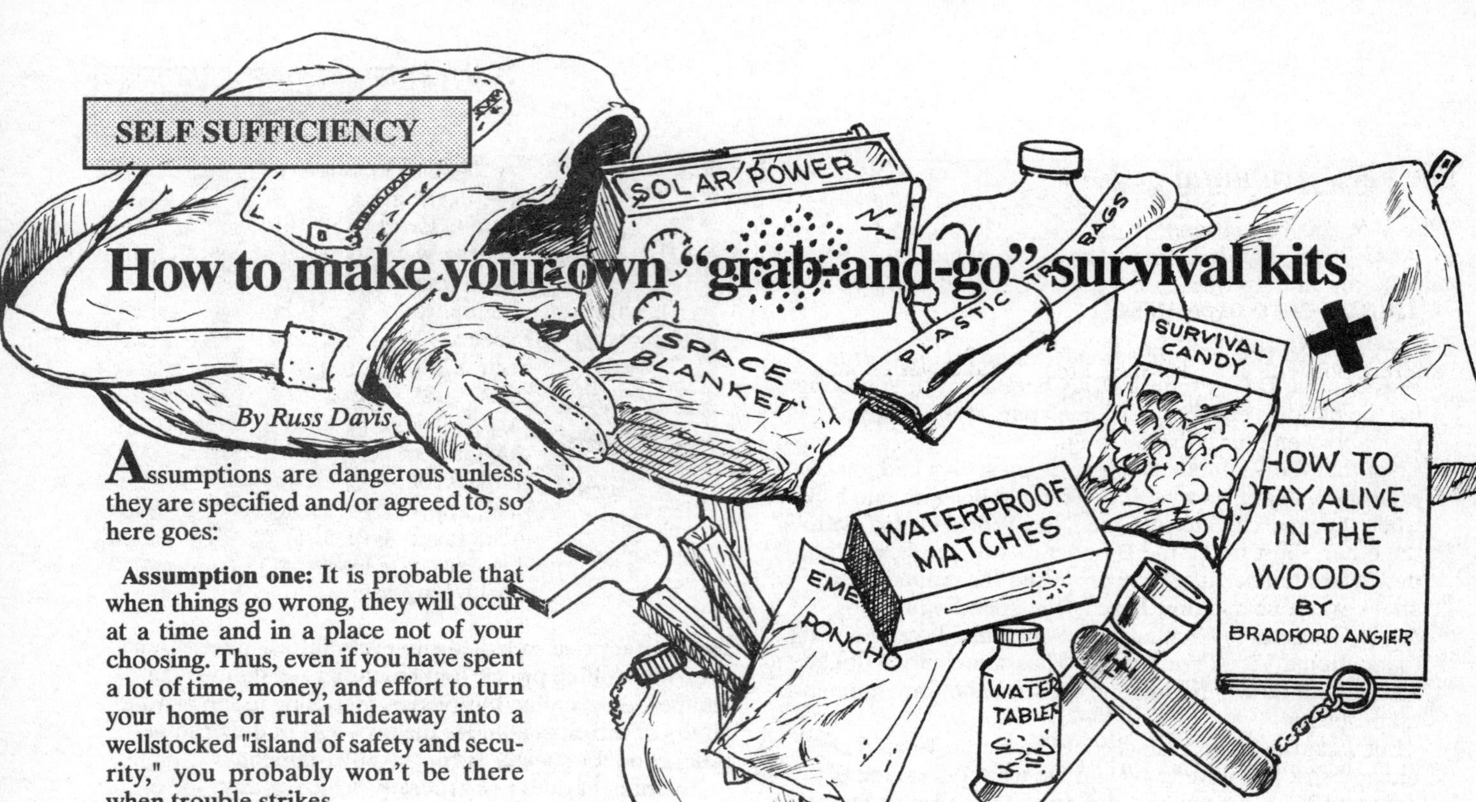

By Russ Davis

Assumptions are dangerous unless they are specified and/or agreed to, so here goes:

Assumption one: It is probable that when things go wrong, they will occur at a time and in a place not of your choosing. Thus, even if you have spent a lot of time, money, and effort to turn your home or rural hideaway into a wellstocked "island of safety and security," you probably won't be there when trouble strikes.

Assumption two: To get from the area of trouble, danger, or emergency **where you are** to an area of safety **where you want to be** – such as your survival stash/hideaway or to a place not threatened by the emergency – you need to have "stuff" instantly available to you to make it there.

Assumption three: Anyone can minimize the threat of such an emergency by some fairly simple prudent **planning, preparation, and practice** – in that order. The extra time and resources devoted to these additional measures may well save lives.

Define the threats

Define the threats. This requires time and heavy thinking. Don't rush it. Don't be afraid to rethink it over and over again. Call them "threats," "emergencies," "scenarios," "potential dangers," or whatever term you like. They all describe the same thing: situations and circumstances which, based on geography, climate, and a zillion other things, could threaten you.

Examples: urban riots, earthquakes, tornadoes, being caught in a winter blizzard while traveling, crashlanding somewhere in the boonies, a nuclear power plant going critical, getting lost while out in search of the elusive mushroom.

The list goes on and on. Your first job is to develop your own list of potential threats. Once established, this list will determine specifically what you will need to meet each threat.

Put it all down on paper. Analyze it. Revise it. Talk with others who face similar potential threats. Do your homework. Put the information down in order: threat, my response options, what I would need during this time, and finally a column for miscellaneous remarks and comments. Paper is cheap. Give yourself lots of room. Don't try to cram it together or you may well fail to see things clearly and to make all necessary notations.

Let's consider how this plan might look. Take one potential emergency for most of the North American continent: **an earthquake**. The earth does a Rhumba along a fault line. Where will you be? Broadly speaking, there are two possibilities: Either you are at home or you're not because you're off driving somewhere – shopping, working, etc. Your plan should consider both possibilities and the options for each. Below is a sample plan:

Sample Plan

Threat	Potential responses	Needs
Earthquake	A. If at home	
	1. if safe, stay	-rely on existing home survival stash
	2. danger of aftershocks or extensive structural damage: Live temporarily in tent in back yard, weather/circumstances permitting	-all salvageable stuff, **plus** tent, bedding, cooking gear, and access to water/sanitation
	3. evacuate to safe area	-take full grab-and-go kit
	B. if traveling at the time	-car grab-and-go kit (it's always in the trunk)
	1. return to home or 2. go to area of safety	

The key—grab-and-go kits

The plan above mentions "grab-and-go" kits. In its simplest form, it's a water bottle and a couple of Snicker bars dropped into your fanny pack (probably on top of your canister of CapStun, police whistle, kleenex, etc., etc.!) when you go jogging in the morning. Primitive, but—given the circumstances—probably adequate to meet your needs.

Of course, this is **not** a comprehensive kit to meet **all** potential needs. For that, you'd end up with a 60-pound pack on your back stuffed with everything from a snakebite kit to extra ammo for your AR-15, which you would also be toting along just in case you had to fight your way through an Iraqi commando raid on the popcorn stand in the middle of the park! Get serious! The key words here have to be "prudent" and "reasonable".

Grab-and-go kits are as different as their missions, yet they all share one thing in common: each contains a carefully chosen assortment of items selected to get the job done. Broadly speaking, there are two main missions: short term and long term. An example of short term might be the aftermath of a disaster in which the situation can be expected to be stabilized and/or help can arrive from the outside within a maximum period of, say, one to four days afterwards. The recent earthquakes and civil riots in California are typical examples. The other type, long term, means precisely that. Grab-and-go kit considerations for this contingency anticipate the need to be self-supporting for at least one to two weeks, perhaps as long as three to six months. An example of this might be crash landing an airplane in an unsettled area, or—as recently happened in Florida and Louisana following Hurricane Andrew—making do for a longer period after your home and livelihood has been destroyed.

Beyond being mission-specific, kits also can be configured according to your pocketbook and/or desired comfort levels. Recently, several commercial packagers have begun to market so-called "**72-hour survival kits**." These run the gambit from a simple kit contained in a couple of cans which you could stick in your pockets all the way up to some big deluxe kits which come complete with little stoves and other niceties. They range in price from a under $15 to well over 10 times that! You pays yer money and yuh takes yer choice.

Commercial kits are one thing. A home-rolled, mission-specific kit is quite something else. For one thing, making your own guarantees it would contain only the items you feel are important. Secondly, it will cost you less, probably a lot less.

The self-assembled "72-hour kit"

For short term disaster planning, a 72-hour kit seems to be the minimum to consider. Practically speaking, this kind of kit would fit into a single container and be available for instant use, should it be necessary. Prudently, it should be with you, wherever you are, ready to use. That means, for example, having one in each vehicle you own plus one for every other vehicle you might drive. Say you are an over- the-road truckdriver. In addition to a 72-hour kit in your personal vehicle, you should also have one which you stow in your rig.

If this sounds like too much effort or money, then you can get by with one kit, as long as you make sure that you always transfer the kit from vehicle to vehicle every time you drive. A bit of a hassle perhaps, but easily done.

A 72-hour kit takes little room, but provides **big** insurance for the unexpected. Everything listed below (except the water) should fit quite nicely into a small cardboard box or similar container. In fact, if you are a good organizer and packer, the basic 72-hour kit will fit into a good multi-pocketed fanny pack. I have one which I made using one of those Winchester day-glo pink multipacs that I bought at K-Mart for under 10 bucks! The fanny pack approach also has some distinct advantages as a little "wear-around-the-waist-just-in-case-you-get-lost-while-hunting-mushrooms" insurance.

It is my practice to keep my kit inside a 10" x 22" x 16" rectangular plastic storage container with a snap-on lid. (This is pretty much one of the standard sizes of such containers available at any K-Mart, Walmart, Target, etc.) For extra protection, I run heavy-sealing tape around the edge. You could just as easily use a cardboard box and enclose the contents inside a plastic garbage sack. For years, my grab-and-go kit was kept inside a garbage sack-lined cardboard apple box which my grocer was only too happy to give me. (I particularly like apple boxes, since they are very sturdy and have a slip-over lid. The main thing is you want something to keep everything together and protected from moisture and getting banged around by all the other stuff you throw into the trunk. The amounts given below are minimums for one person.

- **1 inexpensive nylon backpack.** One of those "$3.99 and up "K-Mart back-to-school specials is fine. The object here is to have something which holds everything else and is tote-able. Lots of zippered or velcroed pockets is a big plus. This will serve as the container for everything else when you actually have to use your kit.
- **1 copy of your favorite "survival" guide**. Mine is How to Stay Alive in the Woods by Bradford Angier. It's filled with no-nonsense information. Even the title is reassuring. There are many other good books on the

market. You could do a lot worse than the Boy Scout Field Book. It's well-written and a bargain at the price. (currently $7.95) Choose one, but choose carefully.

- **3 large (33-gallon) garbage sacks.** (Glad's Sheer Strength brand is far and away the best in my book.) These can be used to hold things, catch water, act as emergency shelter, even serve as a sort of poncho if you cut a head hole.
- **1 police whistle** (for signaling)
- **1 compass.** A Silva "Boy Scout" type is good. A pathfinder style is even better. Whatever model, know how to use it, Bub!
- **1 mess kit**, Boy Scout style or, even better, one of those German army surplus three-piece kits now readily available.
- **1 canteen** nested in a GI metal cup
- **1 bottle water purification tablets** (Halazone, iodine, or whatever)
- **1 straw-type water purifying filter**
- **1 three-piece nested steel knife, fork, and spoon sets.**
- **2 butane lighters** (so you can start a fire by flicking your Bic)
- **2 packages of waterproof matches or strike- anywhere matches.** Double packaged in zip-lock bags. Damp matches are as worthless as a Congressional promise. (Matches plus fire starters will get your fire going when it's too cold or wet for a Butane lighter.)
- **1 tube of fire starter ribbon or package of military Trioxane tabs**
- **2 (or more) mylar space blankets**
- **1 piece of 6-8 mil plastic sheeting**, about 8 feet square (for tenting, shelter. etc.)
- **50 ft. nylon 550 parachute cord** (or something similar)
- **1 plastic emergency poncho,** preferably in bright yellow or orange
- **1 multi-bladed Boy Scout or Swiss Army knife**
- **1 sheath knife w/sharpening stone**
- **1 "barbed wire" coiled saw**
- **1 dual signaling mirror** (or compact mirror)
- **1 pair of cotton work gloves**
- **1 zip-lock vitamin pack containing:**

  6 one-per-day multi-vitamin tablets
  12-50 mg B-complex tablets
  24 1000 mg vitamin C tablets
  This is actually a 6 day supply. Label: "1 multi daily, 1 B- complex 2 x daily, 1 C 4 x daily." This is a good anti-stress and anti-fatigue regimen which you will need during emergency conditions.
- **4 pkgs. presweetened Koolaide** (to take the tang out of the water
- **1 12 oz. box granola breakfast cereal** (you pick the flavor) **or** 1 6 oz. tin of nuts (almonds, peanuts, cashews, or mixed) **plus** 1-16 oz. box raisins
- **1 16 oz. pkg. of M&M's plain** (nuts may turn rancid more quickly)
- **10 tea bags or packets of instant coffee**
- **1 tube or small jar of bouillon cubes**
- **8 oz. package of hard candy**

Alternative food list

You may replace the above with:

- **2 six packs of candy bars** such as Hersheys or Snickers or 12 Tootsie rolls (even better because they don't melt!)
- **1 lb. homemade trail corn mix** (Heat 1 pound corn meal in a heavy skillet, stirring frequently until it is lightly browned. When it is cooled, add 1/2 cup each of granulated and brown sugar, mixing well together. Maple sugar and/or some malted milk powder make this even more palatable. Store in zip-lock bags. This is a real tummy- filler. One heaping tablespoon downed with 8-16 oz. water will swell in the stomach and cut any hunger pangs.)
- **Or an assortment of military surplus MRE brownies, oatmeal bars, cakes, chocolate-covered cookies, etc.** These are readily available, will last for years, and on an item-for- item basis, don't cost much more than commercial candy bars. (No, they don't taste as good as a Snicker, but the idea is to survive, not to pig out.)
- **1 small first aid kit** – Put the following inside a zip-lock:

  1 triangular bandage (substitute a boy scout neckerchief)
  6 bandaids
  3 4"x4" gauze compresses
  1 tube triple ointment
  1 bottlette merthiolate or iodine
  2 scalpel or X-Acto knife blades (well-wrapped!)
  1 small tube sun screen/lip balm
  24 Percogesic or Ibuprofen tablets
  4 Imodium A-D tablets (in case you get diarrhea)
  4 Duclox tablets (in case you don't!)
  1 2" Ace (rolled elastic) bandage
  an adequate supply of any medications you normally need
- **1 small "possibles bag"** with the following inside a zip-lock:

  4 sewing needles
  2 paper bobbins of sturdy thread
  1 assortment of buttons
  6-8 safety pins, assorted sizes
  1 coil (50 feet) 3 strand .015 dia. nylon-coated wire leader cable
  3 long-burning votive candles
  1 small bar of soap (Ivory is more versatile than some others)
  1 toothbrush plus a tiny tube of toothpaste (Wait until you get caught out in the Boonies someday and you'll thank me for this one!)
  2-3 purse-sized packages of tissues (or a partial roll of toilet paper, flattened down)
  1 small roll "50 mile-per-hour" tape (substitute duct tape)

In addition to the kit itself, you should stow some water in your vehicle. (You should **always** carry water in the car. It is prudent practice to carry a gallon of premixed water/antifreeze, too, just in case of radiator troubles, but then that's another article, right?)

- **1 2.5 gallon plastic water jug w/spigot filled with water.** Add to this a couple drops of ordinary chlorine bleach or water purification tablets. The water will need to be changed once a month or so to keep it potable. For the cost conscious, you could save old chlorine bleach bottles and use them. Water with a slightly bleachy taste is not great drinking, but it's a lot better than no water.

Optional items

(Nice to have, space and budget permitting)

- **1 small pocket size, spiral-bound note pad**
- **2 wooden pencils**
- **detailed topographical maps of your area**
- **1 magnesium "match"**
- **1 small magnifying lens** (to start fires, help locate slivers, etc.)
- **1 Esbit Boy Scout folding pocket stove with heating tabs** would also be very nice. They are cheap, light weight, and can cook up a cup of hot brew pretty fast.
- **1 machete** – Choose a South American short heavy-bladed one and you've got a multi-purpose implement with which you can clear brush, chop trees, dig holes, and generally make life more bearable. It can replace a saw, axe, brush hook, and who knows what else.
- **1 small flashlight** with extra batteries and bulb
- **1-2 pairs heavy socks** (wool is best or cotton)
- **1-2 pairs of extra shoelaces**
- **1 hat or cap**
- If you are a smoker, **a small supply of tobacco** (You'll have enough to worry about without going through withdrawal, too!)

Changing the "72-hour kit" into the "7 to 30-day kit"

Changing the scope of the 72-hour grab-and-go kit into something more suitable for an extended time of up to 30 days (and beyond) is simple. You already have all the of basics in the 72-hour kit so all you have to do is add all the items on the options list above plus a few extras. Like my ole mom used to say when unexpected company dropped by at meal time: "Guess I'd better add a little more water to the soup!")

Beyond a couple of days, you need to equip yourself with more substantial bedding and shelter, additional food, and a few other supplies. You also need to beef up your first aid kit and possibles bag. Here are some suggestions.

- **1 pair coveralls** or other change of durable clothing (plus whatever other clothes seem appropriate)
- **1 stocking cap**
- **1 GI style nylon poncho**
- **1 9' x 12' nylon reinforced tarp** would be nice
- **double or even triple your vitamin supplies**
- **1 collapsible Swedish camp saw** with 2-3 extra blades
- **1 folding GI shovel**
- **First aid kit.** Triple everything in the basic plus add:

  1 tube antiseptic-anesthetic eye ointment

  1 pair tweezers

  1 bottlette oil of cloves (for toothache)

  1 thermometer

  1 chapstick

  1 pair pointed scissors

  1-2 large military carlisle style wound compresses (individually-wrapped sanitary napkins work fine!)

  1 bottle insect repellent

  1 tube cortizone rash/itch ointment

  2-3 curved surgical needles with ligatures attached to close stitch up wounds. (If your pharmacist gives you any static about these, just go to any farm store. They are easily obtainable in the veterinary section.)

  1 pair mosquito nose forceps to use when suturing

  10 day supply each of a general antibiotic and a strong oral analgesic (prescription items – ask your doctor.) Also ask your physician about other meds. Don't forget a supply of any regular prescription you are currently taking.

  1 squeeze bottle of a cleansing/disinfectant

  3-8 oz. table salt (use as a gargle, disinfectant, to remove leeches, as a dentifrice, etc. It also can flavor any game or fish you catch.)

  1 snake bite kit

  1 small (half-pint) flask of brandy
- **Possibles bag** – Add:

  an additional bar of soap

  another roll of toilet paper

  1 roll 1/2 inch filament tape

  1 pair of pliers

  1 small tube fast-drying, all-purpose adhesive

  1 small metal file (to sharpen knives, etc.)

  1 piece of bee's wax

  2 oz. powdered rotenone (available from any garden store.) It is a natural insecticide, but mix it into a quiet stream or lake and it'll stupefy and/or kill fish. To give you some idea of how potent it is, 1 oz. properly used in a stream 25 feet wide will zap every fish downstream for at least a quarter of a mile! It deprives them of oxygen, but they are perfectly safe to eat. Works best in quiet waters, not rapidly flowing streams. Mix into a paste before you pour into the water.

  1 assortment of 10-15 fish hooks

  1-2 bobbers

  5-10 sinkers

  50 feet 12 lb. test line

  1 or more spinners or spoons. Red Devil spoons work well.

  1 trot line (25-50 feet of stout line with 3 foot lines and hooks

at approximately 3 foot intervals. These can be purchased pre-made or fabricated by you. They are great for extensive fishing.)

20-30 feet of aluminum foil (for cooking, protection, etc.)

3-4 additional stubby candles

3-4 horse blanket safety pins

- **extra food** – as much as your container will hold in addition to whatever else you have included. Choose "iron rations," that is, foods which have long shelf life, are fairly "dense" (pack a lot of calories for their size and weight), and which can withstand the rigors of temperatures, etc. Candy, nuts, dried fruits, are all good examples of this. This is especially true if they come sealed in vacuum packs. Under some circumstances, other good choices would include caramels, crackers, RyKrisp, peanut butter, cheese spreads, and canned tuna and sardines. I would also consider a box of sugar cubes or perhaps a plastic squeeze bottle of honey. Check out the shelves of your local supermarket, keeping the rules of caloric denseness and durability in mind. Another good choice is to buy surplus MRE's. They can be purchased at any gun show, Preparedness Show, or by mail.
- **Weapon(s)** – for protection/foraging. Whatever you feel comfortable with. You might feel a slingshot is adequate, or then again, you might want something a little more sophisticated.
- **A one person tent plus sleeping bag** may stretch the concept a bit, but would be extremely prudent especially in more isolated areas and/or less friendly climates.

With all of these additions, your small cardboard box-sized 72 hour kit has now just about doubled in size. But that's still reasonable.

Well, there you have it. The fixings for both a short term 72-hour grab-and-go kit and a long term save-yer-buns version. Of course, you are free to add and supplement the list, but – at the risk of sounding a little conceited – don't delete anything unless you have a damned good reason.

A final note: Since I live in the snow belt, during winter, in addition to a 72-hour kit, I always throw a couple of blankets and extra food in the trunk along with a shovel, chains, tow cable, jumper cables, etc. Yep, winter out on the plains is nothing to mess with.

(Russ Davis has spent more than 50 years camping, hiking, canoeing, and hunting. A family therapist and clinical hynotherapist, he is also an Iowa Law Enforcement Academy-certified instructor and is active in teaching and training police officers. His widely-varied teaching experiences range from boy scout camp wilderness cookery to graduate level courses for counselors. He has authored a number of books including two outdoor cook books and several technical books for law enforcement to train tactical teams and hostage negotiators. He also writes for police, gun, and outdoors magazines. He has a Bachelor's degree in foreign languages, a Master's in Counseling, and a Ph.D. in Counseling Psychology.) Δ

Lonesome Butterfly

Lonesome, lethargic old butterfly,
Why do you continue to linger?
Don't you know what is coming?
You'll die in the cold, I fear.

Look, see the clear autumn sky,
Shouldn't your bright-patterned wings
Start climbing the chill-crisped air?
The frost comes at night, like a thief!

—Or do you deliberately barter
This last chance for your escape
To remain where you playfully fluttered,
By the tulips in the dazzling light?

Richard Lee Rose
British Columbia, Canada

A BHM Writer's Profile

Anita Evangelista had been writing for over a decade when she and her family made their move from Los Angeles to the deep Ozark backwoods 10 years ago. Previous sales to such places as *GQ* and *The Los Angeles Times* had been financially rewarding, she says, but life was missing that "something".

Evangelista, her husband, and two kids finally found that "something" on a farm in the hinterlands. It was the same kind of painful change that many back-to-the-landers undergo, and it was, she says, "the best thing that could have happened to us. We converted to self-sufficiency with a vengeance."

Through the years, the Evangelistas have raised chickens and other foul, rabbits, goats, sheep, collies, hogs, horses, and a cow. They've made their own cheese, wine, bread, and shoes; spun wool and woven rugs. They learned car repair, plumbing, electrical wiring, and solar energy applications. "I believe we did everything except learn to tap dance," she says.

Evangelista continues to write, with three published books behind her and two more in the works, and numerous articles in many livestock and farm magazines. Husband Nick also writes. Both kids are homeschooled teenagers, and, she says, "You couldn't ask to know nicer people."

The forest king is returning

By Robert L. Williams

At the turn of the twentieth century, the uncontested king of the forests in America was the chestnut tree, a tree so large and so incredibly varied in its uses that no other tree in the nation could rival it in terms of sheer beauty or as a natural resource.

While not the largest tree in the land, the American chestnut was big enough that the trunk of a single tree could yield enough lumber to fill a box car completely with superior grade timbers and boards. The chestnut tree was soft enough that it could be cut with ease but strong enough that it could be used anywhere oak was needed.

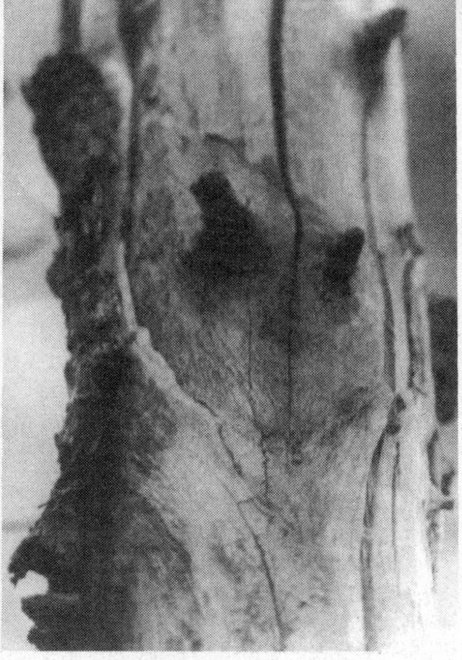

Dead chestnut tree shows canker growth remnants that destroyed the cambium layer and prevented nutrition from the soil through roots to the upper parts of the tree.

It was light enough that it could be handled with relative ease and yet so decay resistant that it could be used as fence posts and would last for half a century or longer in moist soil. It was the equal of the redwood in that it could withstand heavy loads and could serve as football bleacher seats, railroad ties, trestle timbers, and telegraph poles.

The wood was highly prized for making musical instruments, and chestnut furniture was valued highly all over the country. It was also used for plywood and wall paneling, among its dozens of other important roles in American life.

Every fall the trees yielded huge burrs, some of them nearly as large as a tennis ball, and inside the burrs was a delightfully delicious nut so much in demand that entire boxcar loads of nuts were shipped to large cities all over the continent. Songs and poems were written about chestnuts, and countless Christmas and other holiday turkeys and geese were stuffed with chestnuts.

Every spring the trees bore large creamy white blossoms that made entire mountainsides look as if a sudden late season storm had dumped inches of snow on the ridges. Much taller than most of the other forest trees, the chestnut totally dominated the landscape throughout the year.

In winter wild turkeys, deer, squirrels, bears, and other woodland creatures feasted on the nuts, which were among the favorite foods of the passenger pigeons that were so numerous that when they roosted in the trees at night the weight of the thousands of birds broke limbs from the strongest trees.

Then, without warning, tragedy hit.

In 1904 a shipment of nursery stock arrived in the New York harbor, and a tiny spore-like growth was imported, unseen, into the country on the small

Chinese chestnut trees that were to be used as decorations for Long Island streets.

Before anyone was aware of the problem, the fungus spread to native American trees, and during that first year the chestnut blight spread over a radius of nearly fifty miles.

There was no known way to stop it, and each year the blight killed thousands upon thousands of trees. Soon the bleached white trunks of dead chestnuts made the formerly beautiful mountains look like enormous graveyards.

By 1950 virtually every American chestnut tree was dead or dying, with no hope in sight. The roots of trees were not damaged by the blight, but as soon as new seedlings appeared, by the time the tree was one or two years old the blight would strike and cause a canker growth on the trunk of the tree. Within weeks the canker would cause the bark to split and the cambium layer to deteriorate.

The tree limbs and leaves received no nutrition from the soil and roots, and quickly the upper part of the tree died, leaving the roots to try vainly again and again to send shoots upward only to die as the fungus struck relentlessly.

Then, several years ago, Ted Harrison, of Mooresboro, North Carolina, was walking in his woods one day and saw some of the huge chestnut burrs lying on the ground. He looked upward and saw the limbs of a chestnut tree that was estimated to be between thirty and forty years old.

A closer examination of the tree revealed that the blight had attacked it years earlier and somehow, miraculously, one day, the tree managed to "cure" itself of the disease that was so much more virulent than Dutch Elm disease had been.

Almost at the same time another tree was discovered in another part of North Carolina, and this tree, too, had been able to cure itself.

Immediately volunteers of the American Chestnut Foundation rushed to the scenes of the discovery and began to try to cross-pollinate the two trees. Previously, the trees had not been able to produce nuts, only empty burrs, because no pollinators were near enough to serve to fertilize the blossoms.

Larry Nolen holds empty chestnut burrs. No nuts developed because the tree had no nearby pollinators.

Ted Harrison shows the tree that cured itself and which might be the key to saving the American chestnut trees. When researchers learn how this one immunized itself, they can help others do the same.

Meanwhile, the American Chestnut Foundation, with offices and research farms in Virginia, Vermont, and other parts of the country, had begun to work furiously toward finding a way to defeat the blight and restore the chestnut trees, which once accounted for 25 per cent of all trees from Maine to Georgia, to the forests.

In 1983 the foundation was given a research farm in the Virginia community of Meadowview, and the farm has 3,000 chestnut trees in the ground. The purpose of the research is to develop a strain of disease-resistant trees through hybridization. The original time frame was thirty years.

Because of the remarkable discoveries at present, that time frame has been reduced to 5 to 8 years, with breeding completed in 15 to 25 years.

The New York Chapter of the Foundation has received an $80,000 grant to pursue genetic engineering at the Syracuse College of Environmental Science and Forestry. Grants have also been made to the Lyndhurst

Larry Nolen holds a branch from an immunized tree found forty miles away. He is attempting to pollinate the Harrison tree artificially.

Foundation of Chattanooga and the Laurel Foundation of Pittsburgh.

A new method for discovering or detecting genes for blight-resistant chestnut trees, called RAPD (pronounced "rapid") for short, is Random Amplification of Polymorphic Deoxyribonucleic acid. This is being used in the screening against blight susceptible plants and to aid in the development of second-and third-generation hybrids, a cross between American and Chinese chestnut trees.

As early as 1993 Dr. Fred Hebard at the Meadowview facility will begin producing chestnut trees that are fifteen-sixteenth American chestnut and one-sixteenth Chinese chestnut. Within ten years the first completely blight- resistant trees are scheduled to be produced.

The next steps will culminate, it is hoped, in the renewed establishment of American chestnut trees in forests all up and down the eastern states as well as many western states.

The Chinese chestnut is an orchard tree and cannot grow tall enough to become a forest tree. Its upper limbs will never be high enough to receive the light needed for proper growth. And while the Chinese chestnut fruit is somewhat larger than American varieties, the taste is not equal to the original chestnut of American forests.

At least as importantly, the Chinese chestnut is not valued highly as a lumber tree, while the American chestnut was one of the most valued timber trees in the world. And it will be again, if the Chestnut Foundation can continue its work.

Persons interested in having a part in saving the American chestnut tree can join the American Chestnut Foundation at Post Office Box 6057 in Morgantown, West Virginia 26506. This is a non-profit organization and dues are tax deductible.

Seed kits and planting instructions for planting the pure American chestnut seeds (not a blight-resistant type) are available through the foundation. Primary and secondary public school classes are being provided with similar seed kits so that students can be made aware of the problems and possible solutions facing the public and the private sector in the fight to save the trees.

The foundation urges persons who are familiar with the trees to inform them of locations and status of existing trees in the wild.

"I learned about chestnut trees on my grandfather's lap," said Larry Nolen, one of the volunteers who works with the foundation and who remains ready to leap into his car to pursue any leads that may help find the solution to the problem. "Every story he told somehow worked its way around to a chestnut tree. I'd like to be able to tell my grandchildren the same stories. But if there are no chestnut trees for them to see, what is the point of the story?"

Nolen adds, "We have lost the passenger pigeons that once numbered in the billions. Now every one of them is gone from the earth. We don't want the same thing to happen to the chestnut tree, which is one of the finest friends in Nature that the human race has ever known. It is worth the effort it takes to save it." Δ

Nolen and Harrison examine a seedling growing within 10 yards of the adult tree. The seedling has already been hit by the blight and nothing can be done to save it, but the larger tree nearby, with a circumference of 42 inches, somehow resisted the blight that has killed millions of other chestnut trees.

Insulation and vapor barriers

By Martin Harris

Houses in this part of the country (Vermont) date from the early 1800's, and most of them are insulated. Not with Fiberglas, but brick. My point is that insulating buildings against outside temperature extremes is nothing new. Today the materials are new and some of the problems are new, but the principles are unchanged from what they were when ancient Babylonians made their mud-brick houses thick enough to store daytime solar heat gain against the cold desert nights.

It's not my intent here to extol brick as an insulating material: it would take about nine feet of thickness in a brick wall to equal the insulating value of modern wood frame construction with Fiberglas insulation between the studs. It is my intent to take a close look at what's been happening in recent years as Americans, responding to energy costs, have raised building insulation to a high science and have created buildings so well insulated that a range of new problems has surfaced.

Today, of course, the insulation of choice is Fiberglas, not the brick or sawdust or newspapers or hay used by our New England forebears. It works by creating untold millions of tiny trapped-air spaces, thus resisting the transmission of heat that would occur if the surface of the warm area (usually inside, at least around here in the North Country) were separated by only a single thickness of some dense construction material from the outside ambient (usually lower) temperature.

Its effectiveness at resisting heat transfer is measured in terms of R values. Fiberglas doesn't have the highest R-value around – at a rating of 3.12 per inch of thickness (a 3 and 1/2 inch-thick batt has an R-value of 10.92) it's less than half as effective as isocyanurate foam with an R-value of 7.2 per inch of thickness. But Fiberglas is relatively inexpensive, fireproof, easy to handle, manufactured to fit conventional wood frame construction, even available as a blow-in material; no on-site chemical mixing and spraying, no worries about toxic fumes or bio-degrading over time.

Isocyanurate is a lot more expensive and difficult to handle – indeed it's prohibited for residential construction in some states because of health-hazard fears – but it's ideal for applications like refrigerators and high-tech construction where space is at a premium.

Most of the non-high tech insulation materials–Fiberglas, cellulose, beadboard, and so on – are in the 3 to 4 range for R value. There's a slightly less effective product called vermiculite – a kind of shredded mineral-which rates at 2 to 3. Vermiculite and Fiberglas are fire-proof, the others not so unless specially treated. Fiberglas and beadboard are structural, in the sense that they can be placed in upright openings and not collapse to the bottom; the others are pourable or blowable, and therefore will flow or settle to some extent. All can be used, some more easily than others, to insulate housing to modern standards: R-19 in the walls, R-38 in the cap or attic.

Americans, responding to energy costs, have raised building insulation to a high science and have created buildings so well insulated that a range of new problems has surfaced.

These high R-value numbers are part of the reason why we now have new problems associated with insulation that we didn't have years ago when R-values rarely got into double digits. The other part comes from new construction material practices, all of which combine to insure that housing is more air-tight (less drafty, if you like) than it used to be.

Buildings used to be sheathed in 6-inch boards under the finish siding; now it's 4x8 sheets of plywood or waferboard. Finish roofing used to go on over 1x3 nailing strips 4 inches apart; now a solid deck is the norm. Windows and doors were installed with an air-space between the finish millwork and the rough-stud opening; now that opening is carefully filled with insulating caulk.

All this technology change means one thing: there's a lot less outside air circulating through the structure today than there used to be. And this drop in natural ventilation means that a formerly insignificant problem – condensation moisture – is now a major concern. That's because now, once once such moisture gets into the walls or roof structure, it can't get out.

Condensation moisture – dew – happens when air temperature drops. Warm air can hold more moisture, in invisible vapor form, than cold air; but most building materials are now airtight. As you sit in your heated kitchen, the warm air in the room is migrating outward through the walls toward the cold outdoors. The temperature within the wall varies: equal to the kitchen air temperature on the inside, equal to the ambient air temperature on the outside. At some point on its travel through the wall, the escaping inside air will chill enough to drop some of its moisture.

In the old days, that didn't matter: there was so much uncontrolled outside air blowing through the thickness of the structure that any dew thus deposited would be quickly evaporated and removed. Today that's not true any more, and condensation, once deposited, stays and accumulates, with destructive results. The solution is obvious enough, in theory: make the warm inside surface of the wall air-tight.

In practice, that's not easy to do: popular building materials like sheet rock are nowhere near air-tight. So the industry has gone for the next-best thing: we put a thin plastic vapor on the backside of the sheet rock, so that moisture-laden air can't penetrate deep into the wall, into the insulation layer, and there lose its moisture because of cooling. Usually we specify a 6-mil plastic vapor barrier to be secured on the warm side of the wall studding or the ceiling joists before the sheet rock is installed.

The insulation industry also recognizes the problem; manufacturers offer batt insulation, to be stapled between studs or joists, with a built-in vapor barrier for the warm side. They also offer beadboard with a vapor barrier on one side.

You'd think that any of these solutions would be enough, but, increasingly, we're learning that they're not. First of all, we've learned that vapor barriers aren't really barriers: under pressure from the legal industry, manufacturers now call their products vapor retarders, admitting that some moisture will get through even if installation is perfectly by-the-book. Second, we're having to admit that in the real world of construction, vapor barriers—oops, retarders—are sometimes installed with gaps, sometimes pierced during construction, sometimes develop leaks after construction. Third, we're learning that making construction air-tight on the outside with new materials—plywood sheathing, metal roofing, vinyl siding, silicone caulking, acrylic paints—calls for new concerns about vapor and moisture build-up on the inside.

So, we in the design end of the construction business are facing reality: we're now designing into buildings the structural ventilation that used to occur automatically. No, we're not going back to board sheathing and we're not giving up on space-age caulks. We are making sure that there's an air space behind (on the cold side, that is) every thickness of insulation, and that these air spaces are connected to the outside world so that outside air will circulate through them either naturally or mechanically assisted. The intent is to restore the natural ventilation that used to occur, so that moisture won't accumulate.

In most design situations, this has been pretty easy. The construction industry now has inexpensive metal vents for use on soffits (the underside of roof cornices), for roof ridges, for gable ends. They come in a wide variety of shapes and sizes, and are easy to install. More traditional wood vents are also available. The rule of thumb for ventilation is that the clear vent opening (not counting cross-slats) for, say, an attic, should be usually 1.5% of the area of the attic floor. A 1,200 square foot house, for example, would most likely have a 1,200 SF attic, and should have a total of 18 SF of ventilation arranged so as to encourage outside air to flow through from one side to the other. Some building codes allow that amount of ventilation to be cut in half if soffit and ridge vents are used, under the theory that soffit and ridge vents supposedly work better than gable-end vents.

The industry has lightened its ventilation load in another way; by declaring that walls aren't a problem. Standard wood frame construction doesn't call for vents on the back side (the cold side) of each stud space, even though the cold air in that wall is really trapped there and moisture can't readily escape. I suppose that we in the industry get away with this because it usually works; if it doesn't in your situation, I'd suggest that you install small button vents at the top and bottom of the outside wall covering each stud space in the problem area, and see if that doesn't help.

Sometimes the industry doesn't get away with it. For a long time we believed that cathedral ceilings required no ventilation on the cold side of the insulation, because there was virtually no free space up there above the insulation and below the roof deck. Now we've learned that doesn't always work, and so now we're careful to design cathedral ceilings with an air space above the insulation and provision for an unobstructed flow of outside ventilation air through each rafter space.

Sometimes we as individual designers learn things before the industry recognized them as true. I've learned, for example, that batt insulation designed to be stapled between the studs and rafters comes with a built-in vapor retarder that doesn't always work. Maybe that's because there's a break at each framing member; I don't know. I do know, that for large cathedral-ceiling buildings like churches and community halls I won't depend on the insulation vapor retarder and will specify unbroken sheet plastic instead.

Sometimes it works the other way: the industry tells us individual designers what in-the-field problems they've seen. That was the case with attic insulation being installed so that it blocked the flow of ventilating air from the soffit vent, up into the attic, then out through the ridge vent. Some builders, it seems, thought it good to stuff each rafter space with insulation at the cornice level, thereby making the soffit vents worthless. Now we call for the use of light-weight snap-in-place sheet Fiberglas "insulation dams" in each rafter space to make sure an airway is kept open. I've never known a builder to make that installation error, but it must be happening out there somewhere.

I shouldn't end this discussion without some comments on air-conditioning. If it's needed, it means that the whole design process designed above is reversed: now the warm, moisture-laden air is on the outside and the cold side is the inside.

Under these conditions, putting the vapor retarding membrane in the "normal" place isn't going to help much: warm air will infiltrate through the outside walls and condense somewhere in the thickness of the insulation.

The infiltration will be worse if the air conditioning is fan-driven and is creating a slight negative pressure inside the occupied rooms, thus drawing more outside air through the walls. Under these conditions, logic suggests that there should be a vapor retarder on both sides of the insulation, on the outside for air-conditioning and on the inside for normal heating. To follow that logic would create an insulation layer that is completely unventilated (and quite difficult and expensive to ventilate), so the industry follows its own logic and pretty much ignores the problem.

How much of a problem is air-conditioning? Statistically, not significant, explaining why there are no widely accepted design standards for moisture control in air-conditioning situations. (Maybe it helps that almost all the U.S. areas which use air-conditioning heavily don't experience really high humidities.) But even here in Vermont we see, particularly on unusually warm days in early spring, situations where moisture-laden outside air gets into a cold masonry structure and the condensation comes down like rain. Theoretically, it's possible to design for both air-conditioning and heating—the double-vapor-retarder situation—but I wouldn't do it unless other air-conditioned structures in your own neighborhood are pretty clearly having problems.

One final thought: how can one possibly go back into an old structure, say one with blow-in insulation and no vapor control, and solve the problem? Surprisingly easy: just apply an interior paint with the highest-possible perm rating (vapor retardance) to all interior surfaces. It may not be perfect but it will be close enough.

(Martin Harris is a Vermont architect, cofounder of The New England Builder, and author of numerous home building articles.) Δ

Llamas guarding sheep?

Not such a far-fetched idea!

Lightning, a young llama takes a break from the sheep to say hello to dog Brandy. (Photo by John and Karen Northey)

By Karen McGeorge Sanders

It seems that farmers always need an extra pair of hands, but finding the money to pay the extra help is often impossible. You need the help to make money, but you need money to pay the help. Faced with this problem when they added a few head of sheep to their operation, Joy and Brent Crawford, a Montana ranching couple, found a unique solution.

The need for more help occurred when Joy Crawford decided to add a little more diversity to the family's cattle and wheat ranch by running a small herd of sheep. Although the sheep were kept in pastures close to the ranch house, coyotes were still a problem. There weren't enough sheep to justify the hiring of a sheepherder, and the dogs weren't able to stay with the sheep 24 hours a day. What they needed was a guardian to live with the sheep that didn't require a paycheck.

After a long search, Joy found the solution to her problem in the form of a llama gelding named Gus. Waking or sleeping, Gus spends all his time with his woolly charges. An aggressive guardian of his flock, Gus frightens off predators and strange humans with a noisy combination of stomping hooves, blowing nostrils, and the famous llama spitting. Lastly, Gus's pay is easy on a farmer's wallet. The gelding's price was less than what it would cost to hire a sheepherder for a month, and Gus's only upkeep expenses are food and an occasional vet check.

Of course, using a llama to guard sheep, instead of the more conventional dog or human, makes for some interesting adjustments. For instance, Brent and Joy have to make sure all gates are securely latched as Gus has shown a talent for finding open gates and leading his flock into new pastures.

Gus's alertness and intelligence is also in evidence at sheep shearing time. Although llama wool is quite valuable, Joy generally doesn't shear Gus but simply separates him from his charges before the shearing begins. Then as each sheep returns to the herd, Gus finds it necessary to sniff his newly shorn companion from head to toe. Joy says, "It's as if he's trying to figure out what in the world happened to his flock."

Single gelding works best

For the purpose of guarding sheep, Joy has found that a single gelding works best. Two llamas will keep each other company and ignore the sheep, plus geldings are cheaper to purchase than breeding stock and don't try to mate with the sheep. Although it is possible to train llamas to guard sheep, Joy has found that Gus's natural desire for companionship has made schooling unnecessary. Other than halter breaking, Gus has been left wild, so as to encourage him to bond with the sheep instead of humans. Also, it is necessary to keep Gus and his flock in close to the house so that the Crawfords and their dogs can hear Gus warn of any danger. Although Gus is an excellent "watch llama," he can not be expected to protect the sheep against some of the more dangerous predators that might threaten the herd.

"Not every llama makes a good sheep guard. In my experience, only about 50% of the geldings tried make it as guard llamas," says Cy Colarchik of Belt, Montana who uses his llama Glenn to guard a herd of about 100 sheep. He offers the following hints to

Glenn, a guard llama, watches over his flock. (Photo by Robert McGeorge)

give your guard llama the best chance of success:

Don't make your llama a pet. Allow it to focus its attention on the sheep.

A herd of sheep that stays together offers the best chance of success for a guard llama. Otherwise the llama is forced to choose one group of sheep and ignore the others roaming about the pasture.

The International Llama Association says that llamas live approximately 15-29 years and that geldings cost between $500 to $2,500 depending on area and age. For more information or the names of llama breeders in your area contact the International Llama Association at: P.O. Box 37505, Denver, Colorado 80237, (303) 756-9004.

Extra hands are hard to find. So, if you find yourself with a herd of sheep that need watching, you might want to consider some helping hooves, llama style. Δ

Try buying at auctions to save money for just about any item

By Charles A. Sanders

When folks like us set out to equip the homestead with the tools, livestock, machinery and other things essential to our effort towards self-sufficiency, we are usually limited by the amount of working capital on hand. The cost of new tractors and implements, registered breeds of livestock, or fine new tools is usually high enough to keep them well out of the reach of most of us.

As a part of the self-reliant homesteader's country economy, public auctions and estate sales will prove to be valuable in helping to equip the farm and home. From tractors, implements, and livestock to pots, pans, appliances and home furnishings, country auctions can be a great asset to the homesteader. I have made some really good buys at auctions, and enjoy going to them. If you keep your eyes open and use your head, then you, too, can haul away some great deals and some badly needed items for your own place. Here are some tips on making you a successful auction-goer.

First, you need to locate a good sale to attend. To locate country auctions in your area, pick up a copy of the local or area newspaper, especially a Sunday edition or a late weekday edition, say, a Thursday issue. These are most likely to have advertisements for upcoming auctions. Look, too, for handbills posted in or near places of business such as feed stores, groceries, etc. Once you've spotted a sale that interests you, plan to arrive at the site a half hour or so before the scheduled starting time. This will allow you plenty of time to look over the items listed. You can better check the make, condition and suitability of an item before the bidding starts.

Auctioneers operate on a percentage basis. That is, they normally get a certain percent of the total amount of money brought in at the sale. In my area, auctioneers usually get from 3% to 5% on real estate sales, 10-15% on household auctions and only around 2-3% on farm sales. (As one auctioneer told me, "It takes only about as long to sell a five to six thousand dollar tractor as it does a $100 table." Hence the lower rate charged on farm sales.). As a rule, the seller foots the bill for any advertising and for paying the clerks and ringmen, which around here pays about six dollars an hour.

Country auctions are busy places, often quite informal as to bidding and generally a pleasant atmosphere for all. Often, the auctioneer knows many of the "regulars" on a first name basis,

and even knows what items they will be interested in. When you get to the sale site, you will need to pick up a bidder's number, usually a card with an assigned number. This is done at a table or other spot where the bookkeeper is located. Identification, such as a driver's license is usually sufficient to get a buyer's number. However, when particularly valuable items are being sold, a letter of credit or a reference from your bank is sometimes required. With approved identification or letter of credit, a personal check is usually acceptable for payment.

Once the bidding starts, your bid is usually acknowledged by ringmen—spotters working with the auctioneer—who scan the crowd for willing bidders such as yourself. Raising a hand or a nod of the head are usually sufficient to get noticed, but in some cases, you may have to speak out with your initial bid. Don't be bashful, get in there and make a bid. From there, the ringman will watch for your bid and perhaps—no, usually(!) urge you to go a bit higher if you stop bidding. Once you get your sought after item, the auctioneer or the spotter will ask for your number which his recorder will write down along with the name of the item bought and the selling price. As the recorder's sheets are filled up, they are relayed to the payment counter, usually the same place where you picked up your number. It's a good idea, especially if you are buying several items, to jot down the name and the price you paid for each item. Often, the back of your bidder's card is printed with lines and columns just for this purpose. This will help to prevent mistakes and being charged for items which you did not purchase. Too, at most sales, you can merely put all of your booty in one spot until the sale is over. Theft is generally, and I say **generally**, not a problem. Of course, if you have a small and particularly valuable item, I'd either carry it with me or lock it up in the truck until the sale is over.

A few other things should be remembered when visiting an auction. First, remember that most every auction is conducted on the basis that the buyer knows what he is buying and that each item is sold "as is". The old phrase "Caveat emptor" definitely applies here—"Let the Buyer Beware!"

Second, know what item you are bidding on at a given time. Now, that may seem rather basic, but many are the folks who were caught not paying attention and have bought an item when they thought they were bidding on something else. Often, one of the ringmen may hold an item up for the crowd to see, but once the sale really gets rolling, items, especially small stuff, sell fast, and you may find yourself bidding on an item that just sold or on an item that is not up yet! If you do this once, you'll generally break yourself of the habit! There is little harm done if it is a dollar or two item, but even mistakes like that can add up.

Third, know the name, quality, and condition of the item you are bidding on, as well as you can, of course. Just about every auction-goer has gotten "skinned" once or twice in their career. Just learn from the experience. Here is another place that there are usually plenty of folks who are willing to help you evaluate an item prior to bidding. Too, don't be afraid to bid a dollar (or sometimes even less!) for a box of "junk". Many are the times I have bought a box of junk bolts, nails, or whatever, and have been pleasantly surprised to find an unexpected item of much greater worth. Once, I bought a box of old bolts, nuts, washers, and other assorted hardware for about a dollar. I had looked briefly through the box and was sure that I had more than gotten my money's worth. I was very pleasantly surprised to find amid the rusty pieces, a clevice to fit my tractor drawbar, one that I'd been needing. Too, that box of bolts and fasteners has been a great help around the 'stead. I haven't even tried to figure up the savings which that purchase has made for me.

Fourth, have a limit on the amount that you are willing to pay for an item. This can be one of the most important rules of auction going. Again, at one time or another, most of us have gone above and beyond our "limit" on an item in our bidding, and kicked ourselves in the posterior later. Almost any country auctioneer will try to get you to go just a little higher, then a little higher! It's all done in good spirit, and any higher bid he can get means more income for the seller and ultimately for himself, as well. Watch, however, for the unethical auctioneer who will use someone in the crowd to help run up the price on an item. I once witnessed just such an incident at an otherwise good farm sale. The farm owner had a really nice old Ferguson tractor that was selling. A young man and his wife were bidding on the tractor, along with a couple of other folks. As the bidding dropped down to two bidders, including the young man, I noticed the auctioneer give a wink to the other bidder and the price of the tractor ended up going up and up to a point several hundred dollars more than it should have. This second bidder was across the crowd from the other, so it was easy for the auctioneer to swing towards him, so that his gestures were not visible to the young man. I left that sale soon afterwards, and to this date, do not attend sales conducted by this auctioneer. I figure if he cheated that fellow, he'd take me if he had the chance.

Auction-goer's survival kit

Here are some tips to keep in mind when heading to an auction:

- **1. Look over local newspapers, etc. to spot upcoming sales.**
- **2. Arrive early to look over the merchandise. See if it is what you need and check its condition. "Caveat Emptor" applies.**
- **3. Know what you are willing to pay for an item and stick with that amount.**
- **4. Know what similar items are selling for generally. Don't end up paying more than you can buy it for new!**
- **5. When buying several items, jot down the name of the item purchased along with the price paid.**

Another type of auction is the auction house, or often known locally as the "sale barn." This type of sale is usually held regularly, often weekly, and in the same location. The sale is conducted on a consignment basis, which means that items are brought by the seller, sold during bidding with the auctioneer or auction house getting a percentage of the selling price. These types of sales can be general item sales, or be specifically held for horses and tack, feeder cattle, etc. The one I often go to is a combination of general sale and livestock sale. The general sale begins at 6:00 P.M., and the livestock sale promptly at 7:00 P.M. If the general sale is not completed by that time, it moves outside. These livestock sales include everything but horses and tack (they are held on alternate weekends.) It is not uncommon to see goats, sheep, pigs, and cattle all run through the ring in an evening. The smaller animals such as fowl and rabbits are sold during the regular 6:00 sale. Everything from welding rods, to sacks of apples and pears, and even persimmons are often available at this sale. Often, country folks use these sales as an outlet for surplus or otherwise unwanted produce and small livestock. It's a good place to pick up some chickens for $1.00 each or a sack of home grown apples for a couple of dollars.

These sales are often attended by "regulars," both sellers and buyers. The same rules apply here as with other auctions, but I want to reinforce one of them: know what you are buying, especially when it comes to livestock. Some small-scale stock raisers often bring their surplus to these sales to be sold, and the bidder can often pick up some nice animals. The price being paid will be competitive with going market prices, so the seller comes out well. But watch out for "junk" animals being run through the ring. Get to the sales early, and look the "merchandise" over. Check for symptoms of illness or disease and for deformities. If you are not knowledgeable of these defects in animals, then take a friend along with you who can help guide you towards or away from bidding on a particular animal. Keep your eyes open and you can get some good deals here, just as with other auctions. I know several folks who have bought some older cows or ewes at these sales and by hanging on to the female offspring produced, have built up some pretty nice little herds. Just as often, though, I've heard of friends who have picked up sick, foundered, injured or otherwise unhealthy stock. These animals soon died shortly afterwards or had to be put down. Again, it is "buyer beware". It is a good idea to have your newly purchased critters checked out by a veterinarian after you get them home.

Country auctions and sales can be a valuable asset to the homesteader. They can certainly help to stretch the dollars which we never seem to have enough of. Watch what you are doing and you can come away with needed items and equipment for your homestead at some real savings to you. Glance through the local paper this week and find a good sale to go to. But, you should be warned, they can be habit-forming! Δ

Living with a frozen privy

By Don Fallick

Country life is replete with tales about how tough things were in the old days. Granny's "horror stories" about getting frozen to the privy seat probably have no more basis in fact than Grandpa's reminiscences about walking 20 miles to the schoolhouse through hip-deep snow. That is, there's doubtless a kernel of truth in there somewhere, but it's been "improved" in the telling considerably.

Let's get one thing straight right from the beginning. Living with an outhouse is not a delicate subject, and there's no dainty way to talk about it. If you just can't stomach the thought of dealing with the end products of digestion, better skip to another article.

How a privy works

A properly cared for privy is usually several degrees warmer than the ambient outside temperature, because the bacteria in the sludge cause it to compost. This not only raises the temperature, it also eliminates the odor. A few cups of stove ashes thrown down the hole after each bowel movement will help promote composting wonderfully. You won't need to pour ashes down the hole after urinating, because you don't want to do that in the outhouse, anyway.

Urine is wonderful fertilizer for all growing plants, and in the absence of an actual bladder infection, is sterile when it leaves the body. Pouring it down the privy hole is a great waste of this valuable resource, and actually impedes the composting action of the privy by flooding the bacteria. It breaks down into uric acid and ammonia, which poison the good germs. If you must use a privy for **both** elimination functions, it's a good idea to have a two-holer, and use one hole for bowels and the other for bladder. You can switch holes every few weeks or so. Of course, most people do both more or less together, and there's no need to get up and move. Just trying to keep your functions separate will help a lot.

Seat strategies

If you have a good composting action going and your outhouse seals well enough to keep the breezes out, it should be warm enough to sit in, but not necessarily warm enough to sit on. I know people who make toilet seats out of plastic foam. Children's toy life-preservers work well, and are smooth enough to be easy to clean. Another strategy is to make your toilet seats removable, and keep them in the house. I never liked this method, as the seats tend to move around when you sit on them, and nailing laths or moldings to the outhouse bench to keep the seats in place makes the bench hard to clean. Laths also trap moisture, which can freeze the seat to the bench. I tried loosely doweling the seat to the bench once, but the dowels swelled and froze in the holes and had to be sawed off, or else they eventually worked their way through the toilet seat and split it. You **don't** want a toilet seat with splinters!

Natural insulation

Eventually we moved to a house with a privy that had integral seats – **no way** to remove them. I thought, from the stories I'd heard, that it would be painful to sit down on them on a cold winter morning. Actually, it isn't that bad. I'm not very fat, but even so, after the first shock of cold, it takes only a moment or two for your butt to get used to the temperature. One might think that God had put padding on the human buttocks for just that reason! Unless it's colder than 15 degrees below zero, you're just not going to stick to the seat, even if it's wet. And even if you do sit on a thin layer of ice, the heat of your body will quickly melt it.

Squatters-right!

In parts of Europe and Asia where privies are still common, cold seats are not a problem because there are no seats. "Squatters" are easier to build, more sanitary, and warmer on the buns than the American style "commode", and promote easier evacuation. Hemorrhoids are virtually unknown in parts of the world where people don't commonly sit down to move their bowels. They do require fairly good aim, however!

If the cold seat isn't a problem, drafts are. Even a slight draft UP the outhouse hole when you're sitting on it is no joke! There just is nothing colder! In the old days, when women wore dresses, this wasn't such a problem for them because the fabric stopped drafts and covered their exposed legs and buttocks. Now that women wear pants too, they are subject to the same drafts men and boys have always had to endure. A thigh-length coat with buttons or a two-way zipper can be a real blessing on a cold morning. So can a "lap blanket" or a shawl to wrap around your waist, to cover exposed flesh and seal the hole behind you.

Winter nights

Another problem with the wintertime outhouse is light. If you are used to looking at the toilet paper to make sure you "got it all," you may have difficulty when the days get short and you have to work by flashlight. I have dropped one down the hole. I believe it's still there. It's a good idea to keep a spare flashlight in the outhouse, along with a spare roll of toilet paper. You can shout for a long time before anyone in the house hears you! A privy candle or lantern works well too.

Children

My experience has been that small children just won't go to the outhouse after dark. For some, it's the long (for them), scary walk outside in the dark that's the worst part. Others imagine monsters coming up out of the hole. I've raised five youngsters (all girls) with a privy, and every one was too scared to use the outhouse after dark at some point in her life.

Unless you don't mind accompanying kids to the privy to do their business at bedtime and maybe once or twice a night, or changing wet beds, you'll want to own some kind of a chamber pot. This can be anything from a plastic bucket with a lid, to an expensive "chemical toilet." We've used a plastic bucket with a homemade commode box over it for years. This is just a bottomless plywood box made to fit the bucket. Some folks make their commode just the right height to fit over the bucket. Others make the hole to fit the bucket and depend on the bucket's lip to keep it from falling through. In any case, you don't want there to be any room between the top of the bucket and the top of the commode, or urine can get through. The commode we used for years had a regular hinged toilet seat.

Keep the lid on

We used the toilet seat to hold down the piece of cardboard we used for a lid. Now that the girls are all old enough, we just use a bucket with a tight-fitting lid. The buckets don't last long with all the bleaching and scrubbing they get, and it's helpful not to have to find a source for buckets that fit our commode exactly. Anyone caught leaving the lid off becomes the new "official" in charge of emptying it.

Emptying the bucket can be a story in itself. If your bucket does not have a tight fitting lid, as ours didn't at one time, and if your outhouse path gets icy and slippery, as ours does regularly in the late winter, the scene is set for disaster. I won't say who it was, but they went down, the bucket went **up**, and **then** the lid came off! Not all of Granny's and Grandpa's stories **need** improving.

How to build a commode box

Parts list:

- **1/2" exterior plywood**
- **4 pieces as high as bucket and 1 1/2" wider than widest part of bucket for sides**
- **1 piece square, 1 1/2" wider than widest part of bucket for top and lid**
- **1x2 4 pieces 3/4" shorter than height of bucket**
- **1x4 4 pieces cut to 45 degree triangles**

Hardware:

- **3 handles (2 for commode, 1 for lid. (May use pieces of 1x2 if desired)**
- **1 toilet seat with hinges**
- **1 5 gallon, plastic bucket with tight-fitting lid**

Directions:

- **1. Select a plastic bucket with a tight-fitting lid.**
- **2. Cut out four pieces of 1/2" A/C plywood for sides of box. Each side should be exactly as high as the bucket (not including its lid). Each side should be as wide as widest part of bucket, plus 1 1/2".**
- **3. Cut out top of box. It should be square, with each side 1/2" smaller than the sides of the box, and with a circular hole the exact diameter of the inside of the top of the bucket, centered in the box top.**
- **4. Cut triangular corner braces for box top from a piece of lx4. Cut 4 mounting brackets 3/4" shorter than box sides from a 1x2.**
- **5. Assemble parts with glue and screws as shown in drawing. Self-countersinking "trumpet-head" screws work best. Cover with vinyl wallpaper if desired, or paint with enamel, etc. for easy cleaning.**
- **6. Mount toilet seat. Remove all splinters from edge of hole. If you mount the seat with regular toilet seat hinges, and remove the little rubber bumpers from the bottom of the seat, there will be just enough room under the seat to seal against a lid made from the center of the hole you cut out of the top of the box in # 3 above. Since the commode is fairly heavy and must be lifted off the bucket to dump it, it's a good idea to add handles to the sides, and perhaps another to the middle of the plywood lid.**

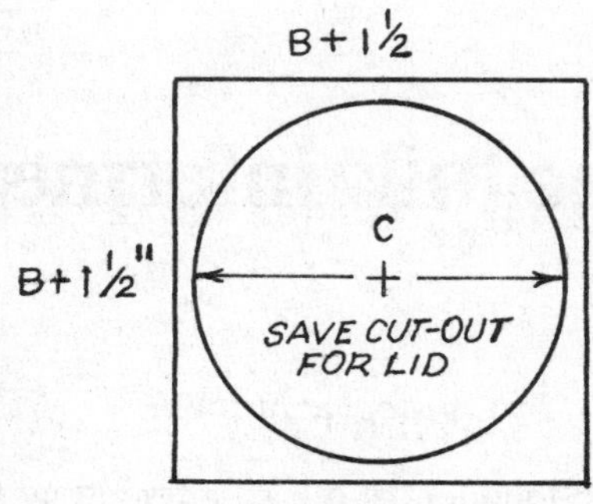

Commode top. Make one. C=inside diameter of top of bucket.

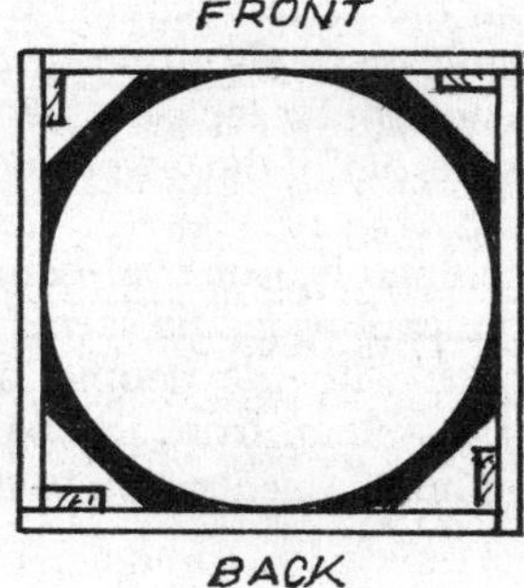

Bottom view. Note 1x2 corner braces and 1x4 triangular top braces.

To use, place box over bucket. Make lid of cardboard or plywood to fit under toilet seat, or remove box and cover bucket with its own lid between uses. Dump and clean out bucket frequently and never keep bleach or other chemicals in bucket during use. Δ

COMMENTARY

The fully informed jury can restore the Bill of Rights

By Christopher Maxwell

The founders of our country left us several tools to help the people keep their government under control. The best known of these are freedom of speech and the right to vote. The hope was that the people would be able to communicate freely, organize opposition to unpopular measures, and "vote the rascals out" if the government quit listening.

Unfortunately, our over-centralized communications media seems to have lost touch with the people, and the electoral system, from the parties to the nominating procedure to the laws controlling and limiting who can or can't get on the ballot, is under the control of the people we want to throw out.

The founders recognized the possibility that legislators might still pass laws which were unjust despite the protections in the Constitution and the Bill of Rights. They left us another way to overturn unjust laws without having to fall back on the Second Amendment.

While few today are aware of it, the jury can prevent the enforcement and implementation of unfair, unjust, or unpopular laws. A jury can refuse to convict persons who have clearly violated the letter of the law.

It only takes one juror to refuse to convict. If the jury votes for acquittal, the case is closed; the State cannot try again.

If enough juries acquit defendants who have clearly violated the law, the State will eventually give up and quit trying to enforce that law.

This happened with the Fugitive Slave Act before the Civil War. Northern juries refused to convict people for assisting escaped slaves in such numbers that the government gave up and quit trying to prosecute those people.

The jury has the power to prevent the government from usurping powers and functions and from enforcing laws to promote the interests of small, powerful groups in society.

In recent years juries have acquitted defendants who openly admitted violating laws they considered unjust.

Homeschoolers, draft resisters, tax resisters, cancer patients arrested for marijuana possession, gun owners, and others who felt their rights were being trampled by our runaway government have managed to convince a jury that they were right and the government was wrong.

If enough juries acquit defendants who have clearly violated the law, the State will eventually give up and quit trying to enforce that law. This happened with the Fugitive Slave Act before the Civil War. Northern juries refused to convict people for assisting escaped slaves in such numbers that the government gave up and quit trying to prosecute those people.

Most of these heroic juries didn't even know they had a legal right to judge the law. They simply voted their conscience. Many of them had been instructed by the judge to ignore the issue of whether the law in question was fair or not and simply vote the facts of the case.

However, once the jury votes to acquit, the judge has no recourse and must declare the case closed and the defendant free.

How many more defendants would be freed if juries knew they had the right and duty to judge the law as well as the facts?

How many unjust and unfair laws would be dropped if everyone knew that no jury would convict for violations of unjust laws?

America leads the world in percentage of population behind bars, police per capita, and number of laws on the books, way ahead of second place South Africa. The problem is not that we don't have enough courts or prisons; we have too many laws.

In the last century it was common practice for judges to inform juries of this duty in their instructions to the jury after all evidence had been presented. Toward the end of the 1800s, as the special interests became more powerful and the laws became more complicated, judges began to usurp all the power in the courtrooms.

While murderers, rapists, and robbers can receive probation or early release because of prison overcrowding, they always seem to have room for tax resisters, gun owners, and people who refuse to send their children in for government brainwashing, i.e., to public schools.

Judges not only quit telling juries about their right and duty to judge the law, many began instructing the juries to vote only on the facts of the case. Some even began to lie to the juries, telling them they had no right to judge the law, that they had to vote according to the letter of the law.

Amazingly, the U.S. Supreme Court has held in decisions that a judge does have the right to lie to the jury, and that he can forbid the defendants attorney to inform the jury of their rights and duties.

Jury trials now are a farce. The jury sits as a helpless audience while two prima donna lawyers play word games before the Presiding Judge. Whichever lawyer is more skillful at manipulating the rules to conceal information from the jury will most likely be declared the winner.

Judges and prosecutors routinely exclude any prospective juror who will not agree to blindly follow the judges' instructions. Jurors are asked if they think the law in question is objectionable, and are excluded if they do. Any juror who gives any hint that he or she knows that the jury does not have to follow the judges' instructions will be excluded.

Few Americans accused of a crime ever receive a jury trial anymore. The courts are so overburdened by the number of cases that most of them must be settled by plea bargains and out of court settlements.

America leads the world in percentage of population behind bars, police per capita, and number of laws on the books, way ahead of second place South Africa. The problem is not that we don't have enough courts or prisons; we have too many laws.

Courts are also showing an alarming tendency to take crimes against the government more serious than crimes against people.

While murderers, rapists, and robbers can receive probation or early release because of prison overcrowding, they always seem to have room for tax resisters, gun owners, and people who refuse to send their children in for government brainwashing, i.e., to public schools.

Our elected legislators and the unelected bureaucrats who have the power to write regulations which are as binding as law have become increasingly arrogant and out of touch with reality in recent years. They now see the public as an obstacle to their plans rather than as their employer.

The laws and regulations they pass have little to do with reality or with the public will. They are not getting the feedback they would receive if juries were fully informed of their duties to judge the fairness of laws and regulations.

If juries voted to acquit everyone charged with violating some new law or regulation, the people who wrote the law would get the message quickly that they were out of touch with the public will.

Fully-informed jury amendment

The Fully Informed Jury Association (FIJA) is the organization that has started the fight to resurrect the knowledge of the jury's power and responsibility. The Libertarian, Populist, and Taxpayers Parties have added the Fully Informed Jury Amendment to their national platforms. The Democrats and Republicans have not.

The fight is moving along on several fronts. Referendums are proposed in several states to require judges to inform jurors of their rights and responsibilities. Sympathetic legislators in some Western states have introduced legislation for the same purpose.

The most important thing about these proposals is that they can be effective even if they are not passed into law. If they get enough publicity and stir up enough controversy, potential jurors will have been informed of their rights even if the laws are voted down.

Publicity is growing in the FIJA movement, mostly favorable, including an article on page one of the Wall Street Journal.

Opposition scare tactics

Not surprisingly, those who oppose jury rights are the same special interests whose laws would be thrown out by any sensible jury.

They try to scare their readers with thoughts of racist bigots voting their prejudices, and ignorant juries carried away by emotional appeals.

Interesting to see what these government stooges think of us, isn't it?

The fact is, racists and other irrational people will vote their prejudices if they get on a jury, whether they know about jury rights or not.

It's the sensible, responsible people who believe the judge when he tells them they have to vote against their conscience if the law says so.

Another scare tactic is to raise the prospect of murderers, robbers, and rapists being set free by juries. This is so ridiculous it doesn't even deserve an answer.

It's judges who set dangerous criminals free, not juries.

At any rate, we win any debate about the fully informed jury, because the potential jurors who hear the debate know their rights and duties when called to jury service.

FIJA activists

Another successful tactic has been to pass out pamphlets in the parking lots and entrances of courts. When a FIJA activist is arrested and the concept of Jury Veto is explained on the news, or in court as a fact of the case, we win.

If they don't arrest the activists, every juror entering the court gets a pamphlet explaining the rights and powers of the jury. We win either way.

It's going to take a lot of work, and a lot of people who are willing to take the chance of being arrested, but we can let the public know there is still a way to take control of the laws back from the lawyers, judges, legislators,and bureaucrats and put it in the hands of the people where it belongs.

Fore more information

For more information about Jury Nullification, or to find out how you can help, contact FIJA at: P.O. Box59, Helmville, MT 59843. (406) 793-5550.

"The jury has a right to judge both the law as well as the fact in controversy." —John Jay, first Chief Justice of the U.S. Supreme Court, 1794.

"If the jury feels the law is unjust, we recognize the undisputed power of the jury to acquit, even if its' verdict is contrary to the law as given by a judge, and contrary to the evidence." —U.S. 4th Circuit Court of Appeals, 1969. Δ

Using water hydraulics to help install your house grounding rod

By Bruce Allison

When I had underground power installed, one of the local electric companies workmen came to my door and asked if he could have some water. I said "sure" I would get him a glass. But he said "no!" He didn't need a glass. But if I could fill his hard-hat with about a quart of water, that would be just fine. So I gave him his water.

Now this struck me as kind of funny! So I followed him out to the transformer site. What he did is one of the most interesting things I'd seen in a long time. He grabbed hold of the ground rod (1/2"x8') and stuck it into the ground about 4 inches. He then poured a little water onto the edge of the rod which flowed down into the ground, he then raised the rod about 3" and then pushed it down. With an up and down motion he was able to push the rod a few more inches deeper.

By adding small amounts of water, and using an up and down motion an even penetration into the ground was achieved. It didn't take more than five minutes to sink it to the proper depth. He left about six inches exposed.

I called one of my friends about a year later just to talk. But he said he didn't have time because he was going to install a ground rod. So I told him I knew of a better way. By using a quart of water in a mason jar, instead of a sledge hammer, he bought into this idea. When I checked in with him later in the day, I asked him how it went and he said great.

Now this is a great technique, but I can't guarantee that it will work in all ground conditions. I have seen this done in the soils and clays of the Pacific Northwest. Δ

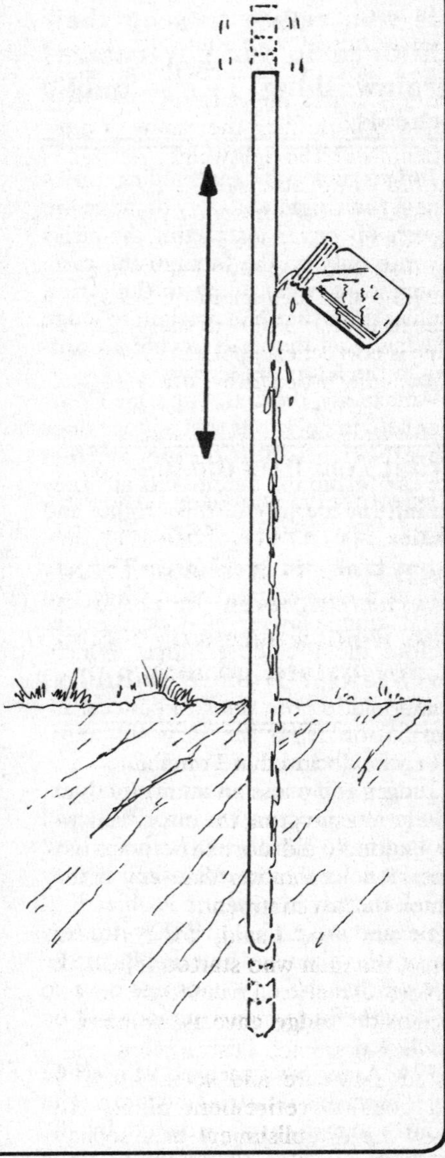

Doesn't anyone remember Tom Paine?

Tom Paine

By Robert L. Williams

Many years ago, before I came to my senses and left public education for good, I was teaching on a college campus when one of the administrators approached me and asked the topic of my lecture that day.

"Tom Paine and the Rights of Man," I told him.

The administrator sneered, managed a look of utter contempt, and asked, "Do you mean to tell me that you are still defiling the minds of our students with the lightweight works of that filthy little atheist?"

Thinking of Rousseau's comment that the Holy Roman Empire was an appropriate title except that it was neither holy, nor Roman, nor an empire, I responded, "Your description of Paine is correct except that he was not lightweight, little, filthy, nor an atheist."

What Tom Pain did hate, and passionately, was Big Government. He wrote, "Society in every state is a blessing, but government, even in its best state, is but a necessary evil; in its worst state, an intolerable one."

I went on to add that Tom Paine was, according to no less an authority than George Washington, the man who single- handedly did more to help win the American Revolution than any other person on this continent.

"He was also," I said, "for better or worse, the man who started the Bank of North America, invented the metal suspension bridge, gave us the idea for a selective service draft system, suggested medicare and social security and pension retirement plans. He urged the establishment of a society for the prevention of cruelty to animals, campaigned vigorously for international copyright laws, and donated to the cause of the American Revolution the money that was earned by The Crisis, America's first genuine best-seller in literature."

Before my prey could escape, I added, "And, incidentally, he was the man who named this country. He was the first person to use, so far as anyone knows, the phrase, "The United States of America."

"He was still an atheist," the administrator added, walking away with the smug assurance of all authoritarian leaders who remain convinced that whatever they say or do has the blessings of God and the approval of the Congress.

And today, two hundred years after the appearance of the Rights of Man, on February 17, 1992, most Americans have never even heard of Tom Paine, and the few who have cannot tell you anything about him except that he was "a filthy little atheist" and enemy of Christianity whose writings defile the minds of all who read him.

To clear the air, Paine was not an atheist in any sense of the word, and it would have been perfectly all right if he had been one in every sense of the word. In point of fact, he wrote in The Age of Reason, "I believe in one God and no more, and I hope for happiness beyond this life. I believe in the equality of man, and I believe that religious duties consist in doing justice, living mercy, and endeavoring to make our fellow creature happy."

Strange words, indeed, from a man who allegedly hated Christianity and harbored no beliefs in God!

What Tom Pain **did** hate, and passionately, was Big Government. He wrote, "Society in every state is a blessing, but government, even in its best state, is but a necessary evil; in its worst state, an intolerable one."

He hated the idea of an uncontrolled welfare state and stated his feelings, clearly when he wrote, "Those who expect to reap the blessings of freedom must, like men, undergo the fatigue of supporting it."

When American troops were being soundly defeated on nearly all fronts during the American Revolution, Paine, who was serving without pay as aid-de-camp to Nathanael Greene, became impatient with the complaints of the soldiers who did not win the war as easily as they had hoped.

And Tom Paine then wrote some of the most memorable lines in the history of the English language: "These are the times that try men's souls. The summer soldier and the sunshine patriot will, in this crisis, shrink from the service of their country; but he that stands is **now**, deserves the love and thanks of man and woman. Tyranny, like hell, is not easily conquered; yet, we have this consolation with us, that the harder the conflict, the more glorious the triumph. What we obtain too cheap, we esteem too lightly....Heaven knows how to put a proper price upon its good; and it would be strange indeed if so celestial an article as Freedom should not be highly rated."

Paine describes a prosperous American businessman who held a child by the hand and, after expounding on his reasons not to fight for this nation and its freedom, concluded by saying, "Give me peace in my day."

Paine fairly bristled with anger as he retaliated. "Not a **man** lives on the continent but fully believes that a separation (of American from England) must some time or other take place, and a generous parent should have said, "'If there must be war, let it be in my day, that my child may have peace.'"

Amen, and amen!

On the topic of religion, he insisted that he did not believe in the creed espoused by any church that he knew of. "My own mind is my own church," he wrote, and later he established a brick and mortar church of his own, the Theophilanthropic Church, whose major creed was that the greatest religious faith is that of good works to our fellow creatures.

He disliked organized religion and held firmly to the faith that the right **not** to embrace an organized church is at least as sacred as the right to attend the church of one's choice.

"All national institutions of churches," he wrote, "appear to me no other than human inventions set up to terrify and enslave mankind and monopolize power and profit.

Jim Bakker should be thankful that Paine is not alive today. Tom would attack the televangelists in their own pulpits.

At the same time he denounced national religious organizations, he modified his position by saying that he did not condemn those who disagreed with him: "They have the same right to their belief as I have to mine. But it is necessary to the happiness of man that he be mentally faithful to himself. Infidelity does not consist in believing or disbelieving; it consists in profession to believe what he does not believe."

In his Rights of Man Paine set forth the arguments that civil rights are merely an extension of the natural rights of man as they existed in pre-governmental status. He argued that these natural rights include the maximum freedom compatible with the rights of others and that civil government should not interfere with the freedom of man except to insure and protect the happiness of the majority of the people.

Not long after his declarations of human rights, Paine was arrested and sentenced to die for his role in the French Revolution. In a bizarre turn of events, he was spared because of chronic diarrhea.

His jail cell door was marked with a charcoal X so the executioner would know whom to behead the following day, and Paine's cell smelled so bad that the door was left open and the X was turned to the wall and Paine was spared until Jefferson and other friends could help him escape to America.

Then, in the land he named and helped to free, he was denounced by ministers as an atheist (and still is denounced by college administrators who would do their jobs if they knew how) and died in disgrace. He was buried on his farm in New Rochelle, New York, but enemies continued to denounce him until finally he was exhumed and his bones were taken to England. A friend at the exhumation snapped off the final joint of the little finger of Paine's right hand and slipped the bone back in the grave so that some part of Paine would remain on American soil. The remainder of his remains were sold as souvenirs, made into pipe bowls and paperweights, and eventually lost.

And today, exactly two hundred years after Paine published his Rights of Man, he is among the most neglected writers and thinkers of the Revolutionary period. High school history books, if they mention Paine at all, award him a vague mention of a propagandist. Preachers continue to vilify him, and everyone else neglects him totally.

Only a few hack writers (like me) who admire and appreciate Paine's mastery of the English language and his dedication to the cause of individual freedom of thought and actions scribble articles like this to remind others that if it had not been for Tom Paine, America as we know her today might never have existed.

So, thanks, Tom, two hundred years late but from the bottoms of our hearts and the depths of our souls, for making us free and inspiring us to try to stay that way. Δ

A BHM Writer's Profile

Therese Reid lives on a small farm in Northwestern Illinois with her husband and seven children. She was raised in Chicago and was a city girl until she and her husband decided to leave the hustle and bustle of city life. They moved to their farm in 1990 and have slowly learned what farm life is all about.

"One of the first questions I asked the farmer we bought the farm from was, 'So how do you get the eggs from the chickens?' I have since learned the answer to this and many, many more questions," says Reid.

In addition to raising her children, Reid is a free-lance writer. She writes a weekly fix-it column for the Journal Standard, and has been published in several national magazines. "I feel very blessed, having the best of both worlds," she says. "I am able to stay home and raise my children, and I am also able to earn a living doing something I love."

How to stop an invading army . . . TERMITES!

By Grover Brinkman

The area home was less than five years old. A reputable carpenter had built it, using top-grade materials. And yet the owners were suddenly facing a survival trauma situation. Tiny insects were suddenly crawling out of the woodwork, inside and out, the floors and window sills.

The distaff member of the household suddenly was terrorized at what she saw happening to her immaculate home. "It couldn't be termites . . ."

"I don't think so. The house isn't old enough."

This photo of a crawl space shows the tunnels used by the termites to work upward to the foundation of the house. Notice the wood shoring (center) almost completely macerated by the insects.

"But they look like termites!"

"They most certainly do."

"This is survival confrontation! How do we get rid of them?"

"Keep your cool. We'll call in a good termite man."

That little scene very well could be fiction. But it was a fact!

If you as a home owner never have had any experience with termites, give yourself time. The odds are good that eventually they'll find you.

It is not the intention here to grow dramatic. But most of the nation is overrun with termites of two types—the subterraneans and the top-floor dwellers, often referred to as drywood termites. The latter are found mostly south of the Mason-Dixon line. The subterraneans do about 95% of the damage to any wood construction.

The termite must have moisture to live, so a favorite habitat is in damp places, under patio cement at the base of foundations, and in damp cellars. If you suspect termites, get a good flashlight and carefully check the foundations and sills, foot by foot. If you spot what looks like small mud tunnels leading up from the ground to the building proper, the bugs have invaded. Termites travel up and down these tunnels to reach their cutting zones.

Oddly, this ant-like insect with the hard snout seldom attacks living wood. They prefer the dry lumber in the building itself. As one termite eradicator explained: "Dry wood is chocolate candy to the termite. Usually the builder, rushing a job, doesn't clean up too well. Many small pieces of wood are buried near the house. Sometimes it is easier to bury than pick up. This is all the termite needs."

Often termites can be detected in early spring when one sees flying insects coming from a basement window, from the edge of a concrete wall, or even inside the house itself.

Don't be fooled. These aren't "flying ants" as so many people suppose. Instead they are winged reproductive forms called alates that leave mature termite colonies each season, swarm like bees and mate. In other words, if you spot these winged insects coming from your woodwork, you have termites, the "advance men" of the insect army. So get busy!

There are many old wives' tales to the effect that termite men carry live insects to the scene to get a job. Nothing could be further from the truth, if you are dealing with legitimate exterminators.

If the termites have invaded, the exterminator will spot the tunnels. If you do not have them, he'll also tell you this heartening fact.

How are the varmints stopped?

Basically, get down to their nests even if it involves crawling, digging or other hard labor. That might mean drilling numerous small holes through concrete or base timbers, into which is injected an approved chemical under pressure. Some of the strongest chemicals are no longer available to the lay person but licensed termite firms have access to them, and know how to use them safely and effectively. The right chemical will stop the termite cold and make a complete kill. These chemicals are also good bug deterrents, killing most types of crawlers, roaches and spiders that invade homes new and old. Any approved chemical will have a long kill-life after application.

One-half inch holes were drilled through the concrete, following the house foundation, through which the chemical was forced. Lastly the holes were closed with cement. This one house required the drilling of more than 100 holes for complete protection.

In treating the "new" home mentioned here, the terminite people used a hydraulic drill to pierce the concrete slabs in the breezeway and porches, also in the garage floor. One- half inch holes were drilled, spaced two feet apart. Into these holes, the chemical was forced under pressure, each injection timed with a watch, so each hole had the same amount of chemical. Afterward, the holes were plugged with concrete and were hardly noticeable.

Next, the entire outside of the house was treated, using a hollow probe that put the chemical down into the soil for at least 2 feet apart.

"One reminder," the termite man said, "don't plant any flowers or shrubbery near the foundation walls, for the soil is sterile. This sterility lasts for several years."

If termites have already invaded the building, interior treatment must be resorted to as well. But if detected in time, outside treatment should be sufficient. One can do all of this without calling in a specialist, providing a hydraulic drill and an injector device is part of one's tool kit. But the termite man, a professional, usually does it better.

The legitimate termite exterminator, after treating your property, will also offer a service contract that insures an annual return visit to recheck. This inspection fee is nominal, and adds to one's peace of mind.

In treating the house mentioned here, the source of the termite invasion was traced to wooden shoring left underneath porch and breezeway floors by the contractor. When building, the owner would be wise to pick up each piece of waste lumber, and see that none is left as shoring in crawl spaces. Don't bury it, as is so often done. Burn it!

Treatment for termites is also available as a new structure goes up, usually cheaper than waiting for an invasion. If the basement walls and sills of a dwelling are treated at time of erection, the cost will be far less due to easy access of all areas.

The ecologist will assure you that the termite is not all bad, and of course he is right. The insects chew up millions of fallen logs, put the humus back in the soil, just as nature intended. But as far as this insect is concerned, your home, barn or any outbuilding is nothing more than an old log, to be chewed into oblivion. It seems uncanny that this tiny insect, not much larger than an ant, would have the ability to fully macerate the large foundation joists of a house, but such is the case. In time the termites turn into sawdust the entire piece of lumber, working from the inside, leaving only a thin shell. Termite men will tell you of old buildings, so eaten by termites, that one walks across a floor, and suddenly finds it caving-in underfoot.

In this war on termites, it is important to recognize the insect on sight. Perhaps the number one imitator is an ant. Termites have erroneously been called white ants, but in reality they are closer to cockroaches in origin.

Remember, the subterranean termite must have contact with the soil to live. So attack them at ground level and below. Dig up a rotting stump and you'll see the termites far below ground level, in the root tips. In your home, tear down any tunnels that you find cemented to the woodwork or concrete walls.

It is the duty of every home-owner to check periodically for termites. Remember they cost Americans millions of dollars in repairs annually. Paradoxically, the termite is useful in nature's plan, converting dead wood into humus. Don't forget, that to a termite, your home is just another log to be chewed into sawdust.

The termite has been around for millions of years, as evidenced by fossil insects found in archaeological digs. Remember, this insect has a soft, pale abdomen broadly joined to a thorax (chest) and its head possesses a pair of bead-like antennae. Ants on the other hand are darker, with a narrow pedicle between abdomen and thorax, and their antennae are elbowed.

Like bees, the termites have kings and queens – different castes do different jobs. It is the worker caste that

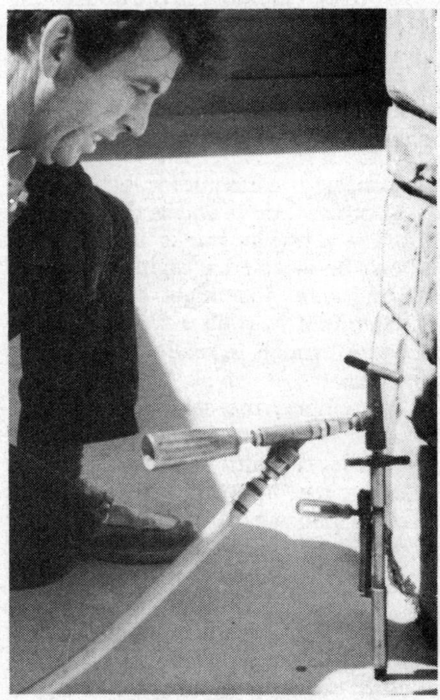

Here a solution of toxic chemical is being forced into a hole drilled in patio concrete. Holes were spaced so there was full concentration of chemical under the patio. Here it was that the insects started.

does the damage. A termite also is easily recognized by its massive head and mandibles. Remember, the subterranean termite, which does 59 percent of the damage to buildings, is found in every state in the union, although the northern tier of states have fewer than areas in the south due to rigorous winter climates.

The termite works with great sly skill, and many times the inroads of the insect is unnoticed until great damage is done. Modern home heating permits the termites to work all the year round.

The winged adult reproductive termite, commonly called "swarmers," can land in your yard at any time, and soon invade your home for their food supply. This is why a home might be entirely free of termites today, and several months later be infested. Termites have been with us since the beginning of time, but for many years their damage was referred to as "dry rot," until the insect was discovered and their habits ascertained. Today, termite eradication is a science, badly needed.

This article should cover the basics concerning termite invasion and eradication, but if you're still confused or troubled, remember the Department of Agriculture has authoritative literature on the termite and its control. Any library also has books on termites. Don't be alarmed at sight of the first "flying ants" you might see. It takes about three years after first infestation for the termites to really damage your home.

Remember, the sole purpose of a termite's life is maceration of wood. Don't let this little insect with the big head chew up your home because you're ignoring the problem. Once the foundation is gone, you're in trouble!

We talk of survival tactics in our lifestyle. Sooner or later, most people face these traumatic moments in their lives. Usually it's some physical violence, man, or nature. One seldom thinks of a tiny insect as an army of destruction. But that is the case. Once termites invade a building, floors crumble and foundations sag in a very short time. The termite has a voracious appetite and wood is its diet! Δ

A BHM Writer's Profile

Ilene Duffy is the business manager for *Backwoods Home Magazine*, but she also has written articles and book and video reviews. As the main proofreader for each issue, she is responsible for the remarkably low number of typographical errors that appear in *BHM*. A former bilingual kindergarten and first grade teacher for nine years in California, she originated *BHM's* very popular "Just for Kids" pages.

Ilene gave up teaching to become *BHM's* business manager shortly after she married the magazine's publisher, Dave Duffy. She says the biggest benefit of working with the home-based magazine is being able to stay at home with her three young sons and to raise her family in a quiet, country setting.

FARM AND GARDEN

Your garden has a history

By Dianne L. Beetler

There is an interesting story behind many of the vegetables we plant in our garden. When Columbus and other explorers came to the New World, they discovered many new plants and carried them home.

South American Indians were growing potatoes in the Andes Mountains when the first explorers arrived. When they took some back to Europe, the potato was regarded as a curiosity, but it soon became an important food item. Before long, it was a staple crop in Ireland. The Irish potato became known by that name in the American colonies when Irish settlers in New Hampshire first planted it in 1719.

Another important food crop which originated in the New World was corn. Columbus found the Indians growing maize. Corn was sometimes used as money by the settlers. Sweet corn was a development from field corn. The first recorded reference to sweet corn was made in 1779 when a variety called Susquehanna was planted near Plymouth, Massachusetts.

Peanuts, also known as goober peas, originated in South America. This plant was also taken to Europe, and then was sent to America as food for slaves. Peanuts were not regarded as an important commercial crop until near the end of World War I.

George Washington Carver found more than 300 uses for this plant and its fruit. The shells can be ground to powder and used in wallboard and plastics. Peanut oil is used in shampoo, shaving cream, cooking oil, and paint.

Central American Indians first grew the tomato. When it was taken to Europe, the tomato became involved in superstition. Some people believed it stimulated love and called it the love apple. Others believed it was poison. Usually it was grown as an ornamental plant, but between 1820 and 1850, people accepted it as food.

Peppers were also first grown in the New World, and Columbus discovered them in the West Indies.

Beans were cultivated by the Indians and eaten by the explorers during their travels. When dried, they were lightweight and easy to transport. The large lima bean was developed in South America and is named after Lima, the capital of Peru.

At the same time that explorers and settlers were finding new plants in the New World, they were introducing plants from the Old World. The Spanish are responsible for bringing eggplant, artichoke, and onion to this continent. Columbus brought lettuce with him. Before that, lettuce had been used as food by Romans and was a favorite dish of the Persian kings.

Two plants native to Africa are okra, sometimes called gumbo, and watermelon. Parsley first grew in Sardinia and southern Italy. The Romans used it to form garlands to crown their heroes, and the Greeks used it at funerals and other important occasions.

Some of our present-day foods were once considered medicines. Asparagus was both food and medicine for the Greeks and Romans. Although they didn't eat carrots, they used them for medicine. Spinach, considered a special food in Europe, was used as medicine by the Persians. Before the 1500s, horseradish was also used for medicinal purposes.

Besides the lima bean, the names of other plants give a clue to their origins. Brussels sprouts came from Belgium. Cantaloupe is a type of melon that came from Cantalupo, Italy around 1890. Swiss chard was grown in Switzerland as early as 350 B.C., but didn't arrive in the United States until 1806.

Another comparative late comer to our country is rhubarb, also called pieplant. This plant, native to central Asia, was grown in Britain but reached this country from Italy in the late 1700s.

The stories behind our plants are many and varied. The next time you harvest food from your garden, stop a minute and think about the history of the plant. You may be about to eat the favorite dish of kings! Δ

A Fish Story

Some fishermans on Lac St. Pierre
Bout half mile from the shore
Fish real hard for two tree hour,
Byembuy they fish some more.

Some time they fish with ole dry bait,
Some time they fish with wet.
They give the fish that ole dry bait,
Themselves--the wet--you bet.

Long time no fish did never come,
Then two tree four pass by;
They see and smell that ole dry bait,
And wink their other eye.

Byembye one big ole bass
Bout seventy leven pound weight,
So old he never see or hear,
He take that ole dry bait.

That fisherman he stand so still,
And reel out yards of line;
He's work that poor blind bass
So very very fine.

Byembye that fish he start to pull,
And then he's pull some more,
And then was fun on Lac St. Pierre
Bout half mile from the shore.

That fish he's plunge like one mad horse,
And then he's pull like ten;
He's tow that boat nine mile an hour-
Big boat and tree big men.

Soon that fish did faster go,
The boat she speed up more;
That fish he's turn off to the right;
By gar, he's head for shore.

He's don't know where he's going
Either now or then;
And up he runs himself on shore
So's he can't swim again.

The men jump out and grab that fish;
He's leave one great big hole.
And now when you look at the lac
All you can see is shoal.

At Lime Kiln Crossing it get so low
That boats they cannot pass,
And Lac St. Pierre fall four-five feet
When they take out that bass.

Lorne S. Inglehart

Handgun choices for women who want to provide their own defense

By Michelle Richards

It is my somewhat radical belief that any handgun of any caliber that you shoot well, with relative comfort, is a viable defensive weapon. This is a radical concept because for years I have been reading and discussing with men the merits of guns and I've found myself trying to understand their views, but never really have. Men seem to approach guns with the bigger-the-better theory, and yes, that has its merits, but it does not take into consideration such natural phenomena as flinching (the body's **natural** reaction to **sharp** loud noises) which many men say they aren't afflicted with, but are. I know it's so. I've watched them. Men believe they must overcome the flinching message their nervous system sends, whereas women seem to do the opposite.

Women are not afraid to say they dislike a gun they feel is just too powerful to control. They can't hit the target. This seems to be the crux of the issue to me. But if you use a lesser kicking handgun that you control well, you will hit your target. And that in a nutshell, is the point of having a handgun for your defense.

The most important consideration I see for women is size of the handgun. It must fit you. My hands are fairly large for a woman my size yet many guns produced today are just too big for me. I cannot get my hand around the grip comfortably nor can I reach the trigger with any comfort. I'm going to give you the measurements of my hand so you can compare your hand size to mine. If your hand is very much smaller than mine some information may not be of value to you, but if your hand is larger than mine you will be able to have more choices available to you. Okay, the measurements are as follows:

- **Base of palm to end of trigger finger = 7"**
- **Across palm, above thumb joint = 3 3/4"**

With these measurements in mind I'll discuss calibers and what I believe are good choices as far as reliable and well-made handguns that are available on your dealer's shelves. I make these recommendations solely based on the fact I am a gun dealer, but please remember I've not had every make and model go through my hands nor personally tested them all. Because I believe very greatly in keeping Americans working I will advise you that I will have as my first choices guns made by American firms, i.e., Smith and Wesson, Colt, Ruger, Charter Arms, etc. I also know some foreign manufacturers make excellent guns for less money. Taurus Manufacturing from Brazil makes excellent handguns with a lifetime warranty and they run approximately $75-100 less than a comparable American manufactured gun. One bright spot is that Taurus just opened up a new factory in Florida and has put some Americans to work.

Women seem to be under the impression that handguns bark loudly and will jump out of their hands and bite them. Ain't so gals but it is necessary to have the mind set that you are "taming the beast." Handguns do bark, but with a positive attitude and practice they do not bite. I personally love 357's and 44's. The harder they kick the more I like it. It's a challenge to me to control and tame the beast. I just plain love hard kicking handguns. But you may not.

The solution, then, is to get you into a handgun you can be **comfortable** using and enjoy shooting. The problem lies in the fact that the larger the caliber, the more recoil there is and the gun must be made bigger and heftier to withstand the forces that imparts on the metal in the handgun. So we have a problem in that to fit your woman-sized hand it must be manufactured smaller in size and lighter, thus the recoil can be tremendous. Many women have reported to me that gun shops try to sell them basically two types of guns—.25's or .38 Special Snubbies. The .38 Special Snubnose (short 2" barrel) is a little monster to shoot. The blast due to short barrel length is dazzling and the recoil is sharp and and in my hands the gun seems to torque sharply. If you've read prior articles of mine in *BHM* you know I don't find many merits in .25's. The .38 is a very good self-defense caliber and is available in many guns that fit women superbly, but it will take practice, a great tame-the-beast attitude and I suggest a 3" barrel.

There is much controversy in gun circles as to which is better—an autoloader or a revolver. Basically, I believe it is a personal choice. For myself, I have chosen 90% of the time revolvers as my concealed carry guns. But, I also have a Colt Government Model .380 autoloader I carry when it is necessary to carry one that is very thin. I've chosen revolvers for their simplicity of operation. Revolvers in the double action style are safe and simple to use. Point and pull the trigger. There is no rack to slide or safety lever to remember. Point and shoot. But today manufacturers are making what's called Double Action Only autoloaders that are as safe and simple to use as revolvers. The slide can be racked thus putting a round in the chamber, and the decocking lever is used like an older style safety. The trigger pull is harder than the older style single action, because the trigger must work the hammer through its full arc. Basically I think of Double Action Only autoloaders as revolvers without cylinders. The advantage of autoloaders is their higher capacity of "firepower." The controversy of revolver versus autoloader will go on. Choose what suits you best.

At this point I'd like to pass on some advice. If you chose any autoloading handgun of any caliber please run various brands and types of ammunition through it to test for reliability. One brand may feed better than another. I personally fire any autoloader with at least 100 rounds, and if it malfunctions I will not use it for defense purposes.

Now on to the calibers...

.22 caliber: Many scoff at the idea of a .22 caliber gun as a self-defense tool. I disagree so much that I carry a .22 caliber Beretta Model 21 as my everyday buddy. It is small, easy to conceal (check your local concealed carry laws), and I have 8 rounds immediately at my disposal. This is a medium-priced, well-made little autoloader that I suggest especially for women with small hands and people who have arthritis or other disabling injuries or health concerns. This pistol has a pop up barrel and can be loaded by inserting the ammunition directly in the chamber, thus someone with arthritis or weak hands does not have to "rack the slide". The gun can be carried very safely this way as the trigger must be pulled through a full arc before it will fire. Taurus also makes an autoloader with the tip up barrel feature and is worthy of your consideration. Other choices are American Arms PX-22 and CX-22 of conventional design. In revolvers the Taurus Model 94 has a 9-shot cylinder and the Ruger SP101 Model with a 6-shot cylinder. All the above suggestions fit the average woman very well.

.22 magnum caliber: There's only one choice in an autoloader here. AMT makes the Automag, a pistol that is small enough for a purse or concealed carry. The advantage is of course the extra muzzle energy it produces over the .22 revolver. Taurus 941 9-shot 3" barrel is a good revolver choice.

.25 ACP caliber: This caliber is for autoloading pistols only and generally has been marketed to women. Across the board I find them poorly made. There are only two I'd use if I chose .25 caliber as my choice—KBI, Inc. PSP-25 and Beretta models 950 and 21. These are expensive compared to other brands, but I'm worth it and so are you. I personally would choose a .22 caliber over the .25 ACP as the ballistics are virtually the same and .22 ammunition costs 1/4 of the cost of .25 ACP, thus allowing me to practice and not break my budget.

.32 H&R magnum caliber: This caliber historically has been a good choice for women. The guns are usually built on a small frame so they fit the average woman very well. The .32 caliber, whether it is the S&W Long Cartridge or the H&R Magnum Cartridge, shoots easily. The recoil is very manageable and muzzle flash is negligible. Ammunition in this caliber is more readily available now than in the past, and comes in enough bullet types to make most people happy. There has been a certain amount of debate as to whether a .32 H&R Magnum is a legitimate self-defense round or not. Comparing muzzle energy for factory ammunition, I find the .32 Magnum turns out 200 to 225 foot pounds, depending on gun and load. The Standard Velocity 158 grain .38 special load is listed as delivering 200 foot pounds of energy in a 4" barrel. So, for women who find recoil and blast to be irksome, yet want more power than a .22 or. 25, this caliber is a honey. My choices in this caliber include Smith & Wesson Models 631 and 632, Ruger SP101, and, if on a very tight budget, NEF (New England Firearms) makes two .32 caliber revolvers that retail at well under $150.

.38 caliber: This caliber probably is the most often chosen as a self-defense caliber. Most anyone can learn to shoot this caliber with practice. The recoil and noise is tolerable and the ammunition choices are vast. It is my personal favorite based on ballistics and guns available to fit my hand. I chose the following .38 Special revolvers for you to consider—Ruger SP101, Taurus Model 85, Smith & Wesson Models 640, 64, 36, Lady Smith 36, to name a few. Smith and Wesson makes over 20 .38 special revolvers, many of which you can try for a good fit. In a relatively inexpensive category, Rossi choices include Models 68 and 88. In autoloaders, my suggestions are: Beretta Model 86 Tip-up barrel for those with arthritis, Colt Government Model .380 and Mustang Model, AMT .380 Backup Model, Taurus Model 58. This 38 caliber section also includes the .357 magnum. I shoot and handle a .357 just fine, but they are large heavy guns and not too useful for concealed carry or purse carry. I understand Smith & Wesson has just marketed a .357 in LadySmith configuration. I have not seen or handled one, but it should definitely be considered. Also, Ruger's SP101 comes in .357 caliber. This caliber with 125-grain Jacketed Hollow Point bullets is considered to be the best "manstopper" on the street. It is a very good choice if you can handle the noise and recoil. These guns also shoot .38 Special ammunition.

9MM caliber: This is today a very popular caliber. It is mostly produced in autoloaders and its advantage is the gun can store 13 and even sometimes 15 or more rounds in the grip. Unfortunately for women this generally makes the grip too fat. Here I'd suggest Smith & Wesson 3900 Series, Ruger Model P85, Taurus Model 92C.

.40 S&W caliber: This is a relatively new caliber and I have virtually no experience with it, and can make no recommendations. Many police departments are considering it presently.

.44 Magnum and .44 Special Caliber: This caliber is in my "whopper" category. The guns are big and heavy with long barrels. It will be hard to find a gun that will fit you here. The only choice I see may be two new guns out this year by Taurus and Rossi, both .44 Specials. (.44 caliber size, but less powerful than magnum). To reduce size and weight these manufacturers have reduced the cylinder size from 6 rounds to 5 and shortened the barrel. If you see one at your dealers, try it on for size.

.45 caliber: This autoloading caliber I believe is one of the best and amazingly it fits the hands of many women. Yes, it's big and heavy, but the gun most associated with this caliber is the old tried and true workhorse, the Colt Government Model 45. It is my theory that in the early 1900's when this gun was designed, men were smaller and thus their hands were smaller. A .45 Colt Commander Model fits me like a glove, but I have to practice diligently to control the recoil and it takes some muscle to rack the slide.

Ammunition:

I believe ammunition is important and have some suggestions. The major ammunition manufacturers have researched and developed some very good ammunition for self-defense purposes. I believe these are excellent choices:

- **Hornady XTP (Extreme Terminal Performance)**
- **Winchester Black Talon**
- **Federal Hydra-Shok**
- **Eldorado Starfire**
- **CCI Lawman**
- **Winchester Sivertips**

If you choose .22 caliber there is no manufactured ammunition expressly designed for self-defense. I suggest CCI Small Game Bullet as it is designed for penetration.

Also, here I'd like you to consider two accessories or after- market items – ear muffs and grips. Not only will ear muffs save your hearing, they also help you avoid flinching by muffling the sound. If you don't hear the loud blast your body's nervous system won't react. Grips are now made for most guns as accessories because manufacturers make generally wood or plastic grips to fit the average male. I find the "average" grip too large and too slippery. Any gun I have over .32 caliber wears a set of rubber-like grips without a backstrap. This gives me a very comfortable padded grip that is virtually slip-proof and shortens the distance from the back of the grip to the trigger. Ask your dealer to install a set for you to feel, it could mean the difference between the gun feeling great in your hands or not fitting comfortably at all. I personally use Pachmayer Professional Grippers on my revolvers as they are designed for smaller-handed police officers, and other brands such as Hogue or others for grips on other type pistols. They really do help smaller hands with the control they may need. If you live in the boonies and have no local dealer, I suggest a mail order firm for these items: Midway, 5875-B W. Van Horn Tavern Rd., Columbia, MO 65203, telephone 1-800-243-3220. Call or write for a free catalog.

If your favorite gun is not included here, that's okay. If it fits you and you shoot it well, it will do the job it is intended to do. My attempt here was to present to you some viable choices based on size, weight, concealability, economics, and what I believe are good choices out in the market place. I did not include single-action firearms, sometimes called Cowboy Guns, not because they aren't good weapons, but because they are usually large and heavy and one must cock the hammer back before each shot. If you have a single action revolver and use it for home defense and are accomplished with it, you have my blessing. I attempt today only to help the neophyte owner to get into a handgun that will fit her and make it possible for her to enjoy shooting and ultimately, if necessary, defend her life. Δ

A BHM Writer's Profile

Lon Gillas owns E-MOTION, a company specializing in high performance electric automobiles, parts, and service. He serves as a government and electric utility consultant on alternative vehicle issues, and is president of the Oregon Electric Vehicle Association. Gillas has been involved with electric vehicle racing for over five years. He coordinates and oversees The Electron Run, Portland General Electric's high school EV-racing program.

Gillas is also associated with alternative power systems for self-reliant living. He developed a reconditioning program for industrial nicad batteries, which can also be used in home power systems. He markets and designs solar and other home power systems.

Gillas has a Bachelor of Science degree in Marketing from Brigham Young University, and has written several articles on electric vehicles and alternative energy for national magazines and newspapers. He is married and has four children, and can be found in McMinnville, Oregon, behind the wheel of an E- MOTION electric car.

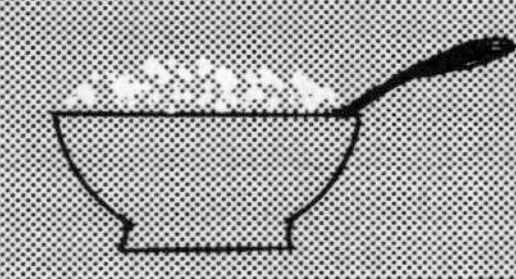

Hearty winter breakfasts

By Jennifer Stein Barker

It's a winter morning. You crawl out of bed and cringe as your feet hit the icy floor. Wrapping yourself in the blanket, you stumble into the kitchen to find your loved one has prepared a breakfast that will warm you from the inside out. You fall in love all over again.

Homestyle potatoes

serves 4:

4 medium potatoes
1 tablespoon canola oil
1/3 cup chopped onion
2 oz. fresh mushrooms
2 tablespoons tamari soy sauce
1/8 teaspoon Tabasco

The night before you want to make this, scrub the potatoes, cut them into quarters (do not peel), and steam them in a basket over boiling water until they are just tender when pierced with a fork. Save the steaming water for soupmaking, and set the potatoes in the refrigerator to chill overnight.

In the morning, slice the potatoes 1/4" thick, chop the onion, and slice the mushrooms. In a large, heavy iron skillet, heat the oil and add the onions. Saute over medium-high heat, stirring frequently, until the onions are transparent. Add the mushrooms and continue cooking until the mushrooms are tender and begin to brown. If they start to stick, add an ounce or two of water instead of using extra oil.

Add the sliced potatoes and cover the pan. Continue to cook on medium-high, checking frequently. As the bottom begins to brown, turn the potatoes with a spatula. When the potatoes are browned and hot through, mix the tamari and Tabasco and sprinkle over the potatoes. Stir to coat the potatoes with the seasoning, and serve.

Hot fruit compote

1 teaspoon minced fresh ginger
1/2 cup boiling water
2 or 3 large apples
fruit juice as needed
1/4 cup mixed chopped dried fruit: raisins, apricots, pears, prunes, pineapple, etc.

The evening before you want to eat this, put the ginger and dried fruit into a medium sized saucepan. Pour the boiling water over them, and let sit overnight. In the morning, add as much fruit juice as necessary to make the liquid in the bottom of the pan about 1/4" deep. Core and cut the fresh apples into chunks (do not peel). Bring the mixture in the pan to a simmer, add the apple pieces, and simmer just until they are tender. Add more juice during cooking if necessary to make an applesauce-like consistency.

Apple oatcakes

These pancakes use only one egg, and are high in complex carbohydrates and soluble fiber. They also taste great!

Serves 3-4:

1 1/2 cups whole wheat pastry flour
1/2 cup rolled oats
3 teaspoons baking powder
1/2 teaspoon cinnamon
1 apple, finely chopped
1 1/4-1 1/2 cups milk
1 egg
2 tablespoons oil

In a medium bowl, stir together the flour, oats, baking powder and cinnamon until very well blended.

In a large bowl, beat the egg and then add the apple, milk, and oil. Add the liquid mixture to the dry mixture and beat with a spoon until well-mixed.

Heat a heavy griddle or skillet over medium-high heat until a drop of water thrown on it will sizzle. Oil the griddle lightly and ladle the batter onto it to make pancakes the size you want. When the top surface is covered with bubbles and the cakes are beginning to set around the edges, flip them over with a spatula. When they are golden brown on both sides, remove them to a warm platter. Repeat with the remaining batter.

Molasses honey

Mix 1 cup of honey with 1 tablespoon dark molasses. Pour into a syrup pitcher and warm by setting the pitcher in a pan of hot water.

Creamy 7-grain with fruits and nuts

If you put dates in your hot cereal, you don't need brown sugar on top of it.

3 cups rolled 7-grain cereal
1/4 cup chopped dates
1/4 cup chopped dried apricots
1/4 cup chopped walnuts
1/4 cup raisins

Keep a pot of boiling water handy to add to the cereal as it cooks. Put all the ingredients into a medium-sized saucepan, cover with water one inch over the grains, and bring to a boil. Turn the heat down a little and cook, stirring frequently, until the cereal thickens. Now turn the heat to your lowest setting. The cereal will continue to cook even if it does not boil. Stir frequently, adding a little boiling water if it becomes to thick. If it sticks, just add a little water and remove it from the heat for a few minutes. The longer this cooks the creamier it gets. When it is cooked to your taste, or you're too hungry to wait any longer, serve as is or with the fruit compote over the top. Δ

Fireplace cooking cures the winter blues

By Robert Williams

Several years ago we experienced a prolonged winter storm that left power lines down and thousands of people without heat, hot water, and operative cookstoves. And for the better part of the week they learned to live a little like the pioneers of old.

The idea was exciting until people realized that the pioneers didn't have electric blankets, toaster ovens, microwaves, compact discs, television, and thermostatically controlled heating systems.

A pot of stew, baked potatoes under the coals, and a warm fire add up to wintertime pleasures.

For the first time in the lives of many of them, they did not harp and harangue at their children to try to be more like the nation's founding fathers. The founders of this country, they now realized, endured more than a few hardships like not having a McDonald's or Burger King to run to when wild turkeys are scarce.

I'm not talking about the elderly and the physically impaired but about the young, active, and physically able people who had devoted their lives to driving to the office or shop, putting in their eight hours, and driving back home to their television sets and electric comforts.

We (I'm almost embarrassed to admit) had a ball. Earlier in the year we had laid in a woodhouse full of good firewood; we had harvested from our garden and small orchard fruits, vegetables, and other edibles; and on a trip to the supermarket we had bought flour and other necessities.

Our old house had four fireplaces, and in one room we had a huge woodburning stove. We knew that heating would be no problem, and cooking would be a snap.

We set about making out menus. For breakfast we wanted bacon, eggs, stewed apples, hot biscuits, and coffee. So I quickly rolled out some dough and cut it into biscuits, placed the biscuits in a huge cast iron frying pan, and covered the fry pan with an old aluminum pie pan.

Frying pans make good bread pans, and even the cat enjoyed the bread.

We placed the pan-oven in front of the bed of coals and tilted it toward the heat by placing a small piece of wood under the back side. Then we raked out coals onto the hearth and set another pan on the coals to fry the bacon and eggs.

In a pot placed over another small bed of coals we chopped up apples and added a tiny amount of water and several spoonfuls of honey from our beehives. A coffee pot replaced the apple pot when the apples were ready.

Within minutes we had our breakfast and more. The bonus was the inspiration to try other dishes, to be adventurous and to risk total failure, if necessary, in order to learn more.

For lunch we decided to prepare onion bread, grilled chicken, baked potatoes, and grilled apple rings. (We like apples and eat them three times a day and for between-meal snacks.)

I used some bricks I had left over when we built a patio and made two stacks, one on each side of the fireplace grate. Then we laid the grill from our regular charcoal grill over the bricks so that the grill itself was a foot or so above the flames.

This time we started the chicken early, let it grill for an hour over the

A home-made cooking rack (made from old conduit sections) is the perfect place for cooking stew, biscuits, fish, burgers, chicken, onion rings, and special breads.

hot coals, and then I added the onion bread which was made simply by rolling out dough into the shape of a fat hot dog and slipping onion rings over the dough.

We placed the dough-dogs on the grill and let them start to cook. As the bread baked (or grilled!) the onions were cooked also and the juices seeped into the bread, giving it a most delightful flavor.

While we were at it, we grilled carrots and other onion rings along with the apple rings. A salad (my wife absolutely refused to let me grill the salad) completed the meal, except for a layer cake I baked in the coals.

To bake the cake, I used the regular batter, consisting of two cups of flour (plain), baking powder, a cup and one third of milk, two eggs, a cup and one half of sugar, three fourths cup of margarine, and a couple of teaspoons of vanilla flavoring. We used regular cake pans for the batter and turned an aluminum pie pan upsidedown over the cake pans, slipped the layers under the coals, and let them bake alongside the potatoes we had wrapped in aluminum foil and placed in the coals.

For icing we used a basic seven-minute recipe featuring egg whites, granulated sugar, and vanilla flavoring, the latter to be added after the mixture was removed from the heat. Because the electric mixer was useless, we held the pot near the fire and stirred with a spoon until the icing was fluffy and stiff.

During the week that we lived without power, we managed quite nicely without the television set and its blaring mind-insulting commercials about the heartbreak of psoriasis, the embarrassment of hemorrhoidal itch, the advantage of one maxipad over all the others, and why we needed a luxury car costing more than our house to make our lives complete.

Similarly, we did not miss the stereo and its cacophony of banging and clattering (although we admit to missing our favorite classical music station) and lyrics about how the singer knew it was just puppy love because the mate's nose was cold.

Instead of re-runs of "My Mother, the Car" we watched the birds feeding on the crumbs we threw out for them and the soft hang-gliding techniques of the huge snowflakes and the swirls of frozen whirlwinds caused by the sudden gusts of arctic air.

In lieu of music we talked, told stories, exchanged ideas and opinions, sang (talk about cacophony!), and enjoyed the silence. When the snow let up for a few moments, we listened to the pecking of the sleet against the windows and the howling of the wind that drew us closer to the fire and to each other.

We read books, outlined in pencil ideas for future stories for some of the publications we work for, and developed story lines for book-length works for future months.

Cooking hot dogs when the stew isn't appealing to young palates.

Our major problem was water, and we were able to get five- gallon jugs full from the woodland spring below the house. We used the spring water for cooking and drinking and coffee, and when we needed water for the bathrooms we melted huge potfuls of snow over the fire.

We learned that we could bake pies, an astonishing variety of cakes and other desserts, several types of breads (including a hot corn bread with caliente peppers and bits of onions and chunks of ham mixed in with the batter), and in general enjoyed essentially all of the foods we could have prepared on the kitchen range, if it had been working.

When appetites differed, we found that we could prepare fish, chicken, steak, burgers, hot dogs, or spaghetti sauce—whatever each of us wanted—so that we had a variety of entrees and side dishes. We found that we could grill many vegetables, such as potatoes sliced wide and thick, peppers, broccoli, cauliflower, and tomatoes simply by placing an aluminum pan over the grill and letting the heat produce a delightful version of stir-fry vegetables.

Our favorite meal was a barbecued rabbit that we prepared by rolling the pieces in a mixture of corn meal, flour, black pepper, and whatever else we felt like putting on it. When we built the fireplace we installed a pot holder so that we could prepare soups and stews handily, and we used the holder more in that one week that we had in any month previously.

We learned that roasted peanuts and popped corn came off the hot coals in a delightfully tasty manner. We enjoyed wiener roasts and marshmallow roasts along with the heartier dishes.

And when the storm ended, we were delighted that the sick and physically troubled people in our area, as well as the truckers and others whose duties required them to be out in the weather, could resume their normal lives.

As for us, we were sad to see the storm go and the electricity return. What we experienced was wonderful in a number of ways, and very little of it had to do with cooking food over an open fire. After all, every aborigine worth his salt learned to do that tens of thousands of years ago.

No, what we learned and felt and reaffirmed was that there is a closeness created and required by the loss of modern gimmicks and conveniences that is unparalleled in our collective lives under normal circumstances. We as a nation or as a community or family find that we must talk during commercials or between innings or between telephone calls. The ice storm was a curse to many; to us it was a very special blessing, and we couch it in terms of fireplace cooking because we have to talk of things rather than feelings and ideas. And the experience was so great that I find myself wishing for another ice storm that would hit only the people who can benefit from another forced opportunity to grow closer to the ones they love. Δ

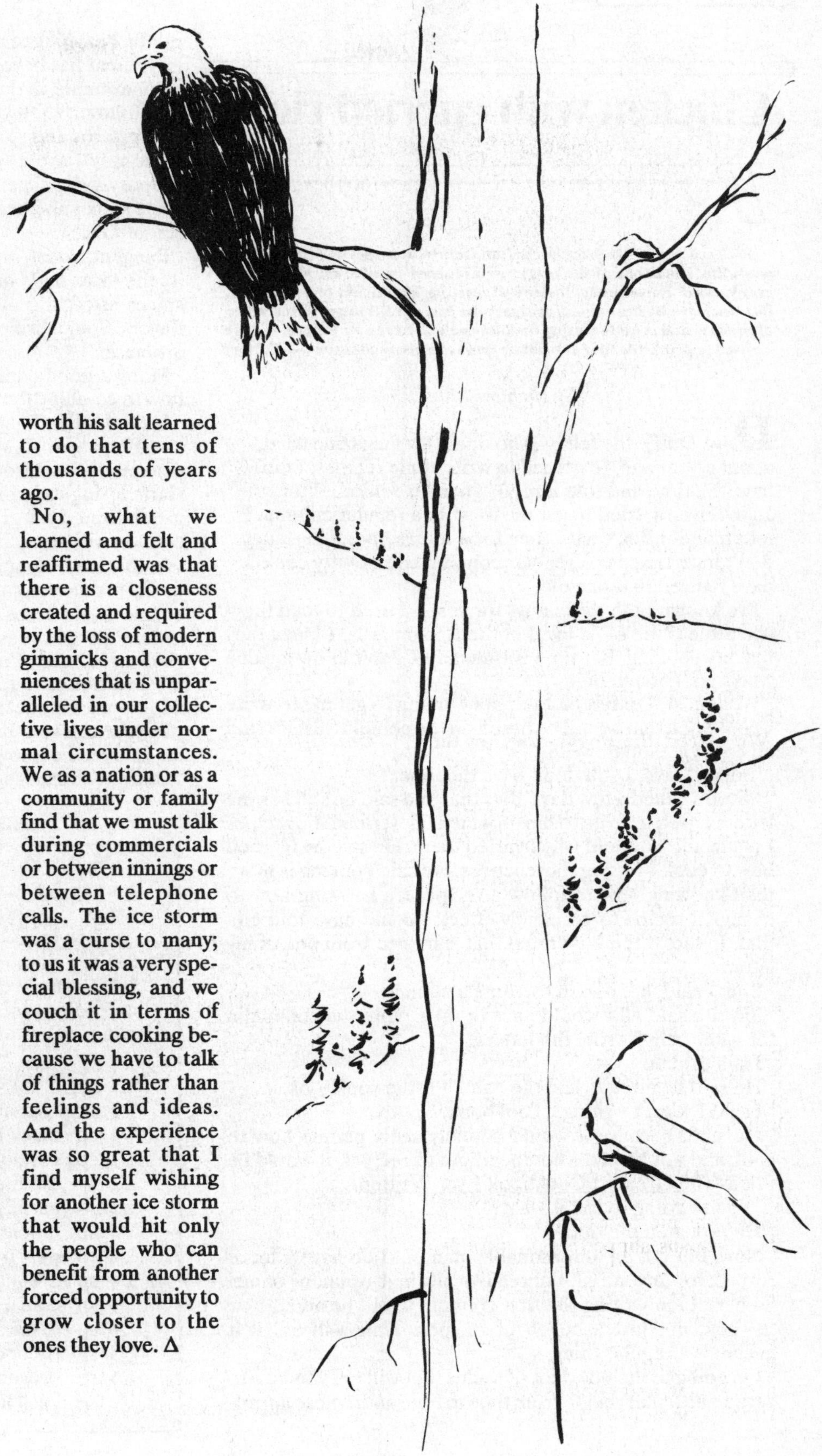

RECIPES

Chicken with curried rice

(Richard Blunt has been a chef or dietary manager for most of his adult life. His is one of the brightest and most creative minds we have ever known. Fortunately, instead of wasting his talents on something like nuclear physics or neurosurgery, he has used it to grace the world of cooking and is quite simply the best cook we have ever known. We are pleased to print this first of what we hope are many columns. — Editor)

By Richard Blunt

Dave Duffy, the fellow who does this magazine tried, about a year ago, to get me to write some recipes. I didn't have the time and told him so. Then his senior editor, John Silveira, tried to get me to write a regular column. I told him, if I don't have time for a few recipes, I certainly don't have time for a regular column. Even Duffy could have figured that one out.

I've known both these guys for years. I used to feed them when the three of us lived in the Boston area. I know they like my cooking, but time is time and I don't know anyone who's got enough of it.

Well, next, Duffy's on the phone trying to get me to write a cookbook that would be based on the column Silveira said he could get me to write.

"Sorry, Dave, I still don't have the time."

Silveira called a few days after that and said he still has the letters I used to write to him in which I described the recipes I made and how and why I varied them. He said he learned how to cook by using those letters. He said cooking is more than knowing how to follow a recipe, it's knowing how to change a recipe to get a new effect. I could have told him that. In fact, I think he lifted that sentence from one of my letters.

Still, I said, no, I wasn't writing a column.

Silveira said all I would have to do is write the column in the same vein I wrote the letters.

I still said no.

He said he already had the name for the cookbook.

I said I wasn't writing a cookbook.

He said, because it would actually show people how to cook and not be just a compendium of recipes, it would be titled, The Greatest Cookbook Ever Written.

"You're going to call it what?"

He repeated the title.

Now, I'm not an unreasonable man but I do have a lot of respect for anyone with unrealistically high opinions of me. So here I am writing the first column. It will be about **how to cook**, not just a bunch of recipes. Time will tell if it becomes a regular thing.

I'm going to include a lot of asides that will tell you how to vary a particular recipe from time to time and, where appropriate, I'm going to include remarks telling you why a certain ingredient has been included in the recipe.

For example, in the list of ingredients for the seasoning mix that follows, I tell you what the principle property of each of the herbs and spices are.

The way I see it, you taste herbs and spices in four very simple ways: pungent, sweet, bitter, and aromatic. Of course some spices and herbs contain more than one of these taste sensations.

Pungent, sweet, and bitter herbs and spices affect primarily the taste buds on the tongue while aromatic herbs and spices affect the olfactory (smelling) nerves and enhance flavors. Some, like oregano, are both pungent (slightly) and aromatic.

Many a good cook is good just because he or she knows how to combine the herbs and spices to get a desired affect.

Incidentally, though grinding your own spices may seem an affectation to some, if you grind your own, you will discover a world of livelier flavors. Pepper, for instance, starts losing its aromatic qualities within minutes after it's ground and if you grind your own for both cooking and table use you will bring livelier flavors to your food.

In this lead-off column I'm going to show you what wonderful results you can achieve with just a little understanding of spices and herbs.

Many people season their flour or batter when they fry chicken but what I'm going to show you here is how to apply the seasonings directly to the chicken before frying. In addition, I include a lightly curried rice that I use to accompany the chicken. If you're counting calories and saturated fat, this recipe is low in both.

Okay, with that said, let's get started.

Chicken with curried rice

1 chicken (2-3 pounds) with the skin and excess fat removed. By removing the first two joints of the wings, skinning will be much easier. Cut the chicken into eight pieces.
3/4 cup all purpose flour
1-1/2 cup olive oil (Each cook has his or her favorite cooking oil. For taste and healthful properties, mine is olive oil.)

Chicken seasoning:

1-1/2 tsp salt (salt blends the flavors)
1/4 tsp black pepper (light aromatic)
1/2 tsp cayenne pepper (very pungent)
1/2 tsp dry mustard (pungent)
1/2 tsp garlic powder (lightly pungent)
1/2 tsp onion powder (pungent)
1/2 tsp paprika (sweet)
1/4 tsp ground cumin (aromatic)
1/8 tsp cinnamon (sweet)
1/4 tsp thyme leaves (lightly pungent)
1/8 tsp rubbed sage (aromatic)
1/4 tsp oregano leaves (sweet aromatic)
1/2 tsp basil leaves (sweet aromatic)

Lightly curried rice:
1-1/8 cups uncooked white rice (do not use the quick cooking type)
1-1/4 cups beer (The hop and barley malt flavors of the beer are important to the flavoring of the rice. I do not recommend any of the light beers. To achieve the characteristic light taste, the breweries significantly reduce the amount of hops and barley malt while increasing the amount of rice and other grains which produce only alcohol without imparting flavor.)
1 cup chicken stock, homemade or canned. (Many people insist on making their chicken stock from scratch and show prejudice toward commercially canned products. I have, over the years, often used canned stocks and have never failed to achieve excellent results with them.)
3 oz. sweet green pepper, diced fine (if you want to add some heat to the recipe, substitute 2 oz. of diced fresh chili peppers
3 oz. onion (diced fine)

1. Combine the seasonings together and blend well. Mix 2 tsp of the seasoning mix with the flour and pour it into a large sturdy paper bag. Sprinkle the remaining seasoning on the chicken pieces coating the chicken on all sides and lightly rubbing each piece with your hands to spread it evenly. Place the chicken in the bag and shake vigorously to coat the chicken evenly with the flour mixture. Set the chicken aside, at room temperature, for about an hour. This will let some of the seasoning penetrate the meat.

2. Heat the oil in a large skillet until it reaches frying temperature, about 350 degrees. The smoking point varies among the oils so watch it closely. A handy rule of thumb is to drop a piece of celery or carrot into the heated oil and if it sizzles immediately, the oil is hot enough to fry with. Brown the chicken on both sides. Don't try to cram it all in the pan. Fry a few pieces at a time to avoid cooling the oil which causes the flour and seasoning to wash off the chicken. Keeping the oil hot also prevents it from soaking back into the chicken. When it's done, place the cooked chicken on paper towels to drain.

3. After all the chicken has been cooked, carefully pour the remaining oil into a small metal bowl and wipe the pan with a paper towel to remove the sediment.

4. Return the pan to the heat with 1-1/2 tablespoons of the oil you used to fry the chicken. Bring the oil back to frying temperature. Add the diced onion and pepper and saute them until the onion becomes translucent, then add the curry powder. Continue to saute for about another minute. To prevent the curry powder from burning, stir the mixture constantly with a wooden spoon.

5. After about a minute, add the rice and continue stirring until the rice has absorbed the oil and has become a light brown. This process of sauteing the curry powder and rice are important. Curry powder must be fried to properly blend its various spices and release their flavors. Sauteing and browning the rice prevents the rice from sticking together when you add the liquid. Browning the rice also adds a wonderful nut-like flavor to the finished product.

6. Add the chicken stock and beer to the rice and vegetables, bring the mixture to a simmer, then remove it from the heat.

7. For the final step, return the chicken to the pan with the rice, cover the pan with foil and put it into a 350 degree oven for about 45 minutes or until the rice is tender and has absorbed all the liquid. An alternative is to put the rice and liquid into a large casserole, add the chicken, and proceed as above.

When it's done, serve it.

If you like the nutty taste of ciccioli (that's cracklings in Italian) leave the skin on the chicken when you prepare it and experience another taste sensation.

If you really feel adventurous, and want to build the recipe from scratch here are recipes for a chicken stock and a curry powder. You could also make your own beer, but we will save that for another time.

Chicken Stock (about 1 quart)

3 lbs. raw chicken trimmings (necks, backs, wings, etc.)
3 qts. cold water
1 onion (peeled and quartered)
1 clove of garlic (whole and unpeeled)
2 ribs of celery (cut into large pieces)
1 carrot (unpeeled and cut into large pieces)

Combine all of the above ingredients in a pot and bring to a boil. Reduce the heat and simmer for at least two hours—four hours is preferable. As the stock boils down, continue to add cold water maintaining about a quart of stock in the pot. When the stock is done, strain it and spoon off the fat. If you aren't going to use it immediately, refrigerate it until you do.

Curry Powder

This is an all purpose curry powder and it's slightly aromatic. To increase the aromatic quality, add a little fenugreek and a little allspice. Let your own taste be your guide.

1 tbs tumeric
1 tbs ground cumin
1 tbs ground coriander
1-1/2 tsp ground ginger
1-1/2 tsp freshly ground white pepper
1/4 tsp ground cardamom
1/4 tsp cayenne pepper
1/4 tsp mace
1/4 tsp dry mustard
1/8 tsp ground clove

Blend, and you have a fine curry powder. Δ

Just for Kids — rainy day magic

By Lucy Shober

Sometimes at this time of year, it seems that the sun has just given up on trying. Day after hazy day of rain and drizzle have kept you hostage 'till your brain itches, and homework has suddenly become interesting. These are the times to employ some rainy day magic.

You'll just need a tad of adult help, and a little preparation, so follow these instructions to create an extra special day for yourself.

- **Step 1. Get delighted! The weather is in your favor for a great adventure.**
- **Step 2. Follow recipe for "Can't Stand to Follow a Recipe but Sure do Like to Eat...Granola" fill a plastic bag with as much as you want, and put it into your right hand raincoat pocket.**
- **Step 3. Before adding chocolates and syrup to granola recipe, remove several hands full of the mixture and put them into a plastic bag. Put the bag into your left pocket.**
- **Step 4. Ask your adult friend to please heat up a pot of apple juice or cider for you. (You'll need this later.)**
- **Step 5. Prepare yourself! There's nothing worse than being unprepared for a walk in the rain. If you have leaky shoes, then put some bread sacks on your stocking feet before you add the shoes. Find a hat and bundle up under your rain gear.**
- **Step 6. Lets go!!!**

Some things to notice on a rain walk

Though it might seem that nature curls up and sleeps these sloshy days, things are just as busy as ever—you just have to look in different places. Something that you might notice right away is that the world seems to be full of robin birds. Whole armies of them show up on drizzly days, then disappear when the sun shines again.

Rainy days are a robin's paradise. Earth worms which usually burrow deep into the earth during cooler weather, must come to the surface on wet days. Their tunnels become flooded and they have to surface in order to survive. They creep along just below the grass line, and as they wriggle, they make tiny scratching sounds. Notice how the robin cocks it's head before plunging that long strong beak deep into the soil to pull up lunch?

As you stroll, munch on the granola from your right hand pocket. If you spot a small hole in the ground or under a rock ledge, sprinkle some of the left pocket granola into it and around it. A damp chipmunk or field mouse might enjoy a special treat on a day like this!

Look into the trees. At the fork of a branch, you might find an example of one of nature's raincoats. Try to locate a gray squirrel. Chances are that you will find one huddled up under his custom made poncho. See how he curls his tail up and over his back? Each hairlike strand of fur guides the raindrops away from his dry body and onto the ground below.

Raccoons, foxes and even pet dogs come with a ready made raincoat too. They have long waxy hairs which form the outer coat to keep water away from the soft downy inner coat.

Now stoop to the ground to notice tiny rivers of water formed by the drops of rain. Follow these little paths of water and notice how they merge with larger and larger ones. As they become enlarged and more forceful they carry heavier bits of dirt with them. This erosion is one way that the earth was carved millions of years ago. As the streams become torrents of water, they are able to etch huge valleys and crevices.

See how far you can follow your own little river. As you creep alongside it, take time too to notice rainy day artwork. Spider webs left from summer look like silver necklaces studded in raindrop diamonds. The misty air softens edges and makes you feel a part of some forgotten fairytale. Perhaps by now you notice that your stream has broadened and deepened enough that a piece of bark with an oak leaf sail can be floated upon it. Someday, you could return to this spot and find a deep gorge, a reminder of your first rain walk.

By now you are probably out of granola, and in spite of the best of preparations, more than a little damp. This is the time for the best part of your adventure. Look until you find a comfortable log or rock to sit upon, and do just that...sit. Sit and listen, with your eyes closed take a deep sniff of the moist air around you. The drip drip drop, and the rich earthy aroma of damp earth are memories that you will want to keep forever.

When you return home to that hot mug of cider, and a warm blanket, feel your pink frosty cheeks, and make plans for your next rainy day adventure.

Making yummy granola

Have an adult preheat the oven to 350 degrees for you.

Use a large ungreased rectangular cake pan with deep sides on it.

Spread uncooked oatmeal over pan, until it is about half way full.

Scrounge around the kitchen for any of the following treats: peanuts, sesame seeds, wheat germ, favorite breakfast cereal, raisins or other dried fruit (unless you hate raisins and other dried fruit) chocolate chips or chocolate covered peanuts, walnuts, hulled sunflower seeds, etc.

Stir these ingredients into the oatmeal, adding more of what you like and less of what you don't. But **don't** add the dried fruit or chocolate candy yet!

Find some pancake syrup and drizzle it over this concoction, but don't get carried away! Add just enough to make your mixture kind of sticky. (about a cup would do nicely.)

Stir again then stick it all into the stove and cook it for about fifteen minutes, then get your grown up buddy to stir it for you. Cook it for fifteen more minutes, then take it out and let it cool off.

Now...add the dried fruit. (If you had done this before you cooked it, it would have made crisp black cannon balls in your lovely granola.)

Last of all, add the chocolate. As you pour it in, accidentally sneeze, or loose your balance and fall down so that you will have an excuse for dumping as much in as you want. (Probably the whole bag would do well.)

Store this in an air tight container for as long as it lasts, which won't be too long, because most of the time it's **really** good!

There are 22 words in the above paragraphs which are related to "That Rainy Day Feeling." Can you find them?

Make up some words of your own to describe the way you feel on these wet days. Two examples are: **squimmy** and **snurdly**......Have fun inventing your own rain talk to use when you take friends on the next rain walk!

The 22 wet words are: rain, rainy, hazy, drizzle, drizzly, raincoat, leaky, sloshy, streams, water, wet, flooded, poncho, rivers, torrents, raindrops, misty, stream, damp, floated, moist, and drip.

Below, color in the three rainy-day explorers. Δ

Preparing your photovoltaic system for winter

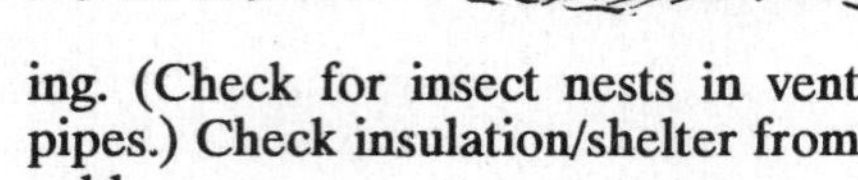

By Windy Dankoff

The winter season puts a solar power system to the test. You need the most energy for lighting, but have the least amount of solar power available. Fall is the time to inspect your system and make adjustments and improvements to prepare for winter's challenge.

The following items should be checked, where appropriate:

Photovoltaic array: Inspect/tighten mounting bolts & wiring, test output, tilt for winter angle. <u>Trackers</u>: oil bearings, check mounting and shock absorbers.

Gas generators, wind generators, hydro-electric: Consult your dealer, manufacturers, instruction manuals, etc.

Charge controller: Check regulator voltage settings; check voltmeter accuracy with digital meter. If batteries may reach a temperature below 55 degrees F, they should be allowed to rise to a higher voltage (14.8V min. on a 12V system). If your charge control has a "temperature compensation" feature, the temperature sensor should be attached to one battery so this can happen automatically. If it does not have this but is adjustable, you may raise the voltage by hand, then lower it again in the spring (to 14.3V). If your controller is not adjustable, then keep your batteries warm.

Batteries (lead-acid types): Test each cell/each battery with digital voltmeter or hydrometer to spot potential failures and check need for equalization. Set up equalization charge if necessary. Ask your system supplier how to do this if you don't know how. Wash away accumulated moisture and dust from battery tops. (Use baking soda solution to neutralize acid deposits.) Clean or replace corroded terminals and coat them with petroleum jelly. Check water levels & refill with distilled or deionized water. Inspect venting. (Check for insect nests in vent pipes.) Check insulation/shelter from cold.

Wiring: Check for proper wire sizing, tight connections, fusing, safety.

Grounding/lightning protection: Install/inspect ground rods and connections, ground wiring. (See *BHM* #17)

Loads/appliances: Check for "phantom loads" and inefficient usages. Examples: Wall cube transformers and TVs with remote control that use power all the time they are plugged in. Does your furnace thermostat hold your inverter on 24 hrs/day? – See below!

Lights: Look for blackening incandescent bulbs; consider more efficient Quartz-Halogen or fluorescent replacements. Clean the dust from light bulbs and fixtures.

Inverters: Check adjustments, settings, connections. Note: Inverters with Battery Charge Option should have charge voltage set around 14.5 (or 29) volts if a generator is to be used for charging. See your manual.

Water supply: Check freeze-protection, pump maintenance, pressure tank pre-charge.

Battery temperature

Lead-Acid storage batteries lose about 25% of their storage capacity at 30 degrees F. If fully discharged, they can freeze at 20 degrees and be destroyed. Summer heat is also destructive. For these reasons batteries should be protected from outdoor temperature extremes. Batteries are safe indoors, if installed properly. See <u>The Solar-Electric Independent Home Book</u> by Jeff Fowler, <u>The New Solar Electric Home</u> by Joel Davidson (*BHM* sells them on page 97), or other installation manuals, and the National Electric Code.

Freeze protection and heat tapes

Electric heat tapes are a popular way to prevent water pipes from freezing under mobile homes, on solar water heaters, in well sheds, and other places where they may be exposed to cold. Where heat tapes are a necessary evil, here are some tips to minimize their energy usage:

Insulate!!! Use foam pipe jacketing, Fiberglas, anything that insulates, and plenty of it. Be sure cold air and moisture are sealed out. **Use less heat tape** than recommended with fewer, wider-spaced coils. With extra insulation, you won't need much heat.

"Frostex" round heat tape is most efficient, but you may wish to add a Line Voltage Thermostat to disconnect it in warm weather. If you use a conventional flat tape, be sure it has a thermostat on it. The thermostat may be tucked into the insulation closer to the pipe so it won't turn on until cold penetrates into the insulation.

Also, **use an inverter** that is efficient for running **small** loads like your heat tape, or **convert heat tapes to 12 or 24 volts!** If you're not afraid to cut and splice, here's how to make a low voltage heat tape:

1. Buy a conventional **flat** heat tape **with thermostat.**
2. For 12V, measure 1/10 of its length from the thermostat end and **cut**. For 24V, use 1/5 of its length.
3. Strip the cut end and connect the two inner wires together using the barrel of a crimp terminal. Be careful; the wires are thin and delicate. Protect the end with silicone sealant and/or tape.

You now have a low voltage tape with thermostat. It will draw the same wattage **per foot** as the original. The neon indicator light won't work, but an ammeter will indicate current flow. The remaining tape may be cut into more low voltage tapes by splicing lamp cord to one end and tying the other end together (using crimp connectors). You will need to add a thermostat if desired. One Line Voltage Thermostat can switch many tapes on and off.

Install heat tapes, even where you don't expect a freeze. They make it easy to thaw surprise freezes without digging, ripping out insulation, etc. Thermostats are optional on these "back-up" tapes.

Furnace and controls

Thermostat circuits and **power usage:** Most central heating systems use a low voltage circuit through a wall thermostat to tell the furnace when to turn on and off. The low voltage is derived from a small transformer which is powered constantly. It consumes only a few watts, but in an alternative energy system that may be a significant load—if it is the only AC device that's running, it is adding constant additional draw just to keep the inverter "up." That amounts to the wintertime energy output of 1 to 3 PV panels, costing over $300 each, plus battery capacity to match!

If yours is a system where the inverter spends most of its time turned off (relatively little AC power usage), it is worth the small modification of adding a Line Voltage Thermostat to your furnace circuit. You may order one from a heating or electric supplier. Have it installed **in the AC line** to the furnace controls. (Also bypass the original thermostat.) This way when heat is not needed, all power is cut to the furnace transformer. A small "limit switch" thermostat may also be added to sense heat in the furnace and keep the blower on until "left-over" heat is exhausted. Material cost of these modifications is under $40, and wiring is simple.

Low temperature setting: When nobody's home you may need your furnace only to prevent your home from reaching freezing temperature (so that water pipes, fixtures, and bottles won't freeze). Most heating thermostats stop at 50 degrees F, but a lot of fuel may be saved if the temperature can be lowered to 40 degrees or less. Electric power is saved too, since the furnace blower will run much less. I suggest replacing common thermostats with a Line Voltage Thermostat listed below.

A "line voltage thermostat" is one that is designed to handle power directly from 120 VAC. A recommended one is Dayton 2E158, available from W.W. Grainger or from any electric or heating supplier. Like most other switches, it will also handle its rated amperage (22A) at 12 or 24 VDC. Its 35 to 90-degree range makes it appropriate for use with heat tapes and furnaces, and coolers and fans as well. The Dayton 2E158 allows switching power on or off with temperature rise, so it also works for switching **fans** on at high temperature for circulation of solar or wood heat.

Being your own power company has its rewards and its responsibilities. Extra attention paid in preparation for winter time will reward you with greater energy independence for years to come. If you are uncertain about working on your system, contact your dealer or a qualified electrician. Δ

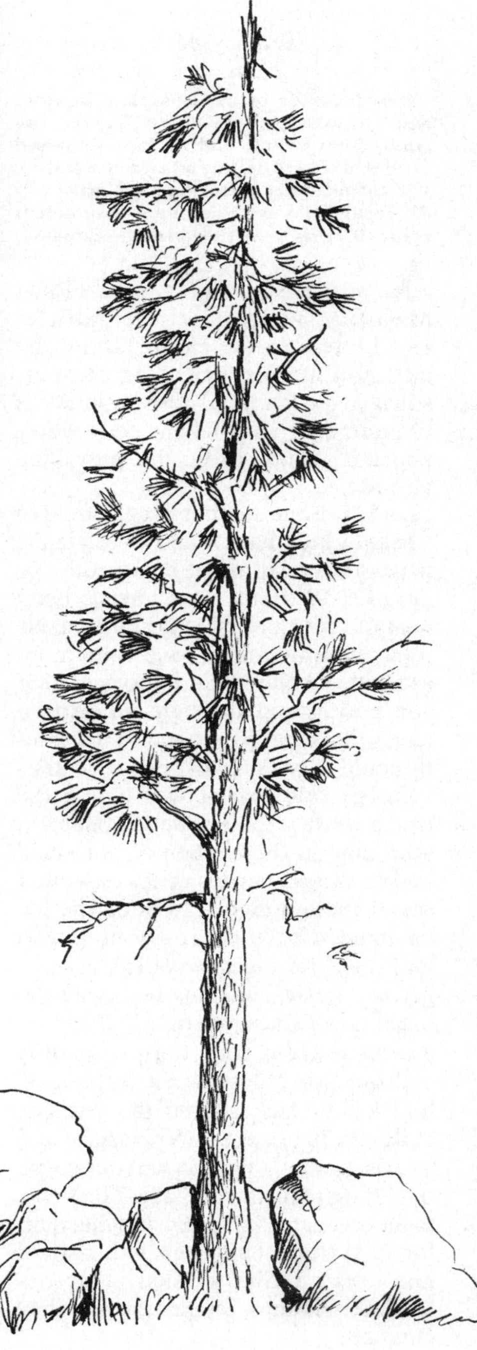

Guilty by default? One family's tragedy and a mother's warning

As told to Shelby Taylor

(The following events took place in rural New York state, in the Southern Tier area. The family is in hiding, and we have promised them that we will destroy all evidence of their whereabouts after publishing this article, in the event BHM is visited by a government agency bearing a search warrant. —Editor)

As readers of Backwoods Home Magazine, we regularly see articles and Letters to the Editor about the intrusion of government on our personal lives. Personal responsibility is discouraged, and "let the feds worry about it" seems to be the prevailing attitude.

I, a lady homesteader, single mom to 5 healthy kids, have found myself in the precarious position of being guilty by default. Without ever having been charged with a crime, my children, my rights and my future have been jeopardized. I believe it's important that you understand through our experiences that what happened to our family could very easily happen to yours.

Earlier this year, I was typing the rough draft of an article I'd been researching in the kitchen of our small mobile home, our living space while I saved enough money to build the log cabin we'd been dreaming of. It was early in the morning, and the kids were getting dressed, making beds with the usual noise and horseplay that can be expected from four happy, healthy children. My eldest daughter, then 12, had left for school and the younger children, Laura age 5, Willie age 4 and Travis, age 2 1/2 were in varying stages of getting ready for the day. The baby, Rebecca, age 15 months, had been up for hours and had been fed, bathed and dressed. She toddled along behind her siblings, laughing when they laughed.

As I worked in the kitchen, I heard a loud "Bang!". What??? I thought to myself, as I toppled the chair I'd been using and raced to the other end of the trailer, about 15 feet away.

The family portrait, taken in early June 1992 while staying with friends. The children in the photo are, from left, Laura, age 5, Rebecca, age 14 months, Kristen, and Willie, age 4. (Photo by R. L. Atkins)

Baby Rebecca stood in the bedroom doorway, crying. Laura stood behind her, wide-eyed, staring past me through the open doorway into the next bedroom. I scooped up the crying baby and did a cursory check of her body—no obvious blood, no bruises. Must have been the noise that scared her.

Looking again at Laura, I followed my little girl's horrified stare and met the frightened eyes of Willie, my 4 year old. He seemed alright but frightened, as did Laura.

"Where's Travis?" I asked, fear beginning to creep into my voice. Travis was our mischievous 2 1/2 year old, always into trouble. He was the only one unaccounted for. I peeked around the corner of the doorframe, following my son's horrified downward gaze and saw Travis on the floor, face down, still wearing his blue footed pajamas.

"Oh my God. What happened to him?" No one seemed to have an answer as I turned him over and looked into his face. His eyes were closed and there was a tiny spot of blood on the front of his pajamas. I scooped him up, shouting directions to the children as I ran to the garage for the car.

"Willie and Laura, take Rebecca and go next door to Rachel's house! Do it now!" The children, drilled since they could walk on emergency procedure, instantly took the baby's hand and went out the back door to the neighbor's house, some 100 feet away. Though we lived in a very rural area, our land connected very close to the houses. There wasn't a house for a mile in either direction, but ours were 100 ft. away. It had not been my choice to have such close neighbors, but on this day it was a godsend.

I raced to the car with Travis in my arms. Placing him on the front seat of our little car, I held his head in my lap as I started the engine. I could see the original spot of blood on his pajamas, but nothing more. Seemingly still breathing, his skin had taken on a waxy, pale effect. Stroking his fine blonde hair, I talked to him as I slammed the car into gear.

"It'll be okay, Travis. Mama will make it better. You'll be okay pretty soon, Honey." I stroked his head, tears in my eyes, aware that for the first time ever, the time when it really mattered, Mama probably couldn't do a damned thing to help him.

As I roared out of the driveway, I saw the other children going into the neighbor's house. I knew they'd be safe. Now, I had to get Travis the 13 miles—all on dirt roads—to the nearest hospital.

We raced to the hospital, covering 13 miles in 7 minutes. The ER nurses gasped when they saw my son, sweeping away with him for emergency care.

Fifteen minutes later, I was told that Travis was dead as the result of a gunshot wound through the heart. He had been dead upon arrival—he'd died with his head in my lap.

Even though I had five kids, none of them had even required so much as stitches. They were a bright, cute, healthy bunch and I had always considered myself blessed. I'd known people who'd lost children, both through death and divorce, and I'd believed that the loss of a child had to be the ultimate in unbearable pain.

Yet, here I stood in a private office in the hospital, a cup of black coffee in my hands, waiting for the Sheriff's Detectives to arrive to investigate the accident. Standard procedure for an accident involving a gun, hospital officials told me.

After they'd taken Travis for treatment, I'd called the neighbor to make sure the other kids were safe. Now I called to tell them I'd be longer than I thought and would be home as soon as I could.

see the children at the neighbor's house and broke the news. The Detectives interviewed them, determining through demonstration that neither child was strong enough to work the bolt and load the gun.

When she was brought to the neighbor's house from school, the detectives interviewed my eldest daughter, Meredith, 12 asking if she had loaded the gun. Fearing punishment, she said no. That left me as the suspect. However, the detectives said they didn't believe I'd loaded the gun and didn't feel I'd been irresponsible and not to worry.

And I believed it. I believed with all my heart that if I just told the truth and cooperated with the officials, everything would be all right.

The view from our house, standing in front on the road. Taken in the fall of 1992. (Photo by R. L. Atkins)

The Sheriff's Detectives interviewed me, asking about the gun and how it had been stored, took fingerprints and did a resin test to see if I had gunpowder on my hands. I had absolutely no idea how the gun had been loaded. I never kept it loaded and kept the shells out of the children's reach in the other end of the house. Finally, we agreed to meet at my house to look for "evidence".

Back at the house, I saw my .22 single shot, bolt action rifle lying on the bed where Willie had apparently thrown it in shock when it went off. We never found the bullet.

After the Detectives had satisfied themselves that they'd gotten all the information they needed, we went to

The kids all came home briefly before the detectives left, and the baby sat in her high chair, eating a cookie. Another set of neighbors came and took the oldest children, while a neighbor girl came and took the baby. I went to make funeral arrangements, select a burial site and other gruesome details.

Returning from my errands, the phone rang. It was the neighbor watching Rebecca. "Can I bring her home now?" She asked. "I can't get her to stop crying."

When the baby came home, I held her and she stopped crying almost instantly. Sitting with her on my lap, I held her against me, smelling her freshly shampooed hair and trying to relax. I shifted position and felt, under her little baby nightgown, a bandage on the back of her right leg. Humm, that wasn't there this morning. I lifted a corner of the bandage and gasped.

Through the front and out the back had gone Kevin's bullet. What I saw on the baby's leg was a gunshot wound.

Off to the hospital again and we discovered that her bone had not been damaged, and that she'd be fine. However, we had to wait again for the Sheriff's Detectives for yet another interview.

We came home and, about this time, Child Protective Services caseworkers showed up, wanting to do their investigation. It was about 9:30 p.m., but I answered their questions and showed them the house, doing my best to be brave and cooperative.

By the next morning, the newspapers had gotten wind of the accident. The tiny town where we lived was in an uproar. An accidental shooting was excitement enough, but a child dying and another shot was enough to incite riot.

The phone began to ring with a bizarre mixture of consolation calls and threats. These were no radical extremists — these were my neighbors. People who, like me, had kids and owned guns.

Our family obtained overnight notoriety. We became the topic of newspaper articles, TV news clips, radio talk shows and letters to the editor. The TV news people from the nearest large city, 120 miles away, camped out in our driveway, and on the day of the funeral, the media was so thick and hungry for tidbits that we couldn't get in to get fresh clothes for Travis's body.

We'd spent the previous night at a neighbor's, in an attempt to get away from the harassing phone calls and the press. Slowly, it started to dawn on me that my children were in danger here. We couldn't go home because of the threats and the media. And, to top it off, I'd heard from a reliable source that Child Protective Services was planning to remove what was left of my family and put the children into foster care homes, pending further investigation of my suitability as a parent.

We—friends and I—made plans to get the children out of the possible grasp of Child Protective Services. I loved my children, had made great sacrifices to give them a decent life, teach what I considered to be decent values—honesty, loyalty, commitment to family. I absolutely refused to let some government agency get between myself and my children for the sake of their paperwork justifications.

So, we ran. The kids got out first and then I followed after the funeral. We have never been back.

The press stayed on the grounds of our house for another couple of days. Vandals trashed the house, stealing whatever they could carry off, even the woodstove. People who had agreed to feed the children's pets until they could find new homes failed to do so, despite 50 lbs. of dog food in the garage. The dogs literally starved to death on their chain outside our home, with people walking by them everyday. The dog warden came for them before they died, but they couldn't be saved.

My mail was stolen and we ultimately lost everything, even the land. The child who'd loaded the gun eventually admitted her mistake to officials, but by then they thought she was lying to cover me. I had arranged before the funeral for her to stay with her father, my ex-husband, where she could get counseling and the security of re-entering school, being with friends, etc. Later, Child Protective removed her from her father's care for a short time, eventually releasing her into his care, though they retained custody.

A criminal investigation was staged, with the objective charge being "Criminally Negligent Homicide". That investigation was ultimately closed several months later when it was decided that there was no basis for a case. Charges were never even filed.

Child Protective Services felt differently about me, however. They initiated a "Petition of Neglect". This petition gives them the right to remove the children from the custody of the parent in question until the parent is found innocent. Yes, Gentle Readers, it's up to you to prove your innocence, **not** up to them to prove your guilt. And in our home state, Child Protective Services is accountable to no higher authority.

If we continue to refuse to cooperate, the court could give custody of my children to Child Protective Services, "in abstentia", without my knowledge or consent or even my presence. If I continue to withhold their location, refuse to make them available, I could be facing Federal kidnap charges, in addition to the bench warrant that already exists for my refusal to attend court.

Travis playing in the creek, his favorite occupation, with brother, Willie, in the fall of 1991. (Photo by R. L. Atkins)

I could be a fugitive from local and Federal charges for simply protecting my children's best interests.

Because we went "underground", so to speak, the children were never removed from my care and are now just as happy and healthy as they can be. They are slightly paranoid about the "bad people", which encompasses anyone and everyone who is not intimate family. I'm not totally convinced that it's any worse than teaching children not to take candy from strangers, but it was certainly not the way I'd intended to raise them.

We may never resolve the issue with Child Protective Services, since I refuse to hand the children over for interrogation and examinations. I also refuse to attend the hearings, with or without them. Remember the news story about the lady who went to jail for 2 years for contempt of court because she refused to divulge the location of her daughter? Who would care for my children if I went to jail for contempt of court?

The point of this story is that it could happen to you. The older child had played with the gun without my knowledge with the 4 year old. The Petition for neglect was based on so many irrational absurdities that it read like a B-movie. Their rationale—1) a gun in the house, despite the fact that it was legal and very common for my area, 2) that we had a hand ax, even though we heated with wood, 3) that we had kitchen knives hanging in a butcher block holder on a wall and 4) that my mail was indicative of a "radical survivalist"—I'd gotten copies of, yep, you guessed it, *Backwoods Home, Countryside,* and a sample issue of the *Survivalist Newsletter*.

Based on these principles, every single one of you has the potential to be victimized by a neighbor or enemy who doesn't like the color truck you drive. One call to the local child protection people, claiming that you are neglecting or endangering your children is all it could take.

Take precautions. Know what might be damaging so you have an answer if you are questioned. Do you have an ax, a saw, a rifle for hunting? Has your child gotten a bruise in a suspect place? Have you spanked your child? Do you know that some localities consider a spanking—the flat of your palm on the child's bottom, without welts, bruises or other damage to be a form of abuse?

Teach your children caution. They may never, I hope, have to use the extreme caution that my children have had to learn. Nonetheless, teach them the theory of laying low. Never discuss what goes on under your roof anywhere but under that roof, with family only. Never, never, never encourage them to tell people that you have weapons or a year's supply of food or that you've taught them how to shoot. Just do it and keep quiet.

Homeschool if possible and if you're so inclined—they will benefit from a better education and less outside influence.

And most importantly, remember that what happened to us could happen to you. With or without a gun. As one parent to another, please take our story to heart. Δ

Using and storing wheat at home

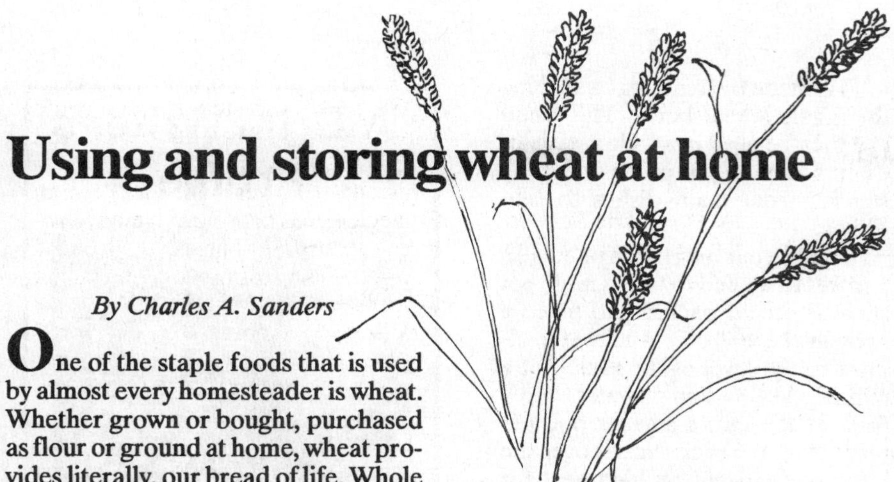

By Charles A. Sanders

One of the staple foods that is used by almost every homesteader is wheat. Whether grown or bought, purchased as flour or ground at home, wheat provides literally, our bread of life. Whole wheat can be made into hundreds of tasty and nutritious breads and foods and is deserving of that prominent place in our diet.

With most of today's store bought flours bleached, enriched, softened and saturated with preservatives, grinding your own flour can not only make good economic sense, but make good health sense as well. Home wheat storage is practical, as wheat flour that is stored at room temperature for over a month loses practically all of its food value. With your own supply of stored wheat, you can easily and quickly produce a week's worth of fresh whole wheat flour. For those of us interested in self-sufficient, self-reliant living, wheat offers much in helping us to sever unnecessary ties to the "supermarket economy", as well as providing more nutritious food for our families and ourselves.

Let's take a look at some good ways for the homesteader to obtain, store and use this golden grain.

For the homesteader who wishes to obtain their wheat in bulk, unprocessed form, I offer the following suggestions:

First, locate a good source of the grain. If you can grow your own, so much the better. You will then have total control over your wheat from seed to finished loaf. Growing, harvesting, processing, and using wheat on the home scale may be impractical for many, due to acreage, time, or desire. However, if you live in an area where wheat farming is common, you can usually work out a deal with one of the farmers to purchase a few bushels from him. If you are a stickler for using organically grown grain, you will probably have a more difficult time locating a source, but keep looking. They're out there, and becoming more common. Commercial suppliers of bulk grains and foods are popping up, providing another source of wheat. Check a few of these out and compare their products, prices, and shipping costs.

Possibly more important than how the grain is raised, is the type of wheat you have and how it is stored. For the homesteader's use, a dark hard winter or spring wheat is probably best. These types tend to store best.

To prepare the wheat for storage, you must first be sure that it is clean enough for human use. To do this, I have used old fashioned wind power to clean the wheat from the chaff. Called winnowing, shovelfuls of wheat are tossed into the air on a windy day, or in front of a large fan. The chaff is simply blown away and the whole grains will drop onto your tarp, plastic sheet, or whatever. You may have to do this a few times to obtain grain clean enough to suit you. The method works well, and I don't know of a better one to clean your grain.

Next, you must make sure that the grain is dry enough to be stored. For home storage, wheat should contain no more than 10% moisture. This low moisture content will help to inhibit insect infestation, as well as prevent molding and spoilage. To dry the grain, you may use a food dryer, however, the time involved in drying such small quantities at a time might make the method prohibitive. I have taken large quantities of cleaned wheat and spread it out on a sheet of black plastic on the deck located on the south side of my house. After a hot afternoon, the direct heat and air combined with the reflected heat from the house lowered the moisture sufficiently to allow me to complete the storage process. I checked the moisture percentage on an ordinary moisture meter which most grain farmers have. If the drying process takes more than one day, merely cover the grain with another plastic sheet come evening, and resume drying in the morning. Note that wheat draws moisture, so watch to keep your grain from being exposed to very high humidity.

Now that we have the wheat cleaned and dried, we are ready to place it in storage. I recommend using 5-gallon plastic buckets for this purpose. They will hold usable quantities of wheat, and are light enough to handle easily. Their round design allows air to circulate between them and they usually have a gasket lining the lid which provides an air tight seal. Finally, you can usually get all of them you need for little or nothing from local restaurants, delis, or bakeries, which purchase bulk food supplies.

I do not put the wheat directly into the buckets, rather I prefer to put it into a plastic bag first. To do this, I bought some non-deodorized 13 gallon kitchen-sized garbage bags. Line each bucket with one of the bags, folding the excess down over the top of the bucket for the time being. Pour in enough of the cleaned and dried wheat to come within a couple of inches of the top.

At this point, I took an ordinary cotton ball and added a dozen or so drops of carbon disulfide. This chemical was obtained from a local drug store (as with any chemical compound, exercise caution in the handling, use, and storage of carbon disulfide). I then placed the dampened cotton ball into an ordinary baby food jar and secured the lid, through which several nail holes have been punched. The jar was placed, with the bottom end up, into the wheat itself, just so the bottom of the jar was exposed. By inverting the jar in the grain, the fumes were able to spread throughout. I then gathered up the excess plastic bag and, removing as much of the air as possible, twisted it shut and attached a wire tie. The lid was placed atop the bucket and tapped firmly into place. This fumigation treatment should take care of any residual creepy-crawlies which might lurk in the grain. Wheat which has been treated in this manner and kept in a cool dry place should remain good for years. Before using the fumigated wheat, I remove the jar and allow the grain to air out for about 24 hours.

Obviously, the home miller will need a method of grinding the wheat into flour. There are dozens of different grain mills available. From hand cranked steel burr mills to electric powered stone mills, you can spend just about any amount you want on a wheat grinder. I have used an old Corona hand powered mill with steel burrs for several years with great results. The only change I have considered is to possibly add a small pulley and set the mill up to use with bicycle power! As with many purchases, you will need to evaluate the amount of use that you expect the grinder to see, compared to the cost of the machine. Decide whether you can use the steel burr grinder or want to get stone ground flour. Do you want an electric model or will a hand-powered one do the job?

Wheat is a surprisingly versatile grain. Of course, far and away its most popular and most suitable use is for making browned and fragrant loaves of fine bread. However, this cereal can be used in other ways.

One of my favorite uses of wheat comes as a by-product of the grinding of a batch of fresh wheat flour. After I grind up a quantity of wheat into flour, I often sift it and remove the coarse leavings. Setting the sifted flour aside to use in breads and cakes, I take the coarse "siftings" and either let them soak overnight in water, or start it directly in the morning. Take about two cups of the coarse cereal and add about six cups of water. Set it on the stove to simmer for about 40 minutes. Once it has thickened nicely, spoon it into bowls, add a dollop of butter, some honey and sit down to a real stick-with-you breakfast! This makes one of the best hot cereals I've ever tasted.

Another good use for wheat is to use the whole kernel or berry to make bulgur. This wholesome and versatile food is made by steaming or soaking the whole wheat berry. The result can then be used in a wide variety of dishes, from soups to crunchy snacks, from main dishes to side dishes.

To make your own batch of bulgur, you will first need to take a large pot such as a cold packer and place a rack in the bottom. Add water almost to the level of the rack. Put a cup of wheat, a cup of water, and a dash of salt into a smaller pot and place it on the rack. Next, cover the large pot and put on high heat for about 15 minutes. Reduce heat and steam until the wheat absorbs all the water in the smaller pot. Once the wheat kernels have fluffed up nicely, you may remove and use them or store them for up to two weeks in the refrigerator.

Bulgur may be used as a hot breakfast cereal by adding milk and sweetener. You can also make a very tasty snack by lightly seasoning a couple of cups of bulgur, spreading it out on a cookie sheet and toasting it in a moderate oven until it is lightly browned and crunchy. Bulgur can be added to any dish which calls for rice or barley with good results. Many soups and salads are enhanced by adding this ingredient. Use your imagination in utilizing this healthful food.

Of course, the most widely accepted use for wheat is for the making of bread. This basic food can be easily prepared at home and is satisfying, not only in its preparation but in its nutritional value as well. Your own rich brown loaves of bread will bear no resemblance to the pasty slices which come from the supermarket.

To make two loaves of whole wheat bread, you will need the following ingredients:

1 tablespoon dry yeast
2 1/2 cups warm water
1/4 cup plus 2 tablespoons honey
3 tablespoons oil
6 cups whole wheat flour

First, dissolve the yeast in warm water. Add to 1/4 cup honey in a large mixing bowl. Then add the oil.

A BHM Writer's Profile

John Silveira is a mathematician, poet, short story writer, and unsuccessful novelist who, when he has to spend nights alone at the offices of *BHM*, won't go outside to the outhouse in the dark without a gun.

Add the flour to the liquid mixture. Knead the dough until it is smooth, then cover and let it rise until it is doubled in bulk.

Punch down the dough and form into two loaves. Place the loaves into two greased 9x5 inch loaf pans and allow to rise again until doubled in bulk.

Bake the loaves in a preheated 350 degree oven for about 30 minutes.

This is a good basic recipe to which can be added other ingredients to provide flavor and texture. Consider adding some cinnamon, a few raisins, sunflower seeds, bulger or chopped dates to give the bread a different and tasty twist.

There are many more recipes and uses for wheat. Your own experimentation will yield great results in cooking with this great cereal grain. If you would like to learn more about wheat, wheat storage and use, I would recommend looking for the book Making the Best of Basics – Family Preparedness Handbook, by James Talmage Stevens, published by Peton Corporation, P.O. Box 11925, Salt Lake City, UT 84147. This excellent book deals with a wide variety of topics for self reliant living. Δ

Raising fishworms as a business

By Robert Colby

Do you remember the movie "Heroes" starring Henry Winkler? Henry played a Vietnam veteran whose dream was to go to Colorado and start an earthworm farm. His friend, played by Sally Fields, thought he was crazy.

Maybe the idea of having a worm farm seems crazy to you too. But it's not. For one thing you can make a good living raising earthworms, with annual earnings capable of ranging from $20,000 to $50,000. Another thing to consider is that it's not too difficult. In fact, it's quite easy to get started.

It does take work, just like most legitimate, legal, and honest businesses. However, we're not talking about back breaking work.

A worm home

To get started you need to prepare a home for your worms. You can start in any kind of container that will hold your bedding material and that will have good drainage. You can use an old wash tub, a 55-gallon drum cut in half, an old wood barrel cut in half, or a plant propagation box. These containers are good for starters, but eventually you'll need to graduate to full size pits made of concrete block, brick, cement, or wood. If you've got room you can just skip the smaller containers and build pits from the start. Make sure you put drainage holes in the bottom.

You can make your own propagation boxes, and you should construct them in uniform size so you can stack them. Once you have your propagation boxes, fill them as shown in Figure 1.

For larger scale production you will want to build pits or bins to raise your stock in. Depending on the area of the country you live in, you will build either indoors or outdoors. If you live in a cold region and want to continue production during the winter you should build indoors. If you live in a warmer climate like Florida or where I live—Arizona—you can build your pits outdoors. Once your pits are constructed, fill the bottom with 3 to 4 inches of gravel. Above the gravel put 12 inches of bedding material. An easy starter bedding material is made up of half peat moss and half manure. The manure must be decomposed past the heating stage to prevent burning your starting breeder stock.

Breeder stock

Once the bed is prepared, place your breeder stock on the surface of the bed. You can get breeder stock from an established earthworm farmer or bait shop in your area. There are mail order sources as well. Coverage should be 100 to 200 breeders per square foot. They will quickly burrow down into their new home. Sprinkle down your bedding with water every day or two depending on climate and how quickly your bedding dries. Don't let it get too dry or your worms will die. The idea is to moisten the bedding, not saturate it.

The worms will feed on the bedding for a while so you won't need to feed them at first. After a week or two, put manure on the surface in a ditch down the center of the pit. Do this daily depending how quickly the manure disappears. Ground grain feeds used sparingly on the surface will help fatten them up for harvest. Water down the surface lightly after spreading a thin layer of grain over it. Spade your bed every 21 to 30 days with a manure fork to loosen your bedding. If you've recently put grain stock on the surface, rack it back to prevent mixing in with the soil. Mixing it in can sour the soil, making it unsuitable for the worms.

Harvesting

You can harvest your first crop in three months if you started your stock with mature breeders. You can tell they're mature enough to breed by the appearance of the clitellum ring around the torso. But if you want any kind of volume to sell you'll probably want to wait a year before you begin sales.

You can keep dividing your stock from one pit into two pits every three months. Every six months you should change your bedding with new compost.

Earthworm soil

Don't throw out the old bedding because it makes great soil for growing your plants or for selling to your local nursery. In fact, if you ask a gardener or nurseryman what the richest potting soil is he will tell you it's earthworm-castings and waste products add high concentrations of nitrogen, phosphates, calcium, and magnesium because they are water soluble and easy for plants to absorb. Earthworms naturally loosen the soil as they move through it, grinding it up in their in-

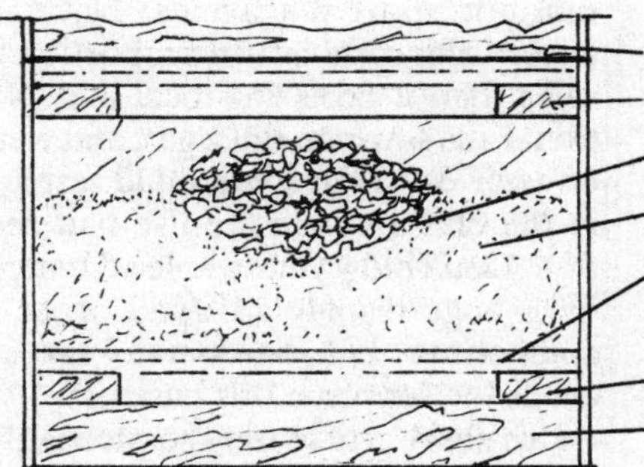

Figure 1. Propagation box

nards. Nurseries will buy the bedding soil the earthworms have so efficiently and naturally processed. There are millions of gardeners in the U.S. and Canada that are waiting customers.

Selling the worms

For containers to sell your bait worms, use ice cream or cottage cheese cartons from your local dairy farmer. Be sure to poke some holes in the lids with an ice pick so the worms can breath. You'll need a variety of sizes starting at half pint all the way up to one gallon containers. Check with your local paper company for boxes to ship the containers in when selling by mail order. Use some moist peat moss to pack them in for shipping.

Be sure to squeeze the excess moisture out of the moss. Too much water can cause the worms to literally cook in their containers. To determine what price to use for different sizes of cartons, call some local bait shops to get an idea of what they are charging.

You can market your products to fishermen if you're strategically located near a lake or stream. Gardeners will buy earthworms for soil enrichment. Contact some local nurseries to sell your used bedding. You can also sell worms to other secondary markets like zoos, aquariums, and poultry farms. You can even sell wholesale to other bait retailers.

If you raise earthworms in conjunction with other animals, you help process the animal waste products. Earthworms are a perfect match for raising rabbits. The earthworms feed on the manure and neutralize the odor of rabbit urine. In addition to rabbitries, your customers would also include poultrymen, game bird breeders, fish hatcheries, zoos, aquariums, frog farmers, and laboratories. Zoos and research institutions use the earthworms for food and in soil research, and they are used in aquariums to feed the fish.

In spite of many new competitors in the earthworm raising market each year, there is much more demand than the producers can keep up with. In fact, your competitors may be one of your best friends. Why? Because they are good prospective customers. And in turn you will be a customer of theirs at some point.

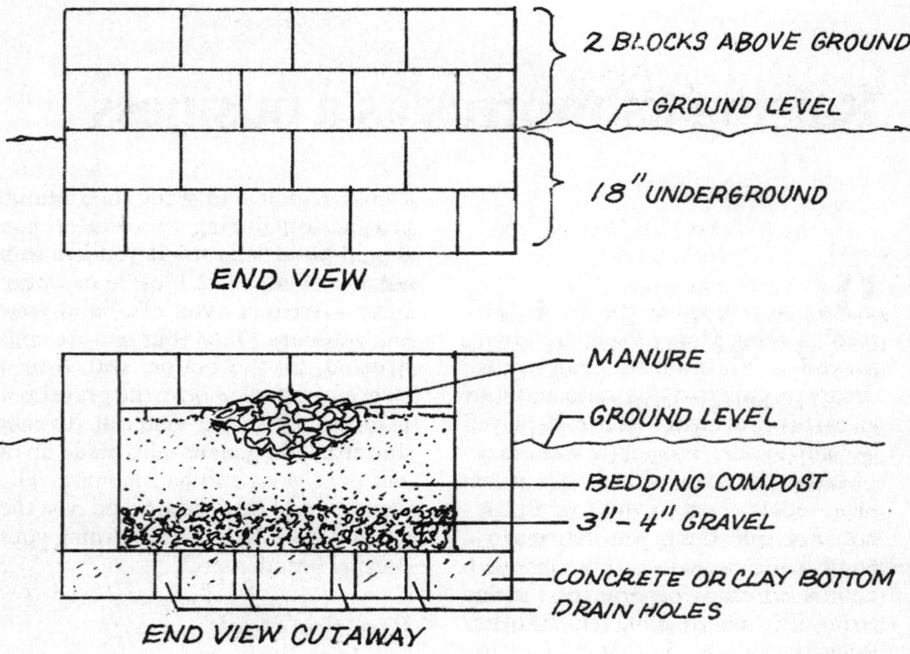

Cinder block pit

When you first start up, you very likely will sell all of your first harvest before your customers stop requesting your product. Your competitors will sell you additional stock wholesale should they have a short term surplus.

Mail order worms

If you want to grow your business you need to do mail order sales. Eighty to ninety percent of all earthworm sales in the U.S. are by mail and the other ten to twenty percent is to local customers.

To advertise, start with one or two outdoor sport magazines. National advertising costs less in proportion to sales than it costs for local ads. National ads save you time, gas, and wear on your car. Run some small test ads in the classifieds in the live bait section. Don't blow your whole ad budget on a huge display ad. Mail order is competitive, but the demand far exceeds the supply in this business.

This short article only scratches the surface on worms; it is meant to whet your appetite. I recommend reading every book you can find on this subject. Start at your local library. Several books were reviewed by Mary Ann Hubbell in Issue No. 16 of *Backwoods Home Magazine*. They were: There's a Fortune in Worms by Hank Haynes, and several by Hugh Carter of the Carter Worm Farm in Plains, GA 31780, namely, 18 Secrets of Worm Raising, What to Feed and How to Feed the Hybrid Red Wiggler, How to Raise the African Red Worm, Over 300 Questions and Answers on Worm Raising, and How and Where to Sell Fishworms and Crickets.

(Robert Colby operates Dreamworks Hatcheries, 5037 East Keresan, Phoenix, AZ 85044, (602)893-3988.) Δ

Calling earthworms ????

By Rev. Dr. J.D. Hooker

Why bother to write about calling earthworms? Better yet, why bother to read an article about calling earthworms?

You can find plenty of printed information remarking on, or offering tips, and information regarding calling everything else from red-squirrels to antelope, and from waterfowl to wolves. Yet, to date, the only printed material that I've ever actually seen concerning the practice of "worm-grunting", as the art of earth-worm calling is nicknamed in Florida, has been a copy of a U.S. Forest Service record of the number of worm calling permits sold for use in the Apalachicola National Forest in Florida's panhandle. About 700 annual permits are sold each year, most of them to professional bait dealers.

Tactics very similar to those used in worm grunting have even been noted in the animal kingdom. Several species of birds, including plovers, seagulls, and kiwibirds, as well as certain varieties of turtles, have all been observed in the act of "calling" earthworms.

The concept is really exceedingly simple. For some reason, vibrations seem to drive earthworms up out of the ground. There are several theories: One has it that vibrations created in worm grunting may simulate those of falling rain, and the worms may be surfacing instinctively to avoid drowning. The second theory maintains that the vibrations may closely mimic those created by tunneling moles or shrews (both voracious worm hunters) and the earthworms are coming to the surface to avoid being eaten. Another claims that the vibrations may somewhat resemble those proceeding seismic disturbances, again causing the worms to surface instinctively.

Actually, any method of sending vibrations through the ground seems effective in driving worms to the surface; it's just that some methods seem to work a little better than others. Probably the simplest, and certainly one of the easiest methods, utilizes nothing more than one smooth stick or board and one notched stick or board. The smooth piece of wood is driven into the ground, then the notched piece is drawn back and forth across it with a saw like motion. It can take any where from a minute or two up to half an hour or so until the worms start to surface.

Josie Hooker, 9, demonstrates worm-calling technique.

Practice and experimentation on the part of the user will definitely increase the effectiveness of this technique, as there are a wide range of soil types, wood varieties, etc., to be encountered. But, once you've mastered the technique, you'll have a pretty reliable method for obtaining fish-bait, chicken feed, or whatever other uses you can find for earthworms.

While this simple, two-stick technique is effective, there are many other variations. Earlier this summer, a close friend of mine (who happens to be a concrete contractor), showed me what he calls, "the mother of all worm grunters." After seeing his contrivance, I tend to agree with him. I've been calling worms for close to 30 years, but this impressed me. He had driven a 4" galvanized pipe about five or six feet into the ground, leaving only about 8" protruding. Whenever he feels like making a weekend fishing excursion, or giving his chickens a little extra protein to boost their egg production, he'll go out and drop the working end of a concrete vibrator down the pipe and turn it on for half an hour or so. Wow!

You can also have a lot of fun sometimes while developing this skill. I've astonished a whole lot of people by proving to them that it really is possible to call earthworms. My youngest daughter likes to astound her friends by inviting them to watch her feed the chickens and then grunting up worms right in the poultry yard, with the chickens, of course, scrambling every which direction snatching them up.

Anyway, whether you're just after an occasional handful of night-crawlers for a quick fishing trip to the creek, or you find yourself considering a part-time (or full-time for that matter) bait business, or maybe an occasional nutritional boost for your poultry, grunting for earthworms is a skill that's not only worth developing, but fun as well. Δ

CRAFTS

Boredom got you tied in knots? Try "string craft"

(James Robertson is half Native American, hence the Comanche name, Naconi. A prison inmate for the past six years (burglary and forgery) in Lovelady, TX, he has been submitting art to "BHM" in exchange for a subscription. He has a projected release date of 1999 but is to be considered for parole this year. Naconi says his parole date is threatened because he refuses to cut his hair, which he claims is a basic part of his religious beliefs. This is his first published article. —Editor)

By James E. Robertson, aka Naconi

We all find ourselves at one time or another with energy to burn and time on our hands. Rather than just sitting around tapping your fingers on the table, why not put this energy to work in a practical way—with "string craft."

It's not a high dollar investment, no tools to purchase, and yet with a few small items you will end up with a work of art, and an item that will please you and make a great gift for any children around.

Let's start by taking a look at the materials needed.

1. Spool of light colored nylon based sewing thread.
2. Spool of dark colored nylon based sewing thread.
3. Two nails (for driving into something for twisting process).
4. One razor blade or sharp pocket knife.
5. One old paperback book (for twisting).
6. One piece of cardboard or the like approximately 4"x8".
7. One old toothbrush.

Making the string itself

This process is not necessary because the alternative of store-bought string exists, but this is for those who want to say, "I made the whole thing, including my string."

I start with rolls of light colored and dark colored nylon- based sewing thread (cotton will break).

First, bang a nail into an immoveable object (wall, tree, etc.) about chest level, then bend it upward to form an "L" shape. Attach the ends of four equal lengths of thread (about eight feet, all the same color) to the nail and stretch all four lengths to their ends. Then take the ends as one and tie them around an old paperback book.

Hold the threads in one hand and take a couple of steps toward the nail allowing the weight of the book to travel toward the floor.

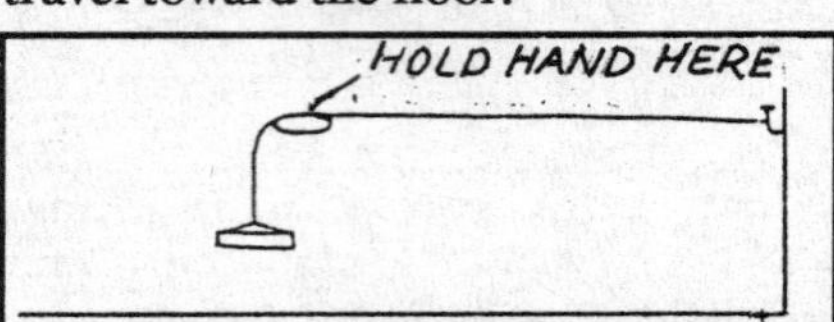

Then take your free hand and spin the paperback book clockwise. While the book is spinning, rotate both hands in a circular motion, hand over hand with the top hand always making contact with the threads. This will form the string, gradually pushing the twist toward the nail.

Repeat this process until threads become one and string is twisted tight against the nail. When string is twisted tight enough, run the paperback between your legs and around the outside of one of your legs at the same time walking toward the nail allowing your body to keep tension on string.

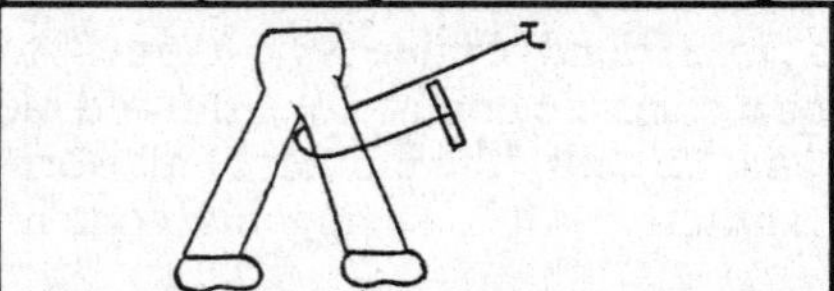

When you have approached the nail where you can reach it, hold string between your fingers at the knot where string is attached to book. Using your razor blade, cut the string on the backside of book freeing it. Make sure you keep your fingers squeezed together at the knot, so as not to allow string to back-twist on you.

After book is free from the end of string, and while string is still running through and around your leg, loop the end of string around the nail, and tie in a knot.

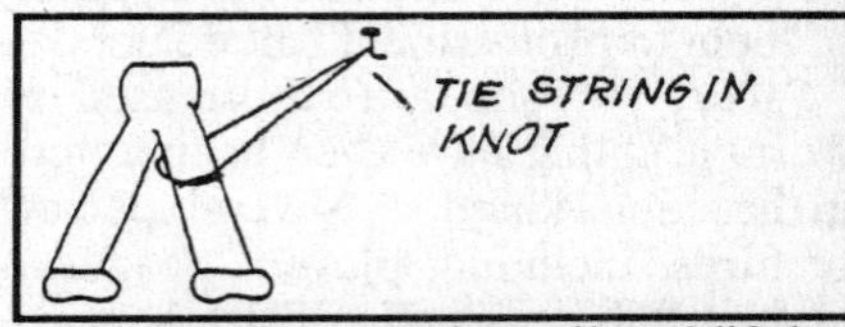

Then walk up to the nail and lift leg out of string, keeping a finger looped through the middle of string where it forms a "U." With the other hand run the string through the palm of your hand keeping the tension stretched and applying pressure to prevent premature twisting.

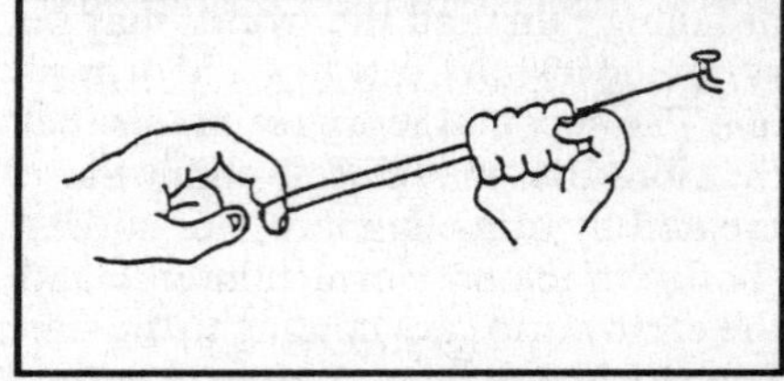

Then move hand toward the end of the string where finger is looped through, applying gentle pressure and pushing twist toward finger. When you are about four inches away from the end, remove finger and string will twist on its own to form your own homemade store-quality string made out of thread.

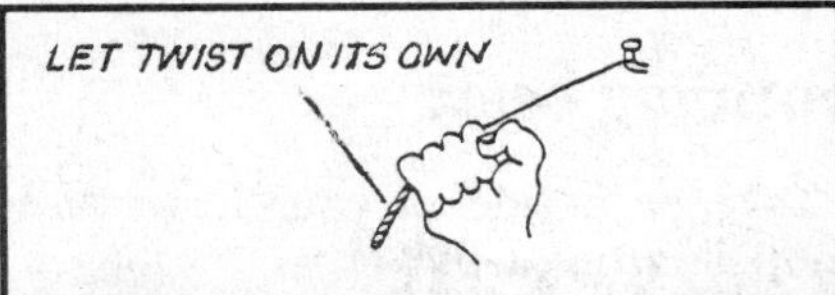

Once string has twisted at the end, run your fingers through to the end a few times to run out any kinks that may form. Grab the string where it has twisted against your hand and apply pressure with your fingers, while releasing your hand to move up toward nail to begin the same process of pushing the twist toward the end, until the whole string is twisted.

After string is completely twisted up to the nail, cut it loose at the nail and tie a knot in the end to prevent unraveling. One of your strings is now finished. Repeat the whole process again, so as to make three lighter colored strings and two darker colored strings. This is what it will take to make your "heart-cross" combo. One of the lighter colored strings will be used as the necklace, so you can put it to the side until called for.

The "heart-cross" combo

For those who do not want to go through the process of twisting their own string, store-bought string will work. As long as you start with two dark colored strings and three light colored strings all cut to approximately 3 feet in length and about 1/8 inch in thickness for the size craft I am making here.

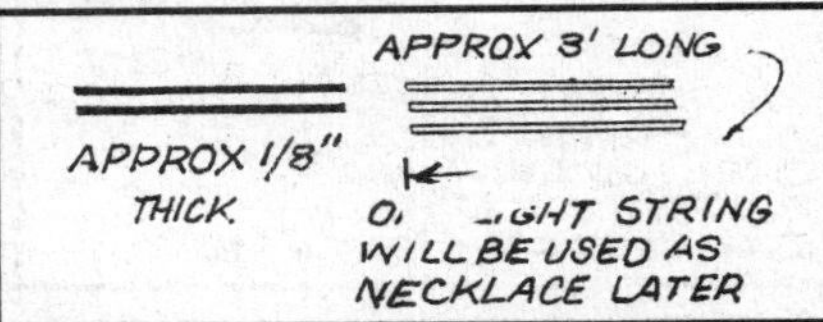

Place your lighter colored string on the bottom with your darker colored string laid over the top to form crossroads. Place the two cross-road patterns side by side because the process that is done in the first set of strings will be done the same with the second set of strings throughout this procedure.

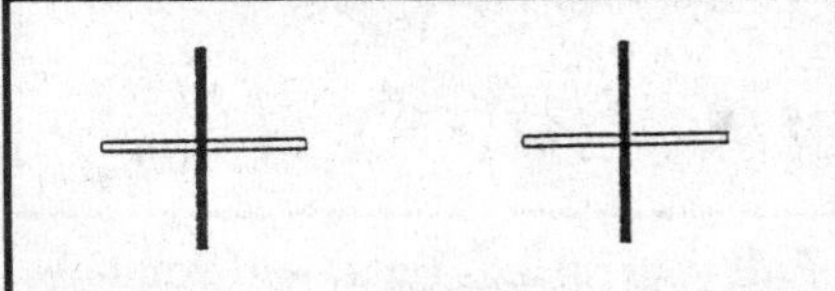

What you are going to do now is form a basket weave process to form the sides of the cross. The process is done exactly the same in both sets of strings.

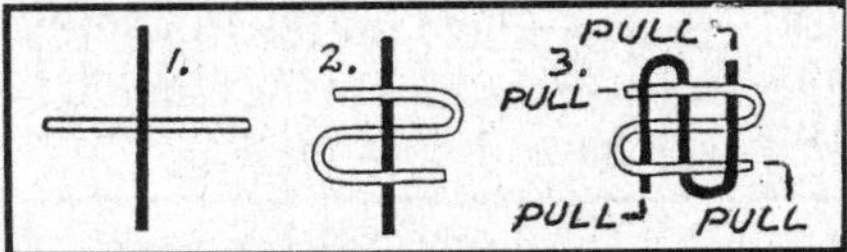

After you get your basket weave formed as demonstrated, take your fingers and pull all the strings with equal tension at the same time watching the center form a checkerboard pattern. Get the checkerboard as square as you can.

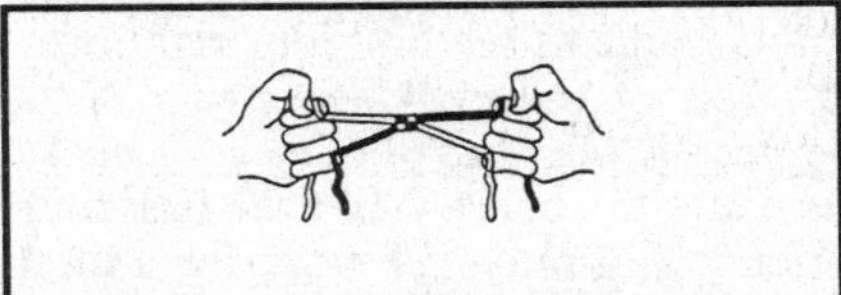

You have made weave number one in which there will be a total of seven weaves for each side. On weave number two and so on, the process is the same, except you have to look at your checkerboard pattern and make sure you begin the next weaving process by crossing the darker string over the lighter string.

After you have done a total of seven weaves on each side, you take each side and line them up with the darker side facing outward, and put them together. When you have both sides lined up evenly, hold the four strings between your fingers on one side to keep the cross lined up and on the other side stretch the four strings outward and tie a small piece of string snug up against the cross (you may need to ask someone for a couple of extra hands, or use your teeth as I do).

Now that you have done this, you are going to repeat the same process that you used to make the sides of your cross. Put the bottom side of the cross where you tied the string downward. Looking at the cross from the top view, repeat the weaving process seven times to form the top of the cross. On the first weave make sure the dark string that will form the stitches in the front and rear view of the cross goes under then over the lighter string.

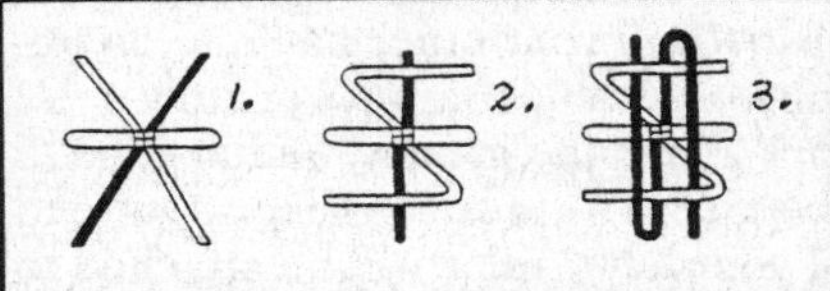

Now you have the top portion of your cross made. Now untie or cut the string you used to line up the sides of the cross and repeat the same process that you used to make the bottom part of your cross. Weave the bottom part a total of sixteen times.

Making your heart filler

Get your piece of cardboard that is approximately 8 inches in length. Using your light colored sewing thread (or already formed string), wrap it around the length of the cardboard until the thickness when combined comes to approximately 1/4" thick.

After you have wrapped the cardboard to form the combined thickness of approximately 1/4 inch, take two lengths of string approximately 1 foot long and run the string under the threads that wrapped around the cardboard and tie in a knot at each end.

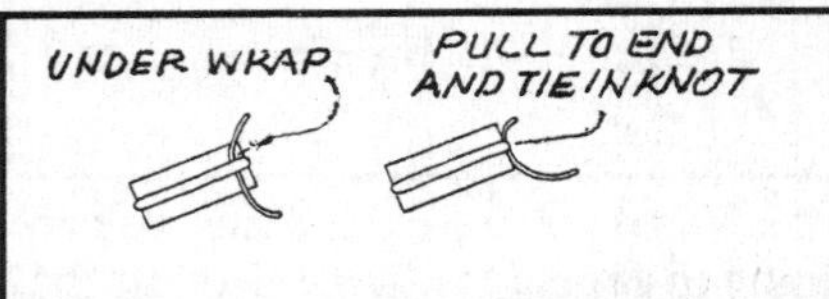

Once your strings are tied off at both ends, slide your heart filler off of the cardboard. Now you have your heart filler.

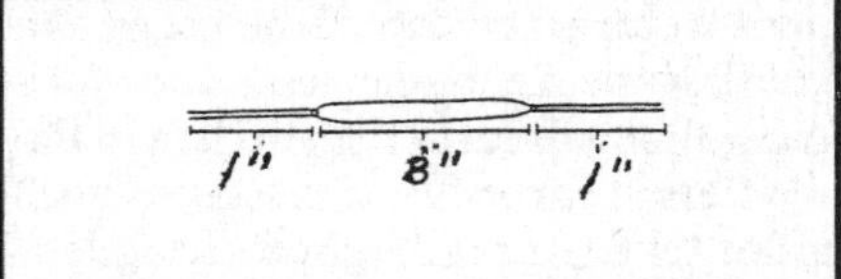

Now nail your other nail into an immoveable object approximately 1 1/2 feet above the ground and also bend this nail to form an "L" shape. One end of your heart filler will be attached to the nail, while the other will loop around your ankle, while you are sitting on the ground to begin the process of making the heart that goes around the cross.

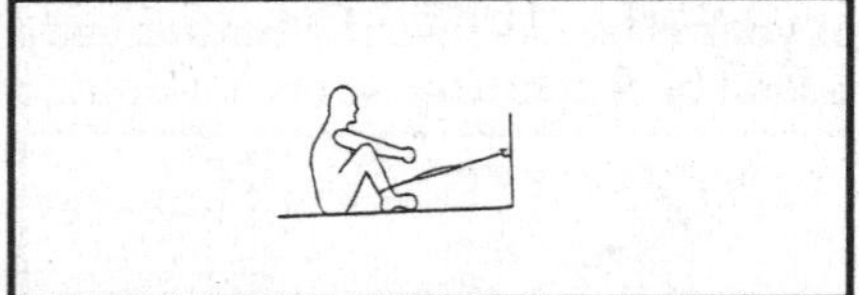

Making the heart

Take your cross and grab a light colored string with right hand coming out of the top of the cross and a dark colored string with your left. Make sure you grab strings closest to you. With the strings in each hand, pull the cross up snug and by eye-balling it, and center cross in the filler.

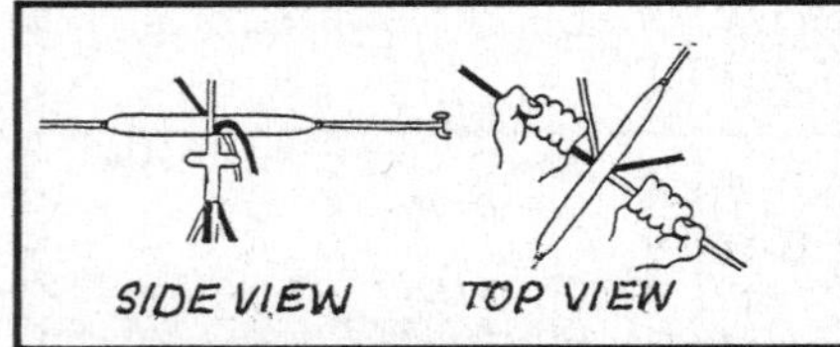

Now, looking at your filler from a top view take your light colored string in your right hand and loop it over the top of your filler. Take the dark colored string and loop it around the outside of the light string bringing it under the filler and up and over the light string loop.

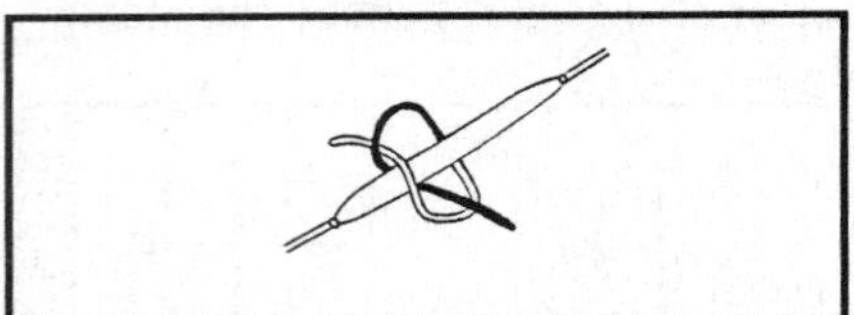

Pull your strings tight, and you have made hitch knot #1. Do this a total of four times, and then get the light colored string that you put to the side for the necklace. Tie one end of it to the end of your filler. Then run the necklace string parallel over the top of the filler and over the tops of the four hitch knots you have already made.

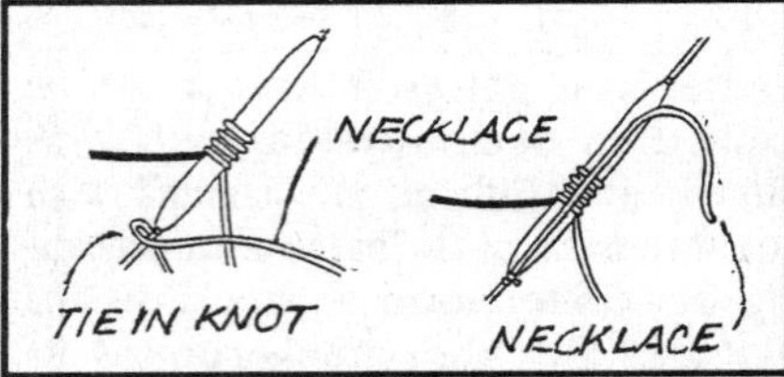

Now proceed to make your hitch knots, same as the first four right over the top of the necklace string. This serves the purpose of tying your necklace into the heart. After the first four hitch knots, make 34 more for a total of 38 hitch knots in all. This will form the left side of your heart.

Repeat the exact same process on the other side. One thing though, after you do your first four hitch knots and go to tie in the other side of your necklace, you have to allow for the necklace to be able to slip over your head. You do this by making the desired necklace size and then hold your fingers on the string at the end of the four hitch knots and stretch the end of the string and tie it off at the end of what will be the other side of your heart.

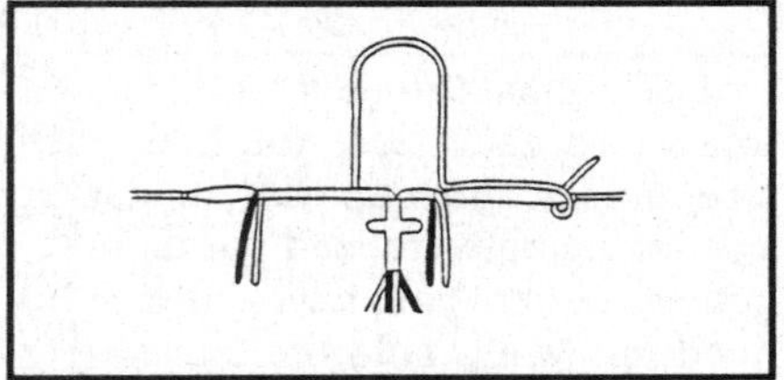

Continue the same process of making your hitch knots right over the top of the necklace string. Do this the same number of times that you did on the other side of your heart. When you have done both sides the same, cut loose the string attached to the nail and your ankle.

Forming heart

Take each side of your heart and loop it around the cross forming a heart, lining up the bottoms of each side of the heart evenly.

Hold in this position with your fingers and tie the two strings coming out of the bottom of each side of the front of the heart together in a tight knot.

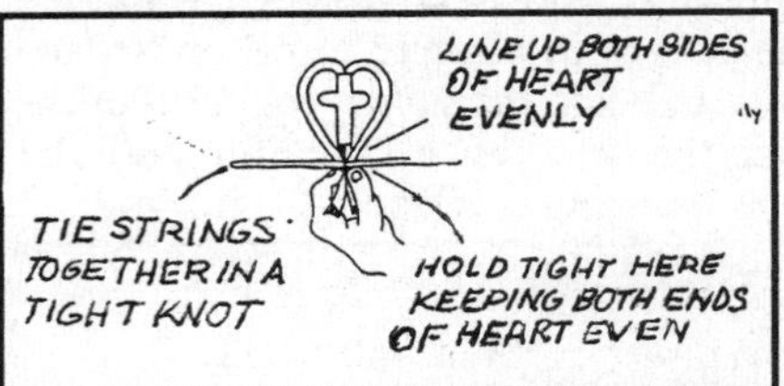

Repeat the exact same process on the backside of the heart.

Tying cross in

There are four strings hanging out of the bottom of the cross. Take the light and dark colored strings on the front side of the cross and let them hang through the outside of the front side of the heart. Do the same with the strings on the backside of the cross. Split your filler at the bottom in the middle and take the two strings hanging in front and the two strings hanging in back and tie them together. As the strings tighten up, it will bring your cross down to the bottom of the heart. Once you are satisfied with the way the bottom of the cross has lined up with the bottom of the heart, tie the strings off in a tight knot.

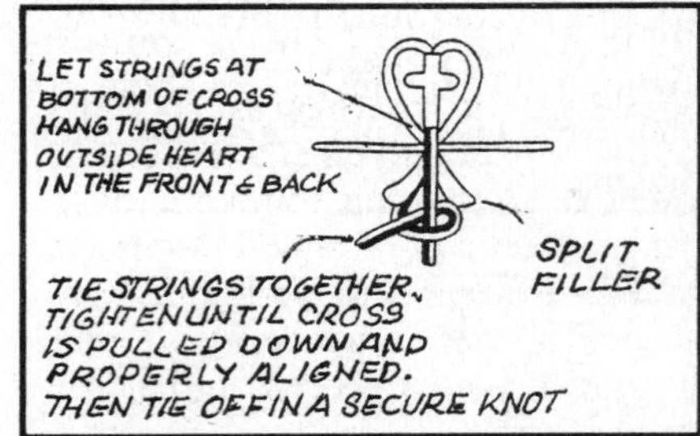

Coil process

Take the two strings in the back of the heart that you used to join the bottoms of the heart together and flip them out of the way. Take all the other strings and filler hanging out of the bottom of the heart and gather them up holding all between your fingers a little ways down from the bottom of the heart. Then take the two strings that are free (that you flipped out of the way) and coil them around the bottom of your heart neatly and tie the coil off on the back side of the heart.

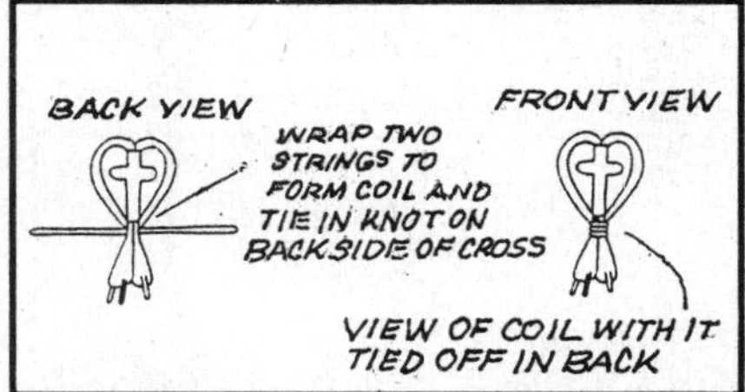

Finishing touches

Take your razor blade and cut off all the ends of the filler and strings hanging out of the bottom of your "heart-cross" combo evenly. Then take your old toothbrush and brush the tassel hanging out of the bottom. This serves to unwind the strings that are hanging out along with the threads, and turn them into threads too.

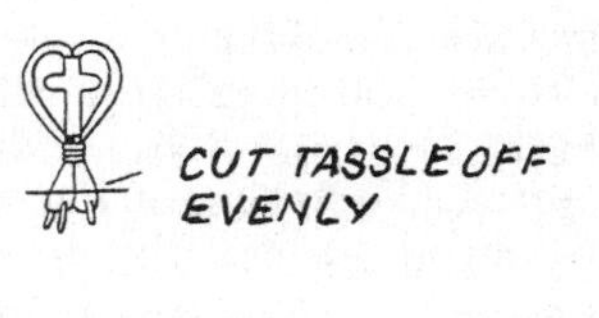

You have now created your "heart-cross" combo, which can be worn as a necklace, hung from the rearview mirror of your vehicle, or used as Christmas tree decoration, or altered to attach to your key chain.

However, the "heart-cross" combo is not the only thing you can make. The potential in creating something with string is unlimited. I myself also make Sacred Circles, hearts with initials inside, celtic crosses, peace signs, etc—all using the same process and a little imagination.

(If anyone has a question about making their "heart-cross" combo, feel free to write the author, James E. Robertson, #425231, P.O. Box 16, Lovelady, TX 75851, or, if anyone would like one of these already made, send me a request and I will make you one on the basis of your word that you will send $4 to me after you have received your "heart-cross" combo, Sacred Circle, etc...) Δ

A night out at the Lady Griz game

By Dynah Geissal

The early morning chores are finished. Now it's time for a hot cup of tea and the newspaper. I shove another log into the cookstove and settle into my rocking chair with my feet propped on the oven door. When I read the sports section I notice that the women's basketball team at the University has a game tonight. It looks as if it should be a good one.

"Hey," I say to my husband, "Do you want to go to the Lady Griz game tonight?"

"Sure," he says. "Sounds great. We haven't gone out in a long time."

The day is busy, as most days are on our subsistence farm. The surplus goat's milk must be turned into cream for us and skimmed milk for the pigs. The horses must be groomed, exercised and trained. Eggs must be gathered, washed, candled and sorted for selling. Baby chicks must be tended several times a day and the rabbits are tended twice. Cheese must be made and sausage, bacon and hams must be smoked for a few more hours. Wood must be split and carried in.

Then it's early evening and the early morning chores of feeding and watering are repeated.

Dinner time! The pot roast has been cooking all afternoon. It's good! As we clear the table, I say to my husband, "Do you still feel like going to the game?"

"Sure," he says, "if you do."

"I'd like to see it, but..."

"Yeah, if it just weren't so far to town, and of course, then there's the drive home afterwards."

"And all the gates to open and close," I say. "I think I'd like to sit by the fire and read tonight. We could make some popcorn. Do you think there's another bottle of that dandelion wine we made last spring?"

"Maybe we'll go to next week's game. It should be a good one too," my husband says. Δ

The Everyday Artist

But what about the people in everyday clothes
The people 'twixt priests and presidents—
what about those?

Billy, who works at the plant, will never make the news.
Tommy, who wants to write songs—who will ever hear his blues?
Betty has three children; she paints when they're in school.
And Johnny Lee the trashman (folks call him a fool),
He sculptures soft warm women in stone hard and cool.

The parents have dreams, but the children must be fed
So portraits go unpainted, Billy's poetry unread.
You struggle and strain 'til the children are gone
Taking your youth, and you feel left all alone.
In the heat of life's struggle you drained your inner well dry
The laborer had to live, so the artist had to die.

Rock your children's children, sing them a lullabye
For loving is an art—..."Baby, don't you cry..."

Jim Watters
Washington, NC

Flowered circlets

By Jj (Photos by Eric Large)

If you can grow, collect or buy dried flowers, you can make flowered circlets for your hair! It's an easy, fun craft idea. Even if you buy all the materials, the circlets are inexpensive to make. Attaching the flowers to the wire form is easy enough that older children can master the technique quickly. And wearing flowers in your hair is fun!

To begin, you'll need an assortment of dried materials—small flowers of different kinds and colors, grasses, whatever you like. I use three or four different dried flowers in various colors for each circlet. Sometimes I include ribbon rosebuds, too. You will need to buy a spool of 20-gauge wire and some "floral tape" from a crafts store. I also use about three feet each of three colors of 1/8" ribbon trailing from the back of each circlet to complete the romantic look.

First cut a 24" length of stem wire from the spool and smooth it into an arc. I hook the ends of the wire around my fingers and draw it along the edge of my worktable. **Caution:** this may damage the table edge. Remove about 18" of floral tape from the spool and begin taping the wire at one end. Floral tape is funny stuff. It's a little stretchy and a little sticky—but only to itself. Getting started wrapping the wire is the hardest part. The tape won't stick to the wire and will want to just twist around and not wrap. Holding the tape in place while you start wrapping usually works. If you can't get it to stay put any other way, bend the wire end back over the first wrapping and continue from there. You will gently stretch the tape and spiral wind it onto the wire until you have covered about a third of it's length.

Now comes the fun part—attaching the flowers! Let's begin with a small sprig of a light, flexible material like Gypsophilia (babies breath). Lay the sprig along the wire, flower end overlapping the wrapped wire and stem end on the unwrapped portion. Wrap another round, snugging the flower stems and the wire together. Careful with the tension! If you pull too hard the tape will tear; if it's not taped tightly enough you won't secure the flowers. Experience will teach you how far down the stem to wrap each sprig. When wrapped close to the flower heads, the sprig will bunch up closely. For a more airy look tape only the very end of the stem.

Different flower materials need different handling. Some brittle materials, like statice, must be taped one small piece at a time. You can gather other more flexible or delicate materials in small bunches and wrap together. Depending on the types of flowered material, the look you want and the size of your sprigs you may wrap just once or use several windings of tape before you add more dried materials. Experiment as you choose sprigs of flowers, lay them on the wire and wrap them in. Floral tape **can** be gently unwrapped if you don't like the effect. I like to use good size sprigs of coordinating or complementary colors next to each other, followed by a third color or different texture of material as an accent. Ribbon roses, when I use them, go in as accents of color or texture. I like the effect of two or three equally spaced along the circlet.

Continue wrapping flower materials until you have about 8" of wire left uncovered. When you run out of floral tape, cut another length and resume wrapping by overlapping the last round and winding once. It **will** stick this time! Cover the remaining wire like you did the beginning, putting a couple of extra twists on the very end before tearing off the extra tape. Your circlet is almost done!

Bend the wire ends back toward the flowered center, to make a "loop" and a "hook". Adjust the wire so that the hook and loop meet properly (at a 90 degree angle) and give the circlet a nice round shape. You adjust the size of the circle to fit the head and hairstyle of the wearer by changing the length of hook and loop. Remember, keep it even! Add the ribbons now, unbending the loop and slipping the looped ribbons onto it.

If you have as much fun making and wearing circlets as my girls and I do, you may want to share the fun. I have found that metaphysical bookstores and renaissance/folk gatherings to be good places to sell your handiwork. Δ

WIN A FREE VITA-MIX *(see page 6)*

Backwoods Home magazine

March/April 1993
No. 20
$3.50 U.S.
$4.50 Canada

... a practical journal of self reliance!

HOMESCHOOLING YOUR CHILDREN

RAISED GARDEN BEDS

WHAT ABOUT GOLD?

BACKWOODS WRITERS

LAND REGULATIONS

HYBRID VEGGIES

HAM RADIO FESTIVALS

DON CHILDERS

Note from the publisher

The Vita-Mix contest

The first winner of our Vita-Mix contest will be drawn March 1 and will be announced on this page in the May/June issue. We will continue the contest for six issues, announcing a winner of a $500 Vita-Mix each issue. The Vita-Mix ad on the back cover of this issue will give you a good idea why they are so useful.

To be eligible for the contest, you must be a current subscriber. All subscribers will automatically be included in the drawings so no need to send in an entry form. We estimate that your odds of winning one of our Vita-Mixes is about one hundred thousand times greater than winning a state lottery, so don't throw your money away on one of those crackpot schemes. Subscribe to BHM.

Independence 2000 changes date, Preparedness Expo changes site

Independence 2000 has changed the date of their Eugene, Oregon show from February 19-21 to April 30-May 2. For details call 1-503-474-6781. Their ad is on page 32.

Preparedness Expo has canceled their Portland, Oregon show and added a second show in Salt Lake City, Utah for May and one in Phoenix, Arizona for November. That makes five shows for the year, which is the most they've ever held. Their ad is on page 53.

Eco Expo has scheduled three shows for this year: Los Angeles, San Francisco, and Boston (my home town for 29 years). The L.A. show is coming up soon – March 12-14 at the L.A. Convention Center. Their ad is on page 52.

We will be at all the above shows.

Vons supermarket

We made this announcement once before but it turned out to be a false alarm. This time it's for sure: *Backwoods Home Magazine* will now be distributed in the 300 Vons supermarkets in Southern California. It's a significant step because Vons is where much of middle-class America shops, and that is our prime target area for subscribers. It's the middle-class that will make or break America. Too bad our politicians don't understand that.

Canadian tax

We may soon raise the already high subscription rates to our Canadian subscribers. The Canadian government has demanded we pay them a Goods and Services Tax (GST) for subscriptions we sell to Canadians. Without all the taxes and fees and increased postal rates we must pay to do business in Canada, Canadians, at the present subscription rate we charge them, would be paying a couple of dollars less per subscription than Americans. It's easy to see why so many of our Canadian readers are so upset with their government. Canada is much farther down the rode to socialism than we are.

Third year book

We are printing a new book called Backwoods Home Magazine – The Third Year. It will be a compilation of Issue Numbers 13 through 18, be about 384 pages long, and be available March 1. An ordering form is on page 89. We had not intended to put out another compilation until 1994 but ran out of Issue No. 13 so are forced to.

Robert joins Annie and Jacob

We are doing our part to restore family life in America. Lenie and I had a second son, Robert Julian, to join our 15-month-old son, Jacob, and my 10-year-old daughter, Annie, in our very noisy home.

Robby has already done me a very great service. Since Lenie is up often in the night feeding Robby, I let her sleep in the morning and I get up with Jake at 6:30 a.m. Together we relax for about an hour listening to Bach or Garth Brooks, eating breakfast, and changing diapers.

This has been an abrupt departure from my usual habit of getting up by myself, sometimes at 5 a.m., and having three cups of coffee with my computer and this magazine. Robby's occupation of his mom has forced me to relax with Jake at the start of each day, and that has done what doctors and pills could not – subdue the stress-related skin rashes that have been tormenting me for two years. And I've developed a nice bond with Jake besides.

When Jake is done with me he goes in and wakes up his big sister, Annie, who plays with him for the rest of the morning while I get to work. It's a great way to start the day. Δ

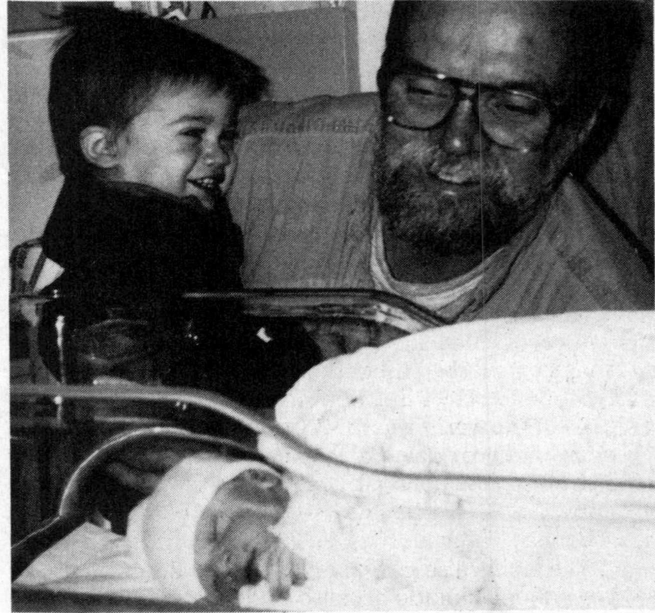

Daddy Dave, Jake, and new son Robby.

My View

The new power of the mass media is eroding the freedom of the press

One of the greatest freedoms a person can have is the freedom to speak one's mind honestly and openly. It's one of the freedoms we have taken for granted in this country, and one of the freedoms that is being steadily eroded in a manner most of us could never have imagined.

Not that we can't still speak our mind most of the time. It's just that we don't get heard very well these days unless we say things that are politically correct to the ears of the mass media, which controls how many people hear us. Since most members of the mass media are liberals, liberal causes get more air time than conservative causes. There are many good examples. The Presidential election of '92 is an important one. The media strongly favored Clinton over Bush so did everything it could to get Clinton elected, such as emphasizing every small bit of bad economic news, like rising unemployment and the growing federal deficit, and ignorning any good economic news. The day after Clinton got elected, the media began emphasizing only the good economic news, as if his very election miraculously turned the economy around. They seldom mention that unemployment and the federal deficit are still growing. In effect they are lying to the people.

Anything to do with guns is always a good example. When some Koreans in L.A. successfully defended their stores against L.A. rioters, the media gave them only passing attention, but emphasized over and over the plight of the poor in our cities' ghettos and how billions in federal money was needed to set things right. That's because the liberal media hates guns, but loves big government spending to cure social ills. If someone uses a gun to commit a crime, it's on the front page; if someone uses a gun to defend his family it is usually not reported at all.

Somalia is another example. The media, being a big fan of globalist ideas like World Government and an all-powerful U.N. police force to enforce human rights around the world, saw Somalia as the perfect example to show how well World Government could work. So they bombarded us with TV pictures of starving Somali children until George Bush, the greatest backer of World Government on the planet, felt "obliged" to send in the Marines. A typical conservative view of this intervention is that it is a new form of colonialism disguised as humanitarianism and that it is merely setting the stage for unwise U.S./U.N. intervention in places like Bosnia Herzegovina, located in that part of the world where World War I was ignited. But you won't hear much of that view in the mass media.

Other examples abound. Feminist groups who still sing the praises of Anita Hill and castigate Supreme Court Justice Clarence Thomas are given all the media play they want. The media also gives ample space to the Hollywood-led boycott of Colorado because voters there voted down a proposal to give gays and lesbians special rights. And environmental pseudo-scientists who still insist that the earth's ozone layer is disappearing still get air time every time they open their mouths, even though real science has shown time and again that there is no evidence to back up their claim. Say anything in favor of Clarence Thomas, Colorado voters, or exaggerated environmental claims, and it will likely be ignored by the mass media.

That's because the liberal mass media is not in the business of informing people with objective news; they are in the business of trying to shape people's opinions by inundating them with selective slices of news that support their political agenda. Their feeling is if they bombard you with enough ozone stories, you'll come to believe the ozone is disappearing, and if they bombard you with enough anti-gun stories you'll believe guns are evil. They got Clinton elected as our President, got us involved in Somalia, and will soon try to pass sweeping environmental legislation that will solve fictitious ecological problems.

There are few conservative publications out there to combat this one-sided reporting. Some names are the *Conservative Chronicle, Insight Magazine, The American Spectator, Liberty magazine, The McAlvany Intelligence Advisor, and Libertarian Party News* (for a stamp we'll send you their addresses), but those publications are simply ignored by the mass media. Seldom are their articles and columns reprinted in the mass media, but let some liberal college rag out of Berkeley or Harvard Square put forth some screwball idea about cow farts causing the ozone layer to disappear and the mass media will put them on the front page.

It's a damn shame. The mass media might as well be the political party that is always in power because their ability to flood the airwaves and print media with their side of the story to the exclusion of the "other" side of the story is driving most of the political decisions that are made in this country. The main reason we are traveling the fast track down the road to socialism is because the liberals who dominate the mass media are at the wheel.

In times past the media often served as the watchdog of government; now it serves as the makers of government and government policy. Just as tyrannical governments of the past once banned freedom of the press, now the all-powerful media giants ban the other side of the story. There's no difference.

They ban the opposition by burying their side of a story deep inside the newspaper, or, more often, by not printing it at all. The ban is as effective as any tyrant's edict to ban all opposition. The mass media has become our modern day tyrant; it is the worst oppressor of freedom of speech this country has ever had.

So what's the solution? Quite simple really. Freedom-loving people who want to hear both sides of the story have got to get into the media business. Not just as news reporters but as owners of newspapers, magazines, and radio and TV stations. If we are to stop this country's deterioration into a socialist state, getting the "other side of the story" back into the mass media is a must. Δ

Dave Duffy

High beds and high production . . . with less work

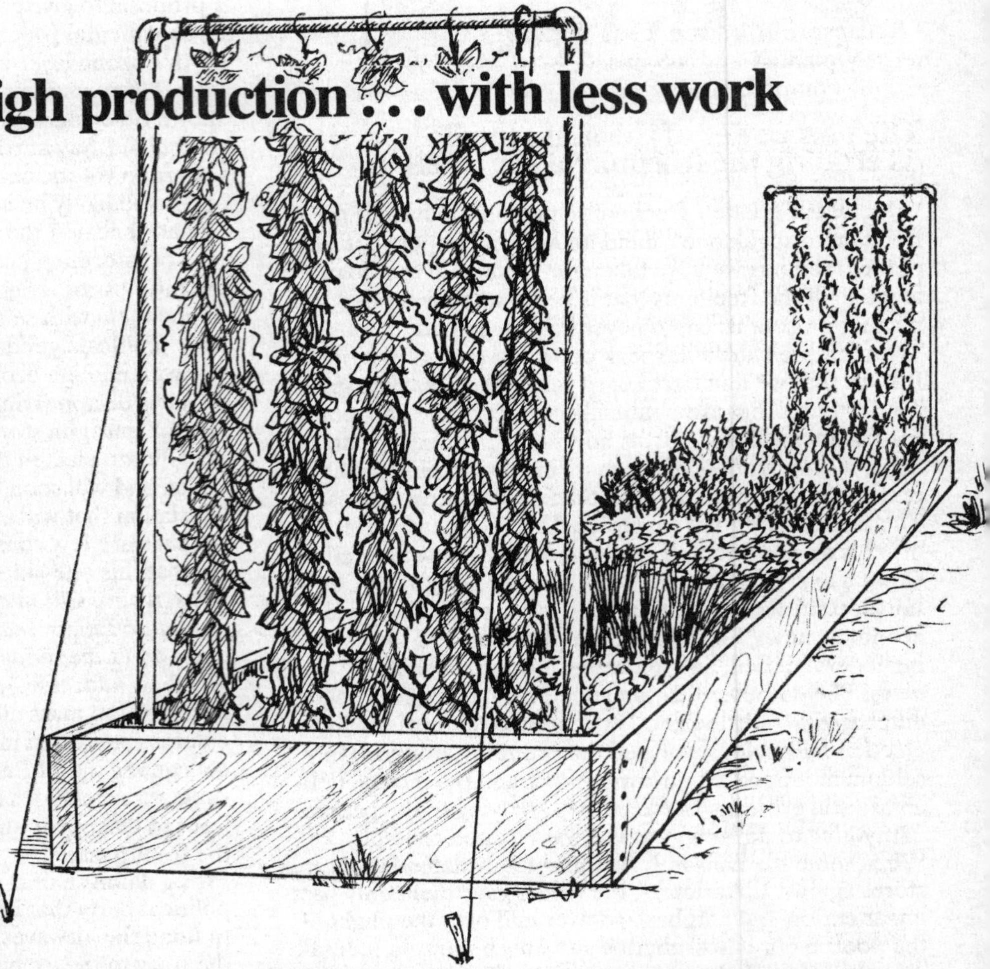

By Russ Davis

Suppose your boss told you that your salary was going to be increased by 400%, **and** you would only have to work one quarter the hours. Would you be interested? Well, your boss probably isn't going to do that, but you can get a similar deal in your garden.

The answer to this is no snake oil salesman's pitch. It's accomplished by combining three tried and true methods of gardening called **raised beds,** and **vertical planting** and **wide row planting.**

What it results in is a smaller garden space which, per square foot, produces easily up to 400% more produce. Because of its intensive planting, weeds don't stand much of a chance. Finally, because of the raised bed and vertical planting, harvesting is a lot easier on the back.

Consider first the so-called normal method of vegetable gardening. It was the same thing my grandfather used and my father used and I used, at least I used to. The keys were till, till, till, then rake, rake, rake. Out with the stakes and ball of heavy string. Drive in a stake, attach the string, move to the end of the projected row, drive in a second stake, tightly stretch the string and attach it. Then hoe a single straight line and plant the seeds.

In my grandfather's garden, God help the carrot that grew up crooked or the tomato plant which wandered. Gardens were judged by straight rows and freedom from weeds. The wide paths between rows gave access to the busy gardener who marched up and down, whacking away at weeds and mumbling dark oaths. It was backbreaking, time-consuming, and down right inefficient. But that was the way a garden was supposed to be. In the fall it was harvest, hoe, and spade under, so the garden plot would be open to the fall rains and winter snows so that next spring you could go out and spade and rake and stake and plant all over again.

Wide row, raised, & vertical is the miracle mixture

Somewhere people who my grandfather would probably have considered lazy and a bit weird, thought about just sort of scattering seeds all over an area and letting the plants grow as they will. French gardeners call this **wide row planting.** More produce from a given area, and less chance for weeds to spring up since the veggies were planted so close to one another.

In other places people started to hoe up little squares and rectangles of soil which ended up being a few inches higher than the pathways between them. This resulted in better drainage and more rapid warming of the soil in the spring. The idea is fairly new in American gardens, but is old as time itself. Worldwide, many people practiced this. In this hemisphere, the Incas and Aztecs, among others, practiced a form of **raised bed planting.**

The third vital component in our little "miracle mixture" is the intensive use of **vertical planting,** such as poles for beans and peas. Thus, a couple of plants in a single square foot of garden space could rocket upwards six or even eight feet, dangling a virtual tower of produce from their supporting poles!

To make this a little clearer, in my garden two blocks, each 1' x 4', provide us with more than enough green beans to meet our eating and canning needs. That's from eight square feet! In fact, our primary garden space consists of four raised beds, three each 4' x 14' and one 4' x 24'. Of course, we also have a few other areas devoted to fruits, flowers, berries, etc., but the primary garden area is more than sufficient to meet all our needs.

Because our raised beds are intensely planted and we make liberal use of compost and a whole lot of mulch, weeds don't stand a chance. During the growing season, we probably devote less than an hour a week to weeding. Since our beds are raised one foot high, grabbing those little pests is a lot easier on my old back. Even in the midst of a drought season, the need for supplemental watering is minimal and accomplished quickly.

In the fall, plant remains are thrown into the compost bin and the entire garden area given a sprinkle of lime and gypsum (to keep the soil lighter) and covered with a three to four-inch layer of good compost. Come spring, the beds are ready for seeding.

Requires less work

You will note that nothing has been said about heavy-duty spading and turning. Once you have established your beds, it is simply not necessary. The most I do these days is to hoe a generous amount of compost and humus matter into the top few inches every now and then. Momma Nature does the rest. Since I am not stepping on the soil itself (**never**), it does not get compacted and require all that churning and turning.

The rules are simple:

- **1. Plan carefully the location of your raised beds.**

Ideally, they should lay along a north-south line to take maximum advantage of sunlight.

- **2. Decide their dimensions.**

My personal preference is for beds which are four feet wide, since that means nothing in the garden is more than two feet away from me. The distance between beds is a matter of personal choice. I prefer to make these access paths four feet wide, as well, so that I can wheel a cart between them. Other advocates of raised beds might suggest narrowing the interval down to two or three feet. You pick it.

- **3. Decide the nature of the raised beds.**

Do you want to simply pull soil up from the pathways, thereby creating beds which are only four or five inches high, or do you want to get some real altitude? My beds are 12 inches high. Most of them are framed with 2" x 12" boards, with a cross support at the midpoint, which creates two 4' x 7' planting areas in the 14' long rectangle. The cross support helps to keep the weight of the soil and the heaving of the freeze and thaw cycle from buckling and bowing the sides.

Using concrete blocks

I am also fond of using a single layer of standard 8" x 8" x 16" concrete building blocks and will probably build all new beds with them. Their "holes" allow for little individual "pots" along the border area—perfect for planting companion plants such as marigolds which act as natural pest repellents.

Of course, if you really want or need more height, you could go two layers high. Whether one or two blocks high, the resulting beds are very functional, even more durable than board-sided beds, and if you decide to change your garden around, concrete blocks are easier to move from place to place.

- **4. Whether you are using wood or concrete block frames for your beds, your next thought should be about the soil used to fill them.**

If you do this correctly, your major soil work is over. Forever. Period. Once the bed is in, all it will require is good husbandry in the form of plenty of compost and organic matter. Other than that, it pretty well takes care of itself. No more plowing, no more spading, no more breaking your back.

Creating good soil

Most of us are not blessed with perfect soil. However, anyone living anywhere can create good soil fairly easily and inexpensively. For most garden applications, you should consider a good loose mixture of rich loamy black top soil, well-composed manure and organic matter combined with a generous helping of sand, vermiculite,

Each of these raised beds is 1-foot high, 4-feet wide, and 14-feet long. A 6-foot high trellis made from common PVC water pipes and used for growing vine crops can be seen at each end. The advantages of raised beds include growing up to 400% more in the same area, and virtually eliminating the drudgery of tilling and weeding. If mulched properly, the need for watering is minimal. These beds are shown after harvesting has been completed and they have been covered with a 4-inch winter blanket of compost. Also note the round rebar hoops permanently placed for cloching each bed to extend the growing season.

perlite, or similar products to help keep the soil light and airy.

Coarse peat moss is also a great ingredient for your soil bed. In combination, these ingredients will also help to maintain proper soil moisture. The last thing a gardener needs is to fight soil which is a sodden sticky mess when it is wet and resembles baked bricks when it is dry. Do it right and you'll only have to do it once. Skip or skimp at this stage and you'll spend hours cussing and toiling.

Probably most of the garden soil in the United States tends to be on the heavier side because of clay content. However, these soils are potentially okay, if you lighten them up.

When it comes to judging the texture of soil, I like to use the "spear" test. I point my fingers into a "spear" and jam the whole hand into the soil. If I cannot penetrate easily up to the knuckles, I would probably consider the soil bed too heavy and would want to begin to lighten it up with generous applications of—yep, you guessed it—composted organic matter, peat moss, vermiculite, perlite, and/or sand.

Naturally occurring sandy soil, such as you find in Florida and the Southwest has the opposite problem of the heavier clays. Sand drains too quickly, requiring an enormous and continuous supply of water. This can be overcome by tilling in a lot of composted organic matter and peat moss. Keep at it and very soon you'll have prime gardening soil.

- **5. Plan for vertical growth.**

Every foot of elevation you gain with frames, poles, or similar devices saves you that much garden footage. Put in a vertical frame five feet high and you've just increased your effective growing area by 500%! What grows vertically you ask? Well, many common vegetables will, either naturally or, if given a chance, can be trained to do so with a little effort. Examples: pole beans, peas, and virtually any kind of vine crop such as cucumbers and squash. Even small to medium-sized melons, if given a little extra support.

Using PVC pipe to build your vertical frames

Vertical frames are simply inverted square-ended "U's." I make many of mine out of common PVC pipe. This comes in 10-foot lengths and can be cut easily with a hacksaw. Since I like my vertical frames to be about six-feet high and four-feet wide, simple math will tell you I use two PVC pipes for each frame. In addition, I also need two 90-degree elbows. I saw each PVC pipe into one four-foot and one six-foot section.

The two six-foot sections are shoved into the soil of the raised beds and become the uprights. Using the two elbow connectors, one of the four-foot sections becomes the cross member. The other four-foot section will be laid directly on the ground to steady the twine I will string from the top.

Nothing is wasted. I have one vertical frame at each end of nearly every raised bed. The cost for each vertical frame comes to about three to four bucks, depending on where you buy the pipe. Make sure you buy PVC which is at least one inch in diameter.

If you are planning on heavier crops such as large squash or melons, go even a little larger. Instead of PVC pipes, you could also use common galvanized water pipe, electrical wire conduit, or wood if you prefer.

Some folks like to train their vertical crops to grow up, through, and around large-meshed fencing attached to the vertical frames. Others prefer to use some sort of netting, either commercial or home-woven. Still others like rigid vertical wires. My favorite, however, is plain old fashioned natural baling twine. It can be purchased at any farm supply store, is cheap, biodegradable, and its roughness gives climbing crops something to cling to.

String it straight up and down, crisscrossed, checker-boarded, or knotted into a coarse net, according to your preference and the crop for which it is intended. I usually limit myself to straight up and down for peas and beans, etc., and knotted into coarse netting for vine crops. At the end of the growing season, I just cut them off, and twine, crop residue and all goes into the compost bin.

- **6. Provide a continuous supply of compost and mulch.**

I throw all my organic wastes, etc. into my composting bin(s). My neighbors are only too happy to give me all their garden waste, grass clippings, and leaves as well. I keep them friendly in that way by a little "bribe" now and then, like some choice items from the garden in season.

Even some of the little kids in the neighborhood pitch in and help in exchange for letting them "play" in my garden. Their parents have often said they think I must be some sort of magician because their kids want to "work" in the garden and often rush home with things they have picked, asking mom to cook up things that they otherwise would never eat at home, like peas and beans.

Composters come in all shapes. You could buy a fancy one (at a fancy price) or make your own. I made mine out of discarded rough oak shipping pallets. Four pallets will make a generous single composting bin. Seven will turn your composting into a three-bin, progressive composting operation which will turn out this black gold at an amazing rate.

Two great books

Over 60 years ago, an old sweetheart named Ruth Stout began to experiment with deep continuous mulching. After taking 40 years to perfect her system, she wrote The Ruth Stout No-Work Garden Book in which she advocated keeping your garden constantly covered with at least six to eight inches of moisture-saving, soil-improving mulch.

She considered old hay, which is worthless to farmers, to be perfect for the job. She was right. Old hay, even old moldy hay, does a great job and can be had for very little. As it does its job as a mulch, it slowly decomposes and adds organic matter and nutrients to your garden soil. Her book is well worth reading.

Another great book is Mel Bartholmew's Square Foot Gardening. He also has a series of TV programs on his gardening techniques which have aired on PBS and cable channels. While I prefer widebed planting to his more orderly square foot methods, he is no-nonsense and covers a lot of basic material very well, including some other ideas about vertical planting techniques.

• 7. Never let space go to waste.

Your planning should include rotating crops both on a yearly and a seasonal basis. Fast maturing cold weather crops like radishes go into the ground early, are harvested early, and a second crop sown in summer for fall harvesting. Many vegetables lend themselves well to a two-season approach.

The other important consideration is to resist your natural desire to plant all of a given vegetable at one time, such as **all** your beans at once. I like to think in thirds: One third of my beans goes in, two or three weeks later the second third, and then a couple of weeks later the last third. That way, I have extended the season and don't face the prospect of everything ripening at once.

• 8. Extend your growing season by cloching.

Cloche is a French word meaning "bell" and refers to the practice of many French gardeners of protecting delicate plants from the cold, both at the beginning of the season and at the end, by covering each plant with a bell shaped glass dome or by covering a whole row in a similar fashion.

My cloche system is simplicity itself. I have purchased 3/8th-inch steel rods, commonly called "rebar," from my local lumber supply house. Normally these 10-foot rods are used to reinforce concrete when it is poured. They are quite bendable and cost a buck or so each. Since my raised beds are four feet wide, it is a simple task to bend these rods into rounded hoops. (Hold on with your hands and press with your foot. Simple.) I then insert these at each end and about every four or five feet of bed space. These stay permanently in my garden.

Early in the spring, I lay a strip of 5-mil clear plastic over the hoops, secure it on the sides and ends with long strips of wood about 1/2" thick and perhaps 1-2" wide. I anchor these strips over the plastic by driving nails part way through the stripping. This holds the plastic securely and allows the stripping to be easily removed to lift up the plastic and air out the beds if the sunlight becomes too warm. My garden soil is warm and ready for planting at least two to three weeks earlier than my neighbors', and without the hassle of spring plowing.

In the fall, I also cloche tender crops to extend their season. Two years ago, we had an early cold snap which sent night time temperatures plunging into the mid-twenties for two weeks steady. That was at the time when my late bush beans were just flowering. On went the plastic. Mornings, after the sun came up, I opened the ends and allowed the air to circulate sufficiently to prevent burning my precious beans. The result: a bumper crop of healthy, tender, delicious green beans. All it cost was a little time and plastic. And the plastic was carefully stored and reused this year.

There you have it. A few ideas on how to make your garden space really work for you instead of turning you into some sort of soil slave. Δ

A BHM Writer's Profile

Richard Blunt is the *BHM* food editor. More than just recipes, his articles in *Backwoods Home Magazine* actually teach people how to cook, whether they are novices or experienced chefs.

He is well qualified for the task. Blunt's career in the food industry spans more than three decades. What began as a desperation job as a teenage pot washer in Cambridge, Massachusetts, developed into a 30-year learning experience that has found him cooking in the kitchens of exclusive restaurants in the Northeast, and he has been a senior manager for three major food management companies. He is currently assistant director of food service at a large hospital in Connecticut, where he lives with his wife and three children.

OWNING YOUR OWN LAND

Land regulations are making it harder to move to the country

By Martin Harris

A lot of people in urban and more recently suburban America are looking to escape to the rural countryside, but it is more difficult now than just a few years ago to find a few good acres in the country.

Not that there's any shortage of land in rural America. In fact the real countryside has been losing population rather than gaining it, and only a tiny percentage of total acreage has been engulfed under the outward sprawl of suburbia.

Maybe no one's out there making more land, as Will Rogers once observed, but in vast areas of the country there are fewer people on it than in any recent historical time. Not only is there plenty of rural land, but acreage prices are – unless you choose to deal with a subdivision company – pretty modest.

The problem lies in an area unimagined not so long ago: regulations governing land use. Land buyers today need to be super-careful lest they end up with a parcel for which the only privilege of ownership is to pay the taxes while trying to enjoy the view.

Land-use regulation, in less sweeping form, has been around throughout American history. The Puritan colonies restricted lot sizes in early New England, and in Spanish California ordinary citizens couldn't buy farmland at all.

Just about all these controls were swept away after the Revolution, and it wasn't until 1916 that the first zoning ordinance in the country was enacted in New York City. Since then, zoning has spread from the cities into the suburbs and then into rural areas; for the last 20 years or so, it's been just about impossible to find a place in the USA where some sort of governmental control over land use (usually exercised through some sort of planning commission) doesn't prevail.

These controls used to consist of things like single-use districts (residential here, industrial there, and so on), minimum lot sizes, and maybe setback requirements or landscaping standards. Now they've grown to include architectural design controls, scenic easements, minimum house size (for tax-collecting purposes), and at the other extreme, even areas where no construction at all is permitted.

Most recently, the Federal government got into the local land-use regulation business with wetlands protection, and most of the states have been quick to follow with their own, even stiffer, restrictions on new construction in vast areas that might be construed to fall under the wetlands rules.

All the new rules and regulations – federal, state, regional, local – add up to one warning: buyers looking for a home site need to be absolutely legally certain that they will be able to build what they want to build, farm, or cut timber or dam a stream, or whatever, on the land before they buy it.

Real estate brokers, working for the would-be seller and intent on closing the sale, can't be depended upon to tell the whole truth (assuming they know it) regarding restrictions on the land they're trying to earn a commission by selling.

Neither, in most cases, can you depend on the seller, or the attorney you retain to handle the legalities of the closing, or even the local building permit official. All these folks may not know about, or even care about, all the requirements you'll eventually have to meet. In short, if you want it done right, you'll have to do it yourself.

Research the regulations before you buy the land

I'd start at the federal level, with the newest and probably most important issue: wetlands. Be aware that land doesn't have to look wet or even be wet in order to qualify as a protected wetland, and that lots of acreage which was legally buildable before the national wetlands regulations went into effect only three years ago is now solidly in the do-not-build category.

Visit your county Soil Conservation Office (a branch of the U.S. Department of Agriculture) and ask to see the wetlands delineation map for the area including your potential home site.

Make sure your prospective acreage isn't in an area shown as a mapped wetland. Make sure it isn't even close: many states add no-build buffer zone requirements to the federal regulations, thereby rendering substantial land areas, although technically non-wetland, unusable.

Make sure your prospective acreage isn't an unmapped wetland, either. Not all wetlands are mapped, and both federal and state regulations reserve to government the right to label a given parcel as a wetland even if it hasn't previously been mapped as one. Land can easily be designated as a wetland – even if it doesn't look wet – if it meets three technical criteria involving soil type, vegetation, and seasonal ground water levels. Any area with heavy soils, annual surface soil saturation, and hydrophytic (moisture-loving) vegetation can qualify. If your land has any of these characteristics, play it safe: get a no-wetlands professional evaluation, in writing, from a recognized wetlands consultant, or go on looking for a different home site.

Make sure your dream-site isn't in a national park, or even in an area on the National Park Service acquisition list. There's a whole group of Americans out there (they call themselves inholders) who, for a range of historical reasons, own homes surrounded by national park land, and they all tell horror stories of NPS efforts to drive them out even though they hold legal tenure. When Yellowstone was allowed to burn a few years back, one reason was to destroy inholder houses in the burn area and thereby "purify" the Park.

Learning whether your dream-site may also be on an NPS dream-list for acquisition may be more difficult. Folks in Maine can tell you about secret (and illegal) maneuvers by NPS in that state to list acreage for acquisition without the owners' knowledge. Best information source: a local property-rights group, such as those that now exist in just about every state.

Watch for buildings and even land on the National Historic Sites Register. Buying into a situation like that can be costly in terms of dollars and even stomach-ache, unless you intend to make no changes in your new acquisition.

Next I'd go on to potential regulatory problems at the state level. These can be checked out at the state capital, usually in an office with some title like "central planning."

Some states now have land-use plans—which carry the force of law—drafted at the state level.

Old buildings are sometimes on a state Historic preservation list. Even pieces of land are sometimes considered historic and therefore unchangeable.

Some areas are considered scenic or environmental resources and in the public domain, even though some hapless private owner is paying taxes on them. Buy into this type of situation and you may be buying a host of problems. Don't repeat the true story of a Vermonter who was sold a small gravel hill which had been acquired by the state—for gravel-mining use—and then had his permit to continue gravel extraction appealed by the same state which sold him the land to begin with.

Don't look at development around you and assume you can do the same on your parcel. In South Carolina recently, an unwary would-be homeowner bought the last two ocean-side lots in a built-up area and had to defend his right to build all the way to the Supreme Court.

Some states have the equivalent of local zoning. Oregon for example, requires that house-lots in the Colombia River Gorge be at least 40 acres. The Gorge is now a Federal park, but Oregon enforces the minimum lot size.

Next, I'd move my investigation to the regional level to find out what regional planning agencies might hold regulatory power over your potential land purchase.

In New York state, for example, there exists an Adirondack Park Agency which controls huge acreages both within the Park itself and a massive buffer zone around it. Under APA rules, types of land use are limited and lot sizes are strictly controlled: they range from 2 to 2000 acres.

Vermont, like many states, has a system of regional planning commissions. These don't usually get involved in approvals for individual house lots, but they have a legal voice in non-residential development down to one acre in lot size, and they have been known to over-rule local zoning and building permits issued by local planning commissions.

Other states have other sorts of regional authorities, ranging from California's Coastal commission to Maryland's Chesapeake Bay Authority. Ask around.

Some regional authorities control rural land from an urban base: Florida's Dade County Metropolitan Authority is headquartered in Miami but its regulatory powers over land use reach out in the County's remote hinterlands. It's not true in the Northeast, but in most of the rest of the country, cities have extensive powers, from outright annexation on down, over contiguous rural areas.

Finally, I'd check out the rules at the local municipal level: the town or township. In some parts of the country, particularly the New England states, these local units are fierce guardians of local control and operate their own planning commissions and zoning boards; but in other areas they frequently abdicate such powers to the county or some regional body.

Maine, for example, has vast undeveloped areas in numbered townships with no local government at all; they're administered out of the state Capitol.

New Jersey and Pennsylvania have a mix of townships and boroughs, all of which guard their regulatory powers jealously.

The local level is where you'll usually find the zoning by-laws which are now traditional across America: minimum lot sizes, set-back requirements, architectural control districts, and so on. Most local authorities incorporate regional, state, and federal mandates into their municipal planning documents and zoning by-laws, but some don't. Some, like a few of the towns within New York's Adirondack Park region which are in open conflict with the Agency, aren't about to legitimize regional mandates they disagree with. That's why it's essential to verify what the rules are (or might be) at all four levels.

Just because I've presented the four levels of government above, in descending order, doesn't mean you have to conduct your information search in that same order. It doesn't really matter which offices you hit first, so long as you know that you're not done until you've hit them all.

One closing note: get your information in writing. Federal level bureaucrats are most notorious for reneging on verbal assurances, as the case of environmental consultant Bill Ellen in Maryland proves. He's headed for jail because he trusted a federal wetlands "expert" and ordered construction in an area subsequently ruled by the same individual to be a wetland. Bureaucrats at all levels are subject to the same failing.

(Martin Harris is a Vermont architect, cofounder of The New England Builder, and author of numerous home building articles.) Δ

Hamfests – overlooked goldmines for hobbyists and collectors

By Bill McLean

Ever hear of a "hamfest?" Most people outside the amateur radio community haven't. Amateur radio operators call themselves "hams." They use the term "hamfest" to describe a unique kind of flea market/antique show/auction that almost always offers real finds for hobbyists, do-it-yourselfers, and collectors of just about everything.

There's a full range of radio equipment at hamfests: transmitters, receivers, components, and the like. But there are also tons of valuable items that often bear no relationship to amateur radio or electronics. You can find old books, magazines, and crafts of all sorts; signs, guns, knives, and collectibles in bewildering variety; even pot holders, homemade cookies, and teargas cartridges!

You can get a working telephone, for example, for $2 to $10, a lifetime supply of solder for a couple of bucks, tools of all kinds for practically nothing, TV antennas, car radios, scanners, and home computers – all at a fraction of retail cost.

General collectors and dealers can often do very well at hamfests. One antique dealer, for example, had a customer in the market for a 1930s Atwater Kent radio cabinet to complete a recreation room decoration scheme. She wanted just the cabinet, not the radio, and she offered to pay up to $150 for a good one. At a hamfest, the dealer found a fine Atwater Kent, circa 1932, with all the innards intact and working. He bought the radio for $40, removed the innards, installed a $25 AM/FM receiver, and sold the works to his customer for $125. At a subsequent hamfest, the dealer sold the original Atwater Kent receiver, without the cabinet, to an antique radio buff for $45. He had realized more that $100 profit for less than an hour's work, and everybody involved was happy with the outcome.

Hamfests are usually pretty sizable events. There are normally a couple of hundred exhibitors and several thousand attendees. They're held all over the country, all year long. In winter months they're typically held at a high school, usually on a Sunday from 8 a.m. to 4 p.m. In the summer, you'll find them at county fairgrounds and 4-H centers. Hint: If you go, go early; the good stuff gets picked over fast.

Hamfests are usually sponsored by a local radio club and admission is $2 to $4. Exhibitors' tables go for $2 to $15, depending on size. Some hamfests permit sales out of vans or car trunks, particularly in the summer. Proceeds from ticket sales and exhibitor fees go to the sponsoring radio club to support public services the club provides for its community. Refreshments and door prizes are almost always offered.

The Big Daddy of hamfests is the annual Hamvention in Dayton, Ohio. Sponsored by the Dayton Amateur Radio Association, it's held every spring for three days at Dayton's Hara Convention Arena and Exhibition Center. It's a mind boggler. Exhibitors number in the hundreds and their wares cover acres.

How do you find a hamfest in your community? They're usually not well advertised, so here's what to do:

– If you know a ham, ask him or her where the next hamfest is. Hams always know things like this.

– Look in the Yellow Pages under "Radio Communications Equipment" for a store that sells amateur radio gear. Call or visit. Such stores invariably keep track of local ham doings.

– Check your local Radio Shack store. There are about 6,000 of them in the U.S. and many keep track of ham activities.

– Check with the radio club or electronics instructor at your local high school or community college.

– Check your local Red Cross office. Many ham clubs are affiliated with the Red Cross to provide emergency disaster communications.

– Write the American Radio Relay League (ARRL), 225 Main St., Newington, CT 06111 for information on hamfests in your area. The League maintains a clearing house for hamfests to avoid scheduling conflicts.

There's bound to be a hamfest in your area soon. Go! You'll have a lot of fun, and you just might find the unusual item you haven't been able to find anywhere else. Δ

Snow Prints

Today I walked shoe-deep in spring grass
That carpets a vale we both know
Where together we once found affection
Surrounded by soft drifting snow.

The trails that we packed with our snowshoes
Held moisture, and now trace our way
With turf that's greener than green is–
Side by side, I saw them today.

When the grass becomes withered and sunburned
Our footsteps will finally fade
But in snow-drifted meadows of memory
The impressions you made will have stayed.

Not time, indifference, nor distance
Will erase one step nor its mark,
Be the clearing all dazzled in sunshine
Or moonless, deserted, and dark.

Richard Lee Rose
British Columbia, Canada

Using hybrids and . . .

Creating your own varieties

By Martin P. Waterman

Creating a new fruit or vegetable variety or any other type of hybrid is not as difficult as it may seem. It does not take a big investment in equipment or detailed knowledge of the sciences. However, you do have to be able to contribute time, have some ability for record keeping and, of course, a level of determination and enthusiasm.

Most gardeners and growers picture hybridising as being the domain of scientists in large laboratories with exotic equipment, but this need not be the case. In fact, some of the most important varieties have been developed by private breeders in their own backyards and greenhouses.

There's no limit to the variety of plants you can breed. This dwarf citrus will be crossed with a lemon.

Why hybridise?

So why develop a new variety? Some may argue that with new technologies, such as gene transfer, conventional backyard breeding techniques are obsolete. In theory this may be true, but due to the expense of gene transfer most of the money available for research is devoted to mapping human genes to solve the mystery of human diseases.

The little funding that is available for agriculture is being used for staple crops such as rice and legumes. Gene transfer and other new technologies are being used for proven crops while innovative and niche crops are being neglected due to the high cost of the research involved. Unfortunately, it is the niche crops that could provide profits for the small grower and lower our dependency on some of the large commodity crops that already are depressed in price because of government subsidies and oversupply.

Squash is easy to hybridise: only one year to wait to see your results. New varities have nutty flavors and are rich in vitamins.

For most breeders, hybridising is pursued to meet a requirement that existing cultivars do not possess. This could include a particular disease resistance, plant or fruit size, ripening time, color, shape, cold or heat tolerance, flavor, scent, or just about any trait you can imagine.

Before you start breeding, you will need to know what you are trying to accomplish. You will also need to know the work that has been done previously in the area you are pursuing. For instance, if you want to breed a yellow cherry tomato – it has already been done. However, if you want to breed a yellow cherry tomato plant that will grow to 10 feet in height, fruit continually throughout the season, and is very hardy in cold weather, then you have a quest.

Time is a very important factor to consider. If you are breeding tomatoes, you can create several generations of hybrids in a year and even more if you have a greenhouse. If you are breeding certain fruit trees, you may have to wait many years for results. These results can be speeded up by grafting cuttings of your new hybrid to an existing tree but this will not tell you how well the new hybrid survives on its own rootstock and how the graft and the tree it is grafted to may be influencing it.

I will give examples of some of the breeding work that I have done. Breeding for the most part is generic, and you can take the knowledge gained by breeding one species and apply it to different species.

Don't reinvent the wheel

The most important piece of advice I was given by fellow breeders was not to try to duplicate work that has al-

These new grape varieties grown from seeds are ready to be planted in a test nursery. The vines that survive two winters and look healthy will be moved to the vineyard.

ready been done. This repetition is usually a waste of time. It is best to build on the work of others and, in most cases, this means working with the latest available varieties so that you can have the best genetic material that has been developed to work with.

How to get started

Every revolution was once a thought in some person's mind, to use a famous quotation. Therefore, you will need to identify the improved cultivar you are trying to create and how you intend it to excel over any of the existing varieties that are available. Perhaps you want to do something similar to what Nolan Blansit did when he bred the first yellow African Violet. Perhaps you want to adapt fruit cultivars that have never been grown before in your area. Perhaps you are already growing a variety but are having a productivity or a disease problem.

When a certain need cannot be met, some growers try to solve the problem, and this is how many growers evolve into being breeders. This is how I got started.

I grew up on the Canadian prairies where you could not grow decent fruit. When I moved east to New Brunswick I was thrilled that you could grow grapes, which I did. In fact, I grew every grape variety that I could find. Still, I was frustrated at the low quality since I found that most were hybrids of native grapes and were far from the quality of those available from California.

I soon decided that if I wanted to grow high quality grapes that I would have to breed my own. The high quality California varieties have no chance of surviving in my cold climate (U.S.D.A. hardiness zone 5) so I decided to obtain the pollen of the high quality grapes and use them on the hardy native hybrids which already had the genes necessary to survive the worst possible winters.

Contact other breeders

I want to interject a very important point here. In my quest, I learned that there were already dozens of private grape breeders in North America and several of them were working on similar projects. Therefore, it is advisable to find out who is doing what in the area you want to pursue.

This is not as difficult as it may seem. By contacting federal, state, provincial, and county agriculture organizations you can quickly learn where breeding is taking place. For instance, orange breeding is being done in California and Florida; lettuce in Salinas, California; and peaches in Georgia, New York, and Ontario, Canada.

Usually where an industry exists, there will be institutional breeders. This is an important resource to be accessed. The work they do appears in various journals, and you can often get copies of their news releases touting new varieties or new methods of culture.

It is important for you to know that as a tax payer you pay for many of these programs so try to get as much of your hard-earned tax dollars back in the form of information and assistance. Most scientists, if they see that you are serious in your breeding efforts, will be supportive. Most institutions have a policy to support private breeders only if they are seriously pursuing their breeding.

Private breeders can be located anywhere and are not usually tied to specific growing areas. For instance, I am doing some banana breeding which may seem out of place for Canada, but more about that later.

The most exciting thing about creating new varieties is the thrill when they fruit and you can taste the results.

By corresponding with other breeders, you can take advantage of their mistakes and successes. You may also be able to obtain useful varieties that will be helpful with your own particular objectives. If you cannot get varieties, you may be able to get pollen which is necessary if the pollen parent cannot or is not growing in your area or is difficult to import because of agricultural restrictions.

When you contact institutions that are involved in breeding, they can usually tell you who the important private breeders are. Once you get to know them you may be able to exchange pollen and plant material and even share seeds so that your breeding program can be more effective and efficient.

After I contacted many grape breeders, I was advised to create a "Mother Block" of grapes. This consisted of varieties that would prove to be hardy enough to survive our winters, which can be as cold as minus 35 degrees and ripen in our seasons that can be as short as 130 days. This was done and close to 200 varieties were tested, of which about 100 remain. From these, maybe 20 are suitable parents because they are reliable enough. We have no grape industry in this province so almost every vine I planted represented the first time it had been planted in this particular climate. I could not have done this without the support of public and private breeders.

Perhaps I erred in choosing grapes since it takes about four to five years for a seed to become a grape-producing vine. However, my first generations are fruiting. I expect to have a seedless grape that can survive regularly in this climate as well as many more improved varieties.

In a normal breeding program, usually less than one percent of new hybrids may warrant release because they excel beyond the level of existing varieties. However, if you are seeking a niche such as a persimmon tree that will survive in USDA zone 4, any hybrid that is likely to survive would probably be a possible selection if for no other reason than for use in further breeding.

Learning basic genetics

You do not have to be a geneticist in order to be a breeder. An excellent place to start is with a high school biology or botany text that has a chapter on genetics. This will usually give you the basic information you need on Mendelian theory and examples using his breeding experiences with pea plants. You will then be able to understand basic genetics and recessive and dominant traits.

Some of the best new rose varieties have been created by simply planting seeds by open-pollination. This particular rose features big edible rose hips ideal for fresh eating, jams, or rose hip tea. Flowers are red, large, and fragrant.

As you progress, you may wish to consider picking up a copy of Advances in Fruit Breeding by Janick and Moore. Your library can be of great assistance in locating horticulture books and addresses of government and private institutions. You will also want to join societies if they exist for the varieties you are working with. This will serve many purposes from understanding the needs of growers to tracking down other breeders.

I started with the simple premise that if I took hardy grapes and crossed them with high quality grapes, then eventually I would get hardy high quality grapes. The theory works, but unfortunately it can take several generations in some instances.

A surprise hybrid grape

There are also many surprises. For instance, I crossed a red and a black grape and ended up with white grapes. This happened because I did not know that both of these grapes each had one parent that produced white grapes. Because this trait was recessive it did not show up until my cross was made.

Basic tools and procedures

My basic tools consist of some fine tweezers, a bottle of rubbing alcohol, paint brushes, and some paper bags. These tools satisfy my breeding requirements and you may be able to adapt other simple tools or procedures for your own particular needs.

In the spring, when I do my grape breeding, I do the following: About three to four days before bloom, I will go out and emasculate a grape cluster before it flowers. I dissect each unopened flower and remove the anthers and thus the pollen. I use the fine tweezers to do this.

By doing this, I have converted each grape flower on the cluster from being a hermaphrodite flower capable of self pollination to a female flower. I then put a paper bag over the cluster so it will not be polluted by outside pollen. When the rest of the clusters on the vine bloom, I will open the bag and brush the desired pollen with the paint brush on the stigmas. I use the rubbing alcohol to clean the brush before I use pollen again so that there is no chance of pollen from a previous cross polluting a new cross.

The pollen I use comes from three sources. It will come from a nearby vine, my freezer (some pollens can be frozen for several years), or it will be fresh from another breeder who is probably in warmer climes. Depending on my objectives, the pollen could be selected for a wine grape, large berries, white berries, seedless berries, hardiness, earliness, high brix, low acid or countless other traits or combinations of traits.

After the cluster is pollinated, I put the bag back over the cluster until the berries set. In the fall I harvest the cluster, plant the seeds in flats, and put them in a cool moist place because they need this stratification in order to germinate. In the spring, the new varieties emerge in the greenhouse and they are planted outdoors. After that, winter, disease, and pests take their toll and what is left standing can be evaluated as a potential new variety. Wasn't that simple?

Seeds can be taken from wild plants, such as these elderberries. Many new selections have been made by simply planting seeds and evaluating new varieties.

A feeling of power

Needless to say, there is a certain feeling of power when you have just created a new variety. As you look upon it, you realize that this is the only variety of its type on this planet and you have created it and nurtured it.

There are some large corporations involved in the fruit industry who have their own private breeders. Any new varieties they develop they use themselves. This gives them exclusivity. For instance, one California fruit company has developed a massive apricot which is delicious and juicy and ships well. It sells for a premium price and will probably never be released.

If you plan on releasing a variety, you may want to consider patenting it. This can give some protection, but enforcement is difficult. Many universities use the patent and then license the variety; an annual royalty is paid as long as the plants are being used.

Besides grapes I am breeding June berries, azaleas, roses, cherries and hardy kiwi. During our long winters, I am breeding dwarf citrus and dwarf banana plants for indoor culture.

Bananas are a particular challenge because the edible varieties are triploids that are not capable of being pollinated, and they have no seeds. However, the edible bananas provide pollen which is used on seeded varieties which are diploids and then hopefully these and/or future generations will be new varieties that will excel over existing varieties and provide fruit in a home setting. There is only about a half dozen varieties suitable for this so far and this is an area that has not been overworked. I enjoy growing bananas indoors so I have another asset going for me – enthusiasm!

A simple way of breeding is to plant seeds by open pollination. This is gambling at best but it requires little effort or planning. Many popular rose varieties have been created just by planting the rose seeds and seeing what new hybrids are produced. If the rose has self-pollinated, you will probably end up with varieties that resemble the parents of that particular rose. However, if another rose has pollinated it you may have a new interesting hybrid that may be worthy as a new variety.

There may be wild fruit in your area which could form the basis for improved varieties for your area or you may already be growing a variety that can be improved.

Breeding new varieties is exciting. You can probably learn new levels in the arts of patience and discipline as you wait with anticipation for seeds to germinate or for plants to flower or produce fruit. In addition, you could be responsible for creating and contributing a new variety that will help you or fellow growers to have more enjoyment in their hobby or to help yourself or others to earn a living. Δ

A BHM Writer's Profile

Bruce Allison says, "I am a user of BSJ (Basic Sound Junk). I haul a lot of other peoples scrap and junk as a side hobby." From this resource, he produces many items he could not otherwise afford. Sometimes inspiration provides the spark, other times devices are gleaned directly from the scrap pile. Because he doesn't earn enough income to buy most things new, one of his rules is: "It's not how much money you can make. What is important is what you really require to give yourself the creature comforts you desire."

Allison originally built his trailer to move the heavy materials to build his house. After he finished that project, he started helping others. He mostly hauls scrap metal and won't haul any wet garbage. By separating his loads into salvageables, scrap, and garbage, he is able to bring in many treasures. "Many people have no idea how to get rid of their excess possessions. Many times I am given new or nearly new items," says Allison.

Besides his recycling, Allison operates an independent energy business called Simple Solar Works. He has been writing for *Backwoods Home Magazine* since 1990. His subjects range from pigs to roto-rooters.

Alternative education — learning in the real world

By Mark and Helen Hegener

Let's start out with a pop quiz: What is education really all about—why do we send our kids off to public school for nine months of the year? Go ahead, give the question some real thought before you read any further.

Chances are, you think that kids are sent to school to learn how to read, to write, and to figure with numbers. The old "readin' and writin' and 'rithmetic . . ."

You're right, that is probably why they're sent to school, but that's not necessarily what they're taught when they get there. And teaching these skills has never been the real purpose of public schooling.

The primary purpose of public schooling was—and remains—to produce a cooperative work force for our industrialized country. The most practical and efficient way to go about this is to round everyone up at the most highly impressionable ages and teach them how to follow directions, how to step in line, how to let others do the real thinking—in other words, how to complacently assume their pre-assigned niche in society.

Jim Hegener attends homeschool with the help of a computer.

In his book, The Night Is Dark and I Am Far From Home (Simon & Shuster, 1990), Jonathan Kozol wrote, "U.S. education is by no means an inept, disordered misconstruction. It is an ice-cold and superb machine. It does the job: not mine, not yours perhaps, but that for which it was originally conceived. The first goal and primary function of the U.S. public school is not to educate good people, but good citizens. It is the function which we call—in enemy nations—'state indoctrination.'"

The "hidden curriculum"

John Taylor Gatto is an outspoken teacher who has become a fierce advocate for alternative education. Recipient of honors from Presidents Carter, Ford, and Reagan, winner of the award for New York State Teacher of the Year for 1991 and New York City Teacher of the Year for 1989, 1990, and 1991, John Taylor Gatto spent 30 years teaching junior high school English in the New York City public school system. He now tours the country speaking before education associations, school boards, homeschooling groups, civic organizations, and alternative educators. He is the author of Dumbing Us Down: The Hidden Curriculum of Compulsory Schooling (New Society Publishers, 1991), and editor of The Exhausted School (The Odysseus Group, 1992).

Gatto writes, "Mass dumbness is vital to modern society. The dumb person is wonderfully flexible clay for psychological shaping by market research, government policymakers, public opinion leaders, and any other interest group. That is the whole point of national forced schooling: we aren't supposed to be able to think for ourselves because independent thinking gets in the way of 'professional' thinking, which is believed to follow rules of scientific precision."

Gatto is not alone in his denunciation of enforced schooling. More and more teachers are recognizing that they've been used by a system that does not have the best interests of the American people at heart. Professor Edward A. Rauchut, a public high school English teacher, announced that he would quit the teaching profession in the October 30, 1991 issue of *Education Week*. He wrote, "Our public educational system is a monopoly founded on anti-intellectualism and bogus theories of learning. As such, real education has always been its enemy, and the single greatest threat to its very existence, a persistent reminder of its failed mission to teach our nation's children. Is it any wonder, therefore, that the educational bureaucracy is so resistant to change? Real education would put the child-detention centers we call schools out of business."

Scores of books have been written about the underlying purposes of schooling. In Don't Blame the Kids (McGraw-Hill, 1982) Gene I. Maeroff, an award-winning education writer for *The New York Times*, cautions, "Make no mistake. Schools have been viewed by Congress primarily as instruments of social change." Paul Copperman, author of The Literacy Hoax (Morrow Quill, 1978), writes, "The primary goals of elementary education—teaching young children reading, writing, computing, citizenship, and basic subject matter—were replaced with a combination of psychological goals and restructured intellectual goals." And Stephen Arons, Associate Professor of Legal Studies at the University of Massachusetts, Amherst, and author of the book

Compelling Belief: The Culture of American Schooling (McGraw-Hill, 1983), writes, "Educators have claimed not only that schooling is the linchpin of democratic process in America but that the schools are the nation's primary agency for eliminating social ills, inoculating against anti-Americanism, and perfecting the personal and national character."

America 2000

Now these goals have been wrapped in new rhetoric and are being shoved down our collective throats as America 2000. Six highly advertised "goals" have been determined, lofty- sounding goals which, when implemented through the rapidly multiplying state and local 2000 plans, will take us a long ways down the road toward complete social control.

In Alternatives In Education (Home Education Press, 1992) Larry and Susan Kaseman examine the implications of the federal government's renewed involvement in public and private education. They write, "In general (the goals of America 2000) are based on using education and schools as the primary if not the sole basis for solving much larger problems in our society such as unemployment, poverty, inadequate health care, and nutrition. When these are labeled 'education goals' and education and the schools are identified as the problem, education and schools can become even more repressive in their role as agents of social control and larger underlying problems that do not relate directly to education are neither articulated nor addressed."

In the Autumn, 1991 issue of *Options in Learning*, published by the New York-based Alliance for Parental Involvement in Education, editor Seth Rockmuller wrote, "At the federal level, at the state level, and at the local level, there is a great deal of energy being expended to define education for the 21st century, to be the leading state in terms of 'true' educational reform or parent participation, or to be the best school district in terms of turning out products (i.e. students) which will fuel our economy. I'm scared to death by all this, and I think you should be too."

Whether we like it or not, whether we're aware of it or not, we and our children are merely pawns in a high stakes game being played by the educational power centers, peopled not only by the school boards and teacher's unions, but also by bureaucrats and politicians and big business interests. The first step will be to inform ourselves and each other. Find out what's really happening in education today, find out what's behind the proposals and the programs. And be prepared for a severe shock.

Jody Hegener reads a book with her rooster.

To learn more about the federal government's plan for education call 1-800-USA-LEARN, and ask for information and their free newsletter about America 2000.

Alternative education

The author and radical alternative educator John Holt was noted for asking questions which rankled the establishment mentality. Questions such as, "One of the main differences between a free country and a police state, I always thought, was that in a free country, as long as you obeyed the law, you could believe whatever you liked. Your beliefs were none of the government's business. Far less was it any of the government's business to say that one set of ideas was good and another set bad, or that (compulsory) schools should promote the good and stamp out the bad. Have we given up these principles?"

Holt's early books on education, classics such as How Children Fail (Pitman Publishing, 1964) and How Children Learn (Pitman Publishing, 1967) are still suggested reading for teachers in training. In 1977, deciding after many years that the school system was hopelessly mired in its own bureaucracy, Holt founded a newsletter for parents and others who might want to explore alternatives to public and private schooling. In his book, Teach Your Own (Delacorte Press, 1981), he wrote, "Why do people take or keep their children out of school? Mostly for three reasons: They think that raising their children is their business and not the government's; they enjoy being with their children and helping them learn, and don't want to give that up to others; and they want to keep their children from being hurt, mentally, physically, and spiritually."

But beyond his campaign to help children and their parents learn and grow, Holt offered another, deeper message. In his book, Freedom and Beyond (E.P. Dutton, 1972), he wrote, "A large part of our problem is that few of us really believe in freedom. As a slogan, it is fine. But we don't understand it as a process or mechanism with which or within which people can work or live. We have had in our own lives so little experience of freedom, except in the most trivial situations, that we can hardly imagine how it might work."

Holt did not believe in perfect freedom. He said that those who saw freedom as the absence of limits simply misunderstood the term. But he was always quick to defend the freedoms of children. He insisted that school was not just a good idea gone bad, but "a bad idea from the word go. It's a nutty idea to believe that we can have a place where nothing but learning happens, cut off from the rest of life."

Hundreds of thousands of parents have agreed, and the homeschooling movement has become increasingly popular in the last 10 years, with national organizations, several national publications, and thousands of support groups providing information and assistance to parents who have chosen to teach their own children at home.

Homeschooling is not simply a new approach to education. For most families it becomes a way to strengthen and build relationships within the family. When they are living and learning together, parents and siblings develop a respect and a bond that simply isn't possible when their attentions are divided by school and its attendant demands. A wise man once said, "We can teach our children to have courage, faith, and endurance; they can teach us to laugh, to sing, and to love."

Homeschooling offers the family an opportunity to guide and encourage children beyond the primary years. It offers continuity and a sense of security that all of us – not only children – need much more than we've been led to believe.

A homeschooling primer

Some of the most common questions about homeschooling include:

What about socialization? Don't children who are kept at home miss meeting and playing with other children?

Homeschooled children have many opportunities to meet and get to know other children in their communities through support group activities, sports, and clubs such as Scouting or 4-H. More importantly, homeschooled children have more opportunities to interact with a wide range of people, and learn at a much earlier age how to be socially competent among adults and with children of varying ages.

But aren't homeschooled children really at a disadvantage without all of the resources of a good school?

John Fee types out an assignment.

Quite the opposite: homeschooling gives children an educational advantage. Supported by caring parents, removed from the pressures and distractions of school life, homeschooled children are free to pursue a more meaningful education, to follow their own interests and to develop a lifelong love of learning.

When should we begin actually teaching our child?

The age of the child is often given primary consideration: it is assumed that children can begin reading at a certain age, should be taught arithmetic concepts at another specific age, and will be ready to start writing at a different predetermined age. However, while this system is convenient for schools in processing large numbers of children, age is not a barometer of readiness. In fact, it tells nothing about a particular child's ability to concentrate, the length of his attention span, the development of his vision and hearing or his general interest in the whole subject of learning.

So how can we tell when he's ready?

Ideally, homeschooling becomes simply an extension of raising your child from birth, and reading or science become no more complicated or difficult to teach than tying shoelaces or riding a bicycle. There's no need to impose a regimented lesson plan when he reaches the age of minimum compulsory attendance. By paying attention to his interests, his activities, and his questions, it will become apparent when your child is ready to pursue more difficult subject material. Many parents delay formal instruction until age 10 or 12, and some never adopt a structured curriculum. Their children are learning every day, for life itself is a learning experience.

What about higher education?

Most colleges and universities have entrance exams, but many of them place much more weight on a student's ability and attitude than on any absence of high school credits or diplomas. Students who were homeschooled all their lives have been accepted at such prestigious institutions as Yale, Harvard, Princeton, and Oxford, and thousands of students go to correspondence high schools, and then on to colleges, universities, and vocational institutes every year. Apprenticeships, or simply finding someone who's willing to let your child learn while helping them for a few hours each week, are also becoming a popular means of continuing a youngster's education.

How can we find out whether homeschooling is legal in our state?

Homeschooling is legally permitted in all 50 states, but the laws and regulations are much more favorable in some states than in others. Keep in mind that homeschooling regulations are subject to frequent change, and the most reliable source of information is your local or state support group, preferably one that has been actively involved in monitoring homeschool regulation. Those states that have not addressed the issue of homeschooling generally apply various other statutes to homeschooling families, such as those for private schools or tutoring. The requirements under these laws may include such provisions as annual testing or another form of monitoring progress, notification of your local superintendent, or comparable or equivalent instruction (which can often be difficult to adequately define). A few states have stricter requirements, and may include a curriculum substantially equivalent to that of the local schools, or a certain minimum number of hours and days the student is taught. Again, an active and well-informed state or local support group is your best source of current information.

For further information about homeschooling call or write Home Education Press, P. O. Box 1083, Tonasket, WA 98855, (509) 486-1351. Or contact the National Homeschool Association, P.O. Box 290, Hartland, MI 48353, message phone: (513) 772-9580.

Alternative and community schools

Alternative schools come in all shapes and sizes. Since 1976 the National Coalition of Alternative Community Schools (NCACS) has coordinated a networking effort for alternative schools, community schools, homeschooling, and free schools around the world. The NCACS Directory describes the typical alternative school: "The schools are small, frequently serving fewer than 50 students total; they maintain low student-teacher ratios. They offer a wide variety of activities to learners as part of the everyday fare: open learning environments, apprenticeship programs, overnight trips away from school, the use of the community as classroom and more. These are alternatives to conventional schooling."

Two of the most successful and widely-respected alternative schools are Clonlara School in Ann Arbor, Michigan, and Sudbury Valley School in Framingham, Massachusetts. Clonlara School's founder, Dr. Pat Montgomery, wrote that she and her husband, Jim, ". . . imagined a place where children of all creeds and races might learn and grow in an unpressured, relaxed atmosphere, free of coercion. A place where the very democratic principles upon which our country was built would become a reality in the everyday lives of students and adults – one person, one vote. No discrimination based on age. A place where parents would share intimately in the life of the school and in the education of their children, where they would be active participants, not passive observers and cookie bakers for PTA meetings."

Daniel Greenberg, Ph.D., one of the founders of Sudbury Valley School, also wrote about democracy: "The idea of personal respect leads almost directly to the concept of democracy as an institutional imperative. Democracy alone is built on the solid foundation of equal respect for all members of the community, and for their ideas and hopes. And so it became a cornerstone of our philosophy to involve everyone, without exception and including the parents, in the full process of running the school."

NCACS publishes a quarterly newsletter, sponsors an annual conference on alternative education, publishes an international directory of schools and educational programs, and offers books, videos, and other resources on alternative education. For further information contact the National Coalition of Alternative Community Schools (NCACS), 58 Schoolhouse Road, Summertown, TN 38483; (615) 964-3670.

Other options

There are over 100 Waldorf schools in the United States, where nature and the arts predominate the curriculum. Waldorf school programs are based on the educational philosophy of Austrian spiritual philosopher Rudolf Steiner, who believed that from birth to seven years of age children learn primarily through imitation; that from seven through fourteen years of age the curriculum should focus on and awaken the child's emerging feelings; and that after fourteen the child's developing powers of independent thought should be addressed.

Textbooks are not used in the Waldorf school; rather, each student makes his own books as he progresses through the classes. Teachers move through the grade levels with their students, and a great deal of attention is given to the spoken language. Eurythmy, an art form created by Steiner in which movement corresponds to musical or spoken sound, is an integral part of Waldorf education.

Information about Waldorf Education can be obtained from Childhood, Route 2, Box 2675, Westford, VT 05494, or from Anthroposophic Press, Bell's Pond, Star Route, Hudson, NY 12534, (518) 851-2054.

Montessori schools stress a prepared learning environment for the child, to assure success for the child at every new task attempted. Over 4,000 Montessori programs in this country alone attest to the popularity of this approach, based on the insights of Dr. Maria Montessori, an Italian doctor and educator who practiced around the turn of the century. Dr. Montessori's "discovery of the child" was a true awakening and advancement in early childhood education. She called the young child's mind "the absorbent mind" because of its great ability to learn and grow from interactions with the world around it. Believing that the child absorbs learning from his environment, Montessori created the "prepared environment," but she was quick to point out that "the environment should reveal the child, not mold him." She stressed the need for beauty and quality in the materials a child was exposed to, and felt that the child should be free to grow in his own way.

For information about Montessori schooling contact Michael Olaf's Essential Montessori, P. O. Box 1162, Arcata, CA 95521; (707) 826-2243.

Combining approaches

Some of the most successful educational programs combine one or more of these approaches: homeschooling with a Waldorf style curriculum, for example, or an alternative school which welcomes families from the community to share their learning resource center. There are alternative schools which utilize Montessori concepts, homeschoolers who have banded together to form alternative learning programs – in short, the emphasis is on finding what works for your own children, for your family, and for your community.

Most of the organizations referred to in this article recognize the effectiveness of such cross-fertilization, and work with each other, forming an "alternative education community" which provides support for families trying to find those programs which best suit their individual needs. Two national organizations bridge the various approaches: The Alliance for Parental Involvement in Education and The Alternative Education Research Organization, both based in New York.

The Alliance for Parental Involvement in Education (ALLPIE), is a nonprofit, tax-exempt, grassroots organization which encourages parents to become involved in the education of their children wherever that education takes place – in public school, in private school, or at home. In addition to their newsletter, ALLPIE sponsors an annual conference on education and provides a catalog of learning materials. By providing information about educational options, family rights in education, current educational trends, and useful resources, ALLPIE works to empower parents. ALLPIE, P.O. Box 59, East Chatham, NY 12060; (518) 392-6900.

The Alternative Education Resource Organization (AERO), founded and directed by education activist Jerry Mintz, produces a networking newsletter, publishes a directory of educational alternatives, and travels across the country and around the world to help those who want to start new educational alternatives in their communities. AERO, 417 Roslyn Road, Roslyn Heights, NY 11577; (516) 621-2195.

(Mark and Helen Hegener are the homeschooling parents of five children and owners of Home Education Press, which publishes "Home Education Magazine," a bimonthly homeschooling magazine, and several books on homeschooling and alternative education, including their newest, Alternatives In Education. They have been featured speakers at homeschooling conferences across the nation.) Δ

A homeschool assignment

By Benjamin Wright

My name is Benjamin and I live in a log house in the woods. My school assignment is to write about everything I did today.

Dad and I got up early and went hunting in the woods around our house. Last week before I could go hunting I had to look up deer in the books and write a story about how they live. I found out what they eat and their habits.

Most of the time when we go hunting we go on our ATVs. When mom goes along we take the truck. My mom doesn't like guns.

It's very cold and snowing so we came home for breakfast. Dad fixed ham, eggs and toast. He drank milk. I had apple juice.

Feeding the animals is my job every morning. Today mom did it for me because I was cold. I played micro-machines and watched a video about exploring caves.

For school we learned about Marco Polo and a fellow named Dias. They both were explorers. Finding the places they went on the map was hard because I had to use latitude and longitude. We marked where they started from and put a string to where they went. Dias went all the way to the end of Africa. After the map work I put their pictures on the timeline we keep on the wall. For math I figured out how old they were when they went exploring and when they died. Reading about people is interesting. Marco Polo learned 9 Chinese languages.

Because we are studying explorers mom taught me how to use a compass. Tomorrow I have to draw a map of where we live.

Dad needed help with the firewood so I loaded some up on my ATV and hauled it to the house. Mom went out to get the eggs and the turkeys got out and started chasing the chickens. I helped mom chase the chickens and turkeys. Tom, the turkey, was fighting with the rooster. She was really mad.

We had lunch and dad read the paper. I wanted to play with my micro-machines but mom got me to help in the kitchen. We made salt-dough figures. I read the recipe and figured out how much flour and salt and water we needed. Mom tricked me because I figured out we were doing math.

While the dough baked in the oven, mom made butter. I sat on the stool and read her my cookbook. She said if I would read 7 pages I could make myself a shake. I figured out all the recipes are in alphabetical order. My cookbook is named Kinder Krunches. I like it because it has good kid food. My shake has 2 fresh eggs, 2 T. malt, dab sugar, 2 cups cows milk, sometimes a little ice cream. I always put a different color in it, sometimes blue or green. (mom says no more eggs for me this week)

We went hunting this afternoon. Mom drove the truck. It's raining and all the deer are hiding. When we do the wash I like to put the clothes through the wringer. I helped hang the clothes on the racks so they can dry. Star Trek is my favorite tv show so I can watch it after my chores are done. Toby and Brandy are my dogs. One is a St. Bernard and he eats alot.

We had stew for supper. I like the bread and butter the best. Pecan pie was dessert, yummy!

After I ate my supper I painted my dough figures. Water colors didn't work as well as model paint.

"Where In the USA Is Carmen?" is my new computer program. I played that alot tonight before I went to bed. My favorite games and books talk about maps and different countries. My mom says I study "map-ology."

(Benjamin, age 10, welcomes pen-pal letters. His address is P.O. Box 1222, Hayden Lake, Idaho 83835.) Δ

What you should know about gold

By Jo Mason

It has been used for coinage for nearly 4,000 years – and long before that for barter. Gold, in fact, was one of the first metals used by primitive man, who made some fairly strange items from it: fishhooks, for instance.

But its price fluctuations seen on the nightly business news hold little interest for the average person. After all, what does it matter to someone just barely getting by that the price shot up from $370 an ounce to over $400 an ounce? If you're like a lot of folks, you're more interested in the price of that other "precious metal," aluminum, and how much you can get for that pile of cans you collected! But if you think gold has no bearing on your own financial situation . . . think again.

First it's important to know exactly what the gold standard was, and how it affected our country until we abandoned it in 1933. How does it work? Two points are essential for the operation of a gold standard:

– Free and unlimited convertibility of gold and gold bullion into gold coin.

– Currency must be directly or indirectly exchangeable for gold coin.

Further, there must be no restriction on the right of gold owners to melt down coin into bullion, to exchange bullion for coinage, or to import or export gold. Also, banks must always hold certain amounts of gold reserves, because **at any time, you would have the right to exchange your currency for gold coins.**

The U.S. had 130 years of relatively stable prices under their system. Under England's gold standard (wartime excepted) the prices of their goods remained stable for about 250 years.

Under that system, the money supply was directly tied to the amount of gold owned by the government. This limited federal spending. The Fed could not, as they do now, accommodate deficits by increasing the money supply. In short, it limited the Treasury's ability to borrow and forced them to limit spending (like you and I must do). The result? Our dollar was sound.

World War I led to a general abandonment of the gold standard, and the U.S. went off it in 1933. Our money then became "fiat" money. (The word **fiat** means decree of the government.) In a manner of speaking, our dollar is valuable because the government says it is.

Some say that the gold standard failed, but the truth is, it worked too well, and against the purposes of certain men who wanted to achieve their own goals. They wanted to create their own idea of an egalitarian state.

This wasn't exactly an original idea. Karl Marx conceived a similar plan when he wrote the Communist Manifesto. He listed 10 steps necessary for transforming a free economy into a socialist one. One of those steps was "centralization of credit in the hands of the state." And that was precisely one of the purposes of the Federal Reserve Act of 1914 – "to establish a central coordinating authority making credit control possible."

Historically, the price of gold rises along with the inflation rate. When the price of gold climbs, it naturally takes more dollars to buy an ounce of gold. Therefore, since gold's value remains unchanged, our dollars are worth less.

The chronic inflation we've lived with for years now is **not** a normal condition for any country. It's the direct result of this debasing of our currency. You might say it's an indirect method of taxation, which takes wealth from you and me and gives it to others.

The government doesn't see it that way. It claims it is able to "fine tune" the economy. Here's what a former head of the Federal Reserve System, Arthur Burns, said in 1977:

"No nation whose history I am familiar with has succeeded in managing the stock of money perfectly; few indeed, have even managed it well. And those societies that have been least successful have paid dearly for their ineptitude. Debasement of the currency had a great deal to do with the destruction of the Roman Empire. In our own time, excessive creation of money had released powerful inflationary forces in many countries around the globe. And, once a nation's money is debauched, economic and political troubles usually follow."

Table 1. Amount of interest an investment must earn just to break even

tax bracket	5% inflation	10% inflation	20% inflation
0% bracket	5%	10%	20%
10% bracket	5.6%	11.1%	22.2%
20% bracket	6.3%	12.5%	25%
30% bracket	7.1%	14.3%	28.6%
40% bracket	8.3%	16.7%	33.3%
50% bracket	10%	20%	40%

Nearly 50 years ago, gold was $35 an ounce. At that time, a dollar could have bought either two adult movie tickets or three to four pounds of ground chuck. Another way of looking at this is that the two movie tickets or the ground chuck cost you 1/35th of an ounce of gold. The current price of gold (at this writing) is $339 an ounce. If we divide 35 into 339, we come up with – you guessed it – today's price of the tickets or the meat, nearly $10, taking into account price variations across the country. Note: this doesn't apply during times of wild gold price fluctuations, such as during the late 70s and early 80s, which were caused by speculative buying. The price did eventually settle back down, like water seeking its true level.

Remember the Red Queen in Lewis Carroll's Alice through the Looking Glass? She told Alice, "Now here, you see, it takes all the running you can do to keep in the same place. If you want to get somewhere else, you must run at least twice as fast as that." When taking into account the double whammy of inflation and taxes, your investment money has to do the same thing. Table 1 illustrates this.

Given today's relatively low interest rates, are we to believe high interest rates or the threat of runaway inflation are things of the past? Jerome Smith didn't believe so when he wrote The Coming Currency Collapse. Although that was several years ago, his book is just as relevant today. In it he says:

> *"Congressmen want to spend, while repeal of existing authorized spending is rarely even considered . . . any interest in the problem . . . is almost always directed not at eliminating inflation but at controlling inflation. This is a wholly hopeless endeavor. Given conditions that exist and the beliefs and motives of the actors, there is no way that the fiat money toboggan ride can be controlled or terminated short of the bottom of the pit."*

Some people believe investing in gold is the perfect way to protect their hard-earned money. Let's look at the two basic ways they do that:

Gold Trivia

"Gold, the precious and magical yellow metal, been known and valued by men and women since the dawn of civilization. Egyptian, Etruscan, Assyrian and Minoan cultures all valued gold. Gold coinage began in Lydia (modern-day Turkey) in 700 B.C."

"Gold is valued not only for its beauty, but for its high resistance to corrosion, malleability and longevity. Gold will not readily combine with other metals. It is one of the greatest conductors of electricity."

"A cubic foot of solid gold weighs about 1,200 pounds. The standard gold brick, or bullion bar, contains 1000 troy ounces, or nearly 68.5 pounds avoirdupois."Δ — *Carl Watner*

Trading and hedging

Trading: If it were possible, I'd sketch a bright red caution light at the beginning of this paragraph. Gold trading is nothing short of pure speculation. It's short-term buying and selling, in which the trader hopes to, ideally, buy at the lowest point on the downside, and sell at the highest point on the upside. This is an extremely risky endeavor. You should only attempt it if you have more money than you know what to do with (I don't know many people who qualify here) and can sleep nights while watching the daily fluctuations of the metal.

And fluctuate it does. In fact, it's known for its wild price swings, because almost anything can affect it, such as trouble in the Middle East or new governmental policies.

Hedging: This is basically the opposite of trading. You buy your gold at the going price and keep it through thick and thin (in a safety deposit box, under your bed, or buried in the back yard). Even should the price of the metal skyrocket, you resist the urge to cash in on your profit. The idea is that you always have a nest egg that retains its value and is there for you in time of need.

Why do we still, as men did ages ago, highly prize gold? Perhaps for the same reasons they came in droves and blasted away mountainsides, literally tearing California apart in search of it. Because the metal will **always** have a certain value, whereas fiat money may not. Because the precious metal is beyond any government.

And, you might say, because it's as good as gold. Δ

The Old Locust Tree
worm-eaten and dead
still stands,
a grey stump
its branches
grotesquely arranged
against the blue sky.
It has its own beauty.

June Knight
Caldwell, Idaho

A chronology of gold in American history

By Carl Watner

1792-The United States dollar was legislatively defined as a unit containing 24.75 grains of .999 gold or 371.25 grains of silver (15 to 1 ratio); US authorized to strike gold eagles of $10 (standard weight 270 grains .91666 fineness, the equivalent of 247.5 grains of .999 purity).

1792-The US Mint, the first federal government structure, was erected.

1795-Gold half eagles and eagles struck for the first time.

1799-Gold discovered in North Carolina.

1802-Gold discovered in South Carolina.

1832-First gold dollar in the United States struck by the Bechtler mint in Rutherfordton, North Carolina.

1834-Standard definition of the dollar and eagle changed. Dollar re-defined as a unit containing 23.2 grains of .999 gold (changed from 24.75 grains). Silver definition unchanged. Standard weight of the $10 eagle changed to 258 grains of .899225 fineness (equivalent of 232 grains of .999 gold).

1837-Gold purity of $10 eagle (and other gold coins) changed form .899225 to .900.

1848-Gold discovered in California. Private gold coins minted for several years before the establishment of the federal mint in San Francisco.

1857-Foreign coins demonetized; no longer legally acceptable in trade.

1861-Gold payments suspended Dec. 21.

1862-Federal government issues legal tender "greenbacks."

1863-Large private outpouring of private tokens to relieve coin shortage during the Civil War.

1864-Private tokens and private gold coinage banned.

1865-First US gold certificates issued.

1879-Specie payments resumed; greenbacks and gold at par.

1900-Gold Standard Act passed. Gold dollar of 25.8 grains, .900 fine becomes the unit of value. $10 eagle becomes 258 grains of gold, .900 fine (equivalent of 232 grains of .999 gold). This confirms usage dating back to 1837.

1913-Federal Reserve Act becomes law.

1933-Treasury calls in all gold. US goes off gold standard. Government prohibits the manufacture of gold coins, private hoarding of gold, and the use of gold as money or in lieu of money.

1934-The price of gold is up pegged at $35 an ounce, up from its former $20.67 an ounce. Under the Gold Reserve Act the dollar was no longer convertible into gold and gold could not be exported.

1942-President Roosevelt issues an executive order closing all gold mines in the US.

1945-Gold backing of US currency lowered to 25% of the total combined sum of Federal Reserve liabilities.

1946-Ban on gold mining lifted.

1961-Presidential Executive Order prohibiting US citizens from owning or holding gold outside the United States issued.

1965-The 25% requirement for gold backing of commercial banks' deposits at Federal Reserve banks was dropped. This released about $5 billion worth of gold for sale to dollar- holding foreign governments.

1968-25% gold backing removed from paper currency in circulation. This freed another $750 million to stabilize the gold market.

1971-President Nixon devalues the dollar, setting a new official price of $38 an ounce, and halts the conversion of foreign-held dollars into gold.

1973-Second dollar devaluation raises price of gold to $42.22 an ounce.

1974-Ban on US citizens' ownership of gold ended as of Dec.31.

1980-Gold price reaches record high of $850 per ounce on free market of Jan. 21.

1986-US Mint manufactures American Eagle gold coins in four denominations; the first non-commemorative gold coins struck for US consumption since 1933.

(Compiled primarily from Coin World Almanac, 1990. Refer to Chapter 12, "A Numismatic Chronology of the United States of America," and Chapter 14, "Precious Metals-Gold Chronology.") Δ

Using a "producer gas" generator to create electricity

By Gene Townsend

While many people today search for a sensible form of alternative energy to produce electricity, one very old method has been all but overlooked. It is a method especially suitable for people desiring to live in remote areas, beyond the reach of power lines, and it is much less expensive than other forms of alternative energy. It is the conversion of biomass fuels to electricity.

The concept of converting biomass fuels, such as wood, straw, corncobs, coal, peatmoss, etc. into electrical energy is very old. Naturally, one would think of burning these fuels to raise steam for a steam plant, or operate a Stirling or other heat engine.

Most people who produce their own home power have need for only a few kilowatts of generated electricity. Steam plants in this size are very inefficient (5 to 10%) as well as dangerous and expensive. Stirling engines are either similarly inefficient or very expensive and nondurable. Take your pick. With either of these, the smoke and soot will coat your equipment and require constant cleaning. There is a better way.

Early days of the gas engine

The gasoline internal combustion engine, known as the S.I. engine, is not normally thought of as burning other fuels, but back in its early days it was operated exclusively on gaseous fuels.

Gasoline was not available before about 1910 when the automobile created a market for it. In that bygone era, coal was the universal fuel, being used for both home heating and early electrical generation plants.

Steam plants during that time – from about 1880 to 1920 – were quite inefficient, requiring much precious fuel. In the United States this wasn't a big problem due to the abundance of coal, but in Europe where fuel was scarce, a better way was found. It was a simple device known as the gas producer, which had been invented around 1820. The Europeans used it to convert coal into a combustible gas, known as "producer gas," that could be used to operate the S.I. engine.

Converted oil drums make up the upright gas producer, right, and gas scrubber.

These power plants would produce about three or four times the power (for a given amount of coal) as the steam engines of the era. The fuel gas consisted of even volumes of hydrogen (H2) and carbon monoxide (CO) gasses, as well as "nitrogen" – the nitrogen and other inert gasses that make up most of the atmosphere.

The tars and soot created by the fuel would damage the engine if allowed to enter, so they were filtered from the gas beforehand, resulting in no smoke being released from the plant. Water requirements were much smaller than steam plants as well.

The "producer gas" plants endured for about 30 to 40 years, but the high efficiency of the high pressure steam turbine, developed in the 1920s, caused its demise. In remote areas of the world, where coal transportation was difficult and expensive, "producer gas" plants that operated on wood or agricultural residue remained through the 1940s.

Any modern gas engine generator can be operated on "producer gas," whether it is derived from wood or other biomass fuels. The cost of the energy so produced is by far the lowest of all alternative energy sources.

The technique of doing this is very simple, but has been forgotten over the years. In modern times, whenever oil shortages are invoked, interest in the gas producer for automotive use is resurrected. Most modern references to this involve automotive applications to which it is poorly suited due to safety concerns and inconvenience of operation. And producers designed for cars are poor designs for stationary use.

The simplest producer is the **updraft type producer**, so named because of the direction of the motion of the flue gases. It is a high temperature, airtight retort with a vertical stack and grate pad, which is usually a gridwork of iron bars at its bottom upon which the fuel rests.

The fuel is broken into pieces several inches square and fed into the stack from the top, while air enters from the bottom below the grate. The opposite directions taken by the air and fuel cause this to be known as the "counterflow" type, which results in greater efficiency. Air entering from below the grate flows upwards where it burns the carbon fuel that it meets and releases much heat that fuels the action of the producer, which is the reduction of carbon dioxide (CO2) to carbon monoxide (CO) which absorbs much heat.

About 70% of the carbon fuel is reduced, the balance being burned. Water released by the fuel reacts with carbon to form hydrogen (H2) gas as well as more CO.

The very hot gases produced in the reduction zone pass upwards through unreacted fuel causing it to heat and

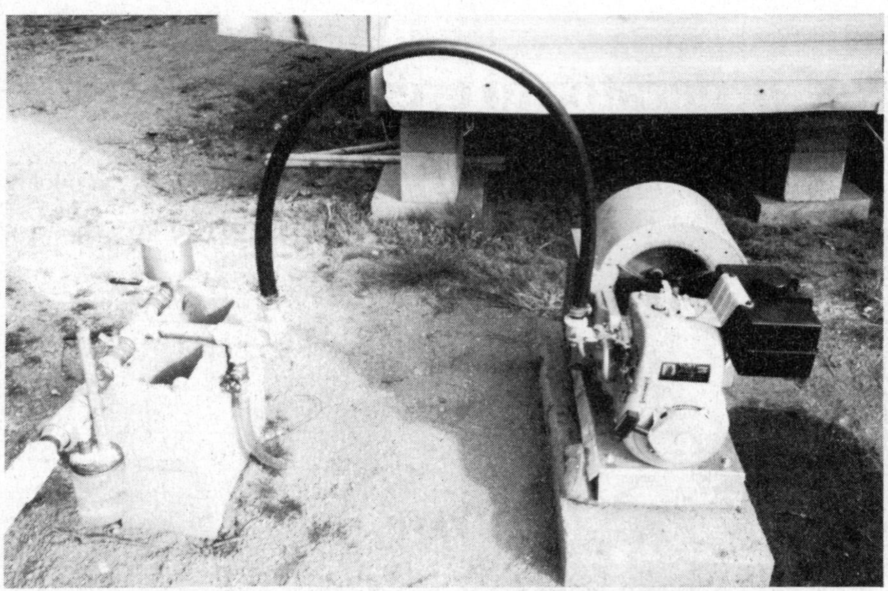

The gas air-mixing manifold at left is attached to a test dynomonitor.

release tars and surface moisture through distillation, also called pyrolysis. This action is unavoidable in the updraft type producer, the distillation gases produced being highly undesirable to the engine. They must be removed from the gases by suitable gas conditioning equipment.

The motion of the gases through the system is caused by the intake suction of the engine attached, so the restrictive nature of the filtration equipment must be minimized to avoid power loss. The gas must be cool as well as clean before it enters the engine manifold. Mixture ratio with air is very close to 1 to 1 for "producer gas." The updraft type can work with virtually any fuel containing carbon, and moisture content is non-critical. So this type has great fuel flexibility, but at the cost of relatively dirtier gas.

The **downdraft type producer** was developed to reduce the tar content of the gas when used with high tar fuels such as wood or lignite coals by burning it in the reactor directly, thus avoiding the need for large filtration units. This was a definite advantage in automotive units, which were mostly of this type. However, operation is optimal only for single fuels, and high ash fuels such as manure and crop residues cannot be used.

The **crossdraft producer** was strictly for use in cars and required charcoal or very high grade anthracite coal fuel. The gas blast velocity is much greater in this type, resulting in much hotter reaction temperatures and faster throttle response—important in traffic conditions. During WW2, Volvo developed trailer-mounted units of this type.

Power output of a gasoline engine will be about half as much with "producer gas," but pollution will be lower due to cooler combustion temperatures. Fuel consumption is about 2.5 lbs. wood per horsepower hour. Compared to other bioconversion processes, such as methane digesters or ethanol stills, a much greater yield results from a lower grade of fuel using simpler equipment. The gas is not stored, but rather produced on demand by the engine as it needs it.

Today, the self sufficient person can produce power at a lower cost than the utilities using this technique—and with very little equipment outlay. It's not nice and clean like PV panels, but it works very well. The gas producer is a carbon-eating animal that needs care and feeding just like any livestock!

(Gene Townsend is the author of the Townsend Gas Producer Manual, a construction and operation manual he sells for $10. If you'd like one, his address is 36515 Twin Hawks Lane, Marana, AZ 85653.) — EditorΔ

A BHM Writer's Profile

Roger DeGroot is an urban dreamer and aspiring backwoodsman. He combines his computer job in Chicago with family life in the suburbs, volunteer work, and teaching in a local college. Somehow, he still finds time to putter in the garden, raise rabbits, and do minor home remodeling projects.

When you're busy all the time, there is a real need for R& R. Five acres in the northern Michigan woods provide the opportunity for the DeGroots. "We bought the land as an investment," says DeGroot, "but the payoff is not the increased value of the land. It is the quiet, peaceful mornings watching the sun come up, with no noise but the gentle breeze in the tree tops and the deer drinking in the pond."

There is always work to be done. One advantage of DeGroot's 30-minute train ride to work is a built-in time to reflect, research, and plan those household projects. DeGroot says, "Anything is easy, if you already know how, or you have a buddy helping you who knows how." DeGroot hopes that through his writing, he can be a buddy who already did it once, for those who don't know how.

Making a living as a writer

By Jo Mason

Why wasn't this article entitled "Earning a living as a backwoods writer?" For the simple reason that chances are you **won't** earn a living writing—not even a backwoods living—not at first.

If you've been counting the days until you can remove yourself from the rat race, and have the time and serenity to write—that's great. If you've been counting on supporting yourself and your family with the income—better reconsider.

Competition among free-lance writers is fierce. The odds are overwhelming that for the first year or several years, you could make better money by working part-time at a fast food restaurant.

That may be hard to swallow; realities always are. But as Robert Ringer's Theory of Reality (*Winning through Intimidation*) states, "Either you acknowledge reality and use it to your benefit or it will automatically work against you." The author also says, "...if I were forced to state an opinion as to what one single factor...is most responsible for failure, my answer would have to be the inability to recognize and/or refusal to acknowledge reality."

Now that you've acknowledged the fact that being a writer requires time, perseverance, and patience, you can use it to your benefit. Already you're one step ahead of those dreamers who sit around in their rose-colored glasses waiting for their "muse," (whatever that is). Now for the good news: Since your business will be conducted through the mail, you can work anywhere you wish. Who else can make that claim? Not doctors, lawyers, movie stars, plumbers, or corporate CEOs. The old story about having to live in New York is a myth. In fact, living in the boonies can actually be a plus.

You set your own schedule, working the hours and days of the week you choose. You'll be your own boss. When you sit down to work each day (and it is hoped that's what you'll do!) you can select among several different projects. If the mood strikes, you can do research for that article about weather balloons, polish up that nearly finished piece on roofing, or maybe make some progress on that historical novel. A lot of doctors, lawyers, movie stars, plumbers, and CEOs would kill for a job like that!

Speaking of plumbers—they earn good money (as we all know who've ever had to hire one) and lead relatively secure lives. A writer, on the other hand, may lead a precarious existence and spend some lean years paying his dues. Then again, a plumber basically has one customer at a time and gets paid by the job. Does he have a chance—as you, a writer would—of writing one book, and selling it over and over again? (and collecting royalties on each sale) Does he have a shot, as you do, at fame and fortune?

Best of all there's the thrill of seeing your work and your name in print, and the pleasure of doing what you love most for a living.

What you'll need to begin

You need a place to work. This can be an entire room for an office, or the kitchen table. Or perhaps there's an old outbuilding on your place you can fix up, or a walk-in closet. The main consideration is that it be a comfortable, well-lit place where you can set up all your equipment and supplies. If possible, try to avoid the kitchen table routine. Every day you must take time to set up your stuff, and take it down again. And who wants to work with toast crumbs and jelly on their desk? Another consideration is your own individual temperament. How much privacy will you require? Can you concentrate with your family carrying on activities around you?

You'll need a typewriter. You might be able to squeak by with using an ancient portable but why begin with one strike against you? The prices on electric ones have gone down considerably since the computer age. As you progress, a word processor would be ideal. Longhand submissions are **out**. You'll want plain 9 x 12 paper—**not** erasable bond. Don't waste money on monogrammed stationery. You don't need to invest a fortune in office furniture. What you need is a comfortable chair (because, if you're serious about this, you'll be spending **hours** and **hours** in it!) and some type of desk (a door placed over two sawhorses will suffice).

You don't have to buy file cabinets. Cardboard boxes or milk cases will do to hold your file folders. But—and trust me on this—buy a huge stack of 9 x 12 folders. Begin your career right by being organized and staying organized. File articles, information, instructions, letters from editors, writer's guidelines, puzzles, poems, clippings, stories—everything.

An important requirement

What else do you need? The ability to blend creativity with practicality. So many beginning writers start out full of impossibly high hopes. Scenario of their ideal first week: Dash off a piece and send to *Field & Stream* or *Good Housekeeping*. Three days later receive phone call from editor saying article has been accepted, check for $1000 is on the way, and can you please send more articles. Listen to me: That is not going to happen.

Here's a more likely scenario – the reality you must acknowledge, remember? You work and write for weeks, months. Every day you check mailbox. Nothing. Finally, there's something: a reject. Later, more rejects. You're crushed. Along with your returned manuscript is an impersonal, printed form that says, "Thank you for sending us your manuscript. Unfortunately, it doesn't fit our editorial needs." Just consider yourself in good company. Successful writers **all** get rejects.

Work and morale

Here's where we separate the men from the boys (or the women from the girls). In order to be successful, you must continue plugging away, day after day, in the face of all these disappointments. Another reason to keep working day after day, is that a rejection doesn't sting nearly so badly when you have a dozen other items "out." As the saying goes, "If you throw enough spaghetti against the wall, some of it's bound to stick."

Due to the nature of this business, it is imperative that you have something to keep you motivated. Try to enlist someone in your family to be your "cheerleader." If no one in your family will boost your spirits during this lonely endeavor, find a writing friend, a pen pal, or join a writer's group. It also helps to tack up inspirational quotations above your desk. Here's a good one: "The way to succeed is to double your failure rate." (Thomas Watson, founder of IBM)

Training, education

A college degree is not necessary. You merely need to be able to communicate with readers, not show off your vocabulary. You do, however, need a working knowledge of good grammar, punctuation, and spelling, and be able to turn a phrase.

Fiction or nonfiction?

Writer's Market says that of the approximately 40,000 books published each year, 85% are non-fiction, 15% fiction. The ratio is probably about the same for magazines. I strongly suggest you **start** with non-fiction. Why not go with the odds? This dramatically increases your chances of getting into print. Once you do, you'll begin to collect those all important published "clips" and **that** will do wonders for your morale. This is not to discourage you from writing novels – for all I know, you could be the next Hemingway. But we're looking at the cold, hard, real world here, because doing so will allow you to succeed.

Poetry

Sorry, once again it's time for one of those hard realities: Do **you** spend money every month on books of poetry? Does your wife? husband? friend? neighbor? I thought not. Don't forget, those publishers are in business to make money – and they won't print stuff no one's going to read. If you want to write lovely verses in your spare time, that's fine. But Chet Cunningham, author of 225 published books, says in a recent *Writer's Digest*, "I don't think there's a single person in this country making a living writing and selling poetry today."

What to write about

Your subjects can be as varied as your own experiences and interests. Do you have a skill, talent, or special knowledge to share? Can you build a birdhouse, carve funny faces on pumpkins, or cater a wedding party? Are you into fitness, diet, or cross-country skiing? There are readers out there who are interested. Next time you pick up a magazine, notice how many of these "how-to" pieces there are.

Maybe you'd like to do "human interest" features (and use your photographic skills). Or maybe you'd prefer to talk about the past. Suppose you find an Indian arrowhead in the woods behind your home. That might lead to a historical piece on the pioneer days in your area. Or you could specialize in travel, humor essays, or inspirational (religious) writing.

Living in a rural area needn't limit you. Take the "human interest" field, for example. Open your eyes to people and events around you, and you'll find scads of possibilities. That 95-year-old neighbor of yours who still works on his farm might make a good subject. Or that lady down the road who makes dolls out of dried apples.

Where to send it

You may have written the most exciting, interesting, informative article ever – yet if you submit it to an inappropriate market, you're wasting your time. You have to learn to slant your work towards each individual magazine. Each one has its own "tone." *Playboy*, of course, doesn't want thrifty recipes; *Lady's Circle* doesn't want sexy stories! But there are more subtle differences, such as those among the "Seven Sisters." *Ladies' Home Journal* has a slightly different readership than does *Family Circle*.

Recommended reading

A current *Writer's Market*. (Writer's Digest Books) This has thousands of publications listed, along with addresses, editors names, requirements, pay rates, etc.

Remember: Time. Perseverance. Patience. Work. Reality. A place to work. Equipment. More work. Slanting to the right markets. More reality.

Going with the odds. Morale. More work. See you in print! Δ

There are things
She does
(Though she doesn't think
anyone is looking)
That make me believe
There are reasons
That flowers in the forest are beautiful
Even if no one
Is ever going to see them.

John Earl Silveira
Ojai, California

Using photos to sell your writing

By Robert L. Williams

All over this nation there are freelance writers receiving rejection slips along with their returned manuscripts. And at the same time, again all over the country, other freelancers are opening envelopes containing checks for their work.

The difference, you say, is that some writers have an inside track, are just more talented, work cheap, or in a dozen other ways sacrifice art for pay checks?

If you really want the truth, the difference in an astonishing number of instances is that the writers who sell their works also include a good selection of quality photographs along with their stories.

Naturally, you must be able to write reasonably well, but writers who can also take good photos stand a far better chance not only of selling the submitted work but of getting a larger number of future assignments than do writers who cannot supply pictures.

I know. For the first couple of years I wrote I was selling perhaps one out of every ten stories I submitted. Then I got smart, bought a modestly expensive camera, worked fairly hard at learning to take appropriate photos (I did not say artistic photos; it has been my experience that good editors want nuts and bolts photos in which people look like people and not like surrealistic art works), spent many hours in the darkroom, and then began submitting the photos I produced.

The difference was astounding. I began to sell at least eight of every ten stories I submitted. In a period of ten years I sent one magazine 125 stories and sold 123 of them. For another magazine I submitted 45 stories during 1992 and sold all 45 of them.

Not only do sales percentages increase, but you also receive a higher pay rate in many (though not all) cases. Some editors will not buy stories without accompanying art. Some others will agree to hire a photographer to do the photos, but if you can supply both art and words, the editors tend to like you and your work much better and your bill collectors will become fond of you as well.

Unusual shots can often be eye-catching to editors.

But isn't photography one of the dark arts, like alchemy or psychiatry or communicating with the dead saints? Doesn't it take years to learn to take a decent photo?

Not at all. First, get a camera that will do the job. You need one with a good body and a good lens or two. There are cameras on the market today that sell for under $250. For this price you get the camera body, a flash attachment, and a wide angle-zoom lens combination. Usually this is all you will need for the basic work you will be doing for newspapers and magazines.

When you shoot photos, be sure to buy the proper film for the magazine in question. Many publications will use only black and white photos, while others insist on color transparencies or slides. Some will buy color prints.

To be safe, shoot some with all three types of film, although many editors will happily use color prints for black-and-white reproduction. Some very helpful editors will use slides for their black-and-white or color reproduction. To get the best possible photos, shoot from several different angles, if possible.

Some useful photo rules

Use very simple but useful rules.

For example, to get the primary subject of the photo in focus and also keep the distance background in focus, close down the lens as much as you can and still have the necessary lens speed.

People and animals make interesting subjects. Notice how light colors dominate in this photo.

In other words, set the camera aperture or opening on 16 or 22, if light permits, and slow the shutter speed down to 1/60 or so, depending upon what your light meter tells you.

If you want the primary subject in sharp focus but don't want background clutter interfering with the quality of the photo, open the lens to its largest setting (2.8, 1.4, or the smallest number on the dial) and raise the shutter speed to 1/500 or whatever the available light will permit.

Observe the rule of thirds: mentally divide the shot from side to side into three segments and do the same from top to bottom. Your finished photo might have a stretch of open sky or clouds for one third, a river for the middle third, and wild flowers for the bottom third.

One third of the photo (from side to side) may be devoted to a dead tree, another third to a man working, and the final third to a boulder or other object.

Use anchor points when you can do so. These are objects in the foreground, either at top or bottom or even on the sides of the photo, to give dramatic effect and perspective. These can be a small pine branch, leaves, blossoms, a roller skate, or whatever is appropriate for your photo.

When shooting flesh tones (people's faces, etc.) set the lens opening on 5.6 and the speed accordingly. To shoot waterfalls, use a shutter speed of no greater than 1/30 of a second so that the water volume becomes thicker, milkier, and more dramatic.

For best color results, use slower speed. Instead of ASA 400 color film, use ASA 100 or even ASA 64 or 25. To capture rapid action or high speeds, use higher ASA 400 or even higher, up to 1000 or 1600.

Best results for black and white photos come from ASA 125 or, second choice, 400. In poor light, reverse the choices.

As a general rule for still life shots, the higher the number on the lens setting (meaning the smaller the aperture opening) the better the quality of your photos will be.

Using filters

You can also improve black and white photo quality greatly by using filters that attach over the lens. You will need a very small number of filters, with a red and a yellow being first choices.

These filters can give much greater contrast (which all editors love) and can cause clouds, blossoms, etc., to appear much more dramatic. The red filter can also be used to give evening or dusk appearance for shots taken at high noon.

If you want a starlight effect on lights, you can buy a filter or simply hold a small piece of screen (as from window screens or screen doors) against the front of the lens.

Your own darkroom

For greatest personal satisfaction, you will want to learn to develop and print your own black and white photos at least. You can also process color slides without difficulty, and if you want color prints, you can use the Cibachrome processing or similar chemicals to convert slides into prints in an ordinary black-and-white darkroom.

It is easy to build a darkroom in a basement corner or to convert a closet. You will need a supply of light and water and the possibility of total darkness. You can buy an enlarger and all of the necessary equipment for printing your own photos for about

This photo was made at high noon, but through the use of a red filter a sunset effect was achieved, and at the same time the water flow was thickened and the rapids were highlighted.

$250 for a modest workroom. This price includes developing tanks, safe light, tongs, trays, and other necessary items.

Developing and printing

To develop your own film, first practice threading a strip of already developed film onto the spools and then putting the spools into the tank. Do this at first with your eyes open, and as you get more facile, try it with eyes closed and then in total darkness.

When you are ready to try it with "live" film, darken the room totally, open the film canister, clip the edges of the film end for easier threading, and load the film. Rinse the film in cold water and then add developer (at 68 degrees for best results) and agitate occasionally and gently for eight minutes or whatever time your chemicals require.

For a stop bath you can use ordinary cold tap water for a two-minute rinse. Then empty tanks, add fixer, and agitate for two minutes before letting the tank and fixer set for another six minutes.

Empty the fixer, rinse, and wash the film for at least five minutes. Use a paper towel or soft cloth to wipe away excess moisture and hang up the film to dry.

When you are ready to print, make a proff sheet first by laying the strips of film over a sheet of paper (with only the safe light on) and expose it to the enlarger light for seven seconds at an opening of 3.5 or eight.

Develop the proof sheet, which will give you negative-sized photos of all the shots on the strips, by putting the sheet in the developer tray (with appropriate chemical mixture) until the images appear and seem sharp. If the sheet is too dark, shorten time or shut down the enlarger even more. If too light, increase the exposure time or open the lens.

Put the sheet into a water tray for several seconds, then put it into the fixer. You need a different chemical for developing but you can use the same fixer for both developing film and paper.

Leave in the fixer bath for at least five minutes, then wash for another five minutes before hanging up to dry.

You can make enlargements in the same manner. Simply raise the enlarger head until the image on the easel surface is sharp and the size you want. Shut down the lens all the way, then back it open a click at a time until you have a good but not glaring light on the easel. A 5.6 or 8 lens opening works well.

Rather than risk ruining a full sheet of paper, there are two excellent and simple tests you can run. First, cut a sheet of paper into strips one or two inches wide. Then, with enlarger off, lay the strip across the easel opening and turn on the enlarger for five to ten seconds. Develop the strip and see if it looks right to you. If not, darken or lighten as needed by increasing or decreasing the amount of time under the enlarger light.

When you get the right test strip exposure, use a full sheet of paper and repeat the process.

The second test is to lay a three-inch strip inside the easel and cover all of it but a width of one to one and one-half

The rule of thirds applies to this photo: The left bank of the stream, the stream itself, and the boy divide the photo naturally.

inches. Expose it to the light for five seconds. Slide the cover down another inch or so and expose for five more seconds. Continue this until you have made five to seven test exposures.

Then develop the strip and select the section that looks best to you. To get the correct time, start counting at the lightest strip and count the number of sections until you reach the proper one. Each section represents five seconds, so if the fourth test exposure is correct, expose the full sheet for twenty seconds.

The beauty of enlarging is that you can increase the size of the photo and cut out all areas you don't want included. If a part of the negative is too dark or too light, you can "dodge" or "burn" by shading the necessary parts of the paper by moving your fingers or a small circle of cardboard until that section receives less light than the rest of the photo.

Remember that a negative is the reversal of what you will see in the completed photo. Dark areas will be light on the photo, and light sections will be dark.

You may need to try a photo several times before you get it exactly the way you want it. Each sheet of paper costs you, but you recoup your expense when you sell the photo.

Recouping costs

Remember that if you invest $500 into equipment you can earn the money back for camera and darkroom with just a few sales to magazines or newspapers.

There is much more, of course, and you may want to take a course or study a good basic book on taking photos and darkroom developing nd printing. I have sold more than 3,000 stories in my writing career, the vast majority of them with photos. I am still studying and learning each time I shoot a roll of film or print pictures.

But the beauty is that I am getting paid while I continue to learn. You can, too. The increased sales will offset your initial investment quickly, and you will be rewarded by increased self-satisfaction and editors' compliments as long as you write. Δ

Barn cleaning

Barn cleaning—the sweet aroma of manure and bedding, the goats and horses watching curiously, companionably for awhile and then going out to graze. Like many seasonal tasks, barn cleaning brings back memories. The job itself allows plenty of time for reminiscing.

When I moved to this farm almost nineteen years ago, I had to work the so-called garden with a pick. The clay soil was fertile apparently as the weeds grew higher than my head, but most of my vegetables were puny. The corn grew only two feet tall and had finger sized ears. Each year the garden got a little better as I added more manure and bedding. For a number of years now I've been able to dig potatoes with my hands.

Tomato plants began to look like shrubbery-four feet high and four feet wide. Our growing season is very short here. We're extremely lucky to get 90 days and frosts in June are common. More than once I've lost the warm season plants in the first week of July. There just isn't time for the tomato plants to grow so large and still produce fruit. My friends scrawny plants produced a ton of tomatoes. My bushes looked like plants from a rain forest but were almost bare of fruit. Time to back off on the manure.

Our small acreage was being overwhelmed by the manure from our many animals. Reluctantly we decided to sell some manure each year. Like most small farmers we don't come by a lot of cash, so this extra income is welcome.

When the kids were little I cleaned the barn myself. As they got older they gradually took over. When they were children they had fun. Their friends came to help. The oldest child was allowed to drive the pickup to the barn and then to the garden. After they were finished, we had a feast to celebrate. I can still see them shrieking with excitement from the back of the pickup as an unexpected blizzard moved in while they were shoveling out the last load.

As adolescence approached, getting the job done became more of a problem. It eventually came down to, "if you don't get it finished, you don't go out!" Shovel handles were broken as raging hormones overcame conscientiousness. Arguments echoed from the barn as they argued about who was working hardest. Even receiving the gross profits from the sale couldn't assuage their dignity.

These days the kids are grown and we all have a good laugh about the unsettling teen-age years. Now my husband and I clean the barn. It's peaceful and rewarding. I like the hard work and when it's finished and the barn floor is covered with fresh straw, I feel real joy. —Dynah Geissal Δ

In praise of the rural post office

By Don Fallick

One of the joys of life in the backwoods is dealing with neighbors who are individuals, instead of faceless bureaucracies. Nowhere is this more apparent than in dealing with the Post Office. Rural letter carriers perform a variety of services for their customers that city dwellers can't even imagine. Need a stamp? The "postman" will sell you one. Of course, you may not be at the mailbox when the mail comes. No matter, just leave change in the mailbox, and the unstamped letter will be stamped for you. Don't have correct change? The letter carrier will make change in a reasonable amount and leave it for you with your mail in a special envelope.

Got a package to mail? Just leave an approximate amount, and the carrier will weigh and stamp it, and either return your change or give you a notice of postage due! Such a notice may accompany mail addressed to you, too. The carrier knows he's your lifeline to the outside world, and will do anything reasonable to make deliveries to you.

Rural carriers who know their customer will sometimes go far out of their way to deliver the mail. A friend of mine who lives more than a mile from his mailbox has sometimes had important "certified" letters delivered all the way to his house, when road conditions permitted. Our letter carrier really does deliver the mail in all kinds of weather. There have been days when my neighbors and I have been snowbound, but somehow or other, the mail carrier got through!

One of the "unofficial" services our letter carrier performs is issuing "road reports" to anyone who asks him, or even to anyone who contacts him on CB radio. I know one letter carrier who successfully relayed a message that a homesteader in the area was having a baby and needed assistance! The letter carrier always knows who's home on his or her route, and will sometimes share such information with customers who need it.

But the Post Office is more than just letter carriers. The rural Postmaster and other small-town postal workers can be just as helpful. When picking up certified mail, the customer is supposed to bring the yellow form left by the carrier. I hate to admit how many times I've forgotten to bring the form to town with me. Every time, the Postmaster has cheerfully made out a new one!

The capacity of small-town postal workers to deliver "undeliverable" mail is legendary. Postal workers in small towns and rural areas know their customers in a way that just can't be duplicated in the city. I have personally received mail addressed to:

The Family with 5 blonde girls
Davenport, WA

Until recently, I thought this was the "topper" for rural mail stories. But last month I heard of a post card that was successfully delivered to the mother of a small child in an equally small town. The only address on the card was:

MOM
Odessa, WA

It seems that the recourceful postmaster tacked it on the bulletin board in the post office, and the appropriate "mom" recognized her son's handwriting. Just another day's work for a rural postman! Δ

A BHM Writer's Profile

Martin P. Waterman, a frequent contributor to *Backwoods Home Magazine*, writes on the science of gardening and horticulture. He also writes on technology such as computers, communications, and genetics, and how these sciences influence our lives.

Waterman is a rural based writer living in New Brunswick, Canada. He spends much of his time writing, gardening, breeding hardy fruit for the north, or on Internet, where he can be reached at Waterman@nbnet.nb.ca.

Cleaning and maintaining your firearms

By Christopher Maxwell

Your firearms will last longer and work better if you keep them clean and lubricated. Many of the malfunctions I have seen with firearms, especially with auto-loading .22 rifles, were simply due to accumulated fouling in the action and lack of lubrication.

Modern ammunition and materials take some of the urgency out of cleaning. Those who learned about firearms during the days when all ammunition was corrosive may remember such sayings as "Don't let the sun set on a dirty gun." The residue left behind by corrosive primers could cause rust to start within hours.

American factories began producing .22 ammunition with non-corrosive priming early in this century, and to the best of my knowledge, no U.S. or Western European plants have made corrosive ammunition for 20 or 30 years.

Bad advice and rank heresy

I do not see any need to clean your guns every time you fire them. I know I will be called a heretic by those who learned to shoot in the good old days, or those whose grandfathers taught them to clean their guns immediately after firing, but I have found this to be true from years of experience. I have never had a firearm damaged from not cleaning every time I shoot.

You should clean your guns often enough to prevent build-up of fouling, and you should clean and lubricate your guns periodically to prevent rust even if you don't shoot them. How often this needs to be done will depend on your climate and humidity and storage conditions.

While modern ammunition is not actively corrosive, powder fouling, unburned powder grains, and fragments of bullet metal can provide condensing points for humidity which will cause rust.

Barrel fouling will ruin your accuracy if allowed to build up, and as stated earlier, built-up fouling in the action will eventually cause malfunctions. This is especially a problem in recoil-operated autoloaders as smoke and unburned powder is blown into the mechanism with every shot. The gas port, gas piston, and/or the gas tube in gas operated autoloaders needs special attention also. These parts should be very clean but not lubricated. The hot gas from the barrel will bake the lubricant onto the parts.

Those who learned shooting when corrosive ammunition was common, along with the military, still practice the same regimen of immediate cleaning after any firing, long after the necessity for such measures is past. The only people who really need to be that concerned anymore are competition target shooters, who think being off by 1/8" at 100 yards is really sloppy shooting. And, of course, those who still do shoot corrosive ammunition.

Corrosive ammunition

If you use surplus military ammunition of foreign origin or American ammunition from the 40s or 50s, you have to assume it may be corrosive. To the best of my experience, all Eastern European military ammunition is corrosive, as is most of the Chinese ammunition being sold regardless of what the box says.

Commercial bore cleaning solvent will not dissolve the mercury salts from corrosive primers. You need to use the old type military solvent or a commercial solvent made for black powder guns or soap and hot water. If you do clean with water or a water-based solvent, you must be careful to dry your gun completely after cleaning. You must clean your gun thoroughly the same day you fire.

Cleaning methods and tips

A good trick to save yourself some work is to take a can of WD-40 to the range with you. Spray some down the barrel and into the action when you are finished shooting to soften and loosen fouling and your cleaning will go faster and easier. Gun cleaning solvent works even better, but nobody puts it in spray cans yet. Some of my stainless guns only need to be wiped off and the bore swabbed with a dry rag the next day after this treatment. WD-40 can ruin ammunition, so be careful to only use it on unloaded guns, and wipe it off thoroughly before loading.

Bore cleaning brushes are available in nylon, bronze and stainless steel. The nylon brushes are durable and will not wear your rifling, but may not remove heavy leading or fouling. The bronze brushes are probably the best for all around use. Do not ever push a dry brush through your barrel. Always wet the brush with solvent first. Do not try to change directions while the brush is in the barrel, push or pull it all the way through.

Whenever possible cleaning rods should be inserted from the breech end to avoid damage to the rifling at the muzzle. If you can't clean from the breech, don't worry too much. Just use a cleaning rod made from aluminum or brass and try to keep it centered in the bore. Rifle barrels are made of very hard steel.

After you scrub the fouling in the barrel loose with a solvent-soaked brush, simply push cleaning patches through, alternately wet and dry, until a patch comes out clean.

The steel G.I. cleaning rod for the M-16 is very useful. It comes apart into sections 7.5" long and is thin enough to fit a .22 but strong enough for larger calibers. You will need an adapter to use civilian commercial cleaning tips and brushes, but these are available at most gun stores or from most surplus dealers. The handle folds into the rod, allowing the entire disassembled cleaning rod to be carried in a 1" diameter tube.

I like Government Issue bore solvent and LSA weapons lube also. Many commercial products are fine, but nothing but the best is good enough for Uncle Sam. Surplus products are cheaper too, if you forget that you already paid for it once.

A toothbrush is very useful for cleaning the hard-to-reach parts of firearms. All sorts of nylon, brass, and bronze brushes are offered at gun stores and gun shows but I have yet to find anything as handy or more effective than a plain old toothbrush.

A product called Gun Scrubber is available at gun stores. This is a very volatile solvent in a very high pressure spray can. It is useful for sub-assemblies which shouldn't be taken apart. Gun Scrubber also removes all lubricants and preservatives, so be sure to replace the lubricant.

Disassembly

Cleaning the action may require some disassembly. If you shoot corrosive ammunition you may need to disassemble your gun to dry it completely.

One of the most important accessories for any firearm is the owners manual which comes with every gun. If you buy a used gun you probably won't receive one, but you should be able to get one from the manufacturer for little or no cost. If you have a military surplus rifle, the proper manual can be found at a gun show or from one of the distributors of surplus or reprint manuals. Ads for these can be found in any gun magazine.

Your owners manual will tell you the proper method to disassemble your firearm, and other important information for operation and maintenance. One tip I can give you is to work in a clean, well lit room with a smooth floor. Small parts always try to escape whenever guns are taken apart and it's really amazing how far some of those little springs and pins can fly.

Lubrication and storage

Lubrication is vital to the operation and durability of any firearm. I use Break Free myself, but there are many good products on the market. All moving parts and contact surfaces should be lightly lubricated to reduce friction and wear. All other metal surfaces should be wiped with a lubricated patch to prevent rust and corrosion.

When guns are to be stored for any length of time, they must be cleaned thoroughly and then all metal surfaces should be heavily greased. Get something at the gunstore that is made for the purpose. Many commercial oils and greases are too acidic and are not made for long term stability.

If possible, it is preferable that all springs be relaxed before storage, especially older shotguns which may have flat hammer springs. With modern coil springs, this is not so critical. Once in my younger and stupider days, I was handed a loaded and cocked GI .45 auto that had been in a drawer in that condition for 30 or 40 years. I took it straight to the range, thumbed off the safety and fired away, without even opening it up to see if there were spider nests in the barrel. It worked fine, but I do not recommend this experiment.

Any firearm should be examined before firing to be sure the parts move freely and the bore is free of obstructions, and this is especially important with any firearm that has been in storage.

Transport cases are not good storage cases for your firearms. Keeping your gun in a gun case locks the moisture in with it. In addition, leather is often treated with chemicals which can be corrosive if left in contact with your guns, so don't store your guns in leather holsters or cases. Δ

A BHM Writer's Profile

Ralph LaPlant is a Brainerd, Minnesota resident employed as a peace officer and emergency medical technician. He supplements his writing by doing freelance writing and photography. His work has been published in local, regional, and national publications.

LaPlant's writing follows his work and interests. He concentrates on prehospital emergency medical care and outdoor camping and survival skills. In photography, his area of concentration is nature. He has travelled to Glacier Park for moose, Wyoming for landscapes, the Boundary Waters Canoe Area Wilderness of Minnesota for its beauty, and twice to Churchill, Manitoba to photograph polar bears.

He currently lives in a two-room log cabin in a remote area. He has no electricity, uses a generator when need be, and pumps water by hand. His future plans include selling the cabin and property and moving to a rural setting with the conveniences of power and water. He says he will never forget his cabin experiences and challenges, but it is time to turn the page.

RECIPES

Smoked turkey and smoked brisket

By Richard Blunt

At first glance, you could have mistaken my previous column to be a recipe to prepare fried chicken. I gave you a fried chicken recipe, but it was really a way for me to tell you about why we use herbs and spices to achieve different flavors.

It is my intention, in these columns, that as you learn why a good cook uses what he or she does, you can carry the lessons over to other recipes. So, in this issue I've included both a turkey and a brisket recipe. With them I'm going to tell you how to combine spices with one of the oldest cooking techniques known to achieve dishes with unique flavors and appearances.

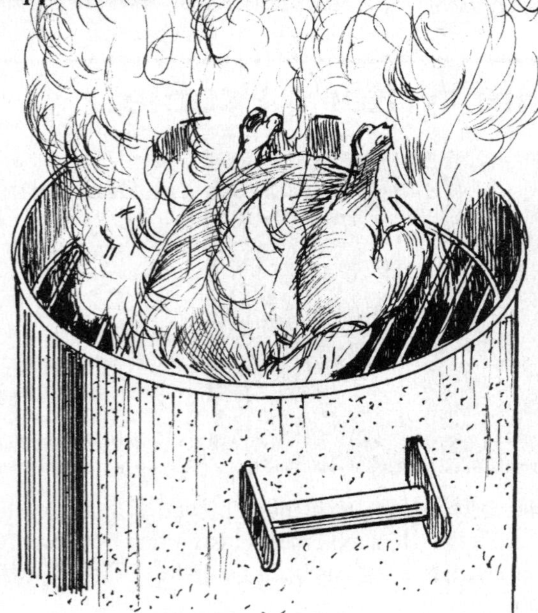

Cooking is like being Alice in Wonderland—a thousand directions to go in with only one to choose. But, if you understand when and why to choose the ingredients, you'll acquire a mental map to guide you every time you get near a stove or—in this case—a smoker.

There are certain rules of thumb you should remember when you cook. I got many of mine from a man I once knew. He was a chef reaching the end of his career and I, barely over 20, was starting my own. His name was Bill Sullivan but I never knew anyone to call him anything but Sully.

Sully was a real character, bad tempered but brilliant, and I could fill a cookbook with just the things he told me. One of the most important was when he once said, "Blunt, flavor is taste, smell, touch and sight combined."

Again and again I watched him put this dictum into practice and, though I haven't seen him in over 20 years, I've always remembered his words and I've made sure everything I cook meets his exacting definition of flavor and, with smoke-cooking, I can easily achieve that standard again and again.

The art of smoking-cooking is older than civilization and goes back to the neolithic age. It's still popular today. With this kind of longevity, you know we must be dealing with something good.

The tools for smoking can be as simple as a plain cardboard box or as sophisticated as a high-tech thermostatically controlled oven. There's a lot to choose from in between.

For the recipes that follow, I used a water smoker and with good reason. The water smoker is the easiest to use and it can be purchased in charcoal, gas, and electric models at reasonable prices. With a water smoker, there's no basting or constant checking of the food. The smoker does a lot of the busy work for me. I like that. It's a real "set it and forget it" way to cook that lets you concentrate on the art of smoking and, with smoking, the methods for imparting flavor to the food are endless.

Among the considerations you must face is the choice of woods used to create the smoke. Hickory is the most popular but I've used mesquite, walnut, aspen, oak, apple, and cherry with outstanding results. Notice, they're all hardwoods. (Don't use soft woods like pine or cedar; they impart a flavor only a termite could enjoy.)

Each wood imparts its own subtle and distinct flavor to the foods being smoked. But I'm not going to suggest any particular type of wood to generate smoke for your recipes. That's something you've got to decide for yourself. My own "scientific" approach to solving this problem is to take a small piece of the wood and burn it. If I like the way it smells, I use it.

Also, smoke cooking opens up a vast new world of herb and spice use and I grow a wide variety of fresh herbs to use in my smoking recipes. But not just herbs and spices can be used. Everything from ginger root to osage orange chunks can also be used, in direct contact with the food or as an enhancement to the smoke.

Finally, consideration must be given to the liquid that goes into the water pan. The liquid serves primarily as a buffer between the heat source and the food and, through evaporation, it creates a moist atmosphere to eliminate basting. But by varying the type of liquid used, it is possible to add additional flavors and subtleties to the food being cooked. I have used beef and chicken stock, fruit juices, beer, and wine, by themselves and in combinations. On one occasion, I combined beef stock, English Ale, and Jack Daniels with a fresh brisket. I've included the recipe here because it's one you must prepare yourself to share the experience.

The following two recipes will get you on your way to smoke cooking but they are just the tip of the proverbial iceberg.

A word about water smokers: They are available wherever sporting and camping equipment are sold. I will not go into how to use the equipment because the instructions that come with them are excellent. If you're new to smoke cooking, follow the manufacturer's directions for setting your smoker up. There are other places to find them. Cabela's mail order house (812 13th Ave., Sidney, NE 69160) has everything I use including various woods packaged for smokers.

Now, onto the recipes. The first one is an herbed whole turkey. I call it Savory Smoked Turkey. With this recipe I give you close equivalents for using fresh or dried herbs. The real difference between fresh and dried herbs is taste. Use fresh herbs once and you'll understand why I grow my own.

Savory smoked turkey

1 12 to 14 pound turkey
2 whole bay leaves

herb butter:

3/4 cup butter or margarine
1 tbsp fresh thyme leaf (or 1/2 tsp dried)
1 tbsp fresh basil leaf (or 1/2 tsp dried)
1 tbsp fresh oregano leaf (or 1/2 tsp dried)
1 tbsp fresh tarragon leaf (or 1/2 tsp dried)
1 tbsp fresh sage leaf (or 1/2 tsp dried)
(if you use fresh herbs, they should be finely minced)
1/2 tsp fresh ground black pepper
1/4 tsp salt
2 minced garlic cloves

for the water pan:

3 cups white wine
chicken stock or water

Prepare an herb butter by melting the butter or margarine and combining it with the herbs, minced garlic, salt, and pepper.

Very carefully slide your hand between the skin and the breast of the turkey to separate them. Brush about half of the herb butter under the skin, then place a bay leaf on each side of the breast, also under the skin.

Allow the turkey to sit at room temperature for about an hour.

Pour the wine into the water pan and make up the difference with the chicken stock or water.

Brush the remaining herb butter over the outside of the turkey just before placing it in the smoker to cook.

It will take about six hours for the bird to cook. Add more chicken stock or water to the pan after the first three hours.

When the meat thermometer reaches 180 degrees the turkey is done.

For the second recipe I had to make a difficult choice between Smoked Fresh Brisket and Smoked Oriental Style beef ribs. I chose the brisket. I decided that ribs got more involved because the ribs require a marinade and I wanted to save marinades for a later recipe. Plus, though the brisket is easy to make, people unfailingly enjoy it.

Smoked brisket

1 fresh brisket (about 6 lbs) Remove all excess fat.

seasoning sauce:

2 tbsp Dijon mustard
1/2 tsp dry mustard
4 tbsp dark brown sugar
1 tsp Worcestershire Sauce
1 tbsp dry sherry or other dry white wine (if you really like the flavor of Jack Daniels or other whiskey, substitute an equivalent amount for the sherry)
1 clove of fresh garlic, minced
1/4 tsp cayenne pepper
1/2 tsp salt
1/8 tsp freshly ground black pepper
1/2 tsp dried basil leaf (or 1 tbsp fresh and minced)
1/2 tsp dried thyme leaf (or 1 tbsp fresh and minced)

for the water pan:

1 qt. good ale or beer – light or dark. Don't use the light bodied beers like Bud Light or Miller Lite. They just don't have enough flavor for cooking.

Combine all the ingredients for the seasoning sauce and mix well. Place the brisket in a suitable bowl or dish that can be covered and rub the seasoning sauce all over the meat. Then cover and place it in the refrigerator for a minimum of six hours. I suggest overnight.

Prior to smoking, bring the brisket to room temperature. Allow the beer or ale to come to room temperature, as well.

Soak at least four of the wood chunks you plan to use, in warm water, for 30 minutes.

Pour the beer or ale into the water pan and make up the difference with water. (Once in awhile, I use all beer and no water.)

Cook the brisket for four hours then check the temperature. The meat is done at 130 degrees; if you like it medium rare and at 145 degrees, it's medium. I never make it well done. But, if further cooking is necessary, check the liquid in the water pan and add more if it's needed.

If you like corn on the cob, you'll love it cooked this way.

Peel back the husks and remove the silk from several ears of corn. Brush the corn with melted butter and fold the husks back over the corn. Tie the ends of the husks with string to seal them. During the final hour of cooking, place the corn in with the brisket. This makes one hell of a meal.

Give this cooking technique a try. I think you'll discover an expanded world of flavor. Δ

Soups and stews for late winter

By Jennifer Stein Barker

By mid-February, the produce section of most grocery stores is looking pretty thin, and your creativity just isn't sparked by the usual selection of winter vegetables. This is a good time to get out the dried legumes and grains and start experimenting with different combinations. Use mushrooms, herbs, and wine for seasonings. Serve with homemade bread or biscuits for a complete meal.

Lima bean and fennel stew

A subtly different vegetable stew with a delightful flavor. Fennel bulb is a winter vegetable that looks something like a round celery, but tastes milder and with a hint of anise (sometimes fennel bulb is called sweet anise in the stores).

Serves 4:

1 cup dried baby limas
3 medium potatoes, diced 1/2"
2 large carrots
1 tablespoon olive oil
1 large onion, diced 1/2"
1/4 teaspoon fennel seed
1/2 teaspoon dried thyme
1/2 teaspoon dried marjoram
2 cloves garlic, chopped fine
1/2 cup dry white wine
1 tablespoon olive oil
4 oz. mushrooms, sliced thin
1 small fennel bulb, diced 1/2"
1 bay leaf
1 tablespoon tamari soy sauce
1 tablespoon lemon juice

Pick over and wash the lima beans, and soak them at least six hours or overnight. Discard the soaking water and place the limas in a large stew-pot with 4 cups of fresh water. Bring to a boil, then lower the heat and simmer gently for one hour.

Scrub the potatoes and carrots. Dice the potatoes. Slice the carrots in half lenghwise, then slice crosswise 1/4" thick. Add the potatoes and carrots to the limas. While they are cooking, saute the onions in the olive oil until they are a rich golden brown, adding water an ounce at a time to prevent burning.

Crush the fennel seed lightly in a mortar and pestle, and add it along with the thyme, marjoram, garlic and 2 tablespoons of water to the onions. Cook over low heat for 3 minutes to blend the flavors. Add the white wine, and simmer until the liquid is reduced a little. Scrape the mixture into the bean mixture, and return the skillet to the burner. Add 1 tablespoon olive oil and the sliced mushrooms to the skillet, and saute until the mushrooms begin to turn golden around the edges. Scrape the mushrooms into the stew, adding more water if necessary to keep from sticking.

Add the diced fennel bulb, bay leaf and tamari, and simmer until the fennel bulb is just tender, about 10 minutes. Add the lemon juice and serve immediately.

Country mushroom soup

Serves 4:

1 large onion
1 tablespoon olive oil
1 oz. dried porcini mushrooms
4 oz. fresh brown or white mushrooms
1 clove garlic, chopped
2 tablespoons tamari
1 medium carrot
1 medium potato
1 1/2 teaspoons fresh thyme leaves (or 1/2 teaspoon dry)
1 bay leaf
1/2 cup white wine

Cut the onion in half vertically, and then slice across the grain in thin half-rounds, so you have thin strips when the layers separate. Heat a heavy-bottomed dutch oven on medium-high and add the onion and olive oil. Saute the onions until they are a rich deep brown, stirring frequently and adding a little water just as necessary to keep from burning.

Meanwhile, soak the dried porcini mushrooms in boiling water to cover. When they are rehydrated, wash them carefully to remove any dirt, then chop them coarsely. Strain and save the soaking water for stock.

Clean and thinly slice the fresh mushrooms. Add them with the chopped soaked mushrooms and the garlic and tamari to the browned onions. Continue cooking, adding a little water only if necessary to keep the mixture from sticking (the fresh mushrooms will probably release enough liquid of their own as they cook). Saute and stir five minutes, or until the fresh mushrooms are done and their liquid is reabsorbed.

Scrub and slice the carrot thinly on the diagonal. Scrub the potato, but do not peel it. Quarter it and slice the quarters thinly. Chop the thyme leaves coarsely. Add enough water to the mushroom soaking stock to make 4 cups, then add it with the carrot, potato, and thyme to the onion-mushroom mixture. Add the bay leaf and the white wine. Bring to a boil and simmer for 15 minutes, or until the carrot and potato are done.

Serve immediately.

Split pea and barley soup

A hearty high-protein soup. Try to find barley that has not been pearled, as pearling removes many of the nutrients.

Serves 6:

2 cups dry green split peas
1 cup barley
1 bay leaf
1 tablespoon tamari
1 tablespoon olive oil
1 medium onion, chunked
2 cloves garlic, chopped
1/4 cup thinly sliced celery
3/4 cup dry white wine
1 medium carrot, thinly sliced
1/2 teaspoon Dijon mustard
1/2 cup fresh or frozen peas
1/4 cup chopped sorrel or parsley
1/4 teaspoon Tabasco
1/2 teaspoon dried thyme

Wash the split peas and barley under running water in a sieve. Place them in a large stockpot or Dutch oven along with the bay leaf, tamari, and 6 cups of water. Bring them to a boil, then reduce the heat and simmer till the peas are soft, about 3 hours. Check frequently to stir, and add more water if necessary to keep from sticking.

When the peas are cooked, heat a heavy skillet over medium-high heat with the olive oil, onion, and garlic. Saute and stir, adding a little water if necessary, until the onions are light golden. Add the sliced celery and the wine, and reduce until the liquid is **almost** evaporated, then add to the soup.

Add the sliced carrots. Dissolve the Dijon mustard in 1/4 cup warm water, and add it to the soup. Simmer gently until the carrots are tender, about 20 minutes.

When almost ready to serve, add the peas, sorrel or parsley, Tabasco and thyme. Simmer gently until the peas are **just** tender, then serve immediately.

Whole wheat biscuits

Makes a dozen 3" biscuits.

1/2 cup whole wheat bread flour
2 cups whole wheat pastry flour
2 1/2 teaspoons baking powder
1/4 cup oil
3/4 cup milk

Preheat oven to 450 degrees.

Sift together the flours and the baking powder into a medium bowl. Drizzle the oil over the flour mixture, while tossing with a fork to distribute the oil in droplets throughout the mixture. Add the milk all at once and stir in with the fork. You should have a fairly soft dough, but it should not be too wet to handle.

Turn the dough out onto a lightly floured board and knead gently 6 times, then pat out 3/4" thick and cut into circles with a cutter or the top of a glass. Pat the leftover dough into biscuit shapes. Place the dough rounds on an ungreased baking sheet and bake for 10 to 12 minutes, until the biscuits are golden on top. Serve hot or at room temperature. Store in an airtight container in a cool place. Δ

The Buck

Thirty years ago, I would a' shot him.
Wouldn't leave the house without a gun,
But today, I'm glad to just have a silent chat,
Me sittin' on this rock, and him standin' there
Like an icon on his favorite bluff.

No youngster, this old boy,
His rack looks like my genealogy chart.
I suppose, in his day, he would a' snorted
An' sprung away before I even spied him.
He seems content, now, contemplatin' the valley I thought I owned.

Some things get better with a little age,
Old fiddles, good wine, fine woodwork, and such.
It all depends on what you want.
He'd probably be a little tough to chew, by now,
But he sure is grand to look at.

I didn't even bring my camera.
Maybe, it's just as well.
Nothing that acetate and chemicals can do
Would be able to capture
What I'm seein' right now.

Must a' got his fill of human company.
Just turned and sorta sauntered off,
As if to say, "See ya 'round sometime."
Why, I'd no more pull a trigger on him,
Than I would my neighbor, back down the road, there.

Richard Lee Rose
British Columbia, Canada

Just for Kids — help for nature's nursery

By Lucy Shober

Warm weather is springing! With this season comes the chitter chatter and pitter patter of wide-eyed newborn wildlings. Maybe in the past you have come across one of these little creatures who has been in need of help.

Perhaps you have stumbled upon a young robin with a broken wing, or a nest of baby squirrels washed from their nest by a violent spring storm. Though it's best in some cases to leave these animals alone, there are times a helping hand means the difference between life and death for a grateful orphan.

Clip this page and save it so that you can use these guidelines the next time you find yourself having to play nursemaid to a box full of wild critters!

You can try to help if:

Before you **even touch** them, you get the permission of your parents.

The laws in your state permit it. Sometimes it's O.K. to care for orphans in your home until you can get them to a veterinarian or a rehabilitation center. (Rehabilitators raise orphaned and injured animals, then teach them how to survive before returning them to the wild.)

You are **sure** that they need your help. Some animals are obviously in trouble, but some are just in their fledgling stage. (Fledglings are sort of like human teen-agers...they are old enough to leave the nest, but still need mom and dad for support.) Fledglings will be almost adult size, but rather scruffy looking. Usually, the parents will be lurking close by, maybe even chattering at you to ask that you leave the baby alone. Often times an orphaned sparrow, horned owl, or deer fawn will be adopted by another mother or aunt in the woodland neighborhood. If they look healthy, it's much better to leave these types of wildlings where they might be raised by their own kind. Then they will learn the secrets of survival from experts!

When you take an animal from the wild, it's because it is in distress...not because you think that it would be fun to cuddle or play with!

It is best to leave them alone if:

The animal is a healthy fledgling, not in danger.

You find animals of prey (like fox or coyote pups, owls and hawks, wild cats etc...animals of prey are the ones who need to eat other animals in order to stay alive). If you feel that one of these animals is in trouble, it's best to remember where you found it and contact a wildlife officer to help you decide what should be done. Wildlife officers are usually found in the blue or government listings section of your phone book.

You find a water bird other than a duck. Most shore birds have very special diets and ways of eating which would be hard for you to handle at home. Here again, except for first aid kinds of treatment, it would be best to get help from an expert.

Most of these animals (animals of prey and shore birds) are protected by the laws of your state or the federal government. That means that it's against the law for you to have them unless you possess a special license. This is so that people won't take them from their homes in the woods to make pets of them or sell them.

The treatment:

First slowly warm the orphan until it's body temperature is about the same as or a little warmer than yours. You can slip it into an extra large old sock, and keep the sock next to a jar of warm (not hot) water, or wrap an electric heating pad with a towel and put the sock onto it. Inside the sock, it feels safer and more like home to most wild babies. They should always be warm when you touch them, but not overheated!

When the animal is warm and comfortable, it is time to think about feeding. If you had tried to feed the baby when it was cold or wet, it might have choked and become even more distressed.

Most mammal (have fur, drink milk, not hatched) babies thrive on a warm pudding made from wheat bread and human soy bean-based baby formula. Use the lid of a mayonnaise jar as a cookie cutter on the wheat bread. Leave the bread in the lid and soak (really **soak**) the bread with the warm milk. Gently push the orphan's nose onto this pudding. After a few tries, the baby should start "nursing" the bread. The milk can be sucked out of it, then the bread eaten. If this doesn't work after a few tries, you might have to use a plastic eye-dropper full of the formula. Just dot it on to the nose of your patient to let it know that it's supper time. Soon you can wean the baby to the pudding mix. Feed your wildling five or six times a day, then be sure to wipe it clean so that its fur won't become gloppy and sour.

Speaking of wiping . . .

Yes, even a wild mother has the problem of changing dirty britches! She must gently lick her baby's privates to encourage it to eliminate (use the bathroom). You can do this by wrapping your finger with a warm moist towel or napkin and lightly brush **that** area back and forth. You might be really surprised at what happens next! Remember, though...it's all a part of nature, so be gentle.

When your orphan charges have settled into the new lifestyle, you can begin to add bits and tads of their adult food into the box. At first, these might be used as toys, but then your healthy babe will catch on to the trick of eating "real" foods.

For the birds . . .

If a baby bird tweets frantically at you with its beak wide open, or if its beak looks to you like a large triangle, it's probably what scientists call **altrical**. This means that the mamma pokes food down into her child's mouth with her beak. Robins, blue jays, and cardinals are some altrical birds. For these, simply take dry cat food and soak (really soak) it in the soy formula. When it becomes puffy, break bits off and poke them into the back of your screaming baby bird's beak. **Boing**! they should disappear, and the screaming will start again. Feed until the bird looks comfortable, but plan on coming back a couple of times an hour at first, then maybe 10 or so times a day as the bird grows older.

Never give baby birds water from an eye dropper. It is too easy to choke them and that could turn into pneumonia. If you feel that the babe is thirsty, dip your finger into water, and let it drip onto the tip of the beak. It will roll into the right place.

Precocial birds (like quail, chicks, and ducks) do best on bits of finely crunched whole wheat crackers mixed with oats, wheat germ, or a good quality breakfast cereal sprinkled over the floor of the cage. If you can find live ants, they would make a great dessert and give your baby target practice at the same time. Make water handy in a jar lid. Scrape up some gravely sand for these little birds to eat too. They swallow this grit and it acts as teeth to grind the food. You might have to pick up and drop the food several times so that it catches the eye of the chick. This is like what its mom does in the wild.

A baby dove or pigeon reaches its bill into its mother's throat to find food. Since you wouldn't want to duplicate this yourself (auggghh!), you can roll wheat bread into be-be sized pellets and poke them deep into the young bird's mouth...with a finger drip of infant formula on the tip of the bill to wash things down. Do this until your dove gets old enough to peck at grains on the floor of his box.

If the baby is injured: try and contact a professional, just give it the first aid listed above, and then ask for help!

Play this animal first aid guessing game:

True or False?

1. If you touch a baby bird to put back into its nest after a fall, the mother will not take care of it any more.
2. It takes about the same amount of time for broken bones in mammals and birds to heal.
3. Sometimes if a nest of baby mammals has been blown from its tree top perch, the mother will rescue the babies if they are placed in a warm basket under the tree.

Answers:
1. False
2. False. (Hollow bird bones take only about two weeks to heal, but mammal bones can take six weeks or more.)
3. True. Δ

The sensible, integrated photovoltaic energy system

By Windy Dankoff

The integrated photovoltaic system works as a whole which is greater than the sum of its parts. It contains subsystems that optimally work with each other and with your needs as they change through the seasons and the years. The integrated system is an attempt to combine multiple energy sources, storage, and usage systems for optimum economy. A well planned "whole system" can temper the feast or famine extremes of alternative energy and reduce or eliminate the need for a backup mechanical generator.

Integrated system design is very specific to **your** situation and climate. To get started on the right track follow these basic principles.

- 1. Recognize your essential needs.

Your need is not for electricity; it is for light, water, preserved food...electricity is **one** way to provide for these needs.

- 2. Minimize the steps of energy conversion.

Every time energy is gathered, converted, stored, transferred, or otherwise processed, a significant amount is lost. Consider the most direct approaches to meeting your needs.

- 3. Tie all systems together.

Make all systems function together as efficiently and as simply as possible.

- 4. Balance needs against solutions.

Use what we have when we need it.

The typical consumer's home is a model of disjointed energy practices. In summer, inefficient light bulbs and refrigerators generate hundreds of watts of waste heat, causing air conditioners to work overtime. In winter

while cold abounds, refrigerators keep working hard to overcome the home's added heat. Electricity used for heating consumes hundreds of times more energy than other uses. Purified, pressurized, quality drinking water is used to flush toilets and water the lawn. The alternative energy household does not have the "unlimited" energy supply that the utility line provides, and cannot afford such carelessness.

Applying principles 1 and 2, we utilize windows or skylight to let in daytime light, and we store vegetables in a cool pantry or root cellar. We can divert rainwater from the roof to a storage tank to supply garden and trees by gravity flow. We use direct solar heat to warm our home in winter and simple solar collectors to heat our water, with gas or wood fuel backup.

We use electricity for those functions that it can do best. Use battery direct DC power directly where feasible, rather than converting it all to AC through an inverter. If we must rely heavily on a gas generator, we use an efficient gas refrigerator, rather than converting the fuel's energy through an engine/generator to power an electric fridge.

Applying principles 3 and 4, we might use the sun for pumping irrigation water and/or refrigerating (high summer loads). The reduced demands in winter liberates plenty of energy for the extra winter lighting load. To make this possible, the pump and the home run off the same energy system.

There are endless variations to system design, with new possibilities opening as the technology advances. Assess your needs, read all you can on the subject, talk to PV users and dealers, and use your imagination!

Utilizing excess energy

No matter how well balanced your system might be, there are many times when more energy is gathered than is immediately required. Your battery bank becomes fully charged and your voltage regulator will simply "waste off" excess energy.

Fact: an alternative energy system designed for year round use will produce excess energy **most of the time.**

A system providing mostly lights will produce lots of excess in the summer, when days are longer. A system providing irrigation water will produce excess in the winter. Your system must be designed to see you through worse than average conditions. The rest of the time, you have excess energy. Utilizing this excess energy may as much as **double** the effective value of your system.

Overload diversion

The idea is to automatically switch excess energy to another load. A device that will use energy in an effective manner. Ideal overloads are those that incorporate a form of **storage**, such as:

- 1) second battery bank
- 2) water or preheater
- 3) water pumping into a storage tank
- 4) home ventilating or cooling, which uses excess solar power exactly when it is needed most.

A second "reserve" battery bank solves three problems by providing a place to dump excess energy, enough backup to reduce or eliminate the need for a backup generator, and a way to enlarge or replace your battery bank without discarding the old batteries. You should not combine batteries of different types or ages in the same set, so maybe you'd want to use an aging battery bank that has lost capacity or is too small for expanding needs as the "reserve" battery bank.

Overload water heating can contribute a saving of fuel in the AE home, although it has serious limitations. To understand this limitation, consider that a typical (rapid heating) AC electric water heater of 40-gallon capacity draws 9000 watts, while the average home AE system has only a few hundred watts to dump intermittently! If you have a solar thermal water heating system, you will already have hot water by the time your PV system is ready to dump. If not, an ordinary electric water heater can be refitted with low voltage heating elements to supply more or less warm water for direct use or preheated water to save gas. Or a gas heater can be fitted with an electric element to save gas. A 150-watt (12 amps at 12.5 volts) heating element will heat one gallon of water from 55 to 125 degrees F. in 1.25 hours. This is a useful amount of heat. Excess energy is **free**—we might as well use it!

Water storage for irrigation has enormous potential for making the most of solar power, especially because the most water is required when there is the most sun! It is ideal to store at least a two week supply of water. When your storage tank fills, allow it to overflow to some trees; the ground stores water/energy too! Use drip irrigation, mulching etc. to minimize evaporation losses.

House or attic ventilation or cooling is a perfect way to "blow off" excess summertime solar power during hot weather.

Control of overload energy

This need not be complex. The simplest "human regulator" is simply a voltmeter, a switch, and you. When you see or anticipate your battery voltage approaching 15 volts (12V system), you flip the switch. The switch transfers all or most of your array to your alternate load or turns your well pump or cooler on. When your voltage drops to 12.5 or so, then there is no longer excess energy so you flip the switch back to the normal full charge position. A control system can do this automatically for you, switching automatically as clouds come and go, appliances turn on and off, etc. If your control system does not have overload diversion, it may be added without altering existing controls.

By the way, PV modules run cooler when they are connected and working (energy is being removed from them). Modules that are disconnected by regulation that does not use their excess energy actually get a little hotter. The decades may reveal that modules that are used constantly last longer than those that are often disconnected!

'Growing' a system

Many people cannot afford, or do not need, to buy a complete energy system all at once. You may be constructing your homestead gradually, expanding your energy system as your enterprises or your family expand. A system designed for growth from the start will be integrated with your needs and will save you a lot of money when the time comes to expand. Balance these suggestions against your budget limitations.

Rule: build a heavy infrastructure:

This refers to the parts of the system that form its foundation and are difficult to enlarge later.

Wire sizing: If you are burying wire from your PV array, or concealing it in walls, use large enough, heavy gauge, wire to carry sufficient current for your future, enlarged array (or put your wire in oversized conduit so that more, or larger wire may be added easily). Add a "pull me" rope to conduits so that more wires can be added later.

AC distribution: When you wire a new house, distribute AC power lines to receptacle boxes in every room even if you don't plan to make extensive use of AC power. Inverters will keep improving and getting cheaper. Consider who may live in your home years from now. Future generations or prospective buyers may not accept the limitations you have imposed on them. Hallways tangled with extension cords are **not** a good option! Nor is ripping walls open to add wiring, or adding lots of surface conduit. You may leave unused receptacle boxes unwired until ready for use.

Array support: It may cost only a little more to buy or build an array frame or tracker of twice the capacity that you need initially. Future expansion will be easy, less expensive, and better looking.

Battery bank: When you connect new batteries to old ones you are inviting problems. Oversize your battery bank and avoid using its full capacity until you expand your array. Or, leave enough space in your battery area for a second, larger bank of batteries to be installed next to your old set.

Consider a 24-volt system: 12 volts is a vehicle standard. It is still ideal for a modest home system that does not need to run large motors or inverters and does not have long runs. But, a 24-volt system is more efficient and economical for larger systems and for small systems designed to grow. A dual 24/12 volt system need not be complex or costly.

Note: Fortunately, there is no strict need for compatibility among PV modules, old and new; different types and power ratings may be mixed into your array.

A photovoltaic system is unique in that its "generator" is composed of small modules and can be expanded over time. This is one of the many factors that make PV power the most liberating energy technology ever developed. Make the most of it by employing integrated system techniques and designing for future needs.

(Windy Dankoff, photovoltaic systems specialist, is an energy systems supplier and industry consultant. He also teaches courses for the Solar Technology Institute in Carbondale, CO. If you wish to contact him regarding your PV needs, his address is P.O. Box 548, Santa Cruz, NM 87567. Phone: (505) 351-2100) Δ

FARM AND GARDEN

Roll your own biofertilizer

By Walt Foster

As many "third world" communities have been discovering, there is a simple bioconversion system that results in an uncomplicated method of producing a liquid, organic fertilizer. This far-cheaper fertilizer is in many other respects superior to common chemical fertilizers. The bionutrients can improve the structure of soil where chemical fertilizers are ineffective. Chemical fertilizers leach out of the soil more easily because they don't bind to the soil as these organic fertilizers do.

This bioconversion process converts organic matter to ammonium (NH4), which attaches readily to soil particles. It is then available for plant use in ammonium or nitrate form. Bioconversion, an anaerobic fermentation process, is fully self-contained. It will not allow any leaching of soil nutrients, and the nutrients will be completely recovered.

Depending on the raw materials placed in the bioconversion system, the digested biomass contains critical elements essential to plant life: nitrogen, phosphorous, and potassium. Trace elements of metallic salts (indispensable for plant growth) such as boron, calcium, copper, iron, magnesium, sulfur, and zinc are also produced during the bioconversion process.

The digested fertilizer contains nitrogen mainly in the form of ammonium (NH4). For many land and water plants ammonium may be more valuable as a nitrogen source than oxidized nitrogen. In the soil, ammonium is much less apt to leach away and more apt to become fixed to exchange particles (clay and humus). The liquid produced from the bioconversion process increases soil nitrogen concentrations comparable with those of inorganic fertilizers when applied in equivalent amounts.

The bioconversion process itself takes place in the absence of oxygen. A satisfactory operating temperature for the process to take place is about the temperature of the human body (95-98 degrees Fahrenheit).

The process starts by loading in grass clippings, pet manure, table scraps, or some other organic material to fill the bottom third of the barrel. Water is then poured in to fill the barrel half full. The barrel plugs are screwed into the barrel which then acts as an anaerobic digester.

The organic matter combined with the water in an airtight container permit the anaerobic bacteria to build up a population to eat the carbon in the organic material, converting the organic matter to bioproducts including the liquid bionutrient and the solid biomass.

The materials I have used to construct this simple bioconversion system are easy to find and quite inexpensive.

The first component part is a used, plastic, vinegar barrel I purchased for eleven dollars at a bakery. (I used two types of recycled plastic barrels: the larger one is 55 gallons in size, the smaller one holds 15 gallons.) The second part is an airlock used for the fermentation of beer or wine. I purchased mine at a home brewers' store for ninety cents.

To fit the air valve onto the barrel, I made a modification to the valve to make it fit the standard barrel plug.

I bored a hole in the barrel plug to accommodate the gas pipe (See Figure 1). Next, silicone sealant was used to cement the gas pipe into place to prevent any future air leaks.

To start the digester, use one of the simple recipes in Figure 1 as starting points. Experiment with the ratios; modify them to incorporate your own organic wastes for your personal backyard production rates.

The procedure is as follows:

- 1. Locate a sunny spot in the back yard.
- 2. Set the recycled barrel on a level spot.
- 3. Modify one of the barrel plugs for the air lock.

MATERIAL	PROPORTION
chicken manure	100%
chicken manure newspaper	50% 50%
chicken manure grass clippings	50% 50%
cattle manure	100%
cattle manure grass clippings	50% 50%
pig manure	100%
newspaper *kitchen garbage (fat free)	50% 50%
newspaper *grass clippings	50% 50%

*Start with a coffee can full of fresh manure

Figure 1. A few biofertilizer recipes.

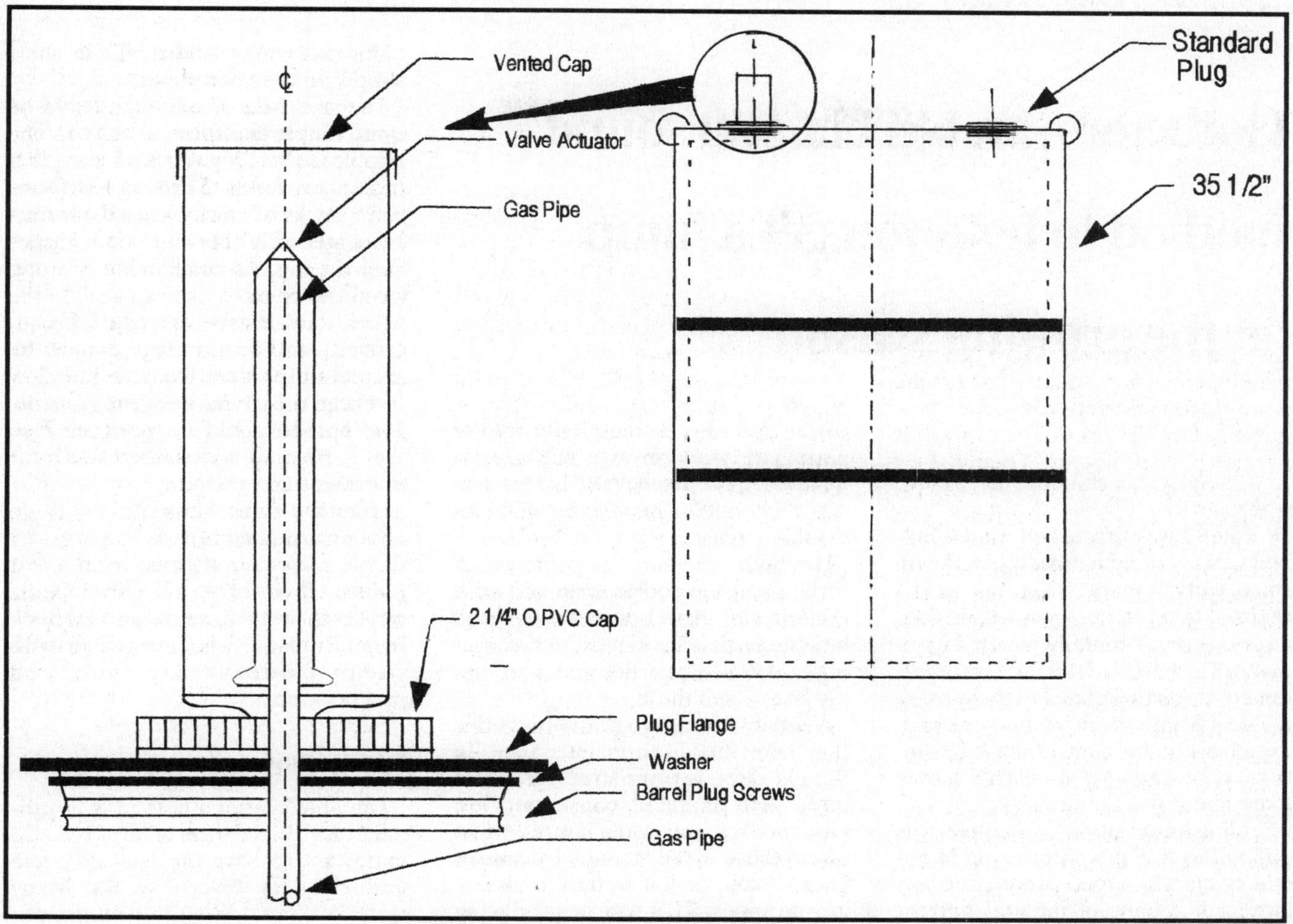

Figue 2. Bioconversion unit and gas handling valve.

- 4. Shred newspaper with a lawn mower and place in the barrel.
- 5. Shred fresh grass clippings and place in the barrel.
- 6. Add pet wastes.
- 7. Add water to the half full mark.
- 8. Replace modified barrel plug with air lock.
- 9. Let the sun warm the biomass.

Check the process as you pass the solar-powered back yard digester. As soon as the fermentation stops, the bioconversion process is complete. This usually happens within 60 days. If it takes longer than 60 days, it is because the anaerobic bacteria population takes time to build up sufficient numbers. Recycle a gallon of your digested liquid next time to speed up the back yard process. Another reason the process could take more than 60 days is starting too early in the year. If you start in the spring before those hot summer days and nights have had a chance to accelerate the process, the conversion will take longer.

You can pour off the top, clear liquid bionutrient and store it in recycled milk containers and take the resulting biomass solids to the garden. To use the liquid bionutrient concentrate, add one tablespoon to one gallon of water. To kill weeds, spray the concentrate directly on the problem weeds and they will die from overfeeding. You may also add a cup of concentrate to your septic tank system once a month to revitalize the bacterial activity which helps keep your underground pipes clean.

Now you can use some of the remaining digested liquid to revitalize the next load of biomass. The cycle repeats.

(Walt Foster teaches and develops bioconversion technology and has been working in this field for 20 years. For more information contact him at 4002 Wise Lane, Billings, MT 59101.) Δ

The land! That is where our roots are. There is the basis of our physical life. The farther we get away from the land, the greater our insecurity. From the land comes everything that supports life, everything we use for the service of physical life. The land has not collapsed or shrunk in either extent or productivity. It is there waiting to honor all the labor we are willing to invest in it, and able to tide us across any dislocation of economic conditions. No unemployment insurance can be compared to an alliance between man and a plot of land.

Henry Ford

FARM AND GARDEN

Hotbeds—an old but still sound method to help you get a jump on the growing season

By Martin P. Waterman

When I was first asked what a hotbed was my mind naturally toyed with some witty remark. This was until I realized that the question was, in fact, a serious one. I humbly pleaded ignorance. The basics of this almost forgotten art of starting plants early by using the heat from rotting manure was then explained to me. Since then it has intrigued me and I set about to discover more about this unique process.

Finding information on hotbeds was difficult as hotbeds were made in another time when food production was more commonly an integral part of daily existence. None of the recent books had much information except for the odd passing reference. I knew from this that there were only two ways that I was going to find out anything. These included seeking out some old historic gardening texts and talking to people, mostly older people, who had knowledge of, or had experience using a manure hotbed.

Eventually, I was fortunate enough to find some people—one of them a sheep farmer—who still practice this method of gardening. The process is relatively simple and it works.

Hotbed basics

The basic principle behind the hotbed is the use of fermenting organic matter, such as manure, to keep plants from freezing. Thus, growers are able to start their plants where they would normally freeze in the cool spring or to extend the season in the fall. Heating of the soil also increases the rate of germination and growth and gives a head start, producing food for the season after winter when fresh vegetables would be scarce.

Hot beds were once very widely used throughout the cooler areas of North America but have now been replaced by systems that use electric soil-warming cables. Some garden and seed supply houses sell these.

Another advantage of the hotbed is they take very little maintenance. In the old days, various structures were built such as small conservatories, plant houses, and green houses. Most often these were heated by smoke flues, steam, or hot water circulating in iron pipes. This way of producing heat needed constant attention, a commodity that was usually in short supply on the homestead.

The structure of a hotbed could be quite simple and from talking to some people in their 70s and 80s I learned it took many forms. The simplest forms were stacks of hay arranged to form a rectangle with old windows or sashes over the top. An old blanket or wood planks were often used as well. In the warm days the covers could be removed—in the evenings, when the temperatures were likely to go below freezing, the covers were put back on. The hotbed could be positioned so that it pointed and slanted south for optimum sun exposure.

Here are some hints on how to go about starting a hotbed. The majority of this information came from a text published in 1894, an encyclopedia published in 1910, an old garden book from England, and interviews with some modern day hot bed practicioners.

Long heat

The objective of a hotbed is to produce an artificial form of heat. It is also important to have the heat continue uniformly for several weeks. Many materials, in addition to manure, can be used. Fibrous materials are added to manure such as hay as long as it will

Manure-heated hotbeds at Carter's Grove, Virginia, an old plantation on the James River.

ferment to bring about the results needed. The result should be that the materials will ferment in sufficient time to allow the seeds or cuttings to grow. The soil and the atmosphere around the soil should remain at a temperature of about 20 to 40 degrees above the freezing point. The hot beds are covered with a sash to regulate the heat. A glass on the sash usually has to be opened during warm days so as not to overheat and cook the vegetable plants before they can mature. (The glass was often attached to the sashes with just a soft putty to allow for the effect of the freezing and thawing).

Horse manure beds

The hotbed itself is prepared some time before it is to be used. When material such as leaves are used, they have to be gathered in the fall so that they have time to be turned several times during the winter to prepare them for the hotbed. The best material by far is horse manure with a little fibrous material such as hay or leaves added to it. When using manure, it should be taken as fresh from the stable as possible. It should be piled to ferment, and all coarse lumps should be broken into pieces. Do not let it dry or it will become burnt and musty. Water must be added to prevent this drying. The manure is worked over to give it an even texture throughout. The pile should be turned so that the outside layers are moved to the center. It should be worked every few days. When the manure is worked over, a portion of leaves not to exceed half the quantity of the manure can be added. Remember that the more leaves or similar material that is used, the milder the heat will be.

Choosing a site

The site of the hotbed should be on dry ground. Make an excavation at least one foot deep and one foot larger than the hotbed frame. Spread the mixture of manure and leaves about six inches deep and beat it down evenly with a fork. Do the next layer the same way. Continue until the pile is two to three feet deep. By spreading the mixture in layers, a more uniform degree of texture and temperature will be the result. The manure around the edges should be banked up against whatever you are using for the walls, be it lumber or hay, to keep the cold out and the heat in. If you are sowing directly into the hot bed, a layer of soil should be put on top of the manure. Four inches is usually the amount placed on the manure. If soil is not added, pots and seed flats can be placed on top of the manure.

I have heard of hot beds being used with no covers at all. They produced enough heat to actually start the garden as early as a month before the last frost. The hot bed would not only produce enough heat to protect from frost, but even a light snow would melt as it hit the warm earth.

Steamed up

The most secure and successful way to make a hotbed is to have it as air tight as possible. After the hot bed is secure and the manure in, close it very tightly. After about four to six days it should steam up which is the signal that the hotbed is ready to be used. A thermometer can be placed in the soil; when it reaches about 75 degrees the seeds can be directly sown.

The inside of the hotbed should be kept humid. The warm soil will cause the plants to form superior root systems so that when it is time to transplant them they will have up to two months or more growth on the seeds that would be normally planted after the last of the late frosts.

Properly done, a well constructed hotbed can provide continuous heat for two months. It should be timed to run out just as the weather is warm enough to allow plants to survive outside the hotbed.

Manure tea

One of the best alternatives to buying fertilizer is brewing your own manure tea. To start, of course, you need a big tea bag. A burlap sack will work well and I have even seen big tea bags made of window screen material. The finer the holes the better, for this will prevent weed seeds from getting into your mixture and thus your garden.

For the tea pot an old cleaned out oil drum filled with water works very well. A rope is tied from the tea bag (full of manure) to a pole which suspends the tea bag (which should always be submerged). Once this is done, let it steep for about a week. It is also a good idea to tug on the rope every few days to help brew the tea. Don't forget to cover the drum with a board or a cover to contain the odor and prevent evaporation and keep out insects.

To use this potent mixture, the tea should be diluted with water so that it does not burn your plants. It should not be applied to foliage, and if it is dark in color it will probably need to be diluted even more. How much you dilute depends on how strong the mixture and what plants you are fertilizing.

One of the great benefits of manure tea is that it can be saved longer than manure.

Manure in the compost bin

Manure is probably one of the best ingredients that can be added to your compost heap or bin. It contains a large percentage of bacteria which will help break down surrounding material. Manure also provides adequate heat to kill weed seeds in the manure. This is important if you are like myself and throw all your weeds into the compost bin.

Manure quiz:

How much do you really know about manure? Here are some questions to test your manure knowledge.

(1) A single hog will produce how much manure annually? (a) 300 pounds (b) 1,000 pounds (c) 3,000 pounds (d) 10,000 pounds

(2) Approximately how many million farm animals are there in the United States? (a) 75 million (b) 175 million (c) 275 million (d) 475 million

(3) Manure can have as much as ______% of its mass consisting of bacteria and micro-organisms? (a) 5% (b) 10% (c) 20% (d) 50%

(4) Which manure is the hottest (richest in Nitrogen, Phosphorus and

Potassium)? (a) horse (b) swine (c) rabbit (d) chicken (e) sheep

(5) A medium sized dairy cow will produce how many tons of manure in a year? (a) 7 tons (b) 13 tons (c) 16.5 tons (d) 20 tons

(6) When is the best time to spread manure on the field?

(a) Before a full moon
(b) Before the wind picks up
(c) Before a rain
(d) Before a barn dance

(7) Manure is best stored when piled up against the north side of the barn. True or False?

(8) Should fresh animal manure be aged before adding it to the garden. Yes or No?

(9) What time of year is best for adding non-composted manure to the garden. (a) winter (b) spring (c) summer (d) fall (e) no difference

(10) Animal manure described as being green is: (a) envious (b) rich in organic matter (c) ripe (d) fresh

Answers are below.

Scoring 8-10 = Excellent, 6-8 = Very good 5 = Average

<u>Manure answers</u>:

(1) (c) 3000 pounds
(2) (b) 175 million
(3) (d) 50%
(4) (d) chicken
(5) (b) 13 tons

(6) (c) Manure should be spread before a rain so the nutrients will wash where they are needed and will not dry out.

(7) False. The wood of the barn will rot faster and the manure will lose nutrients to the air and the rain.

(8) Fresh manure should be aged at least six months. Among other things, fresh manure has high levels of ammonia which can be toxic to plants and there also could be weed seeds.

(9) (d) fall or (a) winter
(10) (d) fresh Δ

Recycle those old clothes into a braided rug

By Marjorie Burris

One of the challenges in living a simpler life style is to make your home comfortable and eye-appealing without a lot of cost. A time honored way to dress up a room and make it warm at the same time is to cover the floor with your own handmade braided rug. And it is down right sole-satisfying to turn cast off and non-repairable clothing into a practical rug that can also be called a work of art.

A 9 x 12 handmade wool rug in the living room of Marjorie Burris' homestead.

The materials

Although wool makes a beautiful and long-lasting rug, contrary to popular belief, other materials can be used satisfactorily. Cotton soils quickly, but is good for a small scatter rug which can be washed easily. I have an attractive and durable throw rug 2 1/2-feet by 4-feet made out of old jeans which has been used since 1975—first as a pad for a rocking chair, then as a protector for a heavy traffic area between the kitchen and the living room, and now as a mat in front of the kitchen sink. I need a mud rug on the back porch, but as yet my jeans rug refuses to show enough wear to be relegated to the outside. I just finished braiding a lovely 7-foot by 9-foot oval rug for my son's home, and it is made out of 100% polyester clothes. My two small grandchildren use it as a play-rug in their family room; spills and spots come out easily with a swipe of a soapy cloth.

I must admit, though, that my pride and joy is the 9 foot by 12 foot wool rug we have used on our living room floor since 1979. And, although all braided rugs are reversible for a double life, my wool rug does not look worn enough after 13 years of hard homestead traffic to turn it over.

My husband has two city friends, owners of a hectic business, who periodically arrive on our door step looking worn and weary and make one request: May we take a nap on your rug?" For the next couple of hours or so I step over snoring bodies on my way through the living room. When they wake up, they thank us profusely for a wonderful time and start their 90-mile journey home looking rested and refreshed. Husband and I are always amazed; the request is never, "May we take a nap in your cool mountain air?" or "May we take a nap in your peace and quiet?"—it is always the rug they mention.

You can start looking for the raw materials for a rug in your own closet, then ask your friends and neighbors for their discards after their spring cleaning. My dozens of cousins regularly supply me with old clothes, blankets, coats, whatever, and like to see a favorite piece of clothing having a new lease on life in one of my rugs.

After collecting all the freebies you can, the next place to look is thrift stores and rummage sales. Many rummage sale and garage sale people are glad to get rid of all their clothing at the end of the day and will sell everything for a small price. You don't have to be fussy; you are looking for material, not size and style.

The charity thrift store nearest me has a liquidation sale every three months, and I can get all the clothing I can stuff into a large size grocery sack for $2 a sack. By rolling the clothes tightly "sailor style" I can get from 18 to 20 pairs of trousers in a bag. The 7 x 9 rug I made has 44 rounds in it and each round, on the average, took 3 to 4 pairs of trousers; less was needed for the smaller rounds, more for the larger rounds.

Since I used approximately 176 pairs of trousers in the rug, the raw material would have cost me a little less than $20 if I had had to buy it all. But, when I got the bags home, I washed all the clothes, then tried them on. I found two pairs of slacks I could wear and my husband found a pair of trousers and a jacket he could wear. We will wear the clothes for awhile, then I will put them in a rug. I like trousers and slacks because I can get the material from them, but I won't pass up coats or dresses, either, if they are the right material or color. Old blankets are great if they aren't threadbare.

The only caution to take in choosing material is not to mix kinds of fabrics. A rug should be made entirely of one kind of material.

Preparation

Wash all clothes, even the wool ones, before starting to work. Washing the wool won't hurt it, especially if you use cool water. You don't care if it shrinks some because shrinkage simply compacts the material for longer wear. After the clothes are clean, rip them apart at the seams so as to get the most material from them. A bonus is the buttons, elastic, trim, linings and zippers you can remove for your sewing box.

Cut out any threadbare places such as worn elbows, pants seats, and knees. You don't want to start with a ready made weak place in your rug. You can tell how worn a piece of fabric is by holding it up to the light and looking through it.

Most materials make a springy, full braid approximately 1-inch wide if they are cut into strips 3-inches wide. To make a braid even, cut thinner materials into strips 3 1/4 to 3 1/2 inches wide; thicker materials work in well when cut into 2 1/2-inch strips. Rarely will you have a piece of material so thick it will need to be cut into 2-inch strips.

A set of cardboard patterns cut into the various widths and about 12 inches long will help you to mark the material for even cutting. I have found that using a different colored cardboard for each width pattern helps me not to get mixed up and use the wrong size pattern.

Lay the pattern on the flat fabric and mark off lines with a pencil or contrasting chalk or pen. You can cut the strips either lengthwise or crosswise, but not diagonally because fabric cut on the bias will stretch and make an uneven braid. I cut ravely materials with the pinking shears. Wool and cotton can usually be torn after marking.

Completely cut up one garment and put the strips together in a box or bag before starting on another garment. This makes it easier when you begin to sew the strips together into one long piece.

Sew the strips together with a bias seam: with right sides together, overlap two strips at right angles and sew diagonally across the corner on the wrong side. (See Figure 1.) I sew these on my old treadle sewing machine, but you can sew by hand using strong thread. Trim away the excess corner. Because your strips will be of various lengths, alternate long and short strips so you won't have a series of seams close together. When you have one garment cut and sewn into a single long strand, roll it into a ball. Sort the balls by colors. You can begin to plan your rug pattern when you see the amounts of each color in the balls.

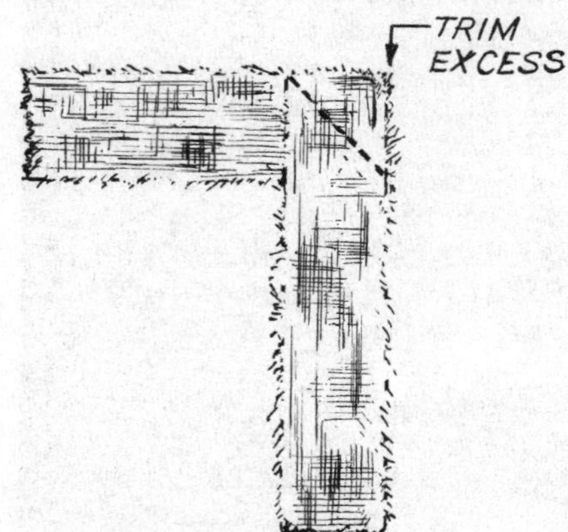

Figure 1. Bias seam joining strips.

Plan the pattern

There are two interesting patterns for a braided rug. One pattern starts with a light colored center then gradually gets darker as the rug gets bigger. The other pattern starts with a dark center, then has light colored stripes working into dark stripes and finishes with a few rounds of color the same as the center. Most braided rugs use a round of a solid color to separate broad bands of mingled colors and finish the rug with one or two rounds of the same solid color, setting the color tone of the rug. For example: in the 7 x 9 rug I made for my daughter-in-law, Lori, I used solid navy blue stripes to separate wide bands of pinks, purples, blues, and greens and finished the rug with two rounds of solid navy blue. This compliments Lori's house which is decorated in these same colors. (See Figure 2.) My own 9 x 12 rug has greys, yellows, oranges and greens separated by solid rounds of black because I happened to have so much black wool.

Figure 2. Grandaughter on 7 x 9 play rug.

Both patterns are pleasing, but the amount of each color you have usually decides your pattern. Another suggestion—go to the store and study the patterns in the "braided" rugs there. Your hand-made rug will be much prettier than a store-bought rug, but you can get some worthwhile ideas about patterns and the lay-out of the rugs.

Beginning the braid

Select three balls of the color you have chosen for the center of the rug and fold the top or loose end of each strand to the inside to eliminate raw edges. Next, fold each strand end into fourths so the raw edges of the sides of the strand are on the inside. (See Figure 3.) Now, sew the three strands together with the left and right strands fanning out on either side of the middle one.

Start to braid and continue to roll each strand into fourths with the raw edges to the inside. There is one difference between hair braiding and rug braiding, though—be careful to fold the loops of the braid around so the open side of the now four-thickness

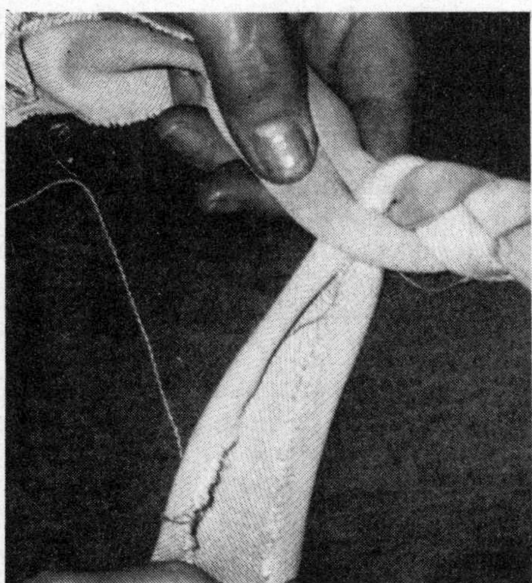

Figure3. Folding strands while braiding.

strand is always on the same side of the braid. (See Figure 4.)

Continue to braid until you come to the end of the ball, then sew another ball onto the first ball in the same manner you sewed the strips together.

For the first few feet, the braid will flop around and be awkward to handle unless you put tension on it. In the absence of a willing friend to hold the beginning of the braid, push a piece of string through a loop of braid and tie it to a chair, or clamp the braid to a clothes line. After a while the length of the braid will hang over your lap and its own weight will pull it tight enough to keep it straight. Try to pull each loop tight with even tension so the braid will be smooth.

To keep the balls from tangling up as you braid, sit where you can drop one ball to your right side and another ball to your left side. Hold the third ball in your lap. About every other loop you will need to thread the lap ball back through the other two strands. This sounds complicated, but it is not, and will soon become so automatic you will not realize you are making the motion.

A word here about those metal tube-shaped braiding so-called aids – they are not a help in my opinion. They clank, they slide out of place and they won't go over the seam where two strips are sewn together. I don't bother with them. I simply roll each strand into fourths as I braid.

When you want to lay down your work, be sure to pin the three strands together at the last loop so your braid will not come apart. It is enough to braid a rug once.

Lacing the rug

I will talk about an oval rug here, although braided rugs can be round, or even square or elliptical. For an oval rug, which is the most common shape, the center braid is always the difference between the length and the width of the finished rug. For example a 5 x 7 rug will have a center braid 2 feet long as will an 8 x 10 rug. A 9 x 12 rug will have a center braid 3 feet long. I allow an extra inch or so to make up for the slight shrinkage of the braid when it is laced together.

For lacing material I use 30-pound test flexible monofilament fishing line. This flies in the face of tradition which shuns the nylon because old timers say the nylon cuts the braid. But I have used my nylon laced rug for over thirteen years without problems and the fishing line is cheap. I've had to repair my first rug, my jeans rug, which I put together with button thread and kite twine several times, but as yet I have not had to repair the rugs I put together with the monofilament.

As a carrier for the lacing, I use a bodkin my husband made out of a measuring spoon which had an eye in the end of the handle. He removed the bowl of the spoon and ground that end into a smooth, blunt point. You could do the same with a tooth brush if it has a hanging hole in the handle. A large safety pin or even a large bobby pin can be used in a pinch. Just so the eye of the instrument is large enough to carry the lacing being used. However, a sharp needle does not work well because the point keeps piercing the braid.

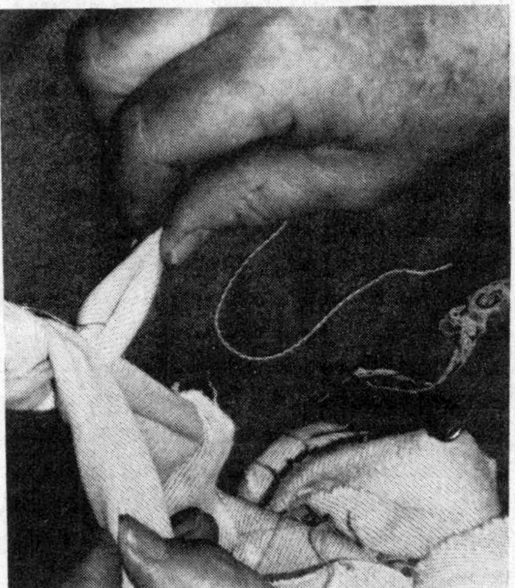

Figure 4. Braid up close.

Make a double strand of lacing about a yard long and knot the ends together. Stretch the lacing out and thread the looped end opposite the knot through the bodkin eye and then pull the lacing down over the end of the bodkin and back up to the eye to keep the thread in place. You do not cut the lacing when you add more. Simply pull it back over the bodkin and out the eye. When adding more lacing, tie the knot of the new piece around the loop of the old piece making a continuous line. At no point does the bodkin or the thread puncture the fabric of the braid.

Lay the completed braid on a hard, flat surface and measure off the length needed for the center of your rug. Next, form a gentle, flat "U" turn in the braid and double it back to the starting point. Pin the two pieces of braid together forcing the "U" turn to stay flat. Keeping the braid flat is important – the test of a well-made braided rug is how flat it lays on the floor.

Now, poke the threaded bodkin through the bend of the "U" between the braid loops and tie the lacing onto the braid so you can pull the knot out of sight under a loop. I use a crochet hook to pull the knots inside.

Finally, lace the two legs of the braid together by first pushing the bodkin between loops on one side, then between two loops on the other side. (See Figure 5.)

Continue lacing until the two legs are joined. The loops of the braid will not necessarily be directly across from one another on the two legs of the center braid. The essential part is that the braid lays flat. When you reach the spot at the beginning of the braid where you first sewed the three strands together in a fan shape, curve the continuing braid around the starting point and keep lacing the third row onto the two center rows. Again, the loops of the braid will not necessarily be directly across from one another – in fact, to keep a rug from "cupping" at the rounded corners you will occa-

Figure 5. Lacing braid.

sionally have to skip a loop on the outer braid thus sewing two loops on the outer braid to one loop on the rug body. It's a mathematical principle – it takes more braid to make the larger outside curve.

Marjorie Burris concentrates on braiding a rug.

By keeping your rug on a hard, flat surface, you can force the braids flat and lace them together where they lie. I start a rug on a table, then as it grows, I either extend my table with long boards or move the rug to the floor.

Keep right on braiding and lacing until you have the size rug you want. If you do not have enough material you can go ahead and use your rug and keep adding rounds as you make more braid. You will enjoy watching your rug grow.

If it appears that the rug won't lie flat, take the time to unlace back through the problem area and do it over. You lose nothing but time – even the thread can be used again, and you will not be forever plagued with a bunchy rug which trips you and isn't pretty. A braided rug takes lots of time to make and it is worth the effort to make it right.

When at last you have the right size rug, trim the end of each strand to a point and whip them together and then to the body of the rug using a regular needle and a strong thread the same color as the braid. This is the only time you will pierce the braid with needle and thread.

Cleaning the rug

There you have it – a beautiful rug you have put hours of yourself into – but don't be afraid to use it. Of course, you want your floor covering to stay nice so an occasional cleaning is necessary apart from regular vacuuming or sweeping.

I clean my wool rug in the winter time when it snows. I collect a bucket full of fluffy, not icy, snow and cover a small area of the rug at a time. Then I quickly sweep up the snow with a broom before the snow melts. The snow is black with dirt and dust and my rug is bright again.

If the polyester rug gets too dirty to wipe clean with a cloth, we plan to drag it out to the driveway, brush soapy water over it, then hose it down. As long as the rug stays flat it will launder nicely that way.

I throw my jeans rug into the washer regularly, but hang it outside to dry. Tumbling the rug in a dryer only makes it come apart more readily.

Braiding a rug is an ideal project for cold winter days when it is too bad to work outside. So why not dig out those old clothes and start recycling them. You'll be proud of your labor. Δ

Winter running

I head up the first icy hill, feeling the absurdity of sliding backward one step for every two I take. I can't help laughing. At the top of the hill, I hit the blast of polar wind that feels like I've run into a glass wall. It takes my breath away. The dry, cold air evaporates sweat as quickly as it forms. In the low places, I combine running with strength training as I pick up at least an inch of mud. And, finally, the exhilaration of glissading down the last ice covered hill toward home, a warm fire, and a hot shower.

– Dynah Geissal

Farm ethics

By Dynah Geissal

One thing about farm life—a person's ethics, philosophy or whatever is always being called into question. I guess it's because we live so close to the earth, to life and to death. We're responsible for the births of animals and often for their deaths. Most importantly, we're responsible for the quality of their lives.

Twenty years ago I didn't know much about those things. I was twenty five and had just come to Montana from the Bay Area of California. I had never lived on a farm, never cared for livestock. I was concerned about chemicals in my children's food so I learned to garden organically. I was successful with root and cole crops the first year as well as chard and other greens. The kids ate turnips like apples and chard stems for celery. Each child above the age of three was allowed to cut up vegetables (under supervision, of course) for their own consumption. This was a great incentive to eat large quantities of carrots and cabbage especially.

I tended toward vegetarian because of the horrible stories I had heard and read about the treatment of animals destined for market as well as the hormones and antibiotics their bodies contained. The kids, however, craved animal products. I believe strongly (as I still do) that, given a choice of healthy foods, children will choose what they need. Raising animals for meat was not something I was ready for but a few hens for eggs seemed like a good idea. The first hen was a Christmas gift and laid her first egg under the Christmas tree on Christmas day.

In the spring I acquired more hens and was very pleased with them. Then one day they started squatting down whenever I entered the chicken house. I asked about this at the feed store. "Do you have any roosters?" the woman asked. "Sounds as if they need a man around the house."

We acquired a rooster and the hens did seem much happier. Eventually one hen managed to hide her eggs well enough to hatch a clutch of chicks. When they grew up I convinced myself that if one rooster was good several roosters would be better. Everything was all right for a while but then the chickens stopped laying. Back to the wise woman at the feed store. "How many roosters do you have?" she asked. "Why, my goodness, those roosters are running those hens to death. They don't have energy left to lay eggs."

I gave away a few roosters but this was starting to seem pretty stupid. I had it "on the hoof." It was organic. But should I kill them? Could I kill them?

About this time I was preparing dinner in our outside summer kitchen. A friend had given us a butchered chicken from his grandmother's farm. I threw a piece of skin to a dog but a chicken snatched it up instead. That did it! If chickens could eat chicken, why was I worried about it?

Goats were the next step and I admit I went through a similar process before accepting the necessity of killing some of them. It took a while longer to get to the point of raising pigs and rabbits which were solely for meat. That was many years ago. It's been a long time since I worried about the ethics of killing for food. I know that they've had the best life I could give them and in the end a quick and humane death.

When animal liberationists from the university came to talk to me about raising livestock they left with a new understanding of the relationship between animal and caretaker. They realized that not eating a turkey for Thanksgiving does not save a turkey's life, that most livestock is raised for market and would never otherwise live at all. They marveled at the contentment of my animals and the harmony in which the various species live together. I think they understood that I care very much for my animals.

So these questions are long since past, but always there are more. Like today. I raise dogs as well as livestock. Last year one puppy out of a litter of eleven was not right. He had little sucking instinct, was always apart from the group, and cried continually. I made the decision not to go to heroic means to save him. I make the same decision with triplet kids if one is weak, apathetic, and small. I believe it is the right thing to do because in the past if I managed to save one, it was never much good and never really healthy.

This time is different. Out of a litter of eight there is one puppy that's not right. He's strong, healthy, energetic; perfect in every way but one. Part of one foot is missing. It's not genetics; he was born with four feet but lost a part of one in a freak accident on his second day of life.

What to do? He has a strong will to live. Does this matter? Should this affect my decision? Will he be in pain all his life? Probably not. And he'll probably adapt. Is it right to let an imperfect animal live? Is it right to kill him? My heart aches for the little guy. If he just didn't have such a strong spirit the choice would be easy. Then I think of him growing up and living a whole life crippled. Will he be able to work and play? I think so. But will anyone choose him to be part of their family and part of their lives? Will anyone think he's special? I hope so. My feelings say to give him a chance to live. I hope it's right. Δ

Friendly alternatives for insect and pest control

By Martin P. Waterman

With the concern today about pesticides, herbicides and fungicides, many people are looking for safer alternatives to control insects and pests in the garden. This is especially true when there are children and pets who can be very sensitive to the chemicals that are often used. Following are 35 interesting control tricks that may allow the gardener to ward off and eliminate would be garden nibblers and uninvited insect pests in an environmentally friendly way.

1. Many frustrated gardeners want to know how to keep small animals out of the garden without resorting to poisons or traps that will kill or injure the animals. Here is a solution you may like to try. Try to locate the entry areas that rabbits and other small animals use to get into the garden. Sprinkle some ground cayenne pepper (or any hot pepper) on the path they take. The animals step on it and when they lick their paws they get a harmless hot tongue and remember the garden as an unpleasant place to dine.

2. Decoys can be effective as well. A plastic owl can keep away certain birds and rodents. It is good to move it around every few days. There is also the old standby, the scarecrow which has proven itself effective against birds and animals.

3. Some gardeners have had success by placing a plastic dish flush with the soil line. Then they fill it with beer which can attract some harmful grubs and caterpillars who end up drowning (albeit happily) in the mixture.

4. Slugs normally take a toll on vegetables such as garden peas. By moving the place where I plant my peas every year, I have had good results. When I plant peas in the same place every year, I usually have had bad infestation. If the outbreak is minor I don't do anything. If it is a major outbreak, I take the salt shaker and sprinkle salt on the slugs. This kills them quite quickly.

5. Chewing tobacco is an age old remedy which has proven to be effective. It is placed in small piles throughout the garden. Many insects are attracted to it because of its sweetness. They feed on the tobacco which kills them quite quickly.

6. Ashes from a wood stove can be effective. I often take a can and punch many holes in a can with a nail. I fill it with ashes and sprinkle cabbage, broccoli and potato plants. I find in most cases it controls a number of damaging insects.

7. Garden cleanliness is a good preventive step. By gathering fruit that has fallen, piles of garden cuttings, and those messy areas, you eliminate the hiding and overwintering places of many damaging insects.

8. Check to see if there are resistant varieties available to you in your area. Many vegetables such as tomatoes are bred to be resistant to a number of diseases and other problems.

9. Giving the garden a rest or rotating the place where you plant your garden, can help with the insect problem. Certain insects and pests will not travel very far especially if they are the kind of insects that live in the soil.

10. By growing all kinds of vegetables, flowers, and plants, you set up a mini ecosystem which will not only encourage a variety of insects but a variety of predator insects that will feed upon the insects that you want eliminated. This creates balance. When the population of damaging insects increases, so do the predators.

11. If you continually have a problem with certain vegetables or other garden varieties, the insects may be too entrenched to be eradicated. By not growing the vegetable for a while this could be the best solution because the insects will move on to other areas.

12. There is another way to keep wildlife out of the garden. It is so simple it should be obvious. A dog! There is one drawback, however – skunks!

13. Live animal traps can be used to safely capture small animals such as rabbits and squirrels. This should only be done as a last resort. Try not to trap small animals in the spring when you may be separating mothers from their young. The animals can then be taken on a picnic or a trip where they can be released in the wild. Remember to check the cages daily and to handle all creatures with care.

14. Garden netting can also be useful. It can be moved around the garden as needed. For instance, it can cover strawberries, then cherries and then other crops as they ripen to keep out certain birds. One has to be careful as in some areas birds can get tangled up in the nets.

15. Talk to older gardeners and some senior citizens. They gardened before most of this new- fangled gardening stuff was invented and are a wealth of ideas. They are one of the least utilized resources. It is also advisable to see what your neighbors are using, then you can learn from their mistakes and duplicate their success.

16. Grow heirloom and historic seeds. Many of the seeds our forefathers (and mothers) used were closer to the wild form. They may not have the same crisp photogenic supermarket appearance but most excel in disease resistance and flavor. Most seed catalogs contain several varieties which are usually listed as historic or heirloom varieties. There are also organizations devoted to saving these historic seeds such as Seed Savers Exchange (Box 239, Decorah, Idaho, 52101) where you may still be able to find that special seed from a plant that grandpa or grandma used to grow.

17. Are you bothered by weevils which can prey at the bases of such plants as rhododendrons? Try wrapping the base of the plant with Rhubarb leaves. If anyone has success with rhubarb leaves in other applications, please let me know.

18. Certain animals (and insects) will feed at night during the summer. A

simple garden light has proven to deter animals and may trick a few insects into thinking they should stay in their beds and not your garden's.

19. Certain flying insects can not easily be detected until they have done their damage. Certain types of traps are available that work on a number of different principles. Some use color such as the apple maggot trap which is usually a red croquet ball covered with a sticky substance such as tangletrap. By hanging this apple on an apple tree, you will attract the apple maggot fly. It will think the trap is a big juicy apple and an ideal place to lay her eggs not being able to recognize it for the sticky situation it really is. Other traps use sexual attractants which are chemicals that imitate the sexual attractant of the female of the species that you are out to control. The male insects are attracted and killed. The females do not produce young. These traps are usually called "Pheromone traps" and are commonly available for a number of different moths, maggots and worms. Check your local nursery. They can usually suggest what is best for your area.

20. The idea of feeding the birds so they will stay in the area and hopefully eat the insects has been kicked around and practiced for some time. In principle the idea is great; in practice it does not always work. What happens is that the birds get lazy and do not feed on the insects. If you use this method, do not feed the birds every day or at predictable intervals so that they will by forced to get a balanced diet of your food and the insects as well.

21. Using dishwater or dish washing liquid (diluted 40 to 1 with water) can be a good way to control the outbreaks of aphids and some other types of insects. It really breaks down fairly easily, does not harm most plants and it usually kills the bugs before they realize that they are soaking in it.

22. Don't forget your hands. Potato bugs can be gathered and their eggs squashed. Caterpillars can be squished but you may want to wear your gloves if you are squeamish. I would always squeeze the leaves that had leaf rollers in them before they would drop to the ground. One day, while squeezing a half rolled leaf with a plump big green caterpillar between my fore finger and thumb he burst and I got squirted in the eye with bug juice. Yuck! I now pick off the leaves put them on the ground and step on them.

23. Use your library and local merchants to find what your alternatives are before using any pest program. Most sprays do not discriminate between harmful and beneficial insects. After spraying, the harmful ones usually rebound in greater numbers than the beneficial insects because the harmful insects usually have shorter life cycles. Before the population of the beneficial insects (that naturally feed on the harmful ones) rebound you may have to spray again and you can find yourself hostage to a spray program with bigger infestations all the time. So remember, some times the cure is worse than the problem.

24. Many of the commercial strawberries in California have adopted a new way to control pests. Rather than applying chemicals as they did in the past to eradicate insect pests, they have a new machine that they use. As it passes over the strawberry rows, the machine vacuums up the pests from the plants. This may have been the inspiration behind some other techniques about which I have been hearing. Gardeners are now gathering potato bugs with a vacuum cleaner or a dust buster.

25. Many farmers have had problems with deer nibbling more than their fair share of the crops. Two solutions seem to work well. The first is to put pails of human urine at the corners of the field. The second is more recent and definitely more civil. This method involves hanging bars of soap in different spots around your property. It is believed that deer have learned to recognize hunters by the smell of soap. One California farmer, after testing, finds Dial soap the best. It may be a good idea to ask the hunters in your area what type of soap they usually use.

26. It is a good practice to leave your grass clippings on your lawn. You will have to add 30% more nitrogen to maintain it. In addition, by returning the clippings to your lawn, they will form a blanket of mulch which will mean less watering and a healthier lawn. As the clippings break down, they add organic soil to your lawn and this promotes earthworms which aerate the soil and help prevent the build up of thatch. By using less water and using less fertilizer, you will be conserving energy and resources. In addition, a healthy lawn is less likely to succumb to pests and diseases which may need to be controlled.

27. Many gardeners are starting to plant wild flowers. Most wild flowers (available from almost every seed company) are naturally drought and disease resistant which means low maintenance. In addition, wild flowers will attract birds, butterflies and other wildlife. Proponents of growing wild flowers argue that most traditional flower gardens are similar to hospitals; if the flowers do not get their beds weeded, their fertilizer doses or their regular watering, they soon perish whereas wild flowers are almost always healthy and vigorous despite neglect.

28. Many organic gardeners have known for some time that garlic is a natural pest deterrent. One popular mixture is to put a few cloves of garlic in a blender with some water and to blend it. The mixture is then sprayed on your plants that are being eaten. There is currently research being done to find out more about how garlic can deter pests.

29. According to Dr. Charles E. Hess, Assistant Secretary for Science and Technology at the U.S.D.A., there is a new safe and effective home pesticide that has been developed by scientists at the Agricultural Research Service. It is available to everyone. Many home gardeners are familiar with the mixture of water and detergent which is successful in killing many species of unwanted bugs. The scientists found that by adding some cooking oil to the concoction it becomes even more effective and toxic to insects. For humans, it is safe, nontoxic, simple to prepare and costs only pennies per application. To make the mixture, you take 1 cup of oil (peanut, safflower, soybean, corn, sunflower, etc.) and add 1 teaspoon of detergent. This is your base concentrate mixture. When needed, take 1 or 2 teaspoons of the

concentrate and add it to 1 cup of water and spray on your plants.

30. Cornell University in New York reports that sodium bicarbonate (yes, baking soda) will act as a fungicide which is effective against powdery mildew and black spot. The best combination tested so far (and only on roses with black spot) was to mix .5% baking soda with water (200 parts water to 1 part baking soda). Researchers still do not have an understanding on how or why this mixture works.

31. One of the best cures for certain insect infestations is the use of chickens. Many orchard owners have found that not only will the chickens find and eat many of the insects and insect larvae on the ground, they will also provide valuable manure for the soil. Some organic plum farmers go around their orchards and shake the trees which causes the plum curculios to roll up into a ball and fall to the ground where the chickens soon gobble them up.

32. One of the best methods for a natural control of insect infestations is to strive for a micro-environment in your garden. It has been found that the more varieties of plants you grow the more chance there is for beneficial predator insects to call your garden home. If you just grow plants that harbor harmful insects, you may have difficulty controlling them even with pesticides.

33. Here is another way to get aphids off your most favorite plants. A high pressure hose will dislodge them and slow down the damage from infestations.

34. For those who have problems with raccoons, the following is supposed to work. Place a radio in a corner of the garden and leave it on all night. The sound is supposed to scare away raccoons.

35. If you lack predatory insects in your garden there is a solution. They can often be ordered by mail from companies that specialize in predatory insects. Check the advertisements in the back of organic gardening magazines to find out more about these mail-order predatory bugs. Some of the varieties available are predatory wasps, lady bugs, and the Praying Mantis. Δ

A BHM Writer's Profile

Born in a small Missouri town in the depths of the Great Depression, Richard Lee Rose has dreamed of becoming self-sufficient since his youth. After earning a teaching degree, Rose began teaching high school in Seattle, Washington, where he commuted by ferry from a rented farm on Vashon Island.

Unable to buy the farm, he and his wife Dorothy bought an isolated quarter-section without buildings near Houston, British Columbia. Self-sufficiency was necessary for survival. Building the house and outbuildings demanded long hours of hard work. "Without conveniences like electricity, telephone, and mail delivery", says Rose, "the most important asset a wilderness family can have is a hardy, determined wife/mother."

Their house was destroyed by a forest fire in 1983. Fire insurance was unavailable, but with the help of many generous volunteers, the family pitched in and rebuilt their home in the same spot.

Since retiring in 1989, Lee has completed a two-masted sailboat and a novel, while continuing work on necessities like harvesting and snow removal. He wonders, sometimes, what people mean by "leisure management."

WIN A FREE VITA-MIX ***(see page 6)***

(see page 6)

Backwoods Home magazine

... a practical journal of self reliance!

ne 1993
No. 21
0 U.S.
$4.5 anada

Understanding the Environmental Movement

Alaskan Gold

Home Birthing

Building Fences

Ahhh! Goat's Milk

Drill your own Well

Houseplants for Clean Air

Note from the publisher

First Vita-Mix winner

Mrs. Margaret K. Letterman of Goldendale, Washington is our first Vita-Mix winner. She won it in a random drawing from among paid subscribers. We'll continue giving away a $500 Vita-Mix for each of the next five issues. You must be a paid subscriber to be eligible.

A Backwoods Home Magazine index

Jeff Aylor of Columbus, Ohio has produced a comprehensive index for our book, Backwoods Home Magazine: the Best of the First Two Years and issues 8 through 18. He's selling it for $3 ($4 for Canadians). I've seen it and it is an excellent, easy-to-use, quick reference index to our first three years worth of issues. The index is arranged by subject and even includes detailed sections for poems, book reviews, and recipes.

So if you've been having trouble finding articles on a particular topic that was covered in a past issue of *Backwoods Home*, I recommend this index as a great tool. *BHM*, by the way, has no financial interest in this index. Jeff Aylor's only connection with *BHM* is that he asked for and got my permission and encouragement to produce the index. Order it from Aylor Research, 7034 Brafferton Place, Columbus, Ohio 43235.

Midwest Renewable Energy Fair

The Midwest Renewable Energy Fair will be held June 18-20 at the Portage County Fairgrounds in Amherst, Wisconsin. We were supposed to be there for last year's show but had to cancel, but we'll definitely be there this year.

This is probably one of the most worthwhile shows in the country. Much of it consists of displays of alternative energy technology such as photovoltaics, wind machines, electric cars, etc. Plenty of workshops. If you're interested in an alternative electrical source for a remote site, try and catch this show. Their ad on page 55 will give you the details.

Preparedness Show

The Preparedness Expo moves to Salt Lake City, Utah May 20-22. As usual we'll be there. I always like going to Salt Lake City. It's clean and mugger-free.

Waldenbooks/B. Dalton

Waldenbooks and B. Dalton bookstores are planning to open their doors wider for us. They have been testing the sales strength of *BHM* in their stores for about a year and a half and have concluded *BHM* has what it takes to be a strong seller on a regular basis. So they are expanding the number of stores we are in fourfold by summer. We wouldn't mind it at all if readers walked into some of their stores and urged them on.

Dave Duffy

We keep growing

Backwoods Home Magazine has experienced some rather dramatic growth during the past two years. Our print run is running 65-70,000 copies per issue, our paid subscription number is nearly 7,000, and many of our advertisers have told us we are their best advertising option. It all adds up to success for the magazine.

It is especially gratifying to have achieved the success without having had any initial financial backing and without having to dish out product endorsements in exchange for paid advertisements.

The credit goes to the many writers who have contributed the several hundred articles that have appeared in our first 21 issues, and to the readers who had the good sense to recognize a quality magazine, then support it.

It is no small task to maintain the quality of a magazine. The publication of each issue is preceded by two months of hard work. The last week before printing is the toughest. The phone is always ringing and problems you never anticipate always keep cropping up. This issue owes a lot to Christopher Maxwell, who flew out from Illinois for a week to help edit the articles going into the issue. He also wrote the editorial. Lance Bisaccia of Ashland, Oregon, edited and put most of the articles into Ventura Publisher, the desktop publishing system we use. Jan Cook of Camarillo, California, used a scanner to capture 90% of the articles on computer so we wouldn't have to type them. John Silveira of Ojai, California, modemed his article into my computer at the last minute. Lenie, of course, typed 'til she dropped. Δ

My View

Control government, not guns

Terrible events fill the news as this issue goes to press. Terrorists bomb the World Trade Center in New York. Cult members shoot it out with BATF Agents in Texas.

Predictably enough, politicians and journalists tell us "Something must be done." New Jersey Governor Florio was on TV a few days after the New York bombing calling for more gun control to prevent similar incidents. Not one reporter asked him just how gun control would prevent car bombs. No one has offered to explain how gun control would have prevented the cult in Texas from acquiring .50 caliber machine guns and grenades, which are only manufactured for the government.

But shouldn't we control guns anyway? Even if gun control wouldn't have prevented these incidents, many well meaning people will be inclined to go along with the politicians' call for new restrictions due to the intolerable crime rate in our country.

According to the FBI Uniform Crime Statistics for 1990, firearms were only fired in 4% of all violent crimes reported. In another 8%, victims were threatened with a firearm, or something that looked like a firearm. Between 88% and 96% of all face-to-face, violent, personal crimes reported would still have been committed even if firearms had never been invented.

The criminals who rob, rape, and kill with kitchen knives, ball bats, and bare hands would surely commit more crimes if not for the probability that some of their potential victims are armed with firearms.

The idea that life would be safer if there were no firearms may be true for politicians and the rich who have bodyguards. Firearms can reach past bodyguards where an assailant with a knife or club couldn't. But the rest of us can easily be attacked, robbed, or killed by gangs of criminals without firearms.

Should the people give up their right to own the means to defend themselves and resist tyranny so that politicians and the rich can feel safe? Is this what America is about?

Eliminating firearms will never be possible as long as there is a demand. Putting ink on paper is not magic. Gun control laws will not cause steel objects to disappear.

Firearms and ammunition are manufactured by ordinary people, using common materials, machines, tools, and knowledge. These materials, tools, and knowledge will not vanish no matter what new laws are written.

Weapons will continue to be stolen from military arsenals. War souvenirs will be smuggled home by returning servicemen. Guns will be stolen from factories producing for the military and police, and purchased from corrupt police and military personnel.

A ban on firearms for civilians will create an illegal market in firearms which may rival the illegal drug market. Like all illegal markets, the prices will be much higher. This will not deter drug dealers, murderers, terrorists and other criminals who intend to use guns, or gang members and other losers who want guns to prop up their egos. Those who intend to misuse guns will pay the price.

Those who most need to defend themselves and are least likely to misuse firearms, the working poor, the elderly, and women, will be the only ones unable or unwilling to pay the higher black market prices.

There are about 22,000 laws in the United States regulating the manufacture, importation, transportation, ownership, sale, possession, carrying, storage and use of firearms. More gun control laws are passed, with no visible effect on the increasing rates of crime and violence.

The histories of ancient civilizations show us that when moral values, respect for society, personal responsibility, social accountability, and family ties declined, crime and violence increased.

We need to address the root causes of violence in our society, rather than waste our time and effort on useless diversions like gun control. Gun control will not eliminate lack of opportunity, irresponsibility, poverty, ignorance, hopelessness, lack of positive role models or the political rhetoric of envy, victimization, and race-hatred.

Until we deal with these problems, crime and violence will continue to increase, with or without gun control.

What scares me more than guns is the idea of the government using gun laws to persecute unpopular political and religious groups. The Branch Davidian cult in Waco, Texas were not suspected of terrorism or violence.

What led the BATF to Waco? Couln't they find any criminals in the cities? Why did BATF keep trying to buy guns from Randy Weaver in Idaho? Maybe he was a racist, a nazi, and everything else he was called in the media. But he was not imposing his opinions or lifestyle on anyone else. He was not a suspect in any violent crime. Doesn't the BATF have anything more urgent to do?

Political and religious fringe groups fear persecution. This causes such groups to acquire weapons. This is well known in law enforcement circles. These operations may have been an attempt to improve their statistics by going after what they hoped would be easy targets. All agencies need statistics to justify their budgets. This may be why some think BATF concentrates on honest collectors instead of violent criminals. A violent criminal may only have one gun, but if BATF can trick some collector into a mistake in his paperwork, they can show they took 40 or 50 guns "off the street." The fact that these guns were never "on the street", and would have never been used for crime doesn't appear in the statistics, or on the news.

Then again, these operations may be attempts to eliminate fringe groups by targeting them for investigation. Nixon used to harass his enemies by sending the IRS after them. A cult, or a self-sufficient family with no measureable income, could not be targeted by the IRS. But almost anyone who owns, buys, or sells firearms can be targeted by the BATF. There are more laws on the books than anyone can keep track of. We don't need any more gun control, we need government control. Δ

Christopher Maxwell

Use houseplants to improve your indoor air quality

© by Martin P. Waterman

New scientific research is revealing facts that many have suspected for a long time to be true: houseplants are good for your health. The primary benefit appears to be their ability to filter the air, but there are also other important benefits. Few realize that even in the worst smog-polluted cities, the air inside their own homes could be more poisonous than the air outside. This can be true for the backwoods home as well.

During the oil shortages of the 1970s when there was uncertainty over energy prices and supply, building practices were changed for office buildings, houses, and even rural homesteads in order to make these buildings more energy efficient. Even older buildings were converted so they were airtight. Unfortunately, by keeping this heated or air conditioned air inside, the result has been the trapping of many unhealthy contaminants, some of which you may be breathing every day. Most of these contaminants come from synthetic building materials that are used in the construction and furnishing of buildings. As most builders are aware, it is almost impossible to build a home without using some synthetic materials. This is especially true of the furniture and appliances that may be used to furnish your home.

A wide selection of houseplants can brighten as well as filter the air in your backwoods home. It takes about 15 to 20 plants to clean the air.

The effect of this accumulation of toxins from synthetic building materials has been named "Sick Building Syndrome" because of the high number of people who are experiencing ailments such as headaches, respiratory irritation, fatigue, nausea, and dizziness.

The National Aeronautics and Space Administration (NASA) has been leading the research into the filtering capabilities of houseplants at the John C. Stennis Space Center in Mississippi. NASA has been facing the same problems experienced by building dwellers with respect to a clean indoor environment in their space program. NASA needs to find ways to keep the air clean for their astronauts to function in confined spaces for extended periods of time. The results are preliminary, but the research has already shown that all plants filter the air. Some of the common toxins that the plants were successful in removing were benzene, formaldehyde, and trichloroethylene. Benzene is commonly used in such products as inks, paints, plastics, and rubber. Trichloroethylene is used for dry cleaning, in inks, paints, lacquers, and varnishes, and formaldehyde is found in foam insulation, particle board, consumer paper products, and glues. Formaldehyde is also found in cigarette smoke and heating and cooking fuels.

In some cases, certain house plants removed up to 90% of these dangerous toxins from the air. Some plants proved to be better at filtering certain pollutants than others, so that a wide variety of plants may be needed to obtain maximum results. In addition to the plant's foliage filtering the air, it was found that the plant's roots and soil microbes also play an important part in filtering and cleaning the air. According to NASA, 15 to 20 plants should be adequate to clean the air in an area of 1800 square feet.

Houseplants need not be boring. Try growing indoor citrus, bananas, cacti, herbs, or whatever you fancy.

In addition to their value in providing clean air, there are other ways in which houseplants can contribute to our well being. Hospitals and treatment centers have used horticultural therapy programs for more than a century to relieve a patient's distress. Growing, propagating, and tending houseplants provides stress-alleviating relaxation.

Small houseplants can become big houseplants. This jade plant is 16 years old.

An interesting study was done at Texas A & M University in which 120 students were subjected to a very stressful film about work accidents. This was designed to induce stress as measured by such responses as muscle tension and blood pressure. After this film, the same students were subjected to different films aimed at reducing stress. The students who were shown a film focusing on natural scenes recovered from the stress more quickly and completely than those who watched the other films about traffic and a shopping mall.

Those who have walked into an office building (or home) with no plants often feel that there is something missing. The calming effects of plants can be used in many ways by providing color, texture, flowers, and interesting "plantscapes," which have become popular among interior decorators. In fact, indoor landscaping has become very popular. This is illustrated by the growth of the plant rental and maintenance businesses.

Some of the other benefits of houseplants include such things as their ability to absorb sound. They can also be used as barriers to help direct office or home traffic flow.

Many chefs and cooks have known for some time that some fresh herbs can be grown in an indoor environment. Others have taken this practice further, creating in effect a type of indoor edible landscaping. Certain fruit and vegetable plants not only provide beautiful foliage, but also produce fresh healthy food while simultaneously filtering your air.

No matter what use you have for your houseplants, whether for culinary, medicinal, or aesthetic value, you can at least know that they are improving your health by removing toxins from your air. Δ

(For further reading on improving your indoor air quality, see BHM's article, "Building for indoor air quality," in Issue No. 10.)

A BHM Writer's Profile

Frances Jablway is a writer, editor, and workshop presenter. She has always loved words and has been writing since she was old enough not to eat her crayons. Topics covered in her work range from cooking, to sports, to size acceptance. To date, she has published 11 articles, one short story, and 12 poems, and has completed two novels.

Currently, Jablway is managing editor of *Poetic License*. She teaches writing related workshops through the St. Charles Illinois Park District and has spoken at writers gatherings. She has lived in the Chicago area for 10 years.

Janet Coates displays the medicinal aloe vera plant, which will help heal your cuts and burns as well as clean your indoor air.

Four ducks on a pond,
A grass bank beyond,
A blue sky of spring.
What a beautiful thing
To remember for years,
To remember with tears.

—William Allingham

Drive your own well for next to nothing

By Roger DeGroot

Water is the staff of life. Without it our gardens will not grow, our kitchen recipes will not be complete and we will remain thirsty all day. For though we can drink milk, wine, and many other mixtures to please our palate and nourish our bodies, it is cool clear water to which mankind turns when thirsty.

Thus, a well is one of the first things one thinks of when one begins to move to the backwoods. And so it was for us. We found a small piece of land, just five acres, with a small frog pond. The nearest water supply was 1/2 mile down the road.

The first thing to do when starting any project in the country is to talk to your neighbors—especially if you don't know anything about the topic. They were there before you and probably had to learn all the same skills you will need. Books and magazines like *Backwoods Home* can provide lots of good information, but there is nothing like the pleasure of learning a new skill while sharing a cup of coffee or lifting a cool one with friends.

Only one of the homes within a couple miles of our land had had a professional company bring a drilling rig to install a deep well. Their well is 167 feet deep and has better tasting water (almost tasteless) than we have in our city abode. Everyone else has a driven well.

Simple equipment

A driven well is a simple thing, made with a length of steel pipe with a drive point on one end. The drive point has small holes or slots on the sides with fine screening covering them. When driven into the earth so that the point is in an underground water source, the holes let in the water but not the surrounding earth and sand.

After spending some time talking to the experts in the area, the second step is to gather the tools and other equipment. You need a couple of pipe

Ron Scholten, left, and Barney Townes pump water from a well they drove.

wrenches and some extensions for their handles. You will be connecting several lengths of galvanized steel pipe to each other as you drive the well, and it's important to get the connections as tight as possible. Two or three foot long pipes (plastic pipe will do fine) work well as extensions and provide the extra leverage you need to get the pipe joints tight enough. You also need at least two strong bodies (more if possible) that are willing to be sore for a couple days afterwards.

The consumables include enough 5- or 6-foot lengths of pipe, cut and threaded, to reach far enough into the ground. In our area most driven wells are between 25 and 40 feet deep—so we started with 50 feet of pipe just to be safe. You also need pipe couplers for each joint and pipe joint compound to help seal the joints. The drive point itself will be 3 or 4 feet in length. At the top of the well, you will need an old-fashioned pitcher pump with a check valve just below it. The check valve will keep the water in the pipe when you have pumped it up high enough.

Location

Another basic step is planning where to put the well. In this part of the country, only 20 miles from Lake Michigan, the ground is largely sand. It's almost like an endless beach. The water table is relatively high. I wonder sometimes what great lake covered this part of the land so many years ago and slowly gave way to plant growth. To decide where the well is to be located is largely a decision of convenience. The county code requires the well to be at least 50 feet from any existing pond and 50 feet from any septic system. Likewise the location should be convenient to a building—either to lessen the distance to a hand pump or to be close to the location where the electric pump and pressure tank will be installed. For a driven well, the pump is normally located above ground in a building. If there is no building conveniently located, consider building a small pump house to shelter it from the weather.

In other parts of the country, there are many other considerations in selecting a location for the well. If you can find someone with a good reputation for divining a well, you might consider asking them to assist. Of course, with a witch hazel or other appropriate divining rod, you can do it yourself. In my case, after deciding where I wanted a septic system, I just picked a convenient place for the well, built a shed to shelter the pump and ran some electric service to it.

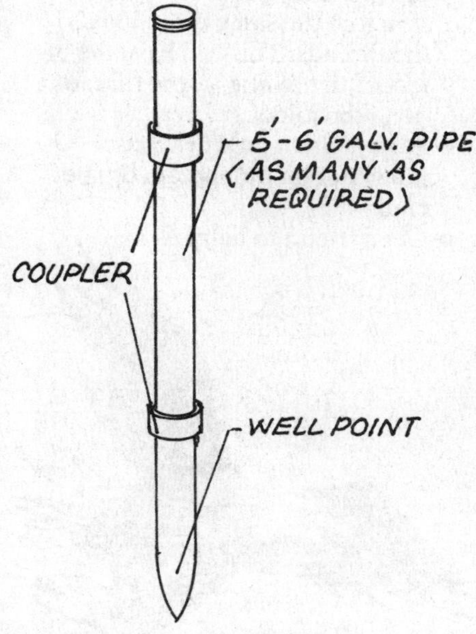

Figure 1. Drive point

Starting

Start the well by attaching one of the lengths of pipe to the drive point and sticking it in the ground (See Figure 1). It is important to start with the pipe exactly vertical. The pipe can be driven with a sledge hammer or with a special driver which can be rented from most well supply shops. The driver weighs about 40 pounds and is basically a steel tube with one end capped. Handles on either side make it easier to lift (See Figures 2 and 3). The process is quite simple. Lift the driver up, then let it drop. The weight of the driver does all the work. You only lift the driver. Obviously, after you have done this a couple hundred times, the driver seems to weigh a lot more than 40 pounds.

As the lengths of pipe slowly get driven into the ground, you must add new lengths of pipe to the top and then lift the driver onto the end of the pipe again. Progress is not always consistent. On our well, the first 14 feet of pipe went down in about a half hour. The next 5 foot piece of pipe took almost an hour to drive. We must have hit a layer of clay or other hard material. Just don't give up.

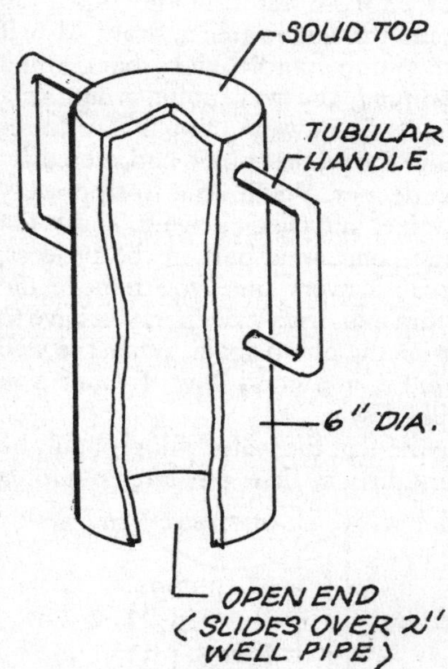

Figure 2. Well driver

Testing

In our region, the county code called for a well to be at least 25 feet deep. After you have driven enough pipe to be 25 feet deep, you can test if there is water in the pipe. Drop a weighted string into the pipe until the weight no longer keeps the string tight. Then pull up the string and check how much of the string is wet. If there is some water in the pipe, you can attach the pitcher pump and try to pump water. It is necessary to prime the pump when you start. That means you have one person pour water from a jug or a bucket into the top of the pump while another person pumps like crazy (See Figure 4).

If you do it right, in a couple minutes of pumping, the water will be drawn up into the pump and you will be pumping from your well. However, if there is not enough water in the pipe, the pump will not be able to draw. Also, if the pump handle kicks back when pumping, the well point is not in a good vein of water. You'll have to remove the pitcher pump and keep driving deeper. You'll want to stop every few feet and check it again. This is the time consuming part of the process, because every time you remove the pump and drive it deeper, you have to prime the pump again. When the well point is in a good flow of water, you will know it.

Note that the water will probably be very dirty at first. But after pumping

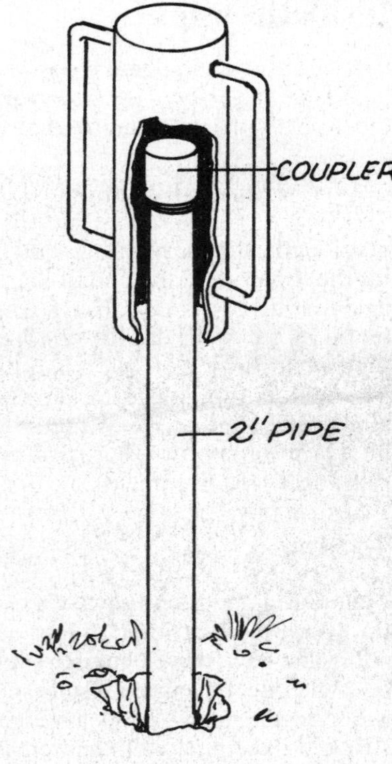

Figure 3

for about 5 minutes, the water will have cleared up nicely. If it doesn't, the point may have been damaged. Keep pumping for 30 minutes or so. If the water does not clear up, you may have to pull it up.

You can rent a well puller, or you can rely on a simple lever. Get a long piece of 2x6 and put a large rock near the pipe. A large chain, wrapped around the 2x6 and the pipe, should grab the pipe as you lift. Successively pushing down on the long end of the lever and sliding the chain down the pipe while lifting the end of the 2x6 should allow the pipe to be slowly lifted.

Obviously, each length of pipe will need to be uncoupled from the next piece as it is removed from the ground. After all the pipe is removed from the ground, check the well point for damage. Sometimes the brass screen will buckle and crack. This will allow sand or dirt to enter the pipe unchecked. The only thing to do is go back to your plumbing supply house to get a new one. They will probably give you one for free, as the points are not supposed to break.

The second time you drive down the same hole will be slightly easier. But don't expect a cake walk. The layers of clay will still be difficult to drive through.

Finishing

At 25 feet we had about 12 feet of water in our well. With the pump attached we were able to draw water, but the handle kept kicking after the downstroke. So we took the pump off and drove another length of pipe. Our well ended up at 31 feet. We found a good vein of water, and after a few minutes of pumping the water cleared up nicely. It doesn't taste quite as good as the nearby well which was professionally drilled to a depth of 167 feet but my $200 investment paled in comparison to their $2500 well.

Some words of advice

- Get a friend who has done it before to help. Most of your neighbors will have some experience. It sure helps your confidence level when the "expert" tells you, "You're making good progress...keep it up!"
- Get several friends to help. A well can easily be driven by two people—but more friends to help with the lifting makes the job go much quicker.
- Keep each joint tight—that means really leaning on the pipe wrenches as you tighten each coupler onto the piece of pipe.
- When each pipe length is halfway down, stop and tighten the coupler. It is amazing how quickly the couplers will loosen as they are being pounded by the driver.

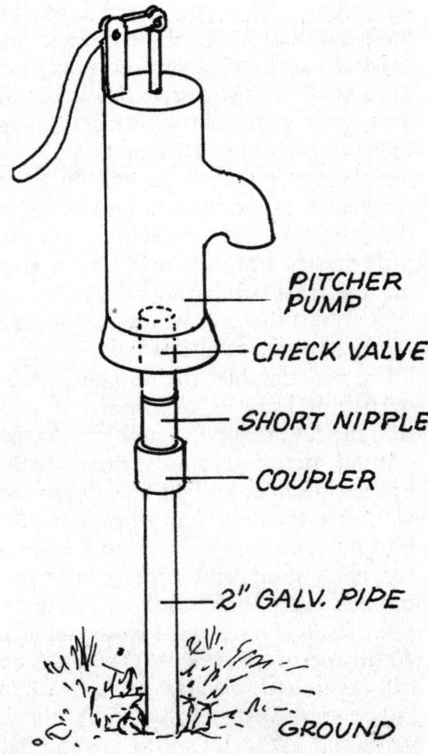

Figure 4

- Tighten the entire pipe occasionally as it goes down. Grab the pipe with a pipe wrench and turn it in the same direction as the threads. This will have the effect of tightening all the threads of all the joints.
- Always drive on a drive coupling, not on the threaded pipe end.
- Get a friend to help. Δ

Sweet Alaska gold

by Barbara Landi
(Photos by Linda Cordle)

There's a new little gold mine tucked away near Eagle River in Alaska, about 20 miles north of Anchorage. The "gold" is clear, sweet, and syrupy, and it is "mined" during the summer months by millions of workers from several hundred colonies that live in hives.

Former Alaska State Legislator John Liska and partners Charlie Klicker and Jerry Hoskins have turned their hobby into the Alaska Honey and Pollen Co., which turns out honey of the rarest kind and highest quality.

Honey is unique. It is a natural substance that man has never been able to duplicate. It doesn't need to be vacuum packed and it will never spoil. It does granulate after time, but can be restored to its liquid state by placing the container in hot water. The bees put natural enzymes into honey that prevent the growth of bacteria. Honey can even be used as an antiseptic.

Bee pollen can also be collected in the process of honey production. A special screen with a series of small openings scrapes the balls of nectar and pollen off the bees' legs as they enter the hive. Pollen is the protein food of the bees, and a valuable health food for people, too.

Insulated hives

Honey production has always been a challenge in the far North because of the difficulty in sustaining bee colonies

Looking down the side of a frame.
These are workers making more cells, working the wax.

throughout the long winter. But Liska and Klicker have devised a system modeled after a method pioneered by beekeepers in Saskatchewan, Canada, of keeping the hives covered and insulated in the field.

Bees don't freeze to death, but they can starve. Some beekeepers feel the expense of feeding the bees over the winter is too great, so they opt for letting the bees die and ordering new ones in the spring. Liska disagrees, and only orders new bees to increase his total "work force."

In springtime, even spilled syrup on top of the hive is not wasted. Hungry bees gather around to drink every drop.

Fireweed honey

In May, the hives get transported to a recent "burn" area in Tok, a little town on the Alaska Highway close to the Canadian border. Serious beekeepers look for a place where there was a recent forest or brush fire. Two years after a burn, a dense blanket of fireweed will cover the area all summer, and the bees will use it to manufacture the clear and delicate fireweed honey that is coveted all over the world. The honey is equally coveted by the local bear population, so Liska and Klicker will have to stay close by to guard their investment.

Their honey is classified as "water white," which means it is the very top of the line in quality and as clear as water. It took top honors at the American Honey Show in San Diego in 1992. Liska and Klicker are deservedly proud to show off all the ribbons and awards their honey has brought them. They also produce clover honey, creamed honey, comb honey, beeswax candles, and beekeeping supplies.

Their honey is sold in Fred Meyer, JC Penney, Hilton Hotels, and the Clarion, to name just a few U.S. outlets, and has been sold outside the U.S., too. The Alaska Honey and Pollen Company's biggest problem now is to keep up with the demand. Δ

The queen is at the center. She is climbing out of a cell, having just laid an egg. She is surrounded by workers.

Beekeepers carrying buckets of sugar syrup in spring to feed bees in hives. This will tide them over until they can fly, when warmer weather comes.

How to build your own beehives

By Gary Hutchins

Beekeeping as a business is ideal for the backwoods individual. Honey, beeswax, and pollen are easy to sell, and swarms of bees are free for the taking. The major drawback is the cost of equipment to house the industrious little creatures.

If you are interested in beekeeping but can't afford to buy commercial hive bodies and frames, here is a simple method of making your own bee hives. This design is not only inexpensive, but it is also compatible with commercial equipment.

Building your own equipment is not as hard as it might seem. You can save hundreds of dollars while using scrap boards that seem to litter everyone's garage. The design of the equipment that is currently mass produced was developed over seventy-five years ago. During the early years of development a good quality wood glue was not available. The lack of a good glue made it necessary for the builder to use a locking joint in construction so that each joint could be held together securely with nails alone.

Since the advent of modern carpenter's glue, nails are used primarily to hold the joint together while the glue dries. Modern glues allow you to use basic joints and still achieve a joint that is stronger than the wood itself. You should use glue on all joints during assembly to ensure that your equipment doesn't fall apart while you are working your bees.

In the construction of bee equipment, a bee space of 1/4 inch to 3/8 inch is critical. If it is less than 1/4 inch, the bees will fill the gap with propolis (bee glue). If it is greater than 3/8 inch, the bees will fill the space with brace comb. A space of 1/4 inch gives the best results.

Your equipment can be made from any scrap 3/4 inch thick lumber that you have on hand. Plywood is great, even wafer board is good, but particle board tends to fall apart when it gets wet.

Start with your bottom board. Cut a piece of plywood (any thickness will do) 15 3/8 inches wide by 22 inches long. Now cut 3/4 inch by 3/4 inch lumber into two pieces 22 inches long and one piece 13 3/4 inches long. Now glue and nail all three pieces to one side of the plywood (See Figure 1).

Now you can build the brood chamber. Start with 3/4 inch lumber that has been cut into boards that are 9 5/8 inches wide. Cut two pieces 15 3/8 inches long and two pieces 19 5/8 inches wide. Take the two 15 3/8 inch pieces and cut a rabbet joint 3/4 inch wide and 3/8 inch deep across the grain on both ends. These rabbets are to allow you to join the boards to form a box. This joint minimizes the exposure of the end grain of the wood

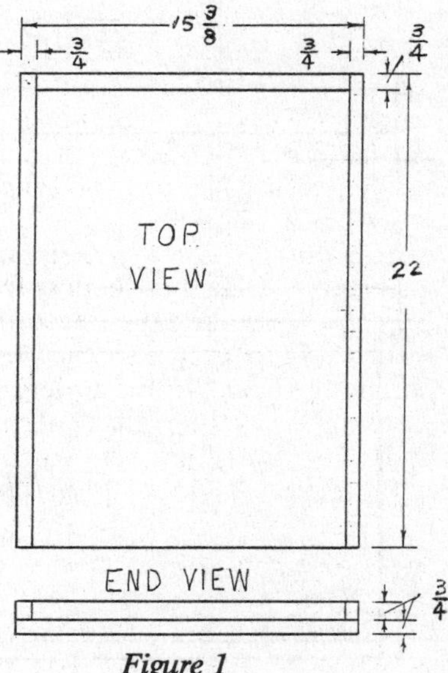

Figure 1

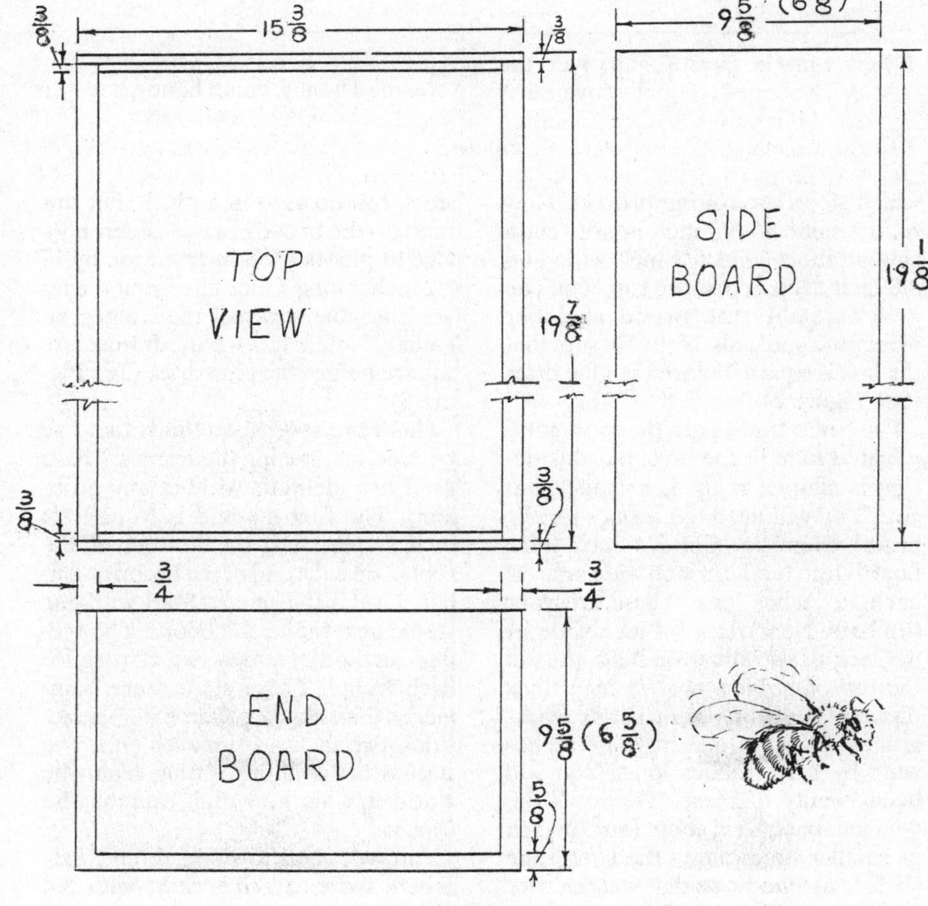

Figure 2

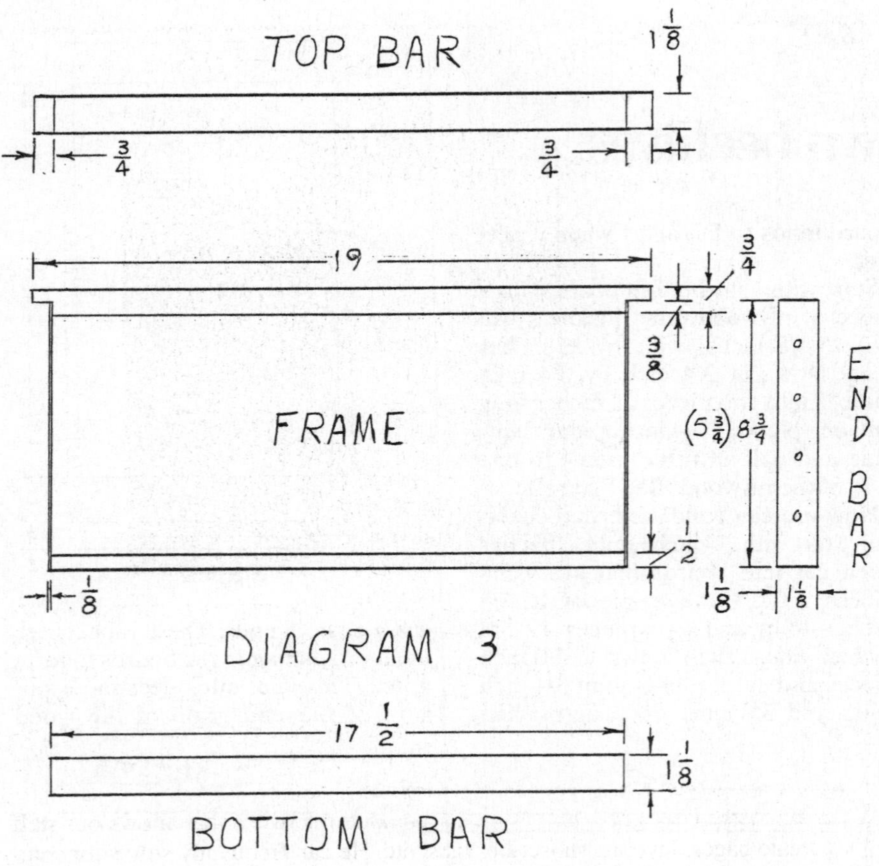

Figure 3

which slows the rotting process. Now on the same 15 3/8 inch boards cut a single rabbet joint 5/8 inch wide and 3/8 inch deep across the top. You can now assemble the brood chamber using glue and nails. Note: Be sure that the box is square before the glue dries (See Figure 2).

The comb frames are the most complicated item in the hive, but this design is simple, rugged, and inexpensive. You will need ten frames for the brood chamber. Cut 3/4 inch thick boards into ten 1 1/8 inch wide boards, each 19 inches long. These are your top bars. Next cut a 3/4 inch wide by 3/8 inch deep rabbet on both ends of the top bars. Now cut 1/8 inch thick plywood (paneling or masonite works great for this) into strips 1 1/8 inches wide by 8 3/4 inches long. You will need twenty of these. These will be your end bars. Drill about four 1/8 inch or smaller holes along the centerline (before assembly) so that you can wire in the wax foundation. The bottom bar is cut from 1/2 inch stock (3/4 inch stock can be used in a pinch, but this reduces the brood area considerably). Cut 10 pieces 1 1/8 inches wide by 17 1/2 inches long. Once all of your pieces are cut, glue and nail the frames together. Note: Be sure the frames are square before the glue dries (See Figure 3).

There are several methods that can be used for spacing the frames. I have used two methods without any problems. The first method is to nail 1/4 inch staples into the bottom of the rabbet on each end of the brood chamber, 1 1/8 inches apart. Start with one staple next to the sideboard. The second method requires two staples for each frame. These staples are hammered into the top bar on opposite sides, two inches from each end. The staples are left protruding from the wood 1/4 inch, which spaces the frames.

You will need to build three to six supers for each hive. Start with 3/4 inch lumber that is 6 5/8 inches wide. Use the same directions as for building the brood chamber (See Figure 2).

To build the frames for each super, use the same directions as you did in building the frames for the brood chamber, but cut the side bars 1 1/8 inches wide and 5 3/4 inches long (See Figure 3).

The inner cover allows you to use a telescoping top cover without the bees gluing it to the hive. Start by cutting a 1/8 inch thick piece of plywood or masonite 15 3/8 inches by 19 7/8 inches. Now cut 3/4 inch thick boards into 1/4 inch wide strips. Cut these strips into two 19 7/8 inch and two 13 7/8 inch long pieces. Glue these strips to one side of the plywood. Drill a hole one inch or larger in the center of the inner cover (See Figure 4).

The telescoping outer cover is the last item that you need to build. Start by cutting a piece of plywood 17 3/8 inches wide by 21 7/8 inches long. Cut 3/4 inch by 1 1/2 inch lumber into two strips 21 7/8 inches long and two strips 15 7/8 inches long. Glue and nail these pieces to one side of the plywood (See Figure 5).

Cover the outer cover with aluminum sheet metal, tar paper, or whatever you have on hand that will shed water. You should paint the outside of your hive to protect it from the ele-

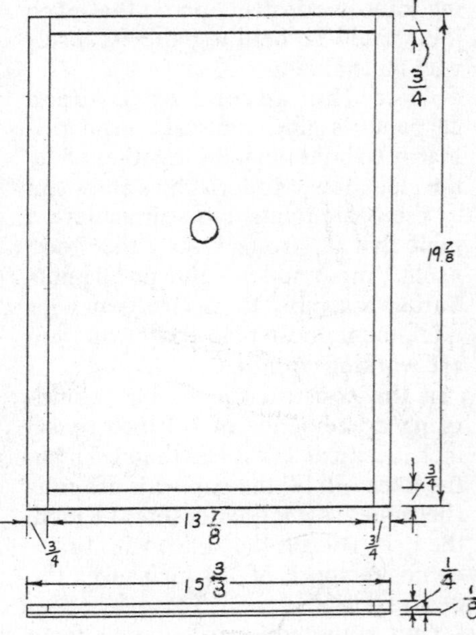

Figure 4. Inner cover.

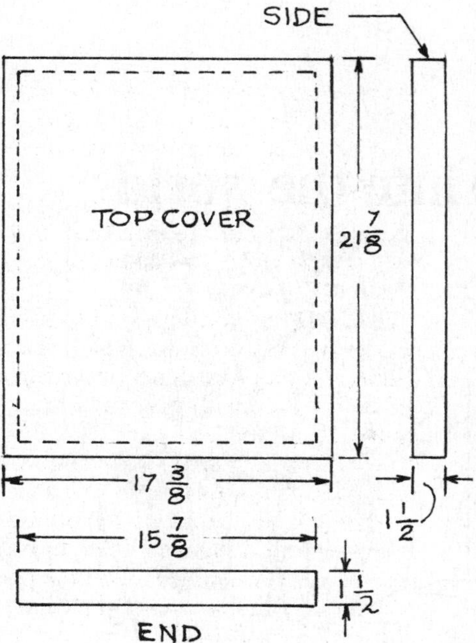

Figure 5. Top cover.

ments, but never paint the inside of the frames.

Building your own equipment not only saves you a lot of money, but you also become a little less dependent upon the commercial suppliers of bee equipment. Who knows, you may even find yourself making your own pollen traps, honey extractors, and smokers. It can be done. Δ

A BHM Staffer Profile

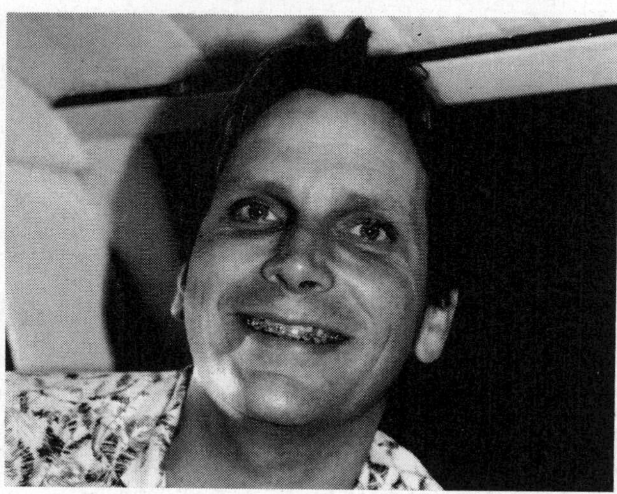

Tim Green is more than just *Backwoods Home Magazine's* computer wizard. Without his faith, encouragement, and financial assistance *BHM* might never have been started. Years ago when Dave Duffy, *BHM's* founder and publisher, was an aspiring carpenter he remodeled a large garage for Green, turning it into a rental apartment. Little did Duffy know that he would be living there two years later while starting a magazine. The first issues of *BHM* were put together on the floor of Tim Green's garage.

Later, Green designed and set up the computer network that allows our staff to create pages, layouts, subscriber lists, etc. He can frequently solve our computer problems by phone. Green is a partner in the magazine and he and Duffy are personal friends. Tim Green lives in Ventura, California with his wife.

HEALTH

Homebirth – a natural way to come into the world

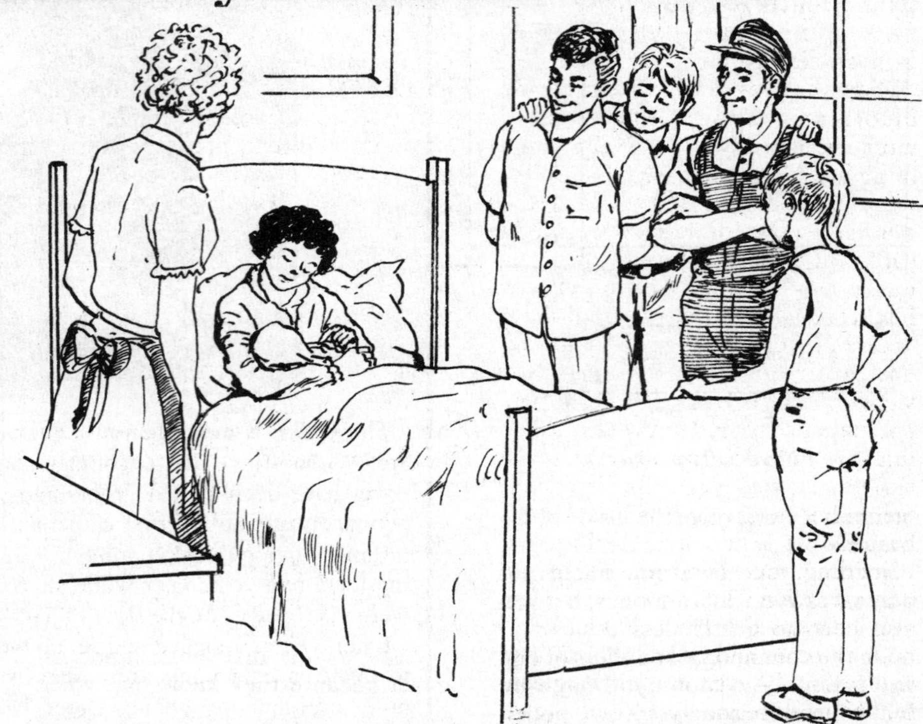

By Julie Pfeiffer Watner

"The fire crackling and sighing in the great stone fireplace both warmed and lighted the little log cabin as we moved quietly about setting up instruments and supplies. Kneeling beside the bed in the far corner of the room, Sam grasped Beth's hand and murmured encouragement as she breathed her way through yet another contraction. Candles and kerosene lamps were lit and everything was in readiness for the new little life about to enter the world. We strained our ears to hear the sounds that would announce the arrival of the midwife."

Does that read like a page from a 19th century novel? Actually, it is an entry in my journal recording a birth I was privileged to attend in September, 1992. Admittedly, it was a bit unusual to attend a birth in a remote cabin which had neither electricity or indoor plumbing, but whether in a log cabin or a city-dwellers apartment, homebirth is alive and thriving in the 1990s.

Until the early part of the 20th century, having their babies at home was the only "practical" choice for women, even here in the United States. After all, hospitals were for sick people, and the incidence of "child-bed fever" was far greater in the hospital than it was at home. Even as late as the 1950s and '60s, few women in mountainous and rural regions went to hospitals to deliver their babies. Gradually, however, with scientific advances making hospitals safer (more sanitary), and ever-increasing case loads making doctors' time more valuable, American women began going to hospitals to deliver their babies as a matter of course. Today over 97% of all American babies are delivered in hospitals.

And yet, shockingly, the infant mortality in the U.S. is higher than it is in several other less technically advanced countries in the world. One common thread that links all the countries with infant survival records better than ours is that there is little or no medical intervention in their birthing practices.

Home-or-midwife-assisted births (and once-in-a-great-while, doctor-assisted homebirths) may not be for everyone, but since 95% of all children **are** born without any delivery problems, it may be worth consideration. Naturally, for the 5% or so of mothers who have complications, an obstetrician and hospital are prudent choices. But for those who do not have complications and who believe that "childbirth ought to be a warm, family-centered experience, not an impersonal operation to be carried out in a cold assembly-line-like atmosphere," birthing your child at home provides a wonderful alternative.

The benefits of homebirth

One of the main benefits of a homebirth is that the parents are allowed to remain in control of the situation. The father is able to hold his rightful position of importance, as he participates in the process of assisting his wife in her travail and welcoming his child from the very moment of his or her birth. And the mother is truly able to be, as our midwife is fond of saying, "queen for a day!" She can do whatever she likes for as long as she likes prior to the birth; then she can choose her own place and position for the birthing, changing as her needs change...all of it in the comfort of her own home and in the company of people she loves.

A nurse-midwife is a person who has received special medical training in the field of pregnancy and childbirth. Most often a nurse-midwife is the only kind of midwife allowed to deliver babies in U.S. hospitals, and they always work in tandem with a medical doctor. Lay midwives are those whose knowledge has come largely from their own study and lengthy apprenticeship. They may be nurses, teachers, mothers, or come from any walk of life. Although prepared for the rare emergency, lay midwives don't "practice medicine," because they don't perform obstetrical procedures; rather they advise the parents, and "catch" the baby. Each state has its own laws concerning the licensing of midwives; some are more restrictive than others. (The government is with us literally from cradle to grave!)

Midwives provide the warm, steady emotional support the birthing mother needs, as well as the continuity of physical care to ensure that everything is in order. They are at the mother's side for "the whole nine yards" of the actual birthing process, unlike most doctors, who are usually just in and out to check progress. Since "normal" is different for every woman, and even different for the same woman with each child, it takes time and patience to find out what is "normal" for each delivery. Midwives take that time, and they are philosophically committed to giving non-interventive care. Most homebirth families are convinced, with good reason, that in normal deliveries the fewer the drugs and interventions, the healthier it will be for mother and child. If you deliver in a hospital—even in a birthing center—where the medical technology is available, the temptation to use the equipment and the pain-killing medication is often too great to resist. Medical intervention is more often for the convenience of the doctor (and, believe it or not, some mothers!) than it is a necessity. (The increasingly litigious nature of our society in general, and of malpractice suits against doctors in particular, also plays a large part in the use of technology in maternity wards, but that is for another article, at another time.)

If unforeseen problems do arise, and transport to a hospital is necessary, most often the midwife will accompany the parents. Immediately after the home delivery of my second son, it seemed advisable to transport me to a local hospital because of a delay in the delivery of the placenta. (The baby was perfectly healthy and stayed at home.) Contrary to the horror stories we had heard regarding the treatment often given transported home-delivery patients, we were given excellent, courteous care. In fact, the doctors and nurses treated our midwife as an equal when they sent me home with an I.V. in my hand.

As a rule, a home delivery is a lot less expensive than a hospital birth, but I don't believe that that is the primary motivation for most families. The cost of a home delivery usually ranges from about $400 in rural areas to around $1200 in metropolitan areas. Midwives are midwives because they like to help deliver babies. They are certainly not in it for the money!

Is it safe?

Homebirth parents tend to be more prepared for the "blessed event" precisely because they are accepting greater responsibility for their own health care. The vast majority educate themselves as to the birth process, possible complications and solutions, nutrition, and pre-natal care. Many midwives offer birth education classes to their clients, and make attendance a precondition to their service. Many homebirth mothers fully prepare themselves for this most important event because they know that when mothers are unprepared, fear sets in (it does seem as if strange and unusual things are happening!), and fear is strictly a "complication enhancer," or even precipitator. In recent years, hospitals have begun to realize the benefits of birth education and now often offer pre-natal classes. This will only improve their record.

A strange prejudice

One of the strangest things about American birth is the widespread prejudice against homebirth. The medical profession has helped foster this because of their vested interest in destroying the competition. When a newborn dies in a hospital it is a tragedy, but when and if a newborn dies at home the tragedy is compounded by accusations of child abuse, neglect, and even murder. This is one of the reasons why midwives are trained to carefully screen their clients. Any needing specialized obstetrical care are asked to get it. Many midwives prefer that each mother find a "back-up" doctor, in case medical help becomes advisable, and most carry emergency equipment (oxygen, for example). So often health problems including infection, drugs, post-partum depression and a host of others are caused by hospital and obstetrical routines. Midwives have an excellent success record—they can't afford to have anything else.

My husband and I and thousands of other couples like us firmly believe that it is a mistake to treat the birthing process in the same way we do illnesses and surgical procedures. We believe that homebirth is a natural, healthy, and wholesome alternative to what is now considered "traditional" birthing in the United States.

Meanwhile, back in the little mountain cabin the midwife arrived and, before another hour had passed, a beautiful baby boy was born into a grateful and loving family. There is nothing that can quite match the incredible thrill of seeing a baby come into this world, take his first breath, and make his first cry. We put another log on the fire, and stayed long enough to see the little one swathed warmly in blankets and elfin cap, held by his triumphant mother, with his proud father looking on. There was a wondrous sense of shared achievement, of joy and of love in that humble little house that night. We departed in the darkness of early morning knowing that for the miracle of birth, there is no place like home!

Information Sources

Sheila Kitzinger, Homebirth: The Essential Guide to Giving Birth Outside of the Hospital, New York: Dorling Kindersley, 1991.

Marion Sousa, Childbirth at Home, Englewood Cliffs: Prentice- Hall, Inc., 1976.

Cascade Birthing, Box 12203, Salem OR 97309. Tel. 1-800-443-9942. Major supplier of homebirth supplies.

(Julie Pfeiffer Watner is the mother of three children, all born at home, residing in Gramling, SC. Her husband, Carl Watner, wrote "Walking the Last Mile with a Loved One...A Guide to Caring for Your Own Dead" which appeared in Backwoods Home Magazine, May/June 1992. She asked for an opportunity to "balance the scales" by writing about the beginnings of life.) Δ

COUNTRY LIVING

The first slaughter

By Therese Reid

As novice farmers, we went through a lot of "firsts" during the eighteen months we had lived on the farm. The first eggs from our own chickens, the first salad from our own garden, fresh mulberry syrup from our own mulberry trees, and now I was to experience the first time one of our steers was slaughtered.

We had worked out a deal with an area dairyman that we would raise the four steers and split the profits. As we got further into the year, we realized that raising four growing steers was very costly, especially if you had to buy all of your feed. To offset the cost, we sold "shares" in our beef, each share being equal to a quarter beef. These quarters would be divided up at some time far in the future, something that we did not dwell on.

During the eighteen months that we raised the steers, they never became "pets", but they did eat apples from our hands, follow us around the pastures, and occasionally get brave enough to let us scratch them behind their ears. My family and friends would always comment when they visited us on the farm, "How will you ever be able to kill them?" And I would assure them that we all knew from the beginning what they were there for.

When the summer came and the time for slaughtering was imminent, I had some doubts, but I was able to rationalize all of them, saying to myself, "They are not pets, they are raised for a purpose, they have had an excellent life, and we simply cannot afford to have four twelve-hundred pound pets!"

I called a butcher in the area that was recommended to me. This shop sent someone to your home to slaughter the steer. (This was necessary for us because we don't own a cow trailer.) I asked if I needed to be present and he said that all I would have to do is have electricity and water available for him and point out the cow. "I could do that," I thought.

I went outside about twenty minutes before the appointed time. I hooked the extension cord into the barn and brought the hose over. Then, like a Judas goat, I filled up a basket of corn and brought the steers up from the lower meadow to the barnyard. I was literally leading them to the slaughter. I felt like I was betraying their trust in me. And again I went through all of the familiar reasons that this had to happen.

When the butcher arrived he looked like an executioner. Sitting in his truck, he was wearing black stretch pants, a sleeveless shirt, a weight-lifter's belt, and tall boots. He looked muscular enough to pick up one of the steers, casually throw it over his shoulder and heft it into his truck. In his hands were a knife and a sharpening rod that he efficiently ran back and forth together. My heart jumped a little.

He climbed out of the truck with his rifle in hand. My heart pounded a little harder. I pointed the steers out to him and told him which one was to be slaughtered that day. He said that since he couldn't drive into our barnyard, I'd have to lead the steer out. Swallowing hard, I pushed open the gate and all of the steers rushed forward. "Run, you stupid beasts, run!" my mind shouted as I backed off the rest and let one slip past me. I squeezed my eyes shut and waited for the crack of the rifle. When I heard it, my heart stopped for a moment. I turned and looked and saw the steer down on the ground, totally still.

I was ready to make my exit. I certainly didn't want to see any more. Luck was not with me that day, however. I found, to my dismay, that the power in the barn was not strong enough to work the butcher's winch. While I tried to hook something else up, he proceeded to work on the steer.

I learned two things that day. As I was forced to walk past the steer, I looked into its eyes, totally expecting to see condemnation. Instead, I saw nothing. The animal that I cared for was gone. The spirit had fled with death, and the thing that the butcher was working on was simply a carcass. The second thing I learned was that it was okay to mourn the passing of any life, even a farm animal. It might seem hypocritical to some, because I was the cause of that death (or rather, my hired hit man), but I feel that the steer's purpose was fulfilled and this was the natural process of his life.

We will continue to raise a steer for our family needs, and we will continue to treat it with respect and kindness during the time it is with us, but we will also realize that death is a natural progression and not the villain that we often make it out to be. Δ

FARM AND GARDEN

Choosing superior bedding plants

By Robert Callahan

Good plants make for good gardens. It seems to make perfect sense, yet each year, many people choose plants which are inferior to those left behind. What makes one plant better than another? How do you know if you're buying inferior plants?

According to Douglas Green, a professional greenhouse grower from Athens, Ontario, there are some guidelines you can follow.

1. Look out for plants that are stretched out. If a plant is more than six inches tall, pass it up. Because of its size, these plants will take longer to recover from transplanting.

2. Healthy looking, dark green stems and leaves are important. Especially pay attention to leaves on the lower part of the plant. If they are dropping off, it is a sure sign of improper feeding. Because of this, the potential for stunting of the plant's growth exists.

3. Most plants start off in artificial soil, and if this soil is permitted to dry out, it is difficult to re-wet. Thus, watering is critical to the plant's natural growth, before and after transplanting. This drying out is especially common in the bargain packs where only a small amount of soil is used for each plant.

4. When selecting tomatoes, choose the plants that have the most soil per plant. Research has proven that the more soil the tomato has, the greater its chances of surviving a transplant and the earlier it will fruit.

5. When looking for geraniums, you want to find plants that are short and bushy, and which have several branches for every two inches of plant height. Furthermore, all of the leaves should be intact and possess a dark green color. If the leaves are not this color, or if there are signs of stretching (spaces of one or more inches between leaf nodes), you should immediately disqualify this plant from consideration.

6. Avoid heavily flowering plants if they are grown together in a single-cell pack, since it will be necessary to cut apart the roots for transplanting. Although they look nice, these flowers are detrimental to the plant because they greatly reduce re-rooting and recuperation. If, however, you purchase a multi-cell pack, where each plant is set off individually, the flowers are not a handicap, as in the previous case, and may in fact be desired.

7. Always count the number of plants you get in a pack and remember it is likely that one or two plants will die during the transplanting process.

8. When buying plants from a greenhouse, check the insect level of the greenhouse by examining the pepper plants. If there are any insects, on the pepper plants is where they will be found. In particular, you want to keep an eye out for aphids or mealybugs. Aphids can generally be found on the underside of the leaves, while mealybugs are generally found where the leaf stem and main stem meet. Under no circumstances should you purchase peppers or tomatoes which have curly leaves. Leaves in such a condition are a sure sign that aphids have transmitted a virus to the plant.

9. Finally, if you're a gardener with strict organic needs, ask the greenhouse grower for information concerning which insecticides, fungicides, and other chemicals the plants have been treated with. In some cases, you may be better off seeking smaller growers who can provide detailed information concerning the amounts and variety of chemicals the plants have been exposed to. Δ

A BHM Writer's Profile

Lucy Shober is 42 years old, has three children, and is currently living out her childhood fantasy—to live on a farm with lots of room for any animal that needs a place to stay, have roly-poly babies that play in the dirt, and have a husband who loves her anyway. Perhaps the foundations of this dream were laid during her childhood on Lookout Mountain, Tennessee, where she and her 11 brothers and sisters kept pet monkeys, goats, pigeons, and coons.

Shober majored in art in college, but worked in wildlife rehabilitation and environmental education. She began writing children's columns for local newspapers. Now she splits her time between working the farm, writing and illustrating for *Backwoods Home Magazine* and other publications, and part time work at a child care center, along side of her two-year-old, roly-poly, dirt player.

Shober and her husband John run The Flying Turtle Farm in Cloudland Georgia, where they raise and sell organic vegetables, minor breeds of poultry, and Irish Dexter cattle. She likes to wander around among cattle, sheep, pigs, goats, horses, all manner of poultry, cats, and a three-legged dog who can still hit 20 mph after being caught in the garbage.

FARM AND GARDEN

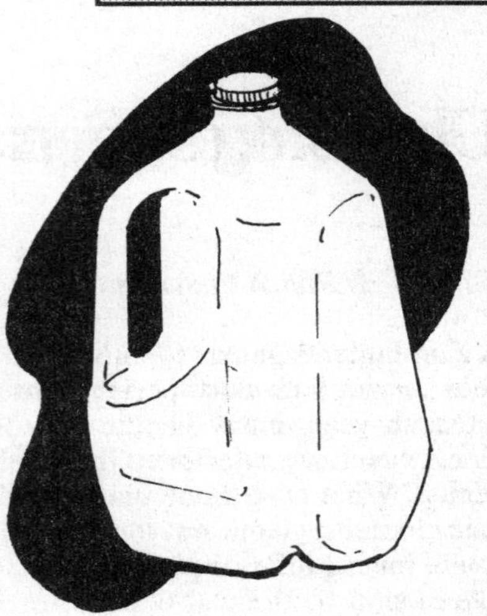

Keep those empty milk jugs

By Bruce Bair

One of the most useful tools I have found in my garden is the humble one-gallon plastic milk jug. They're free, and a family produces an almost endless supply of them. Not only do they provide cloches for my young plants, but also a no-cost drip irrigation system, and a system for starting many seedlings.

To make cloches, simply cut the bottoms off. I usually do so with an old pair of scissors, cutting along the line about an inch from the bottom of most jugs. I then place the jug over freshly planted tomatoes or peppers, which gives me an extra three weeks of growing season, and protection to temperatures as low as 26 degrees so far. To make a super cloche, fill six jugs with water and place them tightly around one with the bottom cut out. This will protect plants to temperatures at least as low as 20 degrees. Simply placing a water-filled jug on the north side of tender young plants when the weather man predicts a freeze provides an amazing amount of protection. I've had potatoes come through such events completely undamaged, while unprotected ones lost all foliage. And incidentally, the bottoms make ideal watering trays for small pots.

Want a fool-proof seed germination system for cucumbers, squash, pole beans, and other crops placed at wide spacings? After planting, fill a jug with water and poke a hole in it with a sewing needle. The tiny stream of water produced wets the ground in an almost perfectly circular spot, and it falls so gently, no crust is formed.

Now comes the best part: the irrigation system. When you plant a tomato or pepper, or a small tree, poke a hole about the size of a dime in the bottom of a jug, and plant it right beside the transplant. Use a posthole digger to plant jugs alongside plants started from seed.

It takes ten seconds to fill each jug from a water hose. Last season, I put out about 100 jugs, which required about a quarter of an hour to fill. When I did so, I checked each plant for insects and other problems. I filled the jugs as needed. In mid-summer, that meant once a day for tomatoes, and every other day for peppers. I found that on very hot days, tomatoes would require up to three gallons of water per plant, so I kept a few extra jugs around each. Placing the extra jugs at a distance from the plant helps develop the root system.

The number-one benefit of watering through milk jugs is water savings. My water bill was about the same during the gardening season as it was during the winter. Using the jugs, nothing gets water but the plant. No water reaches the surface, so weeds can't germinate. It's the same as an underground drip system...but it's free!

At the end of a season or two, the milk jugs become brittle, partially destroyed by sunlight. Only then do I throw them in the recycling bin. Often by then they are so brittle, a good stomping shatters them. Δ

A BHM Writer's Profile

Robert L. Williams is the author of 21 published books, more than 3,000 stories and articles, and 10 television scripts, in addition to his regular contributions to *Backwoods Home Magazine*.

Born in Hayesville, North Carolina in 1932, Williams has been a U.S. Army tank mechanic, professional baseball player, and educator. He devoted 30 years to teaching English and literature—first in high school, then on the college and university campus.

In 1989 Williams saw his pre-Civil War house demolished by a tornado. He and his wife Elizabeth and their son Robert III used a chain saw to build their new house from trees uprooted by the storm. The first story published about their house appeared in *Backwoods Home Magazine*, issue No. 16. Their story is the subject of a book called Starting Over, available from *BHM*.

FARM AND GARDEN

The incredible non-biodegradable food service pail

By Martin P. Waterman

Being an avid gardener and small-scale farmer, I am always on the lookout for anything that will help me to do my chores more effectively and efficiently. This means that anything that will help me to increase my productivity and save me extra work is very valuable indeed. This is especially true if there can be big savings in time. I have discovered a garden implement that, although simple, has so many uses that I am constantly surprising myself with its versatility. The implement is just a simple 5 gallon food service pail.

For those unfamiliar with the 5 gallon food service pail, this is a pail that is very commonly used in the food service industry. They are used to ship every kind of food from pickles to flour to shortening. Unfortunately, many of these restaurants send hundreds, even thousands of these pails to their local dumps. This is indeed a shame and a terrible waste. Many of these restaurants will give you some of these pails if you simply call them up or visit them and ask for them.

I have accumulated about 100 food service pails over the years just by asking for them at various restaurants. Before you think about offering money for them, be sure to call every restaurant in town. If they seem unwilling to give you any, ask them if they throw them out. Guilt is a good motivational tool in procuring these garden workhorses. Below, I have listed a dozen of the many uses for these pails.

1. In the early spring, I use the pails to cover tomato and pepper transplants. This allows me to put them outdoors up to a full month early or more. In addition, the pails are large enough so that they will often fit over a tomato or pepper plant in the autumn, to extend the season by at least another month when the frost season arrives. I am often asked how I can have tomatoes and peppers so early. I guess my secret is out now.

2. If you have certain favorite plants that you like to grow, yet have trouble containing them, these pails are very valuable for this use. Simply cut out the bottom of the pail or at least poke some large holes, then bury the pail. Then you can grow plants such as Jerusalem Artichokes, mints and other plants that have a tendency to take over the garden.

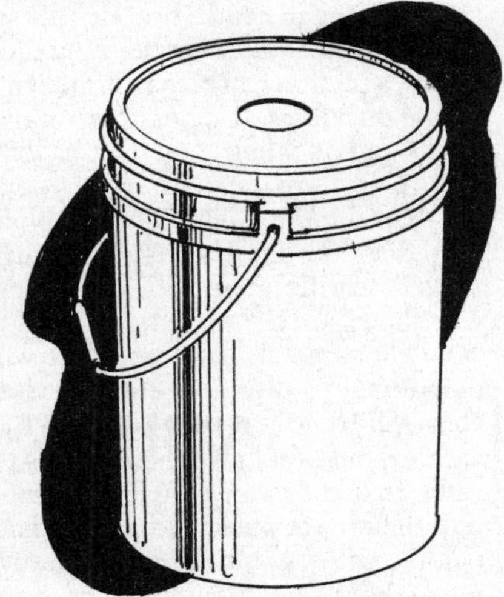

3. If you have a problem with moles or gophers going after certain plant roots, the pail can be buried and the targeted plants grown in them. Again, if the bottom of the pail is not removed, you can poke holes in it with a large spike and a hammer to permit drainage.

4. I often find myself transplanting young shrubs or trees from one area to another. I find that the pails offer an ideal temporary home for the plants. I have also grown certain plants in these containers for several years while I procrastinate or try to figure where I am going to plant them.

5. If you have difficult areas to water where the hose won't reach, these food service pails have strong handles and are ideal for hauling water. Several pails will fit neatly into your average wheel barrow. In addition, the pails are sturdy enough so that you could attach a spigot and a hose at the base of a pail for a slow drip irrigation system.

6. In the spring, I also like to use the pails to start new plants from cuttings or seeds. Pots are very expensive unless you are prepared to order them by the truckload. I start tomato transplants in the pails, and when there is a chance of frost I simply move the pail into the greenhouse or into the garage. This allows me to extend the season for fresh peppers, tomatoes and herbs by as much as two months or more. If you like container gardening, you will probably not be short of additional applications for the pails.

7. The pails are also excellent for harvesting fruit and vegetables. When harvest season begins, it is handy to have several pails with sturdy handles to bring in potatoes, apples, carrots, squash and beets. Another advantage to harvesting with the pails is that you can give them a good first cleaning by simply putting a hose in the pail. This will give the vegetables or fruit a good first wash before they hit the sink and are ready for processing or cooking.

8. I also find the pails excellent for weeding. They will hold a lot of weeds on the way to the compost bin. You will be pleased to know that the pails can also be used to compost small amounts of material.

9. The pails are excellent for food storage. I take pails with holes in the bottom and them hang them in the cellar. Because the handles are strong, I can hang them on a hook from the ceiling joists. This keeps them off the ground where there is dampness and permits good air circulation.

10. The food service pails are good for transporting almost anything. I use them to transport soil, mulch, compost, clippings, rocks, almost anything that needs to be moved around or to and from the garden.

11. I place at least a dozen of these pails full of water in my greenhouse during the spring and fall. During the day, the water absorbs heat which it will release at night when the temper-

atures drop. This is further frost protection for my plants. I often put the plant flats on top of the pails, which also elevates them away from the cool ground and gives some heat radiation from the water below.

12. For use as a pot, the food service pail can be sawed to any height. For those who are artistically inclined, the outsides can be painted. The food service pails are tough. I've left some of them outdoors for five winters now and they show no sign of being brittle or breaking down. Perhaps that can be another use: if they continue to hold up, they just may become family heirlooms.

These are but a few of my gardening uses for food service pails. They have literally hundreds of other uses from hauling feed to storing parts to taking stuff to the dump. Friends of mine use them to make sauerkraut and brew wine and beer. When I am gardening, I often use one as a chair. I have even used two of them to stand on in order to prune branches I can't reach or to wash windows. I am continually finding new uses for them. The pails have truly become as valuable as gold and are now so much a part of my gardening and other chores that I don't know what I would ever do without them. Δ

A bit about ducks

By Dynah Geissal

Ducks are fun to watch, easy to raise, and great eating, too. If you have been considering raising some of your own, you may be interested in what I have learned over the years.

Ducklings can be ordered from a hatchery or bought at the feed store. Ads can be found in the paper for grown ducks. If there is a creek running through your property, confine adult ducks for a couple of weeks or they may just drift on down the line.

Ducklings will need a brooder for six weeks. If you have a brooder house for chicks, a section can be partitioned off for the ducklings. It is possible to raise chicks and ducklings together, as long as the chicks are the same age or younger than the ducklings. The problem with that, though, is that ducklings make a terrific mess with the water. Wet chicks are the result.

Ducklings need a waterer that will allow them to dip their entire beaks. They will try to wet themselves in the waterer, but don't give them access to water that they can actually get into until they're six weeks old. If they had a mother, they could swim right away, but without one they could become chilled. Besides providing her warmth, she also provides oil from her feathers.

Feed duck and goose feed if possible. Chick starter will work if it is not medicated. Keep the temperature in the brooder at 90° for the first week. Lower by 5° each week. At three weeks they can run out into a pen if it is sunny and warm. From four to six weeks maintain 75°. At that time they can be given free range. Butcher at 10 weeks.

If you want to keep some ducks for breeders, choose your biggest ones. Keep only one drake for every six ducks. Too many drakes will really run your ducks ragged.

Ducks will lay way more eggs than they can hatch, so "hatching eggs" can be marked and the extras taken for your use or to sell. Ducks are usually excellent setters. They aren't distracted and they hardly ever give up too soon.

However, they are frequently terrible mothers. For this reason you may want to take some of the newly hatched ducklings and raise them yourself. If you let the duck keep a couple of them, she will show you whether she can be trusted with more the next time. Ducks are unable to fend off predators. If the ducklings are hatched before there is much ground cover in the spring, they are very vulnerable.

Although any hunter should be able to distinguish wild ducks from domestic ones—and although it is illegal to shoot ducks on the water—I lost every duck that swam a little too far downstream during hunting season until I bought white ducks. That solved the problem.

A setting hen will hatch ducklings for you if you wet and turn the eggs several times a day. She will mother the ducklings too, but she should be confined away from the other hens who would peck at the strange "chicks." When they're old enough to swim, she will be upset about it at first, but will come to accept the odd behavior of her "brood" and go about her business.

Ducks are very hardy, and they can live a very long time. I have two that are 12 years old. Ducks are not monogamous, but they often do have a special friend. The companions are almost always together and can be of the same sex or of the opposite sex. Except in this friendship situation, males do not participate in child raising.

Adult ducks can be maintained on pasture with free access to whole barley. Although ducks can live without water for swimming, fertility may be lowered. Certainly they are much happier with water.

Ducks are easy to pluck if they are old enough not to have many pinfeathers. Heat the water to 170° and scald for three minutes.

Ducks are really fun and productive. I hope you'll give raising them a try. Δ

How to build the fence you need

By Don Fallick

Rural fences have many purposes. They can be used to fence animals in or out, to cross-fence pasture, to define spaces, for ornamental purposes, or even to use up rocks in a field. Construction of fences depends on their purpose and on the materials available. Common materials are barbed wire, woven wire, welded wire, electric wire, rails, slabs, milled lumber, stone, and combinations.

Quartered sections of old telephone poles make adequate fence posts, though they have to be replaced after a few years. Just how long such posts will last depends mostly on how moist the ground is. In fairly dry soil, an untreated softwood post may last 3 to 5 years. The strongest wooden posts are triangular sections split from large-diameter trees. Osage orange, black locust, catalpa, northern white cedar, and red cedar will all last 20 years or more in average soil. In general, the softer the wood, the shorter the time it will last. Pressure treated wooden fence posts, available in lumber yards or from supply stores, cost about as much as metal posts, but don't last as long. They look nicer, though.

The overwhelming factor in deciding what type of stock fencing to build is the type of livestock to be fenced in or out. Cattle require very strong fences. Deer and goats need high fences, pigs and sheep, very tight ones. The old timer's adage about building all fences "horse high, bull strong, and pig tight" applies only if you don't know what you're going to be keeping behind it, or if you have an unlimited supply of labor and materials. It's far cheaper to build a four-foot-tall, four-strand, barbed wire fence for horses, a four-foot-high, three strand fence for cattle, a solid wood fence for goats, and a pen of welded "hog panels" for pigs, for example, than to try to build one fence that will do for all of them.

Country folk all have their own ideas about the best types of fencing to use for different purposes. Before believing anyone's ideas, check with your local Extension Service agent to see what's recommended in your area for your kind of livestock. I have my own ideas based on my own experience. Sometimes I disagree with the "experts."

Wire fences

If you have 15 or 20 acres of rich grass per cow, most any kind of fence will do for cattle, as long as it's stout and strong, four feet high, and visible to the cattle. Most ranchers who keep cattle have found that electric fences work best. Cattle quickly learn to respect the fence, especially if rags are tied to it every 10 feet so they can see it. Cattle don't have very good eyes, but after a few shocks they'll learn to avoid the area.

It's not a good idea to depend entirely on the live wire, though. If the juice is off for some reason, or a cow or bull breaks the wire, there will be **nothing** to restrain them from going wherever they please. It's amazing how much damage even one cow can do in a very short time. Three or four strands of barbed wire strung with the electric wire can prevent a lot of grief. Use wooden posts set eight feet apart, with the electric strand set about 3 1/2 feet high, between the top two strands of barbed wire.

Many ranchers build two fences – an electric fence set about two feet inside a stout barbed wire fence. There are different kinds of electric fences and fence chargers, even solar powered ones that require no electric hookup. "New Zealand" fence chargers seem to be getting more popular. They give a stronger shock than the traditional kind. Too strong, some folks believe. I've never heard of one killing a cow but I have seen one kill a mule deer. My personal feelings are that anything that can kill a large deer is not safe to have around dogs or children. Check with local experts to see what has worked in your area.

If you are not going to use electricity, you'll do your cows a favor by using nine-gauge woven wire fencing. Cows sometimes develop the habit of scratching themselves on fence posts, and barbed wire can tear up their udders. Barbed wire has even been known to entangle and kill horses. Woven fence with 12 inch wide rectangles is fine for cattle and horses but **not** for goats or sheep. They'll get their heads stuck in the fence. Sheep are so dumb they may not think of pulling their heads back out, and can starve to death! Goats will chew on the wire until it breaks and pokes holes in their cheeks. The experts recommend six inch mesh for goats and sheep, but I won't use any kind of wire fence for small stock.

Posts of cattle fence absolutely must be the strongest you can afford. If you are using metal posts, use only the heavy duty kind. They can be driven into most soils with a driver made by cutting the end off a truck drive shaft. The hollow shaft fits over the post, to be lifted up and slammed down repeatedly until the post is driven. Round wooden posts are not generally suitable for cattle. They are usually made from small diameter trees, which have a high percentage of the soft heartwood. Use splits or other hard posts.

Wire can be stretched tight with a ratchet fence stretcher, available at farm and ranch supply stores, or even by tying or chaining them to a tractor or pickup truck. The idea is to grab onto the wire several inches before it reaches the corner post, so there will be enough slack wire to wrap around the post and twist around the tightened wire. Then go back and staple the wire loosely at each intermediate post. This supports the wire, while allowing for future stretching and re-tightening.

Woven wire fences can be stretched the same way, but you may need to use a couple of fence stretchers together. One way is to wrap the end of the fence around a board or short post, then pull the post with fence stretchers, tractor, etc. After stapling the fence to the

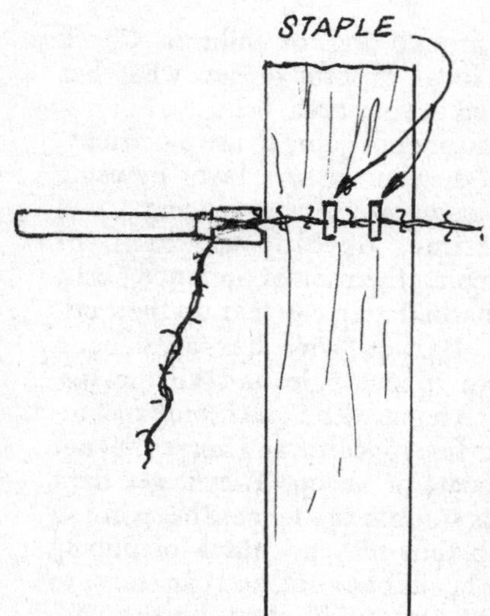

Use a claw hammer to stretch barb wire for stapling to a fence post.

corner post, the horizontal wires of the excess fence can be cut free with pliers, and wrapped around the post and themselves. Fence pliers are very handy for dealing with wire fencing, but very heavy wire cutters and a couple of claw hammers make an adequate substitute.

Wire fences for horses and goats need wooden rails at the top, or the animals will break them down and just walk over them. Any kind of wire fence needs special bracing at the corner posts. These should be the stoutest posts you can get.

Used railroad ties in good condition make good corner posts. They are treated against rot, and can be purchased for $5 to $10. Stout as they are, they still need bracing. One way to do this is to brace the corner post on the diagonal, with a short post notched into the top of the corner post. The other end of the brace can rest on a flat rock on the ground.

A variation of this which I think is stronger, is to place the first line post four to six feet away from the corner post and notch the bottom of the diagonal brace into the line post near the ground. A double strand of wire is then wrapped around the top of the line post and the bottom of the corner post. A stick is thrust between the two strong, twisted tight, and secured. Protect the tops of corner posts from rain and snow by tacking sheet metal flashing over the ends, or at least cut them at an angle, so water will run off.

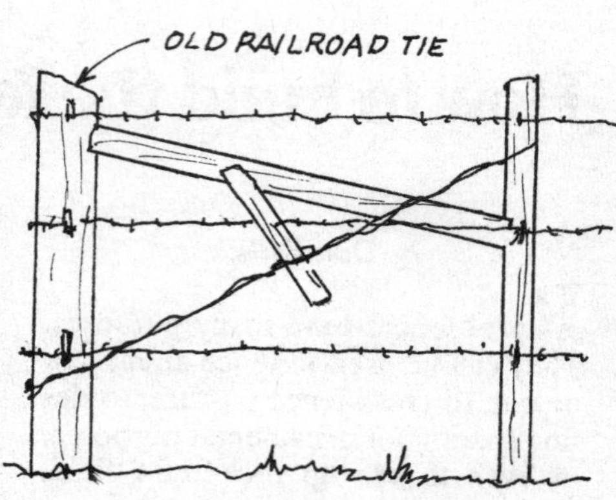

Properly braced corner post.

Since cattle like to rub against fence posts, the posts must be checked regularly and replaced when needed. A broken post can be jacked out of the

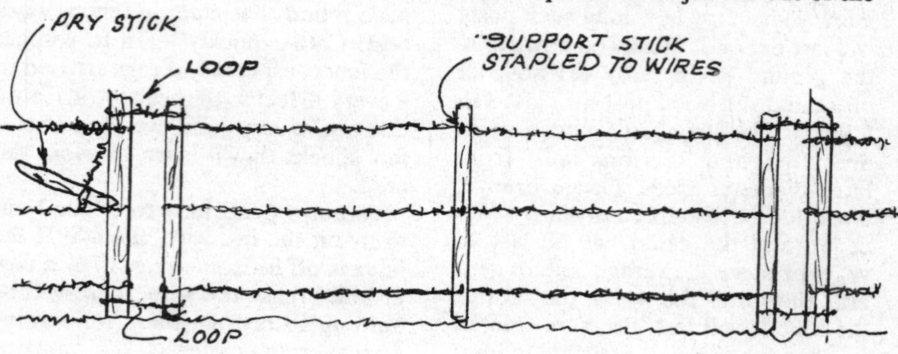

Barbed wire gate with movable support stick hanging by wire from gate post is used to stretch gate so wire loop can be slipped on and off. Wire loops are loosely stapled to gate post so they can move freely without slipping down.

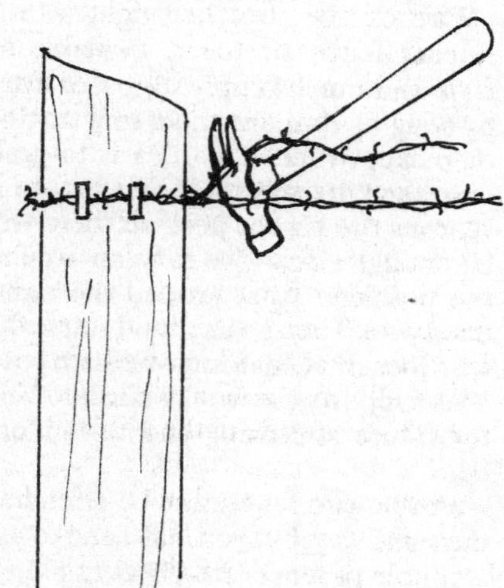

Using claw hammer to twist end of wire around the post and wire.

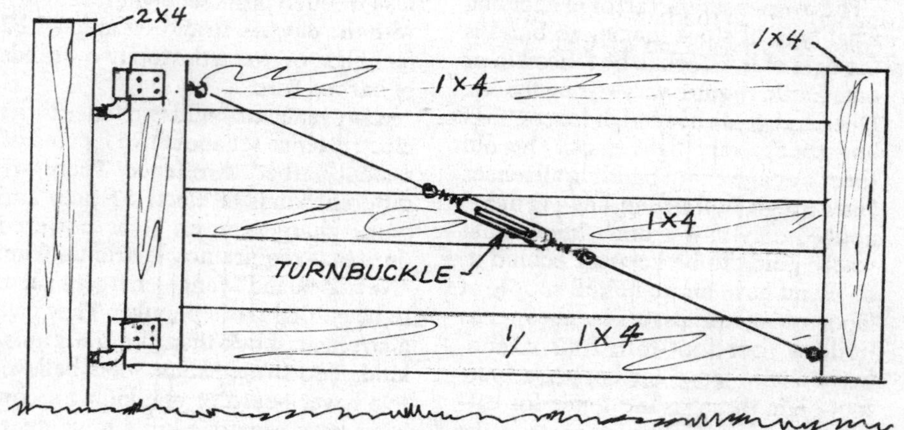

Wooden gate. Gate post is capped with sheet metal, aluminum flashing, or newspaper printing "plate."

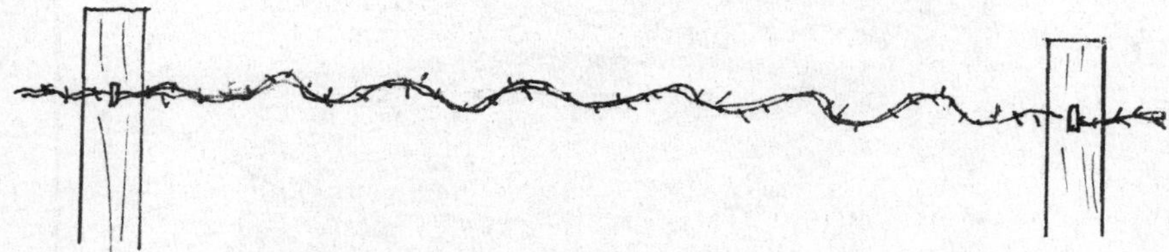

Barbed wire crimped into a zig-zag patterns with a claw hammer to temporarily tighten the wire.

ground by tying or chaining it to a horizontal post, which can then be used as a lever. Sagging wires can be tightened temporarily by crimping them into a zig-zag with the claws of a hammer. Two framing hammers can be used to permanently tighten a strand of barbed wire. Hook the claws of one hammer over the line at one of the barbs and use the handle as a lever to pull the wire tight, just like pulling a nail. While holding the wire tight with one hammer, use the other to pull the free end around the post and wrap it around the tightened strand.

The simplest gate for a wire fence is one made as a freestanding panel of wire, secured to the gateposts with removable loops of wire. The gate can be stretched to a reasonable degree by making it just a bit too short to reach. The bottom of the gate endpost can still be hooked in the bottom wire loop by leaning the endpost at an angle. The top of the endpost can be pried toward the gatepost with a short stick, attached to the gatepost with a short length of wire. Even the lightest wooden gate is too heavy for normal hinges. The best kind of hinges for wooden gates are the kind which have a single, metal loop on the gate and an L-shaped hinge pin that screws into the wooden gatepost. They'll last forever, and you can easily compensate for sagging gates by lifting the gate off and screwing the pins in or out. Metal gates are light and strong, last forever, are readily available in many sizes and cost plenty. You get what you pay for.

Wooden fences

Nothing beats wooden fences for keeping horses or goats. For horses, you need three or four 2 x 6 rails equally spaced, with the top of the top rail four to five feet high, depending on the height of the horse. The top rail should be capped by a 2 x 6 rail laid horizontally, for strength. The horses will lean on it. Posts should be 8-inch diameter, or 6 x 6 square stock, every 8 feet. If you're going to spend this kind of money on a wooden fence, it's silly not to buy pressure-treated posts and top rails. They'll have to weather for a year before you can paint them, though.

That's the ideal fence for horses, but few horse owners can afford that kind of expense. Peeled poles of three- to six-inch diameter will do fine for fence

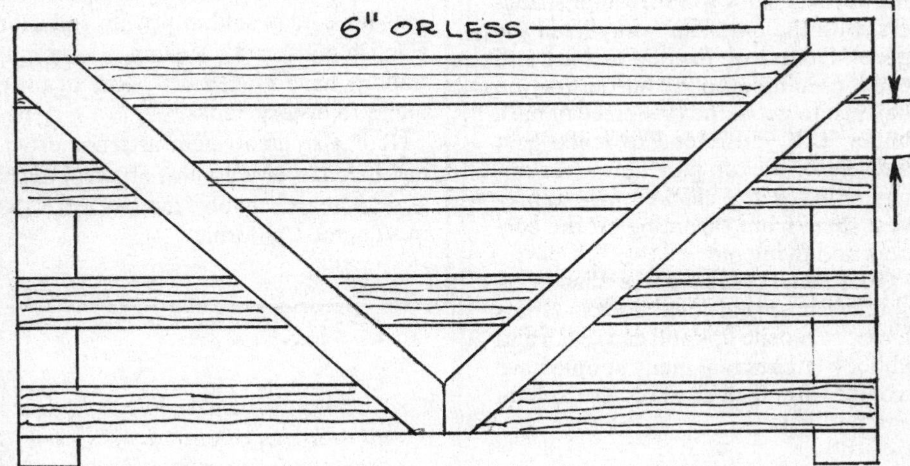

Portable sheep fold panel. Make at least six from rough cut or green 1 x 6. Wire or tie together to form pen. Move as needed. Keep nail points away from sheep.

rails, if they are inspected often. Lumber mills sometimes sell "slabs" (the outside portion of the tree, with the bark still on) really cheap. They look "rustic" and may be plenty strong. Watch for thin spots, though. Trees work really well as fence posts. Nail the rail to the inside of the post or tree with 20d nylon coated sinker nails.

Rail fences for goats don't work well, unless the rails are so close together that a goat just can't get through. Even then, the goats can see through, and may jump right over even an eight-foot fence. But goats (and deer) won't jump a fence they can't see through or

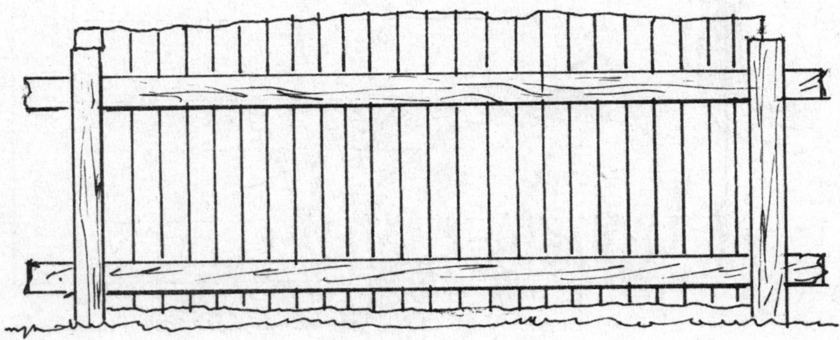

"Stockade fence" for goats. Bark side of slabs must face away from goats.

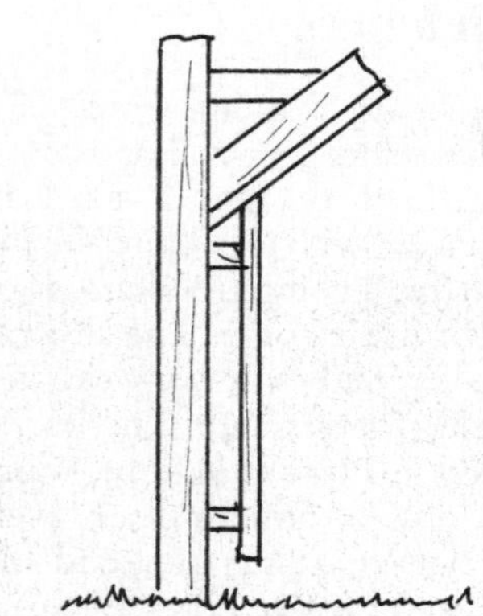

End view of goat kid fence showing inward-leaning top panel (plywood).

over. Many goat breeders have found a solid wood fence five feet tall keeps their goats at home. If you decide to build a solid goat fence from slabs, nail the vertical slabs to horizontal stringers, with the bark side **away from the goats**! Goats love to chew on bark and can loosen up even the hardest driven nail just to get at the tiny piece of bark under it. If you intend to fence goat kids, make the top panel inward-sloping, or make it of chicken wire to prevent them from caroming off the corners and flying out.

Goat fences need gates that hook shut with spring-lock hooks. Goats have prehensile lips and can reach and unhook latches that many people have trouble with. If all else fails, use a chain and padlock.

Stone walls

Much of rural New England is divided up into picturesque fields surrounded by stone walls. The walls, for the most part, began simply as something to do with the stones that constantly surface in the fields. The farmers had to haul them to the edge of the fields anyway, and building walls there served as a boundary and used up the rocks without having to cart them further. If you are cursed with such a field, you might adopt the same plan for dealing with the stones. I can't honestly recommend any other good reason for building stone fences. Δ

A BHM Artist's Profile

Don Childers is the artist who paints each of *BHM's* scenic covers. He also draws most of the illustrations between those covers. Until recently, he did all this on the side, while working full time drawing airplanes and missiles for a Defense Industry contractor. Now he has retired, to spend his time drawing for *BHM* and his own art projects.

Childers sold his first drawing while still in high school. Many of his paintings have been sold to private collectors around the country. Several hang in English pubs, and one is on exhibit in the Dijon Museum in France. His illustrations have graced the pages of everything from top secret defense documents to history books.

He is also an amateur astronomer who builds many of his own telescopes, and inventor of a graphic arts tool to sharpen X-acto knives. Childers studied at several art schools, and has a BA degree. He and his wife of 26 years live in Ventura, California.

Understanding the environmental movement

By John Silveira

Right around Christmas, Dave Duffy's friend, O.E. MacDougal stopped by my house. I hadn't been expecting him and I asked, "What's up, Mac?"

"Fossils."

"Fossils?"

"You said you wanted to go out and hunt for fossils some time."

"Today?" I asked.

"Sure."

"Where?"

We got into his car and he drove us up into the mountains above Ojai, California. I've lived in Ojai for seven years but I didn't know there were fossils up in the hills and we spent most of the day finding various specimens — lion's paws which are shellfish that resemble giant oysters, little corkscrew type shellfish Mac called turritella, mussels, and even one crab's claw.

In explaining why there were marine fossils in the mountains, Mac waved his arms around us and said, "All this was once under water. It was the bottom of a warm shallow coastal sea."

I'd seen the elevation signs along the road on the way up and I knew we were over a mile above sea level. "Where'd these mountains come from?"

"The collision between the edge of the Pacific plate, called the East Pacific Rise, and North American plate. The collision threw all this stuff up millions of years ago to create the mountains we're standing on now."

"A collision?"

"Of course the mountains didn't go up all at once. They took millions of years, too."

"Oh."

He knows quite a bit about the geology of this area and most of the day he gave me a running commentary explaining its features. When sunset was on us and the discomforting chill of the evening air outweighed the excitement of finding more fossils, he drove us back down Highway 33. The conversation was no longer about fossils or geology; it was about dinosaurs. Mac knows a great deal more about them than I would have thought.

He talked about the great fossil finds at Como Bluff in Wyoming, along the Two Medicine Formation in Montana, and the finds in Alberta, Canada. The conversation was all his. I just listened.

And suddenly we were in Ventura.

We stopped outside a small yellow house and he gave me a strange look. "I forgot to drop you off in Ojai," he said.

"I was wondering where we were going."

He looked up at the house as if making a decision. "You gotta be anywhere?"

I shook my head.

"Come on in," he said.

I'd never been to Mac's home before. In fact, I didn't even know where it was. He owns a little house in the hills above Ventura, and when we walked in my first impression was that I was in a rather comfortable and conventional home, not the kind I would have expected of a man who made his living playing poker.

As soon as we walked in, I heard a shower running somewhere deeper in the house. He listened a second, then said he'd be right back and left me alone in the living room.

I looked around at the shelves and tables. The books were about biology and evolution, genetics, mathematics, physics, computers, and chemistry. Not the kind of books one finds in most homes.

There were racks of CDs. Hundreds of them. I recognized some of the names: Beethoven, Mozart, Tchaikovsky, Brahms, etc. There were others I did not recognize: Barber, Britten, Telemann, and a whole slew of others. There were names I recognized only because I'd heard Mac talk about them: Ives, Mahler, and Shostakovich.

The CD player was on but played out. I pushed the button and it opened revealing a carousel full of disks. He actually listened to them.

I closed the carousel.

The furniture was arranged to face a corner where a TV should have been but there was none there.

When he came back, I asked, "Is your TV missing?"

He glanced toward the corner and vaguely grimaced, "I took it in to be fixed."

There were books on the table where a TV would have been. They looked comfortable there.

"How long ago did it conk out?"

"About a year ago."

"A year? When did you take it in?"

"The same day." He looked at me and shrugged. "I never went back for it."

I thought, "If you didn't want it, I'd have loved it." I didn't say so.

I returned to our earlier conversation. "Did the fossils we found today come from the time of the dinosaurs?"

"They're from something called the Vaqueros Formation," he said. "That formation is only about 13 to 16 million years old."

He looked at me and saw the puzzlement on my face.

"The last dinosaurs disappeared around 65 million years ago," he said.

"Oh." I was a little disappointed. It took a little glow off my finds. I had imagined them once being under the feet of the dinosaurs.

"What made the dinosaurs extinct?" I asked.

"No one really knows; climatic change, volcanoes, a nearby supernova, competition with mammals, some sort of plague. A whole bunch of theories have been advanced, but the front runner, today, is that it was either a huge asteroid or a comet colliding with the earth."

"I guess there's never been an extinction like that," I said.

"Actually, if you go on the basis of the percentage of life-forms that disappeared, something like 50 to 70 percent of all species disappeared at the end of the cretaceous period—that's when the dinosaurs disappeared—but about 96 percent of all species disappeared at the end of the permian period which occurred some 200 million years before that."

"96 percent? Geez, it sounds like life came dangerously close to being wiped out completely."

"It would seem that way."

A woman poked her head in through the doorway. Her hair was bundled up to dry in a towel. "Are you John?" she asked.

"Yes," I replied.

"A fellow named Dave Duffy called earlier this afternoon. He was looking for you or Mac. He wants you to call him."

I nodded and she disappeared.

"She's pretty," I said.

"Is she?" Mac asked.

"I heard that, Mac," she yelled from the back of the house.

He smiled.

"Are you writing something for the next issue?" he asked me.

"Dave asked me to do something about the environmental movement."

"What are you going to do?"

"I don't know. I can't think of anything new to write about it. I mean, you can hardly pick up a magazine without finding an environmental article. So, what's there for me to write about?"

He nodded and noticed the power light on the CD player was on. He opened the carousel and looked at what was in there. Then he changed the disks and hit the play button.

"Some of the stuff that's happening is real pathetic," I said referring to the environmental articles I'd been reading lately. "I read an article in the L.A. Times, just the other day. It said farmers and businessmen are secretly killing off endangered species or destroying their habitat to avoid costly government restrictions that the government is imposing to protect those species. It's disgusting."

"Why do you think they'd be doing that?"

"Doing what, killing them off and destroying habitat?"

He nodded.

"Because they're greedy."

He shrugged and sat down. "Have a seat," he said. "I have coffee brewing. Carol's going to make us sandwiches."

"Thank you," I said.

"Your welcome," Carol yelled.

"Well, why do you think they're doing it?" I asked.

He stared at me.

"Killing off endangered species," I said.

"Oh, that." He thought a minute then said, "Take it from a farm owner's point of view. Under current laws, farmers have lost access to their land because it has suddenly taken on some environmental aspect. It could be because his fields are suddenly inhabited by some endangered rodent, or because his property has been designated as wetlands. In the case of a farming community just north of here, in the Santa Ynez Valley, farmers, a few years ago, were prevented from taking flood control measures because environmentalists claimed that the creek beds they wanted to clear were nesting areas for an endangered bird. To the farmer, the question is, 'Why should I have to risk everything for a bird someone else wants to save?' Would the environmentalists insure him against loss? Of course not."

"The possible extinction of a species is more important than any farmer's business," I said.

"A person can even lose access to his house," he added, as if dismissing what I had said. "If he finds an endangered bat, toad, or rodent has taken up residence in his house, and if the environmentalists or the government find out, he could lose access and definitely lose sale value. What's he going to do?"

I didn't reply.

"I'll tell you what he's going to do. To protect his own interests, he's going to set traps."

"It seems pretty stupid to me," I said. "They're not seeing the big picture."

"To them, it is the big picture and it's very rational behavior."

"But they're breaking the law," I said knowing I'd hit on something good. "And the law's the law."

"Yes, they are breaking the law. It's ironic that we romanticize the women of Elizabethan England who were hung for stealing a loaf of bread to feed their starving children but we criminalize the man or woman who kills a rodent because, if it's found on his land, he could lose everything he's worked for all his life.

"I think what environmentalists have missed is what's really important to the average person – the welfare of their families and the security of their incomes. The survival of a frog means less to a man than the survival of his children and the welfare of his family."

"Still, the law's the law," I said. "Are you encouraging breaking laws?"

"Some laws should be broken."

"I can't believe my ears, Mac. Are we going to encourage people to take the law into their own hands? That's anarchy. We can't be making heroes out of lawbreakers."

He shook his head. "We do all the time. Washington, Jefferson, Madison. We'd still be an English colony if they hadn't broken various English laws. Susan B. Anthony, Rosa Parks, and Martin Luther King were all in violation of the law. We have a long and honorable history of law breakers we revere.

"On the other hand, we hung and imprisoned people in Germany after WW II for following so-called 'legal' orders. We said it is a criminal offense to follow laws we know are wrong and the Nazis were, in effect, guilty of adhering to laws we said were wrong and we said they should have opposed them. The law itself is not always right. And keep in mind, Christ himself was legally executed for being in violation of the law."

"I never thought of it that way," I said, "but remember, he was in violation of Roman law. He was in accordance with a higher law."

"That obviously wasn't the Romans's point of view."

"So, are you telling me you advocate the breaking of environmental laws?"

"I think what I'm really telling you, John, is that the way we're doing things now, people are going to do just that and feel justified. Consider how someone feels when he breaks a law. Do you think bank robbers feel the same moral imperative to rob banks that a woman who stole bread to feed her children felt? Or that the poacher and the businessman who is trying to save his business – as well as the jobs of his employees – feel the same way?"

"Well, why do we have these laws then?"

"The environmental movement has captured much of the legal and cultural machinery in this country and they're forcing their point of view without either validating it scientifically or weighing it against other people's needs."

"What do you mean the cultural machinery?"

"Look at their influence on Hollywood. The latest villains in movies and television episodes are hulking armed thugs who are dumping toxic waste. Does anyone really believe that businessmen are going around like armed drug dealers to dump waste?

"The environmental movement has captured much of the legal and cultural machinery in this country and they're forcing their point of view without either validating it scientifically or weighing it against other people's needs."

"And look at the legal machinery. What happens to politicians who disagree with the movement? When John Sununu was Bush's Chief of Staff he became one of the movements favorite targets simply because he pointed out, again and again, that the claims environmentalists made about global warming, holes in the ozone, and such had little or no scientific basis. And his crime was not that he was against the environment but that he was pointing out that, though the environmental movement cloaked itself in scientific clothes, they had very little scientific basis. He said, in effect, the emperor wasn't wearing any clothes. And, to make matters worse from the environmentalists point of view, he said we couldn't make public policy on speculation. He said billions of your tax dollars would be wasted just to make the environmentalist feel good about themselves.

"He became their public enemy number one for these attitudes. But I don't believe he was against the environment any more than I believe that the politicians who suck up to every environmental speculation are helping the environment. That's like saying if you're a television evangelist, it means you're religious."

"But," I countered, "consider the consequences. Let's say we are creating global warming and that it might lead to an environmental disaster. Wouldn't it seem prudent to err on the side of safety?"

He looked at me funny. "That kind of reasoning is the criteria for proving anything you want."

"What do you mean?"

"I can use the same argument to 'prove' just the opposite. For instance, what if someone says that by creating all these controls to prevent global warming we might create unemployment, economic hardships, slower economic growth in the third world that leads to higher infant mortality, less medical care, violent wars and terrorism that could result in World War III, etc., then shouldn't we err on the side of safety and **not** invoke these restrictions and laws?

"Sununu was against using that kind of argument – one that employs logic that can prove both sides of an argument – to make public policy. He wanted facts and he pointed out that, though environmentalism is being dressed in science, there isn't even a consensus in the scientific community as to whether many of the so-called problems are real."

"What about the greenhouse effect?" I asked.

"The greenhouse effect – global warming. It's a perfect example. Sununu said there's no evidence that it's taking place. In fact, evidence supporting exactly the opposite exists but it is now politically incorrect to talk about it."

"What do you mean?"

"Civilization has more to fear from the next ice age than global warming, though you'd never know it from the way we act."

"Ice age? Mac, are you losing it?"

He smiled.

"We not only don't know if global warming is taking place, but there's a lot of evidence that points to a future ice age that's coming."

"What evidence is that?"

"Since the dawn of civilization, the world's been getting cooler. We know that growing seasons in Roman times were longer than they are now. We know that when the Norse discovered Greenland, it had verdant tracts along its coast. There's also a good deal of historical evidence to show that the world has been getting colder in just the last three hundred years.

Like everything else in life, environmental issues are a series of tradeoffs. Not every species is going to survive, whether we want them to or not. It's never happened in all the earth's history and I'm not sure mankind has the means to do it now. You've got to realize, more than 99 percent of all species that ever existed are now extinct.

"And we know that there have been at least eight ice ages in the last 750,000 years. Some have lasted 100,000 years."

"Eight?"

He nodded.

"And you think another one is coming?"

"I'd say it's inevitable."

"When will it get here?"

He shrugged.

"But, once it hits, we'll feel its full effects in less than a lifetime. The geological evidence is that England went from a climate much like the one it has today to being buried under hundreds of feet of ice in less than 20 years."

"That fast?"

He nodded again.

"What would cause another ice age?"

"We don't know what caused any of them but they were probably all caused by the same thing—variations in the sun's energy output, variations in the earth's orbit, volcanoes, changes in the greenhouse gasses, or maybe a combination of these things. We just don't know which one or what combination.

"We do know from the fossil record, however, that the earth has at times been very tropical over much of its surface while at other times, there's been widespread glaciation. We also know that in the last several million years that the earth has usually been a lot colder than it is nowadays."

"This is all news to me. How come no one talks about an ice age, now?"

"They used to talk about it a lot."

"Are you saying this as an indirect way of saying the environmental movement is a fad?"

"It has a lot of the features of one."

"What would happen if another ice age arrived?" I asked.

"Civilization would be shaken to the core. And I think it's conservative to say that 90 percent of the world's population would die out in the first two decades."

"Starvation, war, and what have you?"

"Yeah. Growing seasons would be seriously altered; there'd be shortages of resources; millions, if not billions, of people would try to migrate in the direction of the equator."

"Well, maybe you're right," I said. "But let's stick with what they're talking about today. What do you think the environmentalists should be doing about the environmental movement?"

"I would think, if they really wanted to ensure the survival of endangered species, they would press for programs that made it rewarding for farmers and businessmen to encourage their survival. Think of how many aluminum cans would still be on the side of the road if, instead of making it rewarding to recycle them, we just made it a felony to throw them out our car windows."

"Okay," I said. "But tell me, do you think we can save all endangered species?"

"Frankly, I don't think we can. Like everything else in life, environmental issues are a series of tradeoffs. Not every species is going to survive, whether we want them to or not. It's never happened in all the earth's history and I'm not sure mankind has the means to do it now. You've got to realize, more than 99 percent of all species that ever existed are now extinct.

"But the first thing we have to do is decide what we want and what we can't afford."

"We could lose everything that way," I said.

He shook his head. "I don't think so. I think we may find out we'll keep an awful lot. More than Nature's ever been able to. In fact, with a rational approach, we may be able to keep almost every species we've got left in this country. But as far as the rest of the world goes, we're going to find out it's a negotiable item.

"Something else I would have thought the environmentalists would do is achieve a consensus of what the problems are, what kind of environment we should have, and how to go about getting it instead of using a cowboy mentality of 'good guy vs. bad guy' to force their ideas down our throats."

"A consensus by whom?"

"Government, science, and business."

"But you can't bring business into the loop," I said. "They **are** the polluters."

"If you really feel that way, it would seem even more imperative to bring them in," he said.

"Let me take a John Sununu tack, then," I said. "Just give me one instance where business really helped to clean up the environment."

I would have sworn this would stump him, but he said, "The Japanese realized they had a pollution problem several years ago, and they called together representatives of the government, science, **and** business. Then they spent 10 years analyzing the problem. What they were trying to acheive was a consensus as to not only what the environmental problems are but how to correct them. By using this approach, they're now on the road to cleaning up their environment.

"Okay, Mac, then you admit there **are** environmental problems in this country?"

"Of course," he said. "Consider where you came from, Boston. Dave Duffy told me that as little as 20 years ago, the two of you used to catch fish in Boston Harbor and eat them. No one would do that today unless they had a death wish.

"However, what are they doing in Boston to correct the problem? Talking, creating patronage jobs, and collecting higher taxes. But they're not getting people together and they're not working together. "But what would have happened if Boston were a Japanese city? Community leaders, business leaders, and scientists would have sat down together, analyzed the problem with the Harbor, determined what the sources of pollution are, then determined how to clean it up without creating unemployment.

"But we're not going to see this approach in this country. And that's because the environmentalists have concluded that they alone can determine what the problems are and what the solutions should be. They've enlisted sympathetic politicians and scientists and they excoriate anyone in politics or science who disagrees with them or even suggests they may be wrong. More importantly, businessmen and industrial leaders – the people creating most of the wealth and jobs in this country – are excluded because they've been hailed as the enemy."

He lifted his cup and looked into it. "More coffee?" he asked.

I nodded and he went back to the kitchen.

He returned with the coffee pot and filled both of our cups.

"How much coffee do you drink, anyway?" I asked.

"I stop just short of drowning myself."

As he put the pot on a coaster on the coffee table between us and sat down again, Carol came out of the kitchen with a tray of sandwiches and placed them beside the pot. Then she left without a word.

"Who's she?" I asked.

"I don't know," he said.

"I heard that, Mac," she called from the other room.

He smiled. "Gotta keep them on their toes," he said. "Now, where were we?"

"Well, I was going to say, you make it sound like environmentalism should be a series of tradeoffs and it can't be," I said.

"Let's assume it isn't, and most environmentalists would agree with you. But by putting farmers, loggers, and businessmen in a situation where it's to their advantage to get rid of the critters or lose their businesses, the environmentalists have created tradeoffs these farmers and businessmen act on, and the rest of us, including the environmentalists, have very little say in how these tradeoffs are played out. If they did what the Japanese have done, and made environmentalism a public issue, and ensured compensation to those who are put at risk for public policy, they'd also ensure that the public would have a say in how endangered species are treated. As it is, they leave it all in the hands of the farmer setting the traps, a farmer who all too often feels he has an economic stake in seeing a species exterminated – at least on his own land.

"As a consequence, environmentalists have unwittingly become active participants in the extinction of many species because, for them, environmentalism is not a negotiable issue."

"If you're right about what you've been saying," I said, "I think it's fair to say the environmentalists are just misguided."

"I'm not willing to be that charitable," he said. "Those in the environmental movement appear to have the same means to their ends that social and religious reformers have always had; they are willing to sacrifice the lives and property of others for their ideals. Notice that environmentalists are rarely looking for encouraging laws. They want **tough** laws. We are conducting political environmentalism in this country the same way the communists and socialists used to practice economics in Eastern Europe: They didn't encourage the citizens of their respective countries to comply; they created a series of economic crimes. Here, the environmentalists have created environmental crimes."

"Why do you think the environmentalists don't think this way?" I asked.

He shrugged. "Because for them the environmentalism issue is not really a scientific issue, it's a political issue. For the leaders of the movement, environmentalism is not about the environment anymore than communism is about the worker or the Inquisition was about religion; it's about politics and power. And for the man on the street, the environmental movement is the survivalist movement of the '90s. It's the same siege mentality.

I laughed. I looked at the window. It was dark outside.

"Well, I've got to say, I never realized there could be another side to the environmental arguments. But I've got to be getting home."

Mac stood up. "I'm taking John home."

"Okay," the woman called back.

We got in his car and Mac drove me back to Ojai.

"Have a good weekend," he said when he dropped me off.

"I won't. I still have to find something to write about on the environment."

"Do something on the movement itself and what it means to the people who are alienated by it." Δ

Lumber regulations that purport to protect consumers really protect big business and keep lumber prices high

By Martin Harris

American consumers and builders ae being bilked out of billions of dollars every year by government regulations that purport to protect the interests of consumers but actually protect the profits of big business.

If you've ever wondered what Washington lobbyists do to earn their tasselled loafers and super-thin attache cases, the lumber industry and their political lobbyists provide a good example. The lobbyists remain invisible – that's part of their job – but their clients are not, and neither is the effect of their lobbying on the lumber prices the average American pays. What they've done, in the corridors of power, is to make sure that the lumber used to build housing and small business for middle America must come, not from local sawmills, but from the giants of the forest-products industry.

In Vermont, for example, a state with a substantial lumbering industry, any wood-frame building financed in whole or in part with federal funds is prohibited from using the production of local sawmills in its construction. Many of Vermont's banks use the same prohibition on construction they finance. The result: lumber for the vast majority of wood-frame construction in the heavily-timbered Green Mountain State comes by rail or truck from the Far West or the Deep South, from the mills of such corporate giants as Weyerhauser, Potlatch Forest Industries, and Louisiana-Pacific.

Another result: Building owners pay about 50% more for the imported product than they would have paid for the local product. That's a mathematical fact which can be verified by simply comparing prices at local building-supply retailers, which stock corporate lumber, with prices at local sawmills.

What isn't mathematical fact, but simply the professional judgment of those in the construction business, is that native lumber is every bit as good quality-wise, as the corporate product and that frequently it's a lot better.

Why, then, (and how) is its use prohibited? Here's where the carefully-orchestrated tap dance begins. The why of this situation is easy enough to understand: corporate lobbyists earned their fees making sure that the rules of federal agencies in the construction-finance business require builders to purchase lumber only from the mills of those forest-products corporations who employed the lobbyists. The how is a little more complex.

. . . corporate lobbyists earn their fees by making sure federal rules require builders to purchase lumber only from the forest-products corporations who employed the lobbyists.

Clearly it wouldn't do to simply prohibit use of the output of local mills; that might stir up the locals. And, in fact, if you ask at the state offices of such agencies as Farmers' Home Administration, the headquarters of the State Housing Authority, or similar agencies, you'll get a vehement denial that any such boycott of local product exists. Don't believe it.

The boycott is hidden. No outright prohibition on native lumber, but rather a fine-print requirement that all lumber used be visually inspected or stress-graded in a certified grading process and each piece then grade-stamped before shipment. Only four mills in Vermont are large enough to afford this expensive process, and only a relative handful throughout the entire Northeast, according to the records of NELMA, the Northeast Lumber Manufacturers' Association. The vast majority of New England production goes to builders who are quite capable of knowing a poor 2 x 4 when they see one, buy their lumber from local mills, and don't need a fine-print federal regulation to protect them from themselves.

The same situation prevails throughout the country: wherever there's a local lumber industry, local builders or do-it-yourselfers have a choice, whether they realize it or not, to buy corporate or buy local. The scales are tilted to favor corporate, but no matter; once you know how the prohibition is set up, you can avoid it if you wish.

That choice won't be made any easier by those who make a dollar selling or using corporate lumber: they have a long list of supposed short-comings of the native, locally-produced, product. Usually, it's something like this: .

1. Native lumber is lower in quality than corporate. Maybe so, in some isolated cases; but local mills have repeat customers to please, and they can't afford to try to peddle junk. Warped and twisted sticks, knots and checks, waney edges and end splits are even more likely to be found, in my own personal experience, wearing a corporate label in the local mill yard where they wear no label at all. In any case, visual grading of lumber isn't exactly rocket science: if you see a defective piece, just reject it from your purchase.

2. Native lumber is full-dimension. In other words, a 2 x 4 is a full 2 x 4, not 1 5/8 by 3 5/8. Why getting a heavier and stronger stick should be a shortcoming is hard to understand, but the industry argument focuses on the idea that some other building products, like door and window frames, are sized to the reduced dimension of "dressed" lumber. This argument conveniently overlooks the fact that, with

the arrival of a range of wall thicknesses for energy conservation reasons, millwork manufacturers have responded by including jamb extensions, split, and adjustable jambs as part of their product line.

3. Native lumber is not kiln-dried. Usually so, sometimes we refer to the greener pieces as pond-dried. Corporate lumber is kiln-dried, but it shrinks after construction too. All "natural" lumber shrinks after construction; that's because the standard kiln-drying, or air-drying process doesn't take out enough moisture before construction. But it doesn't matter. I've built with both corporate and native lumber, and I've seen no worse shrinkage problems with one than with the other. I've seen no evidence to support the somewhat hysterical claim that sheetrock will practically fall off the walls and ceilings if you dare to apply it to green native lumber framing.

4. Native lumber is rough on your delicate hands. True. There are very few local mills which will mill all four sides of a stick and round the edges for you. If you prize the surface smoothness of framing lumber,then the corporate product is for you.

5. Native lumber is weaker. This one is outright nonsense. No engineering degree is needed to understand that a full-dimension stick has more strength-creating material where it's needed—out at the edges—than a thinner dressed stick. Of course, if you compare, say, native hemlock of a given size to imported douglas fir, then the native stick is weaker; but folks who make this comparison know well enough that all species of wood have different inherent strengths, and that stick-for-stick comparisons should be made only with samples of the same species.

6. Native lumber is dimensionally inaccurate. Unfortunately, this one is sometimes true. It's not as true as it was years ago, when it seemed as though a lot more operators were out there trying to get another year or two out of worn-out equipment; but there are still a very few local mills who put out uneven product. Again, it doesn't take a rocket scientist to measure a sample of product to see whether dimensional accuracy prevails. Most mill operators today know that lumber used for housing and light commercial has to be sawn right.

7. Native lumber is more subject to rot and decay. Sure, if you're comparing native pine to, say, corporate yellow pine, or untreated wood to preservative-pressure-treated wood. But it's not true if you compare, fairly, within species and within treatment guidelines. All modern lumber is more subject to rot and decay than the product our grandparents used; that's because virtually all lumber today is third or fourth growth, frequently plantation raised and thinned for maximum rapid growth. These conditions create coarse grain spacing, a condition much more conducive to rot than the tight-grained nature of wood from mature, virtually zero-growth, climax forests.

8. Native lumber is less profitable. I'm uneasy about raising this point, because it raises the kickback issue, one that we would rather didn't exist within the construction industry. Nevertheless, here it is. Fact: native lumber costs less per board-foot than corporate; that's true here in New England and probably everywhere else. Fact: Builders and contractors who are repeat customers of building-supply yards, customarily get a discount (unavailable to one time retail buyers) on lumber purchase. Fact: a high percentage of residential and light commercial construction is priced time-and-materials, where the builder has the opportunity to bill the owner for lumber at list price while he actually buys it at discount. Given these facts, of course some folks in the construction industry claim that native lumber is less profitable. It is: for them. It's not, for the home- or business-owner.

What all of the above sugars down to, I think, is a ringing endorsement for the use of native lumber in those parts of the country where it's available and for those projects where it's legal. How easy will it be to go this route if you agree with my assessment. Let's look at the obstacles.

1. Your lender doesn't like it. If your lender is Federal, you have two choices: corporate lumber or a different lender. If your lender is a private bank using federal construction rules, you have a fighting chance of talking him out of this particular guideline.

2. Your local building inspector doesn't like it. Building inspectors are not entitled to make up their own rules; if he prohibits native lumber, ask to see where that prohibition is printed in the rules he is obliged to enforce. Be aware that if you win on this one, he may retaliate by giving you a hard time on everything else—bureaucratic minds work that way.

3. Your builder doesn't like it. Get a new builder. Maybe you can talk him into it; more than one builder here in Vermont, who at first resisted doing native-lumber construction for me now shows photographs of that solid-looking framing as part of his promotion brochure.

4. Some of your sub-contractors don't like it. This is most likely to happen with gypsum board (sheetrock) specialists, who charge surprisingly low per-square-foot fees to ply their trade, and won't take a job they suspect to be overly time-consuming because of inaccurate framing, not plumb, square, and true.

Your framing, if it's done right, ought to meet those criteria. If it's not done right (something that can happen with corporate lumber, too) you'll probably end up doing your own sheetrock.

I couldn't end this little report without pointing out one specialized area in which native lumber really shines. I'm not thinking here about cost savings, or keeping money in the local community, or extra framing sturdiness or any of those other advantages: I am thinking about renovation work on old structures, mostly built back before the turn of the century, back when dimension lumber was not yet standardized at two inches thick and multiples of two inches deep. If you're dealing with an old structure, filled with 3 x 5 studs and 2 1/2 x 9 rafters, forget about matching them with corporate lumber. Just go to your local sawmill and tell the owner-sawyer what you want. A few clicks on his machinery, and he'll cut out whatever you need.

(Martin Harris is a Vermont architect, co-founder of "The New England Builder," and author of numerous home building articles.)

Δ

Visiting Laura

By Fran Jablway

Once upon a time, a little girl was born in Western Wisconsin. As she grew up, her family moved by wagon to Kansas, Minnesota, Iowa, and Dakota Territory. When she reached the later years of her life, she realized that she and her family had participated in an exciting time in U.S. history known as the Westward Expansion, and she wanted to preserve her memories for children. With that thought in mind, Laura Ingalls Wilder began writing her popular "Little House" books.

Laura Ingalls Wilder

Her family was one of the first to settle in DeSmet, South Dakota. She taught school and started a family in this little town. Just as Laura wanted to preserve her memories of early DeSmet, DeSmet wanted to preserve its memories of her. The Laura Ingalls Wilder Memorial Society was started in 1957 to pay tribute to one of the founding settlers.

This little town on the prairie has seen few changes since Laura left for Missouri. Driving into town on U.S. 14, one change is obvious: the stretch going through town has been designated the Laura Ingalls Wilder Historical Highway. The original homestead site, located about a mile and a half east from the downtown area, is now the location of the pageant celebrating Laura's works every summer.

The surveyor's house

Going north on Calumet Avenue, signs point the way to the Surveyor's House, the start of the tour. At the reception area and gift shop, visitors receive a map of DeSmet with sites that are mentioned in the books marked. Some, such as Loftus' store, are still in operation. Others have gone the way of the buffalo.

Who would make the pilgrimage to this little place 40 miles west of Brookings and with what looks like a view of the end of the world? According to Susan Behm, a tour guide, visitors come from as far away as Japan. "We print a list in the paper every week," she says. Most of the visitors on my tour hadn't come quite that far—just from Illinois, Kansas, and Minnesota, according to the plates on the parked cars. Fans of Laura's writings of all ages and occupations (writers, teachers, and one engineer who's also the indulgent husband of a certain freelancer) came to pay homage.

In On the Shores of Silver Lake, Laura described the house as a "mansion." Actually, the front room is no more than 15 feet by 15 feet. While the house primarily provided the railroad surveyors with a place to stay and to store their tools, it also served as a way station for newcomers in the process of staking their claims. Up to 15 people slept on the floor at one time. The railroad gave Pa Ingalls use of the house in return for keeping an eye on the equipment.

Later settlers moved the Surveyor's House to town from Silver Lake, which lies northwest of town. The L.I.W.M.S. acquired the building in the late sixties and renovated it, using as many of the Ingalls' possessions as possible and filling in with other pe-

The gift shop

riod pieces. At the back of the house is a model of the Brewster school where Laura taught the first of her three terms.

A few blocks away lies the house that Pa built after Laura's marriage. Where possible, the house has been preserved and where not, restored. Downstairs in the parlor are some of the Ingalls' furnishings, supplemented by replicas. One room holds glass cases filled with drafts of Laura's works and some of her possessions.

Ma and Mary lived in the house until their deaths, making a living by taking in boarders. Now the extra bedrooms upstairs hold the books, typewriter, and desk of Laura's daughter, Rose Wilder Lane. Rose herself was a novelist and war correspondent. At the time of her death in the 1960s, she was preparing to leave for Saigon.

Like Rose, many little girls and a lot of little boys have looked to her mother as a role model. When I started school in 1967, the great majority of children's books had either male or passive female main characters. I read the "Little House" books cover to cover and back again, mentally roaming the vast prairies with the Ingalls family, relieved that there might be more options for girls than nurse, flight attendant, or mommy.

While walking the grounds of the Surveyors' House last summer, tears of gratitude for her work, and the way it opened up possibilities, prickled behind my eyes. In one brief moment, the efforts of her family and all the others to open the country became tangible. For about 15 minutes, I said very little as I waited for the lump in my throat to clear.

Talking with some of the younger visitors, I learned that Laura's books are as popular today as they were when originally published almost 50 years ago, and not just for the first-hand accounts of life in pioneer days. Her books gently illustrate the timeless values of self-sufficiency, independence, family, and simplicity, concepts that structured society then and could be used to restructure it today.

The "Laura Festival" is held annually the last weekend in June and the first two weekends in July. Guided tours are available daily from 9 to 5 from June 1st to September 15th. The rest of the year, tours are by appointment. Also, books by and about Laura and her daughter Rose are available by mail order from the gift shop. For more information, send a self-addressed, stamped envelope to Laura Ingalls Wilder Memorial Society, DeSmet, SD 57231, or call (605) 854-3383. Δ

The Pa & Ma Ingalls home & museum

Stocks — as important as herbs and spices

By Richard Blunt

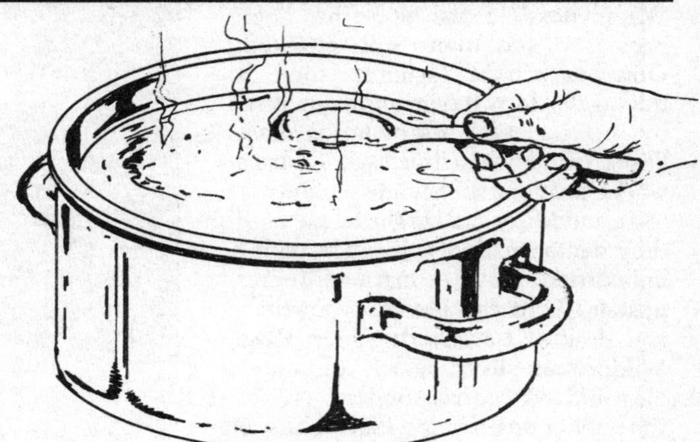

Last night, as I sat here in my kitchen doodling, my mind wandered back to the late '60s when I worked at the Smith House Restaurant in Cambridge, Massachusetts, under the tutelage of an irascible old chef named Sully. One of my most vivid memories of working there is the constant presence of two large stainless steel stock pots that sat on the back of the stove. They went on the heat every morning at about 6 and stayed there, at a barely perceptible simmer, until about 3 p.m. when they were removed, strained, and immediately refrigerated.

In one pot was a basic brown stock and in the other was a chicken stock. Many of the dishes that hit the tables in the dining room had their start in those stock pots. The stocks were used by all of the cooks in the restaurant to make soups, sauces, stews, and a wide variety of entrees. Knowing how to make and use the stocks was a requirement to get a cook's job at the Smith House.

Sully, in one of his softer moods, once told me, "A well made stock is as much of a flavoring agent as good herbs and spices." He leaned toward me and, in an avuncular voice, said, "Richard, the flavor a stock imparts to your cooking has no substitute." I was surprised by his tone because most of the time Sully sounded like Hitler when he was telling his generals how he wanted Norway invaded.

Now, once you've tasted a soup, sauce, stew, or an entree with a well made fresh stock, you'll see that Sully, in stressing the importance of a stock, was right.

The good news is: there's nothing complicated or elaborate about the preparation of a good homemade stock. Yet, it can become a cook's personal signature on a food item—that magic ingredient that will seem to be missing when someone else tries to duplicate one of your recipes. Think back to the times you've tried to duplicate a dish you first had at a restaurant, a neighbor's dinner party, or at your elderly Aunt Clara's house, and, when you tasted your own concoction, your first reaction was disappointment because it was not as good. Something was missing.

Very often, the cook's secret was a stock that was developed and personalized over a period of years. I'm going to give you two master stocks you can use just as is or, by varying the amount and variety of herbs, spices, vegetables, and meat, you can change the flavor the stocks to suit the tastes of you, your family, and your friends. As I said in earlier columns, I'm not going to just give you a bunch of recipes; I'm going to show you how to cook.

But before we get to the recipes, here are a few rules that apply to the preparation of all stocks. Most of them help to maintain the stock's clarity: The clearer the stock, the wider the variety of uses it will have, whereas stocks that are not clear have limited uses. For example, stews, sauces, and many entrees don't require clarity so a clear or a cloudy stock will serve for any of them, but many soups, like French onion, and all consommes, require clear stocks. Also, just because a cloudy stock looks like it has more in it, it actually doesn't have any more flavor.

Now, the rules:

- 1. Avoid aluminum pots. Clarity is the issue and aluminum pots tend to make stocks cloudier.
- 2. Do not allow a stock to boil for an extended period. Extended boiling will produce a very cloudy end product. The rule is a slow simmer. (The difference between a boil and a simmer is the amount of agitation at the surface of the liquid. As soon as agitation begins, you have a boil. Minimize this agitation and you have a simmer.)
- 3. As the stock first heats up, an albuminous grey mass will appear on top. Skim this greyish mass off as it appears with a wooden spoon, removing as little of the liquid with it as possible, or better yet, use one of the fine mesh ladles that are used for this purpose in Chinese cooking.
- 4. Trim any excess fat from the meat and bones. Fat is of no value in a stock.
- 5. Do not use any salt. As the volume of the stock is reduced during the slow simmering period, the salt is concentrated and no one has yet figured out a good way to get the salt out once too much is in. Save salting for when you're going to use the stock in a recipe.
- 6. When the stock is done, strain it through a fine mesh sieve lined with three layers of cheesecloth. I suggest ladling it into the sieve rather than pouring it because ladling seems to ensure the clarity.
- 7. Last but not least, cool the strained stock as quickly as possible. This will prevent souring and maintain the fresh taste.

Basic brown stock

Ingredients:

5 lbs. raw beef bones, it helps if some of them are meaty, and neck, shin, shank, leg, or knuckle bones all work well
5 qts. cold water
2 large carrots, chopped
3 ribs of celery, chopped (If you decide to use the leaves, avoid the green ones, because they turn bitter with long cooking, but the yellow leaves in the middle are fine.)
1 medium onion, chopped
1 cup fresh tomato, chopped
1 small white turnip, chopped
6 whole black pepper corns
4 sprigs fresh parsley
1 clove unpeeled fresh garlic
1 tsp. dried leaf thyme
1 bay leaf (If you can find imported bay, from the Mediterranean, use it instead of the usual California bay. California bay has a strong flavor that doesn't flavor stocks as well as the milder imported bay.)
6 whole cloves

Preparation:

1. Preheat your oven to 450 degrees.
2. Mix the chopped onions, carrots and celery and place the beef bones along with one cup of this chopped vegetable mixture in a roasting pan. Arrange the bones and vegetables into a single layer. Place this in the upper part of the oven to brown. Turn the bones and vegetables a few times to ensure even browning. Browning should take 30 to 40 minutes.
3. Transfer the browned bones and vegetables to your stock pot and discard all the extracted fat.
4. Add the water, along with the remaining chopped vegetable mixture and the other ingredients, to the stock pot. Transfer about three cups of the water to the roasting pan, after you have discarded the fat, and bring this to a slow simmer on top of the stove. While this is simmering, scrape the bottom of the roasting pan with a wooden spoon until all the brown glaze on the bottom has dissolved into the water and transfer this liquid to the stock pot.
5. Bring the stock to a boil over high heat then immediately reduce it to a slow simmer. Remember to remove the grey mass as it appears.
6. Place a lid on the stock pot so that it covers about 3/4 of the pot. Continue the slow simmer for four to five hours.
7. Remove the stock pot from the heat and taste it. If it isn't flavorful enough, return it to a simmer and reduce it some more. When it tastes good strain, and cool it.

Variations:

This and the next recipe are good recipes for a basic brown stock and a basic chicken stock. There are, however, an infinite number of variations on them. I'm going to give you seven that will give you an idea of how to go about changing these stocks so you can find one you can call your own.

1. To sweeten the stock, add more carrots.
2. You can give the stock a sharper, and some would say, more acidic, flavor, by increasing the tomatoes.
3. To give the stock a saltier taste, increase the celery.
4. Add two or three dried allspice (pimento) berries to enhance the flavor of the cloves.
5. A warm, pungent flavor can be created by the addition of a few dried juniper berries which can be found in a well stocked grocery or specialty food store.
6. To get a stronger herb flavor, increase the amount of thyme—but be careful not to add much as thyme can take over the flavor and ruin the stock.
7. The addition of 1/4 tsp. or less of savory will add a clean, fresh, balsamy flavor to the stock.

I could go on endlessly, but we have limited space in this column. A rule of thumb, however, is that you may decide on stronger stocks when using stronger tasting meats, like venison and lamb, and lighter flavored or sweeter stocks for meats like veal and chicken.

The fresh stock can be kept in the refrigerator for up to three days or it can be frozen for several weeks. I use self-sealing plastic storage bags for freezing. They work great without leaking. After the stock gets cold in the refrigerator for a day, it becomes slightly gelled and this makes it easy to scoop into the plastic bags for freezing.

Also, after you have refrigerated the stock, all the fat that has risen to the top congeals and is easy to remove before freezing or using.

Making the chicken stock is almost the same as making the brown stock. But, since chicken stock is almost always a light stock, the browning process in the oven is eliminated. However, once again, the recipe is not engraved in stone and you can vary it to suit your taste and make it your own. Use the tips I gave you for varying the brown stock to do that.

After you have an educated idea of how you want your stocks to taste, and know what to add or take away to achieve that taste, there is a world of culinary delight in your future. I, myself, while experimenting with Oriental food, created a number of special chicken stocks from the basic chicken stock that follows. They include recipes for Corn Soup (Shantung), Garlic Pork with Vegetables (Szechuan), and Chicken with Walnuts (Canton) and they are just a few of the delights that make use of these special stocks. You will find more on your own.

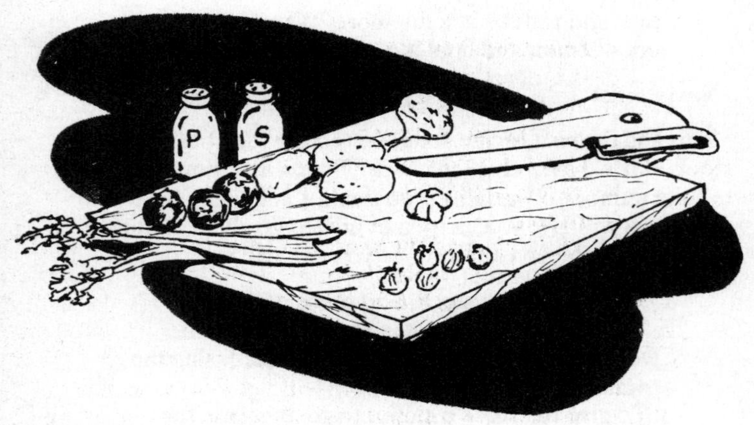

Chicken stock

Ingredients:

5 lbs. chicken backs, necks, and wings. (I don't recommend using livers and gizzards in your stock because I personally don't like the flavor they impart.)
4 qts. cold water
Extra water for par boiling
1 medium onion, chopped
3 ribs of celery (remember what I said about the leaves)
1 medium carrot, chopped
1/2 tsp. dried leaf thyme
1 bay leaf (imported, if possible)

Preparation:

1. It doesn't matter where you buy your chicken, but raw poultry can have a number of residues that adversely affect the flavor of a stock. Par boiling will eliminate them. To do this, place the chicken in your stock pot and add just enough water to cover it. Bring the water to a boil over high heat, then reduce the heat to a simmer for two minutes. Next, remove the pot from the heat and discard the water.
2. Now, add the four quarts of water listed in the recipe, along with the rest of the ingredients. Bring this to a boil over high heat then reduce the heat until you have a slow simmer.
3. Do not cover the pot. Simmer for three hours, or until the liquid is reduced to half its original volume.

This stock can be varied the same way you vary the brown stock and if Duffy and Silveira convince me it's still worthwhile doing the cookbook, I'll go deeper into the variations there.

But for now, there you have it, two balanced stocks with plenty of flavor with several suggestions on how to vary them. And here are a couple of recipes that you can try them out with.

Blunt's beef stew

Ingredients:

2 1/2 lbs. lean beef diced into 1 1/2" cubes (I use chuck, top round, or bottom round as these cuts don't fall apart during cooking.)
1/4 (more or less) cooking oil
2 1/2 qts. fresh brown stock
1 1/2 cups peeled and seeded fresh plum tomatoes
2 ribs of celery, diced 3/4"
1 small (6 to 8 oz.) white or yellow turnip, diced 3/4"
12 to 16 fresh white pearl onions, peeled
3 medium red skin potatoes, unpeeled and diced 3/4"
1 clove fresh garlic, peeled and minced
1/4 tsp. dried thyme leaves
1/4 tsp. dried basil leaves
Salt and fresh ground black pepper to taste

Preparation:

1. Dry the diced beef with paper towels. Wet meat will not brown properly.
2. Heat the oil in your stew pot or a large frying pan. Add the meat in small batches and saute it until it is browned. (I'm going to give you a quick lesson in browning: You brown the meat in small batches because trying to brown it all at once results in leeching the liquid from the meat, and you wind up parboiling and drying it out instead of searing it. Browning in small batches allows the meat to retain more of its juices and more of its flavors. This is why you should also pat it dry before browning it.) If the oil becomes low during browning, add more. A few minutes before the last batch is ready, add the minced garlic.
3. If you did your browning in a frying pan, you should now transfer the meat to your stew pot, then use a cup of brown stock to deglaze the frying pan.
4. When the browned meat is in the stew pot, add the stock (including the stock used to deglaze the frying pan, if you used one), and tomatoes. Bring this to a boil, reduce the heat and simmer it until the meat shows signs of tenderness. This usually takes about one hour. While simmering, have the lid about 3/4 of the way covering the pot.
5. When the meat starts getting tender, remove the lid from the pot and add all the carrots, celery, and turnips. Continue simmering until the celery shows signs of tenderness.
6. Add the onion and potatoes and simmer until they are tender.
7. Add salt and fresh ground black pepper to taste.

I don't thicken this stew because I feel that the vegetables thicken it enough. Should you want an even thinner stew, just add more stock. But, if you like a thicker stew, combine 1/4 cup of cold stock with 1 tbsp. of flour and stir it into a smooth paste. Gently stir this paste, a little at a time, into the stew, until the desired thickness is achieved. After adding the paste, allow the stew to cook for at least five more minutes, before serving. This cooks the flour and prevents a starchy taste.

Here is another interesting recipe. The original recipe, from which I adapted it, is from South Africa, and is meant to be eaten as a stew. I, however, have served it as a meat casserole, with rice or noodles and, once, with mashed potatoes. As either a stew or a casserole I think you'll enjoy it, especially if you like venison. You also get a chance to use both stocks in this recipe. However, if you use only one, make it the brown stock and use two cups instead of 1 1/2. I call this recipe:

Stewed venison with mushrooms and braised garlic

Ingredients:

- 2 lbs. venison (chuck or rump); trim off and discard all the excess fat and dice the meat into 1 1/2" cubes
- 1/4 cup (or more) peanut oil (The amount is explained in step 2 of the preparation.)
- 1 cup onions, diced to 1/2"
- 1 cup celery, diced to 1/2"
- 1 clove garlic, peeled and minced (this is the first garlic in the recipe)
- 1 1/2 cups fresh brown stock
- 1/2 cup fresh chicken stock
- 3/4 cup white zinfandel or other young red wine
- 1 1/2 tbsp. soft butter or margarine
- 2 tbsp. flour
- 1 tbsp. lemon juice (no seeds)
- 4 whole cloves
- 1 medium bay leaf (imported, if possible)
- 1/2 tsp. dried thyme leaf
- 1/8 tsp. cayenne pepper (1/4 tsp. if you like spice)
- 1/2 tsp. salt

Braised vegetable ingredients:

- 6 large garlic cloves, peeled
- 12 whole medium mushrooms
- 1 tbsp. butter or margarine

Preparation:

1. Dry the venison with paper towels.
2. Heat the oil in a frying pan then brown the venison, a few pieces at a time, turning the piece to brown on all sides without burning. As each batch of meat finishes browning, place it into a four or five quart oven casserole.
3. When all the meat is browned, discard all but two tbsp. of the oil. Return this oil to the pan at medium heat. Add the onions, celery, and minced garlic. Saute this until the onions and celery are soft.
4. Add both stocks and the wine and bring these liquids to a simmer while scraping the bottom of the pan to free the brown glaze that was left by sauteing the venison.
5. Mix the flour with the softened butter (or margarine) to form a smooth paste without lumps. Blend this with the simmering stock mixture, stirring constantly to prevent lumping. Continue simmering until the mixture starts to thicken.
6. Add the cloves, the bay leaf, thyme, cayenne, salt, and lemon juice. Continue simmering for five more minutes.
7. Combine this sauce you have now made with the meat in the casserole. Cover it and place it in a 325 degree oven and bake it for two hours or until the venison is tender.
8. While the stew is baking, you have plenty of time to decide whether you want braised mushrooms and garlic. If so—
9. Place six to eight large peeled whole garlic cloves in a small pan with one tbsp. of melted butter or margarine. Cover and cook over a low heat for five minutes then add the mushrooms and cook for another five minutes. Ten minutes before removing your stew from the oven for service, add the garlic, mushrooms, and liquid to the stew and blend.

Depending on your preference, it is also possible to adjust the thickness of this stew/casserole. Just follow the same procedure described in the beef stew recipe. If thickening, remember to return the casserole to the oven for five more minutes of baking to prevent a starchy taste.

This can now be served with noodles, rice, or even as I once did, with mashed potatoes. Δ

Just for kids – Have a chat with your cat

By Lucy Shober

"Nnnnnnn...RREEEEE-OOOO OWWWWW?!! Rrrrr" Loosely translate these words from feline (cat talk) into the English language, and you will probably come up with the following sentence: "Uh-oh...WOULD YOU PLEASE GET YOUR BIG FOOT OFF MY TAIL?!! (Sometimes I'd like to scratch some sense into you.)"

"Fggll, YAT-YAT-YAT-YAT-YAT-?" when translated from canine (dog) into human, means "C'mon fellas, the mailman has arrived...shall we taste his socks again?"

These animal words are easy for us to understand, but would you like to know more about what your pet friends are trying to tell you and each other? To do this, simply think about the world in the way they would. Sometimes if a dog wants you to know that he respects you as his friend and boss, he will lie down and show you the most tender part of his body (his tummy) while wagging his tail and sporting a wide grin. The reason? When a mother dog washes her puppies, she rolls them over and licks their stomachs clean. A puppy respects its mama and shows the same respect for you by presenting that tender area for you to pat. You probably know that cats and dogs raise the fur on their backs when they feel threatened, so as to seem larger than they really are, and that they mark their territories when leaving their scent (by using the bathroom) on all of its borders.

Has your pet cat ever driven you crazy by rubbing her cheek and back along your leg for what seems like hours at a time? Aside from telling you that she really likes you, she is also saying to other cats, "Keep away, this is my person! Can't you sniff my scent all over this leg?"

In the barnyard, too, little conversations are always going on. A sharp "BOK! BOK! BOK!" from a rooster, along with some fancy foot scratching will bring a screaming hoard of chickens to his side. "Look girls!" he says, "I've found all of these grub worms here, and I'll scratch them up for you!"

When he would like a little romance with a new member of the flock, the

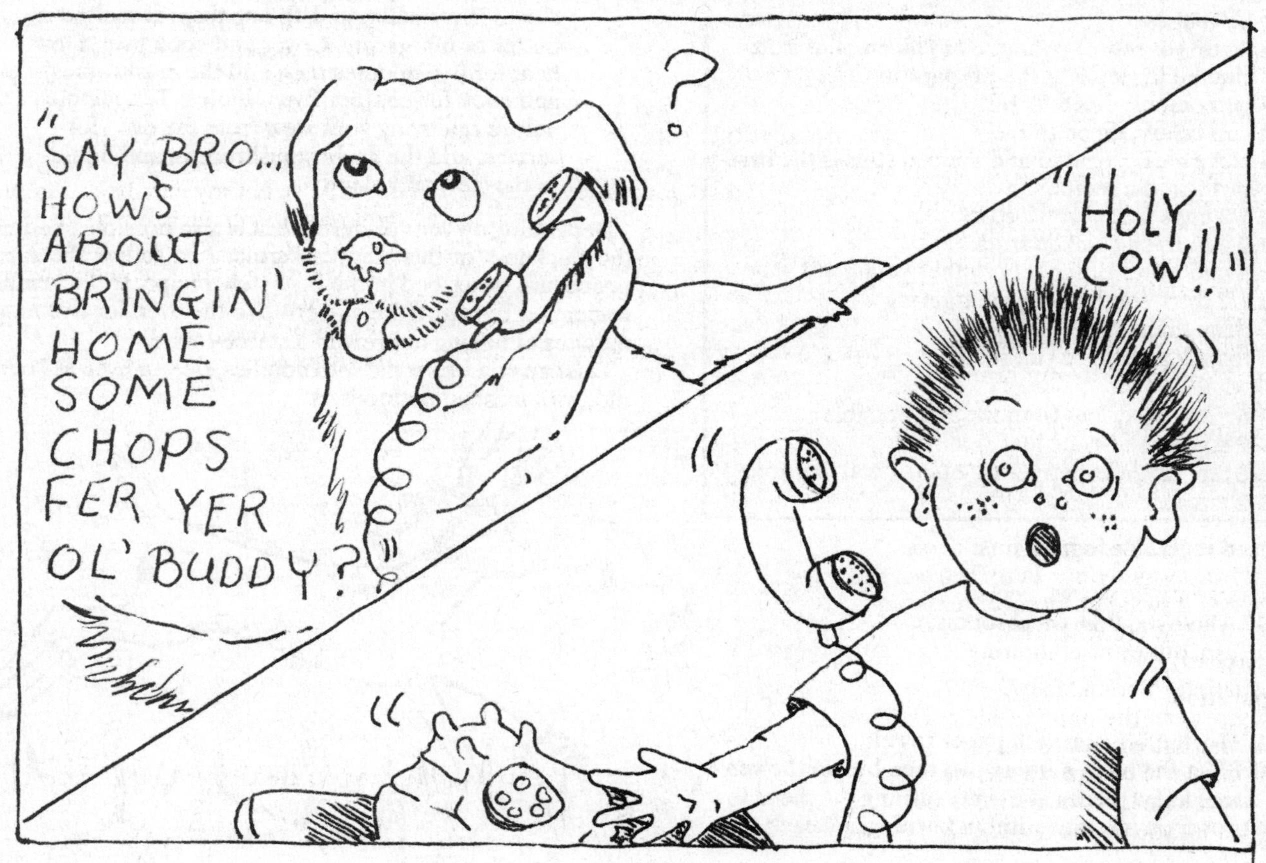

rooster will dance in a circle around her, hopping on one leg, and scratching the ground with the other...his wing stretched out waving to the hen of his dreams. "Oh, Lawrence...I'd sooner be fried," she might reply by stalking away with a few sharp cackles.

There is no sound in nature more heartwarming than hearing a mother duck drop that raucous "WAK WAK WAK!" in exchange for a gentle, high pitched "weeble weeble weeble" as she coaxes her hatchlings to climb out of their shells and greet the world. "Come on now, I'll be here for you," she seems to say.

It's probably not very wise for you to try and have a close conversation with your neighbor's Angus bull, but you can observe and understand the lan-

guage he uses for the rest of the herd. Remember these bovine language tips the next time you find yourself at a loss for words while facing the neighborhood steam-snorting hulk.

Bull talk: "MMMMMMMMMmmmmmm mmm....MMMMMMmmmmmm," (spoken softly).

Translation: "I know I'm big, but I could really like you, you know."

Bull: Rests his head over the back of a nearby cow.

Translation: "This is my wife, I'm totally blown away by her curly brown forelocks. I'll swat her flies forever."

Bull: "UH-WHEEEEEEE!" (very high-pitched).

Translation: "Scram...fast."

Bull: Presents the nape of his neck for another bull or cow to lick.

Translation: "You can out-wit me, or you look a whole lot stronger that I am, so I'll just let you be the boss...O.K?"

The more you're around animals, the more you'll see the world from their point of view, and therefore understand their languages. As you begin to understand your pet, try to communicate with it on its own terms. It's fun, and it just might make for a wonderful relationship!

True/False questions

A. When you feel threatened by an animal, just stare directly into its eyes to scare it away.

B. To greet a horse, gently breathe into its nostrils.

C. Baby chicks can have nice conversations with their mothers even before they've hatched from the egg.

D. Some types of wild dogs gnaw on tree limbs and rocks to leave their scent, and mark territories.

True/False answers

A. FALSE!! Don't do that! To stare directly into an animal's eyes is sometimes interpreted as a threat. Instead of staring, avert your gaze, and slowly back away while using soft reassuring words to calm the frightened creature.

B. TRUE. That's horse talk for "Let's trade breath, I'd like to get to know you better."

C. TRUE. In this way, a baby gets to know its mother's reassuring voice even before it hatches. This ensures that after hatching, the babies don't run to the wrong cluck!

D. FALSE. Who thought that one up?

Match-up game

Match the animal language below with the pictures on this page.

A. "I see something very interesting....Hmmm...maybe if I just tiptoe....mmmmmmm, looks tasty......"

B. "I'm not gonna try to do anything here....I've got my ears back... In case you want to bite them, they will be out of the way. I know that you are stronger than I am......couldn't we just be friends?"

C. "Boy, have you done it now! I'm furious!" Δ

SOLAR POWER

Idaho utility entry into PV field may be a sign of things to come

By Larry Elliott

For more than 10 years, most of us involved in the alternative energy industry, and people who have remained informed about this emerging technology, have seen steady progress, especially in regard to photovoltaics and their use in residential electrical systems. We have gone from a simple backwoods cabin system consisting of a few crude lights and perhaps a 12-volt TV, to systems that duplicate electrical power supplied by utilities. It seems only natural then that the utilities themselves would begin taking a serious look at this new technology.

Idaho Power and Light, an electric utility based in Boise, Idaho, has gone from taking a look to actually getting directly involved in this emerging new industry. In September of 1992 this utility received approval from the Idaho PUC to set into motion an innovative three year pilot program that most likely is the first in the nation. The utility will supply photovoltaic equipment to those customers who are not now served by Idaho Power's utility grid due to the high cost of extending electric lines into these remote locations. These systems will be complete packages, designed, assembled, installed, and maintained by utility personnel. The systems will not be sold outright, but will be leased to the customer and paid for on a monthly basis, similar to customers served by the utility power grid.

According to information supplied by the utility, a typical small residential system is projected to cost $10,000 and have a monthly charge of $160. In addition to the monthly charge, an initial payment equal to five percent of the total installed cost of the photovoltaic system will be required prior to installation. Initially this program will be limited to six different applications. These six will be residential electric service, stock watering, sign lighting, general lighting, communication sites and cathodic protection, all of which are limited to remote sites. The utility has limited the three-year program to an investment of five million dollars and individual PV systems to less than $50,000.

Even though the program is less than six months old, it has already had a positive impact. A rancher in Jordan Valley, Oregon, who is located in their service district, has installed a 2800-peak-watt-water pumping system for stock watering and irrigation. The system has been in operation for several months now and delivers over 10,000 gallons per day. Total installed cost was $42,000. In addition, an Idaho developer is building a residential subdivision with no utility connection, thanks to this program.

Although a round of applause is in order for the progressive and long term responsible thinking of this utility, not everyone sees this program as a positive step forward. Many dealers and installers of photovoltaic equipment expressed anger and frustration over the utility's entry into the market. According to complaints filed with the Idaho PUC, one dealer expressed concern that Idaho Power is overstepping its "authority as a public utility" by selling power to non-grid customers. Similar and more harsh comments have come from others who are involved in the solar electric business.

It is this author's opinion that it is far too early to either heap accolades on the utility or retreat in fear that the small fry are going to be consumed by utility sharks. I do think that those of us who have been in this business for some time and have a good working knowledge of the industry as a whole, can make some well founded assumptions about the positive or negative impact of this program.

One positive outcome of this program will be the change in perception the public will have in regard to photovoltaic technology. No longer will solar cells be seen as simply power supplies for calculators and automotive battery maintainers. Utilities are in the business of supplying reliable and cost-effective electrical power, and the public perception in most cases agrees with that. Would they be expected to do less when supplying photovoltaic-produced electricity?

Also, anyone who has ever installed and used a stand-alone PV system has become far too aware of how grossly inefficient most every electrical appliance sold in this country really is. There are many pitfalls and obstacles the utility will be forced to overcome as they proceed with this program and their personnel become more familiar with the technology. If this and other utilities expect to make these programs a long-term commitment, they will have to serve as a positive influence on manufacturers to make efficiency a priority and not an afterthought.

Many people have complained that lending institutions have been quite reluctant to loan money for alternative energy equipment, demand instead that loan-seekers have their homes be connected to the grid. Idaho Power's program could serve as an example of how much faith they have in the technology and is an acknowledgment that not all homes must be utility-connected to be safe and functional. Also, if Idaho Power or others of their size and wealth decide to sell this equipment directly, banks and other lending institutions may be forced to finance these systems.

I'm sure other utilities are going to watch closely the progress or lack thereof that Idaho Power makes in the next three years. If they succeed as they plan, other utilities will begin to look more favorably toward PV technology and may look into setting up their own programs, perhaps in the area of grid/PV intertie systems for businesses and homes.

I think that any negative impact the program will have will be short-lived and limited. Because of overhead, regulation by PUCs, and the lack of uniformity of system design, individuals and well trained and innovative dealers will be able to compete quite well. Unless the program evolves into one where equipment is sold outright and perhaps financed by the utility at less than market interest rates, it will have a limited impact on the market.

Most people who opt to live in remote areas do so as much for the freedom from outside interference as they do for peace and quiet. Very few people will be willing to pay a heavy lease payment for several years, knowing they have no equity in the equipment. I am reminded of the comments made by one of my latest customers when we finally threw the breakers and solar electric power began flowing into the system. He looked out the window and in a loud voice said "Good God Almighty, I'm free at last!" At first I thought he might just be quoting Martin Luther King, but then I realized he meant he was free from the utility bills he had been paying when living in the city.

For some people there is almost a patriotic or pioneer feeling that comes from this lack of utility umbilical cord. Even so, the lack of individual maintenance will appeal to some, and so will the lack of heavy up-front costs. Still, I feel that if we are all put on a level playing field, with no special-interest leverage, we can all benefit from the activity generated by Idaho Power's program.

For more information, contact Idaho Power Company at P.O. Box 70, Boise, Idaho 83707 or at (208) 853-8526.

(Larry Elliott is the owner/operator of Solar Tech of Bend, OR. (503) 388-2053.) Δ

A BHM Writer's Profile

Jennifer Stein Barker grew up in Vermont, where healthy cooking has always been popular. As an adult living in the Cascade Mountains of Washington, she owned and cooked at Garrison Springs Lodge, a backcountry ski lodge. As her reputation for good food grew, she began writing for *Backwoods Home Magazine* in 1989.

When she met her husband Lance and moved to Oregon, Barker began working on a cookbook (soon to be available through *Backwoods Home Magazine*) and teaching whole foods cooking courses at the Blue Mountain Community College extension in John Day, Oregon.

The Barkers live on 40 acres in the pine woods of Bear Valley, Oregon, with three cats and a three-acre garden. She was last seen digging beets, turnips, and kohlrabi out from under the snow.

How to buy your first dairy goat

By Anita Evangelista

Fresh milk is one of the gentle joys of living away from the city—fresh milk, butter, buttermilk, cream, ice cream, cottage cheese, and a fancy assortment of aged cheeses. All of these delights come to us courtesy of our dairy animals, such as cows, sheep, and goats.

Goats, being the "poor man's cow," lend themselves particularly well to a small homestead. A dairy goat and her offspring can live comfortably in a 20' x 20' corral, with only a small shed for shelter from the elements. Or she can be allowed the run of a pasture or field, so she does most of her own food-collecting.

Best of all, a dairy goat's food requirements are a mere fraction of a cow's: four pounds (a flake or two) of good quality mixed hay or access to pasture, and two to three pounds of mixed grain (corn, oats, alfalfa pellets, molasses), will keep her cranking out around a gallon of milk every day for about ten months of the year. If you bought your hay and grain in the Ozarks, you'd spend around forty-five cents a day to collect that gallon of milk—less if you grow your own foodstuffs, such as pumpkin or corn. Try to find that kind of a bargain at the supermarket!

Okay, you're convinced. Now, how do you find that special dairy goat? Number one and most important is to **avoid** shopping at a goat auction! While many animals sold at auction are quite fine looking, you just plain don't know enough about the animal's history, milking habits, health, or care to risk buying one of these cheap wonders.

Instead, check your local farm classifieds for people selling goats from their own places. This gives you an opportunity to look over the premises and see the condition of the other animals. If the place is dirty (beyond ordinary farm clutter), horribly disorganized, has sick livestock—you get the idea—get out of there! You don't need to buy into someone else's problem.

There is a mild controversy over whether the new goat-keeper should start with adult animals or goat "kids." Some folks believe that if you start with kids, you can accustom them to your farm routines and handling before they become milkers—and kids are generally cheaper than adults. My preference, having started that way myself, is to buy an adult along with her kids. Here's my reasoning: the adult goat has proven that she can successfully produce offspring, she's already milking so you can take a look at the condition of her udder, and you don't have to train her to get used to milking, so there's no wait to get your first glass of milk.

Dairy character

It's also easier to judge the animal when it is in its "finished form"—fully grown. The goat you're considering doesn't have to be purebred; it's better to start with a "grade" or crossbred goat anyway. They're cheaper—about half the price of a purebred, or less—and they're often a shade hardier, being possessed of "hybrid vigor." And you'll feel bad enough making the inevitable mistakes of goatkeeping on a crossbred animal. You can always get high-cost purebreds later.

Take a close look at your potential milker. She should show some degree of "dairy character," the outward physical traits most common in good milking animals. She should look feminine, with a narrow neck (compared to a buck or billy); full, evenly rounded rib cage and belly; long, flat backline; somewhat prominent hip bones; strong, straight front legs; and solidly placed feet. There's a great deal of variability here—some nannies have narrow chests, but milk fairly well, or are a little swaybacked. These are not desirable traits, and ultimately end up reducing the animal's potential milk production. But since you're not going to enter the animal in any shows (crossbreeds can't compete), it doesn't matter if she's not a perfect physical specimen. It's more important that she's healthy.

She should look well balanced and happy; a few ribs may show very, very lightly, but she shouldn't be rail thin. Her hair coat should be clean and shiny, her eyes clear and free of matter in the corners. Depending on the breed, she may have very upright ears, pendulous long ears, or no outward ears at all. The insides of her ears should be clean. She should be free of grape-sized lumps or abscesses under her skin.

She may or may not have horns, either because the horns were removed when she was a kid or she was born without any. Some goatkeepers are adamant about removing horns, believing that goats with horns will hurt each other and damage breeding bucks. There's a certain amount of truth to this – goats butt and will use their hard, sharp horns vigorously. Some does will even batter their fellow nannies' udders mercilessly. If you have woven wire fencing, a few particularly dull horned nannies will persist in poking their heads through and not be able to pull back out, necessitating a series of rescues.

However, horns are also the goat's natural protection, which they will use against marauding dogs and other predators. We've kept goats both with and without horns. The only time we had a real problem was when a doe tried to jump from the milking stand when my husband's attention was on the udder – he got bumped in the forehead by one horn, and subsequently developed a nice black eye. He told our friends that I gave it to him!

Teeth, feet, and udder

Assuming you're looking at an adult doe (or nanny goat), there are three main features you must closely inspect before you part with your hard-earned cash: teeth, feet, and udder. If the goat is lacking in any one of this "triangle" of traits, she's not worth bringing home. Ask the goat's owner to place her in a pen or stanchion so you can take a closer look.

Teeth: Imagine my shock at discovering my newly purchased two-year old doe had no upper incisor teeth! She had a full complement of eight front teeth on the bottom, but where did those top choppers go? Turns out that goats and sheep both simply don't have upper incisors – just a flat, toothless, pad against which their lower choppers work. Those eight bottom teeth must do all the goat's food gathering, so they've got to be in good shape. Hold the goat's head steady by the nose and gently pull or fold back her lower lip. If she's got all eight and they look solid, the teeth are okay. If any are missing, or the teeth appear loose, or have wide spaces between them, or are more than an inch long, then you're looking at an elderly girl here. I'd bypass that older goat until I had more goat experience under my belt.

Feet: Your new goat has to be able to walk from feed sources to the milking stall, so her cloven hooves had better be up to the job. Most goat keepers trim their animals' toenails from time to time, and the feet are generally in pretty decent shape. Beware of "pixie toes" – turned up, overgrown hooves. Those extra-long toenails are just as uncomfortable for the animals as claw-like toenails would be for you – and that'll cut down her mobility and milk production. Pixie toes also suggest less than adequate care for the animals, so should rate a turn-down.

Feel each of the goat's feet – she may not particularly enjoy this, and try to pull away. If any foot feels especially warm, has a slight greenish tinge, or carries an unpleasant odor, this goat is most likely suffering from "foot rot." Ask! The condition is contagious, so you might as well leave this place right now. If there's a hint of foot rot, when you get home you might consider taking your own shoes off in the car and carrying them into the house for scrubbing with a bleach solution. You don't want to introduce foot rot to your property, since it's difficult to eliminate.

If the goat limps, it could indicate any number of things, including a sprained ankle, having been bumped in the shoulder or hip by another goat, a limb deformity, or other foot ailments. Unless you know for sure that the limp is caused by a simple mechanical injury (such as a sprain), this trait would be grounds for refusal. Don't buy problems.

Udder: This is the part of the goat that will cause you the greatest grief or give the most satisfaction. There's a lot of variation in udders – from the high, tightly held round udder to the long, pendulous, nearly-dragging-on-the-ground type. There are udders with two teensy teats, and ones with a pair that would shame a cow. There are udders which are firm and springy, and ones that are like flabby sponges. Here's the first rule of thumb: the udder must be evenly balanced. Both sides of the udder should be about the same size and texture. You can determine this visually, and by feeling the udder. Reach behind the goat and cup each side of the udder in your hand. It should feel body-temperature warm, soft and yielding. There should be no hard spots, extra heat, graininess, lumps, or sores – which are indications of disease, possibly mastitis (infected udder). Reject any goat with signs of udder disease.

The next rule of thumb is: the udder should sit firmly high against the goat's underside. A long, droopy udder can produce a good quantity of just-fine milk – but the poor goat can get that pendulous appendage caught on wire fences, large stones, and can even wind up stepping on it! The shape of the goat's udder is also an inheritable trait, so if you plan to keep daughters from this doe, you'd best avoid problems.

Finally, get ahold of each teat and test your milking skills – squeeze thumb and forefinger gently closed and then close each finger in succession. Some goats object to strangers being this familiar when there's no grain to hold their caprine attention. Forge on anyway. Does the teat protrude slightly from the end of your hand? Milking will be easier and cleaner if the teat's tip clears your palm. If the doe has extra-large teats, feel for "backflow" – where you squeeze the teat and the milk feels as though it moves both out the teat and back into the udder. This isn't necessarily a bad trait; it only makes milking a bit more challenging. If backflow is the goat's only problem and you take her, you can figure you're going to develop particularly strong hands over the next few months.

History and future

If your potential doe has passed so far, you'll need to ask about her personal health history – how old she was when first bred, how many kids she's had at each "freshening" or birthing, if she has ever produced a "freemartin" or hermaphrodite kid (not uncommon, particularly in naturally hornless goats). The more babies she can have at one time, the more you have to sell, raise up into new milkers, or put in the freezer. Remember that in order to produce milk, your doe will have to be bred every fall or winter – and those kids are one of the valuable by-products dairy goats provide

It's interesting to ask how much milk your potential nanny gives. I've never spoken to any goat-raiser who claimed less than a gallon daily for their does – but I've sure met a lot of goats who fall short of this number! Most does are capable of producing a significant quantity of milk, but they must also be routinely de-wormed (either with dairy wormers or by various organic methods), and fed enough to maintain their weight while still cranking out milk. The addition of molasses to feed always ups milk production somewhat – and raw, chopped pumpkin is a super milk increaser!

Most goats will drop milk production when they're moved to a new location, or stressed when being handled by strangers, so even if the goat's owner has kept perfect records, the doe's production will be less than expected. It'll pick up again after a week or two of your tender loving care. Be sure to ask about the animal's feed, milking routines, and vaccination history (have the owner write this down). If the owner has a special type of feed, ask to buy five or ten pounds so the goat has a familiar food for several days.

If this is the nanny who will provide your milk, she'll probably set you back $50 to $150. If she comes with kids, they shouldn't be more than $25 each, unless they are exceptionally fancy.

Your new goat may be "broke to lead," or trained to be on a leash – or she may be "broke to drag," completely without formal training. She might be most easily moved to your car or truck by showing her a bucket of feed, or she might be so freaked by this turn of events that she's near-wild. Try to be calm and patient with this prim lady, talk evenly and gently to her, and use her given name often. It does make a difference.

Some new goat owners will pen their nannies separately for a couple weeks, while they inspect the animal for any signs of illness or health problems. If I could do only three things before I brought a new goat home, I'd ask the former owner to worm the animal in my presence so I could see how it's done, and so that any internal parasites were deceased before we got home. And I'd dip each of the goat's feet, before she touched my soil, into a solution of 25% bleach and 75% water, just to be certain there were no foot diseases coming onto my property. I'd also dust my new goat with a light coating of organic rotenone or the chemical based Co-Ral – so that any stray lice or ticks wouldn't have a chance.

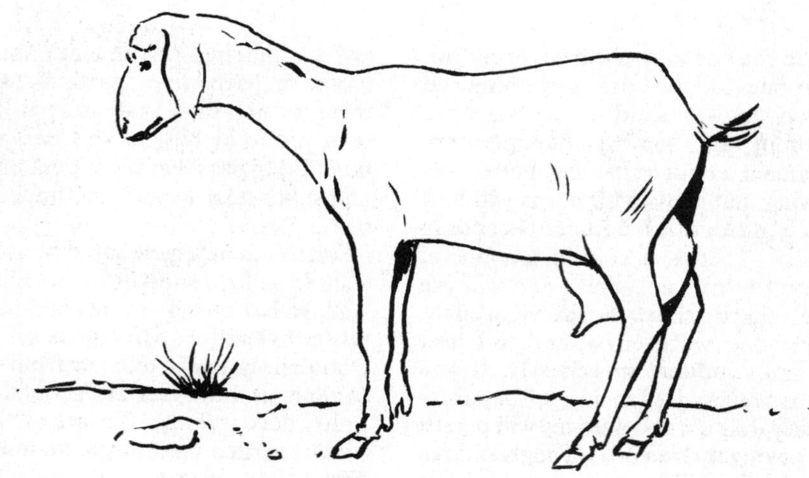

Last but not least, be prepared for your new goat to be lonely and afraid for a few days. She may cry piteously (and drive you nuts), or try to be extra friendly (and drive you nuts). Be sure to milk her every twelve hours, adjusting her schedule to suit your own.

And get ready! Unless you have a household chock full of your own assortment of kids, prepare to be swamped by the best, freshest milk you ever tasted! Δ

A BHM Writer's Profile

Jan Cook grew up in Detroit Michigan and studied to become a commercial artist. That plan changed when she married a Navy man and left home while still in her teens.

Cook has lived on both coasts, but for the last 20 years she's called California home. In addition to her job as *Backwoods Home Magazine's* Crafts Editor, she's a technical writer with the Department of Defense and as part of her duties travels throughout the United States and Europe. Always creative, she picks up inspiration for craft ideas to share with our readers during her off hours. She has been sewing since she was nine, and learned to knit at eleven.

The dairy goat — a gallon of milk a day

By Darlene Campbell

Looking for a way to combine sufficiency with efficiency? The most efficient animal on the place is the goat. It is scoffed at by skeptics, eyed by the curious, and well-loved by those who know. Countless people already know the benefits of goat milk, but in case you haven't heard, the milk from goats contains considerable smaller fat globules, making it easier to digest than milk from a cow. The curd is much softer and smaller, and vitamin A appears in pure form, as contrasted with carotene found in cow's milk.

Adults and infants alike who suffer from allergies, constipation, stomach ailments, and forms of diarrhea can successfully tolerate goat milk. It is wholesome and sweet flavored, and many people use it for making their own butter (a cream separator is needed), cheese, yogurt, ice cream, cottage cheese, and buttermilk. The doe is a clean, odorless animal, and when handled properly, her milk has a lower bacteria count than cow milk.

Few people can use all the milk produced by a cow. On the other hand, a good milk goat can produce approximately a gallon of milk a day for most of her lactation. I say approximately, because she will take several weeks to reach her peak, and will then produce for roughly 200 days, or until she is dried off before kidding again. Keeping two does is desirable — not only do they keep each other company, but you can time the breeding so that one is in production while the other is dry. Not all does produce the expected one gallon a day, so even with two 3/4 gallon milkers, there is adequate milk for the table and the feeding of young kids. When cost is compared, the goat is easily maintained on only one-sixth the amount of feed required to keep a cow, yet she produces one-fourth the amount of milk that a cow does. You can keep six goats for the cost of keeping one cow, and you'll get more milk.

Dairy goats come in six different breeds:

Nubians are probably the most popular; they're easily recognized by their pendulous ears.

French Alpines are recognizable by their contrasting black or gray markings on white, or black and brown bodies with light colored legs.

Toggenburgs are always some shade of brown with light or white stripes on the face.

Saanens are white or cream colored and are known as the heaviest producers.

LaManchas have little or no ears.

African Pygmies are a knee-high breed that not only produce milk well, but also bear kids in sets of triplets and quadruplets as often as twins.

Breeders of purebred goats are found all over the country and are happy to educate the novice. However, if you are looking to purchase a purebred, be prepared to pay a price in three digits. Ask the seller to let you see the goat's production records and records of the goat's ancestry.

If you are not prepared to purchase top of the line, talk to a breeder about buying a grade doe. This is an unregistered doe with many of the attributes of registered stock.

Feeding

Feeding a dairy goat can be as complex or a simple as you make it: complex if you want to raise all your own grains and hay and make your own organic ration; simple if you purchase manufactured rations. Don't, however, make the mistake of thinking that your goat can subsist on brush or weeds and still produce milk suitable for the table. Feed her as a dairy animal.

The dairy goat is a ruminant and requires a high-fiber ration that is also high in protein. Select a ration of at least 16% protein to keep her in good health and peak production. Additional calcium is necessary, as are trace minerals. We have always fed alfalfa hay in combination with a sweet grain mixture containing can molasses. Molasses is a source of iron and other important minerals; it is commonly used in pre-mixed feeds as a binder. The alfalfa supplies needed roughage, as well as protein, calcium, and minerals, and is considered to be one of the ideal types of hay for dairy animals. Clover is another ideal hay.

Other hays are also valued, but they have less protein and calcium, so they must be supplemented with a feed concentrate or quality grain ration. These hays include barley, birdsfoot trefoil, Bermuda grass, lespedeza, marsh or prairie grasses, oat or wheat grasses, soybeans, or any combination of these. It requires about 2,000 pounds of hay per year for each mature animal, if pasture is also available. And it takes only one acre of good, productive land to provide pasture for four producing dairy goats.

Being very clean animals, goats will not eat soiled feed. If by chance a young goat has jumped into the feed bin or manger and soiled it, other goats will refuse to eat. Therefore, keep all hay off the ground and clean the manger frequently. Construct it in such a manner that the goats cannot climb into the hay. During very cold weather, they may not drink enough water to keep production up. The offering of warm water once or twice a day is greatly appreciated by your stock. And should a doe go off her feed and refuse to eat or drink at all, a little molasses added to the warm water is an ideal tonic.

Most of us do not have the available acreage or farm machinery needed to grow all our own feed for livestock, but we can plant the garden or harvest from nature with the dairy goat in mind. To "grow milk" in the garden, simply plant choices that will complement your doe's nutritional needs;

they are not so different from your own. Plant sunflowers (goats enjoy both the seeds and the whole plant), mangel beets, Jerusalem artichokes, pumpkins, comfrey, carrots, kale, and sweet corn for the husks and stalks.

Gather dandelion greens, which are rich in Vitamin A, and nettles, which are high in Vitamins A and C. Bear in mind that these are only fed as treats, or in addition to the grain and hay requirements for production. Since the amount of minerals and protein in such additives are unknown, due to differences in soil types, too many garden greens and wild herbs can unbalance your dairy goat's ration.

Avoid poisonous weeds such as milkweed, locoweed, and bracken, wild cherry after it has wilted, and certain plants that are poisonous during certain stages of growth or after a frost. Contact your local extension agent for more complete information on feeding dairy goats or sheep, as the requirements are similar. Your agent can also give you information about poisonous plants in your area.

Equipment

Heating the barn is not necessary, but it should be draft-free and well ventilated, with plenty of bedding straw. It should also have a separate area for milking and an adjoining pasture, so the goats are free to come and go.

Dairy goats are closer to the ground than cows, so for the comfort of the milker, the doe should be placed on a milking stand. You can construct one from 2x4s and plywood. (Figure 1) An udder wash solution is used to clean the udder before milking.

A pair of hoof clippers or small pruning shears is needed to keep the hooves trimmed short. Many a goat has become crippled for lack of trimmed hooves. The hooves continue to grow and, unless shortened, will curl under. When walking becomes too painful, the goat will go down on her knees and stay there.

A pair of electric clippers will keep the belly hair cut short, and also hair on the udder. This makes for a cleaner goat and cleaner milk. In summer, she can be clipped over her entire body to quickly get rid of long winter hair.

Milking

Milking should be done at the same time every day. The grain ration is fed while the doe is being fed, and not at any other time. The expense of equipment needed for milking depends on whether you intend to sell the milk commercially or only want to produce for home use. Naturally, for commercial use, you should invest in a stainless steel strainer and milk pails. For home use, plastic is satisfactory, if it is kept sanitized and used only for milking. All equipment must be scrupulously cleaned and sanitized after each milking.

Do not use iron, copper, brass, or chipped equipment when handling milk, as they cause the milk to oxidize, which affects the flavor. Immediately after milking, strain the milk through a milk strainer containing a disposable filter. A double thickness of cheesecloth can also be used if it is washed and sanitized in bleach after each use. (This is not recommended for other than home use.) Using a clean, sanitized funnel, pour the milk into glass containers and apply lids. My favorite containers are Gatorade bottles. They hold about a quart and have long necks for easy handling. Quart-size or half-gallon canning jars can also be used, but I find them more difficult to pour from than Gatorade bottles. Always wash and sterilize the containers after each use, so they are ready for the next filling. Refrigerate the milk immediately.

Pasteurization

Home pasteurization is also possible with very little extra work. You can buy a small pasteurizer or invest in a cooking thermometer. Pasteurization is not sterilization; it is merely a heat treatment to kill disease-producing bacteria and reduce the number of other micro-organisms. It destroys harmful bacteria which may have entered the milk through handling. It also destroys the enzyme lipase, which reacts with butterfat in milk, causing it to become rancid and develop a goaty flavor. Fresh goat milk should taste no different from fresh cow milk.

Also, you, as a handler, can be a carrier of harmful bacteria without realizing it. Farms with outdoor toilets are suspect for deadly organisms that cause septic sore throat, scarlet fever, dysentery, Q-fever, gastroenteritis, diptheria, paratyphoid, and typhoid fever. Many infants are fed farm-bought goat milk, and it's very important to make sure that all milk that leaves the premises is safe.

Pasteurizing in the bottle. Place the milk in a bottle that has a cover with a hole punched in it large enough to receive the thermometer. Place the bottle of milk on a rack in a deep pan or pail. A large canner is ideal for this method if you are processing more than one or two bottles. Add warm water to the pan or canner until the water level reaches the level of the milk in the bottle. Place over heat and warm until the thermometer in the bottle reads 145 degrees. Remove from heat and leave the bottle in the hot water for 30 minutes. Continue checking the temperature of the milk; if it drops below 145 degrees, reheat slightly. This temperature must be maintained for a full 30 minutes. After 30 minutes, gradually replace the hot water with cold water, until the milk has cooled. After the milk cools, keep it cold by refrigeration.

Pasteurizing by double boiler. Pour the milk into the top of a double boiler and insert the thermometer. Heat over hot water until the thermometer registers 165 degrees, stirring constantly. When the milk reaches 165 degrees, maintain that temperature for 20 seconds, then remove and cool immediately by plunging it into cold water. Change the water frequently, or add ice to cool the milk. Continue to stir the milk until it's cold. Pour the milk into sterilized containers, cover, and refrigerate. Do not over-process, or a cooked flavor will develop.

Batch-type pasteurization. This method is used with an electric batch-type home pasteurizer. It will pasteurize two gallons of milk or more, or as little as two quarts. These appliances are almost automatic and don't take much of your time or attention. Follow the directions provided by the manufacturer of your particular unit.

Breeding and kidding

To keep the doe in high production, not only must she be fed a highly nutritious ration, she should be bred each year. Some does are known to produce young twice in a year. Kidding usually occurs in the spring, after a gestation period of 150 days, or roughly 5 months.

If you don't have your own buck, notify the breeder who sold you the doe and make arrangements for breeding far in advance. This is necessary because the doe will be receptive for only 24 hours (or less), so you must be ready to transport her to the buck on short notice. To check the doe for receptiveness, place your hand on her back and stroke her down to the base of her tail. If she ignores this gesture or tucks her tail against her body, she is not ready to be serviced. If she wags her tail excitedly, it's time to breed her. This back stroking is the simplest method for detecting heat. Other signs to watch for are redness or a swelling under the tail, a slight discharge, bleating and restlessness.

Each kidding season is a new experience of baby goats and bottles and nipples. Twins are usual, but it's not uncommon to have triplets. When each kid arrives, clean the mouth and nose of membrane and mucus. Cut the umbilical cord and dip the end into a small jar of iodine. We always take the newborn from the mother immediately after allowing it to stand and nurse for a few minutes. This way the mother can be hand-milked twice a day and the surplus milk used on the table. Otherwise, she will produce only enough for her kids. The first feeding is most important, as the kids receive antibodies through the colostrum. The colostrum also works as a laxative to start the immature digestive system working. Colostrum is the thick, yellow substance produced by the doe for the first few days after giving birth. It is wonderful for feeding all sorts of orphans on the farm, and I always keep a pint or more of it in my freezer to save newborn puppies and kittens as well as lambs, pigs, calves, and just about any young thing that needs bottle feeding.

The newborn kids are brought into the house and placed in a box filled with straw. From that point until they are weaned, they are fed from a sixteen-ounce pop bottle with a lamb's nipple attached. At first, they take only two or three ounces every four hours, but as they grow they are soon taking sixteen ounces of milk three times a day and experimenting with grass and grain.

Young goats are clowns. They leap and pirouette as gracefully as any ballet dancer. They love attention but can become a nuisance if allowed to run free. Add to this the fact that they are notorious escape artists and you could have your hands full keeping them out of trouble. Fencing should be of suitable height to prevent them from jumping over, closely woven to prevent stepping through, and made of a safe material to prevent injuries. Barbed wire should never be used to confine goats. Although you may be tempted to step over a low enclosure yourself, don't do it! Climbing or stepping over a fence is a sure-fire way to teach young rascals that a fence can be jumped. Always use the gate and young goats will learn the only way in or out is through that gate.

Because they are filled with energy and curiosity, young goats appreciate a few objects of amusement to satisfy their desire to climb, leap, and perform gymnastics. A platform, a barrel, a couple of old tires stacked one on the other – and they'll never be bored. A tire suspended from a tree makes an excellent opponent in mock combat for an adult buck. A mature does with an udder is less likely to indulge in such nonsense, but don't let that fool you. They may be less likely to jump a fence, but they are unusually canny about going under.

The young bucks are castrated at an early age and used in the woodlot to clear brush; they can also be sold or eaten. The meat is known as chevon and is delicious barbecued. The hide is tanned and made into leather goods. No other farm animal offers such amusement and affection, clears a woodlot, produces fertilizer in convenient pellet form, and places meat, cheese, and milk on the table. So much for so little – naturally. Δ

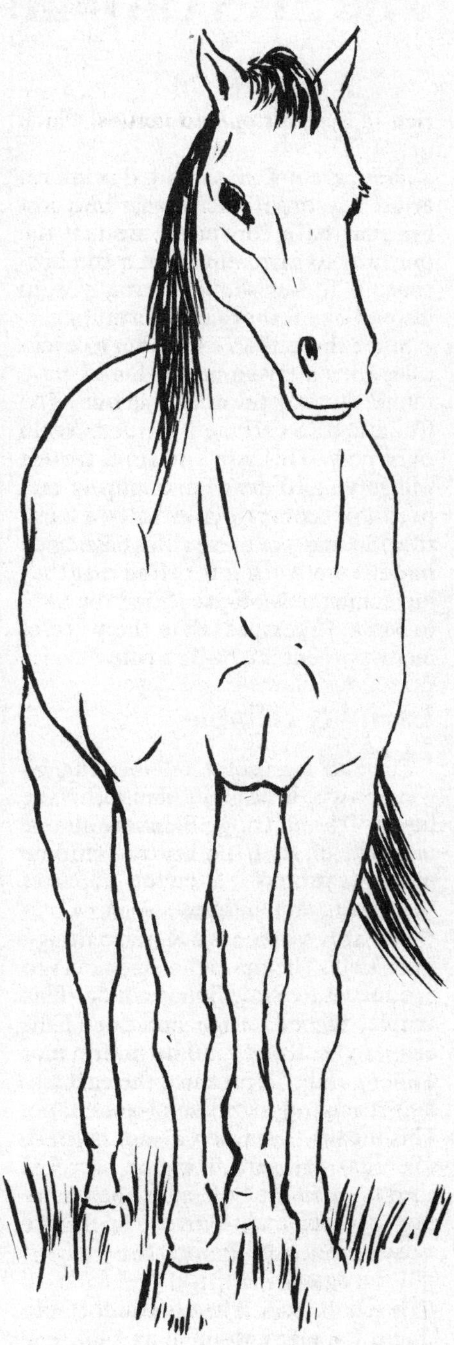

The SKS carbine—an honest bargain

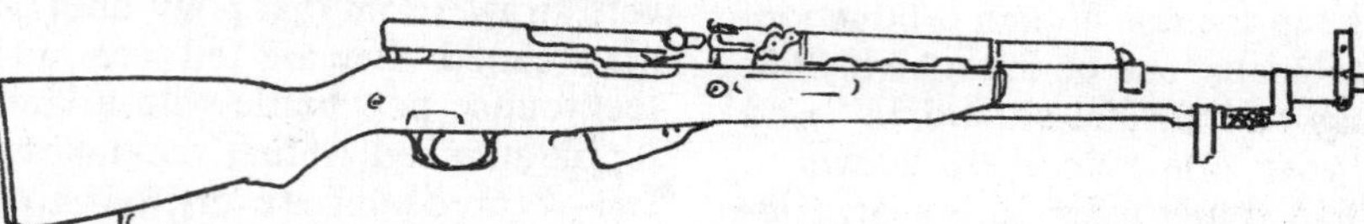

By Christopher Maxwell

There are not many bargains in firearms. My experiences with low cost firearms have convinced me that the only way to save money on a gun purchase is to buy the gun I really want instead of a low priced substitute.

Since there is an exception to every rule, I keep trying and I think I have found the exception to this one. The Chinese SKS carbine is a true bargain right now. This gun and its cartridge will serve as a deer hunting, pest and predator control, and self-defense rifle. So many of these rifles have been imported at such low prices that they are selling new at gun shows for $120 to $150. That is less than the price of many popular .22 rimfire rifles.

Useful & reliable

The SKS is a useful, reliable, rugged weapon within its limits, and within the limits of the cartridge. Jams are almost unheard of, and the bore is chrome plated to protect it from the effects of corrosive ammunition.

The SKS carbine is a Russian design from 1945. They gave the machinery to produce it to Red China in 1956. This simple, rugged design suited the Chinese so well they made more machinery and still produce the carbine. It is a gas operated semi-automatic. This means that when a shot is fired, some gas pressure from the barrel is used to open the bolt, eject the empty case, re-cock and re-load. The trigger must be released before the weapon will fire again.

The short stock is a very comfortable length for many women, and the low recoil and easy hit capability makes this a good choice as a home protection gun for those who are not proficient with handguns and dislike the recoil of shotguns. Many of these are purchased as defensive weapons, for which they serve well.

The carbine measures 40.5" in length and weighs 8 pounds. Some will say the SKS is overbuilt for the 7.62 x 39 mm cartridge, but the weight reduces the recoil to negligible levels.

You probably won't need the folding shisk-ke-bab bayonet unless you plan to finish off the wounded with it or toast marshmallows over the burning rubble of your enemies' villages. The skewer is easily removed; simply remove the pivot screw. There goes about a half pound of excess weight.

The 7.62 x 39 mm cartridge

The Soviet 7.62 x 39 mm cartridge propels a 123 grain bullet at 2400 feet per second from a 20.5" barrel. The Remington soft point loading for this cartridge works very well for deer under about 150 pounds at woods ranges, where almost all shots are taken at under 100 yards, and most shots are less than 50 yards.

This cartridge is slightly less powerful at the muzzle than the old standby .30-30, but the 7.62 x 39 is loaded with pointed bullets so the .30-30 loses its advantage fast. If you are careful with your shot placement, and don't take that shot you aren't sure of, the SKS will do fine for whitetail.

Bargain ammunition too

Practice ammunition is inexpensive and widely available. This is the same cartridge used in the AK-47, which was adopted by almost every country in the world outside of North America and Western Europe. Currently, East German manufactured ammunition is available for about seven cents per round by mail order in case lots. Chinese surplus ammunition is also easily available for less than 10 cents per round. If you shop around at the gun shows or get a copy of Shotgun News you will be able to find plenty of low priced ammunition. The surplus market changes from month to month. In the last two years I have bought cheap surplus ammunition for the SKS made in Yugoslavia, China, Iraq, Portugal, and Czechoslovakia.

This low priced ammunition will all be full jacketed military ball, often steel cored or steel jacketed. This makes it unsuitable for hunting anything but small game, and eliminating pests and predators. As practice ammunition, it's cheaper than making your own.

Corrosive ammunition

All Eastern European and Chinese surplus ammunition I have tried is corrosive. After firing you must clean the bore and the gas port, piston and gas tube thoroughly with hot soapy water or black powder solvent. All parts must be dried completely after cleaning. The bore and the end of the gas piston are chrome plated to protect them from the effects of the chemicals left behind by corrosive primers but I have seen some gas pistons which were badly pitted and corroded right through the plating.

If you are scrupulous about cleaning your gun immediately after use, there is no reason not to use corrosive ammunition. If you are likely to get lazy and not clean until you get around to it, or you are sometimes out in the field for days before you get to somewhere that has hot water, you'd better stick to non-corrosive.

All the major U.S. ammunition manufacturers have begun producing this cartridge. The Remington soft point seems to perform well on game. The others may, I haven't seen them used yet. Non-corrosive military type ammunition is available, made in Portugal and South Korea. This is less expensive than the U.S. commercial ammo and is good enough for training, practice, and pest and predator control.

Easy to operate

This is not a target rifle. The trigger is stiff and does not break clean, and the **intrinsic** accuracy is no better than 3" at 100 yards with any that I have tried. In terms of **practical** accuracy, it is easy to shoot and comfortable for most beginners. I have seen several novices get hits on 100 yard targets with their first shots from these carbines. Since the effective range of this cartridge on predators and small deer is no more than 100 yards, this level of accuracy is acceptable.

Ammunition is loaded from the top of the receiver into a 10-round integral magazine. Loose cartridges can be inserted individually, or 10 rounds can be stripped into the magazine at once from chargers (stripper clips). Some of the Chinese surplus ammunition comes packed on these, and they are available from most of the surplus ammunition dealers.

Once the bolt is closed there is no practical way to "top off" the magazine with extra rounds while firing. The magazine follower holds the bolt open for loading only when the magazine is empty. No manual hold open device is provided. If you want to fully load the magazine, or change the type of ammunition, you must either fire the magazine empty or dump the magazine, then close it and retract the bolt.

Some states hunting laws will require that the magazine be blocked to prevent loading more than five rounds during hunting season. This ten round capacity and the fact that this is not a detachable magazine has prevented the SKS from being banned by any of the "Assault Weapons" laws, so far.

If you need a simple, rugged, reliable rifle for deer hunting at close range, pest and predator control, self-defense, or just something a little more interesting than a .22 to plink with, the SKS carbine may be right for you. The price is certainly right. Δ

A BHM Writer's Profile

Vernon Hopkins is a retired trapper of 40 years, and he has witched wells for the past 30 years with a success rate of about 95%. We profiled his extraordinary life in Issue No. 2, and he subsequently became a writer for *Backwoods Home Magazine*. Vernon brings his extensive knowledge as a naturalist and observer of the natural world to *BHM*.

The right rifle for a woman

By Michelle J. Richards

Previously in *Backwoods Home* I've written articles about firearms for women. First shotguns, then handguns, because they were the easiest to write about, as there are quite a few options for women in that marketplace. Rifles are an entirely different problem.

If you are of average size or smaller, you face big problems getting a rifle to fit you, and at the same time a caliber that is useful for its intended purpose. Once we get out of the .22 rimfire rifle arena, the stocks are too large and the rifles too heavy.

Thus, if a woman wants a centerfire rifle she has two options: buy a nice walnut or synthetic stock rifle and have someone who has the skill cut the stock down and replace the butt pad—or buy youth model rifles. Being rather a purist, I hate the look of a cut-down walnut stock, and the youth models are generally stained birchwood. Personally, I think they both look terrible. Nothing wrong with birch stocks; they are tough and wear well, but they lack class. A firearm to me is a thing of beauty and also a tool.

The other problem is caliber choices. Youth models are generally .243 caliber or .308 caliber. The .243 is a good choice for small to medium deer with proper ammunition and shot placement. The .308 is extremely powerful and can be used on bear and even moose if one is careful. Why the big spread in caliber? And why .243 and .308? The .243 is a good choice for a large youth, but a .308? I know very few women who choose .308 as a caliber of choice. It's hard kicking against a 115-lb. frame, and there's plenty of other calibers out there that are just plain easier to shoot.

I'm 5'7", about 130 lbs. That's just a tad over average size in the U.S. today. I'd like to see manufacturers make a series of rifles to fit people my size. There's lots of men out in America my size or smaller who would benefit from this also. After numerous back surgeries I can no longer heft up and balance out an 8 lb. rifle and get a good sight picture through open sights, nor can I get a steady look through a scope. If you weigh 115 lbs. and have normal muscles in your arms, neither can you. One of the most important things in being a good rifle shot is being steady and having your cheek hit the stock the same place each time you shoulder the firearm. If your eyes are a different place each time, you see the sights differently, and you won't shoot to the same point of aim.

With all this in mind, let's see what we can do for you, with what is in the gun racks at your local dealers. I'm going to attack this first by rifle action, then by caliber.

If you are unsure of what is meant by "rifle action," it just means the mechanical means of getting ammunition from storage (tube, magazine, etc.) to the chamber where it is ready to be fired. We have single shot, lever, semiautomatic, pump, and bolt actions. The single shot is just that: one round of ammunition is all the rifle holds in the chamber. The operator opens the action and places one round in the chamber, then closes the action. After firing, the operator must open the action and clear it, and insert another round. The lever action rifle generally has a tube under the barrel. Think of all the westerns you've seen on TV. Remember the cowboys and their rifles? Generally they were lever action rifles. A lever is used to open the action, strip a round from the tube, chamber the next round and close the action. This can be done repeatedly until one runs out of ammo. The pump is just like a pump shotgun and works

the same way. The bolt action is opened and closed by an arm on the side, and the semi-auto does all the functioning for you. It only requires that you do the first one manually; all the other rounds are stripped from storage and chambered by the gun itself each time you pull the trigger.

"Caliber" is the diameter of the bullet used in the ammunition. Generally, and remember I said *generally*, the larger the diameter of the bullet, the more "powerful" the gun. The way the American caliber system works is this: a smaller diameter bullet can be used in a longer case with more powder and be much more powerful than a larger diameter bullet in a shorter case with less powder. The Europeans use designations like 6.5 x 55, which translates to a .264 caliber in our system. But the second number is length of the case, and that is important too, as the longer the case, the more powder can be used to propel the bullet. One has to study American calibers to know the variations used and to know what is more powerful. Calibers and actions seem to confuse women the most when I talk to them, so as I discuss calibers later in this article I'll try to compare them for you so you can understand better. We'll start off with .22 caliber *rimfire* rifles first, then go to *centerfires*.

Rimfire rifles

In the .22 caliber rimfire arena, most rifles will fit you tolerably well. They are generally designed for kids, and for plinking for adults. Their low power (compared with centerfires) makes it easy for the manufacturers to make them small and of lighter weight. When one is a serious small game hunter, that demands superb accuracy from a rifle. Kimber and Anshutz make expensive, regular sized rifles. But your average hunter can do extremely well with regular production .22s. All the major manufacturers make good .22s, and there are many styles to choose from.

I'll name a few of my favorites in the different action styles for you to look over at your dealer's. First to come to mind in the semi-auto style is Ruger 10/22. This rifle is so popular it's almost a cult item. It's strong, dependable, light in weight and Ruger quality through and through. It has so many aftermarket accessories designed for it, it's a huge business all its own. The Marlin Papoose is also a nifty little rifle. It weighs 3 3/4 lbs. and can be broken down and stored very conveniently for camping or carrying in an automobile. Feather Industries makes a great little .22 that has a military look to it. It holds 20 rounds, weighs 3 1/4 lbs., and breaks down for easy storage and transportation. In bolt actions, Marlin makes quite a few variations and they are very good rifles for the money, but to me are a little heavy. The lightest is Model 880 and it weighs 5 1/2 lbs. In pump actions, Rossi makes a cute .22 model #M625AC that weighs a mere 4 1/4 lbs. That leaves us with lever-action rifles. Winchester and Marlin make very, very good .22s. They are expensive compared to other action styles, but are superb little rifles. They cost the same as their big sisters in calibers such as .30/30. They come in birch, walnut and laminated stocks. They have carbine length barrels and handle like dreams. The Marlin 39TDS weighs 5 1/4 lbs., and is my pick over the Winchester 9422 at 6 1/4 lbs. Those rifles are made to last, and if they're cared for, you can hand them down to your granddaughter and she to hers.

Centerfire rifles

__.22 caliber__: This family of calibers includes the .222, .223 and such and is a "varmint" caliber rifle. They are generally heavy barreled and weigh 8 to 11 lbs. Too heavy for me. But if you're a prairie dog hunter and can use a rest to fire from, you'll do fine once you shorten the stock. I see nothing from manufacturers for women in this category.

__.243 caliber__: This is a caliber women seem to like. It has low recoil, and there are good rifles built for a woman's smaller frame. All major manufacturers make a bolt-action woman/youth rifle in this caliber. This caliber can be used for varmints with 70-80 grain bullets and deer with 100-105 grainers. Browning makes a gorgeous lever-action named BLR in this caliber, but it's a little heavy for my tastes. A friend of mine has one and she thinks it's superb.

__.270 caliber__: Here Winchester makes a bolt action in women's and youth size for you to consider. This caliber is another choice women seem to make regularly. The recoil is manageable, and the .270 is capable of taking down medium game very well. All manufacturers make lighter weight .270s but you will have to have the stock cut to fit you. They generally weigh in the 6 1/2 to just shy of 7 lb. class.

__.30 caliber__: This class encompasses many different calibers. They include the .30/30, .30/06, .308, .300 Winchester Magnum. Now that's confusing as heck, isn't it? So I'll list them by approximate power levels or recoil levels. The .30/30 is an old caliber. The first .30 in the name denotes caliber, and the second is how many grains of powder. The .308 is a .30 caliber, too, with a short stubby case. Then comes the .30/06 which has a longer case with more powder, then the .300 Win Mag, which is the most powerful. I'll discuss the .30/30, .30/06, and .308, as I believe most women will find the .300 Win Mag to be too punishing, and the ammo, if you can even *find* it in the boonies, is expensive as all get out.

__The .30/30__: Tried and true. The American deer rifle. I love this cartridge. It's **cheap** to buy ammo for it. The Winchester and the Marlin lever actions in this caliber are rugged workhorses that fit women very well, and the weight is not excessive. If I had to pick one rifle and one rifle only for a woman to hunt with, it would be a .30/30. The recoil is mild, the gun fits for size and weight, and the ammo is cheap. The .308 and .30/06 come in bolt and semi-auto rifles, but again they will be heavy and long-barreled. I have a bolt action Winchester Model 70 Featherweight in .30/06. The weight is 6 3/4 lbs., but the stock is too long. At that weight a .30/06 kicks like the proverbial mule. My teeth snap together viciously if I forget to clamp them together before firing. Most women will not enjoy a .308 or a .30/06. But if recoil does not bother you and you don't mind cutting down your stock, the Remington Model 7 Light-weight, Winchester Featherweight and Ruger M-77RL Mark II all weigh in the 6 lb. class.

7.62 x 39: Here's that European caliber designation again. This caliber has become quite popular as a deer hunting caliber. It was a Russian military caliber, and lots of surplus rifles have been shipped into the U.S. from foreign countries. Plinking ammo is dirt cheap. These surplus rifles don't interest me as they are heavy, but Ruger has a rifle called the Mini-Thirty Semi-Auto that women I've shown it to liked. It has a rather military look to it, but they liked it anyway. Winchester and Remington both make appropriate hunting ammo for it. Ballistically it is about the same in power as a .30/30, but it can use pointed bullets for a longer, flatter trajectory than the .30/30.

Now that we're done with the usual rifle calibers, I want to go to some oddballs that fit women well. I say oddballs because they are rifles chambered for what is considered pistol or handgun ammunition. This is a nifty benefit, as you may already have a handgun in 9mm, .38/.357, .44 or .45ACP, and you can use the very same ammo. The 9mm, .38 Special, and the .45ACP from a rifle can be used for squirrels, rabbits and fox-sized animals at reasonable distances. The .357 can be used for deer to 75 yards or so and the .44 mag for deer or bear from 75 to 125 yards. These pistol calibers benefit greatly from the longer rifle barrel, as the velocity can improve 100 to 200 feet per second. Please be sure you use hunting ammo in the .357 and .44 magnum, not self-defense or target ammo. Talk to your dealer about what is appropriate. What I like about the 9mm, .357, .44 and .45ACP pistol calibers in rifles is this: There are rifles that will fit you well. Yep, almost as if they had women in mind when they designed them. Let's see what's out there.

9mm: Marlin makes a rifle called the Model 9 Camp Carbine. It's nifty at 6 1/2 lbs. with a 16 1/2" barrel. It's short, light, and could double as a home defense weapon. Feather Industries makes the semi-automatic AT-9, much like the .22 I wrote about earlier. It weighs 5 lbs, has a 25-round capacity, and breaks down for easy transport.

.38/.357: Here we have Marlin and Winchester lever actions weighing in at approximately 6 lbs. with 16" barrels. Rossi also makes a lever model M65SRC which weighs in at 5 3/4 lbs. Another interesting rifle is a pump action .357 called the Timberwolf that weighs 5 1/2 lbs. and can be broken down for transport. It's made by the folks that make the UZI, and I hear they are rugged and reliable as all get out.

.44 mag/.44 Special: Here again we have the same three manufacturers of lever actions: Winchester, Remington and Rossi. They all make a rifle in this caliber that weighs from 5 3/4 to 6 lbs., with short barrels.

.45ACP: Marlin makes the Model 45 Camp Carbine in this caliber, just like the 9mm described earlier. It's short, lightweight, and it's just a little step up in power over the 9mm. Good for small game and home defense.

After reading this far you've realized I'm a devotee of lever actions. It's true, I'm prejudiced as all get out. There are well-made, rugged, gorgeous, hand-down-for-generations-quality rifles out there for any game I need to put in the port, that fit me and other women without resorting to butchering the stocks or buying a rifle that doesn't fit. If you can handle recoil and need to hunt moose or brown bear, the Browning BLR comes in larger calibers such as .308 Winchester and .358 Winchester — and Marlin has the .35 Remington at 7 lbs., and the .444 Marlin at 7 1/2 lbs. These have short barrels and balance well while carrying. They seem much lighter and shoot easily for smaller people. Yep...I'm prejudiced toward lever-actions for women.

The main disadvantage of lever actions is that, because ammo is stored in a tube with the nose of the bullet in the primer of the case ahead of it, only round nose bullets can be used safely. Round nose bullets are not as flat-shooting as pointed bullets, so distance is a very important consideration. Many people shoot 200 or 250 yards across canyons or large meadows for their game, and roundnose bullets are not appropriate for that application. The average distance deer are shot in the U.S. is only 75 yards, so your .30/30 or .44 magnum pistol bullets are satisfactory. If you need a pointed bullet to go 200 yards, don't despair. Browning's BLR has a magazine that can take pointed bullets, so you can get the smaller sized gun that fits you, in lever action style, in calibers such as .243, .257 Roberts, .270 Winchester, and other larger calibers. Look into a Browning if your area requires shooting game at longer distances.

Well, I've tried to cover rifles that fit women and calibers that are comfortable for us to shoot with our smaller frames. I've also tried to choose calibers that ammunition is available for at your local hardware store out in the boonies. There are many calibers that women can enjoy, but getting ammunition for them is tough, or has to be brewed at home at a handloader's bench.

Hope this review of rifles has been of help to you gals who are considering hunting or for you who already are hunting with rifles that don't fit you well. Hunting is a fun, healthy sport that can benefit you and your family by putting healthy lean meat on your table and providing hours outside in the fresh air just enjoying the out-of-doors. Δ

Hummingbird

A stir in the early dawn,
action in a nearby tree;
a blur of whirling colors
looks through the window at me.

Ah, little helicopter
right frisky are you, today.
Any bird that dares invade
is instantly chased away.

Inside a gleaming blossom
of the trumpet vine you drink.
A whirling bit of feathers —
then, gone swiftly as a blink.

June Knight
Caldwell, Idaho

Buying the first horse

By Jan Palmer

Many small farms sooner or later find themselves thinking of adding a horse or two. Maybe the kids want a horse to ride, or maybe the thought of a team to work the garden sounds good to Dad. Maybe you want to clear some area that a tractor can't get into or you just don't want to hassle with a tractor at all. For whatever reason, a horse or pony might fit into your operation.

What kind of horse?

When someone mentions working horses, many people think of draft horses. However, for many purposes, a pony or light horse will be more suitable. Availability of feed is a big consideration. Consider what you plan to do with the animal. Look long and hard at this, and get a paper and pen out to write down some answers.

First, what do you want the animal to do? If your primary objective is tilling the garden and dragging firewood, you don't need a "bombproof" riding horse. If you want a horse to do that, **plus** keep the kids busy and maybe do an occasional cart ride or youth event, your needs will be much different.

Some other questions: Do you have experience with horses? **This is an important question!** If you have no experience, you'll need a much different type of animal than someone who can break a horse himself. What kind of cash outlay do you have available? Would you be interested in raising foals? How much (if any) equipment do you have?

Keep in mind two important things:

- 1) It costs just as much to feed a bad horse as it does a good one.
- 2) A horse can be of more use if it is comfortable and healthy.

This Stardardbred is in training for the racetrack. Often a horse that doesn't cut it at the races might have the temperament to cut it in your operation, for a reasonable purchase price. The horse pictured here is a pacer—note that the legs on the same side are moving together. An advantage of Standardbreds is that they are usually trained to drive.

Factors to consider

There are several things to consider, and many things that will go into the pricing of a horse. Get that pen out and comment on what your needs are in the following factors:

Temperament, or the general attitude of the horse, is a big factor. A horse that is willing and obedient is of much more use than the stubborn, sullen one who refuses to pull against a load. Closely related to this is **manners**, the horse's code of conduct. Horses that bite, strike, kick, rear, run away, shy at everything, or pull back can be dangerous in the hands of someone with little or no experience.

Other such habits (found more in the horse's stall) might be cribbing, wood chewing, kicking, weaving, tail rubbing, and stall walking. More on these later.

Soundness is another consideration. A "sound" horse has no visible or unseen defects that affect its serviceability. An "unsound" breeding animal (for example a mare who won't carry a foal to term) might make a wonderful work animal.

Conformation is the overall structure of a horse, as compared to a standard of perfection. A blue ribbon winning "halter" horse isn't necessarily the best choice for dragging logs, but there are things to look for (which I'll discuss later) which might limit the work life of your animal. If you plan only sporadic use of the horse, or don't plan on breeding, some faults might be overlooked. These faults often lower the price of a horse, but what one person considers a glaring imperfection, you might not mind at all.

Breed or **type** is an important factor. If you want a purebred animal with a pedigree, you have a better chance of getting a decent price should you ever decide later to sell the animal or breed a foal. This is perhaps one of the first considerations you should look at.

Short people will usually have trouble harnessing a 17 hand Shire. If you plan on hauling 10 inch logs, 10 feet long for six months a year, you'd be better off looking at the larger breeds, either a good size draft horse or a good size light horse team.

These ponies look to be of Shetland or Welsh descent, and as a team could do many jobs of bigger horses on less feed and space. (Photo by Dwayne Palmer)

On the other hand, if you're more looking for a riding animal for the kids, tilling the garden and hauling up firewood, and you don't have a large amount of room, a team of ponies might be just the ticket. Ponies have the reputation of being mean. In all fairness, a properly trained pony is no meaner than a properly trained big horse.

Level of training is another factor. Generally, the more advanced the horse is in "show" accomplishments, the higher the price.

Age is yet another factor to decide on. Young horses often are cheaper but lack the training and experience of older horses. Horses in their prime, 5 to 8 years old, generally command the highest prices. Don't overlook a teenager – many older horses have several good years left in them. I personally have a pony who is 30 years old and a quarter horse who is 21. One respected horseman once said horses "don't get smart until they're 12." Older horses often have outgrown silly, childish behavior and are ready to work.

Health is another factor. Auction rings are full of horses who are either starved, overfed, or crippled. Some health problems are permanent and require a lifetime of care.

Blemishes often lower the price of an animal, but many don't affect serviceability. Things such as old cuts, scars, or white spots from old injuries may not look pretty, but if you aren't concerned with pretty the horse might suit you fine.

Color and markings are two things that most people notice first about a horse. These will probably be lower on your list; a good horse can never be a bad color. A fancy colored animal might not have the other qualities you need.

Once you have a list of things you consider important, a price you are comfortable paying, and an idea of what you are going to use the horse for, you're ready to start looking.

There are several breeds available to consider. A few of different sizes are discussed here.

Draft breeds

If you are looking for a draft horse, that is, a large work horse for extensive logging, tilling and so forth, there are several good breeds.

The Clydesdale gained fame as the symbol of Budweiser beer. These gentle giants are usually from 16 to 18 hands tall. (A hand equals 4 inches.) The Clydesdale usually weighs between 1600 and 1800 pounds, with some individuals approaching 2200 pounds.

The Shire often looks like a Clydesdale, averaging 17.1 hands (17 hands, 1 inch). One of the characteristics that is distinctive about the Shire is that the "feathers" (the long hair on their lower legs and feet) is fine, straight, and silky, and there's usually more than on other breeds.

A good-sized pair of light horses that could do most jobs on a small homestead. While most people like matched teams, it's more important that the pair work together and are of about the same size than that they be the same color. This team is well matched. (Photo by Dwayne Palmer)

The Percheron, a French breed, is usually black or gray and most are between 16 and 17 hands and average about 1700 pounds. They are noted for heavy muscling on their lower thighs.

The Belgian is the most popular draft horse in American draft circles today. They are generally the same size as Percherons but are usually sorrel or "blonde" in color, and somewhat heavier muscled than other breeds.

A nice pair of Belgians. Note that the near horse is not pulling even with his partner; the other horse seems to be doing most of the work at this point. A draft team can handle most chores on a farm, just as their ancestors did years ago. (Photo by Dwayne Palmer)

One of the smaller draft horses is the Suffolk, a breed that is always some shade of chestnut (reddish-brown). They average 16 hands in height and have long been prized for their temperament and working ability.

Light horse breeds

Perhaps you don't need a horse that big. Maybe the size is too intimidating, or you don't feel that you can afford one at this time. Another alternative is a light horse breed, that is, a full size horse but not a draft type.

One possible candidate is the quarter horse, a breed that comes in a wide variety of sizes and colors. They are common in America, with over 3 million registered throughout the world. Some are trained to drive as well as ride, and quarter horses can be found to suit nearly any budget.

A medium size POA. A pony this size could haul small logs and do many other chores around the farm. With a partner, he could also till the garden, haul hay and manure, and do most jobs usually required of bigger horses. (Photo by Jan Palmer)

Another popular breed (also an American breed) is the Morgan. The original Morgan was prized as an animal that could work the fields all morning, gather cows in the afternoon, and still pull the buggy with style for an evening on the town. The Morgan is generally 15 to 16 hands and 1000 to 1200 pounds, and they are noted for their good temperament.

Another breed that might be practical is the Standardbred, which are normally raced in harness. This can be an advantage if you want a driving horse, as most Standards are trained to drive. But beware: many are **not** trained to ride.

If you live in an area close to harness racing tracks, you can often find a horse that was too slow or lacking in talent to be a race horse but might be just what you are looking for. Be cautious if you try teaming two together. Horses on the track are trained to outtrot their rivals, and if you get two trying to outdo each other, you could have a runaway team.

Ponies

If the horses I've described are still too large, consider one or two ponies. The most popular candidates include the Shetland, the Welsh, and the POA. The Shetlands are the smallest, often just 40 to 45 inches, and can be any color. The Welsh are found in many sizes, from just over Shetland size to 15 hands. They are usually heavier muscled than the Shetland. The POA (Pony of Americas) was originally formed by crossing the Appaloosa with the Shetland. Today the breed is a 46 to 56 inch pony with Appaloosa coloring and is often handled by children.

Looking

In looking for your work horse, check local feed store bulletin boards, newspapers, and tack stores. Ask around at sales, fairs, and other events, if there are any in your area. Check classified sections of magazines like the *Small Farmer's Journal*.

Once you've found a candidate or two, go looking. Watch the handler work around the horse. If your candidate is represented as being trained to ride and drive, watch him at both (don't take anyone's word for it). If the

Two different sized animals, "imperfect" horses. The smaller pony was a wild-looking yearling when purchased for $25. Owned by the author, he was trained to ride and drive, and haul small logs about 8 feet long and 4 inches around. The larger mare is a Thoroughbred, cast out at a breed sale. The disposition of both is shown by the kids. (Photo by Jan Palmer)

horse is kept in a stall, casually check the stall. Are there fresh chew marks? If so, better plan on buying or hauling in lumber. Are there holes dug in the floor? Are there spots worn away? Is there a small ditch in front of the door? This could be caused by weaving (rocking back and forth on his front feet).

Watch the owner groom and handle the horse. Does he pull his head back to avoid being brushed on his face? Does he allow his ears to be touched? Is he fussy about having his mouth, nose, or eyes touched or wiped off? Are his feet in good shape? Does he lift them quietly and hold them up to be cleaned out? If the owner doesn't clean the feet, why? Is it because the horse won't lift his feet, or because he throws them at you? Is the horse tied up to be groomed? If not, why? Does he pull back when tied? Does he accept being handled easily? Is he busy trying to grab the handler's coat or fidgeting around impatiently? Does he accept the bit easily, or does he throw his head up and run backwards? When the cinch or belly band is snugged up, does he stand quietly or try to bite? Does the owner lead him up a few steps and let him adjust slowly or kick him in the belly and say "cut it out"?

What are his eating habits? You'll have to ask about that. What kind of feed has he been on? If he's thin, beware. Did the owner starve him to make him controllable? Or is he in poor health, or just not getting enough food?

If there are trenches in his stall or pen and he's skinny, you can bet he spends his days pacing up and down the pen rather than working, and runs off any feed he gets.

One mare I got several years ago in Washington state was being given away, and I was suspicious why anyone would give away a 6 year old trained Appaloosa mare who was "a little thin and needed her teeth floated" (filed even by a veterinarian, a $20 job). I went to see the mare, and she was more than "a little thin" – she was starved to a skeleton and nearly fell when I got on her. She seemed well behaved and someone had cared for her somewhere along the line.

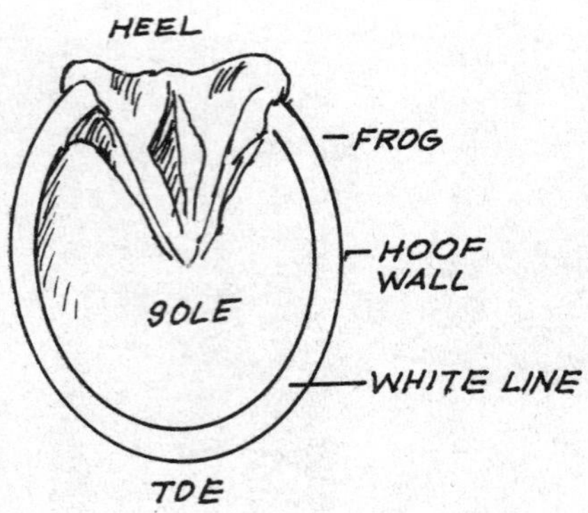

The parts of the hoof as viewed from the bottom. The white line is where nails are driven for shoes on the horse's hoof. If the foot smells and there is a blackish "gunk" in the frog, the horse has thrush, which is caused by the feet being wet or dirty. This is not usually a serious malady and my be avoided by preventive care or cured with a relatively inexpensive medication. Press on the sole to find sore spots before buying a horse.

It turned out that the only thing wrong with the mare and her teeth was that she wasn't getting enough to eat. For six months I thought she was going to die. As she gained weight she became a bit headstrong, and could get pretty evasive when it came time to be worked. As time went on, she turned into a decent little mare, but there are some signs that will never go away.

Feet inspection

When you pick up your prospect's feet, tap the bottoms and the sides with a small screwdriver, and gently press the handle into the bottom part of the foot. Beware of the horse that snatches his foot away from you in pain. With his front foot raised, poke and prod the knee with your hand. Look for signs of soreness.

Hold up the back feet to put quite a bend in the hock (the large joint). Hold it up for about 30 seconds, then have the handler trot the horse off straight. Watch for a horse that obviously limps away. The first step might be weak, but after that it should stride out with no problems. A horse that limps off probably has some hidden soreness inside that might be a problem if you use him for heavy land tilling or pulling logs.

With the horse standing squarely, run your hand down to the hock joint and feel for any softness or swellings. Be cautious about any excessive heat in the joint. Check all four ankles the same way. If the seller is impatient, remember it's your money. Above all else, your horse has to be able to work and has to have a good temperament. If a horse willingly puts up with all this examination, he'll probably put up with almost anything.

Run your hands firmly down his shoulders and legs. Notice any heat, swelling or "mushy" areas. Run your fingers down his back. If he flinches, look closer. Is his back excessively long? If so, it could be something that might get worse. If his back is short and well muscled, ask what work he has done lately. Many horses off the track or coming out of heavy training will be sore, and usually time will take care of it.

Bad habits

Ask about any habits the horse might have. Cribbing, for example, often results in horses that are "poor keepers" – that is, they don't keep weight on very well. They are also more prone to colic due to sucking air into the belly. They feel full when they aren't, so they don't eat well. Sometimes the habit is rooted in boredom, but don't count on it. A confirmed cribber will crib in the pasture or anywhere he can lay his teeth on. He'll rest his teeth on a ledge (fence, feeder, etc.), arch his neck, lean back a bit and make belching sounds. Usually this activity goes on for hours.

Chewing wood on the other hand is not accompanied by the odd behavior of cribbing, but your wood structures will disappear in a hurry.

Tail rubbing is harder to determine. Most horses will rub on trees or stalls if their tails are dirty, if they have worms, or in the case of males if their sheath is dirty. A confirmed tail rubber never has a full tail because it is always rubbed off. If you don't care about the length of the tail or the ap-

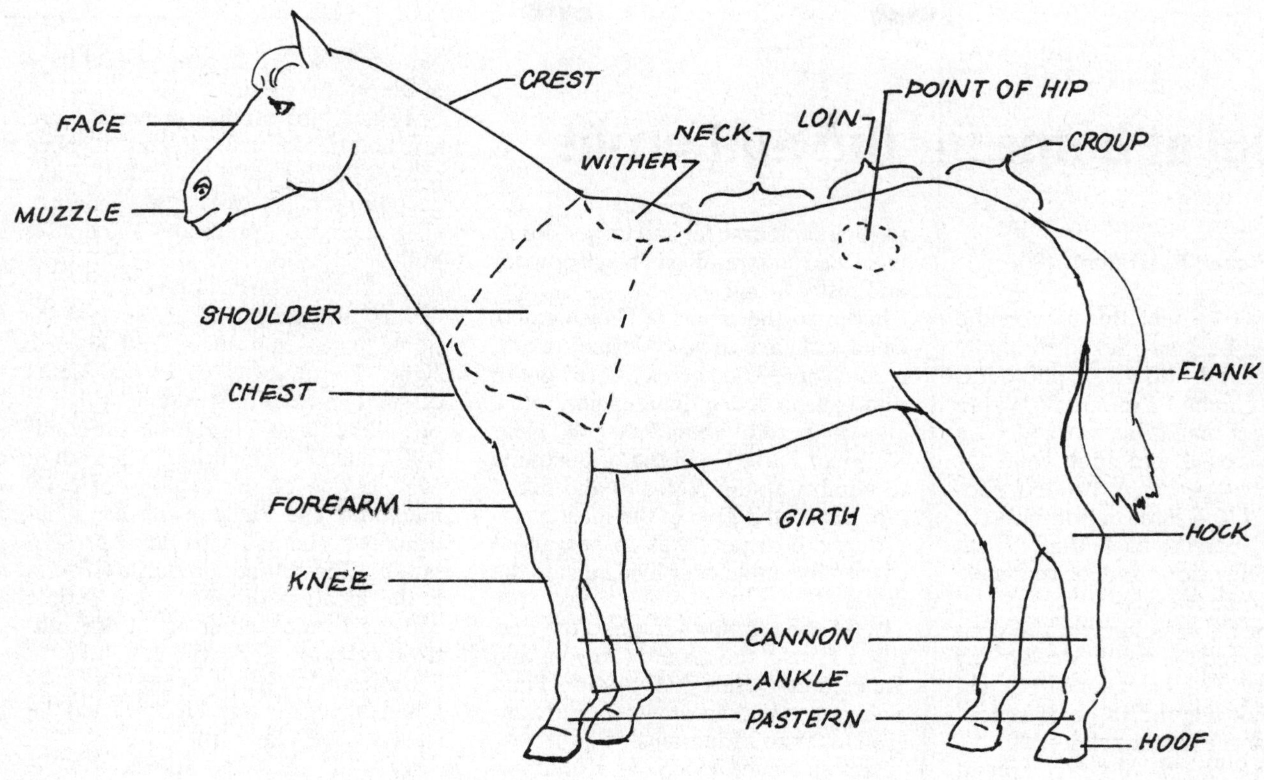

The basic parts of the horse. The height of a horse is measured from the withers to the ground in increments of "hands" (a hand equals four inches). Example: a horse that is 14 hands is 56 inches. These basic points of the horse will be referred to by horse handlers on a regular basis.

pearance of it, this is one habit that might not be a big deal to you.

Manners and temperament will probably take a on greater importance if you're working the horse alone or if you have kids.

You might be in the budget category of having to settle for an imperfect horse—a horse that's so homely that no one else wants him. If his temperament and manners are such that he'll try to learn what you want, or if he's already been used for some of your jobs, you might consider giving him a try.

If you have the time and money to invest in good feed, the horse rescue organizations might be a place to look. Be advised, though, that a starved horse might have problems that need special feed and vet care, and might not live, even after you do all you can do for them. Many starved horses bond with their rescuer, and will do more for that person than any other. However, you must be especially strong on discipline with these horses.

Two ponies I bought at an auction are examples of this. They were registered POAs, but were very thin and had signs of being abused (slinging heads, overly shy of people). I gave them nicknames of Popcorn and Peanut. Popcorn was absolutely terrified of anything that looked or sounded like a whip. He would go into a panic and run over anyone or anything that got in his way. He broke several halters and lead ropes and could not be disciplined at all without going into a panic. It took eight months of quietly being around him and feeding him before he would willingly come to me. Peanut, on the other hand, was a defiant brat determined to never have to do without again. When fed he would grab a mouthful, and wheel and kick or charge at the person feeding. After the second time he charged, I took a whip to him to discourage the behavior.

As can be expected, the attitudes came into play in the "turn-around time." Peanut, being the more aggressive one, was ready to go to work in just a few months. Popcorn, however, took a full year before he trusted me enough to do what I asked. Once he crossed that bridge, however, he'd do absolutely anything I asked.

Finding your ideal horse might take time. If you doubt your abilities, see if there is an experienced 4-H or saddle club member in the area who might be able to go along with you. Follow the basic guidelines outlined here—and best of luck finding your horse. Δ

School at home for fun and profit

By Robert L. Williams III

Last week I spent the day on the Blue Ridge Parkway, hiked to a gorgeous waterfall, did some photography work, climbed a mountain, wrote a story for a magazine, worked on a tool shed, sawed and split wood for winter, developed film, printed photos, cooked, fed information into the computer, played basketball, read, watched television, and occasionally talked to some friends.

I was not on vacation; on the contrary, I devoted the whole week to my school work. You see, I am enrolled in what I think may be the best school possible for me: home school.

It is a type of school I recommend very highly to certain types of people, but not to everyone. Whether home school is, as some people think, the ideal study environment or simply an excuse to keep from learning depends upon two major factors: what kind of teaching you can get at home and how motivated to learn you are.

For me, it is nearly perfect. My classroom may be a waterfall, a mountain range, a photo lab, The Grand Canyon, tourist resorts, restaurants, or a movie theater. I may study in a lab, a forest, my back yard, at a building project, or in a museum. Some days I may be in all of these places on the same day.

In my history study, I made extensive tours of museums of Washington D.C., state capitals, Revolutionary and Civil War battle fields, historical museums, homes of prominent historical persons (including Washington's Mount Vernon, Jefferson's Monticello, and others).

When we studied the American West, we took an extensive trip to New Mexico, Arizona, Arkansas, Colorado, Texas, Oklahoma, and Tennessee, where we visited a number of places of interest. In New Mexico, I spent two weeks at the NRA Whittington Adventure Camp and participated in skeet and target shooting. I also had training in black powder and pistol firing.

In the northern part of New Mexico, I had a chance to visit Vermejo Park, a ranch of 633,000 acres where I got to photograph bears, deer, eagles, and a gigantic herd of about 9,000 elk. Near Vermejo Park, I had the opportunity to climb Capulin Volcano and hiked into the crater. One of the most interesting experiences was to see about twenty-five mule deer living inside the crater.

In Arizona, I photographed the Petrified Forest, the Grand Canyon, and the Painted Desert. In Colorado, I had a chance to see the snow covered Sangre DeCristo Mountains.

Back in New Mexico, we visited Albuquerque, Tucumcari, and Santa Fe.

One of the big thrills of going to the West was to cross the Mississippi River. While on that trip, I saw oil wells and enjoyed the Indian culture of Oklahoma. I was also treated to the sights of Nashville, Memphis, and Knoxville, where I spent several days at the World's Fair.

My textbook studies at home were also helpful. My geometry and algebra classes helped me a great deal in my carpentry class work. In carpentry class, I helped to remodel one house, built a large log tool shed, and then helped build a large house.

Near my home, there are several national parks, museums, and historic sights. I visit these parks and sights often. The Shield Museum, which is one of the finest museums in the country, is one of my favorites. The Hall of Man is one of the exhibits of early mankind. The Planetarium has a nationally acclaimed astronomy presentation. Kings Mountain Battle Ground is the location of what some people call the turning point of the Revolutionary War, and you can hike to Furgurson's Grave, where he was killed during the war. I have visited the sites of Civil War battles.

My study of music appreciation is through radio, television, and live performances, such as the Cornell University Chorus, Mark Twain Tonight, Cats, and South Pacific. I have access to a music library of dozens of Broadway show recordings, operas, classical music, and folk artists.

After hours of academic subject work, I often learn carpentry by doing the actual work. Here I am flooring the deck we built.

My science studies include, in addition to textbook and classroom work, field trips to science museums, extensive nature study on our farm, on mountain ranges, and along waterways. Our subject matter ranges from the highest mountain peaks to the world revealed by the microscope.

One of my science studies was of a vitamin plant food with household vitamins. I was able to make a vitamin which resulted in remarkable plant growth and produce. I grew cabbage heads up to fifteen pounds, pea plants that reached a height of four feet, a tomato patch that produced a hundred pounds of tomatoes each day, and a huge watermelon and cantaloupe patch. One of the best parts was that I had no difficulty with insects. The vitamins acted as sort of an insect repellent.

My study of music appreciation is directed by a professional musician. My "textbook" includes performances by my instructor as well as a library of musical recordings that include classical music, opera, bluegrass, Broadway shows and contemporary music.

Spanish instruction involves the use of textbooks, Spanish tapes, and periodic conversations with persons whose native language is Spanish.

Instead of writing commonplace themes like how I spent my summer vacation, I am writing stories to submit to magazines and newspapers. I also do the photo work for these stories.

So far, I have sold over fifty photos (eight to one market for one hundred dollars each), and I have written and sold three stories (one for $100, one for $200, and one for $300).

At this point I think I should tell you that my instructors are also my parents. I am fortunate to have parents that are willing to pass on part of their experience and education to help me with my education.

Many students leave school because of religious reasons; however, my reasons for asking my parents to teach me at home were very different. I felt more comfortable studying at my own speed, and I can study subjects that I find useful to me, in addition to the required subjects.

Starting home school was the best decision we ever made, as far as I am concerned. I have never for a moment regretted attending home school. I was more interested in getting an education than a piece of paper stating that I had an education.

In home school, I am making progress and learning the material that will help me in the future. Other people may feel that a home schooler is lonely, but I stay in touch with my friends and enjoy spending time with them every week.

We do not think that home school is for everyone, but if a student is unhappy in public school and really wants a good education, I would recommend home schooling to that student. At home there are few distractions that interfere with work and create stressful tension. (We had a distraction as I was writing this: a deer paid us a visit and we took time out to go outside to watch him, but it was a pleasant diversion.)

I now feel better about myself than I have in ages, and I feel that I have a better chance for a good education. My parents are willing to devote the time to see that I understand the material.

In fact, I know what James Garfield meant when he said that the ideal school is Mark Hopkins on one end of the log and himself on the other. The difference is that I have two instructors, and close friends, on one end of the log, and I would not willingly give up my place on the other end of the log.

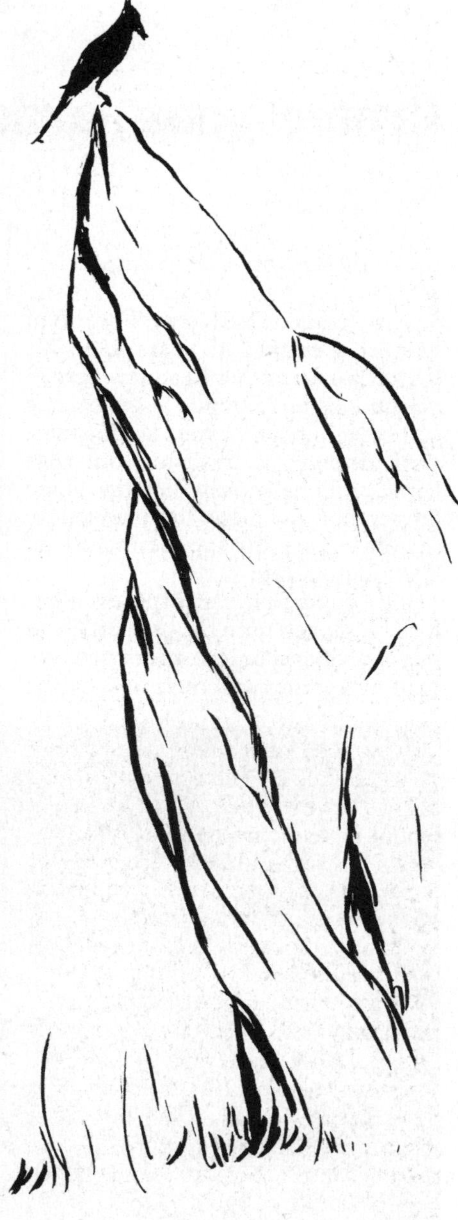

For me, it's the best seat in the best school imaginable.

(Robert L. Williams III is a 16- year-old homeschool student.) Δ

Protect your garden with a homemade trap

By Ron and Carol Oliver

Carol and I moved to our little bit of heaven a couple of years ago. We found two acres that fit somewhere in our budget, and jumped at the chance of becoming tax paying landowners. With dreams of fresh air, our own home, and deliciously healthy home grown food, we made the plunge into the unknown on the peninsula of Washington state.

One of our first concerns, even before we moved onto the property, was our lack of gardening experience. We read everything we could find on the subject. We talked to the State Extension Service, called the "Master Gardeners," and bugged our gardening friends unmercifully as we looked for answers.

Learning experiences

After all our planning and research, the first garden didn't turn out all that well. Some vegetable varieties would not mature, and some just wouldn't grow. It didn't seem to matter to the insects what grew in the garden, it was always on their menu. We had a lot to learn about living with the land.

We had decided the critters and eaters of our garden had as much right here as we did. So lethal poisons and killer traps didn't fit into our plans of getting along with the local inhabitants.

Three-quarter front view with the door open and the trigger set. The trap is ready to bait and place in the garden

Bugs, grubs and other creepy crawling things were controlled with a bit of work and persistence. But the four legged monster called mountain beaver (yes, you read that right, mountain beaver) who waited until sundown to wipe out a row of tomato plants was another matter. To do bodily harm to these varmints was out of the question. We didn't want to hurt them; we just wanted them to take up residence away from our garden.

Fencing a portion of our rapidly shrinking garden was the first thing we tried. Cleaning up some blow-down on the property furnished us with posts, and a timely sale of fence wire at the feed store put a strong barricade between our few remaining tomato plants and the midnight feeding of our rodent looking mountain beaver. It took two days for our tomato loving friend to tunnel under the wire.

We tried all the suggestions friends and neighbors made, including dumping the cat box litter down their holes, and scattering moth crystals around the perimeter of the garden. Nothing worked, although I did notice the beaver's appetite seemed to improve each time I dumped the cat box.

Traps?

Out of desperation, we started talking about traps. I remembered a rabbit trap I used to make as a boy growing up in Arkansas. The bunnies would go into the end of this contraption and a door would drop, keeping them safe from dogs and such until they were removed. This seemed to be a simple solution. Anything caught in the trap would then be relocated away from the garden, and we could sleep at night knowing we had not caused the slow, painful death of some little creature.

2	Each	Wood Screws	1 1/2"X8	Pivot Supports
2	Each	Washers	1/4"	Pivot Supports
		Nails, Box	4D	
3	Pieces	3/8" Plywood	7"X24"	Bottom and Sides
1	Piece	3/8" Plywood	7"X21 3/4"	Top (Rear)
1	Piece	3/8" Plywood	7"X1 1/2"	Top (Forward)
1	Piece	3/8" Plywood	7"X8"	End
1	Piece	3/8" Plywood	6"X9 3/8"	Door
1	Piece	Scrap (Lath) 1/4"	1 1/2"X18"	Lever
2	Pieces	Scrap (Lath) 1/4"	1 1/2"X14 1/4"	Pivot Supports
4	Pieces	Scrap (Lath) 1/4"	1 1/2"X7"	L&R Door Guides
2	Pieces	Scrap (Lath) 1/4"	1 1/2"X5 1/4"	Bottom Door Guide
1	Piece	2"X2"	6 3/4"	Pivot
2	Pieces	Wire, (Coat Hanger?)		Trigger, Door Connector
		Paint or Water Repellent		Weather Proofing

THE DIMENSIONS AND TYPE OF MATERIAL ARE YOUR CHOICE. THE "TRAP" CAN BE SCALED UP OR DOWN ACCORDING TO YOUR REQUIREMENTS.

Materials list.

Searching through the wood pile, I came up with a few little pieces of plywood. Using scraps of lath and a short piece of metal coat hanger, I was able to make a 1992 version of the 1945 rabbit trap. The flexibility of this design allowed me to use available materials and scale the dimensions up or down. Total time of construction—about two hours.

It took a few days to adapt the trapping techniques to fit our particular pest. Once we started thinking like beavers, it was a pretty simple matter to get them to investigate this new addition to their turf. We checked our trap a couple times a day to prevent the catch from being contained too long. We usually checked before going to bed at night and first thing in the morning. Because of skunks in the area, we always approached the trap with caution.

Success

Much to our neighbors' surprise, the trap worked. We caught our first uninvited dinner guest about a week after putting the trap in the garden. When we found our trap "tripped," we turned it upside down and transferred our catch into an old wire cage. We then used the cage to transport the mountain beaver to the relocation area. Our garden has remained untouched after relocating two mountain beavers.

It didn't seem to harm the animals when they were moved. We checked on them a few days later and found fresh-dug tunnels and evidence of their feeding. It probably would have been easier to gas the beaver tunnels, or use spring loaded "killer" traps, but we felt we should really try to live in harmony with our own little piece of Mother Nature.

Carol and I have learned a lot this past year. Our experiences have taught us that it's possible to control some garden pests if we work with nature. We have accepted the fact that some vegetables don't grow well in our area. I guess the most important lesson is that we can get along with the other inhabitants of our two acres—even mountain beavers.

Trap assembly

The dimensions and type of materials are your choice. The trap can be scaled up or down according to your requirements.

1. Nail lath left and right door guides to left and right side plywood pieces.
2. Nail lath bottom door guide pieces to bottom plywood piece. Be sure to center side to side, to leave room for side plywood pieces.
3. Nail right and left plywood sides to bottom, making sure that side and bottom door guide scrap pieces are aligned.
4. Nail top rear plywood (trigger hole piece) to right and left side pieces, even at rear. The front of this piece should end at the door track created by the lath door guides.
5. Nail on end piece as you square up sides. (Hardware cloth can be substituted.)
6. Nail the forward top plywood piece to the top front. This should line up with the door guides in the sides and bottom, creating a slot and track 1/8" wider than the thickness of the door.
7. Cut oval shaped notch into the rear top piece. Make the hole 3/8" wide, 3/4" long, centered side to side and 5 1/2" from rear.
8. Drill a 1/4" hole in one end of each pivot support piece, centered and 3/4" from the end.
9. Nail the pivot supports to the left and right sides, 9" from the front of the trap (the ends with the holes drilled in them up).
10. Drill a centered 3/8" hole 1/2" from each end of the lever.
11. Nail the center of the lever across the center of the pivot piece.
12. Attach the lever and pivot assembly between the upright pivot supports

with 1 1/2" wood screws and washers. Do not over-tighten: the pivot and lever must swing freely.

13. Install wire connector into the hole in the front end of the lever, and into the hole in the top of the door. Slide the door into position through the slot between the front and rear top pieces.

14. Install the trigger in the rear hole in the lever. The sensitivity of the trigger can be adjusted by changing the angle of section "A" (see detail on drawing).

15. Apply paint or waterproofing to protect your trap from the weather. Δ

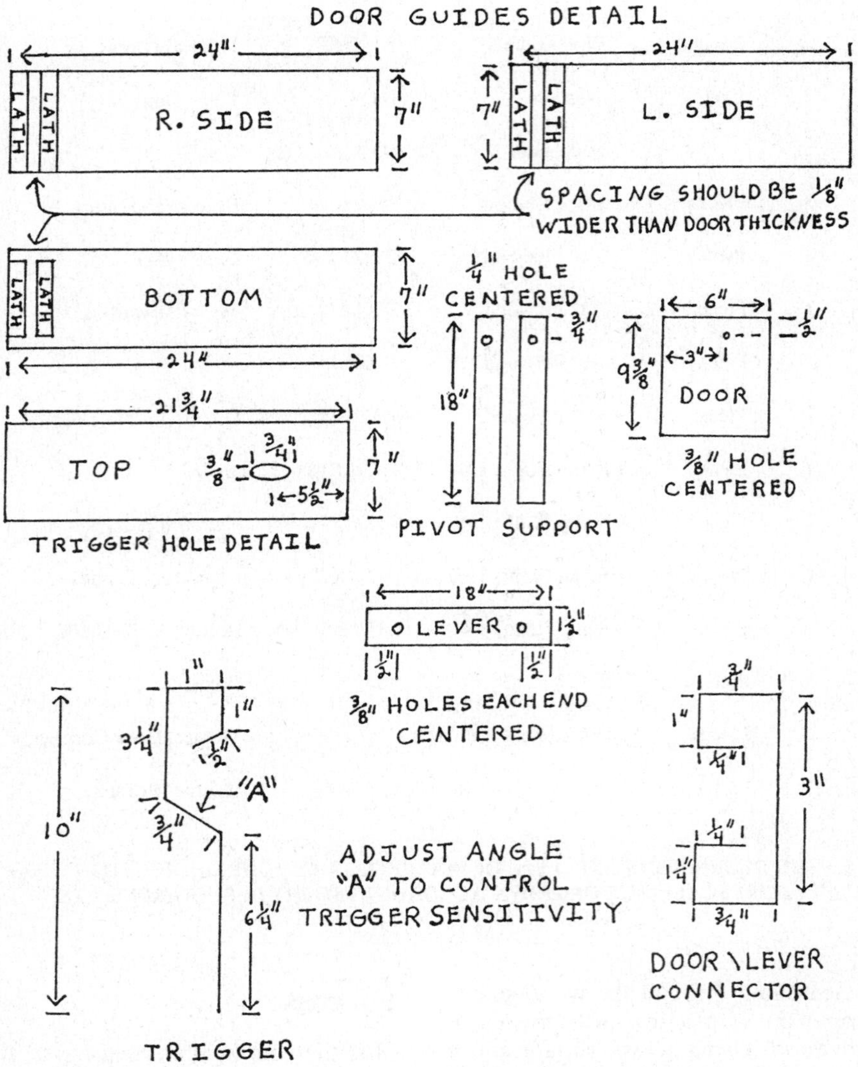

Carol releases a mountain beaver away from the garden. Use caution around any animal you catch. They might look cute and harmless, but don't let their looks fool you.

DOOR GUIDES DETAIL

24" R. SIDE 7" LATH LATH

24" L. SIDE 7" LATH LATH

SPACING SHOULD BE 1/8" WIDER THAN DOOR THICKNESS

BOTTOM 24" 7" LATH LATH

TOP 21 3/4" 7" 3/4" 3/8" 5 1/2"

TRIGGER HOLE DETAIL

1/4" HOLE CENTERED 3/4" 18"

PIVOT SUPPORT

DOOR 6" 3" 1/2" 9 3/8"

3/8" HOLE CENTERED

LEVER 18" 1 1/2" 1/2" 1/2"

3/8" HOLES EACH END CENTERED

TRIGGER 1" 1" 3 1/4" 1 1/2" "A" 3/4" 10" 6 1/4"

ADJUST ANGLE "A" TO CONTROL TRIGGER SENSITIVITY

DOOR\LEVER CONNECTOR 3/4" 1" 1/4" 3" 1/4" 1 1/4" 3/4"

Building diagram.

WIN A FREE VITA-MIX (see page 6)

July/August 1993
No. 22
$3.50 U.S.
$4.50 Canada

Backwoods Home magazine

... a practical journal of self reliance!

SPECIAL LOG HOME EDITION

Solar Energy
Greenhouses
Homesteading

Quilt Magic
Making Cheese and Butter

Note from the publisher

The raw milk of country magazines

Just before going to press with this issue, an advertiser called me to say that he would not advertise in this issue unless I gave his company "some recognition." In other words, he wanted a product endorsement in exchange for his advertising dollars.

I said, "No, I'm sorry; we don't do that." He seemed surprised, as if I must be crazy to pass up a nice fat check for the one-third page ad he had previously committed to. In fact, my heart did sink a little because I needed that nice fat check to help pay the bills for the special promotion that is placing this issue on the front counters of some 1,100 Waldenbooks bookstores and 900 other retail outlets across the country.

But it didn't sink much. When I hung up I apologized to Lance, one of my editors, for losing the commission he would have gotten for the ad sale.

"I understand," Lance said.

And I realized he really did understand, because *Backwoods Home Magazine* really doesn't cater to the monied interests in our lives. Rather than suck up to the people who sell products to our readership, we bow to the people who read the magazine. They want information, and we give it to them, honestly and as accurately as we can. This issue is no exception. It's a special log home issue, but the main article, which begins on page 27, explores the log home warts that go along with that log home beauty. We try and tell you how to deal with those warts, but we will never hide them from you. It's the only way an honest story can be written.

A recent review of us by the *Washington Post* put it rather accurately when it said, ". . . *Backwoods Home Magazine* is like raw milk . . ." compared to other country magazines that are "more of a pasteurized product."

For all you readers who are picking this magazine up for the first time, welcome to the raw milk version of country magazines.

Solar cell pioneer Tony Lamb dies

A special friend of *Backwoods Home Magazine* and a man who played a prominent role in the development of modern photovoltaic (solar cell) technology died recently.

He was Tony Lamb, a prolific inventor who developed the first practical solar cell in 1931. Lamb used the solar cell as part of many of his inventions, including the electric eye and light meter. His first solar cell patent was filed July 14, 1932 when he was 29. He was 89 when he died.

An electrical engineer for Weston Electrical Instrument Corporation in New Jersey and a World War II "critical scientist" during most of his younger years, Lamb moved to Newbury Park, California, in his late 60s where he became one of the nation's most successful senior citizens activists.

Tony Lamb

We profiled Lamb in our first issue and made him our "man of the year" in our second issue. What we saw in him was a fiercely independent man who would buck all odds in the pursuit of what was right.

When he developed his first solar cell, he had to battle industry bureaucrats to market it, and when he became a senior activist he had to battle intransigent bureaucrats and politicians.

In the end he beat them all, and we salute his spirit.

Second Vita-Mix winner

Jim Darlack of Pasadena, Maryland is our second Vita-Mix winner. He was chosen in a random selection from among our 7500 paid subscribers.

We'll continue giving away a $500 Vita-Mix for each of the next four issues. You must be a paid subscriber to be eligible. The Vita-Mix ad on page 33 will show why the Vita-Mixes are so prized by many homesteaders. Δ

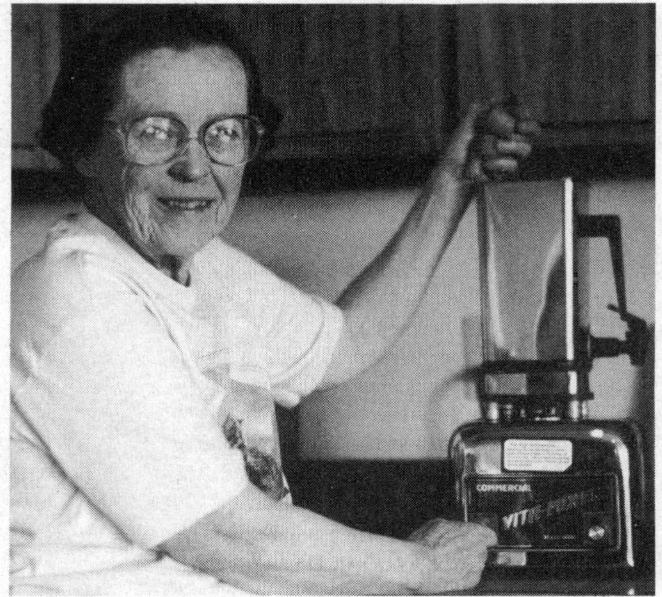

Meg Letterman, 73, was our first Vita-Mix winner. Here she prepares a carrot/nut/raisin salad for one of the pot lucks at Ponderosa Village, a self-reliant community near Goldendale, Washington.

My View

Milwaukee water, self reliance . . .

A few months ago thousands of Milwaukee residents became sick from drinking the city's drinking water, which is drawn from Lake Michigan. The main suspect was a waterborne parasite called cryptosporidium, which is found in the intestinal tracks of animals. Officials suspected slaughterhouse run-off into rivers that feed the lake.

More than a week after the outbreak Milwaukee Mayor John Norquist recommended that about 800,000 people served by the city's water system continue to boil their water. The mayor said they still weren't sure what was wrong with the water. Schools covered their drinking fountains, and their was a run on bottled water at the supermarkets until it ran out.

The story stayed in the nation's paper for about two weeks until the press got tired of it. People in Milwaukee were still boiling their water, but the story was no longer selling newspapers.

I wonder how many of you know what became of the Milwaukee water problem? Did they (whoever **they** are) eradicate the suspect parasite? Was it something other than the suspect parasite that they had to eradicate? Or does the problem still exist today, subdued for the time being but as alive and as dangerous as ever. You should really check into it; what you find out may make you consider storing water in your basement.

The Milwaukee water problem is one of those episodes that come along now and then to remind us of how much we rely on systems that are largely beyond our control and knowledge. Big hurricanes like Andrew in the Southeast and earthquakes like the one in San Francisco a couple of years back also open our eyes to our vulnerability as a society. They're still rebuilding in Florida and California, but who cares beyond some people there. I suppose you would if you drank some of that Milwaukee water or had your life partially destroyed by Hurricane Andrew.

. . . and a cool country drink

It is the premise of this magazine that we should care about the bad things that could happen to us and our families and that we should be prepared to deal with them.

No, I'm not another survivalist wacko from Waco so don't send the BATF and FBI after me. Most of the people who read this magazine are just ordinary folks, mainly living in the country and by and large independent of the vagaries of urban systems that now and then come crashing down. Most of us wouldn't have been bothered much by the Milwaukee water system, or any urban water system, breaking down. We just shake our heads at the sight of all those city dwellers running around in a panic wondering where they're going to get their next drink of water.

Dave Duffy

And I'm not knocking modern civilization. I like the remarkable antibiotics and vaccinations it has given us, the great machines that free us from back-breaking work, and the photovoltaics and computers that allow me to produce this magazine from deep in the woods of the Northwest.

But I choose to do without modern civilization's baggage: crowded neighborhoods where you barely know the person next door, the stress and frustration of urban life, and a system in which all my needs — food, clothing, shelter, transportation, energy, even water — are produced, distributed, and controlled by others.

When something breaks down in the city, I must wait for it to be fixed so I can get on with my life. When something breaks down in the country, I fix it myself because I probably helped build it.

In an urban setting most people work in abstractions, with no meaningful output, no visible finished product. We know more about Madonna than we do about our neighbors. In the country it is just the opposite. We often build our own house and grow the products we consume. Our neighbors may be miles away, but we know them and visit them.

The attraction of this magazine is the attraction of a simpler, independent life, living directly from our own efforts, having control of how we live our lives and of the systems we are dependent upon. The belief in such a life spans all class, race, and political boundaries. It is the natural high of life. Many of our readers and most of the writers of this magazine are living that life.

So if you live in Milwaukee or any other city, I invite you to visit us in the country to see how life can really be worth living. We don't always have all the automatic gadgets of city life, but we have almost none of the baggage. And when our water system breaks down, we just go out to the creek and get us a nice cool, clean cup of water. Δ

Dave Duffy

Homesteading at Hayden Lake

By M. C. Wright

Being a back-to-basics family is our goal, producing our own food, making the things we need. Too many years were spent working every day to pay for shiny new things that after a few weeks lost their glow and all we would have left were the payments. We realized the kids were not going to remember new furniture or the car right out of the show room. The things they would remember are the experiences, the memories of being a family.

We wanted to get as far away from the "civilized" world as possible and still be able to make the money needed to survive. Building our own log house and not having to pay rent or house notes ever again was a big incentive. We try to be as self-sufficient as we can without being slaves to this life-style also.

We moved to Idaho and bought our land in 1975. It's about 60 miles from the Canadian border in the Idaho Panhandle, where we are in the middle of a great forest. The trees are so thick around us that we barely feel the wind. Storms will blow so strong that the tops of big trees will pop off with the sound like a shotgun, but outside at ground level we only get a gentle breeze.

We lived in the small community of Rathdrum, Idaho, about 20 miles from our homestead, while our three older kids were in high school. Then, about six years ago, we sold everything. After a week-long sale, where I was subjected to arguing over the price of my most prized possessions, we were left with the absolute necessities. From a four bedroom home in town, we moved to a 21-foot long travel trailer in the woods.

Peeling logs for the family-built homestead involved young Benjamin, and 84-year-old Grandpa (in hat).

Knowing that we would live in the trailer through the summer and fall while we built our house, I planned for clothes and supplies accordingly. I made lists for each person or function. It made sorting a lot easier. Husband Bill, six- year old Benjamin, myself, the kitchen, the bathroom: each had a page in my list book. Only the things on the list were kept.

Anticipating a backwoods lifestyle, I had kept a wishbook for many years and filled it with every picture, idea, or hint I found that might one day come in handy. With wishbook and trailer in tow, we moved to the wilderness on the 4th of July, 1986. I was fully armed with enough ideas to scare even the most enthusiastic hubby when we began to build our homestead. Probably one of the few things Bill and I agreed on without negotiation was that the house would be as rustic as possible. Furnishings would be as "cabinish" as we could get.

Saving our trees

We planned for the land around our house to be left as natural as possible. Not wanting to cut our big pine trees, we bought logs. Two truck loads (about $1200) supplied enough wood to build the house and heat it for a couple of years. Information gleaned from loggers and experienced builders taught us that logs called "house logs" cost three times what is called "firewood grade" and are usually the same wood. We found firewood grade quite suitable. Tamarack is what we got. There are also a couple of pines in our house somewhere.

We bought our "firewood" in 36-foot lengths. The wood was seasoned, so we had very little peeling to do. We made peeling tools by straightening the shafts on garden hoes. They were cheaper and didn't break as easily as specially-made peeling tools.

Our house-raising crew was family. There was daughter Angie, her husband, David, and another daughter, Stacie. Mike, our older son, helped while on leave from the Marines. Benjamin became chief go-fer. Grandpa Wright, 84, and Grandma, 82, supplied baby sitting and food services. Grandma Wright was chief cook. Driving the Suburban when it was time to raise logs was my main job.

It never rained on us and we never needed a Band-aid. Only one log was dropped, and it made a hole in the kitchen sub-floor that was easily patched, and we just kept on working. There was no real house plan. It started out as a log box, and we went from there. We pre-cut holes for the doors. Window openings were cut only after the roof went on. The chainsaw was an indispensable tool. When it broke, the whole job stopped.

The family room.

We figure our home cost us less than $10,000, everything included. Most of our finish materials came from salvage yards, rummage and yard sales. The inside doors were discovered at a sale at Coeur D'Alene Lake. They are oak, from an old hotel. They still had the room numbers on them. I paid $3 each for them.

Wood heat, natural cooling

We heat entirely with wood. Once lit in the fall, the stoves don't stop 'til spring. We bank them up good at bedtime and they will go all night. Two stoves keep the whole house warm using about seven cords of wood a winter. Once the logs warm up, it is very cozy.

In the summer, windows open at night cool the house. If the doors and windows are shut throughout the hot day, we have natural air conditioning.

Ceiling fans run year around. In the winter, they push the warm air down, and in the summer they supply a nice breeze.

Two of my prized possessions are a 1920s gas cook stove and a claw-foot bathtub. I searched from Idaho to Mississippi to find a perfect old gas stove. It's a green and cream colored

A surprise visitor

After the roof was on the house, we began moving clothes in from the trailer. One morning very early, Benjamin and I showered in the trailer and, with beach towels wrapped around us, ran to the house to get dressed. It was about 50 feet to the house. I got to the front door first, stepped over a two foot board put there to keep the dogs out and found a huge cougar inside! The cougar bounded for a back window. I grabbed Benjamin at a dead run, swung him under my arm, and made a wild dash back to the trailer where we stayed until Bill got home.

What started out as a big log box evolved into a comfortable home by Halloween, 1986, our official move-in date. Floors are all 1-inch by 6-inch planks, most covered with big braided rugs. Animal skins, snow shoes and quilts decorate the walls. A bedroom and bath addition to the back is regular cut-wood. Our building crew (the kids) moved away, and Bill and I decided it would be easier to work with cut boards instead of logs. Its walls are covered with old barn wood. The nicks and knot-holes are still there for the rustic effect.

We have a family room, kitchen, two bedrooms, dining/school room, pantry, loft, bath, and a walk-in closet. I have a built-in desk and a sewing craft area, two features that I considered non-negotiable in the house plan. Most everything else was up for discussion.

Cozy kitchen now houses Margaret's prized 70-year-old Magic Chef cookstove, purchased for $100.

six-burner Magic Chef and I love it. It turned up in the attic of a salvage business in Spokane. We had to climb over boxes and old furniture and there it was, sitting there waiting for me. I was so thrilled it was hard not to look interested. I said, "how much?" He smiled and said "$100." I quickly paid, got a receipt and left with a big grin. Two days later, our propane service man changed the jets and adjusted the valves. It has cooked in spectacular fashion ever since.

I was ready to give up on ever getting the kind of tub we wanted when Angie was late coming to see us one Saturday. She arrived blowing her car horn and screaming. I was afraid to ask why. She had stopped at a sale on the way. The family was moving and wanted to sell all they could, including a claw foot bath tub! Angie bought it for $50. It took less than 20 minutes to go back, unhook the tub from the plumbing, load it into our truck and make off with it.

Benjamin adopted the tub for a bed before his room was finished. He would pile it full of blankets and his sleeping bag. The married kids think it is wonderful to take a nice long bath in "mom's tub." Four grandkids can share the tub and think it's great too.

Doing without

For our first year, we did without electricity, telephone or running water. Water for dishes and bathing was heated on the wood stove. Washing clothes was a real trial. We could do most of them in the washtub with an old scrub-board, but when I couldn't face the chore, we went to the laundromat in town.

Clothes washing is now done with a wringer washer, and I hang them on the line to dry. I think my clothes come cleaner than with any automatic washer I've ever had. Of course, my love for the solar clothes dryer (the clothes line) stops when the dog drags the sheets off the line. And it seems like nothing is more appealing to a bunch of kids than a clothes line. It must resemble a trapeze...and many a small acrobat I've found trying out his expertise on my clothes line. The day the clothes line broke, bringing down three full rows of wet clothes, was enough to bring me to tears. But in a few days, things like that are funny memories and we laugh at them. It does get to be a pain having clothes hanging in the house in the winter, but even that can be kind of pleasant. I have a rack over the bathtub for hanging clothes. Socks, washcloths and the like go on wooden racks near the fireplace, where they dry overnight.

I found a second wringer washer at a yard sale this summer for $20. So now I have an outside washer and an inside washer.

We used an electric generator during the first year. One hour per day of educational video for Benjamin was allowed. The generator was big enough to light one lamp, the TV and our computer for the genealogy booklets I write and sell.

It's not a lot of fun to need the generator in sub-zero weather and have to go out and get that little red monster to bring into the house to warm it up, then haul it back outside and crank, crank, crank. Eventually, it would start, but by then the operator usually was an ice cube. It never failed that when we needed the crazy thing and it turned balky, Bill would be away at work. That was the winter when the Arctic Express brought 40-below temperatures in the daytime and colder at night. It also was the winter the dog decided to have 13 puppies under the house.

Bless that little red generator. It literally worked its little heart out that winter. It died in the spring. We also own a bigger, ugly green Onan generator that we used mainly while we were building. Now it's our back-up power source.

Skins and quilts soften Tamarac log walls in the Wright's Idaho homestead.

Life in the woods

Enjoying a good book by lantern light before a warm fire can be the highlight of a busy day. On the other hand, there can be nothing as scary as a cabin in the woods in the winter— fireplace crackling, lantern light, blowing wind, and some weird noise from the outside that cannot be identified. Several times, I've been close to convinced we were visited by "Bigfoot" or several of his cousins.

One very cold rainy night early in November our first winter, Benjamin got cold and climbed in bed with us. Sometime later, he woke me rubbing and brushing at his face. There were drips all along the ceiling line the entire length of the house. The first layer of tar paper had blown loose up on the roof. Bill had to climb up there in gale force winds and rain to nail on wood strips left over from log chinking. I stood in the rain, parka hood over my face, holding a flashlight so he could see, and handing up things he needed. We got the tin that week and finished the roof quick. Now, as far as I'm concerned, there is no better sleep than a warm bed under rain on a tin roof.

We try to keep all our homesteading projects on a pay-as-you-go basis. Everything we buy is paid for in full. We look for used things in good condition when we can. Lots of our things come from a thrift store and yard sale excursions.

There is a quote I read: "We're here trying to maintain a lifestyle, but we're in a world where we have to make a living."

Bill is an electrician. He usually works about seven months a year. He enjoys his work, and if there is a big industrial job like a new paper mill, he'll work year-round. He did that three years ago. Bill and Benjamin are great buddies. They spend a lot of time together building, fixing and playing.

Homeschooling also allows us to be on our own schedule. After putting three kids through the public school system, we decided we could do a better job. Benjamin is basically in charge of what he studies. We guide him and sneak in the heavy stuff.

Cooking and canning

I use old fashioned (actually antique) cooking utensils. No plastic or Teflon. And nothing just sits on the self because it is old. My cast iron cookware is used all the time. Nothing tastes better than fried chicken cooked in cast iron.

I like to wonder what the lady of the house was thinking about 100 years ago when she used the same rolling pin I'm using now.

Putting away food and wood for winter, making butter, caring for the animals and kids, are continuing chores. All my cooking is from scratch like Grandma did it. No mixes found in this house. But sometimes a U-bake pizza as a special treat.

In deep winter, it's sometimes hard to recall summer's grapes or even where the garden is.

Going to the wholesale warehouse about once a month, we buy as much of our food supplies as possible in bulk. I always keep a couple of extra 50 pound bags of flour on hand. Sugar, brown sugar, honey, spices, corn meal, beans, wheat can all be stored in big white plastic buckets I buy for $1 from local fast food places.

Margaret Wright

Drying and canning my own food are very important to me. I feel like I've really accomplished something when I have a pantry shelf full of food we produced. Nothing is prettier than a row of freshly put up jelly sitting in the kitchen window to cool.

Herbs are very important in our daily life. I've learned a lot of the "old" ways of healing and use herbs for illness and as daily supplements to help maintain healthy bodies.

Every Tuesday and Friday, we buy two gallons of fresh cow's milk from a local gal. It always has a couple of inches of wonderful cream on top that makes the best butter and whipped cream imaginable. Benjamin and I have made butter in an antique crock butter churn my Mom gave me for my birthday several years ago. But most of the time, I use a food processor. Yes, I admit it, I have a food processor.

Gardening, sewing, and home schooling are just a few of the tasks I do. Sewing and needlework are very relaxing for me. Quilt making is a favorite. I've made all the kids and grandkids crocheted afghans. In the summer, I can't do much of the handcraft things because of all the time spent outside. In the winter, after the first snows, I dig out all my projects and life kind of settles down for a few months. We read, do crafts, and make models during the winter months.

We love our home and the land it sits on. Protection of our lifestyle is a priority. Our way of life is not for the majority of the population, but that's okay. This is America and we all can make choices.

Our choice is a cozy log home in the Idaho panhandle. Δ

FARM/GARDEN

How to choose a greenhouse

By Martin P. Waterman

After years of wishing and planning I finally did it. I now have a greenhouse and I am as proud as a new father. Like so many greenhouse owners, I don't know how I ever lived without one. Now, my new greenhouse has become a major part of my gardening activities.

I also learned numerous valuable lessons during the selection process which I am going to try to impart in this article. Hopefully, I can share with you the significance of the planning stage before you buy or build your first greenhouse so that you can avoid some of the mistakes I made and, of course, duplicate some of the areas where I was successful.

Making an accurate assessment about the total greenhouse size that is needed often is more easily said than done. Unfortunately, most will find that their first greenhouse is inadequate. Once they discover that there are so many additional crops and uses that are suited for their greenhouse, their original plans can become obsolete.

I am not going to go into detail on the technical requirements of certain types of greenhouse plants. There is ample information readily available on these topics. However, I have tried to compile a list that outlines about a dozen factors that you should consider before you procure your first greenhouse.

What to grow

This may not sound like an important question, but believe me, it is. I thought I knew exactly what I would do the second I had my new greenhouse. Was I ever wrong! Greenhouses open up more possibilities than you can imagine, so it is good to start to plan as if you already have one.

I had originally wanted my greenhouse so that I could propagate material such as grape vines and fruit trees in the spring and also start seeds for experimental varieties that I wanted to try growing. Of course, when I realized I could start vegetable plants in the spring, have an early crop of peppers and tomatoes and have late-season strawberries into November, I became painfully aware that I had not truly taken the time to consider many of the options that would open up to me once I had my greenhouse. I am finding that I am doing many additional things with the greenhouse beyond what I even thought would be possible. I am starting tropical houseplants and growing bananas and indoor citrus which are moved indoors in the fall. I am growing some flowers, mostly for the simple fact that they smell and look so pretty.

*My pride and joy.
My greenhouse door is open to prevent overheating on a hot day.*

Therefore, when you are contemplating buying or building your greenhouse, take some time and think about all the varieties you want to grow. Then, take some more time to think about the varieties that you may want to grow in the future. Better still, buy or borrow a book on greenhouse growing and study all the possibilities. I was surprised how many books have been written on greenhouse growing and I found our local library had a very impressive selection, since this is such a popular topic. When you are contemplating what you may want to grow, it is a good idea to discuss it with your spouse and loved ones to factor in their favorite foods and flora. When you have a better idea about the things you will be growing, your questions will begin to be answered, and you should begin to get a better idea of what type of capacity you may need. I still find myself considering new crops each week. This is another benefit of owning a greenhouse. You get to scheme about and experiment with new varieties that you could never grow before.

When to grow

The amount of time that you will be using your greenhouse is also an important fact to consider. If you plan to use it regularly and it becomes your entertainment, recreation, and even therapy, you will want a structure that you can use as much as possible. How much time you spend in your greenhouse is also very important. Some people will use their greenhouse only in the spring. They find that by growing their own landscape bedding plants and starting vegetable transplants early, they can save as much as several hundred dollars a year, especially if they have a big lot. Others like to move their houseplants into the greenhouse in the summer or grow an early crop of vegetables. Still others like to grow a late fall crop as well. Obviously, the more you use your greenhouse, the more you may want to invest in it to make sure it is comfortable to work in and able to accommodate all the growing time you want to donate.

Of course, if you use your greenhouse in the early spring and late fall, you may need heat and artificial lighting. You will also have to consider whether or not you want a double layer of plastic, which insulates better than a single layer by trapping warm air. You may also want to consider double pane glass. If you use your greenhouse in the summer, you may also need some type of cooling system.

How big is big enough

This is a very important consideration. I outgrew my greenhouse in the span of a few days. It was a little embarrassing to say the least. I am now working on procuring my second greenhouse, which will be much bigger.

One item you may wish to consider is the expandability of the greenhouse you intend to purchase or build. Many greenhouse kits are expandable and sections can be continually added. The ability to do this so that your structure can be expanded is a very good feature. However, be careful that expansion of your greenhouse does not become more expensive than if you just built or purchased a second structure.

Big can mean many different things to many different people. Do you want it big enough so that you can have good size work benches? This is important if you do not like to bend because if your plants are on the ground, you will be doing a lot of bending. Therefore, benches will be important, especially if senior citizens may be using the greenhouse. Not only can bending to ground level get to you after a while, it is often difficult to get a good look at some of the plants you are growing.

A greenhouse that is too small may not have room for an aisle down the center. Take some time to think about how wide you want your aisle to be, or if you are installing benches, how much room they will take up. A greenhouse should have an aisle big enough so that you can have easy access to all the plant material.

Do you want to put in a heat retention system such as water-filled jars or drums? These will take up room and must be factored into your plans. Do you want room for a hammock or even a chair? A greenhouse is an excellent place to relax, read, converse with friends, meditate, snooze and even hide. My greenhouse is much too small for most of these purposes. It is 8 by 12 and is continually too full of plants. I see that I can usually use three times as much room. This has led me to the discovery of a formula. The volume of an empty greenhouse will always become full since the amount of material you will want to grow will always be equal to or greater than the available space. Height is also an important consideration. If you are growing vines in the greenhouse, you may want a high ceiling. I have some "sweet 100" cherry tomatoes that will soon be over 6 feet in height and growing. I will have to head them back because they are getting too tall for my greenhouse.

A greenhouse additon need not be elaborate. This wood and plastic structure allows hundreds of plants to be started.

If you like the idea of hanging plants, you may also want a high ceiling so that the pots and the plants are not in your face. In addition, you will require a structure that can support this type of weight. Some types of hanging plants, in addition to adding beauty and charm to your greenhouse, will also provide some degree of shading which can be beneficial on hot days. Another reason why I chose the greenhouse that I did is that I can add hanging plants very easily.

Climatic considerations

This is also ignored by many growers but it is important. If you live in an area where you have considerable snow in the winter, you will want a structure that will not collapse. If your area has a history of hail storms, this could also have a bearing on what type of greenhouse and covering you buy or build. Do you live in an area with high winds? If this is the case, you may have to consider anchoring your greenhouse, or else you may have to retrieve it from the next county after a wind storm. I anchored my greenhouse by driving wooden stakes about three feet into the ground around the frame and then nailing the stakes to the wooden base. So far, even on a very windy day, the greenhouse does not budge even when the doors are closed.

The prevalent wind direction in your area will also tell you how to position your structure. For instance, my structure does not have a cooling system. It is not necessary, since I live in a cool Maritime climate with a short season. Therefore, I positioned the greenhouse so that the constant east-west breeze would blow through the greenhouse when both doors are opened. This keeps the greenhouse cool in the summer. It is not an elaborate cooling system, but for my purposes it works very well.

Aesthetics

Some will argue that aesthetics is secondary to functionality in a greenhouse. I would not normally bring up the question of how your greenhouse looks except for three facts. The first is that you do not want a greenhouse that after two or three years of use will look like a shanty greenhouse. Secondly, for those in urban areas, you don't want something that will upset the neighbors or authorities. Having a greenhouse is a status item and status often brings jealousy in our society. Some greenhouses that you can buy look so shoddy that I would be embarrassed to own one.

In addition, many municipalities have become so silly that they require a building permit for anything larger than a dog house and the structure cannot be an eyesore. This is just something to be aware of in the planning stage. My greenhouse is, to my tastes, very good looking and I am very proud of it.

Materials

Should you choose glass, plastic or Fiberglas coverings? There are good and bad arguments for all these materials, and entire book chapters have been devoted to debating this, resulting in many different conclusions. I chose plastic for several reasons. First of all, the price advantage was dramatic. Secondly, I thought that it was the best value and best-made greenhouse I could find. I also decided that if I liked it, I would then buy another one. My next greenhouse will also be plastic and the same style, because I would rather invest the differential in buying a larger greenhouse and plant materials for it.

Should the frame be made of steel, aluminum, plastic or wood? Again, there is much debate about this. You will have to decide what your needs and budget are and choose appropriately. Incidently, my greenhouse has a wood frame which I like very much. The wood is soaked in paint during the manufacturing process and therefore lasts a very long time.

To build or to buy

Originally, I was going to build a greenhouse. I love building things. I have been collecting glass windows from yard sales for years. However, whenever I sat down to draw up plans, I found that building my own greenhouse would probably be more expensive than buying a greenhouse kit. If you are considering building a greenhouse, make certain that your materials list is very thorough, because the project could nickel and dime you to death. Do not forget incidentals such as hardware, sealant and paint, which can add up to quite a bit of money.

If you are building a kit like my greenhouse, make sure that the instructions are easy to follow and you need minimum hand tools and do not require a degree in engineering from MIT to assemble it.

Of course, you can always add a greenhouse to your existing house. By doing this you can benefit by adding equity to your home. The solar heating provided by a well designed greenhouse can bring you impressive savings. A proper greenhouse addition can lower heating bills to the extent that the addition can be paid off in just a few years. There are many excellent books on this topic for those who want to investigate this type of greenhouse.

Hobby vs. commercial

Let's say you start several dozen tomato plants for your own use in January, move them into the greenhouse in March and in May have a hundred pounds or so more than you can use. You talk to your local produce manager, convenience store owner or restaurant and find that they will buy all the fresh tomatoes you can supply. This may sound unusual, but it is just how many hobby greenhouse growers earn money to supplement their hobby and often go on to become successful commercial growers. The types of commercial growing are endless: fresh herbs, cut flowers, rose bushes, fruit trees, bonsai specimens, fruits, vegetables, landscape and ornamental plants, etc. You will also have the advantage of specializing in varieties that are ideal for your market. This alone can give you an advantage over some of the large factory style propagators. Recently, I visited a local garden center. I know the owner and he told me that they could not propagate certain plants fast enough to meet demand even though they have acres of greenhouses. I learned that they were constantly looking for contract growers who could help supply them with big sellers such as Citrosa (mosquito repellent plant) Geraniums, Clematis and several other different varieties of herbs and flowers. Commercial considerations may be the farthest thought from your mind, but when neighbors and others begin to come and offer you money for tomatoes or plants, the temptation to sell a few and grow a few more may be to hard to resist. In fact, it may be downright profitable.

The base of your greenhouse

What are you going to use as a base for your greenhouse? If you have a concrete pad, this is great. It will help store heat during the day and release it at night in the cooler times of the year and can prolong your season. You could put your greenhouse on some turf, but if it is a wooden structure the base can begin to rot after a few years. You may want to look into buying a greenhouse that uses pressure treated lumber for the wood on its base or has a plastic or aluminum base. There are many alternatives to an expensive concrete pad or concrete footings. You can create a pad from levelled gravel which will allow water drainage and prevent rot. You could put down some of those concrete patio squares that are often used for paths and walkways. In any event, you will have to give the type of base you need some due consideration, especially since the cost could exceed your budget. It is best to shop around and price out the alternatives. I found out by accident that it is important not to have any spaces between the pad and your greenhouse. One cold spring night cold air leaked in through a small crack between the concrete pad and the base of the greenhouse. It froze a few leaves on nearby plants. I remedied this by filling the crack with a handful of sandy soil.

To heat or not to heat

This is another big question. I had not intended to heat my greenhouse. Now, to extend the season, I have changed my mind. Heating can be done in so many different ways and different systems that you need to consider how long you want to prolong your season. At a certain point, the cost of heating may diminish the value of any crop you may be growing. Then again, the thought of having green plants and fresh nutritious vegetables into winter may offset the power costs. Therefore, it is important to look at these factors as well. A greenhouse structure, if built on an existing house, can provide heat via solar radiation in the day and be closed off at night where it will not be in jeopardy of freezing. With free standing greenhouses, there are some simple ways to prolong the season, especially if you are just trying to add a few weeks. In my area, the first fall frost can happen as early as September. A local hobby greenhouse grower heats his greenhouse on those nights when there is frost warnings. He uses three brooding lights that are normally used for raising chicks, and they give enough heat to prevent freezing temperatures in his greenhouse well into November. Other growers will buy electric heaters and set the thermostat so that the heat will come on when temperatures approach freezing. Still others I know with greenhouses have a small wood stove which they start before bed and this keeps the greenhouse toasty warm all night.

Electrical requirements

You may not think that you have any electrical requirements, but you may need more than you may think. If you add an electric misting system, lighting, heating or cooling system, or a good sound system to keep the plants growing, you may have to consider at least adding an outdoor outlet so that you can run an extension cord through the greenhouse. An outdoor outlet is always a good idea, since you never know what power tools or appliances you may need to use outdoors. For instance, you may want some music for your greenhouse warming party.

Water requirements

Are you going to run a hose to your greenhouse or have a tap installed? Do you want a misting system with a timer or are you content to hand water your plants with a watering can? If you plan to go on vacation or travel, you do not want to be a hostage to your greenhouse, so you may want to consider a timed watering system. On a hot day, you will be amazed just how soon your greenhouse can go from tropical humidity to being dry as a bone. Drip irrigation can help prevent this by adding a large water drum. The drum will also help retain heat during cool nights.

Greenhouses need water, and if you do not install a tap your greenhouse should not be far from a water source. If you plan to use a watering can carried from the house, you can be in for many trips.

Price

I have seen few industries where there are such large variations in price for a manufactured product. I have seen almost identically configured greenhouses vary in price as much as 200% or more. There are many large and small manufacturers, and the selection can be staggering. You have to weigh the factors that are important for you. For instance, some greenhouses have no base. Building your own base can often cost more than the greenhouse when you factor in what your time is worth. I highly recommend writing and visiting as many greenhouse sellers as you can. Most gardening publications have a large selection of ads from greenhouse companies. If you are a handyman with construction skills, you are in luck. There are several books available on building your own greenhouse and you may be able to save a lot of money and have greater latitude in designing and building your structure. Once you know what requirements are valuable to you, you can start to narrow down the list of possible greenhouses that have the features that you need. I have received many questions regarding greenhouses. My advice to most people who want one is to start with a small, inexpensive greenhouse and see how you like it. This will initiate you into greenhouse growing and give you a better understanding of it and guide you on how much you may wish to expand. When you calculate price, do not forget the extra expenses. For instance, if you order a kit how much will the freight and taxes cost? Be aware of the items the greenhouse you are buying does not have. Many greenhouse manufacturers offer an inexpensive stripped down model. However, once you begin to add on the extras, you may no longer have an inexpensive greenhouse.

Planning hints

Remember, the idea of a greenhouse is to enrich your life and help you to enjoy your hobby. Be careful not to fall into the trap in which you are supporting the greenhouse and the plants, and not the other way around.

Planning is crucial, so I recommend the following. First, go get a pencil, a ruler and some paper. Go now and don't put it off. You've probably delayed too long already. Secondly, make a list of what you would like to grow in the greenhouse. Tomatoes? Okay, how many plants? Is ten or fifteen enough? How many different varieties should be grown? How big will the pots be or how much room will they take? Keep adding to your list and you will get an idea about how much room you will need. If you are like most people, when you finish your list you will probably need a greenhouse about the size of a football field. Now is the time for compromise to bring the size down to suit you budget and, of course, reality. This exercise should tell you much about what type and size best suits your needs. And, of course, remember that needs evolve.

Without exception, everyone to whom I have talked about their greenhouses has told me that they wish they had more space. My next greenhouse is going to be at least 12 x 20 feet (240 square feet) even though I know that it will probably be too small. Ideally, I would like 18 x 30 feet (540 square feet). That way I could have two aisles with a place to relax and work.

Why I chose my greenhouse

I wrote to about two dozen greenhouse companies. I studied all the information that was sent to me. I found there were some very fancy greenhouses at very high prices. I also found there were some shoddy looking greenhouses that looked like they were constructed by children. I learned a great deal of information from the material since I was able to see what features I needed and which ones were useless to me. I strongly recommend anyone contemplating a greenhouse to get as much information as possible. If you know anyone with a greenhouse, ask them what they like and dislike about it. Ask them what they would do differently if they were buying a new greenhouse tomorrow. In other words, do your homework.

After reading all the material that I received, I was not certain which greenhouse was the best for my needs. In a strange twist of fate, I learned that there was a greenhouse manufacturer a couple miles from me. They manufactured a line of quality wood products and had started manufacturing greenhouses a number of years ago.

I chose this company for three reasons. The first thing I liked was the price. For my budget the greenhouse was affordable. I also liked the Gothic Arch style, since we live in a snow belt. Last year we set a record by receiving over 6 feet of snow in about 24 hours. One of the greenhouses built by this manufacturer was almost completely buried under snow, yet suffered no damage. In its price range, the greenhouse kit I purchased was the best looking by far.

The third thing I liked was the quality. Let me explain. I also found another greenhouse manufacturer about 25 miles away. They make a greenhouse with plastic pipe and a plastic covering. Their kit costs almost as much as the one that I purchased but included no base and it looked shoddy and crooked since the frame was not very solid.

The manufacturer I bought my greenhouse from is called Sun Harvest Greenhouses (P.O. Box 165, Petitcodiac, New Brunswick, E0A 2H0, Canada; phone 506-756-2151). I called the owner, John Lewis, and he tells me that they have new models under development, and if anyone writes or calls him, they will be sent information on their greenhouse kits. The greenhouse part of the business was started by John's father, Art Lewis, who is an avid gardener. Word of the greenhouses spread by word of mouth and now they are finding that greenhouses have become an important part of their business.

I purchased my greenhouse because it suited my objectives. Fortunately, as my objectives evolved my greenhouse was able to suffice, except for, of course, the shortage of space. This was my error. I want my next greenhouse to have enough space so that in the spring when greenhouse space is needed the most, I will not have to scale down my plans for lack of room. I also want my next greenhouse to have a double layer of plastic to extend my season.

A misting system is really too elaborate at this point, and I am looking into some hydroponic systems. On the hottest August days, if I soak my greenhouse, it is okay for about four days. If I am gone more than four days, I have someone water it. It's low tech, but it works.

One problem I had was cats going into the greenhouse in the spring and digging up my seed flats. This activity stopped once the plants germinated. I put a few pots to block each entrance which also deterred the cats.

If I had a ventilation system, I could keep the doors closed in the summer, but at this time I cannot justify the expense. Our summers are so short and cool that a ventilation system would only be used a fraction of the year.

Since purchasing my greenhouse, I have looked at even more greenhouses, and I have decided that I am going back to the same manufacturer where I purchased my first one. I am glad I did the research that I did, since I don't think I would have had the same results by building a greenhouse from scratch or purchasing one elsewhere.

Of course, like anyone, I like the aluminum and glass structures, but the prices are so prohibitive I just can't justify spending that kind of money. I think the thing that matters most is the kind of care the plants are getting and not the kind of status you are getting. Again, this is why I was so pleased that I found a plastic greenhouse that looked decent and that I am proud to show.

In the spring and fall, I close up the greenhouse at night to retain heat. In the morning, I enjoy going into the humid greenhouse. The plastic walls are covered with dew so no one can see inside and the smell is just terrific, especially since the citrus is almost always flowering.

It is hard to believe that I was once intimidated by the idea of a greenhouse. Now my greenhouse is a big part of my life. I am still intimidated by hydroponics, though; this is my next project to investigate and conquer. Perhaps I will be reporting soon on my successes and failures in this misunderstood aspect of gardening as well.

Some greenhouse sources

Farm Wholesale, Inc., 2396 Perkins NE, Salem, OR 97303, (800) 825-1925

Fox Hill Farm, 20 Lawrence Street, Rockville, CT 06066, (203) 875-6676

Troy-Bilt Manufacturing, 102nd St. and 9th Ave, Troy, NY 12180

Northern Light Greenhouses, 128 Intervale Road, Burlington, VT 05401, (800) 356-4769

Sun Harvest Greenhouses, P.O. Box 165, Petitcodiac, New Brunswick, Canada E0A 2H0, (506) 756-2151

Gothic Arch Greenhouses, P.O. Box 1564, Mobile, AL 36633, (800) 628-4974

Genesis Horticultural Systems, 64 Airport Road, West Milford, NJ 07480, (201) 728-0781 Δ

Quilts – masterpieces of the heart and windows into women's history

By Marlene Parkin

Many of the quilts of yesterday took a lifetime to make. Perhaps the mystical part of quilts – the aspect that makes them almost human – is the countless hours of work and devotion it took to create a masterpiece of the heart.

Beyond their beauty and usefulness, quilts possess a magic that will never die, for all of life's hopes and fears, loves and hates have been sewn into them. Long ago, a woman whose quilt took her nearly 25 years to finish, remarked, "I tremble sometimes when I remember what that quilt knows about me."

Little is known of the women who stitched the quilts of old; most remain anonymous. The exact origin of quilts is also somewhat sketchy. The name derives from Latin meaning "stuffed sack," which was translated into Middle English as *quilte*, meaning "wrap around the body," providing both padding and blanket. A partial unraveling of quilt history reveals that the oldest example of patchwork, a canopy for an Egyptian queen, dates back to 960 B.C.

Generally speaking, a quilt consists of three layers: the top, the filling, and the back. Wool, silk, or cotton were common fabrics for the top layer and muslin for the backing.

In the earliest quilts, grass and leaves or feathers were used for the filling. After the top had been meticulously pieced together, the three layers were assembled and laid over a quilting frame supported by legs, sawhorses, or chair backs. In the South, the quilting frame was often suspended from the ceiling. The layers were then joined together by quilting, the running of stitches through the three layers of material.

The technique of quilting was used throughout the ancient Near East. When the Crusaders ventured to Eastern lands, they brought back the arts of needlework to Western Europe. The West began importing rich silks, satins, brocades, and lace from the East, and women in all walks of life, from queens to peasants, joined the excitement of quiltmaking that lasted through the Middle Ages and Renaissance. Quilts were coveted and cherished, and often were recorded in ledger books.

Pioneer quilts

Regardless of origin, it was the pioneer women in America whose needles would create a way of life that would influence their whole cultural and social structure. No other art was ever so completely dominated by women or brought so many together to work, including young ladies, for in the 18th century they were rigorously taught that usefulness was happiness. And there was no better way to make oneself useful than to sew.

As early as age four, little girls began practicing their stitches. Holding a delicate needle in their tiny, clumsy fingers, they pieced together simple four-patch blocks of plain and flowered calicoes. One woman described her childhood experience: "Before I was three years old, I was started at piecing a quilt. Patchwork, you know. My stint was at first only two blocks a day, but these were sewn together with the greatest care or they were unraveled and done over." By the time young women were about to be married, the needle had become their constant companion, and they took great pride in the accomplished needlework of their quilts.

Since cloth was not plentiful in the colonies and most women could not indulge in the luxury of imported silks and satins, creating quilts meant making their own cloth or piecing together whatever scraps were at hand. Often inspired by familiar objects and reflections of their new life, quilts were given such names as Windmill, Little Red Schoolhouse, Wedding Ring, Lost Ship, Horseshoe, Lone Star, Bear's Paw, Wild Geese, and Drunkard's Path.

The most popular quilt pattern during colonial times was undoubtedly the Log Cabin, the first ones made of thick woolens, consisting of blocks which always have a square center (red and yellow were preferred, to symbolize a glowing chimney) with strips of material, half dark and half light, sewn next to each other, reminiscent of log cabin construction.

Regardless of the design a woman chose, all quilts had the same basic meaning. They were the very core of a woman's life, encompassing her passions, attitudes, beliefs, noble spirit, anger, and indignities.

There are several variations of the Log Cabin: Barn Raising, Light and Dark, Straight Furrow, and Streak of Lightning – all influenced by the skillfully planned arrangement of contrasting colors. Because of their strong construction, Log Cabin quilts were rarely quilted, but instead were knotted together or tufted.

The Log Cabin was only one of the many patchwork quilt designs – there simply were hundreds of them. Regardless of the design a woman chose, all quilts had the same basic meaning. They were the very core of a woman's life, encompassing her passions, attitudes, beliefs, noble spirit, anger, and indignities.

Of indignities, she suffered many. These were the days when women were not allowed to vote, and a woman's main tasks in life were to please her husband, bear his children,

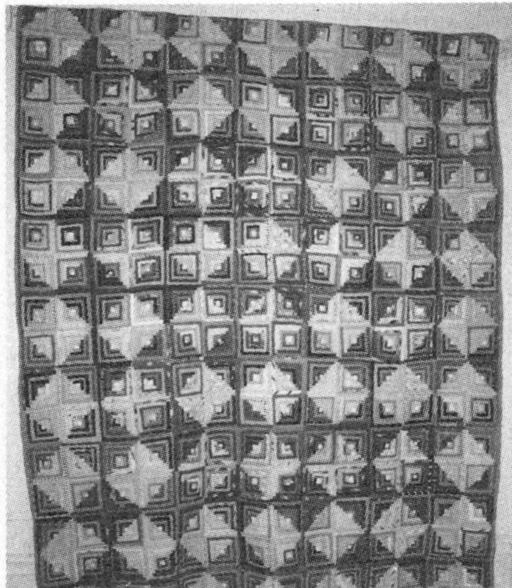

Log cabin quilt.

and keep his house. Yet there always persisted a dogged will to make something extraordinary in the midst of duties, to weave pleasure into toil. There also remained a poignant faith in the future, and the idealism of romantic love never wavered.

All young ladies were expected to marry shortly after their education, possessing a dowry of quilts, usually thirteen—a baker's dozen. Twelve quilt tops were to be finished before her engagement.

The tops usually were not quilted until she was reasonably certain of marriage, for it meant a real outlay of money to purchase the fillings and backings. When a woman was pledged to marry, the thirteenth quilt—called the Bride's or Wedding Quilt—was designed and quilted. Often the most elaborate, many of these were of unrivaled beauty.

Caroline Cowles Richards noted in her diary, dated 1862: "I have been up at Laura Chapin's from 10 o'clock in the morning until 10 at night, finishing Jennie Howell's bed quilt, as she is to be married very soon. Almost all of the girls were there. We finished it at 8 P.M., and when we took it off the frames we gave three cheers."

After a woman had married and settled into "domestic tranquility," she looked for ways to beautify her home. Whether alone or in company, her restless needle never stopped.

As Ellen Birdseye Wheaton wrote in her diary in 1851, "Elizabeth and I spent most of the day in sewing, and accomplished quite a satisfactory day's work. What a busy set of hands to direct and control. Sometimes, I think I shall faint and fall down by the way."

Second only to church meetings, quilting bees were extremely important to women's social lives. With few newspapers and distant neighbors, quilting bees were a chance for women to exchange confidences and affairs of the heart, all the while making painstaking stitches that were performed with patience and a commitment to the humblest detail in creating a handiwork of startling invention.

There were serious discussions, too. As Harriet Beecher Stowe wrote in The Minister's Wooing, quilting bees enabled one to learn "how best to keep moths out of blankets, how to make fritters of Indian corn undistinguishable from oysters, how to bring up babies by hand, how to mend a cracked teapot, how to take grease from a brocade, how to reconcile absolute decrees with free will, how to make five yards of cloth answer the purpose of six, and how to put down the Democratic party."

Red-pieced quilt, unnamed, made in 1882.

As the dust of the westward movement settled, resources expanded, and women had more free time for quiltmaking. The quilts of the late 1800s illustrate the extravagance of the Victorian Age. Pieces of silk, satin and velvet, rich in color and texture, were transformed into the most unusual and handsome quilts.

Enter the era of the Crazy Quilt, which was pieced from materials of irregular shapes, sizes, and colors. In these years of sentimental overflow, quilts were made with bits and pieces of personal pasts: silk neckties and shoe labels, lace from a wedding veil, political ribbons from campaigns.

Crazy quilts added to other ideas of craziness during this time. In 1890, *The Ladies' World* magazine suggested its readers stage a crazy tea party. Mismatched invitations were to be mailed to guests. The hostess's house was to be decorated with crazy quilts, pictures hung upside down, and lamps topped with shades of various colors and sizes. The menu included baked beans with currant jelly and hot, salted lemonade. Ringing a bell every five minutes would signal the guests they must end their topic of conversation and begin a new one.

Like any other types of quilts, crazy quilts were often made as gifts or to mark a special occasion such as a wedding. Many were exquisitely embroidered with flowers, names, and pictures that held personal symbolic meaning.

By the early 1900s the craziness fad had ended: crazy quilts were out and the more traditional cotton patchwork quilt was back in style . . . and quilting was still in the hearts of many women.

Close-up of Crazy Quilt. This was made in 1893 for a wedding. Notice the words, "A wife's loving tribute" and "Faithful and true."

One woman, Clemmie Pugh, made over 400 patchwork quilts since 1900, and gave most of them away: "I always kept a quilt in hand, and then when I'd set down to rest, I'd work on the quilt. My husband said I gave a good living away, but I never lost anything by giving folks something."

Although quilts are timeless treasures of art, never meant to be disposable or forgotten, many have been lost or reduced to the scraps from which they were made. Fortunately, there have always been quilt lovers whose devoted interest in quilts has helped save many from the ravages of time.

Close-up of a sampler Crazy Quilt shows fine detailed embroidery and roses made of silk. Symbolic motifs on crazy quilts were common and roses stood for love.

Aunt Jane of Kentucky, a woman who made many quilts, once gave a poignant reason for her love of quilting: "... when I'm dead and gone there ain't anybody goin' to think o' the floors I've swept, and the tables I've scrubbed, and the old clothes I've patched... but when one of my grandchildren sees one o' these quilts, they'll think about Aunt Jane, and wherever I am, I'll know I ain't forgotten."

The quilts that remain help light the dark corners of women's history, providing a remembrance of their pride and passion. For gazing at a quilt is like reading a history book. Its needlework contains words of wisdom, imagination, philosophy, religion, realism, joy, sorrow, life, death, friendship, and love. And if we could read between the tiny stitches, what stories they would tell. Δ

Caring for an antique quilt

Storing quilts: Wrap a quilt in acid-free tissue paper or roll it up inside a cotton sheet. Quilts need to "breathe," so don't seal or store them in plastic, which causes fabric-staining mildew to form. Folded quilts should be refolded periodically to avoid permanent creases and discoloration marks.

Hanging quilts: Do not hang a colorful quilt in direct sunlight — it will fade. Avoid tacking a quilt to a wall with pushpins. This puts too much stress on the fabric. Instead, hang a quilt with a double-stick tape such as 3M's Scotchmate Hook & Loop Fastener tape, which distributes the weight of the quilt evenly. Rotate wall-mounted quilts about every eight months and hang from the opposite end to avoid concentrating the weight on one side.

Cleaning quilts: How to clean a quilt depends a great deal on type and condition. All antique quilts should be cleaned only when necessary. The least stressful method is vacuuming: Place a piece of fiberglass screening over the quilt while carefully and slowly using a low-suction hand vacuum to remove dirt and dust. Vacuuming is the only recommended method of cleaning for silk and velvet quilts.

Cotton and linen quilts in good condition (generally from the 1920s on) can be hand washed, if necessary, in the bathtub using cool water and a gentle detergent such as Ivory or Ensure. Be sure to test for colorfastness first: rub each piece of different fabric with a damp white cloth. If there are no signs of color, it's safe to wash the quilt. Avoid twisting or wringing the fabric; instead, gently massage. Rinse until water is suds-free. Press water out of the quilt with terrycloth towels. Lay quilt flat on a sheet to dry. If outside, cover with a sheet. A final word on cleaning: most experts recommend against dry-cleaning any type of quilt. This method is too stressful on the fabric. When in doubt about cleaning, consult a quilt expert or conservator. Δ

COUNTRY LIFE

I'm living my log cabin dream

© 1992 by Ralph LaPlant

It has always been my dream to live in a log cabin back in the woods. I can remember when I was a child telling my mother that when I grew up I was going to live in a log cabin and eat rabbit stew. She laughed, with both of us not realizing that when I did grow up I *would* be living in a log cabin, although not necessarily eating rabbit stew.

The reality of my log cabin started back in 1979 when I purchased a log cabin described by the realtor as "rustic," being 16' X 16' and located on 40 acres of land adjacent to county park and a state wildlife management area.

The drive to the cabin is just over a mile long on a logging trail that is off of a gravel township road. The property is located just east of Brainerd, Minnesota. Brainerd is about dead center in the state.

When I first walked into the cabin, I had mixed emotions. Part of me thought of the pioneers who lived in this type of dwelling. I was envisioning settlers and cowboys fighting Indians, but on the other hand me fighting the mosquitoes. The reality of the situation was the work that lay ahead. The cabin was completely bare except for a bird's nest and glass on the floor from broken windows. I was told the cabin was built two years previously, which I believed, as it was in good overall condition. But work still needed to be done.

I bought the land from a very cooperative seller and slowly moved in furniture and appliances. I made bimonthly commutes to the property from where I resided west of the Minneapolis area. This worked out great as my schedule as a paramedic gave me a week on, week off schedule. Over the deer hunting season I would spend three weeks.

In 1984, I borrowed a tractor locally, cut down sap-filled aspen, dragged them to a site near the cabin, peeled them, and let them dry until the following summer. Then I built a 12' wide porch, mainly so I could enjoy the buggy season, as the porch was screened.

Although isolated, the homestead is about 10 miles from two towns, a modern medical facility, and the author's employment.

In the spring of 1991, I'd had enough of my work and present living situation, and decided to move to the cabin on a permanent basis. I had been interested in wildlife, outdoor photography, hunting, fishing, etc., so it seemed a natural move for me to make.

The initial high was terrific, but I realized that I "needed" certain things, one of which was electricity. I purchased a Coleman 4,000 watt generator. This not only powers my 110 volt equipment such as drills, saws, grinders, etc., but powers a 40 amp battery charger. I charge a deep cycle 12 volt battery. This battery powers my lights and a small, rarely used, black and white television. For the first time I was able to vacuum the cabin carpet.

I was very surprised and pleased to discover that a natural gas line runs through the property, supplying a small town to the north. That gives me the luxuries of a cook stove and oven, 28,000 BTU space heater, and an old Servel refrigerator. No longer would I have to lug in 100 pound LP cylinders on a regular basis.

I witched for a well and drove a sand point 28 feet down, using a fence post driver to drive in the pipe and couplings. When I struck water, it was like the movies when they discover oil. I no longer had to carry in my water supply. I use a pitcher pump which pumps some of the finest water I have tasted. The water is stored in 5-gallon jugs, and I keep 50 gallons on hand as a rule.

I use an outhouse, and with the cold Minnesota winters, I use an L.P. fueled sunflower heater to take the edge off, if you know what I mean. I have learned what the word "expedite" means.

Writing, teaching, and being a college student "requires" that I have a computer for word processing, so I have that in my cabin also. When I get visitors, they are thrown for a loop. Not only does the computer seem out of place, I am the only person they know who must pull a rope to run it.

Outside is a small tool shed, work bench, and the generator shed. I store my gasoline in 5 gallon cans. I have a John Deere "G" tractor with a bucket which is my "workhorse" and an old International Scout with a hydraulic blade to plow my driveway which, as I said, is over a mile in length. As you can probably guess, my vehicle is a 4 X 4 pickup truck.

I acquired a two bottom plow, a tandem disc, and a field cultivator. These, along with the tractor, make it relatively easy to plant a garden. The garden is about 75 feet long by 25 feet wide. At the time of this writing, Minnesota is experiencing a drought, so the harvest might be light this fall. It will be interesting to see what crops the deer and raccoon get to before I do.

I have about 60 acres of woodland, so firewood is not a problem. I am in the process of installing a new woodstove, although last winter I heated almost exclusively with a barrel stove.

My total acreage is about 90 acres, including mainly woods, some low land, beaver ponds, and about 10 acres of open ground under some power lines. I obtained an agreement from the power company and was granted an easement to plant Christmas trees. I planted 1,000 Norway Pines this spring and will plant the same number next year. They offer good habitat and erosion control, and who knows, might yield an income in the future.

I reload my own ammunition and have a pistol and rifle range a short distance from the cabin. Last year I was fortunate to have shot a black bear, two whitetail deer, and various small game.

Minnesota is noted for being the "Land Of Ten Thousand Lakes," and our area is especially concentrated with them, so with a little effort, fish are also available for food.

This seems to be the ideal type of living, but the reality is that a cash flow is needed. In my particular situation, I am fortunate to work half time for a local police department as a peace officer and dispatcher. I have written magazine articles, done free-lance photography, and worked part time for a lawn service and an ambulance service. All of this pays the bills and gives me the flexibility in scheduling to travel and pursue other interests.

For those interested in living the "homestead" lifestyle, my only suggestion is to do it. Procrastination is easy. Making the move is also easy. Put your heart, mind, and back into it, and I am sure you will find the rewards never ending.

Whether it is hearing a whippoorwill or a coyote at night without hearing other noises, or seeing a sunrise, or the aurora borealis or a starlit sky without distractions, you will never regret the move. Δ

A BHM Writer's Profile

Born and educated in a small town in southern Mississippi, Margaret Clark (M.C.) Wright still has the accent to prove it. She was raised by her grandmother and a loving nanny while her mom worked outside the home. Wright married her high school sweetheart; they have been together 32 years. She is mother to four children and "Mamaw" to seven grandchildren. Her youngest child, Benjamin, is still at home.

Wright and her family have travelled extensively, following the electrical construction trade. They landed in Idaho 20 years ago and are still there. Wright has worked with several rural ambulance services as an emergency medical technician.

Basically a mother earth type, Wright homeschools her children, cooks from scratch, sews, quilts, gardens, and takes care of the animals. Her favorite attire is a denim skirt, sweatshirt, and Birkenstocks with socks, which she describes as a real fashion statement. She began writing after taking some journalism classes—a hobby turned serious. She says, "I love the idea of other people being interested in my lifestyle, and hope I can inspire them to follow their dreams."

What to look for in a kit log home

By Ken Lefsaker

There are two main types of log homes—green logs and milled kit. Both of these main divisions have variations within them. Here are some pros and cons.

"Green Logs" are simply tree trunks that are peeled and laid horizontally to form a wall. If you like big, round, full length logs, look at this type. Be warned, though, that green logs have inherent problems of shrinking, twisting, and cracking as they dry. The manufacturers of these kits have a variety of ways of coping with these problems. Because of the size and weight of these logs, expensive equipment is needed to deal with them. Also, they are often assembled at the plant and then numbered and disassembled before shipping to the building site. That adds to their cost.

The other type of manufactured log home is the "Milled Kit." These are made from squared-up beams, which are then shaped to produce the desired profile. The most popular is a "D" shaped log, which gives the round log look on the outside but is flat on the inside to form a uniform surface. This type of log can be much dryer and lighter, and can be handled more easily.

Moisture content — the most vital concern

The most important quality to look for in any log is its moisture content. This will determine how stable your home will be.

Logs are stable if the moisture content is above 30% or below 15%. Nearly all shrinking, warping and twisting occurs when the logs are between about 17% and 30%.

The industry standard for dimensional lumber is 19% or less. The 2 x 4 you purchase from the local building center should be 19% or less. It takes 6 months to air dry a 2 x 4 to 19%. Think about this when a dealer advertises air dried logs. It takes up to **four years** to air dry an 8 x 8 log to 19% or less.

There are companies that advertise and sell newly cut green trees. If you try to build with these, you will certainly encounter every problem a log home built from new green logs can have.

Many log home kits are sold "surface dry." This means a moisture content of 25% or less. The surface of the log feels nice and dry, but it is not dry to the center of the log. A house wall built from such logs will settle and move around. Joints may separate, windows may no longer fit, and extensive recaulking may be needed.

The next category is the "dry log." These are supposed to be 19% or below in moisture content **to the center**. If it isn't 19% to the center, they will still be unstable. Testing would require cutting a sample log in half to measure the moisture at the center, an expensive proposition which many companies are unwilling to do.

Many companies calculate the moisture of their air dry logs by very "optimistic" methods. One company that advertises air dried logs has computed the wind drying effects of being hauled at 60 m.p.h. on the freeway. So many miles at such a speed equals so many months of drying. Uh-huh.

Kiln drying

Kiln drying uses an enormous oven to force-dry the wood. If you see a "K" stamped on a 2 x 4, it was kiln dried. It only takes 3 to 4 weeks to kiln dry a log properly, unlike air drying which can take years. This process will bring the moisture content in a log down to 15% or less at the center.

The kiln is slowly brought up to 210 degrees F over two weeks, then this temperature is maintained for another week or ten days. Speeding this process to shorten the time spent causes steam explosions which damage the wood.

Kiln dried logs at 15% or less moisture content are the best to build with. They are stable and are much lighter and easier to handle than other logs. At 20% surface dry, a linear foot of log can contain 4.5 pounds of water. The same wood kiln dried would contain 15 ounces of water.

Insects in the logs

Kiln drying has other benefits as well. Neither insects nor their eggs can live through the process. Molds and fungi, too, cannot survive the heat. Powder post beetles can be brought into the home in almost any wood that has not been kiln dried or preservative treated.

Round logs with the sapwood left on them are more likely to have insect problems than squared logs. Surface applications of insecticides or fumigants will not kill larvae deep inside the log. Logs that are not kiln dried must be treated with a deeply penetrating preservative.

Buy your logs from a company that kiln dries and properly stores logs so they aren't re-wetted. Bug free, dry, heartwood logs are safe from mold and insects if kept dry until construction and then properly water sealed.

You need more than logs

A big question when buying a kit is, what is included with the logs? Some companies charge extra for spikes, caulk, plans, etc. A good manufacturer should have an extensive file of architectural plans for the house, and engineered plans for the foundation, saving you the expense of custom drawn plans.

Independent testing

The best suppliers of log home kits contract with an independent testing company such as Timber Products Inspection Company to inspect their logs. This firm works for Boise Cascade and Weyerhauser. The agent comes in at random times without warning and picks out logs at random to cut in half and test at the center.

The manufacturer of your log home kit should use the services of an independent inspection service, and should be willing to show you test data.

Most companies do warranty their logs for a certain amount of time. Kiln dried logs can be warrantied for the lifetime of the original owner if properly maintained.

Joining the logs

There are many different joining methods for corners and top and bottom log faces . . . too many to enumerate here. The best and most popular method of joining log faces is the single tongue and groove, with the groove cut into the bottom face and the tongue on the top face. Spiked down and with adhesive on both sides of the tongue, along with a strip of foam insulation along the top of the tongue, this method provides the best assurance against air leaks.

Look at other log homes

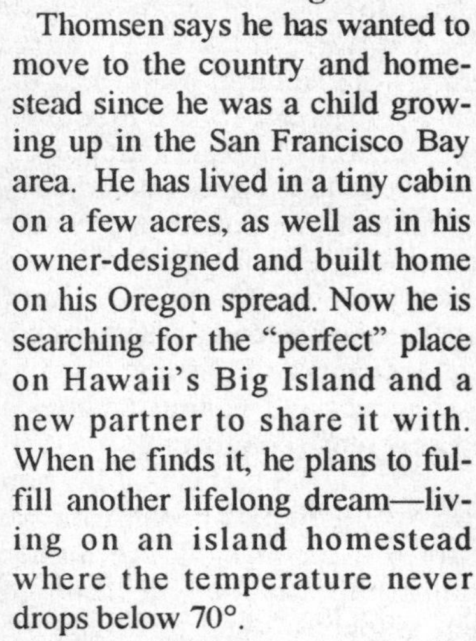

Every manufacturer of log home kits will tell you his system is the best. Every dealer and builder will tell you that the kit he sells is the best. Since your home will probably be your largest single investment, you should be willing to do a little traveling to make sure.

Any log home will look good the week after it is built. Ask the manufacturer for the addresses of homes built with his log kit five or ten years ago. A few days driving or even a few airplane tickets is not an unreasonable expense to make sure you get a log kit that won't cost you thousands of dollars in repairs. Δ

A BHM Writer's Profile

Skip Thomsen is the author of three books and many magazine articles, most of them dealing with independent energy. Thomsen wrote The Modern Homestead Manual and his deisel generator book, More Power To You, to share his experience of more than 15 years homesteading 108 acres in Oregon "from the ground up." Both books are available through *Backwoods Home Magazine*.

Thomsen says he has wanted to move to the country and homestead since he was a child growing up in the San Francisco Bay area. He has lived in a tiny cabin on a few acres, as well as in his owner-designed and built home on his Oregon spread. Now he is searching for the "perfect" place on Hawaii's Big Island and a new partner to share it with. When he finds it, he plans to fulfill another lifelong dream—living on an island homestead where the temperature never drops below 70°.

Besides his frequent articles for *BHM* and other magazines, Thomsen is currently working on a book of photo essays about photovoltaic (solar electric) systems that work. It will be specifically oriented toward Hawaii.

Chinking for log homes

By Jim Talbot

In the handcrafted style log homes, chinking is an integral part of the design. Chinking fills and seals the gaps between the logs, protecting log homes from water and insects. If you can control water, you can look forward to many years of service from a log home. Chinking also eliminates heat loss and air infiltration, reducing heating bills and making the home noticeably more comfortable.

Chinking looks at home in a log house.

A little known fact is that log homes tend to be a bit dark because the wood absorbs a lot of light. An authentic chinking application reflects a significant amount of light to brighten and add life to a log home.

Chinking cannot eliminate structural problems of the log home, other than help the structure recover from abnormal log movement.

Moisture and shrinkage

In a new log home, for example, the logs often contain a high moisture content. Over the first 18 months of a home's life, this moisture level drops significantly as the logs normalize to local atmospheric conditions. The wood cell structure collapses, and the diameter of the logs shrink considerably. The logs may also untwist, causing further stress on the seams. It's not unusual for a log wall to drop four to six inches during this time. Kiln or air drying the logs before building the home can help minimize the amount of initial shrinkage.

After the 18-month period, the logs undergo seasonal variations, shrinking under dry conditions and swelling during periods of high humidity. The vertical walls in a log home, which are bearing walls, continually experience a great deal of movement.

This means that the key attribute of a chinking material is long-term elasticity to accommodate contraction and expansion of the walls. Chinking must have exceptional elongation, and stay flexible over the life of the home. For instance, modern chinking compounds are based on advanced, highly elastic acrylic emulsions. These emulsions provide excellent flexibility over time and good resistance to mildew growth and dirt pick-up.

Aside from elasticity, chinking must also be easy to tool and clean up. Lastly, it must look authentic (like old mortar).

Acrylic chinking vs. mortar and caulking

The first acrylic-based chinking for handcrafted log homes was developed in the early 1980s. Modern acrylic chinking has excellent long lasting elastomeric properties to move with the walls while adhering tightly to the logs. This chinking should maintain a tight seal for the life of the log home.

Prior to the development of acrylic-based compounds, people used all kinds of materials for chinking. Nearly all were unsatisfactory for one reason or another.

Mortar chinking lacks elasticity. With seasonal moisture variations, the mortar often cracks and separates from the log, permitting air and water filtration as well as intrusion of insects. Trapped moisture within the log walls can cause a variety of problems, including damage from freeze/dry cycles and rot.

Caulking works in the short term, but it's not formulated to spread properly and to retain its original elasticity in a large gap typical of log home applications. It "slumps" in such a large gap. In addition, caulking eventually weathers and becomes hardened with time. So it soon loses its ability to accommodate wall movement. Finally, it looks like caulking—shiny, rubbery, and plastic—not like authentic chinking.

A chinking compound must be formulated for an optimum blend of properties. If it's too flexible, it will tend to be soft. A soft chinking will lack durability and tend to pick up dirt easily. It also becomes difficult to apply. The ultimate chinking sticks to wet wood, trowels easily, has the right blend of elasticity and durability, and looks like mortar.

Insulation

Generally, the chinking material is applied with a thickness of about a quarter inch, so by itself it doesn't make a large contribution to R value. But it's always applied on both the outside and inside, against a backer rod. The dead air space between the inside and outside walls usually makes the R value through the chink joint greater than that of the log itself.

Calculating gap size

A 12-inch diameter log will shrink a lot more than a 6-inch log. The larger the log, the more the chinking will have to stretch to accommodate wall movement. So for larger logs, the geometry demands larger chinking gap widths to permit more stretch. Otherwise, the chinking material would have to stretch a high percentage of its overall width, risking damage.

As a rule of thumb, you can divide the log diameter by six to figure the optimum chinking gap size. A 12-inch log requires a 2-inch gap.

Estimating the amount of chinking needed

Simply take the average gap width in inches, multiply it by the lineal feet of chinking needed, and divide by 385. The result is the number of five-gallon pails of chinking required. For example, if your average gap is one inch and you have 1100 lineal feet to fill, then you'll need 1100/385, or roughly three pails.

Application

It's applied over a backing material that is inserted between the logs after the house is assembled. The applicator starts with a bead of chinking over this backing, using a refillable application gun. He then trowels the bead out, taking care to work the material tightly against the upper and lower logs. After troweling, the chinking should be a uniform 1/4 inch thick. Acrylic chinking compounds are generally water borne, so cleanup is simple using soap and water. While it cleans easily when wet, it's almost impossible to clean off after it dries.

It can be applied by a handy homeowner, or there are professional applicators available.

Most manufacturers make chinking available in standard colors that won't change over time. However, after years of service, environmental conditions such as dust, dirt, acid rain, and stain from re-stained logs can degrade its appearance. In these cases it can be refurbished with a specially formulated chinking paint, or a premium grade latex exterior house paint. Remember, chinking has a capacity to stretch, so any paint covering it must stretch at the same rate.

Premium grade chinking is designed to protect the house over the long haul and should last the lifetime of the home itself. However, such circumstances as falling trees, earthquakes, abnormal movement, and remodeling can overstress the chinking and cause cracks. The good news is that typically any cracks that do develop can easily be filled and feathered out with new chinking and the seal returned good as new. Chinking is available in standard "caulking" tubes for these smaller jobs.

Applying chinking.

Chinking needed for many log homes

About 25% of log homes – the handcrafted styles – are designed for chinking. Chinking gaps in these homes run from about three-quarters of an inch for round logs up to four inches for a square log home. In the square log home, the walls are virtually 25% chinking.

Milled and scribe type log homes, on the other hand, make up the balance, about 60% and 15% respectively. Theoretically they require no chinking.

If all goes well with the design and building of these houses, they will be airtight without the need for chinking. But sometimes abnormalities occur. It doesn't take much to cause some discomfort and raise energy expenses. For example, a one-eighth inch gap between the logs all through the house is equivalent in area to leaving the front door and a back window wide open.

Acrylic-based chinking can act as a simple, yet effective, fix in these situations, restoring the home's tight seal, original comfort, and energy effectiveness. It represents a solution to abnormal problems in these log homes in a way that adds beauty. It looks authentic, like it belongs there.

Advanced acrylic-based chinking compounds have contributed greatly to the resurgence of the handcrafted style log homes. They've made it possible to seal any log home in a way that looks authentic and finely finished.

(Article based on information from Rich Dunstan, president, PermaChink Systems, Inc., Redmond, WA) Δ

Haiku Disaster

Love poems
Are like blood stains left
After an accident
Has been cleared.

John Silveira
Ojai, California

Log homes – fact and fiction

By Martin Harris

(Every type of construction has its own special problems as well as its own advantages. Log homes are no exception to this rule. Log homes were originally expedient wilderness construction, usually replaced by other housing as soon as time and finances allowed. Today's log home owner is usually attracted by the image and exterior appearance of a log home, but wants all the amenities and comforts of conventional construction on the interior. Martin Harris, an architect who writes regularly for BHM, shows how the problems peculiar to log construction can be overcome. — Editor)

It's a fact of history that there's an element of fashion in building design and construction: a little history and tradition, a little local materials and techniques, a little climatics and weather response. These factors come and go over time, with the result that it's tough to predict what style will be trendy next. One style that's been popular over time, for reasons ranging from logic to fashion, is log construction.

Part of the American mythology is the idea that log cabins – walls of horizontal logs, stacked up – are rooted in the distant American past. We no longer need to believe that our Presidents each grew up in one, but Lincoln Logs are still a favorite childhood toy, and log house kits still sell well to folks above average in income and stylishness.

The mythology isn't really true. With the exception of the Swedes, western Europeans who crossed the Atlantic back in the 1600s and 1700s built frame, stone, and brick structures; it wasn't until the 1800s and the movement into northern New England and the near Midwest that Americans (other than Swedes) began building real log housing out of squared or rounded logs laid up horizontally. If you want to argue log housing for the Virginia colonies, you'll have to accept logs set up vertically, palisade style. Real log construction – the kind we immortalize in Lincoln logs – comes from the Swedes, Finns, and Russians, folks who really created the horizontal-log construction system.

And one type of real log construction survives today, not as a low-cost do-it-yourself construction technique for new settlers in heavily wooded areas, but rather as pre-fabricated kits for buyers who are willing to pay a premium for the design appearance such construction creates. The kits are manufactured in a few wooded areas around the country, where the right size logs are available; detailed to incorporate modern standards of energy efficiency and mechanical systems; sized to be used in an infinite number of floor plans; and even designed to be used as surface treatments on top of other types of construction.

These kits, whether they're structural or decorative, draw on the Swedish/Russian log tradition, where the basic round shape of the tree trunk remains unchanged; the logs are

Maybe log cabins once had stone foundations or no foundation at all. Today, the cabin walls start on top of a conventionally framed dimensional lumber platform on a concrete foundation.

stacked horizontally, and they're joined at the corners in a variety of interlocking systems with various lengths of log overhang beyond the joint. If there's an American log-construction tradition, this isn't really it.

The English settlers of Virginia used a lot of log construction, mostly for defensive palisades but occasionally for buildings. It was in the vertical mode, where logs are stood up side-by-side in a trench and the dirt backfill keeps them in place. And then there's a handful of examples of horizontal log construction, where the logs are carefully squared on all four sides before being set in place, the smooth exterior and interior surfaces thus created making an easy base for exterior clapboarding and interior lath and plaster. In northern New England, such examples of horizontal dressed-log construction are far more common: one, in northern Vermont, is even the reputed birthplace of a President (Chester Arthur). Palisade logs were used for fortifications around here, before the Revolution, but not for housing. We don't have any examples of English settlers in northern New England using Swedish-type raw-log construction.

None of this matters to the modern log-housing industry, which focuses exclusively on round logs for its kits and on slabs taken from round logs (or cut to look like round logs) for exterior log-style siding. I suspect that's because historical accuracy matters less to the customer than a construction material which conveys an image of reality and solidity in an age when just about everything else is false or plastic or both. And there's no question that real-log construction is, in fact, real and solid.

In a way, that's its major problem. Solid log construction has inherent problems in energy efficiency, in multi-story or large-room design, and of course in concealing the pipes, wires, and ducts that are an essential part of modern construction standards for occupant comfort and convenience. It even has something of a problem in sheer weight, considering that log buildings are no longer axed or adzed out on site but are transported long distances from point of manufacture to point of use. There's a lot more pounds of wood in a log house than in a frame house of the same size, and that weight costs money to move around.

Let's look at each of these areas in turn.

Energy efficiency

Log walls are thick – usually 8 inches or more – and they're not terribly high in insulating value. Compared to ordinary Fiberglas insulation, which has an R-value (a measure of heat retention) of about 3 per inch of thickness, raw wood has an R-value of about 1.5 per inch. That's somewhat better than the R-value of window glass. What it means in practical terms is that an 8-inch-thick log wall, which, being rounded, is maybe 6 inches thick at its narrowest point, has an R-value of about 9. In contrast, a standard 2x4 wood stud wall, with clapboard on the outside, sheetrock on the inside, and 4 inches of insulation in between, has an

From the inside, the logs make a flat wall surface. If the owner wants to keep the logs exposed and doesn't add some interior insulation, the R-value of the wall will be about R-9. That's half of the R-value usually considered desirable in modern wood frame construction.

R-value of 11 to 13. By way of comparison, R-19 is pretty much the minimum that architects and engineers like to design into building walls today.

If log walls aren't terribly good in terms of heat-loss by conduction, they're excellent in terms of heat loss by convection; in other words, the better kits are virtually draft-proof. That's because they're not built in the traditional way: raw logs with mud in the chinks. They're built, instead, with each log milled to create a flat surface of the top and bottom faces, and a groove cut into each face so that a wind-stop and insulating spline can be used to connect each log to its counterpart above and below. That pretty much stops wind infiltration through the wall, probably better than ordinary wood frame construction which contains a multitude of possible wind-infiltration joints.

The rest of log construction—roof, foundation, doors and windows—is built much like ordinary construction and can be insulated just as well. If you want R-38 overhead, the normal standard in the northern half of the country these days, achievable with 12 inches of Fiberglas, you can build it into the roof assembly as easily with a log structure below as with a wood frame structure. Your foundation will most likely be concrete or masonry, full-basement or slab-on grade; insulating it with foamboard is just the same as for more ordinary construction. And, of course, doors and windows are different only in the jamb treatment, which needs to be a lot deeper than "normal" because of the extra thickness of the log walls.

Multi-story or large-room

Nothing describes the potential problems in this area better than a child's Lincoln Logs house kit. Assemble one according to your own floor plan choice, and then push on its walls and gables ends gently to simulate the lateral forces of wind or even earthquake (we need to design for both, these days). What you'll see is that log construction, unless subdivided internally into fairly small rooms which provide lateral bracing for the overall structure, is not real good at resisting these forces. What you'll see is that it's extremely difficult to erect structures more than a standard log in length. What you'll see is that lateral strength is created only at the joints, and that, for the rest, the more door and window openings you have, the weaker the structure becomes. What you'll see is that there's some tendency for the stacked logs to roll a bit, one atop the other, so that cumulative movement at the top of a wall can be substantial. This pattern shows clearly in old log structures out in the countryside, and even the introduction of modern spline connections doesn't add much structural rigidity in this particular area.

This isn't an overwhelming problem, of course. It's quite easy to build lateral reinforcement into log construction, using methods ranging from interior partitions at right angles to the exterior walls, all the way to vertical steel, anchored in the concrete foundation, as a stiffener for the log walls. Do most log kits and designs incorporate these or similar needed engineering devices? Yes—but a few don't.

This particular kit has a spline design that's about three inches wide. If you look carefully toward the left-hand edge, you'll see a strip of compressible filler which acts as a weather-strip.

Window opening sizes don't always match up with even log numbers. Sometimes most of a log must be cut away, as we see here, to create the rough opening for a particular piece of millwork.

And the larger the rooms in your design, and the higher the structure, the more you will need such engineering reinforcement.

Concealing mechanicals

Solid logs, clearly, don't naturally provide a concealed space for pipes and ducts and wires the way wood frame construction does. There are three solutions.

1. Run these mechanicals, exposed, wherever they're needed, on the inside of the structure. Maybe you can pretty them up a little by neatening the installation, using colors, and so on.

2. Drill out the logs to provide concealed chases for wires and piping. Ducts, even the smallest, are too big for this avenue to concealment; you'll have to give up wall-register duct-fed hot-air-heating in favor of pipe-fed hot water.

3. Build a stud wall inside the log structure, thus providing a space for at least four inches of Fiberglas insulation, wires, pipes, and ducts. The disadvantage to this option, of course, is

that you paid a premium for log construction and now you won't see it unless you're out on the front lawn. You'll see sheetrock and window trim, just as if you were sitting inside a tract house in some subdivision.

All of which raises an interesting question: if the most practical way to bring modern levels of energy efficiency and concealed mechanical systems to a log structure requires the concealment of the logs on the inside, why not take the next logical step and build a conventional wood frame house, finishing it on the outside (and maybe on the inside too) with wood siding cut to look like logs?

It's the same question faced by people in this part of the country (New England) who want to build a heavy-timber, exposed frame house, only to discover that such designs are tough to insulate, and even tougher to pipe and wire and heat without all the hardware showing. And yet, concealment of the hardware results in concealment of the handsome (and expensive) framing as well.

Here's my view on this matter: I'm an enthusiast for "real" buildings, where the brick or wood or steel structure is out there in full view to serve as a kind of functional and yet decorative framework. It's worth, in my opinion, paying a modest premium for. Even the best fake log cladding on the market doesn't fool the owner or his guests into believing that they're in a real log house, just as the best fake beams in an imitation New England Cape-style cottage won't fool those looking at them.

Since the exposed structure gives us such admitted esthetic pleasure, it seems a little counter-productive to cover it with sheetrock so as to create hidden spaces for mechanicals and to raise the R-value a few points. What's so bad, in fact, about designing the mechanicals for full exposure on the inside of the building? Properly organized and installed, brightly painted and maybe even labeled, mechanicals can be an attractive part of interior design. (Bonus: it costs less to solve the problem this way, as compared with full concealment).

A closing thought on costs: log cabins may have been the low-price housing of choice in Northern Russia or the American Frontier, but it isn't any more. You'll pay something of a premium for this traditional construction technique today, and your return-on-investment will be esthetic rather than monetary. It's a do-it-yourself possibility (logs cut from on-site trees, that is) in only a very few parts of the country, where the right trees are still standing, a kit-type project everywhere else. The question – is it worth the extra cost – is the same one asked of other Americans at other times, who built houses with Greek columns across the front, with Victorian gingerbread porches and turrets, with brick veneers over wood frame construction, with slate roofs rather than asphalt shingle. The answer: if you like it, it's a buy; and you'll probably recapture your extra investment on re-sale.

Where the logs overhang, on the outside corners, the spline system is readily visible. Here the builder has planed off the projecting spline (top of the lower log). The matching recess shows two logs up. It's easy to see that moisture will cause a maintenance problem over the years with this style of overhang.

(Martin Harris is a Vermont architect, cofounder of the "New England Builder," and author of numerous home building articles.)

Δ

Electric car racing — what a gas!

By Lon Gillas

Electric cars now have the sleek lines of their gas counterparts.

Imagine going to the race track for a typical day of auto racing. When you arrive, there is something wrong. There is no blue haze coming from the cars, there isn't even a roar of engines as some of the cars go by at speeds of over one hundred miles per hour. The concessionaires are crying about the lack of earplug sales. None of the cars have decals from auto companies or oil products. Instead, these cars are sponsored by utility and battery companies. As the owner of an electric vehicle (EV) race team, I'd like to welcome you to the world of electric car racing.

Modern electric car racing has been on the track for the last three years. Previously there were some small road rallies sponsored by local (EV) clubs. In December, 1990, an organization called the Solar Electric Racing Association (SERA) announced the inaugural Solar and Electric 500 in Phoenix, Arizona. It was to be held at Phoenix International Raceway on April 5-7, 1991. The idea behind the Solar Electric 500 is the same as the early days of auto racing: to present and test new products at the race track. On the track different electric car technologies could be tried and tested against their contemporaries. Competition is the master of innovation at the race track. In the first year of the Phoenix Solar Electric 500, 13 electric cars in two classes and nine solar cars competed in races. In the electric car class, the highest single lap average speed was 69 miles per hour. The winning car of the two hour endurance race averaged 54 miles per hour, traveling 108 miles.

Two years later, in March, 1993, the Solar Electric 500 hosted 55 electric cars in seven classes and two solar cars. Top speed for a single lap in an electric car was 104 miles per hour. The winning car of the two hour endurance race averaged over 61 miles per hour, traveling 122 miles. Since 1991, additional EV races have been organized, like the Pikes Peak Solar/Electric Challenge in October, 1992, and the Clean Air Grand Prix in Atlanta, Georgia, in May, 1993. EV racing is a great educational medium for the public. Seeing EVs race around the track at speeds of 70 to 100+ miles per hour quickly dispels the old image of EVs being glorified golf carts. The public is also surprised to note that most of these cars look surprisingly like the ones already parked in their driveways, with the exception of the electrical outlet where the gas cap used to be.

E-Motion's entry into the Solar and Electric 500 in Phoenix.

Racing electric cars is still a new sport. The race track stretches the vehicles' limits, and the drivers push that limit at a controlled facility. Racing accentuates many problems that might not be noticed in conventional driving. At the 1992 Phoenix event, a 25 mile sprint race was introduced. Four of the 20 cars had their circuit breakers overheat and open due to the extended stress of high current over an extended period. Tom Sneva, the 1983 Indy 500 winner, burned out his electric motor in the 25 mile sprint race at the 1993 Solar Electric 500. He came back in the two-hour endurance race to place second. While experimentation on the track is frustrating and costly, it is far less trouble than having EV customers experience like problems on our streets.

Rapid technology advancements are being made by EVs on the race track. In some races we see battery changes taking only nine seconds. Let's see an Indy car refuel that fast. Other cars are getting 50% recharges in three to four minutes. In the garage charging area, the electric cars are plugging into modified parking meters that have built-in receptacles for charging—something we will see on the street in the next few years.

Presently, most of the major components for EVs are off-the-shelf items. The DC controllers are manufactured by a company that makes a similar product for electric fork lifts. Several aerospace companies are getting involved in the EV industry to help replace their sagging military and commercial aircraft business.

Notably absent at the race track have been cars produced by the traditional auto manufacturers. Representatives have been there in person, and some of the races have been sponsored by auto manufacturers. No one has a definitive answer for the lack of these vehicles. I have contacted several manufacturers, both American and foreign, for sponsorship, without success. I see the auto manufacturers in a sort of Catch-22 with EV racing. If they race and lose against our small time EV teams, everyone will ask them what they have done with the millions of EV research dollars they have spent over the past 30+ years. If they win, everyone will ask why they are stalling in getting EVs out to the public, when they have a superior product.

What is needed to improve EV racing and EV in general? More races, more teams, and more sponsor dollars. The lack of EV races in the U.S. doesn't justify professional race teams. Virtually all the EV race teams are hobbyists or part-timers enjoying the fun and the challenge and paying their own way. We have raced against a team where the entire race team members are rocket scientists for an aerospace company. Again, not your typical racing experience. Part-time racing, with fewer than three races a year, makes it really hard to obtain the sponsors needed to participate and to continuously research and improve new developments in EVs. New batteries are always being introduced with increased performance. The EV industry is still waiting for the "super battery" to arrive. About once a week, people contact me with new ideas about how to improve EV performance. I can't rely on this year's experimentation, because next year's technology is going to win the race.

Sponsors are crucial to the survival of EV racing. Without the sponsorship of materials and money, we cannot do the research and testing that is necessary to improve today's EVs to go faster, farther and safer. We are constantly improving motors, wheels, batteries, charging systems, aerodynamics, brakes, power controls, etc. All of this research is directly related to our consumer EV business.

The largest group of sponsors for EV racing, with the most to gain, are the utility companies. Most EVs are driven during the daylight hours for commuting and running around town. My wife and I plug our cars in at night, when all electric utilities have surplus capacity. EV recharging can be a terrific load leveler, with the potential of being able to charge over 50,000,000 cars in the U.S. tomorrow without building a single new power plant. This means added, unexpected revenue for the utilities, cleaner air for the nation, and lower transportation costs for the car owner. EV technology can also be used on the homestead. There are trail bikes and all-terrain vehicles available with electric power. They could give us silence in the hills, with the batteries being charged by any alternative electric energy source.

(Lon Gillas is the owner of E-Motion, an electric vehicle conversion company, 7025 Riverside Dr., McMinnville, OR 97128. Tel 503-434-4332.) Δ

A BHM Writer's Profile

Don Fallick has been writing for *Backwoods Home Magazine* since issue number eight, but he's been reading *BHM* since the first year. He built his own home on his first homestead in western Colorado in 1976. Since then, Fallick has lived in Wisconsin, Washington State, and Utah. His homesteading activities have included owner-built construction, homeschooling, independent energy, horse-power, harvesting wild foods and game, home-based business, cooking, and raising everything but his standard of living.

Fallick and his bride Barbara have 10 children between them. All have been homeschooled. When he is not writing for *BHM*, Fallick works as a surveyor and substitute school teacher. At one time or another, he has also been a carpenter, handyman, nurse aide, factory worker, locksmith, editor, and commercial pilot. He has a wide range of interests, and says that he tries to do everything that interests him. Current projects include a lengthy "how to" book, three books of guitar music, and two children's books.

Selecting the right PV voltage

By Windy Dankoff

The independent home power system is based on storage batteries and direct current (DC) electric power. Batteries are low voltage modules that may be assembled in 6, 12, 24-volt or higher configurations. Voltage is the electrical "pressure" at which the system operates, and part of the battery's job is to maintain this pressure at a fairly constant level. Thus, a "12-volt" battery maintains a working voltage within the range of about 11 to 14.5 volts—a **standard**. A 12-volt appliance will run properly within this range of electrical pressure.

While the voltage remains fairly constant, the **current** (measured in **amps**) varies according to the power required by the appliance. As more lights are turned on in your house, more current is drawn from your batteries. A large bulb draws more current than a small one. Some appliances draw different amounts of current at different times; a circular saw draws more current cutting 2" wood than ½" wood, because the motor works harder.

Twelve volts is the most common standard for alternative energy homes only because it is already a conventional standard—for vehicles! As we progress to higher voltages, less current (amps) is required to deliver the same amount of power (watts/horsepower). Wire, switches, and other in-line components are sized according to the **current** they carry; the voltage has little bearing on their sizing. Therefore, a 24-volt home electric system is less costly to wire—it requires half the wire size, and less labor to install. Control systems and inverters contain components that the current must pass through, so they too can be smaller and less expensive in a higher voltage system.

To confirm this for yourself, compare prices of 12 and 24-volt charge controllers and inverters. The 24 volt models handle far more watts per dollar! Efficiencies also tend to increase with higher voltage/lower current. To see an extreme example of relative wire sizes, look under the hood of your car and see the big wire that goes from the battery to the starter. A typical circular saw requires as much power as your starter, but look at the **little** wire it uses! The saw uses 120 volts, and requires $^{1}/_{10}$ the wire size to carry the current.

The common voltage standards for independent-powered homes are **12 volts** and **24 volts**. Your choice of standard is based on these factors:

1. Overall system size: Small, cabin-size systems standardize on 12 volts, which offers the widest choice of small DC appliances and small inverters. Medium to large homes generally cost less to set up on 24 volts, for the reasons below.

2. Inverter size: Inverter requirements beyond 2,000 watts or so indicate 24 volts, for lower cost per watt and higher efficiency.

3. DC well pump or other large motors: Motors above ¼ HP often necessitate the use of 24 volts, whether they are DC motors or AC run by inverter. Large motors are more efficient at higher voltages. High current is required to start most motors, so both wire and inverter need to be oversized. So the potential savings are especially great in going to higher voltage for motor circuits.

4. Wiring distances: Long wire runs from PV (photovoltaics, or solar cells) or (especially) wind or hydro generators, to a DC well pump, or to other buildings, can be very costly at low voltage/high current. The longer the distance, the larger the wire must be to reduce losses. So cutting the current in half by using twice the voltage can cut your wire cost by nearly 75%.

5. Plans for future growth: If any of the above indicate a requirement for 24 volts in the **future**, set up for it from the start so you won't be left with obsolete equipment (such as electronics) on a 24-volt system. High quality 24-volt lights are nearly as common as 12. Many large DC motors and pumps are not available at all in 12 volts, because the lower voltage motors are less efficient and require costly, over-sized wire, breakers and switches.

We do not go to 48 volts very often, because we cannot get DC lights, refrigerators, and well pumps at that voltage. Most PV dealers and users agree that DC power still has its place for running the specialized, super-efficient DC appliances made specifically for independent power. Direct use of DC in well-engineered appliances reduces both energy consumption and inverter requirements.

We are maintaining 12 and 24 volts as our DC home standard because it is safer and less costly to use than higher DC voltages. (1) Less battery cells are required (they are 2 volts each) with less connections between them. (2) High DC voltage from batteries (120 volts) poses a serious shock hazard (twice that of 120 volt AC). (3) High DC voltage poses more fire hazard (it causes much bigger sparks) than AC power at the same voltage. Low voltage virtually eliminates these hazards. 120 volt DC is used in industrial power systems, but generally not in homes. Our use of high-efficiency appliances and our elimination of electric heating devices keeps power consumption low, so wire sizes in our DC homes need **not** be 5 or 10 times oversized for low voltage!

A system dedicated to one specialized purpose need **not** conform to the common 12 or 24-volt standard. When a solar system is designed only to power a well pump (with a motor range of ½ to 1 HP) we may go to 60 or 120 volts DC if that optimizes economy and efficiency.

Remember, the final product of your energy system is not volts—it's light, water, communication, mechanical energy, etc. The voltage selected should be that which produces these ends at the lowest overall cost, with a high degree of safety and reliability. Δ

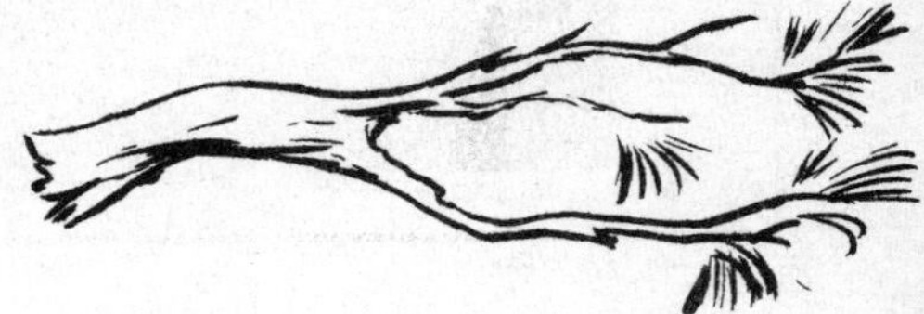

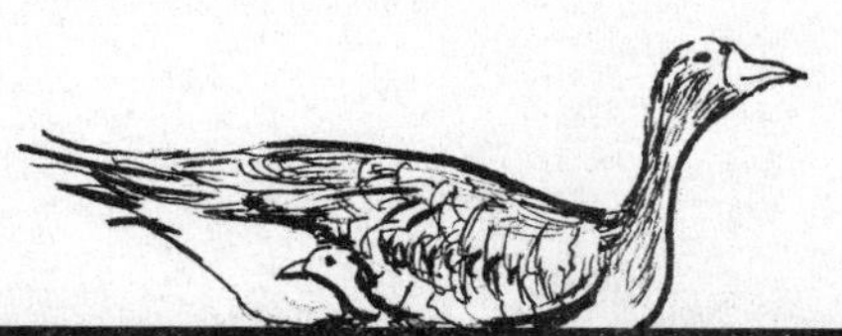

Father goose

By Dynah Geissal

I had two pairs of geese for many years. Two years ago, one goose stuck her face through a gap in the pig pen fence. The pigs pulled off her beak. It was a gruesome sight and, of course, we had to butcher her.

We kept one of the goose's daughters, who seemed to be a special favorite of the surviving gander, in hopes that they would mate. They didn't, but the young goose did mate with a male that had recently been given to us. The lone gander became part of an inverse trio with the old couple.

The young goose made her nest very early the next spring. It was so early that I marvelled that the eggs did not freeze. The nest appeared to be in a good place – in amongst the cattails by the creek. I worried, though, about spring breakup.

Spring was late, and I began to hope that the goslings would hatch in time. The water began to rise, and still they needed a few more days. Then one gosling hatched, but by then the water was only a foot from the nest. The goose had elevated her nest above the marsh; still, it would be inundated soon. The sun shone all day. The water kept rising. Too late for the eggs, but the goose wouldn't leave her nest. The gosling swam round and round and called morosely, then frantically.

The lone gander seemed to ponder the situation and then to make a decision. He swam purposefully out to the gosling and coaxed him to shore.

The gander tended the gosling for the rest of the day, but I wondered what would happen at night. As evening approached, the young one tried to move underneath the gander, who seemed uneasy about it at first but then finally permitted it. Later I looked out and found that the gander had settled down and the gosling was peeking out from under him.

For two weeks, the goose stayed on her flooded nest and the gander cared for the gosling. Then one day the goose came to reclaim him. No way. The gander chased her away. She tried for several days to get the baby back, but the gander would not allow it.

Eventually the goose resorted to following way behind the two who were so devoted to each other. I wondered if perhaps the gosling were a female and if the gander had claimed it as his future mate. But it was paternal devotion. The gosling was a male. Δ

A BHM Writer's Profile

The day he celebrated his third birthday, Robert Leonard Williams III made his first national television appearance as a photographer. Tom Brokaw, then host of NBCs Today Show, described Williams as the youngest published photographer in history. By the time he was five years old, Williams had been featured on more than a dozen TV shows. At age five, Williams had a one-man photo display at the Las Vegas Convention Center and was under contract as a photographer with the Vivitar Corporation.

When Williams was 12 years old, he wrote his first published magazine article. At age 16, he wrote his first article for *Backwoods Home Magazine*. He has written for a number of other magazines, and is co-author of a book on hiking in the North Carolina mountains.

Currently, Williams is working on his first novel, a fictional version of the aftermath of a natural disaster. He is also sawing lumber with a chain saw and working on a $30 tractor barn and a chain-sawed three-car garage. He is still taking photos and writing magazine articles.

FOOD

How to make cheese and butter

By Dynah Geissal

If a dairy animal has become a member of your farmstead, it will soon be time to investigate various ways to use the surplus milk. Feeding it to calves, pigs, chickens and turkeys are all possibilities, of course. Before long, though, learning to make various dairy products for the family will become more and more attractive. Here are some ideas.

Making cheese

Making cheese is an adventure and is a great way to preserve milk for later use. When I first began to make cheese, I used recipes that consisted of many pages of directions. It was overwhelming and time consuming. Fitting the many steps into a day full of many other chores, I would still be working on the cheese by evening. That is not necessary! You can bet the early herders who made cheese to preserve the milk didn't use elaborate recipes. You can graduate to involved cheeses after you've been successful with simpler ones.

The simplest cheese is made from soured milk. The jar of milk is left in a warm place, as for making yogurt or bread. I use the coolest part of the warming shelf on my woodstove. (When making cheese use glass, stainless steel or food grade plastic.)

When the curds and whey separate, drain the whey into the pig bucket. When it is free of whey, add salt, pepper and any herbs you like, such as garlic or chives. It can be used as cottage cheese or cheese spread. This is a very soft cheese. It can be made firmer by heating the curds and whey to 180° before draining it.

To make a fast soft cheese, heat one gallon of milk to 180° and add ½ cup vinegar or lemon juice. Stir. Continue heating for 10 minutes. Drain. Tie up in a clean cloth and hang over a bowl to drip for two hours. The cheese can then be crumbled for use in lasagna, salad dressings or dips.

Another ricotta type cheese is made a day before it is needed. To one gallon of 88° milk (the approximate temperature of fresh, warm milk) add one cup yogurt and ¼ rennet tablet or 40 drops of liquid rennet. (Rennet can be bought or ordered from an old style drugstore that carries such things as home remedies and vet supplies or from a well stocked natural food store.) Let it set for 12-18 hours at room temperature. Drain. Use in cooking or add herbs and eat.

Ready to try a hard (as in solid) cheese? As a rule of thumb, two gallons of milk is a minimum. One quarter rennet tablet or 40 drops liquid rennet are used for two gallons of milk. The curd is usually heated to a maximum of 102°. Two tablespoons of salt to the curds made from two gallons of milk are added before pressing.

Here's an easy method. Take two gallons of 88° milk and add ¼ rennet tablet or 40 drops liquid rennet dissolved in 2 tablespoons of water. Stir. Cover with a cloth. After about 40 minutes lift a bit of curd. It should be the consistency of store bought yogurt. If it isn't firm enough, wait a little longer. (If your house is cold, place the bucket of milk into a large pot of warm water to help maintain heat.)

When the curds have set, stir gently (I use my hand). The idea is to break up the curd into equal sized pieces but without beating or squeezing. The curd is fragile at this point. Let it sit undisturbed for fifteen minutes. Drain. Then tie up in a cloth to drip.

Adding one step will produce a slightly different cheese that will keep a bit better. After the curds have rested, the cheese bucket is placed into a large pan of water. Heat slowly until the curd has reached 101°. Stir often. Drain as before.

A cheese that is going to be preserved for more than a week needs salt. Salt can be added to any of the above recipes at the rate of 1 tablespoon for each gallon of milk that was used. The salt is added just after draining off the whey but before hanging up to drip. I've tried using less than the amount of salt called for, and it results in a poor quality if it is kept for any length of time.

Pressing the cheese is the next step. A simple method is to place the curds in a bowl with a plate resting on the curds. Put a weight on top of that. Pour off the whey as it forms. Another easy method is to place the curds in a cloth and to put a weight on that.

Eventually such makeshift arrangements will no longer seem satisfactory. Then it's time to get a real cheese press. A press can be purchased, but they are not too difficult to make.

There needs to be a mold to hold the curds (a coffee can will do), which must be secured to a drain board that allows the whey to drain from the curds. The follower pushes into the mold and presses down onto the curd. On top of everything is a board on which to put the weights to press the cheese. There must also be a way to hold every part of the press together. My cheese press looks like the photos.

To press the cheese, first break up the warm curd into pieces the size of a quarter and put them into the mold. Sprinkle salt onto each layer, using 2 tablespoons in all if 2 gallons of milk were used. One of the goals of pressing is to remove more of the whey, but it must be done gradually. When the dripping has slowed after the press has been loaded, put on the follower. When it slows again, put on the top board. Next place a brick or similar weight onto the board. Repeat until there are four bricks. Let press 12-18 hours.

When the cheese is removed from the press, it can be eaten immediately if desired. At this point it is called a green cheese. If the cheese is smooth with no cracks and is not crumbly it could be aged. To age it, let the cheese air dry in a cool place. Turn it every day. If any mold forms, rub the cheese with salt or vinegar. When a rind has formed, daily turning is no longer necessary. Just turn it every few days, checking for mold at the same time.

A cheese press

Sample the cheese at one month. For a stronger flavor, age the next cheese for two months. Cheese can be aged for a year or more, but I suggest trying one additional month at a time with each new cheese until the desired flavor is achieved.

Using starter is another step along the cheesemaking "whey." Starter will give fresh milk more character. If the milk is a few days old, it will already have enough bacteria for character on its own. Another reason to use starter is that it inoculates the cheese with desirable bacteria so that there are more of those than there are of any stray "bad" bacteria. Clean raw milk usually sours pleasantly, but it doesn't hurt to add starter and I usually do it. I add whatever homemade dairy product I have on hand – sour cream, yogurt, buttermilk or whatever. Add ⅓ cup to 2 gallons of 88° milk and let sit 30 minutes before the rennet is added.

Good hard cheese cannot be made in warm weather without a root cellar or other cool place. If the temperature is warm, bad bacteria will overcome good whether you add starter or not.

Skim milk can be made into cheese, but it should only be for immediate use. It will easily acquire a strong taste if it is aged. All the flinging around in the separator and the exposure to air causes it to break down. It can be eaten fresh, though, and is just fine for that.

Cheesemaking, like breadmaking, requires getting a feel for the job rather than just following directions. Here are a few tips, though, for likely problems. If the cheese is crumbly, one of the following is probably the cause:

(1) the milk was too sour,
(2) the curd was heated to too high a temperature,
(3) the curd sat too long in the whey.

If mold gets into an aged cheese, don't automatically throw it out. Some molds make a very good cheese. Others can be cut out if they are objectionable. Cheese can be inoculated with such delectable molds as those in blue cheese. Add a small amount of the store bought cheese to the curds as they are placed into the mold. This method is not reliable but is fun to try and sometimes makes an excellent cheese.

A very dry cheese may be the result of incomplete separation of the curds and whey. You will notice that the whey looks creamy. That is usually caused by the cream separating somewhat from the milk and not setting up properly. Remedy that problem by beating the milk with a wire whip before adding starter or rennet.

I hope you will give cheesemaking a try. Start with the simplest procedures and gradually add the more esoteric steps as you gain confidence. Even the most basic cheeses are very delicious, and cheesemaking can add a new dimension to the goal of self sufficiency.

Making butter

How easily butter can be made depends a lot on whether the milk came from a goat or a cow. Butter is made from cow's milk by skimming the cream from milk that has been refrigerated for two days. In that case, skip ahead to the actual process of buttermaking. Goat milk users will first have to obtain the cream.

Goat milk is naturally homogenized, so the cream does not rise to the top in the way the cream in fresh cow's milk does. A cream separator is, therefore, almost a necessity. In a pinch you can do without, however. My cream separator blew up last summer and I continued to make butter. The method is messy, takes up a lot of space and is inefficient; but it does work. Here's how:

Keep a couple of gallons of milk refrigerated for two days. During that time, some of the cream will rise to the surface. Pour the creamy part of the milk into two baking pans. Use the remaining thinner milk for cheese or livestock feed. It isn't really skim milk, because relatively little of the total amount of cream has been removed. Refrigerate these pans for two more days. Skim off the cream and proceed with buttermaking.

Not all cream separators will work for goat's milk, so find out before you buy. I have had two made by McCormick Deering, and they worked very well. The cream adjustment screws are very sensitive, so only change them by ¼ turn when trying to change the thickness of the cream. Both screws should be adjusted out the same number of turns. If a book comes with the machine, it will tell how to adjust the screws for making butter. If there is no book, just experiment. Heavy cream is not necessary for making butter. A nice medium consistency is fine.

Milk should be at room temperature for best separation. That is easy with cows or a large goat herd, because the milk is separated right after it leaves the animals' bodies. With a small goat herd, the milk may have to be saved from several milkings. In that case it isn't always practical to warm it to room temperature, and I don't worry too much about it. When the milk has all been separated, pour back a couple of gallons of skim milk to flush out the remaining cream.

Ideally, butter will form from cream in twenty minutes or less, and there are many ways to accomplish this. The butter churn is traditional, of course, but I don't have one, so I've tried many other methods.

Kids that are old enough to stay interested for the required amount of time may enjoy shaking a jar of cream until the butterfat separates from the buttermilk. The jar should be large enough to allow for expansion in volume as air is incorporated.

Some blenders will make butter, but mine heats up too much. I begin with an egg beater and switch to a wire whip and then a wooden spoon as thickening occurs. When finished, the liquid will clearly separate from the solid butterfat.

If the cream has been beaten for twenty minutes with no results, don't go on and on. There are several possible explanations. If the milk was fresh that day, it may be that there is not enough lactic acid in the cream. A butter starter could be added, but I think it's easier just to refrigerate the cream for a couple of days and then make the butter. In a cool house, the cream can be left out until it is just slightly tangy. Then proceed.

Another reason that cream may fail to turn to butter is its temperature. If the failed butter is returned to the refrigerator, it may form butter, with buttermilk underneath, all by itself. If that happens, the cream was too warm. The fat had separated but was so soft that it didn't solidify.

If the cream is too cold, it will take way too long to form butter, and when it does form it will not completely separate from the buttermilk. It gives a poor quality product that doesn't keep well. The ideal temperature will vary between 50° and 60°, depending on the outside temperature and also the stage of lactation.

When the butter has separated from the buttermilk, pour off the liquid. Save it for cooking or drinking. It is a superlative by-product. Begin rinsing the butter with cool water. Save the rinse water for the pig bucket. The butter should be worked with the hands as it is rinsed. When the rinse water remains clear, all the buttermilk has been removed.

The butter is then slapped and patted by hand or with butter paddles (if you're lucky enough to have them) to extract the water that has gotten into the butterfat. It is important to get all the water out to preserve the keeping quality as well as the cooking quality.

I don't pasteurize any of my dairy products, so it is necessary to add a little salt so that the butter does not sour too quickly. It doesn't take much. The butter is then shaped. A butter mold could be used, or the butter can just be poured into a bowl. I usually shape it with my hands and put it on a plate. Refrigerate for a few hours before using.

Homemade butter is wonderful. The only exception is when bad cream is used. Don't even bother trying to make butter from very sour cream. It's not worth it. Give buttermaking a try and before long it will become second nature.

Making yogurt

Homemade yogurt is easy to produce. It is delicious and can be used in many dishes. This product is not exactly like store-bought and should be judged on its own merits.

In the beginning it is best to buy a live yogurt culture which can be purchased at a health food store. It is expensive, but only has to be bought once unless something happens to kill or contaminate what you have made at home.

The goal is to inoculate the milk with the proper bacteria and then to incubate it at a temperature that encourages rapid growth of that particular bacteria.

Heat fresh clean milk to the boiling point. Then cool it to 100°. Stir in the starter and place in a clean container. Don't screw the lid down tight, because it needs to breathe. Contain the heat for about 8 hours or until thick. There are many ways to do that. A wide mouthed thermos will work. The cool part of the warming shelf of my wood cook stove is what I use. The jar of yogurt should be placed on a pad so that the bottom doesn't get too hot. Placing the jar the proper distance from my heat stove works fine too. I've even put it into the brooder house on the baby chicks' warmer when my house has been very cold. That worked great.

After the yogurt has been made, save a bit for the next batch. Two tablespoons is sufficient for a quart. It's like sourdough starter in that it will eventually become your own with its individual characteristic flavor and consistency. If it gets an off flavor or no longer thickens the way it once did, buy some more starter and begin again. I haven't had to do that for years, though.

Some people dissolve gelatin in the milk to give the final product a stiffer consistency. Honey, vanilla and other flavorings can be added at the beginning, too. Goat milk yogurt sometimes isn't very thick, and that can be remedied by simmering the milk until it is ¾ of its original volume before cooling and adding the culture.

Keep the yogurt refrigerated. It can be used in place of sour cream for a lower fat result, as a topping for cereal or eaten by itself. It can be served with fruit, nuts or toasted wheat germ. The yogurt also can be poured into a cloth and left hanging to drip. That will produce a yogurt cheese which is similar to cream cheese. It is wonderful.

Yogurt is an excellent producer of healthful bacteria in the body. Ingestion of yogurt is especially important after the use of antibiotics, which don't differentiate between good and bad bacteria.

Homemade yogurt can be used in so many ways that once you start making it you'll want to have it on hand all the time. Give it a try!

Making sour cream

Sour cream is made by one of two methods. The easier method is to let some cream sit out. The optimal temperature range is 75° - 80°. Depending on the freshness of the cream, it will take 24-48 hours to thicken. Leaving it longer may make it thicker, but the quality will be lost as other less desirable bacteria increase.

The second method is to add some lactic acid to the cream at the beginning of the process. This can be in the form of yogurt or it could be buttermilk if the buttermilk is sour. Fresh cream buttermilk won't have much lactic acid, so there's nothing to gain by using it. Sour cream starter can be bought, but almost anyone making their own dairy products will be able to come up with something sour. Be sure that it's "pleasantly" sour, which means the good bacteria are predominant.

After starter is added, proceed as above. Heavy cream is not necessary. Light cream is fine, although the heavier the cream, the thicker the consistency. Some people add powdered milk at the beginning for a result more like store bought.

I make sour cream in batches of eight pints when I have plenty of cream. Believe it or not, it will keep as long as a year refrigerated. Don't open the jars until they are to be used. There may be mold on top, but that can usually be scraped off. I opened a jar the other night to serve with tamales. There was an unattractive layer of pink on top, but it was excellent underneath. I had made that sour cream nine months before.

I hope this has helped you to get started on new ways to use your excess milk. Δ

A BHM Writer's Profile

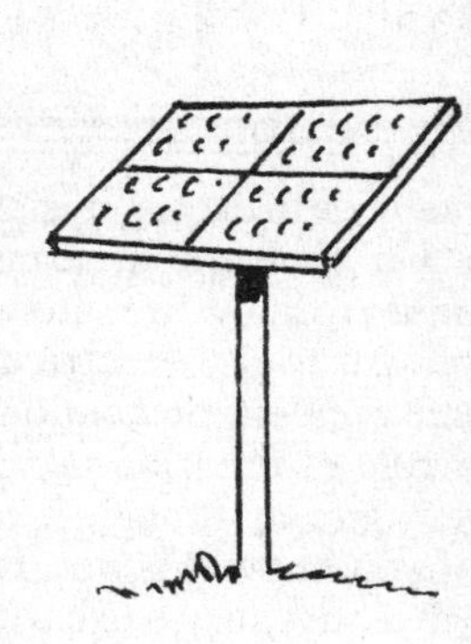

As a boy in the 1960's, Windy Dankoff was fascinated with all things electrical, but saddened to see wild places destroyed by technology. Then he heard about wind power. After teaming with Michael Hackleman (of electric vehicle fame) to learn all he could about the old wind generator technology, Dankoff moved to New Mexico in 1977 and began producing and selling wind generator parts using wind powered machinery. It was pioneering with no industry support, but it worked.

Says Dankoff, "Photovoltaics (solar electricity) was a dream then. It worked for the space program, but was too expensive for us." In 1980, when cheap PV panels became available, Dankoff switched from wind to the more reliable solar panels. Soon he was running power tools, an arc welder, and a solar car. But pumping water was a tough problem. Dankoff developed the Solar Slowpump™ in 1983. Today his pumps are used by independent power producers from Africa to Maine, while Dankoff Solar Products, Inc. supplies solar electric systems to remote homeowners in the norhern New Mexico area.

Windy Dankoff is still interested in preserving the quality of the environment by helping others develop their own independent power systems. His articles in *Backwoods Home Magazine* and other publications cover power systems of all types.

They are not just "HIS firearms"

By Dr. Stephenie Slahor

It might sound sexist in this day and age, but some women still have the idea that firearms in the home are the man's domain. Whether the man is husband, father, uncle, brother, or son, some women look to him as the one who keeps, maintains, and uses the firearms.

Quaint as that notion may be, it is an unsafe notion. Even if a woman does not want to be a shooter, she must know the basics of firearms so that she knows the safe way to handle or store firearms. Whether she chooses to hunt or target shoot is her decision, but if she is in a home with firearms, it is as important for her to learn firearms safety as it is for her to know fire safety, safety with power tools, electrical safety, and home accident prevention.

The cardinal rule of firearms safety is to treat every gun as though it is loaded, even if you know it is not. In that way you will always keep a firearm pointed in a safe direction. A firearm must never be pointed at anything you would not want to shoot and kill. It's that simple. By thinking that the firearm is loaded and ready, you will treat it with the respect due it.

The person in the household who owns or uses the firearms may be the one to instruct all the non-shooters about the safety rules, but non-shooters should also attend a hunter safety course or a firearms safety course offered by a local sports club or police.

Nearly all firearms have some type of safety mechanism, but this device is merely mechanical. Like all mechanical things, it can fail. A safety lock may be used as a supplement to help assure safety, but it should never be trusted completely.

Even in those households where a woman says "They're his firearms," there are still responsibilities and safety considerations to make to keep things safe. Like saws, scissors, knives, axes, and other tools, firearms deserve respect from all family members whether they use them or not. Δ

A BHM Writer's Profile

Jan Palmer and her husband Dwayne live on 10 acres near Grove, in northeast Oklahoma. An Illinois native, she grew up on a farm, studied agriculture at Black Hawk Community College in Illinois, and lived in Washington State for eight years before settling in Oklahoma.

Small livestock is the backbone of her farm, including milk goats, horses, a donkey, chickens, ducks, geese, sheep, and once in a while a pig. With the city moving closer, a couple of breeder pigs will become permanent residents in 1995. Grove specifically prohibits pigs, but allows other animals to be kept within city limits. If the farm is annexed, a grandfather clause will be in effect as long as pigs are on the property, but once disposed of, they apparently cannot be replaced.

Palmer writes for *Backwoods Home Magazine* and several other magazines. A flair for unusual and rare breeds brings interesting livestock to the Palmers farm. They have Dominique chickens, Barbados Blackbelly sheep, and other, less common breeds on the place.

Long range antennas for the homestead

By Jeff Butterfield

I moved from the hustle and bustle of southern California several years ago to a small Texas community of 3000 people. I have never once missed the pollution, noise, traffic nor the crime, but I quickly found that I missed the variety of television and radio programming that I was used to (news, talk shows, music, etc.). The entertainment that is provided by these media is not all bad, and I was frustrated that I couldn't pick it up when I wanted to.

After looking into a satellite system for my house (cost = $2,000) and a professionally installed T.V. antenna (cost = $250), I decided there had to be a better way. Figuring that my electrical engineering degree had to be worth something, I set out to design an antenna system that would pick up fringe area television and F.M. radio signals and A.M. signals from all over the region by day and all over the country by night. I am still a student, so my budget was limited. After some preliminary sketches, I figured that I could do it all for less than $50.

The final set cost less than $25, plus a trip to the hardware store and a Saturday morning to set it all up. Today I regularly pull in T.V. stations from a number of cities and listen to radio stations from all over the state. At night I catch my favorite syndicated talk shows from places like Chicago, Denver, Louisiana and San Francisco on my A.M. radio. The system I am going to describe is simple to set up, inexpensive and doesn't require an engineering degree to figure out. Best of all, it is extremely flexible and forgiving and can be tailored to most homesteaders' situations.

What antennas do

An antenna is the link between transmitters and receivers. On the receiving end, the antenna captures the signal from the atmosphere and routes it to your T.V. or radio. Many people overlook this critical link and either suffer with poor performance or look to more expensive ways to get around the antenna deficiency. (C.B.'ers sometimes add illegal amplifiers to boost their effective range when a legal antenna might do a better job.) If you live in the middle of some big city, you can get away with the whip antenna on your radio or some rabbit ears on top of your T.V. This is because you are so close to the transmitter that you don't notice the inefficiencies in the antenna.

In a more rural setting, the amount of radio signal that passes your way will be far less than if you lived downtown. To compensate for this reduced power, you need an antenna system that is (1) outdoors and away from power lines and other obstructions (your house impedes clear reception), (2) up as high as you can get it (altitude has a dramatic effect on reception), and (3) designed to receive the frequencies you want.

A quick and effective T.V./F.M. antenna

This antenna was designed primarily for U.H.F. channels, though it will do a good job on V.H.F. channels (Ch. 2-13) as well. The reason I designed

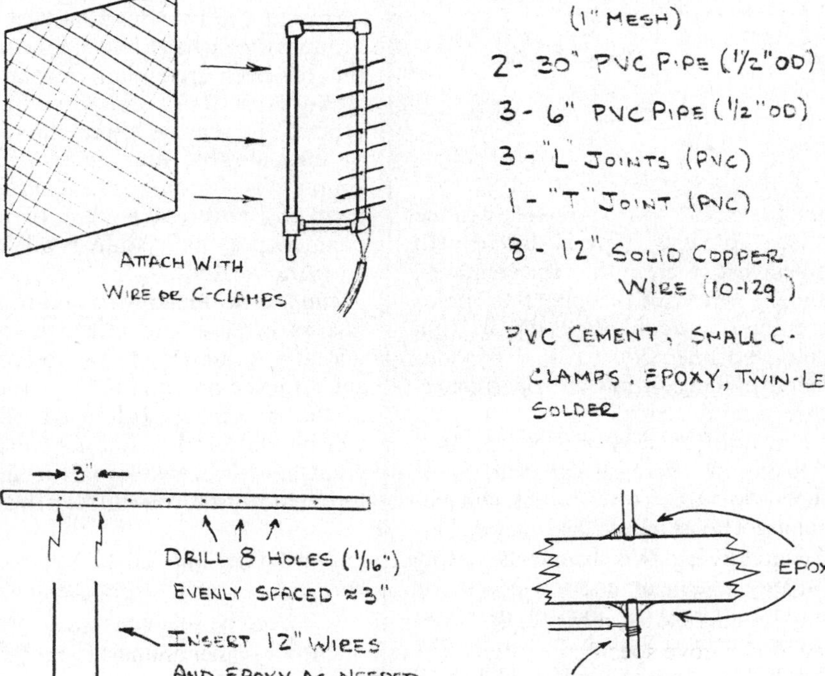

the antenna for U.H.F. is because many rural residents are completely out of range of most television stations and instead receive translator stations which relay and re-broadcast the material from the larger stations in their state. So as not to interfere with the main station's transmissions, translator stations all operate on the upper-U.H.F. channels.

The antenna is made of some scrap PVC pipe, some T and L fittings, a piece of chicken wire, some 10 gauge solid copper wire, and a few miscellaneous nuts and bolts. The antenna can be fastened to a mast made of copper pipe or electrical conduit.

The PVC pipe is fashioned into an O shape frame. Individual antenna elements (known as dipoles) are arranged along one side of the frame,

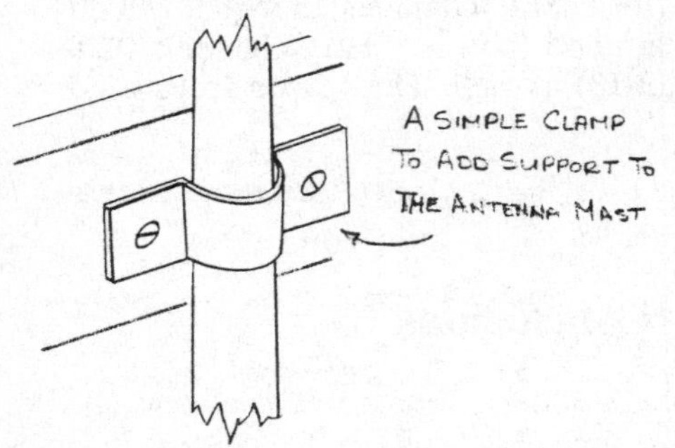

and the chicken wire is fastened to the other. The PVC pipe is drilled with holes slightly larger than the elements, and the wire is fed through. If the holes are tight enough, then the friction might be adequate to hold the elements in place. If not, a drop of epoxy should do the trick.

The chicken wire mesh acts as a reflector to increase the amount of signal that passes over the antenna elements. The chicken wire may be attached to the PVC frame by simply twisting some wire at a few points (or C-clamps could be substituted). If you live in an area with high winds, you may want to unravel a wire coat hanger and mold it around the perimeter of the chicken wire to reinforce it.

The antenna elements make up what engineers call a phased-array. This means that they are connected in such a way as to maximize the signal they can pick up and deliver to your receiver. To make the phased-array, you need to solder two feed wires (any size wire will do nicely) alternately from element to element (see diagram).

These two feed wires are then connected to a length of 300-ohm twin-lead antenna wire (available at most T.V. shops, discount and hardware stores) which is run to the T.V. If you have your antenna mounted outdoors, you should also attach a lightning arrestor to the twin lead and run the ground wire to a 4-foot copper pipe that has been driven into the earth.

The mast itself can rest on the ground and may be fastened to a tree or the eaves of your house using a simple pipe fastener (see diagram). I gave my antenna a coat of clear enamel spray paint to help protect it from the weather.

Run the twin-lead wire in through a nearby window and attach it to the antenna terminals of your television set. Aim the antenna in the direction of the transmitter (often translators will be clustered in one location). If you want to receive signals from different locations, you can turn the mast by hand when you change channels or invest $50 in an antenna rotator. You can use this antenna for several T.V. sets and an F.M. receiver by buying a signal-splitter for $5 at your local T.V. shop or Radio Shack.

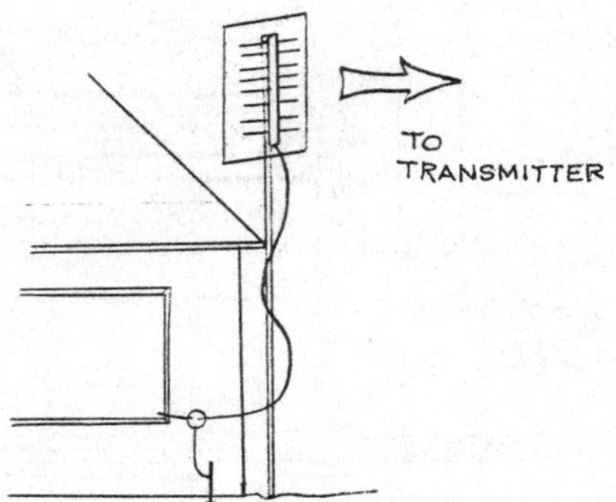

A BHM Writer's Profile

A published writer since 1960, Jj began homesteading in 1975 in Western Colorado. Several moves later she landed in Washington, in a remote rural cabin. Involvement with the ecology movement of the 60's, raising a family of five daughters, and a frequent lack of money have honed her survival skills over the years. Jj feels deeply connected to the earth and its elements through gardening and living near the wild. She also enjoys crafts, including painting Pennsylvania Dutch barn signs.

An easy A.M./short-wave antenna

Some people say that A.M. radio is dead; I couldn't disagree more. It is still the preferred medium for news, weather, talk and informational programming. These are the kinds of things that farmers, homesteaders and those living in rural areas would likely want to receive. Another interesting characteristic of A.M. signals is that at night they have the ability to bounce off of the upper layers of the atmosphere and be heard hundreds or thousands of miles away. To maximize our A.M. reception, we will use a different antenna design than for T.V. reception. If you have a small shortwave receiver, this antenna will work great as well.

The technical name for this type of antenna is a Windom, and it will provide excellent reception while, at the same time, being easy and flexible to build. You can make the antenna any length you'd like. Obviously the size of your property will be the constraint you have to consider. As shown in the diagram below, the antenna is merely a length of stranded copper wire (a piece of lampcord from the hardware store will work well) strung between two trees, the eaves of your house, or masts made of electrical conduit. An

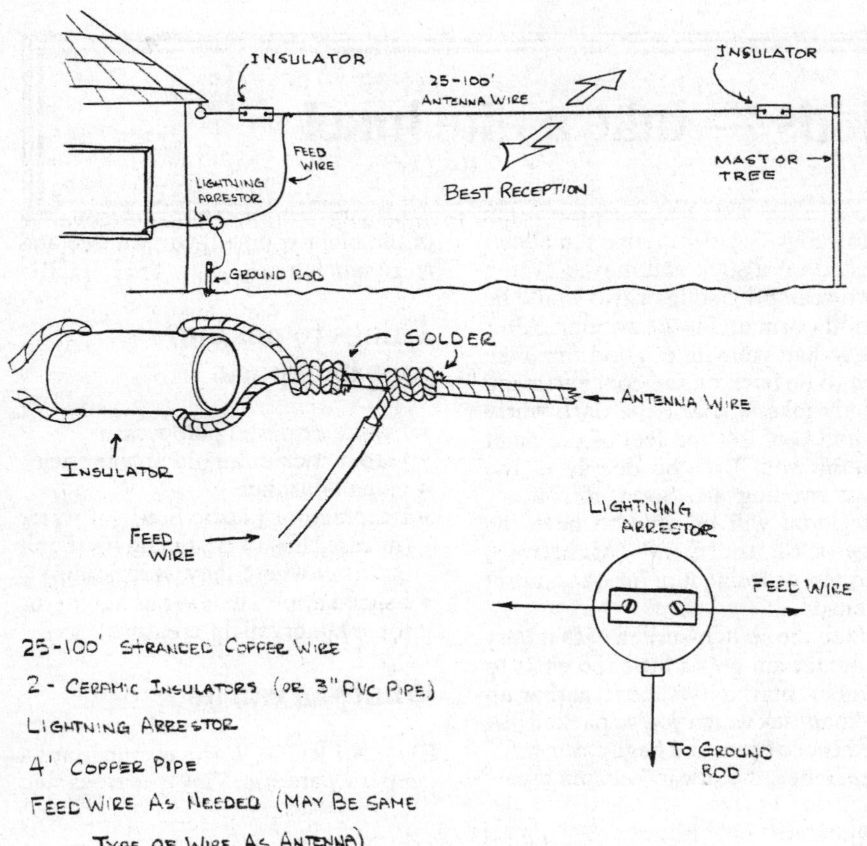

indoor version could be made by running the wire from one end of your attic to the other. This line is insulated from its connection points by ceramic insulators (Radio Shack sells them) or a couple of 3" pieces of PVC pipe. A feed wire is attached to the main element at some convenient point and runs through a window to the receiver.

The antenna works best for receiving signals that pass perpendicular to it. So, if you want to pick up a station to the north of you, it would be best to run the antenna east-west. If you are going to use the antenna for general A.M. or shortwave, then any convenient direction would be acceptable. I ran my antenna from south-east to north-west, so that I could pick up shortwave stations from both Europe and South America. As with the T.V. antenna, you should always use a lightning arestor and ground rod.

Coupling the A.M. antenna to the receiver can be done in several ways. If your receiver has an antenna terminal on the back, you can attach the feed wire directly. Some radios have the telescoping whip antennas. If this is the case, you can attach an alligator clip to the feed wire and clip it to the whip antenna. If your receiver has an internal antenna and no external connections, or if you find that the direct connection tends to overload the receiver, then some indirect coupling is needed.

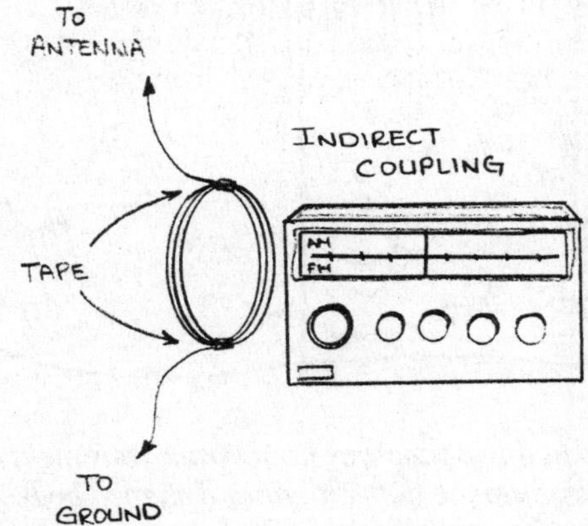

To indirectly couple the antenna to the receiver, we need to make a set of loops in the feed wire. The loops can be any dimension, 6-8" being acceptable. Make a set of 5-10 turns in the feed wire and tape the loop at several points to keep it from unraveling. The end of the feed wire should then be grounded; your ground rod, a cold-water pipe or the little screw that holds the face plate on the electrical outlet are good possibilities. Tune your receiver to a weak station, put the loop behind the receiver and move it around until the signal is strongest. You might want to tape the loop in place to keep it from being moved.

What is happening here is that the antenna is picking up the signal and running it down the feed line. By grounding the other end of the feed, we create a path for the received signal to flow. The loops in the wire radiate the received signal for a short distance, and by putting the receiver in the middle of this field we enjoy good reception without any direct connections.

Conclusions

A good antenna makes all the difference in reception. This is especially true when we live some distance from the stations we want to receive. You will be amazed at how many more stations you will be able to pick up when you install these outdoor antennas. If you get really serious about your radio reception, General Electric makes a Super-Radio that is specially designed for extra sensitivity and selectivity. You can call them at 1-800-626-2000 to find out who sells it locally.

As with any do-it-yourself project, remember that safety should not be ignored. DO NOT install an antenna near power lines, and always use a lightning arrestor and ground rod. Both of these antennas are easy to build, very forgiving if the dimensions are not exact (or even close) and work incredibly well. Best of all, they can be put together with scrap materials that are probably out in your garage or that can be easily scrounged. Good luck and good reception! Δ

Just for kids — take a nite hike!

By Lucy Shober

How many times have you lain awake in your bed on late summer nights listening to the symphony of creatures outside? Sometimes do you imagine what it might be like to become a part of that chorus yourself? If you get permission from your grownup, you might just be able to join in the ruckus—take a nite hike! It's best (and more fun) if you invite a quiet buddy or two to go along with you. Perhaps you might even wangle your favorite adult friend into giving your hike a grand start by helping you to make a camp fire supper.

Hot-dogs... cider... marshmallows roasted on a stick and maybe even a rowdy campfire song or two would be a good warm up for the evening. After you've had your fill of good fun, take time to lie back on the cool earth and quietly take stock of the dark world around you. Let the feel of the night envelop you. Breathe deeply of the moist evening air. Soon, if you are quiet, you will be able to hear the chorus of nocturnal (nighttime) animals warming up for the sunset serenade.

When the scritch-scritch of that busy carpenter ant gets a little too close to your ear, maybe it's time to gather up the knapsack which you've packed just for this occasion, and begin your walk. Remember, if you can become a part of the night yourself, you will see and learn much more, so... SSHHHH!!

Things to put into your backpack

- 1 white or pastel pillow case
- 1 stout stick or an old broom stick
- 1 small flashlight
- 1 canteen or plastic bottle of water (in case those marshmallows didn't quite get where they were going!)
- 1 sliced apple (to leave as a treat for some hungry night creature)

What you can do

BUG A FROG! Warm evenings are a peepers' paradise. Tiny tree frogs sing

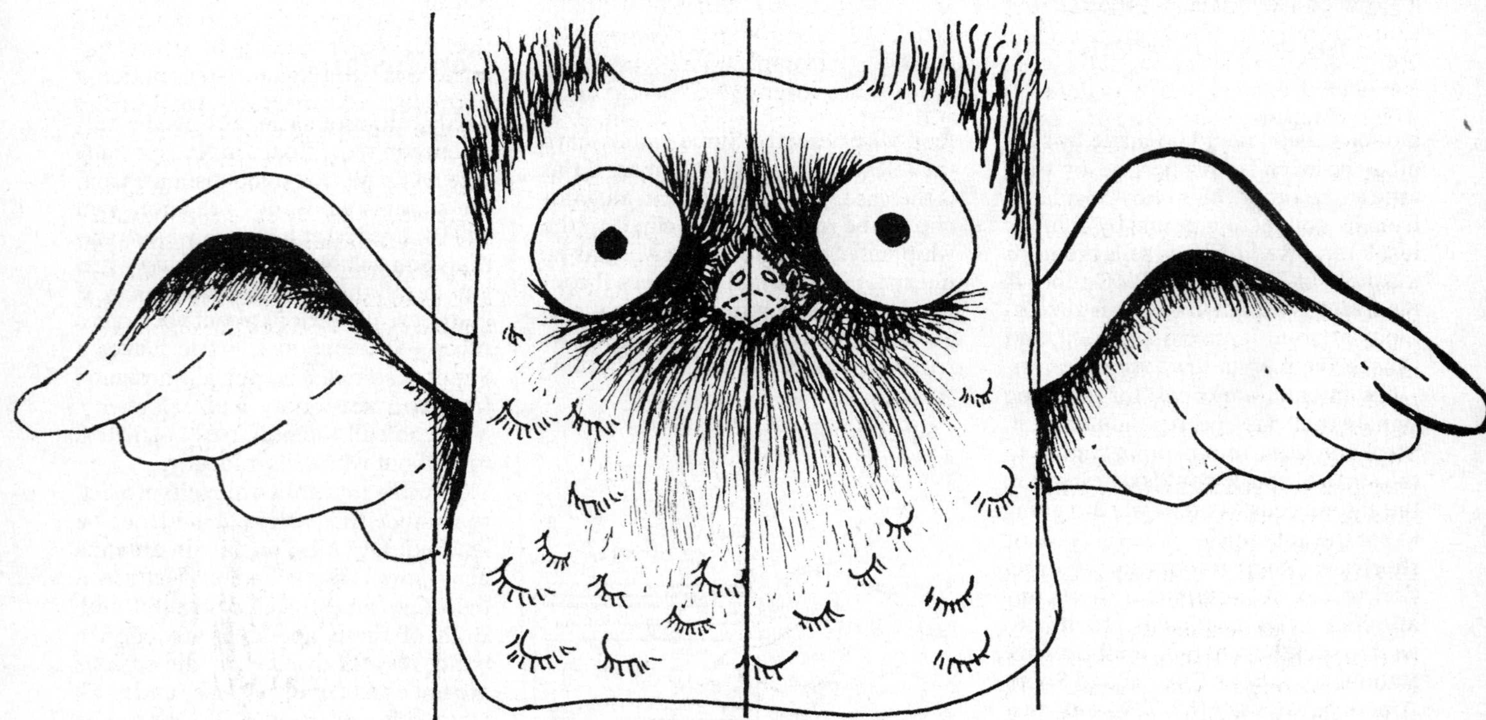

Need an obnoxious buddy to keep you company on the way home from your night hike? Cut out this poor screech owl who seems to have a walloping case of larengitis. Snip the dotted diamond shaped beak. Fold his wings and middle so that he fits over your mouth as shown in the picture on the opposite page. Then squeeze the paper with two fingers and blow. You might like to trace this picture onto several other thicknesses of paper until you achieve the obnoxious scree that is most undesirable.

to each other throughout the forest, perched on branches and leaves as they chat the night away. You, if you are careful enough, might be able to sneak up on an amorous peeper. When you hear the high-pitched squeak of one of these little fellows, tip-toe toward it. If you get too close, the peeping will stop. So YOU stop. Be quieter than you ever thought possible. When the singing begins again (because the frog thinks that you've gone away), inch a little closer. Each time the singing stops, you stop, until you are able to pinpoint which bush or tree your friend is using as home tonight. Then (and only then) you turn on your light and try to spot the little fellow! What looks like a surprised mound of bubble gum will be your reward for patience. These delightful critters will be very thankful if you simply enjoy without touching them. (Imagine how you might feel if a finger the size of an elephant wanted to give YOU a gentle pat!)

FROG A BUG! When you have said goodbye to your little green buddy, choose as your next night spot, a leafy tree branch with low-hanging leaves. Now, with one of your human pals, stretch the pillow case out flat. Hold it as close as you can to the leafy tree branch. With your stout stick, give the branch one good crack, and then quickly, another. When you shine your light upon the pillowcase, you might be surprised at what's happened . . . you have just interrupted nature's cafe! How many different kinds of bugs have fallen onto your case? On a good night, you might find as many as ten different types of insects feeding on a single branch. Imagine how many millions of these little feasters must be munching away all around you. Some come for the leaves, and others come for the leaf eaters. What's on the menu tonight?

DIAMONDS IN THE LEAVES! The forest around you is rich with treasure. Would you like to explore a little further, and discover the secret diamonds of the night? Take your flashlight now, and place it EXACTLY between your eyes, on the bridge of your nose. It might take a little practice and a lot of giggling before you master the technique, but if you look straight down the beam of light into the leaves of the forest floor, the tiny diamonds will begin to show themselves. They glisten so brightly in the dark . . . hat could they be? Gently push aside a clump of leaves to uncover even more of these glimmering jewels. This treasure though, is rarely gathered up by pirates. Why? Because it BITES!! Did you guess? What you have been hunting is really SPIDERS. As they stare up at you, their tiny eyes reflect the beam of your flashlight.

Be the night

By now, you are probably about to burst at the seams from being quiet for such a long time! So just let it all go now . . . take time out for a quick holler! Screech and roll on the ground, whoop and snort. Grab up a big handful of that good rich earth and inhale its delicious fragrance. YUM! Do two somersaults, put your flashlight on the ground, run twenty feet into the dark night then return to its safe glow. Feel better? O.K. It's quiet time again. Slowly and quietly walk away from your noisy spot. Keep walking until that nighttime feeling of peace has come over you again. Now, notice a particular nook or cranny, maybe a flat rock or mossy log which seems to invite YOU over for a sit. Now do just that. Cozy up to your buddy, get comfortable, take three deep breaths. Turn your flashlight off. Let the night seep into your clothes, into your hair and even into the pores of your skin. Quiet...quiet. Become the night. Δ

Fitting in with your new neighbors

By Susan Betz

Eight years ago, my husband and I went for the dream and moved to the country. We now have good jobs, a working farm, and a lot of good, solid friends. I have recently been elected to a second term on the Town Council here. In short, we have managed to fit in.

We made a few mistakes. I have seen other city folks blunder terribly without even knowing it. Often they left their dreams behind, themselves the objects of scorn, without a clue as to why it didn't work out.

First mistake

Let's start with the day you move in. It is a country tradition in most places to stop by and meet a new neighbor, if not help them move in. Our neighbors stopped by when they saw the van and helped us unload. We made our first mistake when we offered to pay them for their help. They were insulted. Did we think they had offered to help for money? Did we think they could be bought? Were we just throwing our money around to show off? We did not even realize that this offer was insulting until much later. They just politely and firmly refused.

If your neighbors do not take the initiative, you should stop by at least once and let them get a look at you. Don't dress up. Don't stay too long on a working farm...you are probably keeping them from chores. Some people will simply not neglect a guest. I found to my embarrassment, and I must admit, annoyance, that some people will talk to you all night, then complain to others that you don't know when to go home. Leave before they want you to go. If the town is small enough, and you stay long enough, you will find out these things. It is best not to have to find out the hard way.

Beware

While such things leave one feeling awkward, the people mean no harm. If anything, they are over-polite. Unfortunately, there are some folks you should beware of. Almost all of these people will find you, often by showing up with helpful advice. One type will give you bad advice, in the hope that you will take it, fail, and go back to the city where you belong.

One of our neighbors noticed my husband and me in the field, checking the condition of our mown hay. Fortunately, and unknown to her, we had helped someone else bale their hay already. Our hay was still far too wet to bale. Baling at that time could not only have caused our hay to mold, the heat of fermentation could have caused a fire by spontaneous combustion. More than one barn has burned due to wet hay bales. This neighbor enthusiastically urged us to bale immediately in fact, she almost insisted. Watch out for such people. She has given us really lousy advice before and after this occasion. At first I figured she was just ignorant. I later found that she has been baling hay and such all her life. I eventually had to face the fact that she knew what she was doing, and what she was doing was lying.

Beware of anyone who seems to have plenty of time to tell you how to run your farm. Successful farmers are too busy running their own places to stand over the shoulder of every newcomer and make sure they get things right.

Finding good advice

If you want good advice, successful farmers are the ones to get it from. So how do you find them? Look for a busy place where the livestock and plants are healthy and the buildings well maintained. Stop by and ask when would be a good time to come over and ask for advice. Chances are that you will get a warm reception. After you get your advice, you might stop by again when you don't want something. It wouldn't hurt to come with baked goods or the like, either.

Another type of person who will show up is someone who wants to use your land, or buy something like your timber, cheap. Be careful that you don't get skinned. Consult experts. One of the best ways to find out about local rents and prices is no, not your broker, but a long term successful farmer. It is best not to say exactly why you want to know, you are just wondering. Many people are reluctant to get involved between two neighbors making a deal, and thus may not tell you that you are being swindled. Needless to say, but I will anyway, don't tell the party you are negotiating with where you got your information, no matter how many times they ask. It will get back to your source, and you may be blamed for causing a feud between two long-time residents.

Bargains

Next, there are those friendly folks with something to sell. This may not be mentioned the first time, but things that are poor quality or overpriced will often be eagerly peddled to people with no experience by a crafty few. Anyone who has something of good quality at a fair price doesn't need to try to palm it off on a newcomer.

Don't be so eager to get that first tractor, set of plows, or whatever. Look around quite a bit. Tell your new friend you aren't ready. City folk are known for paying too much for stuff. This not only has the obvious drawback, but a neighbor who needs the item and is willing to pay a fair price may resent being outbid by someone who barely knows what to do with it.

Trespassers

The last group I want to warn you about are trespassers. If you want to maintain control of your property, you will have to be very vigilant, especially for the first few years. Our biggest problem was hunters, but once we looked out and saw an entire Boy Scout troop sledding down our hill! When confronted, the troop leader explained that they had always sledded there, every year. Another woman told us how she planned to race us for the apples on our trees.

All the above were firmly told, as often as necessary, that the property was under new ownership, and while we didn't mean to be unfriendly, we wouldn't have bought it and wouldn't be paying taxes on it if we didn't intend to use it all in our own way. We intend to limit hunting, sledding, and food gathering on our property to ourselves and our friends. Those who had to be told twice were reminded that there are laws against trespassing and theft, and we would resort to calling for enforcement if pushed.

Having said enough about the rotten apples, I want to assure you that there are only a few, and that standing up to them will not ruin your relationship with your more desirable neighbors. The decent people in the community do not approve of such shenanigans any more than you do. Be calm and firm and you will be respected for it.

More blunders

Number one on the list is talking about how great things are in the city, or complaining about how crude things are in the country. Part of this stems from the fear that you will try to do something about it. Do not get involved with anything that will raise taxes or regulate the unregulated. If you like zoning laws and building regulations and hate manure, pesticides, or any other aspect of farming, move to an area that already has the kind of laws you want. Violate this and you will be almost universally resented by long term residents. Rural government does not provide a city level of services and regulation. If you cannot live without them, country life probably isn't for you.

Know-it-alls don't get a lot of respect or help, either. Never tell anyone how to do something unless asked, even if it is your profession. On the other hand, if you ask for advice, don't argue with it. You can ask questions to understand, but don't argue. If you don't like the advice, say thank you and then ignore it.

Do not brag about your income or live in an ostentatious or flashy way. We all know money isn't everything. Be careful not even to appear to think that you are better than the locals if you have surplus cash.

Don't whine about your work or about your aches and pains. It may be considered amusing. After all, didn't you want this country life? Did you think it would be easy?

The nicest thing a country dweller can say about someone is that they are a hard worker. This is the ultimate compliment. Hard work is valued as an end to itself. Laziness is condemned.

It is a myth that outsiders will not be accepted. It is true that many are not. The reasons are varied, but always seem to center on a few social blunders. If you can avoid these, you will fit in just fine. Δ

A BHM Writer's Profile

The rugged, wooded hills of southern Indiana are home to Charles A. Sanders, his wife Patti, and their three children. Sanders built the heavily-insulated, south-facing, wood heated house in 1979. In 1992, they added to the house and to their family as well. They have 39 acres of timber and pasture, where they grow timber, a few cattle, and hay. They can, freeze, and dry hundreds of quarts of vegetables from their large garden each summer. The Sanders raise their own beef, and augment it with small game and deer from the surrounding woodlands. Their orchard keeps them in apples and pears. They keep bees for pollination and honey.

Sanders' interest in the land carries over into his occupation. He has been a conservation officer for 19 years, and serves as a district firearms instructor. Sanders spends his vacation time as a member of Indiana's Inter-Agency Wildland Fire Crew, and has fought wildfires in Oregon, Idaho, Montana, Minnesota, and Kentucky, as well as his own state. Writing is an especially strong interest. Besides writing for *Backwoods Home Magazine*, Sanders is writing a common-sense, down-to-earth, present-day homesteader's guide. His other interests include trapping, reading, radio, and winemaking.

How to make money with wild crayfish

By Gene Check

In recent years a lot of interest has developed in the money-making potential of crayfish – not only the huge multi-million dollar crayfish industry that exists in Louisiana, but exciting markets opening up for crayfish in other parts of the U.S. as well.

While farming crayfish can offer excellent income possibilities, (see July/August '92 *Backwoods Home Magazine*) it also presents certain drawbacks. Farming crayfish necessitates owning land and building ponds. Commercial crayfish ponds also require large water pumps, etc., to manage ponds for decent production. Furthermore, raising crayfish for food purposes is only practical in certain warmer areas of the U.S. This is because virtually all crayfish farming is done with a species called the Red Swamp crayfish (*Procambarus clarkii*). Red Swamp crayfish are used because they thrive in pond culture and can be grown to a 3-inch or bigger eating size in 3 to 6 months.

The problem with swamp crayfish is that they are raised in shallow ponds that are periodically drained. This means commercial crayfish farming is mostly limited to temperate regions such as the southern U.S. and areas of both coasts.

Fortunately, there is another way to cash in on crayfish which is available to virtually anyone in most parts of the country. This is simply harvesting crayfish in the wild. While crayfish trapping does require an investment in traps and other equipment, it's easy to start out small and add equipment as you go.

Louisiana is the state most famous for its crawfish. (In Louisiana the term "crawfish" is used, while the rest of the country uses "crayfish".) The harvest is upwards of 100 million pounds each year. What many people don't realize is that roughly half of this total comes from crawfish caught in the wild. In Louisiana, most wild crawfish are caught in the Atchafalaya flood basin (off the Mississippi River) which is roughly 18 miles wide by 80 miles long.

In California, Signal crayfish are harvested in the Sacramento River from Colusa to Rio Vista, with up to 500,000 pounds taken yearly. Swamp crayfish are also starting to get harvested in the rice growing regions of California, where they are considered a pest because of their burrowing activities.

While not on the same scale as California, other western states such as Oregon, Washington, Utah, etc. also support a commercial harvest of wild crayfish.

In my home state of Wisconsin, crayfish have been commercially harvested for various markets for decades. Despite this, I've found that in Wisconsin, Minnesota, and other areas of the midwest, crayfish are seriously underharvested. Last summer I couldn't find enough trappers to trap the areas I knew about, despite the excellent income to be made.

I've also received reports from the Northwest and other areas of the country where there are reputed to be excellent populations of crayfish with little or no harvest occurring.

What species

While there are dozens of different crayfish species around the country, only about 6 or so have major economic importance. This is because the most lucrative crayfish markets are for food purposes. A crayfish has to be at least 3 inches long (Figure 1) to be considered suitable for eating.

Very few crayfish species grow large enough or plentiful enough to be commercially harvested. In any one region of the country, there are likely to be only one or two species worth considering.

In Louisiana and the rest of the South, about 90% of the wild and farm-raised crayfish harvest consists of Red Swamp crayfish (*Procambarus clarkii*). Young swamp crayfish have a greenish brown color but turn red as they grow older. A mature specimen will be purple-black on top and dark red on the sides and claws.

White River crayfish (*Procambarus acutus acutus*) account for about 10% of the southern harvest. The young white river crayfish is tan-white with small black spots. The adult is light brown or purplish red with a dark stripe down the tail. Old specimens that are deep red can be distinguished from swamp crayfish by their narrower claws and the absence of a blue vein on the underside of the tail.

If you buy crayfish for eating purposes in any of the southern states they are almost sure to be one of these two species.

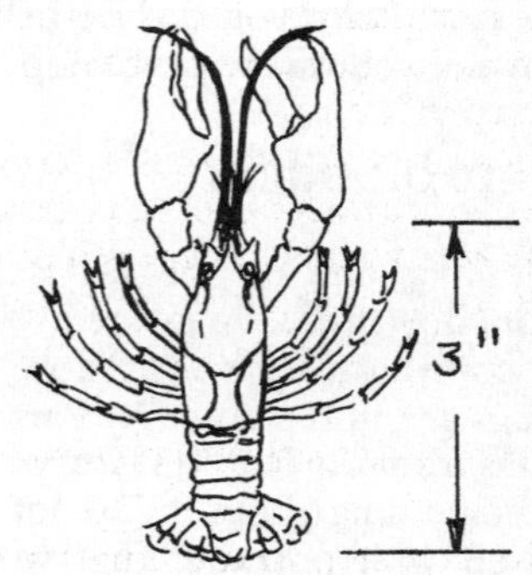

Figure 1. A crayfish should be at least 3" long to be suitable for eating.

In California, the Red Swamp crayfish is harvested in some of the rice-growing areas, but most of the crayfish harvest centers around the Signal crayfish (*Pacifastacus Lenivsculus*), which is harvested in the Sacramento delta region. They're called Signal crayfish because of the distinctive coloring of their claws when lifted in a defensive position. The Signal crayfish is also harvested in Washington, Oregon, Utah, and other western states.

In Wisconsin, Minnesota, and other northern states, the harvest mostly involves two species, the Rusty crayfish (*Orconectes rusticus*) and the Virilis crayfish (*Orconectes virilis*). Of these two, the Rusty crayfish is most often harvested. Rusty crayfish are reddish brown or reddish tan with large claws. They have a dark rusty colored spot on each side of their bodies just in front of the tail. The Rusty crayfish is native to the central states but has been spread to many parts of the northern U.S. by its use as fishing bait. In some northern lakes the Rusty crayfish has exploded in population to the point where they are considered a pest. Where this occurs, I've found crayfish trappers are welcomed with open arms by lakefront property owners to help control the crayfish over-population.

The other northern crayfish which is sometimes commercially harvested is the Virilis crayfish. They can be identified by their blue claws, which have very small white wart-like bumps. They are a native northern crayfish which doesn't reach the super abundant populations of the Rusty crayfish but still can be quite profitable to trap in certain areas.

The easiest way to identify crayfish is to ask a crayfish buyer in your area. If none are available a fishery biologist at your local natural resources office or university should be able to help.

How to catch crayfish

The first step in catching crayfish is to go to your local natural resources department and find out what, if any, regulations there are concerning the harvest of crayfish in your state. Regulations may determine what traps can be used, how and when they can be set, etc.

Crayfish are harvested with traps baited with 1/2 to 1 pound of fish. Traps are made with wire mesh screen. A funnel or funnels made of the same screen are built into the trap to guide the crayfish into it.

Some people believe that rotten fish would best attract the scavenging crustaceans, but I've found that fresh fish works far better. In Louisiana, where crawfish is a big industry, some dried, processed, fish-based baits have been developed, but most trapping is still done using regular fish for bait.

Most commercial crayfish trappers buy rough fish cheaply from commercial fisherman and store the bait in a series of chest freezers or a walk-in freezer.

I know one crayfish trapper who lives in an area where there is some excellent fishing for panfish and other fish. In this area there are some large resorts and campgrounds that provide fish cleaning houses for their customers. The large volume of fish scraps they produce is a nuisance for the resort owners, who are glad to have the trapper pick them up. Five gallon pails with lids are provided for the resort owners who fill them neatly with the fish remains and may even freeze the pails until the trapper has time to pick them up.

Although crayfish trapping has certain similarities no matter where it's done, there are some major differences depending on the species you are after and the habitat where they are found.

Southern trapping

Swamp crayfish are caught from November to May in the flooded backwaters of the Atchafalaya basin and other waterways in southern Louisiana. The best trapping normally occurs in February or March. Some of the most productive trapping is where new areas of backwater are created by the rising floodwater. Trappers check their traps every day or two, depending on how active the crawfish are. This backwater trapping is usually done in fairly shallow water, 3 feet deep or less.

The most common trap used in the South is the pillow trap (Figure 2). This trap is normally made with a 3/4" chicken wire type mesh. Wire mesh coated with black plastic is generally used. The black plastic coating extends the life of the trap and is said to catch crayfish better.

There are various designs of pillow traps, but the most common is 18" to 2' long and has two small funnel entrances at one end, while the opposite end of the trap can be opened to remove your catch and add bait.

If there is any current, the funnel end of the trap is pointed downstream, as the crayfish will work their way upstream into the trap. Many southern trappers feel the pillow traps work better if they are tilted at an angle with the funnels pointed down to make it easier for the crayfish to enter the trap.

In Louisiana, the trapper may run hundreds of traps many miles back in the swamp. The fact that the pillow trap can be flattened and stacked in the boat is a big plus.

Trapping in the west

While swamp crayfish are harvested in California, most of the western harvest still centers around the Signal crayfish. Here the crayfish are trapped in deeper (up to 20') rocky areas of the Sacramento River).

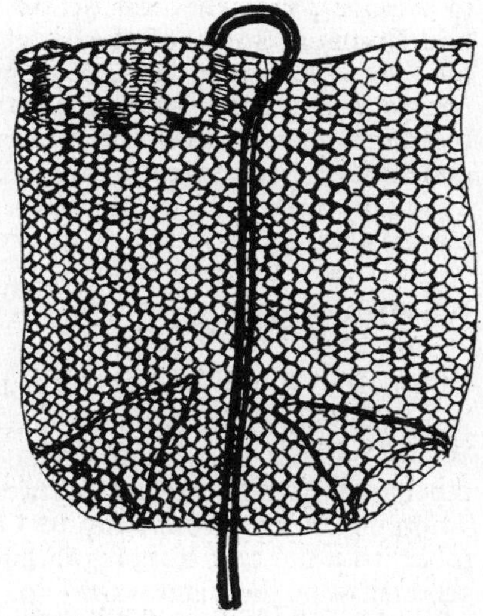

Figure 2. The pillow trap is the most common trap used in the South.

A series of traps are set on one main line with a large float marking each end of the line (Figure 3). Each trap is fastened to the main line with a short line and a clip to prevent tangling. These lines are lifted up into the boat with a hydraulic device. As traps come up, they are unclipped, emptied, and stacked in the boat. When setting the line, traps are baited and clipped to the main line one at a time as the line is paid out. Lines are moved to a new location each time they are checked.

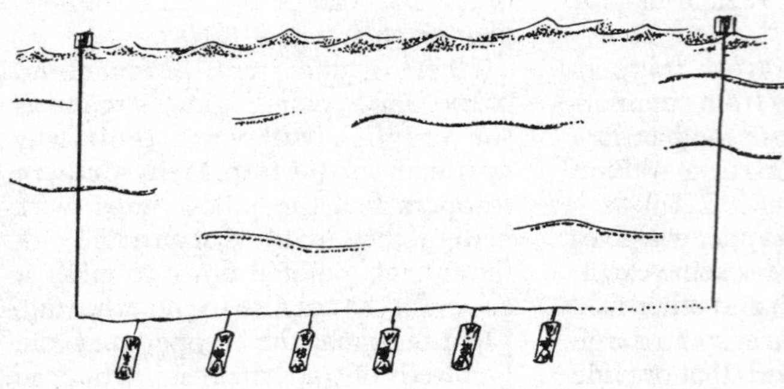

Figure 3. Series of traps with floats.

Winching up traps in these rocky areas can be tough on equipment, so traps are made with heavy-duty 1/2" by 1" plastic-coated screen. Each trap is typically a 10" diameter screen tube with a screen funnel on each end. A door is built into the side of each trap to add bait and remove the catch.

Trapping is normally done from May to October, with the best action in mid-summer. Some of the biggest operators run as many as 1,000 traps.

Signal crayfish are also caught in the reservoirs and rivers of other western states, but here traps are set individually with a rope and float to mark each trap.

Northern trapping

Virilis and Rusty crayfish are commercially trapped in my home state of Wisconsin, and to a lesser extent in other areas of the North and Midwest. Trapping occurs from May to October, with the best trapping in mid-summer when the water warms up.

I've found the best trapping to be in the large, deep, clean lakes of northern Wisconsin. This type of habitat can support good populations of large crayfish. Another advantage of large waterways is that many traps can be set in one area. Commercial trappers run up to several hundred traps.

Not all large lakes contain profitable populations of crayfish. You can narrow your search by talking to your local DNR or fish manager. They are often familiar with lakes that have been trapped in the past. Resort and lakefront property owners often complain to the DNR when they perceive their lakes to be overrun with crayfish.

You can test a large lake by taking 10 traps and spreading them out widely in various spots around the lake. Set traps in five to fifteen feet of water with each trap attached to its own rope and float. Bait them with 1/2 to 3/4 pound of fish and check daily. Avoid shallow, muddy areas. The best spots are sandy or rocky bottoms adjacent to deep water. In a good lake, it's not unusual to get several pounds or more per trap, but what you want to look for are areas of shoreline where the highest percentage of big crayfish can be caught. I would advise you to wait until mid-summer before test-setting, to better ensure that the crayfish are fully active. Once you find a good spot, you'll generally want to set traps about 100 feet apart.

Handling your catch

It's important to handle your crayfish properly while on the water, so they remain in a healthy condition. Try to avoid leaving your crayfish in the sun, as it's very hard on them. I've had the best luck by dumping the crayfish in 48-quart Coleman-type plastic coolers. When the cooler is 2/3 full, the lid can be shut and the drain plug opened. The open drain hole provides all the ventilation required. Crayfish will normally keep well this way until you get home. On hot days, you can throw in a handful of ice before closing the cooler lid.

Grading crayfish

You'll probably have to separate out the smaller crayfish before you can market your catch. If you are dealing with a crayfish buyer, they can tell you how they want the crayfish graded.

I grade my crayfish right on the boat with a small box grader (Figure 4) which is placed on top of a Coleman cooler. This grader is simply a wooden box made of 1 x 6 lumber with rows of conduit fastened inside. The spacing between the bars allows the smaller crayfish to fall through. The bigger crayfish that remain on top are dumped into another cooler. I like to use a 3/4" spacing between the bars. The spacing is critical, as a 1/16" difference either way can make a big difference. If you make a grader, make sure there is absolutely no "give" or shimmy in the bars.

Storing crayfish

If you're lucky, you'll be able to deliver your crayfish to a dealer every day. However, most trappers find it necessary to have some type of storage facilities at home for their crayfish. That way, crayfish can be stored until a worthwhile amount can be taken to market. It's also a good idea to keep some crayfish around during the season to supply any new markets that may develop.

In Louisiana, dealers often store 25 to 50 pounds of live crayfish in large nylon mesh bags which are stacked in large walk-in coolers. This method works fairly well for a few days, but it's beyond the means of the average trapper.

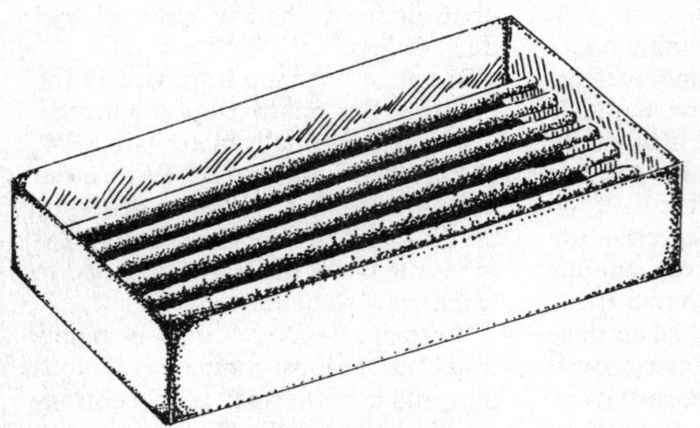

Figure 4. Crayfish box grader.

I've found a much better method: store your

catch in tanks of water (Figure 5). It's necessary to keep enough water flowing in and out of the tank to maintain clear water. Aerators added to the tank will greatly increase holding capacity.

The idea of creating storage facilities may sound intimidating to the newcomer, but here again, you don't have to start off big. Most beginning trappers will probably find they're eating most of what they catch.

Eating crayfish

For those who have never cooked or eaten crayfish, I'll describe the most basic methods. With experience, you can go on to more elaborate meals.

Rinse off your live crayfish and throw them into a pot of very salty boiling water. Let them boil for several minutes. The crayfish are done when they change color and float to the surface.

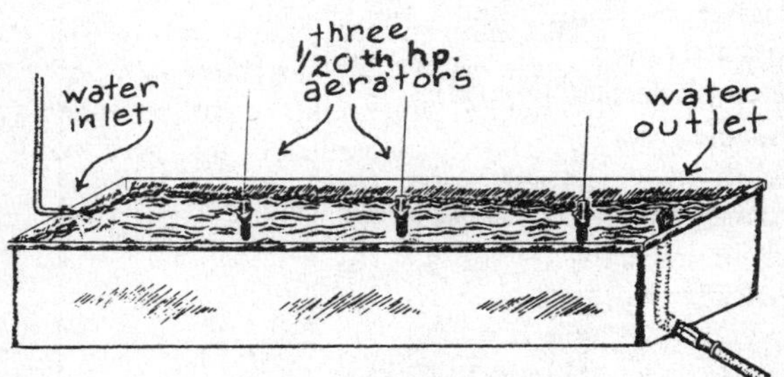

Figure 5. 1000-gallon tank.

Drain the water and let it cool slightly. Grab the body of a crayfish with your left hand, and use your right hand to simultaneously pull and twist the tail off the body. Then you can peel the shell from the tail. Remove the vein that runs along the tail before eating.

On larger crayfish, the claw meat can also be eaten. First detach the claw from the leg. Some people break open the claws with their teeth, but this can be painful. It's easier to break off the small hinged pincer of the claw and then stick the prong of a fork through the opening. By twisting the fork, you can break open the claw and retrieve the meat. After you try fresh-cooked crayfish, your biggest problem may be saving enough for your customers.

How much money can you make?

Crayfish prices and demand can vary greatly, depending on what part of the country you live in. In Louisiana, many crayfish trappers prefer to sell all their catch to one processing plant. Crayfish can bring 30 cents to a dollar a pound, depending on how plentiful the catch is in a given year. That may not sound like much, but good trappers will catch several hundred pounds in one day.

In the West, crayfish trappers get a dollar to a dollar- fifty per pound, with the best trappers making very good money in a season. To do that, they work very hard, and they have to build up a big stock of equipment over the years.

Crayfish have been marketed in Wisconsin for decades in the food, bait, and biologicals markets. Unfortunately, these markets have been dominated by a handful of professional trappers. However, exciting new markets for Rusty crayfish have recently developed which promise to open up the crayfish industry to many more people in the northern states.

Rusty crayfish three inches or longer are in demand for food markets in the U.S. and overseas. Prices for the 1993 season have yet to be firmly established, but they'll probably be in the range of 50 to 75 cents a pound. A serious trapper should be able to make from 50 to 250 dollars per day, depending on his skill and the number of traps he's running.

Marketing is important. If you live in an area where there is no tradition of eating crayfish, you may find that there is not a ready market for your catch. But creating your own markets is not as hard as you might think. With the increasing interest in Cajun cooking, people everywhere are curious about trying crayfish. If you introduce people you know to eating them, many will come back to buy later. Establishing a new product can take time, but this can turn out to be an advantage if you're the only supplier around. Word of mouth will spread quickly with a novelty product that people enjoy.

A couple of notes of caution: Don't try selling crayfish under 3 inches, as it's too much work to eat crayfish that small. And sell your catch for at least $1.50 a pound – it's hard to raise your price once it's established. Some Cajun seafood restaurants will buy crayfish, sometimes paying up to several dollars a pound. But they can be very picky, demanding jumbo crayfish with two large claws.

(For more information on crayfish trapping, trap plans, marketing, cooking, etc., buy Gene Check's 65-page book, Commercial Crayfish Across America. The price is $7.95 (plus $1 P&H) and you can order it from "Backwoods Home Magazine" (see page 74) or from The Real Outdoors Co., 10422 North Rd., Tomahawk, WI 54487.) Δ

Log homes, motorcycles, and good food

By Richard Blunt

Dave, the fellow who publishes BHM, called me about a month ago and said the next issue is going to have a log home theme. He asked if it were possible for me to steer my column to recipes that would reflect that theme.

Log homes and recipes? I didn't see how the two went together. The way I figure it, the uniqueness of food is more related to where you live than what you live in. Still, I gave it some thought and hoped to come up with something.

Nothing. I couldn't think of a thing.

So, I decided another approach was nèċessary and I let my mind wander over my past culinary experiences and I tried to remember where I was when I first had them. Eventually, I started thinking about my cross country motorcycle trip in '71, the people I met, and the recipes they gave me when they found out I was a chef. Pretty soon I had a list of recipes I had picked up on that trip.

It was a great trip. Before nearly killing myself in an accident in Minnesota, I traveled as far south as New Orleans, and as far west and northwest as California, Oregon, and Washington. During the trip I met a lot of fine people and, when folks discovered I was a chef from Boston, many of them insisted on sharing their favorite recipes with me. Without exception, it was all good food. But four of the recipes, that now stood out in my mind, were given to me by people who lived in the more remote areas of Maine, Georgia, North Dakota, and Washington. All of the culinary masters who shared these delicacies with me were free thinking, self motivated types – they had to be to invite a road-dirty motorcyclist from Boston to eat with them. Each of the recipes is basic down home cooking, and suddenly I could visualize myself sitting down to a meal, of any one of them, in a log home with one of those folks I'd met 22 years ago.

North woods baked beans

If you like baked beans, this first recipe is a great variation that was shared with me by two wonderful people that I met in Maine. They were a couple who were on vacation and Bill, the husband, worked for Great Northern Paper Company. One of his company benefits was free use of a lake-front campsite on property owned by Great Northern.

The lake was called the "Middle Unknown." I had arrived there after a thirty mile ride down a one lane dirt road (which I was kind enough to share with huge pulp trucks that seemed to suddenly emerge from the forest shadows like prehistoric beasts) and I was in no frame of mind to doubt the lake's name when he told me. And, the name was appropriate, anyway, because where I stood was completely unknown to me. By my calculations I should have been in Canada. But my mistake proved to be to my advantage. Try these beans and you'll see why.

Ingredients:

2 cups white pea beans (regular, not quick)
1/2 cup diced onion
2 cloves fresh garlic (chopped)
3 tbsp maple syrup
3 tbsp chili sauce
2 tbsp dark unsulphured molasses
2 tbsp dijon mustard
1 tbsp dark brown sugar
1/2 cup your favorite beer or ale
1/4 cup good beef or chicken stock
1 bay leaf
1 tsp salt
1/2 tsp cider vinegar
1 tsp curry powder
4 oz. piece of salt pork (scored almost down to the skin but leave the skin attached)

Preparation:

1. Cover the beans with cold water and discard any beans that float to the surface. Drain the beans and cover them with cold water, again. Now, put them in the refrigerator and let them soak for at least 8 or 9 hours (or overnight).

2. After the beans have soaked, drain off what water remains and cover the beans again with fresh water. Place the beans over a medium héat and bring them to a boil. Now, reduce the heat and simmer the beans for another 30 minutes to soften them. Drain them again but save about two cups of the bean stock for later use in the recipe.

3. Place the salt pork in some boiling water and simmer for 10 to 15 minutes. Remove the salt pork from the boiling water and place it in the bottom of a 2 or 3 qt greased oven

casserole. Next, add the well drained beans to the casserole, covering the salt pork.

4. Combine and mix all of the flavoring agents in a small bowl, and add this mixture to the beans and stir them in.

5. Cover the casserole and place it in a pre-heated 250 degree oven and bake for 7 to 9 hours, when the beans will be tender and have absorbed the flavoring liqueur. Check the casserole every couple of hours. If the beans seem to be prematurely drying, add a little of the reserved bean water to restore consistency.

During the last half hour of baking, remove the cover from the casserole. This allows the mixture to thicken a little bit while still retaining some moisture.

Try these beans with some fresh caught smallmouth bass broiled over an open campfire. Need I say more?

Scrapple

The next recipe is scrapple. Although it's well known and popular in the city of Philadelphia, it's actually a Swedish dish and it was served to me in a campsite in North Dakota by a Swedish couple on their way to Canada. Scrapple is a great breakfast food and I often have it with my favorite omelets. And, since the meat is cooked before being incorporated, it's a great recipe for making use of leftovers.

Ingredients:

1 1/4 lb. good quality sausage meat
1 lb. ground smoked ham (ground cooked veal, chicken, or turkey, can be used in place of the smoked ham)
1 1/3 cups yellow corn meal
4 2/3 cups rich soup stock (beef or chicken, see my last column if you want a good stock recipe)
1 tsp. salt (more or less according to taste)
to taste fresh ground black pepper
2 tbsp. finely chopped onion
1/8 tsp. dried red pepper flakes
3 medium eggs

Preparation:

1. Break the sausage meat into small pieces and sauté it in a large frying pan, over medium heat, until it loses its pink color. Continue to break it up as it cooks. Remove the pan from the heat and add the ham, salt, black pepper, onion, and red pepper flakes.

2. Pour the stock into a sauce pan and place it over a medium heat. Slowly sprinkle the corn meal into the stock as it heats, stirring all the while with a wire whisk. Continue stirring until the mixture thickens and there are no lumps. Then cook it five more minutes while stirring constantly. Now, cover the saucepan and place it in a larger pan of simmering water and continue to cook it this way for another 40 minutes. During the last five minutes, remove the cover and stir the corn meal with a wooden spoon until it holds its shape on the spoon.

3. Combine the cooked corn meal with the meat mixture in a large pan over a low heat and continue stirring with the wooden spoon until it is thoroughly mixed. Then remove the pan from the heat and allow it to cool. Lightly beat the eggs and add them to the mixture, one at a time, stirring them in with the spoon.

4. Grease a loaf pan and a piece of aluminum foil large enough to cover it. Pack the scrapple into the pan. Bang the pan on the counter to remove air pockets. Cover it with the aluminum foil. Place the pan in a pre-heated 350 degree oven and bake for about one hour. When done, the scrapple will be firm and slightly swelled. Allow it to cool, then place it in the refrigerator until cold.

Final preparation:

5. When it's cold, remove the scrapple from the loaf pan and slice off pieces that are about 3/4 inch thick. Coat each slice with corn meal or flour and sauté them in a frying pan with oil, margarine or butter until you've browned both sides. Take my word for it, you're going to like this.

Country sausage

Here's a sausage recipe that was shared with me while I was visiting friends in Woodinville, Washington. This recipe was exchanged while sitting around in the evening, talking, drinking a few beers, and munching on some of this sausage as a snack.

Homemade sausage, at first glance, seems overly simple. Essentially, it is made from meat, fat, and seasonings. Some meats because of their texture, color, and consistency when cooked lend themselves more readily to sausage making.

Pork is one such meat. However I have seen recipes that call for moose, elk, deer and even squirrel meat. Each of these recipes requires a carefully chosen selection and measured amount of herbs and spices.

From my own experience, it is this selection of flavors, along with the ratio of fat to lean meat, that determines the quality and appeal of your sausage. Here's a list of the herbs, spices, and flavorings that I have used over the years.

1. coriander
2. mustard seeds
3. fresh ground black pepper
4. fresh ground white pepper
5. hot/sweet red pepper
6. allspice
7. cinnamon
8. savory
9. mace
10. nutmeg
11. garlic (fresh and dried)
12. IMPORTED bay leaf
13. thyme
14. basil
15. clove
16. paprika

You can see there is a lot to choose from. As I tried to demonstrate to you in my first column (Issue No. 19,

January/February 1993), each of these flavorings has a character of it's own — some more dominant than others. Before you start experimenting with blending these flavors, it is important to have a good handle on their individual characteristics and your own taste.

The sausage flavoring, that I have included with this recipe, is one that I like and it tastes good if you use this sausage when you make the scrapple recipe.

Ingredients:

2 lb. Fresh pork shoulder butt cut into one inch strips
2 tsp salt

Spice blend —
1 tsp ground allspice
1 tsp ground cinnamon
1 1/2 tsp ground nutmeg
1 1/2 tsp ground imported bay leaf
1 1/2 tsp ground clove
1/2 tsp basil leaf
1 1/2 tsp ground coriander
3 1/2 tsp ground white peppercorns
1/4 tsp red (hot) pepper flakes

Blend the above spices together. (This is a basic blend, flavored on the light side. As you become more experienced, you'll want to vary the ingredients.) Use 1/2 tsp of the blend to flavor the sausage. Save the rest for future use.

Preparation:

1. The pork shoulder butt will give you about the correct 2 to 1 ratio of lean to fat.
2. After cutting the pork, put it back in the refrigerator for a couple of hours. This will chill it to the proper temperature to make it easier to grind.
3. When the pork is chilled, put it through your grinder using the course screen. Then, pass it through once more using the fine screen.
4. In a large mixing bowl, thoroughly combine the ground meat, the spice mixture and the salt. If you have a heavy duty mixer the mixing will be easier.
5. To check the flavor, sauté a little until it's cooked. Taste it and adjust seasoning if necessary. Remember your own taste is the judge.
6. Cover the sausage and refrigerate it overnight to allow the flavors to penetrate the meat.

By the way, I make sausage into patties and freeze them because I find making link sausage to be too much work.

Down home chicken dumplings

This is a recipe that was shared with me by a retired heavy machine mechanic, who had been out for a Sunday drive. We met in a gas station off one of the Interstates in Georgia. As usual we got to talking about food. When he discovered that my grandmother came from Georgia and that my favorite food of hers was chicken and dumplings, he just had to take me and my traveling companion over to his house for the original Chicken and Dumplings recipe that my grandmother had stolen from Georgia and taken north. Hey! I didn't argue with him. Free food is free food.

Ingredients:

Dumplings —
1 3/4 cups all purpose flour
3/4 tsp salt
1 1/2 tsp baking powder
3 1/2 tbsp margarine or butter
3 medium eggs (slightly beaten)

Preparation:

1. Mix the flour, salt and baking powder together.
2. Cut the margarine or butter into the flour mixture until the mixture becomes crumbly. Do this is the way that you would when making pie crust.
3. Add the eggs. Mix to form a stiff dough and allow the dough to rest for 20 minutes.
4. On a well floured counter, roll the dough to about a 1/4 inch thickness. Cut dough into strips about 3/4 inch wide by 2 inches long. Set aside in the refrigerator until ready for use.

Chicken and sauce —
1 2 lb. frying chicken cut into eight pieces
1/2 tsp salt
1/4 tsp fresh ground black pepper
1/4 tsp mustard powder
1/4 tsp garlic powder
1/4 tsp thyme leaves
1/8 tsp rubbed sage
1/4 tsp basil leaves
1/4 cup vegetable oil (to fry chicken)
1 small onion (diced medium)
1 stalk celery (diced fine)
4 tbsp margarine or butter
1/4 cup flour
4 1/2 cups chicken stock

Preparation:

1. Mix the salt and spices together. Sprinkle the mixture onto the chicken and rub each piece to coat it completely. Set the chicken aside for 30 minutes.

2. In a large fry pan, heat the vegetable oil and fry the chicken pieces until they are evenly browned on each side. If necessary fry only a couple of pieces at a time adding more oil as required. Set the chicken aside on paper towels when done.

3. After frying the chicken, remove all the oil from the pan and return the pan to the stove and a medium heat. Melt the margarine and add the onion and celery and sauté them until they are lightly browned. Now, add the flour and mix it with the sautéed vegetables and margarine. Cook this mixture for five minutes stirring all the while to prevent burning. Now, while still stirring constantly to prevent lumps, add the chicken stock to this flour and vegetable mixture to form a sauce. Allow it to simmer for a few minutes until it thickens then remove it from the heat. Preheat the oven to 350 degrees.

Assembly and final preparation:

1. Place the chicken pieces in a three quart casserole. Heat the sauce to a simmer again and pour it over the chicken pieces.

2. Arrange the dumplings in the casserole so that they do not lay on top of one another. If you have too many, freeze the excess for later use. Cover the casserole and place it in the oven and bake it for about an hour or until chicken is very tender and the dumplings are cooked.

Serve this with your favorite rice or noodles dish.

And there it is, folks, a column about log homes, motorcycles, and good food. What a life. Δ

There are days
This job makes me feel
As though I could just drain out through
The h
ole
in m
y
s
o
c
k.

John Silveira
Ojai, California

I Turned Left

I turned left,
Instead of right,
As I usually do,
Onto Creek Road,
And stopped.
Morning sun and snow
Lay upon the mountainside north,
And above them, clouds drifted by,
Like young girls
Parading at a prom
Showing off their gowns.

There was no one to share it with,
Except an ocassional car
That blasted by,
Blind to what I saw
Otherwise, they'd have stopped,
Perhaps to have parked
Beside me and watched.

I drove back home,
Rummaged through my house
For a camera,
I couldn't find,
And all the while
The clock turned,
And sun and clouds
Moved inexorably through the sky,
Like bits of glass
Tumbling in a child's kaleidoscope
Impossible to turn back.
And I stopped my search
And ran back down
And watched,
Trying to freeze
The moment before it changed
With that imperfect camera of my mind
And all I have to show
Is this poem.

Look.

John Silveira
Ojai, California

FARM/GARDEN

Peppers for short season growers

By Martin P. Waterman

Growing peppers used to be one of the most frustrating experiences that I would encounter in my gardening endeavors. Year after year, I was disappointed with the results . . . that is, until I learned that there are some simple tricks that can keep you harvesting pecks of peppers, even if you have a short growing season. Using these proven practices you'll hardly be able to pickle or preserve them all.

I love peppers. I used to just like peppers until I started growing them and realized there was more to peppers than I could have ever imagined. I also learned that there is a multitude of uses for peppers other than for stuffing or simply being chopped up in salads or stir fry dishes.

I started growing peppers like most gardening neophytes. I would purchase a dozen green bell peppers in the spring and by fall, I might have a few peppers. I thought that peppers were destined to be a novelty in my garden. I began starting my own varieties from seed and began experimenting. You see, I had been growing a plain green pepper like the varieties they sell in the supermarket. Logic should have told me that every variety that the supermarket sells usually represents a compromise in flavor and other qualities, since it must be pleasing to a wide variety of tastes – in other words, bland! In addition, during the season, pepper prices in our area are quite low and reasonable, so not only did I need a reliable pepper to justify the garden space, I required premium quality peppers and a respectable sized harvest.

Growing peppers

Peppers can be one of the most finicky vegetables you can grow. There are many factors that will influence your peppers and once you understand these factors you can make the necessary adjustments needed to guarantee that your peppers are productive.

The first factor to contend with is that of our short season. For the most part, peppers are a tropical perennial. Therefore, we have to tailor some gardening practices to the natural needs of this plant. Because our season is so short, it helps if you can lengthen your pepper growing season. The growing season here can be as short as 120 days. I therefore lengthen my pepper growing season by starting peppers indoors very early in the season.

I have started pepper seeds as early as the first day of January. This may be a little too early unless you have strong artificial light to use until the days get longer. I now usually start the seeds near the end of February or the beginning of March. There are many benefits to starting the seeds this early. About the time of the last frost, I will have potted plants that are not only flowering but have already set, in some instances, dozens of peppers. When the first warm days appear, I move the peppers outside to harden them off and to speed up their growth. I take them indoors when the nighttime temperatures are cool, because cold stunts their growth and the flowers will not set fruit.

In order to bring the peppers to this level, they are grown in a south window indoors. I grow them upstairs, since this is the warmest part of the house. I do not have to grow many plants, because by the time I put them in the garden they will soon be providing fruit from late June until frost. Using this method, I have produced more fruit from one plant than by growing a whole row of a dozen peppers my old conventional way. When I grew peppers the conventional way, sometimes I had to wait until the end of August before I saw harvestable peppers.

An interesting thing happened when I started growing peppers this way. Because I was able to start with mature plants, I was no longer limited to those very few varieties that are suited to the north. I could now grow peppers from around the world and I often wonder if the person who coined the phrase that variety is the spice of life may have been talking about peppers. I have grown as many as 20 varieties to test in a season. Many of these varieties are unheard of outside the southern United States and Latin America. By starting them early, each plant will have big crops of fruit.

One year, I had several plants that were almost two feet high when I transplanted them. The potted peppers are very easy to transplant. I just dig a hole and slide the pepper out of the pot and put it in the hole. At this age, the soil will stay together because of the developed root system. In late June and early July, when people see my pepper plants loaded with harvestable fruit they turn green with envy.

There are other advantages to growing peppers indoors: it forces me to send away for and read gardening catalogues, as well as to plant the peppers during the coldest and most discouraging months of winter. I find this helps me focus on spring and summer, and the green seedlings remind me that warmer weather is coming.

A head start is very important to growing peppers, but this does not mean that there cannot be success by buying nursery plants. I still buy peppers from garden centers and get good yields from these as well.

Special needs

It is important to understand the metabolism and special needs of the pepper plants. Peppers do not like cold weather. When you buy your plants, they may already have blossoms. If you put them in the garden when the weather or the soil is too cold, they will drop their flowers and become semidormant. This will cause a delay, since the peppers will have to produce new flowers and that will delay your harvest. Also, during rainy periods peppers will also drop their blossoms, and rain can be plentiful in our maritime climate. This is the reason I keep my peppers in pots until we are well into

June and warmer weather and prefer to have some peppers already on the plants when I transplant them. I leave them outdoors but bring them in when the temperatures get cool. On a cool night, you can put them in a garage or a shed. When there is a warm spell for a few days, the peppers really take off.

I can plant peppers, either my own or plants I have purchased, once they have already set fruit because there is no longer the threat of a cold spell delaying fruit set which is one of the problems that used to cause me to have late and low pepper yields. I usually plant my peppers when night temperatures will seldom go below 55 degrees which is in mid to late June.

season. That can have you still eating garden peppers in November.

Peppers can be grown indoors, but when they begin fruiting they have very high light requirements. With the boom in indoor hydroponics systems, peppers are one of the most popular crops and are easy to grow. At the U.S. field station in Antarctica, they grow their own peppers year-round indoors.

Once you have planted the peppers outdoors, there are still a few extra tricks to help you to guarantee high pepper yields. Do not over-fertilize. This will cause blossom drop. When you fertilize, use a fertilizer low in Nitrogen, such as 5-10-10. Some years I

Peppers. (Photo courtesy Alfrey Seeds, Knoxville, TN)

I also use these pepper plants as ornamental substitutes. I put some in large pots and use them as patio plants. Hot peppers such as cayenne peppers are particularly ornamental when the numerous red fruits contrast against the green leaves. It is not unusual for a cayenne pepper to set more than 100 peppers. I would rather grow peppers as ornamentals than potted flowers such as geraniums.

Growing peppers in pots also has some extra advantages. When the first sign of frost appears you can move the pot into the garage and then outside again. During an Indian Summer you can add an extra two months to your

do not even fertilize my peppers. If they get too much fertilizer, they will produce too much foliage and usually no blossoms. One mistake pepper growers make after planting the peppers too early and trying to compensate for stunted plants with no blossoms is to blast them with fertilizer. This does more damage than good. When I do fertilize the peppers, it is after they have set fruit.

In late July or early August, I will harvest almost all the peppers. This can be quite a load. However, it forces the plants to produce a new crop that will be ready in the fall. When a pepper plant is fully loaded, it tends to go dormant. Once you remove all their fruit they will begin to produce another generation.

Varieties, varieties, varieties

If you should decide to start your own peppers indoors, you will have complete control over selecting varieties. For instance, Stoke Seeds has over 60 varieties of peppers, and most of the large seed houses also carry abundant varieties. Commercial growers choose varieties that will appeal to the maximum number of people. My favorite peppers that I grow I have never seen at any garden center. The garden centers like to produce the varieties that are known by their customers and that are reliable.

To simplify selection, there are two kinds of peppers: hot and sweet. When I choose sweet peppers, I like to try to grow different colors and shapes. This makes them more interesting to use in the kitchen. This includes black, blue, gold, brown and white peppers. I like to use different colors in salads, marinated dishes, and omelets, where the colors can be dazzling. I also enjoy experiencing the different flavors.

Hot peppers are, of course, a matter of taste. There are some intermediate peppers that fall somewhere between hot and sweet for those who do not like to dine with a fire extinguisher. I find I cannot live without hot peppers as a food or a spice. They do magic for stir fry recipes and many dishes such as spaghetti sauce, chile and even hamburger dishes. One warning: if you like hot peppers, there is the temptation to grow some of the fiery hot varieties. If you do, be careful. You must wash your hands and utensils after using them. One day, after working with some dried cayenne peppers I accidentally I rubbed my eye. It felt like it was on fire! When cooking with hot peppers, only add a little at a time, as a little goes a long way.

Varieties are a matter of personal choice. Some gardeners like the Hungarian peppers, others the sweet cherry types. I like them all. I have tried many varieties and have many favorites. I am always experimenting to add new varieties. As a matter of tradition, albeit a new tradition, I will grow Jalapeno, Cayenne, Hungarian and several colorful sweet bell peppers. Then I will try some new ones for comparison purposes. If I like them I will add them.

Before you order your pepper seed, consult some recipe books on cooking and preserving. This can be a great guide to help you to choose your varieties. For instance, if you want to make authentic chiles rellenos (peppers stuffed with cheese, breaded and deep fried), you will need Anaheim peppers. After you tempt your taste buds, consult your seed catalogues. They will have several photographs and descriptions to help you make your selections.

Because you may only want a few plants of each, you will have extra seeds or plants. Pepper seed will keep if stored in a cool dry place for up to four years. You can always test seed viability. Place ten seeds in a damp paper towel. If 8 out of 10 germinate, 80% should be viable.

Extra plants are no problem. I usually give the extra ones to friends or neighbors or trade them for other plants.

Storage and preserving

Peppers can be pickled, frozen, canned, dried and made into relishes and jellies. There are so many pepper recipes that you could make a different one every day of the year. Peppers can be roasted in the oven or barbecued and then peeled. They are delicious when prepared this way. Peppers are so versatile that once you begin using them regularly, you will wonder how you ever lived without them. If you understand how to increase the yield and the variety of peppers you can grow, this can open up a whole new world and spice up your gardening from planting to harvest.

Requirements at a glance:

- Germination time for seeds:
  6-14 days
- Best temperature for germination:
  68° F -86° F
- Average time until harvest:
  40-100 days
- Spacing:
  18 inches apart in rows 2 feet apart
- Soil pH:
  6.0 - 6.5
- Fertilizing:
  2 light side dressings during season
- Height:
  2.5 feet
- Other requirements:
  Full sun and moist soil

Pepper seed is widely available from seed catalogues. However, if you feel that you want to try even more exotic varieties, there are some specialty pepper seed houses such as Horticultural Enterprises and The Pepper Gal that you may want to try.

The Pepper Gal, 10536-119th Avenue North, Largo, FL 34643, (200 varieties)

Stokes Seed Company, P.O. Box 548 Buffalo, NY 14240

Horticultural Enterprises, P. O. Box 810082, Dallas, TX 75381-0082

Alfrey - Peter Pepper Seeds, P. O. Box 415, Knoxville, TN 37901 (SASE required) Δ

A BHM Writer's Profile

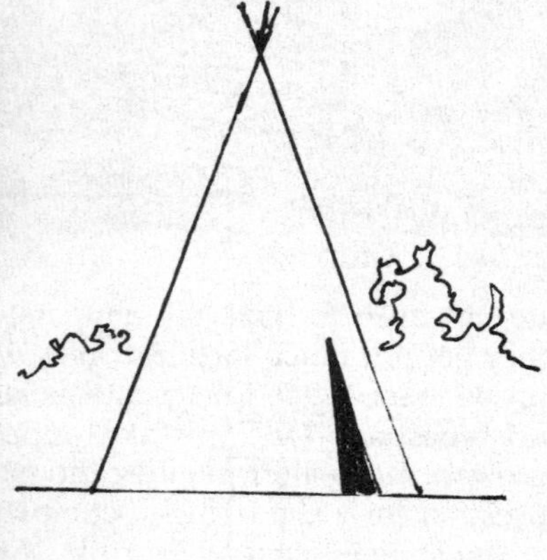

Dynah Geissal is 48 years old, is married, has three grown children, a son-in-law, and one grandchild. She and husband Bob have been subsistence farmers for 21 years and figure they are 90% food self-sufficient.

On August 1, 1994, they bought 40 acres of bare land in the mountains of western Montana. Since then they have lived in a tipi at 4600 feet while building shelters and pens for the livestick and beginning work on their home. They carry water from their hand dug well and their only electricity is from a single solar panel, providing two lights and a radio.

Salads for summer

By Jennifer Stein Barker

During the hot, busy days of summer, nothing beats lightly dressed salads straight out of the garden for pepping up a quick meal. Home-grown vegetables and greens have more flavor and more vitamins than the store-bought varieties. Also, you can grow varieties the stores never dream of carrying. They can only afford to sell vegetables that are able to withstand the rigors of packing and shipping and storage. You, on the other hand, have the luxury of being able to choose a variety solely on the basis of flavor.

So let your imagination run wild. Read the seed packages and pick out varieties you've never heard of. Try greens like mizuna, garland chrysanthemum, claytonia, orach, perilla, pak-choi, chinese mustard. Try lettuces like oak leaf, canary's tongue, sierra, and red sails. In winter, keep a pot of sorrel (high in vitamins A and C) on the windowsill to add zing and nutrition to your winter salads.

Following are some recipes for summer salads that are easy to vary according to what you have in your garden or can find in your store. Try them as they are written, then try the suggested substitutions or start inventing your own combinations.

Simple green salad

Nothing beats this lightly dressed salad for fresh flavor. Use as many different greens as you can find or grow in your garden! Garnish with the whatever vegetables are on hand, or let the variety of greens provide the contrast of texture and flavor. Serves four.

Ingredients:

1 clove garlic, peeled
8 cups mixed salad greens, rinsed, dried, and torn into bite sized pieces
1 or 2 ripe tomatoes
1 carrot, sliced thinly on the diagonal
3 florets broccoli, cut into small pieces
Alfalfa sprouts (opt.)
1 tsp. olive oil
2 tsp. tamari
2 tsp. cider vinegar
2 drops Tabasco
Chopped fresh basil or thyme to taste

Preparation:

Rub the inside of a large salad bowl with the peeled garlic clove. Put the greens in the salad bowl and drizzle the olive oil over them. Toss gently with utensils or your fingers, until the oil coats the greens.

In a small cup, mix the tamari, vinegar and Tabasco. Pour the mixture over the salad and toss gently again till the greens are coated. Slice the tomatoes as desired and arrange the vegetables in the most artistic way you can over the greens. Sprinkle the vegetables with the fresh herbs.

Serve immediately, or chill for up to 15 minutes.

For variety, change the type of greens you use. Change the vinegar. If you don't have fresh herbs, use an herb vinegar, or crush a pinch of dried basil or thyme between your fingers as you sprinkle them over the salad. Use whatever vegetables you have on hand, or whatever looks best in the store. Remember, the vegetables are just a garnish in this salad "the real center of attention should be the variety and flavor of the greens.

Marinated veggies with feta and greek olives

Try other vegies in this salad: yellow crookneck or zucchini squash, any sweet peppers, celery, peas, green beans, even oriental greens! Serves 4 as a side dish, or 2 as a main dish.

Ingredients:

Marinade:
1⁄3 cup olive oil
1⁄4 cup red wine vinegar
1 Tbsp. fresh lemon juice
Freshly-ground black pepper
1 clove garlic, minced
Herbs to taste: thyme, basil, oregano, dill, rosemary (choose 2 or 3, fresh if possible)
1⁄4 lb. feta cheese
1⁄2 jar black Greek olives

Veggies:
1 green pepper
1 ripe tomato
1 stalk broccoli
1 carrot
1⁄2 red onion
1⁄2 cucumber, peeled

Preparation:

Marinade: In a 2- or 3-quart bowl that has a tight-fitting lid, mix marinade ingredients with a small whisk.

Vegies: cut the broccoli into bite-sized pieces. Steam them over boiling water until just barely tender, then warm to the marinade. Dice and add the green pepper, tomato, red onion and cucumber.

Refrigerate the salad at least 4 hours before serving. Stir it about once an hour, and return it to the refrigerator. Just before serving, arrange the salad on a bed of washed leaf lettuce, and decorate it with chunks of the feta cheese, and the Greek olives. The olives can be pitted with a cherry pitter if desired.

Sweet and sour slaw

A fresh-tasting slaw to complement corn bread and barbecues. This salad stands up really well to being packed along on a picnic. Try red or green peppers or oriental greens in this salad. Serves 4.

Ingredients:

- 2 large carrots, coarsely grated
- ¾ cup shredded red cabbage
- ¾ cup shredded green cabbage
- 1 apple, chopped finely
- ¼ cup raisins
- 1 tsp. caraway seed
- 2 Tbsp. oil
- ¼ cup cider vinegar
- 1 Tbsp. orange or pineapple juice
- 1 Tbsp. honey

Preparation:

Toss together grated carrots, shredded red and green cabbage, chopped apple and raisins. Whisk together oil, cider vinegar, juice, and honey until well mixed. Pour the marinade over the vegetables. Sprinkle on the caraway seed, and mix all together well.

Cover and refrigerate at least three hours before serving,or up to 24 hours. Remove ingredients from the refrigerator and toss together at least three times to distribute the marinade. Δ

Going back
Was like a trip in a time machine
That didn't quite work right,
Or how else am I to explain that
Everything,
Once mine,
Was at best, now awkwardly familiar
And I stood before the doorstep
A stranger
In a place I once called home.

John Silveira
Ojai, California

A BHM Writer's Profile

Mick Sagrillo writes wind power articles for *Backwoods Home Magazine* and has regular wind power columns in several other independent energy publications. His company, Lake Michigan Wind and Sun, Ltd., manufactures, repairs, and sells wind generator components and systems across the U.S. and in 29 foreign countries.

An avid tinkerer and realistic environmentalist, Sagrillo is a founder and director of half a dozen wind energy, renewable resource, or environmental organizations. When he's not teaching wind energy workshops around the country, Sagrillo lives with his wife Lynn on their small homestead in northeast Wisconsin.

Living with a plywood floor

By Julia Leiterman

When asked what type of floor covering I chose when I built my house, I just smile and say "North American softwood." What I'm really saying, though, is "plywood."

I built my house on a tight budget that demanded creative planning before and during construction. I chose to invest most of my funds in components that would become focal points in my home or would be hard to upgrade later, and a hardwood floor didn't make my budget cuts.

I could accept living with a plywood subfloor, but I refused to leave it looking like a construction site. Paint was my solution, and it delivered an attractive finished surface at a fraction of the cost of conventional materials.

Planning ahead for this option, and building it into my construction plan, was the key factor in obtaining a surface I'm still happy with four years later.

Raw materials

The quality and durability of any paint job depends on surface preparation, which in this case means filling every nailhole, knothole and seam. It's a lot of work, but its crucial to the finished look and will give you a subfloor smooth as glass.

Use a commercial filling compound that's intended for exterior use to ensure your patch job wears well and stays put. To make the work go faster, buy the filler in quantity and use a trowel to apply it. Follow the product's directions, and make sure you wait the recommended drying time before taking a sander to it.

You can reduce the amount of filling required by purchasing a higher grade of plywood. Standard construction usually calls for "Factory" wood, which comes peppered with knots that can keep you on your knees forever. For an additional $5 per 4x8 sheet I went with "select," which had the knotholes already filled and sanded and left me just seams and nailholes to deal with. If you want perfection, order "good one side," and you'll receive slick sheets without a blemish.

Paint

Painting is the fun part. Start with a layer of primer, because it's cheap and will make your paint go further, even if the manufacturer claims their paint is self-priming. If you're not happy with the meager color selection of premixed "porch paint," just order up an oil-based paint in the shade of your choice and have the shop add urethane to it. Either way, you'll be paying about $35 a gallon and will end up with a tough enamel surface that won't need touchups for at least two years, even in high traffic areas.

Paint gives you a real chance to be creative, so don't feel limited to a single color. Country-style stencils around the perimeter of a room will give it a stamp of individuality, and the use of bold blocks of contrasting color can define space and highlight special features. You can even paint on "throw rugs" you'll never have to send to the cleaners!

Inspectors

I built in a high income suburb with a building inspector who didn't know the meaning of the word "budget," and he refused to approve my flooring until he'd seen the finished product. Once the paint was in place however, he was happy to sign the occupancy permit, and the only real conflict we had was over the bathroom and kitchen floors. The building code decreed they must be waterproof, and though I won the fight over the kitchen I had to put linoleum down in the bathrooms.

Contractors

Don't forget to tell everyone that sets foot on your construction site that the subfloor will be your finished floor, or you'll be faced with a recovery job that goes way beyond filling the nailholes. Post signs, and be prepared for some mishaps despite your warnings. I've got a patch of homemade anti-skid where my bricklayer spilled sand on the freshly painted stairwell, and a couple of holes in the diningroom courtesy of my electrician, who found the floor got in the way when he was running wires. Even my plumber left his mark in one corner, spilling a mysterious compound that tenaciously bled its way through numerous coats of paint until I neutralized it with a special spray-on primer.

My floor turned out so well that hardwood has been bumped indefinitely from my "to do" list. Painting the plywood changed it from an eyesore into a finished floor, and has given my home that elusive aura of completion. So if you're searching for a floor covering that's low maintenance, low cost, impervious to kids, dogs, dirt and looks great, take heart. You don't have to look further than your stack of framing lumber. Δ

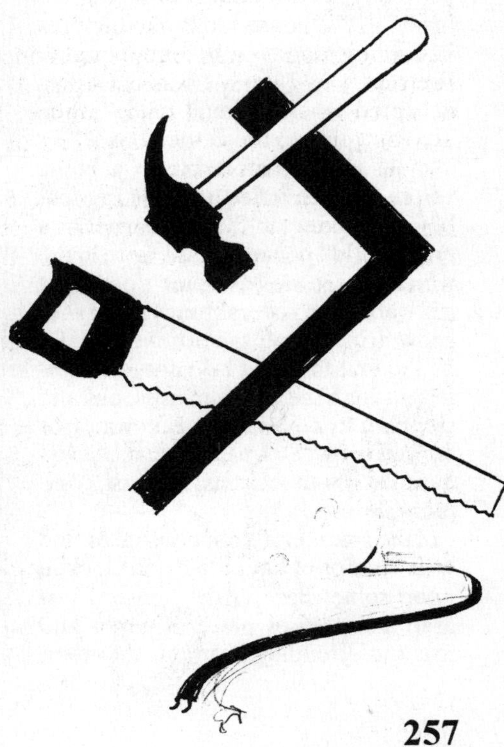

Backwoods lifestyle misunderstood by people living in the "real world"

By Margaret Wright

Six years and a lot of hard work have brought our family to the place in our lives where we are very happy.

We started with a tree-covered 10 acres and now have a nice log home, farm animals, a garden, and a totally self-reliant lifestyle.

Those of us who choose this life-style have got to understand that we are a minority. The people in the majority are the ones in the "real world."

We who choose this alternative life-style have to associate with all types of people. Some will agree with our choices and wish they could do the same. Some will wonder if we are some type of subversive group. Some will wonder if we are just plain crazy.

Some of the people we associate with look at the pictures of our home and smile, with a look of wonder, as if we were telling a bad joke. A few of the yuppie types are honest in saying the inside of the house looks like pictures in *Country Magazine,* but they couldn't live that way. I knew I was not being accepted when an aunt said, "when are you going to finish the house?"

I feel as uncomfortable in a home where I'm reminded to wipe my feet before walking on the fine carpet as a "real world" person would, here in the woods where we have pine floors that get walked on several times a day with snow dripping off the Sorel boots. I'll be the first to admit I do not like coming through the house in my socks and stepping in a puddle of rain water or melted snow. So I usually make sure I have on my moccasins. It's just common sense.

In the summer it's not unusual to find little clumps of hay with dried chicken poop somewhere in the house. I just grab a napkin or piece of paper and toss the offending item out the door. Yes, I do have rugs at the doors. My family is reminded to wipe their feet or take off their boots, but it's a bit of a hassle to take off boots if you're in a hurry to get the flashlight or a tool needed for a quick fix-it job. Not to mention a child in a hurry for a potty-stop.

My furniture gets a good cleaning every spring, but I am not going to stand guard over it and make sure some tired person who has been out working hard does not come and lie down for a short snooze. After working on the car or cleaning the chicken coop, I would object to the transgressor lying on the couch, but the poor soul is certainly welcome to spread out on the braided rug in front of the fireplace. In the "real world," you have to spread a blanket on the floor in front of the TV so the carpet doesn't get mussed up by a child sprawled out playing trucks or watching cartoons.

We who choose this alternative life-style have to associate with all types of people. Some will agree with our choices and wish they could do the same. Some will wonder if we are some type of subversive group. Some will wonder if we are just plain crazy.

It's true that growing and canning my own food takes a lot of time. Believe me, when I'm in the middle of my fourth box of peaches I'm wondering myself if I have lost my mind. Once all the food is on the shelves and I stand back and see what my hard labor has accomplished, though, I know I'm not crazy. Some folks would comment it's so much easier to buy at the store. Yep, they're right. Guess I never was one to take the easy way out.

It took about two seconds to turn down the offer of a new washer and dryer from a very concerned relative. I know it takes a lot of work to wash five loads of laundry in a wringer washer. Hanging them on the clothes line is not a lot of fun either, unless you enjoy being out where the breeze is blowing, birds are singing, and the sound of the chickens proves that things are being accomplished. In winter the ideal decor for most people is not a rack of towels and dish cloths hanging in the family room. I really don't mind. If I happen to have a guest, I just carry the whole thing to the hall, or most often just leave it in full view as sort of a testament to my good work.

One way to stop overnight guests is to tell them that next year you may put in indoor plumbing. Even my own mother refused to stay with us because of this issue. She insisted on going to the nearest motel.

No, I'm not a withdrawn survivalist or doomsday advocate. I live in the woods in a log house, raise my own food and homeschool my children as a choice of lifestyle. Not everyone wants to be a slave to the new car, designer furniture, new carpet, or school system.

My children and grandchildren are **welcome** here. They can play in or out of the house. I'm not running a zoo, but I do maintain a comfort zone that is called a **home** . . . not just a place. Δ

The land! That is where our roots are. There is the basis of our physical life. The farther we get away from the land, the greater our insecurity. From the land comes everything that supports life, everything we use for the service of physical life. The land has not collapsed or shrunk in either extent or productivity. It is there waiting to honor all the labor we are willing to invest in it, and able to tide us across any dislocation of economic conditions. No unemployment insurance can be compared to an alliance between man and a plot of land.

Henry Ford

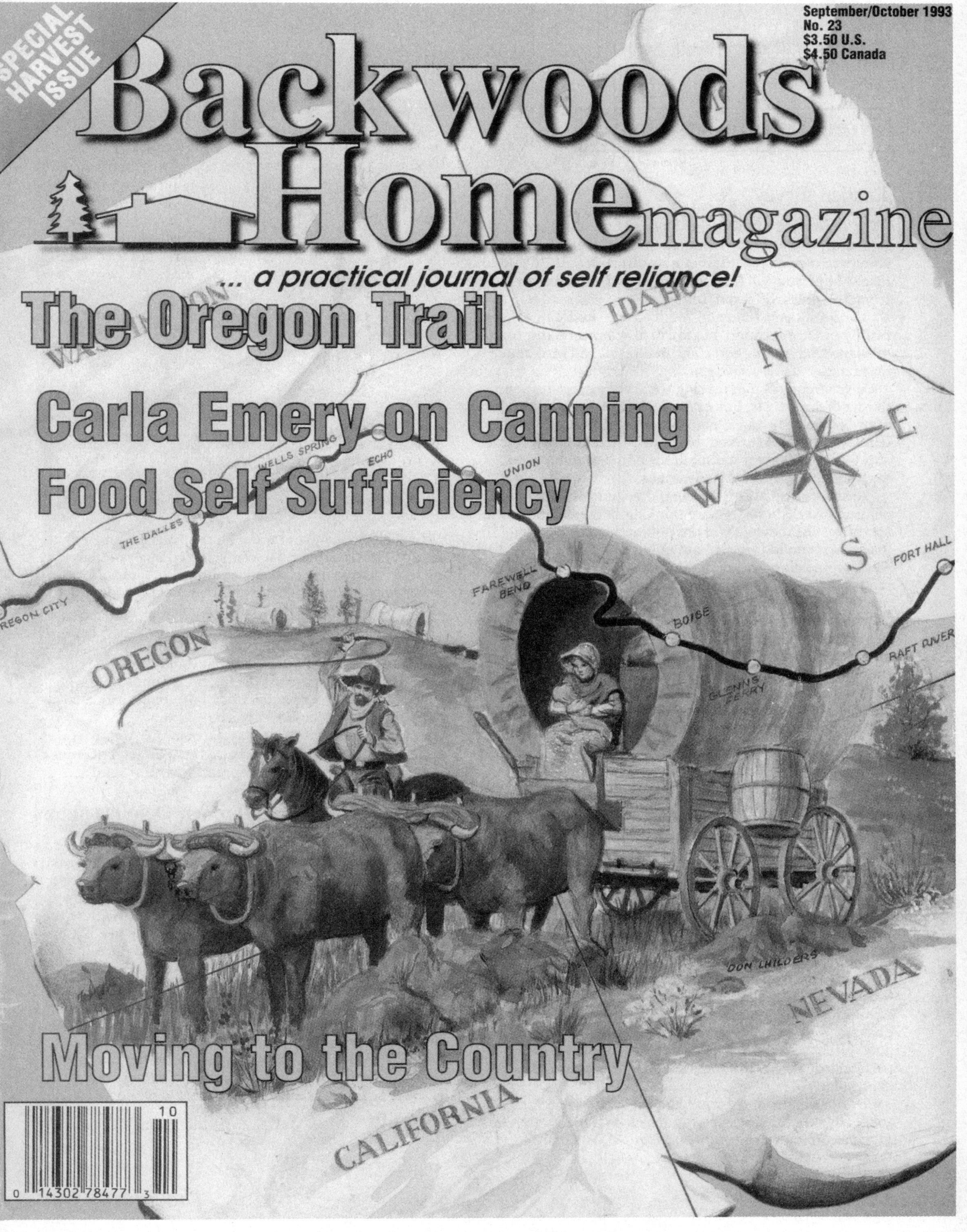

SPECIAL HARVEST ISSUE
September/October 1993
No. 23
$3.50 U.S.
$4.50 Canada
Backwoods Home magazine
... a practical journal of self reliance!
The Oregon Trail
Carla Emery on Canning
Food Self Sufficiency
Moving to the Country
IDAHO
OREGON
NEVADA
CALIFORNIA
N
E
W
S
WELLS SPRING
ECHO
UNION
THE DALLES
OREGON CITY
FAREWELL BEND
BOISE
GLENNS FERRY
RAFT RIVER
FORT HALL
DON CHILDERS
10
0 14302 78477 3

Note from the publisher

Reader survey

The centerfold of this issue contains a reader survey designed to help us better understand what you like best about the magazine and what new directions *BHM* should take. I hope you will take the time to unfasten the survey from its staples, fill it out, fold it, tape it, and mail it in to us. I know it takes time and you'll have to invest in a twenty-nine cent stamp, but it will give you an opportunity to shape what we do here. The end result will be a better magazine.

We've already begun making some changes in response to readers' requests. For example, last issue and this one are what we've been calling "theme issues." Last issue's theme was log homes and this issue's them is harvesting and food. The survey has a question to determine if you like the idea of having theme issues.

The survey also asks if you would be interested in purchasing several books we are thinking of publishing. If the survey results indicate you are not interested in them, maybe we should forget about publishing them.

An important question in the survey asks if you would attend a *BHM*-sponsored self-reliance/alternative energy exposition held in Ashland, Oregon. We don't know if we'll try and hold one, but we definitely won't if not enough people are interested. These shows cost a fortune to put on, so the chance of great financial disaster looms over a sparsely-attended show.

You don't have to answer all the questions in the survey if you don't want to. If you are not interested in some of the articles it asks questions about, just skip those questions. I'd greatly appreciate your help with this survey.

Three for two holiday gift offer

And now for the sales pitch. Page 67 has a nifty offer some of you may be interested in if you want to give *Backwoods Home Magazine* or one of the two magazine anthologies as gifts to friends this holiday season.

Buy any combination of books and/or magazine subscriptions and we'll give you the third one free. Use any combination you like. E.g.: Buy two subscriptions and get a third subscription free, or buy two subscriptions and get one of the books free, or buy two books and get another book free. We'll enclose a gift card if you indicate some of the magazines and books are to be sent as gifts.

Our idea is to increase our subscriber base and get the books into as many hands as possible. It is an extremely good offer from a dollar perspective, and the books in particular make very thoughtful gifts for people seeking knowledge.

We didn't make up a form to be used with the offer, so you'll have to just write up your order on a sheet of paper. This three-for-two offer will end Dec. 31, 1993.

Dave Duffy

Third Vita-Mix winner

Michael McShane of Drain, Oregon has become our third Vita-Mix winner. He was selected in a random drawing from among our paid subscribers. We'll pick three more winners, one for each of the next three issues. You must be a paid subscriber to be eligible.

The Vita-Mix, for those of you who don't know, is about the most versatile kitchen tool you can have. It's basically a super heavy duty food mixer that stands about a foot and a half high. Vita-mix sells them for about $500 and they are worth every penny. Each one comes with a color video that shows you how to us it.

BHM gets the Vita-Mixers as payment for Vita-Mix's ads, and we turn around and give them away in drawings like this. Nice simple way to spread wealth around.

BHM will be at September, October shows in Denver, Boston, Salt Lake, and Seattle

Backwoods Home will exhibit the magazine at shows in four of the nation's best cities in September and October.

They are: Denver, Colorado, Self-Reliance Expo & Fair '93, September 16-19 (ad on page 3); Seattle, Washington, Preparedness Expo '93, October 1-3 (ad on page 82); Boston, Massachusetts, New England Eco Expo, October 1-3 (at the World Trade Center); and Salt Lake City, Utah, Preparedness Expo '93, October 21-23 (ad on page 82).

I am especially looking forward to the show in Boston, because it was my home town for the first 29 years of my life and I have friends and family all over the Northeast. John Silveira and O.E. MacDougal, two other Bostonians associated with *BHM*, will do the show with me. This will be the first show for Silveira and MacDougal.Δ

Dave Duffy

My View

(We're delighted to give this issue's editorial space over to P.J. O'Rourke, who delivered these comments to a gathering of the Cato Institute, a free market think tank. O'Rourke has authored several books, including Parliament of Whores, a best-seller about the U.S. government. This article is reprinted with permission from the July 1993 *American Spectator*. —Editor.)

No ideology, no agenda

The Cato Institute has an unusual political cause—which is no political cause whatsoever. We are here tonight to dedicate ourselves to that cause, to dedicate ourselves, in other words, to . . . nothing.

We have no ideology, no agenda, no catechism, no dialectic, no plan for humanity. We have no "vision thing," as our ex-president would say, or, as our current president would say, we have no Hillary.

All we have is the belief that people should do what people want to do, unless it causes harm to other people. And that had better be clear and provable harm. No nonsense about second-hand smoke or hurtful, insensitive language, please.

I don't know what's good for you. You don't know what's good for me. We don't know what's good for mankind. And it sometimes seems as though we're the only people who don't. It may well be that, gathered right here in this room tonight, are all the people in the world who don't want to tell all the people in the world what to do.

This is because we believe in freedom. Freedom—what this country was established upon, what the Constitution was written to defend, what the Civil War was fought to perfect.

Freedom is not empowerment. Empowerment is what the Serbs have in Bosnia. Anybody can grab a gun and be empowered. It's not entitlement. An entitlement is what people on welfare get, and how free are they? It's not an endlessly expanding list of rights—the "right" to education, the "right" to health care, the "right" to food and housing. That's not freedom, that's dependency. Those aren't rights, those are the rations of slavery—hay and a barn for human cattle.

There is only one basic human right, the right to do as you damn well please. And with it comes the only basic human duty, the duty to take the consequences.

So we are here tonight in a kind of anti-matter protest—an unpolitical undemonstration by deeply uncommitted inactivists. We are part of a huge invisible picket line that circles the White House 24 hours a day. We are participants in an enormous non-march on Washington—millions and millions of Americans not descending upon the nation's capital in order to demand nothing from the United States government. To demand nothing, that is, except the one thing which no government in history has been able to do—leave us alone.

There are just two rules of governance in a free society:

- Mind your own business.
- Keep your hands to yourself.

Bill, keep your hands to yourself. Hillary, mind your own business.

We have a group of incredibly silly people in the White House right now, people who think government works. Or that government would work, if you got some real bright young kids from Yale to run it.

We're being governed by dorm room bull session. The Clinton administration is over there right now pulling an all-nighter in the West Wing. They think that, if they can just stay up late enough, they can create a healthy economy and bring peace to former Yugoslavia.

The Clinton administration is going to decrease government spending by increasing the amount of money we give to the government to spend.

Health care is too expensive, so the Clinton administration is putting a highpowered corporate lawyer in charge of making it cheaper. (This is what I always do when I want to spend less money—hire a lawyer from Yale.) If you think health care is expensive now, wait until you see what it costs when it's free.

The Clinton administration is putting together a program so that college graduates can work to pay off their school tuition. As if this were some genius idea. It's called getting a job. Most folks do that when they get out of college, unless, of course, they happen to become governor of Arkansas.

And the Clinton administration launched an attack on people in Texas because those people were religious nuts with guns. Hell, this country was founded by religious nuts with guns. Who does Bill Clinton think stepped ashore on Plymouth Rock? Peace Corps volunteers? Or maybe the people in Texas were attacked because of child abuse. But, if child abuse was the issue, why didn't Janet Reno tear-gas Woody Allen?

You know, if government were a product, selling it would be illegal.

Government is a health hazard. Governments have killed many more people than cigarettes or unbuckled seat belts ever have.

Government contains impure ingredients—as anybody who's looked at Congress can tell you.

On the basis of Bill Clinton's 1992 campaign promises, I think we can say government practices deceptive advertising.

And the merest glance at the federal budget is enough to convict the government of perjury, extortion, and fraud.

There, ladies and gentlemen, you have the Cato Institute's program in a nutshell: government should be against the law.

Term limits aren't enough. We need jail. Δ

— P. J. O'Rourke ©The American Spectator

History of the Oregon Trail

By John Silveira

Dave Duffy, the guy who publishes this magazine, called me from Oregon the other day. He'd just gotten back from Wisconsin where he'd seen his distributor.

"I was talking to Harvey Wassermann," he said. "He reminded me that this year is the year of the sesquicentennial of the Oregon Trail."

"The what of the Oregon Trail?"

"The sesquicentennial," he repeated like someone who had just learned a new word. "It's the 150th anniversary."

"Oh," I said.

"He said that, since I'm an Oregon based magazine, I'd be dumb not to have something about the Oregon Trail in the next issue."

"He's right."

"Can you write it?"

"Sure."

"Do you know anything about it?"

"Sure."

A few days later, O.E. MacDougal, Dave's poker playing friend, stopped by. It was nice to see him again. When I answered the knock at my door, he was standing there with a stringer of fresh fish. My two cats, Doggy and Phideaux, were immediately at his legs, milling back and forth and rubbing themselves against him.

"They're never that nice to me," I said.

"The next time you want affection from them, rub yourself down with a can of tuna fish," he replied.

"Come on in," I said.

"Got any coffee?"

"There's a fresh pot right there on the stove."

"Great." He followed me in and put the fish on the breadboard in my kitchen. He poured himself a cup and asked, "Are you writing anything for this issue of Dave's magazine?"

"Yeah, I'm writing about the Oregon Trail." I pointed to a stack of library books on the kitchen table. "I'm starting my research, now."

He came back to the table and went through the stack. "You have some good books here. Looks like you have a lot of reading ahead of you."

I nodded. "A week or two, at least."

"Want some fish?" he asked.

"Not really. I won't have time to clean and freeze them."

"They're already cleaned," he said. "What I want to know is whether you're hungry? I'll cook them for lunch, now."

"Sure," I said and sat down at the table.

The cats were now circling him like sharks stalking a victim. Mac started to look though the cupboards. The cats proceeded to get underfoot.

"Pots are under the stove," I said. "Silverware and knives are in the draw to your left. Herbs and spices are in the cupboard on your right."

He found a knife and deftly cut some small cubes of fish and put them on the floor. The cats closed for the kill. He smiled and shook his head.

"I'd hate to be a mouse in this house."

He assembled everything he thought he needed to make lunch as we talked about fishing, the weather, Dave and his magazine, and Bill Clinton. He told me some jokes he'd picked up in his poker games.

He hesitated for a moment and asked, "Have you found much about the Oregon Trail in the books you've got there?"

I shook my head. "I'm just getting started."

"You know," he said, "there was a guy from Boston – same place you and Dave are from – a Harvard graduate named Francis Parkman. He went out west in 1846 and collected his experiences and observations into a book he called The Oregon Trail. It's a famous book. You should read it."

"I've never heard of him," I said. "But I'll look for it."

The cats were milling again, currying his favor with soft whining meows and affectionate caresses.

"The Oregon Trail is one of the most exciting episodes in American history," he said.

"That's what I gather. It's the sesquicentennial," I said, hoping I had said the word right.

"True. We mark 1843 as the beginning of the Trail but it's actually older."

"It is?"

"In 1832, a man named Nathaniel Wyeth crossed it to show transcontinental travel was possible for wagons and, in 1836, Methodist missionaries using the Trail started what would become a great migration of New England Methodists from New England to Oregon. Hunters, trappers, traders, and missionaries used it in that time, too. But it was 1843 that saw the beginning of the regular procession of settlers that would become one of the greatest overland migrations in mankind's history."

"Oh," I said and took one of my steno pads. I was surprised he knew about this kind of thing. "Would you mind if I take a few notes?"

"No, go ahead."

He turned on my oven, then got pots and spices out of more cabinets.

"The Oregon Trail stretched about 2,000 miles," he said. "It ran from Independence, Missouri, to the Willamette Valley in the Columbia River region of Oregon."

"Are you sure of that? 2,000 miles?"

He nodded. "It crossed mountains, rivers, and desert, as well as the American prairie that was once called 'The Great American Desert.' The trip took anywhere from four to six months.

"Today, there are places in the mountains where you can see ruts carved out of solid rock by the wheels of what must have seemed like an endless procession of wagons. And each year the passage became a little easier because earlier caravans had moved boulders, felled trees, and filled gullies and gulches."

He cut off more fish and gave it to the cats. "Do you ever feed these two?" he asked.

"I'll toss them outside if they're bothering you," I said.

"No, they're just fine."

He found some cornmeal. "Do you have any parmesan cheese?"

"In the 'fridge," I said.

He opened the refrigerator door.

"Do you know how the Trail came about?" I asked.

"If you're looking for first causes," he said and turned around holding one of my treasured wedges of parmesan cheese, "Napoléon Bonaparte was looking for cash to support his European wars when he was approached by emissaries from Thomas Jefferson, then President of the United States. Jefferson offered cash for France's claims to the Louisiana Territory in North America, and in 1803 the United States bought the Territory for $15 million, about three cents an acre. The funny thing is, when he bought it, Jefferson had no legal authority to do so, and he knew it."

"Then why'd he do it?"

"For one thing, he wanted to get more territory for this country. The Louisiana Territory virtually doubled the size of the United States. But, even more important, he wanted to eliminate the presence of one of the European powers from North American. He knew they were a threat to the fledgling United States.

"So, the deal was made and this country came into possession of a new territory that stretched from the Mississippi River to the Rocky Mountains."

"And Oregon was part of the Louisiana Purchase?" I asked.

He shook his head. "Though the Oregon Territories were claimed by Spain, Great Britain, and Russia, they weren't actually in the possession of any of those powers. And because of that, the next thing Jefferson did was to commission an expedition, under Captains Meriwether Lewis and William Clark, to cross the new territory. They were to map it and return with a report of what they found. By these actions, Jefferson hoped to legitimize American claims to the new territories he'd just bought as well as the lands in the Pacific Northwest."

He cracked some eggs into a bowl and beat them with a fork.

"There was a lot at stake. The Oregon Territory was as large as all the original 13 colonies combined."

I wrote it down. "I didn't know that," I said.

"Lewis and Clark crossed the continent seeing sites no white man had ever seen before. They traded with the Indians and lived off the land."

"What did they trade with?"

"They brought several hundred hand mirrors, thousands of sewing needles, crates of knives, bells, pots and kettles, and bushels of colored glass beads to trade with the Indians."

"Really?"

He nodded.

"So, Lewis and Clark were the first to follow the Oregon Trail," I said.

"No, they took another route but the trail they followed was of no use to the settlers who came after them."

"Why not?"

"The settlers that followed came with wagons, families, and all the worldly possessions they could afford to pack up. There were deserts, rivers, and one of the world's great mountain chains in their way. They needed a trail that tens of thousands of wagons and hundreds of thousands of people could follow."

"Then why were Lewis and Clark important to what you're telling me?"

"They legitimized the Americans' claim to Oregon."

"Oh. Then who found the Trail?"

"The Oregon Trail and most of the other trails to the Pacific Coast were discovered by a breed of men that is uniquely American – the mountain men.

"To Americans and foreigners alike, the American icon is the cowboy. But the American cowboy, though a figure of legend and romance, is nothing when compared to the mountain man. The cowboy was usually young, a drunk, and almost always worked for someone else.

"The mountain men were different. They often traveled on foot, sometimes on horseback. Most of them were self- employed as hunters, trappers, and traders. And though most of them were of limited formal education, they were extremely intelligent men who learned the languages of the Indians they met along the way. And, oh yeah, they were drunks, too."

"Really?"

"Some of them were."

"Did they leave a written record?"

"I said they were intelligent, not educated. Many of them couldn't read or write and they didn't draw maps of where they went. They kept maps of their travels in their heads and passed the information on to others by word of mouth.

"It was the mountain men who discovered South Pass in Wyoming – the only place along the Great Divide where passage to the Northwest was possible for wagons. Not easy, mind you, but possible."

"Can you give me the names of any of those mountain men?"

"Sure. There was Jedediah Smith. Born in New York state, he could read, write, and even worked as a clerk on a fur trading boat, as a boy.

"There was Hugh Glass who, after he was mauled by a grizzly bear, was left for dead by his companions. They took his weapons and even his clothes figuring a dead man wouldn't need them. But he didn't die and he crawled 100 miles through the wilderness until he reached Fort Kiowa. Along the way, he ate nuts and berries and even scared wolves off a kill so he could scavenge the remains."

"And he lived?"

"Yeah. And when his health returned, he went back to the mountains."

"Another one was Jim Bridger. He was born in Virginia just after the turn of the century and at 17 he went to the mountains for the first time. He joined the expedition of a man named..." He tapped his finger on the counter. I knew he was searching through his memory. I made a note to look it up myself when he said, "... William Ashley. Bridger spent 60 years wandering throughout the West. He was almost always on foot and he traveled as far south as the deserts of New Mexico and as far north as the snow covered mountains of Montana. He was the first white man to see the Great Salt Lake and one of the first to see the geysers in Yellowstone. He could neither read nor write, but he had an incredible memory and never forgot a pass, a trail, or the best place to ford a river.

"He wasn't just a hunter and trapper. He was a businessman. He built a fort on the Blacks Fork of the Green River and it became one of the thriving businesses along the Oregon Trail.

"Was it a military fort?"

"No. Although it was later used by the U.S. Army, like many other forts along the Trail, it was a private enterprise. It consisted of little more than two log buildings with sod roofs, one of which was a blacksmith's shop. Indians went there and traded furs for knives, traps, and ammunition. Later, every wagon train en route to Oregon stopped there."

"What was the name of it?"

"He named it after himself, Fort Bridger."

I wrote it down.

"He had a strange way of running his business, though. He had a Mexican partner and there was a blacksmith whom they hired. But all three were mountain men who couldn't stay put. Wagon trains stopping there frequently found the fort empty."

He mixed some herbs into a bowl with the cornmeal.

"There were other trading forts built along the Trail and pioneers stopped at each to make repairs to their wagons, shoe their animals, and even take on new provisions."

"Bridger became a legend in his own time, not only because he was a great explorer, but because he was a great storyteller who often regaled members of the wagon trains, with incredible tales about himself."

"Could you give me an example of one?"

"Yeah. I can't tell it as well as he did but I'll give it a try. One of them went like this: While sitting around a campfire at night, he would tell the members of a passing wagon train how years before he had been chased by six blood thirsty and well armed Indians. Armed with only a six shooter, he took careful aim and killed five of the Indians while riding at a full gallop. But the best he could do with the last Indian was to kill his horse while in the same instant, the Indian, firing his last shot, killed Bridger's horse. He and the Indian engaged in mortal hand to hand combat with nothing but their buffalo knives. It was the biggest, strongest Indian Bridger had ever seen. First, he had the upper hand. Later, the Indian had the upper hand. So it shifted, all through the night, until dawn.

"He paused. The settlers asked, 'What happened then?'

"Bridger's voice got very low and he said, 'He killed me.'"

I laughed. "He told stories like that? They must have loved him."

He nodded. "Once you met Jim Bridger, you never forgot him.

"Several things were named after him; Bridger Mountain in Montana and Bridger Peak, Bridger Pass, and Bridger National Forest, all in Wyoming. And, of course, there was the fort he named after himself."

I looked at what I'd been writing. "Do you have any idea what travel on the Trail was like?"

"Sure. It was a long, miserable journey. It started in Independence, Missouri. Independence, by any standards, wasn't much of a town then, but because so many people started their westward journey from there, it became one of the busiest towns in the United States. The main part of the town was nothing but a single street of permanent buildings. The rest of the town consisted of tents and wagons belonging to the people getting ready to go west.

"And once a caravan left, it followed the Santa Fe Trail for two days. On the third day, the trail forked and there was a single sign that read:

ROAD TO OREGON

"It was the only signpost on the entire Trail."

He dredged the fish through some beaten eggs and then a mixture of cornmeal, the herbs, and spices. Then he grated some cheese onto them.

"In western movies, all the conestoga wagons are covered with white canvas. But that wasn't the way it really was. There were red, white, blue, and yellow canvas tops. It must have looked like a traveling circus when they started out. But by the end of the Trail, what with the bleaching action of the sun, the dust, the rain, and occasional snow, they were all the same dull dusty brown.

"They were often called prairie schooners because of the image they created as their canvas tops billowed in the wind as they crossed the prairie.

"On a good day, a caravan of wagons could make 20 miles. If the weather was bad, they might make only 10. But on the average, they could expect to make 15 miles a day through open country. This was less than two miles per hour. A child could walk beside the wagons and keep up. In fact, despite the mental images we have of people riding westward in their conestoga wagons, the wagons were usually jam-packed with possessions and there was neither room for passengers nor reason to make the draft animals pull any more than necessary. Most people, men and women, old folks and children, actually walked the entire trip west. Even the men steering the wagons often did so as they walked alongside the oxen, rather than riding up top."

"Oxen?" I asked. "Didn't they use horses?"

"Not if you had a brain in your head. Usually, six or eight oxen were yoked in pairs to each wagon. Oxen are stronger, hardier, and more dependable than either horses or mules, and they were far less apt to be stolen by Indians. They could also forage anywhere and weren't as prone to running away."

He put the fish on a cookie sheet and put the cookie sheet in the oven then he sat at the table with me.

"Families usually each brought a cow or two for milk and, if an ox went lame or died, the cow could be yoked to the wagon."

"Still better than horses," I guessed.

He nodded. "Not to say no one brought horses. Some families did. But oxen and cows were much more important than horses along the Trail."

"It must have been a gruelling trip," I said. "Day after day of relentless travel."

"They didn't travel everyday. Sunday was a day of rest. Though nobody really rested. Women made earthen ovens and baked bread, then did laundry for the coming week. The men repaired harnesses and tended to the animals. On Monday, it was back to the Trail.

"And they didn't work their animals all day long, either. At noon, teams were unhitched, rested, and watered while children took baskets out into the prairie to gather buffalo chips for the evening cooking fires."

"What? I always thought that was a joke."

"What was a joke?"

"Using buffalo chips to cook."

"It wasn't. The prairie didn't have trees and using valuable space in the wagons for carrying firewood was out of the question. Besides, dried dung was a good fuel. It was plentiful and easy to gather, and it burns with a clean, smokeless flame. It was a perfect fuel for the pioneers."

"Well, what did families bring in their wagons?"

"When they left the east, they brought everything they were going to need—food, tools, a rifle, a bible, and the children's school books. There wasn't going to be much to buy when they got to the Northwest, and they were probably going to be broke when they got there, anyway.

"But the trouble was that families often brought too much and wound up jettisoning parts of their loads as they went along."

"Were the wagons dependable?" I asked.

"They were dependable, but they weren't indestructible. All along the Trail, the emigrants passed the ruins of wagons from other parties that had broken down. They passed the bleached skeletons of oxen. They also passed the simply marked graves of those whose trip, because of illness, accident, or Indian raids, ended right there on the Trail.

"And where the Trail grew steep, they passed rusted stoves, plows, and tools, and bags of beans or sugar now spoiled by weather and insects. They passed weathered furniture that had been jettisoned by earlier pioneers who had to lighten their loads if they were to make it over the mountains."

Phideaux climbed up in his lap. Mac petted him.

"But not everyone who brought too much failed. One man, Henderson Lewelling, brought as strange a cargo along the Oregon Trail as anyone—fruit trees. But his trees took a lot of care and their weight was an immense burden to his draft animals and slowed them down. This slowed the entire wagon train down. At first, other members of the wagon train suggested he should dump them. Then they insisted. Later, they pleaded. But he refused. Eventually, his three wagons lagged behind the others and finally he and his family became separated from the main train and had to make most of the trip alone. In the end, they made it to Oregon, trees and all, and he was to found what has become the great apple orchards of Oregon and Washington and he himself became a wealthy man."

"What about all these forts along the way?" I asked.

"The first important stop along the Trail was Fort Laramie, about seven weeks and 700 miles out of Independence. There, the train might stop for five days. The oxen were rested and shod for the rough rocky trail through the mountains ahead, wagons were fixed..."

"They shod the oxen? Like horses?"

"Yeah, but not with horseshoes. Oxen have a different type of foot."

"After Fort Laramie, they reached South Pass, and here they crossed the Great Divide. This was where most families discovered their loads were too heavy and they had to jettison a lot.

"After they reached the top of the pass, it was downhill for miles to come. We take brakes on our modern automobiles for granted, but those wagons didn't have brakes to speak of. Going downhill, men locked the wheels with poles and often tried to hold the wagons back with their bare hands. But, even with the wheels locked, the wheels slipped and slid like runners on a sled, and the poor oxen, often running at a gallop, just tried to keep from getting run over from behind. Sometimes, despite their best efforts, wagons turned over and were damaged or even completely ruined and left to add to the pioneer litter on the landscape. Animals were injured in these accidents and more than one settler's trip ended here with a burial.

"All along the Trail, each wagon had to eat the dust raised by all the wagons in front of it. As a result, positions close to the head of the line became coveted positions, so many of the wagon trains alternated the lead wagon. One day you'd be the lead wagon, the next day you'd be the second wagon and the day after that you'd be third. Eventually, you'd be at the end of the line. But the very next day you'd be up front again."

"Were Indians a danger?"

"Yes, but cholera and accidents were the two biggest dangers on the Trail."

"What kind of accidents?"

"Surly animals, drownings at river crossings, wagon accidents . . ."

"Wagon accidents? How?"

"A child walking alongside a wagon might stray too close to the wheels and get a foot run over. Keep in mind this was in the days before antibiotics and the wagons were hundreds of miles from the nearest doctor. A wound easily became infected, then gangrenous, and injuries were often a death sentence."

"Okay." I was writing it all down.

Taking Phideaux in his arms, he got up and checked the fish. "Not quite done," he said and sat down again.

"Anyway, about 1100 miles out, or halfway to Oregon, was Fort Bridger. Oxen were reshod there and wagons were repaired.

"Incidentally, it was at Fort Bridger that the Donner party, hearing of a wondrous new short cut to California, left the Trail and cut across present day Utah and Nevada. Traveling across country with little grass or water, animals died, wagons were abandoned, and people in the train started to die. Later on, they were harassed by Indians and, when they reached the Sierras, they arrived just in time for the first winter storms. Thirty six of the eighty-some-odd people who started out died."

"But that's not the Oregon Trail," I said.

"You're right," he said and continued.

"After Fort Bridger was Fort Hall. Fort Hall should be interesting to you because establishment of the Oregon Trail owes much to New Englanders and two Bostonians in particular."

"Who?"

"One was the young businessman I'd mentioned earlier, Nathaniel Wyeth."

"What was his business?"

"Actually, he cut ice from ponds around Boston in the winter, and shipped it to the West Indies."

"What did he want to do on the Oregon Trail?"

"Provisioning. After several false starts, in 1835, he finally established Fort Hall, which was to become an important stopping and provisioning point on the Trail."

"Why was it called Fort Hall?"

"Hall was the name of his financial backer, another Bostonian."

"Well, I'm not sure this belongs in my article, so I'll put it in my gee-whiz file," I said.

He laughed. "Fort Hall is located on the Snake River. Here, the California Trail branched off and many of the settlers who changed their minds about Oregon headed south from here to go to Sacramento.

"But in the early days of the Trail, most went on to Oregon. They followed the Snake to Glenn's Ferry where they could cross, and from there they forged on to Fort Boise.

"Two days past Fort Boise, the trail climbed into Blue Mountains and descended into the Rio Rondo Valley. It was the last place they would find fresh water, plentiful game, and good grazing until they reached the Columbia."

"Why, what was there between the Rio Rondo Valley and the Columbia?" I asked.

"A high, dry, windy and almost barren plateau that's hot during the day and cold at night. It must have been miserable to cross. Stock grew thinner for lack of grazing and there was almost no water. And when they finally reached the Columbia, well, in the early years of the Trail, the wagons had to be lowered by ropes down into the gorge and ferried down river on rafts. Later, there was a road cut through the forests of the Cascades. But even the road was dangerous. It was crudely built and at many points it forded rushing rivers where wagons were occasionally swept away."

He put Phideaux down and checked the fish again. "Ready," he said and he took the cookie sheet out.

I got dishes and silverware.

He served it up.

"The Trail ended in the Willamette Valley of Oregon," he said, "and most of the early settlers settled there. Later, many went north into what was to become the state of Washington but which, in the early days of the Trail, was still dominated by the Hudson Bay Company.

"How many people actually traveled along the trail?" I asked.

"It's estimated that 350,000 people crossed over the Trail when it was the road west. Of course, we'll never know exactly how many or how many of them died and are buried along its route.

"There's more you should know. Many other trails overlaid the Oregon Trail. Gold seekers en route to California followed the eastern part of the Trail as far as Fort Hall, then branched down into California. The Mormon Trail, taken by thousands of Mormons, coincided with parts of the Oregon Trail. The Mormons, bringing converts from not only the east, but Europe as well, often did without wagons and came with handcarts."

"Handcarts?"

"Yeah.

"But of all the overland routes west, the Oregon Trail was used the longest. And after the railroads made the wagon train obsolete, the Oregon Trail was still used as a trail for driving cattle and sheep east."

"Can I ask you something, Mac?"

"Sure."

"How do you know all this stuff?"

"You'd be surprised what I pick up from the conversation in poker games," he said.

We ate our lunch and Mac left.

In the afternoon, I started my article.

Tonight, I'm sitting in my living room, drinking a beer and watching Cheers. The books are back at the library. Phideaux is on my lap and Doggy is outside catching something. During the commercials, I think about how easy this writer's life is becoming. Δ

Reliving the Oregon Trail

By Vern Modeland

Harvest time is here and the snow line is creeping down from the high country, but neither event is an excuse to ignore this year's observance of the 150th anniversary of the Oregon Trail. Rather, fall's arrival may be just the justification you need for planning your own involvement in learning more about "The Emigrant Road."

Trail's end

You might want to be on hand for the end of a 73-day journey of walking and wagon travel across 1,000 miles of Idaho and Oregon. Participants are to arrive in Oregon City, OR, on Labor Day weekend for a three-day festival recalling life in the west 150 years ago. Activities planned are a pioneer living history event aimed at both children and adults, stage entertainment, a rodeo demonstration, story telling and hand craft exhibits. A Native American encampment is to honor their presence and role in homesteading the west.

The Trails End Finale at Oregon City comes at the end of major commemorative events and re-enactments that began in January in Missouri. Across Missouri, Kansas, Nebraska, Wyoming, Idaho, Oregon and in Washington, as many as three million Americans will have taken part in activities linked to celebrate the Oregon Trail's sesquicentennial by the time snow once again blankets most of its route, say organizers.

All along some 2,000 trail miles westward from Missouri, pioneer times and methods of travel have been re-created this year. Walking, on horseback, and riding in covered wagons, modern-day Americans and some of their kin from other countries have tried to sample the settlers' experience. Historic drama, music, clothing, and free-lance surprises have colored the strung-out celebration thanks to dedicated historians, preservationists and fun-lovers who live along the trail's route or just like to remember it.

One is Dale Johnson. He farms near Campbell, NE, and collects horse-drawn rigs that he volunteers for events like the trail travel re-enactment caravan that moved across Nebraska in May and June.

Another Nebraskan who apparently likes to get into such things in an extraordinary way is Joe Jeffrey. He's a veterinarian who dressed himself and his horse in Nes Pierce Indian regalia and charged a surprised re-enactment wagon train when it passed through his land south of Lexington, NE, on its way to an overnight stop at a nearby KOA Campground.

Free stuff

An armload of special booklets and brochures has been produced with detailed maps and schedules of activities. Close reading can uncover directions to out-of-the way places and non-events that often turn out being more informative and memorable than the big photo-op stuff. By dialing among the toll-free numbers on the list accompanying this article, you can get in touch with tourism staffers who can help design personalized mini or macro Oregon Trail experiences almost anywhere along its path that you might want to be.

Missouri was the general launching point for the people from other places who 150 years ago were ready to tame the west. At Independence, near Kansas City, is the National Frontier Trails Center. It serves as interpretive center, museum, library, archives and research center for the Oregon, Santa Fe and California Trails. Artifacts, a

Toll free information on the Oregon Trail

Each of the states with claims to the Oregon Trail route is participating in the sesquisentennial celebration this year with a variety of events and activities. To bring to your mailbox the schedules, maps, and a remarkable amount of history and anecdotal information that will aid in your awareness as well as travel planning, here are toll-free numbers you can call:

Missouri.	1-800-877-1234
Kansas.	1-800-252-6727
Nebraska.	1-800-228-4307
Wyoming.	1-800-225-5996
Idaho.	1-800-635-7820
Washington.	1-800-544-1800
Oregon.	1-800-547-7842

Mailing addresses:

Missouri Division of Tourism. P.O. Box 1055, Jefferson City, MO, 65102.

Kansas Travel & Tourism Division. 700 S.W. Harrison St., Suite 1300, Topeka, KS, 66603.

Nebraska Tourism Division, P.O. Box 94666, Lincoln, NE 68509.

Wyoming Division of Tourism, I-25 at College Drive, Cheyenne, WY, 82002.

Idaho Vacation Information. 700 West State Street, Boise, ID, 83720.

Oregon State Tourism Office. 775 Summer St., N.E., Salem, OR, 97310.

Washington Tourism Development Division, P.O. Box 42500, Olympic, WA, 98504. Δ film presentation, the life-size statue of the "Pioneer Woman," and many nearby preserved buildings impart some of the excitement of being at the start of the trail's real starting point.

Major all-season highways generally parallel the Oregon Trail route all the way from Westport to the Willamette Valley. Lesser roads and short side trips will get you closer to the sense of isolation and hardship that met the folks who hoped to make 20 miles a day for five months in the general direction of the sunset. Adventuring on your own beyond the concrete pathway can lead to planting your own feet in the grooves that remain clearly visible in prairie and rock. Those tracks are precise markers of that slow journey thousands of walkers and their wagons made more than a century ago.

Landmarks

Blue Mound was the first major checkpoint they looked for at the start of the Oregon Trail. It is visible today as a 150-foot high hill south of Interstate 70, southeast of Lawrence, KS.

West of Lawrence and Topeka, near St. Marys, KS, a 275 year old elm tree, 99 feet tall and 23 feet around, is acclaimed by Kansans to be the last living witness to the great migration. The tree marks the spot where Louis Vieu operated a ferry for Oregon trailers that crossed the Vermillion River.

Further west, an 80-minute drive north of Interstate 70, or south from Interstate 80, puts you in Blue Rapids, KS, on the way to Alcove Spring. Trail travelers carved their names and dates of passage into the rocks and tree trunks when they rested there. Alcove Spring is now on private property but you might gain permission to visit by contacting the city clerk at Blue Rapids, KS. The zip is 66411. The phone number is (913) 326-7736.

Rock Creek Station, between Beatrice and Fairbury, NE, on U.S.

Conestoga, the prairie super freighter

Conestoga wagons were the super-freighters on the Oregon Trail and other routes across the High Plains' ocean of grass until the railroads came to replace their carrying capacity.

The Conestoga wagon was named for a Pennsylvania town where they first were built around 1725. Its innovative sway-backed design and waterproofed seams allowed a Conestoga to keep a large amount of cargo in place while bouncing over rocky terrain or floating across swollen rivers. Power came from teams of four to six oxen.

Made entirely out of white oak—more than three tons of it per wagon—a Conestoga was 19-and-a-half feet long and 11-and-a-half feet high to the top of a span of canvas-covered bows that afforded some shelter from the elements for the wagon's load of commodities.

The wheels were the most complicated and time-consuming work involved in building a Conestoga, according to Thomas E. "Lucky" Jones, who was crafting replicas at an Ozarks theme park in the 1970s. Wide iron tires and painstaking workmanship were critical to the big freight wagon's serviceability, Jones said. Spacing between spokes had to be precise or a finished wheel wouldn't be truly round. The spokes had to slope away at a consistent angle from the plane of the hub for the assembly to gain maximum stability and strength. The iron band had to be heated to expand it to a carefully calculated fit, then, once it was hammered into place, quickly quenched with water to shrink it and firmly lock the wheel's many parts together.

Jones, with one apprentice, could build a complete Conestoga in two months, sometimes a little less. Working from drawings obtained from the Smithsonian's National Museum of American History, Jones used no power tools, only knives, chisels, mallets and the like, and a forge on which to fashion wheels, hinges, and other hardware. The market for the handful of new Conestogas he built was limited to themed shopping malls and museums. Δ

— Vern Modeland

Thomas E. "Lucky" Jones, Wheelwright

136, was another stop. It's a state historical park today, where 150-year-old wagon ruts are to be seen and a visitor's center with interpretive display is open year-round. A park permit is required.

At Fort Kearny, near Kearney, NE, on Interstate 80, there's another visitor's center with trail artifacts and restored buildings from the period. Again, a state park permit is necessary for admission.

Two major landmarks that gave Oregon Trail travelers a sense of getting somewhere are Chimney Rock and Scotts Bluff up the steepening grade of the North Platt River's valley in western Nebraska. Both are near Scottsbluff, NE, on U.S. 26. The landmarks are national historic sites and have museums.

"Rut Nuts" will find thousands more historic sites on the Oregon Trail route across Wyoming. Towns along the trail have either a museum, a historical society, a chamber of commerce or a Bureau of Land Management office to provide local directions, maps and information, promises the Wyoming Division of Tourism.

The trail's route enters Wyoming at Fort Laramie. Thirteen additional miles west on U.S. 28, near Guernsey a 150 foot tall cliff of soft sandstone is etched with more names and initials of Oregon Trail travelers. Beyond Casper (Fort Caspar) and Independence Rock, the trail went through South Pass. At 7,500 feet elevation, it was the highest point reached on the entire trail. South Pass is 34 miles from Lander on Wyoming 28. From there, the trail squeezed through Smith's Fork Crossing (Cokeville, WY, on U.S. Highway 30) before entering what today is Idaho.

Spectacular scenery

U.S. Highway 30 from Montpelier to Interstate 84, and Interstate 84 on west across Idaho and Oregon, approximate the rest of the route the wagon trains took. The Snake River, the Blue Mountains and the Columbia Gorge form an ever more spectacular backdrop to the journey.

Interstate highways take today's Oregon Trail follower to Soda Springs and Ft. Hall, Glenns Ferry and Boise in Idaho. The state operates historical interpretative centers at Montpelier and Fort Boise.

In Oregon, you can take walking breaks at significant landmark sites along I-84 while making trail-miles west through Huntington, LaGrande, Pendleton and The Dalles on the final leg of the route to the end at Oregon City. There is a Bureau of Land Management interpretive center, open daily except Christmas and New Years, at Flagstaff Hill. It's five miles east of Baker City.

Still celebrating

The 150th anniversary celebration of the Oregon Trail is far from over. Here's a listing of some remaining events:

In Missouri

* "Women of the 1800s—The Oregon Trail," part of a series of exhibits and forums. It's scheduled through all of Sept. at Shoal Creek, 7000 N.E. Barry Road in Kansas City. Phone (816) 792-2655 for more information and the cost.

* Santa-Cali-Gon Days Festival on the square at Independence, MO, Sept. 3-6 commemorates the three trails heading west with arts and crafts exhibits, a carnival and free stage entertainment. Phone (816) 252-4745 to learn more.

In Kansas

* The Plum Creek Fall Festival will be going on throughout Oct. at the Plum Creek Pumpkin Patch and Pioneer Farm, 15415 West 119th Street in Olathe. Phone (913) 782-0032 for information.

* Since 1899, Johnson County Settlers have celebrated annually at Olathe. Entertainment, a carnival, parade, food and arts and crafts Sept. 5-7 with the Oregon Trail's sesquicentennial as this year's theme. Phone (913) 764-1050 for information.

* Historic Ward-Mead Park will be the sight of an Apple Festival with trail connections Oct. 5. The event includes tours of the pioneer cabin, home and related buildings. There are arts and crafts, period foods and entertainment. Contact (913) 235-1633.

In Wyoming

* The 21st annual Mountain Man Rendezvous, one of the nation's largest, will be held at Ft. Bridger Sept. 3-6. Box 35, Fort Bridger, WY, 82933. Phone (307) 782-3842.

* An art exhibit, film festival and a symposium of nationally recognized speakers is to present panel discussions and other events commemorating the Oregon Trail at Central Wyoming College at Riverton, Sept. 16-18. Contact the college at (307) 856-9291.

* At the Casper planetarium, an ongoing program is "Lore and Legends from Around the Campfire."

In Idaho

* The Oregon Trail Run, a relay run of 152 miles, will be held Sept. 11-12. It starts at Massacre Rocks State Park near American Falls and follows State Highway 30 to Three Island State Park in Glenns Ferry. Contact: Idaho Dept. of Parks and Recreation. Phone (208) 327-7444.

In Oregon

* "Trail's End Finale." A celebration at the end of the Oregon Trail held in Clackamette Park, Oregon City, Sept. 4-6. Themed activities, storytelling, entertainment, rodeo demonstration, pioneer craft displays, Native American encampment, and the arrival of the official Oregon Trail Sesquicentennial Wagon Train at the end of 73 days journey across 1,000 miles of Idaho and Oregon. Δ

Harvesting from nature

By Darlene Campbell

One of the most exciting concepts of backwoods living is collecting and preserving food from the wild. Wild foods are high in both vitamin content and flavor, but unlike their domestic cousins from the garden, wild greens and fruits are available during a shorter season of harvest. Why? Because man has not tampered with them genetically to alter size, flavor, quality, or for that matter, made them so tough they can withstand being packed and shipped across the country without bruising. Just the opposite—wild foods are fragile and must be handled gently and prepared quickly to retain their natural goodness.

It is beyond the scope of this article to include all wild foods, so seek additional information on native fruits and herbs available in your area and learn more about them. Also, I do not intend to touch on wild mushrooms or morels since a wrong selection can prove fatal.

Beginning with wild greens—if carefully hand picked when young and tender, they are a delight to the palate, but if picked late in the season they tend to taste bitter. Some greens transplant well and I dig up those found on our land and move them near the house for ease in harvesting year after year. I especially enjoy growing wild garlic and wild onion for soups and salads. These I harvest by snipping tiny bits with kitchen shears when needed, or in the case of wild garlic, I snip large amounts and freeze them in polyethylene bags. Wild garlic does not form the multi-sectioned bulb we are accustomed to seeing in the supermarket. Instead it has a single bulb which is mildly garlic flavored with long slender leaves that are as valued as the bulb.

Wood sorrel and blue violets are not only pretty when planted around the house, but are tasty in salads and make pleasant herb teas. To preserve the delicate leaves, dry them as you would any herb and store in small jars away from light.

Karen, the author's daughter, enjoys learning about wild plants native to the area. The fields and forest are rich with new discoveries.

Many wild greens are harmful or bitter if not cooked properly. Greens such as poke salad, dandelion, sour dock, wild lettuce, lamb's quarter (a wild spinach), purslane, wild mustard and the tops of wild beets require two or three changes of water to make them palatable. Pick only the young, tender shoots and leaves. Wash them in several changes of water to remove all dirt and grit. Place greens in a pot and cover with water. Add salt if desired. Boil until tender, and drain. Add fresh, clear water to the pot and simmer for ten minutes more. Drain a second time and add any spices or flavorings such as onions, bacon or vinegar.

The dandelion is rich in vitamin A, with almost twice the vitamin A content of spinach. The early spring leaves are a delicacy, while those growing later in the season are quite bitter, thus the change of water when cooking, even up to three water changes.

In the case of poke, the root and berries of this plant are poisonous. Only the young tender shoots or sprouts should be used containing the immature stalks and leaves. This wild green is relished by country folks everywhere the herb grows naturally. It is found growing along fences or in freshly cleared fields.

Many seeds from native trees are edible and can be ground into flour. This was a staple of early pioneers and Indians. For example, the mesquite tree of the Southwest desert was prized by early Indians and Mexicans for its long bean pod. By drying and grinding the pod and its contents, a nutritious breadstuff is made. The pod can be cooked while still green and is considered a delicacy. Although I have not tried the mesquite bean, while living in Arizona I experimented with the bean from the palo verde tree, and found it quite flavorful if separated from the hull and eaten raw when still green and tender as one would eat English sweet garden peas. I even ground the dry bean into a flour using a food chopper and mixed the product with regular flour. This produced a more nut-like flavor in home baked bread.

The honey locust produces a similar pod, reaching up to 15 inches in length and spiral shaped. The pod is enjoyed by kids who find it sweet when chewed. This seed pod (sometimes called the Screw Bean) can be infested with insect larvae, so inspect carefully before you harvest it. Insect invasion is evidenced by small holes bored into the pod. It was used the same as mesquite and palo verde by early settlers and Indians, and is believed to be the locust that John the Baptist lived on in the desert.

The roots of many plants are also edible, such as the Jerusalem artichoke, which is a potato-like tuber. The sassafras root is probably the most commonly known, and has become somewhat hard to find in recent years. This root was once in great demand in Europe and was sold for tea and flavoring. Aromatic, the flavor of this tea is unsurpassed. The sassafras is generally a small tree in the northern United States, but grows quite large in the South.

The bark is distilled in large quantities for the oil which is used as a natural flavoring for medicine and candy. It is also used in potpourri. The leaves can be dried and used as a cooking herb for soups and stews, especially in creole cooking. Although I have searched our woods for this common mitten-leaf tree, I have had to rely on a health food store for my supply of sassafras.

The cattail, both broad-leaved and narrow-leaved varieties, yields an edible root which is starchy. The root can be roasted or dried and ground into flour. The young, tender shoots can be peeled and served in salad, or steamed or stir-fried like asparagus. Choose only the youngest, most tender shoots. In the early spring here in southeast Oklahoma, when green browse is still scarce, whitetail deer come nightly to our pond to relish the early sprouting cattails. On these days I arise early and take a walk to the pond. Strolling its boundaries and surveying the animal tracks and paw prints in the mud, I read them like most people read their morning newspaper. They tell me that not only have deer visited the pond, but that a flock of wild turkey and a fox stopped for water.

There are countless numbers of fruiting trees and berries in the wild that offer food for the taking. One has only to remember the time of harvest to collect more than a winter's supply. Wild plums have a very short season. They seem to ripen almost overnight after being on the tree for ages. Once they ripen, they drop. Be ready to harvest and preserve on a moment's notice. I like to make jam from this sometimes tart fruit, or can it with sugar for serving at breakfast on some cold winter morning along with hot waffles and honey.

The staghorn sumac is supposed to make a lemonade drink. The berries are quite sour in the early summer when they exude a sticky substance, and my children love to suck on them. However, it is the root of the sumac —not the berry—which is used for making the drink. I have tried steeping the berries with poor results; perhaps pressing them to extract the sour oil would be preferable.

There are wild fruits and berries for making delicious jellies and fruit leathers, canning with or without sugar, and freezing. Most abundant on our backwoods farm is the wild and sometimes pesky persimmon. I've always heard that the persimmon must pass through a freeze before it becomes sweet. Not so. Just like any other fruit, the persimmon will ripen and sweeten in its time. Since it is a late fall producer, the crop is usually not ripe until after a frost or early freeze. It could be that this is where it received its reputation for not being edible until after a freeze. We have trees on our place that produce large, succulent and juicy fruit, while nearby there are trees that have a much smaller, drier fruit. This is probably due to genetics, as both varieties receive the same amount of rainfall and grow in identical rocky soil. Persimmons are high in potassium and vitamins A and C.

When harvesting persimmons, pinch the fruit gently while still on the tree. If it is soft and yielding, chances are it is ripe and sweet, ready for harvest. Another way ia to shake the tree vigorously. A shower of ripe persimmons will drop to the ground for easy gathering. These are a favorite food for wildlife, so any missed fruit will be eaten by 'possum, coon, bear or fox. Even our dogs and goats enjoy a persimmon or two. And Mickey our pet 'possum relishes these golden sweet fruits in season, almost as much as he enjoys hot dogs.

Another source of vitamin C is the rose hip. Rose hips are more abundantly produced by wild roses than domestic ones. Allow the hips to ripen before harvesting and then experiment with their multiple uses, such as potpourri, jam, jelly, tea, wine or dried arrangements. When preparing the hips for jam or jelly, remove the blossom ends, stems, and leaves. Wash and store in an airtight container in the refrigerator until ready to use.

The hips are used with the seeds removed unless the recipe calls for hips and seeds. To remove the seeds, cut the fruit in half and scoop out the seeds, or remove a portion of the top of the hip and using a sharp knife, carefully remove the seeds. Don't discard the seeds, for they are a rich source of vitamin E and can be used for adding additional vitamin E to other dishes. Grind and boil them in a small amount of water, then strain through a layer of cloth. Use this solution as part of the liquid called for in other recipes.

To make rose hip jam, measure and cook clean rose hips in an equal amount of water. Since vitamin C is easily destroyed, never let it come in contact with copper or aluminum. Use wooden spoons and stainless steel knifes. Cook the hips until tender and mash. Force the resulting pulp through a fine sieve and add one cup of sugar for each cup of pulp. Cook again until the pulp thickens to jam consistency. Pour into sterilized jars and seal.

Wild grapes are almost impossible to harvest because they climb to the tops of the tallest trees. There they stay to feed birds and climbing wildlife. However, we are fortunate to have several wild grape vines growing near the house which climb onto trellises the former owner built for the purpose. Like the persimmon, these grapes offer two distinct varieties— one is small and hard, while the other produces large clusters of juicy tart grapes. The difference here is that the better producing vines are watered by kitchen gray water, while the other must survive on natural rainfall. Wild grapes make excellent juice which can be canned or frozen for later use—or make it into jelly following your favorite recipe.

Another good choice for making jelly is wild cherry. When fermented, it makes a pleasant wine. Although it is delicious eaten fresh, the fruit is small and mostly pit. Birds so love this fruit that they actually become intoxicated when it becomes overripe and ferments on the tree.

When seeking wild edible plants, there are a few things you should bear in mind for the sake of preserving the environment. Take no more plants than are necessary, and harvest only the leaves or fruit when possible, leaving the root to reproduce again. Don't harvest the same location year after year. Don't disturb wildlife dens or homes. Never disturb a member of an endangered species, for it is the only hope that some species have to increase their number. Leave the land and other things as you find them. Don't kick over rocks, rotting stumps etc. Don't cross private land without getting the owner's permission, and when crossing a field repeatedly, always take a different route to prevent a beaten path. Keep dogs under control to protect wildlife.

Above all, do not leave tell-tale signs that might give away the location of a nest of birds or den of wildlife. Don't reveal where you find something interesting, for then it's no longer a secret, and the second visitor may not hold the same respect for the laws of nature as you do.

Even if you never harvest from the wild, the fun of discovery and the knowledge gained of the plants in your area are worth taking time from daily chores to indulge yourself and your children in this natural pleasure.Δ

A BHM Writer's Profile

At age 46, Carl Watner is editor and publisher of *The Voluntaryist* newsletter (free sample copy from Box 1275, Gramling SC 29348). He and his wife Julie homeschool their four homeborn offspring. Julie Watner is also a writer and *Backwoods Home Magazine* contributor. Carl Watner also operates a feed mill, producing and retailing livestock feed in upstate South Carolina.

Watner's interest in death and dying stems from his early work stint in a family-owned cemetery in Baltimore, Maryland. Carl is author of ROBERT LeFEVER: Truth Is Not a Half-way Place; editor of A VOLUNTARY POLITICAL GOVERNMENT: Letters from Charles Lane; and a major contributor to NEITHER BULLETS NOR BALLOTS: Essays on Voluntaryism.

Slaughtering and butchering

By Dynah Geissal

Fall is butchering time, a period of joy in the harvest of the year's work and of sadness that the lives of your beautiful, healthy animals have come to an end. On this occasion the animals should be treated with the same kindness and respect with which they were treated during their lives. Good farmers raise their animals free from fear, anxiety and stress. The animals should meet their end as they lived, without the terror of the slaughterhouse.

Making careful preparations will help you remain calm. After years and years of butchering I still feel a strong adrenaline rush when the animal is killed. Be prepared for that and use it to make sure the death is as painless as possible. A knowledgeable person can direct these strong feelings into doing the job right instead of letting their emotions get the best of them and botching the job.

When the temperature only reaches 40° during the day and the pasture is no longer adequate feed, it is time to butcher. Sheep and goats should be nine months or under. Pigs should be just slightly jowly.

Past wisdom dictated that 250 pounds was optimum butchering weight for a pig, but after your porkers reach 225, the ratio of weight gain going to fat versus lean meat increases dramatically.

After many years of experimentation, I try for 200 pounds. At that point my pigs have no more of a fat covering than my goats. There's still enough fat for lard and sausage, but there's no reason to pour more and more feed into them only to find their kidneys so imbedded in fat that they're hard to locate. I buy my pigs in early May and by mid-November they are eating so voraciously that I know it can no longer be practical to keep them.

Calves are traditionally kept until they are 10-15 months old, but that can be a problem for a family raising their own meat. If the calf was born in February it could be butchered in December. In a place like Montana, however, December is late for butchering. With the temperatures around 0°, your meat would have to hang a very long time to age.

If you decided to keep the calf till spring, you would be faced with deciding whether to butcher it after feeding all winter or to let it grow some on the pasture.

By the time the calf is looking really big, it's midsummer. In a cool climate you could butcher it then if you did it fast, but you would have to pay someone to hang it to age. In most climates, you don't butcher between May and October anyway, if you can help it, because of the fly problem. So then you're up to fall when you have all the other butchering to do. If you can manage it, I think that is your best option.

Here are a few additional suggestions to think about ahead of time. Butchering pigs and cows is easier if you withhold food for 24 hours before butchering. This is not totally necessary, and if you would feel bad having your animal hungry on its last day, don't do it. Just be extra careful with the guts.

When you butcher only certain members of a herd, avoid frightening the others. Don't run through the herd chasing the one you want. Move slowly and calmly. Try not to kill one animal in front of the others. Don't slaughter in the animal's home.

The exception to this is when you are slaughtering pigs. Swine do not care if you kill their companion and will rush over to drink the blood if they can.

It makes sense to leave the pig butchering until last so that they can consume anything that is left over. Don't feed surplus fat to pigs, though. Only poultry can convert fat into useable production calories. That is because of their high rate of metabolism. If you feed fat to pigs, it will provide calories, but it can only become fat, not meat.

Before butchering, decide what parts you will save. I think I've tried saving just about everything, and I think there's some value in that. However, if no one wants to eat it, the value is only in learning and experimenting and knowing the possibilities.

There is a certain satisfaction in using everything. Ears and tail can flavor a pot of beans. Hooves can make gelatin. Stomachs can hold blood sausage and other things. Lungs are edible. Intestines can be used to make sausage casings or cooked in some other additional dishes.

I will describe what I keep, but feel free to make your own decisions about what you and your family would like to try.

A word about using the intestines for sausage. If the situation is such that you have running water in a hose, it is fairly easy to clean them. Otherwise you'll have to do it indoors, which is a lot of work. After that you have to turn them inside out and scrape them.

If you don't scrape them, they'll still be edible but they'll be tougher than you might like. These days I feed the intestines to the animals and buy prepared ones. If you buy them from a butcher house, they're already prepared and quite inexpensive. Try not to buy them in the grocery store, as they demand ridiculous prices.

Be sure to save enough fat for lard, sausage making, and if you're butchering a cow, for ground beef.

A goat is shot in the back of the head. The front is too hard. With a cow or a pig, mentally draw lines from the top of each ear to the opposite eye. Where the lines cross is where you shoot. One shot with a .22 should do it.

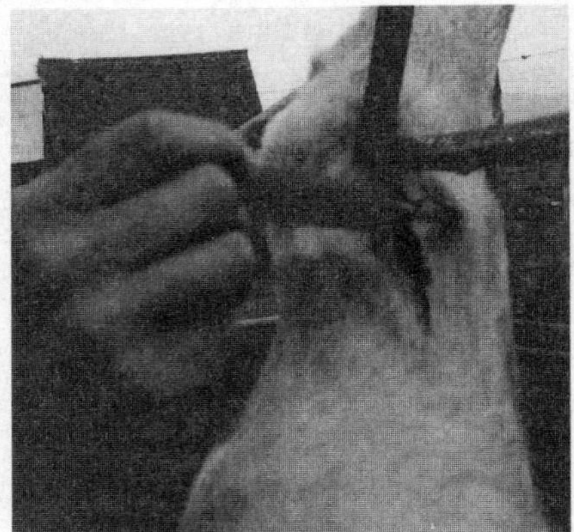

Figure 1. Cutting around the foot.

We shoot pigs in their pen. That is the least traumatic for everyone. If you do this, though, you'll want to get the pig out of the pen as quickly as possible so as to slit the throat on clean ground.

Throw a noose around its neck and drag it out. You want to slit the throat while the heart is still beating in order to get all the blood pumped out.

Stick the point of your big knife into the throat and cut outward through the skin. Never try to cut into the skin through the hair. Make sure you've severed the main veins and arteries.

Any male animal that is to be used as food should have been castrated. If that wasn't done, however, remove the head and testicles right away. That's easy with a goat, but a cow or pig can kick with a real wallop, so be careful. This is done so the meat won't be tainted.

If you are butchering a pig, you will want to wash it down now. A pig is a clean animal in a natural environment but gets pretty dirty when confined. Be especially careful in cleaning the rear feet, for they'll stay on unskinned.

Remove the head by cutting all the way around with your big knife. As always, avoid cutting into the hair. Instead keep your knife between the flesh and the skin and cut out. With a goat, twist the head until the bone snaps. With a pig or cow, use your meat saw.

Make slits between the achilles tendon and the ankles and insert the gambrel. At this point, you could scald a pig but in these days of preserving meat by freezing, there's really no point. In days past, the skin was left on the bacon and hams to protect them. It's traditional, but there's no other reason to leave it on since we don't eat it anyway. And logistically it's just much simpler to skin.

Remove front feet at the joint. Using a pulley for a goat and a come-along for a pig or cow, hoist the animal into the air to a height convenient for working on the rear of the animal.

Slip your short pointed knife (Figure 1) into the slit you made at the achilles tendon and cut around the foot, again cutting out, not in. Be very careful not to cut the tendon. With the knife between the flesh and the skin, slice a line through the skin down each leg to the centerline. Then cut down the body to the neck (Figure 2).

Now take your skinning knife and begin skinning at the junction where the leg cuts meet the centerline. Hold the skin with one hand or your hook and pull hard to create tension as you use your knife to separate the flesh from the skin. Work out from the center (Figure 3).

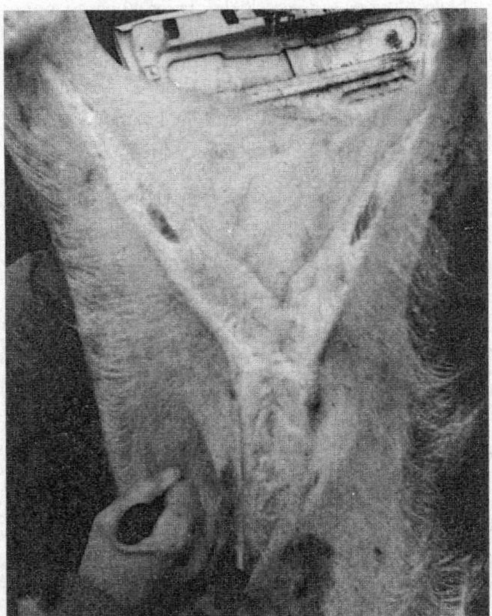

Figure 2. Cutting down the body.

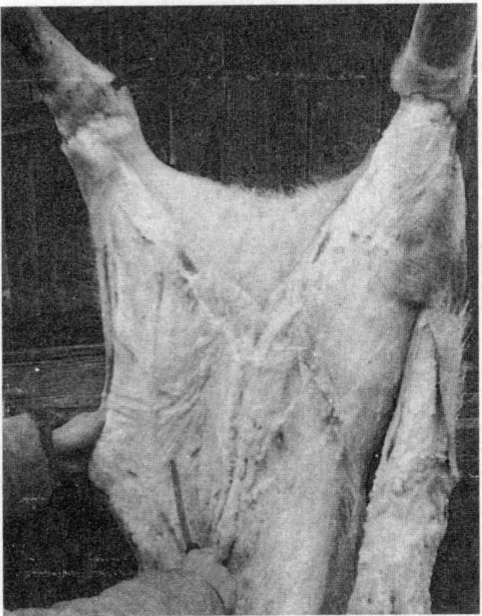

Figure 3. Skinning from the center.

If you are not going to use the hide, you won't have to worry about keeping it intact. Just be concerned about the meat in that case. You'll have to be much more careful if you want to use the hide.

Keep pulling the skin away with your hand or the hook and continue to slice between the hide and the flesh until the belly is skinned. This will relieve the tension of the skin on the rump. Now work around the leg from front to back.

The next step is to start at the top of the "Y" and skin up and over the crotch. The skin is tightest here, so be especially careful if you're saving the hide. Pull skin out and down to create tension on your work while you slice with your knife. A layer of fat makes the animal relatively easy to skin. Leave as much fat on the body as possible.

Work over the anus to the tailbone. Give the tail a sharp jerk and it will separate from the vertebrae. From here on, the weight of the skin practically skins the animal for you. Work all around the body. If there is too much movement on the gambrel, lean against the animal.

Raise the beast when it becomes difficult to reach your work. Bring the work to you and stay comfortable. The forelegs are a bit difficult near the shoulders. Start on the outside of the leg (Figure 4). Work around to the front. Skin the neck and the inner forelegs and shed the skin.

Lower the animal so that you can comfortably work on the rear of it. At this point you want to separate the large intestine from the body. You will begin by cutting around the anus with your short pointed knife. Be careful not to make any holes in the intestine. When it is cut free, pull it slightly out and tie it off. It is helpful to have a partner here. This step (tying) is unnecessary if you are butchering a goat.

Cut down the belly with your pointed knife. Cut from inside out as before. With your other hand hold the guts away from the point of the knife (Figure 5). Cut through the belly fat all the way down to the sternum. Next, cut the meat between the legs.

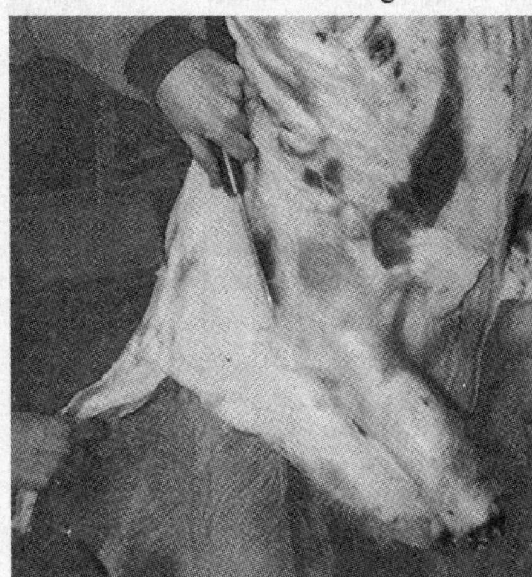

Figure 4. Skinning the foreleg.

If the animal is a male, cut out the penis. Place a large container underneath to catch the guts. By now they will be bulging out of the body. At some point if you are butchering a ruminant, there may be a flow of greenish liquid from the neck. This is just the cud and nothing to worry about.

Cut through the fat surrounding the guts, then sever any tissue connecting them to the rear wall of the body cavity. Pull the anus through to the inside and then out. Separating the intestines from the body is tedious, so take your time. You don't want to spill the contents into the meat.

Be careful also not to rupture the bladder. Some people tie it and then cut it off, but I've found that method to be more likely to cause spillage.

Pull the intestines and bladder out of the body. Most of the stomach will also be free now. You will need to reach in and under to lift it all over the sternum. Some people cut through the sternum, but it's easy enough just to lift the guts out. Most everything will now be hanging out of the body.

Strip away as much of the surrounding belly fat as you can to feed to the chickens. Get out the bowl for the innards you want to keep. Remove the kidneys and fat. Cut out the liver and put it into the keeper bowl along with the kidneys. Sever the remaining flesh connecting the stomachs to the body, and it should all fall into the gut bucket.

Cut out the diaphragm and remove the lungs and heart by severing the connective tissue behind them. Separate the heart from the lungs and squeeze out the blood from the heart. The heart is a keeper, while the lungs aren't.

From the neck end, cut out the windpipe. Be sure the opening is clear all the way through the body cavity. Clean all over with cold water. (Now you see that if you hadn't cleaned those rear feet of a pig, the dirt from them could contaminate the meat.)

Except for pork, we age all our meat from fowl to cow, and strongly advise you to do the same. Pork should only hang overnight to chill, and all meat should be cut up in a chilled state.

A goat should age one week in 40° weather, longer in colder weather. If it's too warm to age it, it's a real shame to butcher at that time, because the meat won't be as tender as it could be. A goat is hung whole.

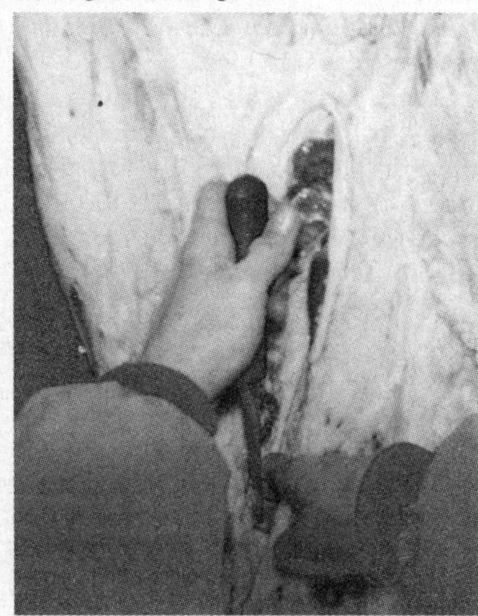

Figure 5. Cutting down the belly.

To halve a larger carcass, face the belly while your partner helps hold the body and helps to guide the saw from the back when necessary. Use your fingertips on the blade to guide your cut.

A cow should be quartered for ease of handling, of course, but also to allow the meat to cool as quickly as possible. Merely cut between the 2nd and 3rd ribs and be ready to hold the fore section. It should be hung for two weeks under the proper conditions.

When you're finished working on the animal's body, it's time to salvage the tongue and brains from the head. The easiest way to get the tongue is to cut under the jaw in the soft space in the middle. When you have slit this open, reach in and cut the tongue loose from its mooring. Working through the mouth is much harder.

Chopping the skull with an axe works for getting out the brains, but sawing it in half with your meat saw gets the job done with a bit more finesse.

If you plan to use the rest of the head, you will have to skin it now. Remove the ears, eyes, nose and anything that doesn't look like meat or bone. Clean thoroughly. You may want to brush the teeth. You could make goat's head soup or you could make headcheese. The only heads I use these days are pigs.

Some people use the jowls for bacon, but if you've butchered before the pig has gotten really fat, there won't be much there. I use the head meat for scrapple, tamale meat and pozole. I used to use some in liverwurst, but we prefer these other dishes.

In any case, you'll need a pot large enough to hold the head. If you cook with a wood stove as I do, just add water to cover, put a lid on and leave it on the stove to simmer until the meat is tender. It's less convenient if you use some other kind of fuel.

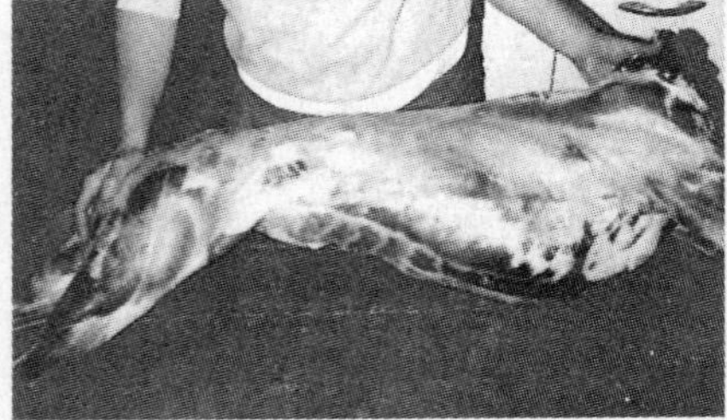

Figure 6. A goat ready to cut up.

Remove the meat and bones from the pot and separate them. Take out anything that looks strange and you're ready to use whatever recipes you've decided on. Boil down your broth to a manageable amount and either use it in your recipes or freeze it for later use.

When you are ready to cut up your meat, refer to the section that applies to your animal. Cutting up a deer or a sheep is the same as a goat.

Cutting up a goat

Cut behind the shoulder blades to remove the front legs. Cut off leg at elbow. These lower legs can be soup bones, but they're not much good for anything else. You can package the shoulder as it is or you can bone it, roll and tie for a rolled roast. You could also cut it up for stew meat.

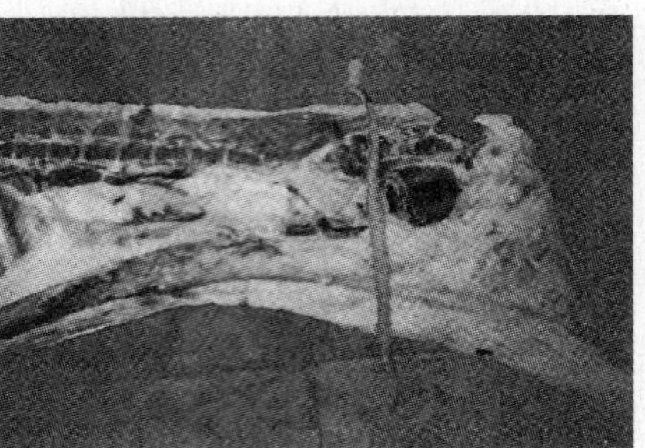

Figure 7. Separating the rear third of a pig.

Take as much meat from the neck as you can. Use that for soup.

You could cut chops if you wanted. You would have to saw through the backbone between every rib to do that. You could bone out the chops to avoid all the sawing. Or you could just cut out the whole muscle bundle along the backbone. It's called the backscrap and is the best meat on the animal (that's what I do).

Next take your meat saw and cut the ribs from the backbone. Then cut them in half with your knife for easy packaging. Underneath the backbone is the tenderloin. Cut that out.

Now for the rear third. Cut off the foot. Next cut off the leg at the knee. These are your shanks. Separate the legs at the pelvis. These are the only roasts I keep from a goat. I use the front shoulders for stew or stir fry. You can package the leg as it is or bone it. Boning saves a lot of space and a rolled roast is a pleasure to cut when it's cooked, too.

That's it except for working over all the bones to retrieve any last bits of meat for your sausage bucket. I save one goat just for sausage and one for jerky. You may want to do that, or you may have other favorite uses. Goat meat (or *chevon* as it's called) is really wonderful when it's properly handled.

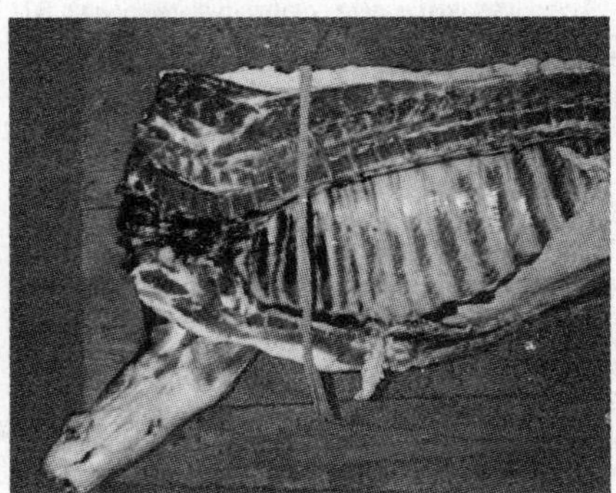

Figure 8. Separating the front third of a pig.

Cutting up a pig

There are many ways to cut up a pig and many ways to cure meat. I'm going to tell you how I do it and why I use this method. If you're doing your own curing, you have the vagaries of weather to contend with. Below freezing and it doesn't cure. Fifty degrees and it spoils.

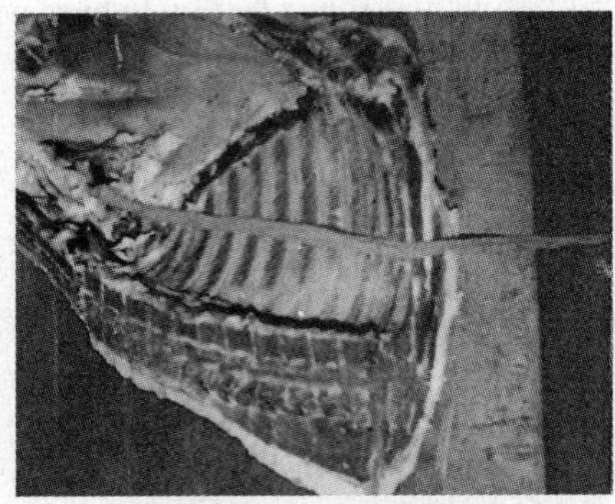

Figure 9. Separating the ribs from the chops.

In my first experiments I used an old fashioned cure. It was very salty. The hams and bacon hung in a cool room all year and didn't spoil. If you don't have a freezer, you could do that.

You can use a dry cure or a brine cure. In the brine cure, the strength of the brine is determined by the amount of meat. Theoretically it can't get too salty that way, and I have found that to be true.

If you butcher when it's 40°, and then it warms up to the 50s, then it freezes for a while, then warms up to 50° again, there's a real danger that your meat will sour around the bone. By the time it's in the warm smokehouse, you've really got trouble. For this reason I bone the hams. I have never had a problem since I began

Figure 10. Rolled pork roasts and the bone they came from.

doing this. Also it makes the ham nice to cut when it's rolled and tied.

Your pig should have hung overnight so that the meat is firm. Now you will want to cut your side of pork into thirds. To do this take your meat saw and cut straight down from the backbone through the aitch bone to separate the rear ham from the body. (Blue tape, Figure 7.) The cut should go right through the ball and socket joint. Remove the foot.

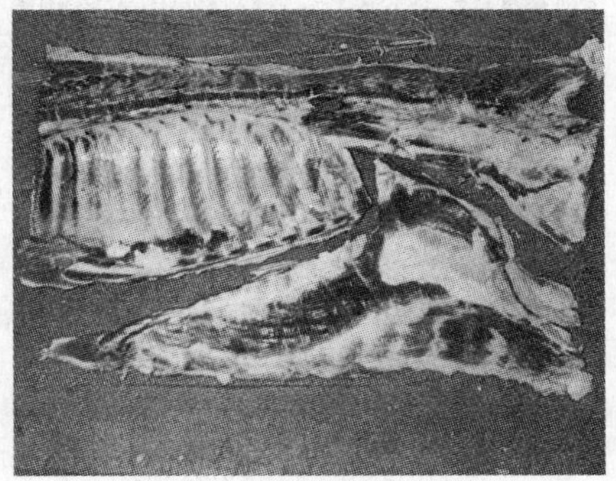

Figure 11. The bacon separated from the ribs.

To separate the front third, cut between the second and third ribs again cutting straight down from the backbone. (Blue tape, Figure 8.) Look carefully at the muscle bundles and try to keep them intact.

Take the middle section and make another cut after the 11th rib. Then cut across the ribs parallel to the backbone to separate the ribs from the chops. (Blue tape, Figure 9.) Look at both ends of the meat to see where to cut. Remove the belly fat and save it for sausage and lard.

Saw through the backbone for chops and finish your cuts with a knife. It's helpful to have a partner to hold it steady. Trim off the extra fat but as always, leave some.

Now trim out the loin. Feel the bone with your fingers and just cut out the muscle bundle as well as you can. This is your best roast. Cut it into whatever size you want (Figure 10).

Figure 12. A pig cut up but not yet boned (front).

Trim the excess fat from the ribs. Decide whether you want extra meaty ribs or if you want to slice off most of the meat for bacon. Cut the bacon from the ribs (Figure 11). Cut the ribs into easily packaged pieces, but leave the bacon whole until after smoking (Figure 12).

Before cutting your hams, you'll have to decide whether you want them large or small and how much meat you want for sausage, stir fry, etc.

Figure 13. Roasts, hams, chops, bacon, ribs & sausage trimmings.

Cutting hams and roasts takes some practice, but don't worry too much. They can always be trimmed to look nice and nothing is wasted. It can always go into the sausage bucket.

Begin two piles of trimmings. One will be for sausage and the other will be better pieces for stir fry. Take the front third and cut off the hock. If you wanted to make this a shoulder roast you could, but the meat is very fatty and not as good quality as the rear. It could also be used for sausage or stir fry.

When you make your roasts, study the muscle bundles and try to keep them intact as much as possible. To bone, cut to the bone and cut around it as well as possible and along the backbone to the third rib. Cut off the front muscle bundle and put it into the sausage bucket. Roll it up as it would be with the bone in and trim it to look nice. Trim off excess fat.

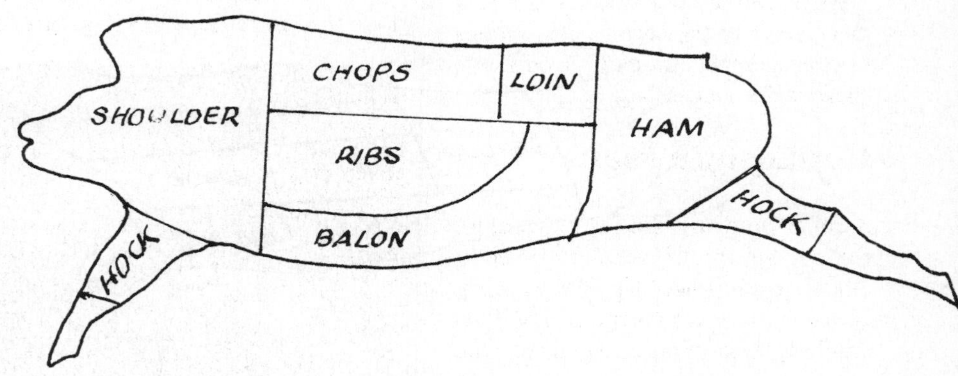

Figure 14. Cuts of meat from a pig.

Take the rear third and decide how much hock you want and cut that off. Bone out the rear hams and trim off excess fat. This is tedious, so just take your time. Make your cut in to the bone and cut it out as well as possible. Trim end for looks (Figure 13).

Put your bacon, hams and hocks into the curing bucket. Be sure to save enough fat for sausage and lard, and you're finished with this part.

Cutting up a cow

Begin with the hind quarter. Cut off the leg by making a cut with the meat saw from the hip to the tailbone. If you cut across the top, you will have round steaks. The first cuts are top round and are the best. Thicker cuts make round roasts. The small, less meaty part near the shank is the heel of round. The shank is a soup bone.

The muscle flap on the belly is the flank steak. Cut that off and remove the layers of fat. The rump roast is the meaty end that was cut away from the leg. Bone it out for a rump roast or just cut it off with the saw.

The top muscle on the remaining piece is all steak. You could cut through the backbone for each steak or bone it out and then cut into steaks. Or the part behind the ribs could be left whole for a sirloin roast. The meat underneath the backbone is the tenderloin or filet mignon which can be removed and cut into steaks (butterfly) or left whole.

Your steaks, beginning at the rear just ahead of the rump roast and moving forward, are sirloin, porterhouse, T-bone, if boned, separate into the filet mignon and New York strip. The rib steaks could be left whole for a rib roast, which would be your best roast.

Everything left on this quarter is stew or burger. Stew meat is the better meat. Remove the fat and anything un-meatlike.

Now we're ready for the front quarter. To remove the leg, lift it up and start cutting underneath until you have cut behind the shoulder blade and separated the leg from the body. The part on the shoulder is called a blade roast. It can be boned or just cut with the saw to the size you prefer. The top part of the leg is chuck and can be made into roasts or steaks. It can be boned or not.

The lower part of the leg is burger or soup bone. There are probably a couple of rib steaks on the remaining piece, so cut these out. The neck meat is stew. The meat at the front that would have been just behind the leg is brisket. Remove that from its bone.

Cut as many ribs as you want for short ribs. Everything else is stew or burger. When making hamburger, use at least one fourth fat.

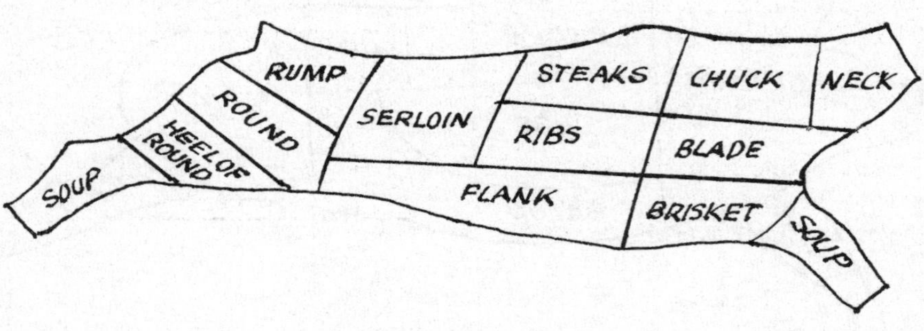

Figure 15. Cuts of meat from a cow.

Curing

Mix the brine before you cut up your pork, so you can just drop it right in. Two five-gallon buckets of food grade plastic works fine for two pigs. The recipe is for 100 lbs. of meat which should also be right for two pigs. Measure out 8 pounds of pickling salt and 2 pounds of sugar, honey, brown sugar or maple syrup. This is the critical part. Dissolve this in water. We add other spices such as cayenne, black pepper, garlic, etc. but this is only for added flavor and not necessary. The use of boiling water aids in dissolution.

Some people add saltpeter (nitrates), but all it does is make the meat a uniform pink, and I prefer not to use this additive. Bacon and hocks will cure in a week at 40°. Hams will take six weeks. For every day below freezing, another day should be added.

Weight the meat so it doesn't come above the brine, adding more water if necessary. Use a plate with a clean rock on top.

Sausage

Any kind of meat can be used for sausage. Just save whatever scraps you have from cutting up meat. You can use as little as ¼ fat, but the sausage is much, much better if ⅓ is used.

Sausage making is one of the most fun of all my projects. But don't rush through it or it can turn into a nightmare. If you've just finished cutting up your pig, give yourself a break and wait until the next day to do the sausage.

I have enclosed several recipes that you might like to try. We like to make many different kinds each year. Whatever you do though, take the time to cook some of each type before you package it or stuff it into casings. It may be too bland or worse too spicy, in which case you'll have to add more meat.

If sausage is being made from pork, only one grinding will suffice but beef or goat should be ground twice using a coarser grind the first time.

Some recipes call for water and some don't, but if you're making link sausage you will have to add some liquid. Add enough so that the sausage is easy to work.

Smoking

Hardwood must be used for smoking so that the meat doesn't get resins in it, as it would from pine. When smoking hams, bacon and sausage, you use what is called a cool smoke. This means that the meat is not being cooked while it is being smoked. You can use anything to hold the meat and smoke. We built a smokehouse out of sheets of plywood, which enables us to walk inside to hang the meat.

We use an old woodstove to provide the smoke, which passes from the stove through a stovepipe with damper into the smokehouse. The pipe should go in fairly low, but not so low as to inhibit draw.

For an hour or so, leave the door ajar to let excess moisture escape. Then close it and try to keep the temperature around 100°. When it's done is a judgement call, but we give sausage approximately 12 hours, bacon 14, and hams 48. The color is the key. It should be the color of mahogany.

Recipes

Scrapple: basic recipe

By weight:
4 parts meat (ground or chopped)
3 parts broth
1 part cereal

Cornmeal is traditional, but oatmeal is sometimes used, as is buckwheat flour. Some people use half cornmeal and half buckwheat flour, while others substitute a little wheat germ for some of the cornmeal.

If using cornmeal, add some cool broth first to keep the cornmeal from lumping up. Then cook with the rest of the broth and the meat until it begins to thicken. Stir often and don't let it scorch.

At this point add the seasoning. Use whatever you like and leave the rest. The amounts given below are about right for the meat from one head (or about 8 lbs):

2 T salt
2 T pepper
1 T marjoram
1 T sage
1 t cayenne
½ T nutmeg
Trace of mace
2 T onion (ground or chopped)
½ t thyme
1 bay leaf

Pour into a lightly oiled loaf pan and chill. Turn out, cut to appropriate size, wrap and freeze. When ready to cook, slice and fry until brown outside but still soft inside. Scrapple is traditionally served with maple syrup.

The cereal-to-broth ratio needs to be pretty constant, but you can use more or less meat.

Pozole (poh-so-lay)

Meat from 1 head, chopped
(about 8 lbs)
Broth to cover
4 lbs hominy
2 T salt
4 T chili powder

Cook 2 or 3 hours. When ready to eat, chop or shred cabbage, onions, and radishes and place in separate bowls.

To serve, ladle soup into bowls and top with the desired raw vegetables. Squeeze lime juice over all.

Tamales

Take the head meat and add cumin, crushed garlic, chopped hot peppers to make a nice spicy mixture. Eat or freeze.

Preparation: Traditionally, tamales are wrapped in corn husks. That's fine if it's summer (if they're dry, soak them to make them pliable). If corn husks are not available, there are plenty of other wrappers to choose from. I go to the garden to see what's available—cabbage leaves, chard, even lettuce. Even in the depths of winter I have something under straw that will do. The advantage is that the whole thing can be eaten.

Make the outer covering of cornmeal (I like to use masa) with some lard worked in and then add some water (like making biscuits). Add some garlic, cumin and cayenne and spread onto the wrapper. Roll up and steam for about two hours and serve.

Sausage: A few basic recipes

As you can see, the amounts of the various seasonings are really arbitrary. Feel free to add more or less according to what you like. Salt is really a matter of preference if the sausage is going to be frozen. Most recipes call for 2 T to 6 T for 10 lbs, but I prefer to stick with 2 T. If you like variety, try several recipes, but if you just want to get it done, go for the recipe for 100 lbs. Pork, beef and chevon can all be used in sausage. Chevon can be substituted in any recipe calling for game or beef. For smoked sausage, increase salt to 2 lbs per 100 lbs meat and add 3-5% water, or enough to make the sausage easy to handle.

Basic country sausage

10 lbs meat
2 T salt
4 t sage
4 t pepper

or

8 lbs meat
2 T salt
8 t sage
4 t pepper
1 t ground cloves
2 t nutmeg, thyme or allspice

or

10 lbs meat
½ t marjoram
1 t mustard
2 T salt
1 T pepper

Spicier country sausage

10 lbs meat
2 T salt
2½ t dry mustard
5 t pepper
2½ t cloves
5 t cayenne
6½ T sage

or

10 lbs meat
2 T salt
5 t pepper
5 t fennel seed
1 t cayenne
2 t garlic

or

10 lbs meat
2 T salt
5 t marjoram
5 t pepper
1½ t garlic

Basic sausage for quantity

100 lbs meat
1¾ lbs salt
2-4 oz sage
2-4 oz pepper
½ - 1 oz cayenne
½ - 1 oz cloves or 1 oz nutmeg

A BHM Writer's Profile

Dave Duffy is the founder, publisher, and editor of *Backwoods Home Magazine*. He built his own home in a remote area of the Siskiyou Mountains of southern Oregon while launching the magazine, and that home served as *BHM's* first office. Since the home was 10 miles from the nearest electric utility pole, Duffy installed a photovoltaic system to produce sun-generated electricity to run the computers and printers to publish the magazine.

Duffy has since moved the magazine 11.3 miles down the road, across the Oregon border and into northern California, where he is currently building a new office for *BHM* on the shore of a remote mountain lake.

Born in Boston, Duffy spent his first 29 years there, where he worked as a journalist for several daily newspapers. He then moved to Nevada and California, working as a journalist for newspapers and later as a writer and editor for the Department of Defense.

Unhappy with working for others and living near cities, he spent several years of vacations and long weekends building his hideaway in southern Oregon. He eventually fled the rat race for the woods. In 1989 he started *Backwoods Home Magazine* to help others do the same.

Harvesting the blacktail deer

By Vernon Hopkins

Since the time of their discovery along the Columbia River by Lewis and Clark, the small West Coast deer are known as blacktails. The changes in the life history of the blacktails has been less drastic than that of the mule and whitetail deer, while they suffered from the inroads of civilization, they are confined to the Pacific coast area and there are no records of having left this range due to man or predators.

Management

Before game laws were established there was unchecked killing by commercial hide and meat hunters. Fish and Wildlife management began to mature in the late 1800s and early 1900s. The first of many regulations were passed in 1901, limiting the number of deer taken by an individual, between August 14th and October 31st to five. That was farther reduced to two of either sex in 1917 and then to one buck only in 1923.

Since deer are so abundant in the Northwest, their range so wide spread and their proximity to or distance from the settled areas so varied, they are hunted in a wide variety of ways. The types of hunts are often determined largely by game department needs in reducing a herd, scattering concentrations, altering sex ratios by killing bucks or does in certain areas. Consequently, there are many types of deer hunts. There is a general, annual season, where a hunter may go to any part of the state and hunt for the entire season. Permit type hunts are usually for harvesting a certain number of deer from a given area or herd. Where heavy concentrations must be reduced, a "Hunter's choice" season, allowing either sex deer to be harvested, may be opened. To assure an adequate number of breeding-aged bucks, some areas may only allow the taking of 4-point (Western count) or larger bucks.

Safety

During the war years, youngsters who normally would have learned about woodsmanship and hunting safety, could buy no new rifles or ammunition. Many who were in the service learned about shooting for the first time, as a result, there was a terrific build up of the desire to hunt. With war restriction over, there was a virtual flood of old and new deer

hunters. Many brought into the woods their contribution of the country's great tide of carelessness, vandalism and getting things out of their system. Consequently, deer hunting is not as safe as it once was.

Some states require the wearing of a red or orange hat, shirt or jacket. Even where not required by law, unless hunting on private land, if wearing red or orange helps in any way to avoid hunting accidents, then it is worth it. Many states require first time hunters to pass a hunter's safety course before being able to purchase a license.

Preparation

Due to the limited opportunities of shots at deer during a lifetime, experience with a rifle must be done on a target range or safe shooting area. Purchasing a license and carrying a rifle into the woods does not give anyone the right to fire a shot at a living animal. To earn that right, one is obligated to practice enough to develop the skill to be certain of making any reasonable shot presented for a sure, humane kill.

Sight in the rifle yourself, as each person sees a different sight picture. A bore-sighted rifle is not a sighted-in one. Bore-sighting merely puts the first shot on the target, the fine tuning is done by sight adjustment. A minimum accuracy requirement from a shooting rest should be a 4" group at 100 yards. Finely tuned rifles will shoot a 1" group, while some custom made rifles are capable of groups of 1/2" or less.

Scope sighted rifles have become increasingly popular, not only in areas where long shots are common, but also where dense cover limits shooting to short range, so hunters can determine sex of deer sighted in brush or shade. The rifle scope is a poor substitute for binoculars when viewing large areas. It must never be used for observing other hunters. It is a very unnerving experience to step out of a brush patch and see someone looking at you through their scope sighted rifle.

The .30-.30 caliber carbine has probably killed more deer than any other rifle. Due to its limited accurate range, it is not considered an all-around deer rifle. A novice will often purchase the same caliber rifle as their father or a friend uses. The veteran hunter who picks his shots, often passing up what would be a bad shot, may harvest his deer annually with a light caliber that would result in wounded and lost game in the hands of a beginner.

The .243 Winchester and 6mm Remington are considered a minimum caliber for deer. .257 Roberts, .270 Winchester, .280 Remington, .308, 30-06 and 7mm magnum are all excellent calibers.

Do it right

To make clean kills in the field requires some knowledge of the deer's anatomy. What kills is the permanent disruption of vital tissues by the bullet. Regardless of caliber, if a bullet does not expand properly, it is a poor hunting bullet. For handloaders, custom-made hunting bullets, while expensive, are well worth their cost. A solid hit in the heart, lungs, major chest arteries, spinal column or brain will put a deer down in its tracks or within 100 yards or less. The first three listed vital organs are grouped together in the largest part of the body, providing the largest target for a quick kill with the smallest chance for errors.

On a straight broadside opportunity aim at the rear edge of the foreleg and

half way up the chest. If it is not a perfect broadside, look for the foreleg on the far side. If the buck is angling slightly away, shoot at the far shoulder, not the near shoulder. If it is angling sharply away, you may have to slip the bullet into the flank, behind the last rib. This calls for real penetration ability of the bullet, but is a common shot.

All solidly hit deer do not drop in their tracks. With heart and lung hits, a deer will often spring high into the air, then take off at a rapid pace. Unless dirt is seen flying above or below the deer, indicating a miss, examine the escape route for at least 100 yards, often the first blood will be found. If it is bright and frothy, it is a heart or lung hit and there will be a dead deer nearby. Dark blood means a gut shot and the trail should be followed slowly, looking for an opportunity for a finishing shot.

It is every hunter's responsibility to make every effort possible to recover wounded game. Obtain the assistance of a companion, or use a hunting dog on a leash if necessary to follow the animal until found dead or until it can be put down with a finishing shot.

A place to hunt

While most hunting is done on public land or that owned by large timber companies, some large ranches have guided hunts or allow hunting for a fee, others allow limited hunting by permission only. If interested in hunting on posted land, do not show up at daylight on opening morning with rifle in hand and expect permission or stop and ask if it is o.k. to shoot the tame deer standing in the orchard.

Contact the ranch owner several months before opening season, offer to help him on a few weekends in exchange for hunting privileges. Checking and repairing fences is a good way of learning an area. The rancher already knows where the deer can be found. If you are a responsible person who doesn't rut-up his fields, leave gates open or allow your dog to chase his livestock, he may even tell you where the deer are. If you are invited back, it does no harm to present the family with a large, dressed turkey a few days before Thanksgiving, a large box of chocolates for the wife's birthday or perhaps a special kind of rose bush, if she is into growing flowers.

Game habits

Game habits fall into predictable patterns which you must understand to hunt successfully. Deer are constantly using air currents to detect danger from man and predators. There are thermal, prevailing and storm winds. They can be made to work for you just as easily as against you in your hunting, once you understand their tie-in with big game activities.

Thermal winds, as their name implies, are air currents set in motion by temperature changes. From late evening until early morning, the trend is down hill, down valley, always toward lower ground. From an hour or so after day light until evening the flow of thermal winds is uphill. Strong prevailing and storm winds cancel out normal thermal and touches off game reactions, which you must base your hunt on to be successful.

With their normal daily pattern changed, deer will be moving and feeding at all hours of the day during stormy, changeable weather. Due to the constant movement of brush, grass and trees, making it difficult to identify objects and sounds, along with the ever changing air currents, deer become very nervous and spooky.

They like to move nose to the wind, hence the inflow and outflow mornings and evenings, between bedding and feeding areas. Their bedding grounds are usually on high, dense growth ridges and hogbacks, one to three miles from their feeding areas.

Hunting methods

There are three generally accepted methods of hunting deer. The "Still Hunt," "Drive" and "Stalk," with many variations of each. The exact method depending upon the terrain, weather conditions, number of competing hunters and deer population.

Except for the elderly and the handicapped, "Road Hunting" is not an ethical means of hunting. With its rapid means of vacating an area, it is the cause of much vandalism, road sign shooting and spot-lighting deer at night. With the ease of having alcoholic beverages handy, the risk of hunting accidents is greatly increased.

The type of hunting clothing is important, both from the standpoint of comfort and brush noises. Wool or knit clothing with a soft finish does not give off harsh scraping sounds in contact with brush. Avoid any material with a hard, slick surface.

"Still" hunting is usually done by a lone hunter, who starts at feeding grounds at day light, hunting into the thermal wind along deer travel ways. Moving slowly, pausing every few steps to observe terrain for any out-of-place color or shape. Seldom is seen the "postcard" pose of a large buck standing broadside in an open area. A flick of an ear, movement of an antler, a twitch of a tail is often the first sight of a deer. By moving slowly and stopping often, any sounds made are similar to those of deer as they travel, stopping to feed while heading toward the bedding area.

"Drives" are conducted by two or more hunters hunting together. The drivers hunt slowly through dense cover, small canyons and below rim rocks to push deer from their beds to other hunters on stands, which are elevated areas giving a good view of escape routes. Noisy drives are less efficient than quiet ones, as deer easily pin-point the drivers and will often sneak back around them instead of moving on by the waiting hunters.

"Stalks" are similar to "still" hunting except, the hunter works quietly near feeding or bedding areas, often sighting deer out of rifle range, then using any available cover to conceal his approach to within shooting distance.

Except during rutting season, does with fawns and bucks stay in groups by themselves. Hunting areas with lots of small tracks seldom produce mature bucks. Bucks are often found in groups of three to six or more.

Hunting "hot spots"

Deer are creatures of habit, everything they do is for a reason. Find that reason and locating deer becomes more than luck. They bed in areas that provide a breeze covering their back tracks, shelter from heat or storms and escape routes. Locate an area with these conditions and deer are very likely to be there. This season, next season and all seasons to come, when a deer is killed at one of these areas, another will move into it. I personally have taken or passed up bucks in some of their "hot spots" for a period of more than 60 years.

Transportation

For many hunters, their first and only thought is to find and shoot a deer, with no idea of how it is to be transported from hillside to their camp or vehicle. On smooth ground or snow, it may be moved a short distance by dragging. If available, a pack horse is an easy method of transporting a deer, even for miles. Except on private land, it is too dangerous to carry a field-dressed deer in the woods, especially, in the "piggy-back" position where the deer is straddling the hunter's back, with the head tied back. As one hunter remarked on arriving at camp, "Those darned hunters don't care what they shoot at. They shot this one twice while I was carrying it out." When retrieving a deer from the bottom of a steep canyon, it is best to skin it out, taking the hams, shoulders, backstraps, loins and any other meat that can be salvaged. Place this in a heavy canvas sack, inside a burlap sack and attach to a pack board. Antlers are removed from the head and tied bottom-side up on the back of the pack.

Sometimes, it is best to just admire the deer in these situations and save yourself a lot of work by not shooting it.

Field dressing

Once a deer is shot, a novice could learn several important details by watching a veteran hunter field dress it. A body shot deer does not need to be bled by cutting the throat. Three things that will taint the meat are; musk from the musk glands, intestinal juices that through a gutshot or sloppy cleaning have touched the flesh, and blood that has been allowed to clot and petrify between the layers of muscular tissue.

The tarsal glands are located at the hock joints inside the legs and are easily recognized by the brown patches of rough hair which covers them. The metatarsal glands are located on the outside of the hind legs about five or six inches below the hock joint. These glands should be removed by cutting away the entire skin at the glandular area. Grasp skin above the gland and peel it away by cutting and pulling. Clean hands thoroughly before proceeding with the field-dressing. One whiff of these glands will tell you why.

To remove the intestines, the first cut is made from vent to brisket just through the skin. The hide will pull away from the underlying tissue. Pinch up a small amount of this exposed tissue near the hind legs, make a slit in it large enough to insert your fist grasping the knife with its blade pointing up. The body contents are pushed away as a cut is made eye to the brisket. Cut through the diaphragm, reach well forward past lungs and heart and cut the windpipe. By pulling on it the entire body contents can be removed. Save the heart and liver.

Turn deer onto its stomach, grasping antlers and tail, pour out any clotted blood in body cavity. The veteran hunter will field-dress a deer within five minutes or less.

If hung and skinned immediately after being field dressed, any blood shot meat can be trimmed away and bloody tissues cleaned with paper towels before blood clots. Most hunters transport their deer home or to a meat processing plant before being skinned. Only a small percentage of hunters own walk-in coolers in which to "age" their venison. Meat processing plants hang their client's deer for a week or ten days before cutting and wrapping it. For most hunters, the hams may be hung in a cool room away from flies, for one to two weeks to "age." Ribs may be barbecued, backstraps "aged" in the refrigerator, shoulders boned out for stew meat, ground for venison burgers or made into jerky.

The final test of all wild game is at the dinner table. Any time venison must be served with a heavy, spicy sauce to disguise that gamey flavor, somewhere between hill and kitchen, a hunter omitted an essential step in handling it. Δ

Solar panel testing and repair

By Donald Koehler

This article will discuss the testing, repair and troubleshooting of photovoltaic panels. We will look primarily at those panels constructed of circular silicon cells, covered by a transparent, resilient rubber-like coating with fiberglass backing. Some panels are found covered with a plexiglass™ like material, others may be backed with a phenolic-like material. Most of the newer panels I have worked with have a backing of metal or are flexible. Some have been made of a cloth-like material and could be rolled up. I will concentrate on the older panels most likely to show up as surplus. Let's start with some basics.

Tools for testing

If you buy used panels, they should first be tested for output. The tools for testing range from simple to complex. I use a digital voltmeter, an accurate ammeter, and an auto headlamp. A rheostat is used to put a variable load on the panel. It also allows the panel to be sized (determine its power output). A load of some kind is required for any troubleshooting.

Normally a panel is sized by testing for both voltage and current outputs under a full sun. The panel's voltage at no load vs. max load (highest current) is important to know. Power is simply determined by use of the math formula P= I x E where P is power in watts, I is current in amps and E is voltage. It's as simple as P I E.

I use an inexpensive digital voltmeter, a high quality 0-8 amp ammeter, and a rheostat to provide a variable load. Analog (pointer needle) voltmeters are fine, but as I describe troubleshooting later on, you will begin to see the advantage of a digital voltmeter. Radio Shack offers several fine units at low cost, making them a worthwhile investment for even those on a limited budget. Any meter you choose should allow for both AC and DC measurements and have a bail or handle to hold the meter upright. This allows you to read the meter while your hands are full of wires and test leads.

An ammeter can be made from some types of old meter movements, however I prefer the high precision type to allow exact measurement of the current available from the panel under test. Automotive 0-15-0 charge meters are all but worthless since most panels under test are less than 4 or 5 amps. Readable accuracy at these levels is virtually impossible. An external meter shunt will allow the use of a common multimeter (VOM) to measure currents up to many hundreds and in some cases thousands of amps. A shunt basically acts as a very tiny resistor placed in line that allows a voltage drop that is proportional to the current passed through it. In most cases a dedicated 0-8 ampere range meter is most useful for testing and general system use.

The bottom line is that more accurate test equipment equals better data. You make the choice.

The rheostat I use is nothing more than a huge wire wound variable resistor in a vented case. When using a rheostat, initially set the resistance to maximum (highest) resistance, then lower it until the current no longer increases. At this point the voltage across the rheostat, and the current passing through it will give you the actual power produced. With power disconnected the resistance of the rheostat can be measure and recorded for future reference.

When troubleshooting, any kind of load will do. I use an old 12 VDC headlamp.

Troubleshooting

The panel under test should be where you can move it about and see the output leads. At this point you don't need to know the ratings of the panel. Locate the output leads, hopefully marked as "+" and "-" or "Red" and "Black." Prop up the panel or have a friend hold it (much better) and attach the load (head lamp or rheostat) with a set of test clips. Polarity is not important since the load doesn't care. Now attach your voltmeter across the load. In this case polarity does matter. Most digital voltmeters won't be harmed if connected backwards but an analog could be damaged. Be careful. To avoid harm to an analog meter, you can turn the panel away from the sun or set the meter to a high voltage range and look at the direction the needle takes. If it tries to move backwards or beyond zero you have the polarity reversed. Once you have determined polarity and other data, remove the load and record the voltage with no load or as it is commonly known "open circuit voltage."

Note: Ammeters are polarity sensitive. They must be connected so that current goes through them. They become part of the current path. Never connect one across a panel or load. Damage will result.

Troubleshooting a panel is easy but requires some patience on your part. A panel with low output current and usable (high enough to charge a battery, etc) voltage may be usable as is. A panel with low voltage and current will need to be repaired to be usable. To troubleshoot a panel you will need the voltmeter and load described earlier, as well as several long (3 inch) needles, some clip leads and a pair of heavy gloves or ViseGrip pliers. A good magnifying glass will help also.

Connect the sick panel to a load such as the auto headlamp. Connect the negative (black or -) lead of your voltmeter to the panel (observe polarity) and with the panel facing toward you determine which cell is last in the string to be connected to the ground or negative terminal. (Hint: The cells are connected like tiny batteries, some in series strings to increase voltage, and some connected in parallel to increase current. Cells are normally connected together with a foil like conductor.) With your pliers, insert a needle into the transparent covering until the needle just touches the foil conductor at this first cell. Now connect the positive lead from the voltmeter to a needle with a clip lead. Insert needle through covering to make contact with positive side of cell. Expose the panel to the sun and if the cell is good you should see about .6VDC or just over half a volt. Now you can see the value of a digital voltmeter.

If the cell is good continue on up the cell string. As each good cell is added the voltage will rise about .6 volts. You may find an entire cell string that is good with a bad cell in an adjacent string causing trouble. If a bad cell is found place a needle above and below the cell and use a clip lead to jumper around it. Mark all bad cells with a magic marker or any opaque washable marker. Once all bad cells have been marked and jumpered test the panel output. This will give you worst case output assuming the cells or connections cannot be repaired. On panels with plexiglass™ type covering the needle may have to be inserted from the rear of the panel. Be careful not to tear the foil conductor between cells. Use this information and common sense for checking other types of panels.

Damaged panels

Panels with obvious damage, corroded conductors or backs that are delaminating are rarely worth the effort to fix. If the panel has a gunshot hole through a single cell it may be worth the hassle to repair. Some panels may be thermal damaged at the cell interconnects but have good cells. This thermal damage is caused by the covering and backing having different thermal expansion rates that cause a movement that pulls the foil conductors from the cells. Repair in this case is tedious but inexpensive. If you have the patience, older panels can be repaired.

Additional tools and materials will be needed—a pencil eraser (pink), a small piece of fine grit sandpaper, a sharp X-ACTO knife or razor blade, a low wattage soldering iron with low temperature rosin core solder, and small pliers or tweezers. In addition you will need some glue or fingernail polish. To seal work when finished use clear silicon RTV or bath tub caulk. I prefer to work indoors so I use a 100 watt spot lamp as my sun substitute.

Your first step in repairing any panel is to isolate the fault. In a panel with the older resilient transparent covering take a magnifying glass and carefully look at the suspect cell and connections. Is the cell broken. Is the foil conductor lifted from the cell or broken. If the cell is broken (i.e. bullet hole) or has major cracks, it most likely is not repairable. To try and replace with a new cell is really not worth the hassle. If you only have some broken connectors or only minor cell cracks and want to bring the panel back to life, proceed to the next step in the repair process.

Repairing panels

Take a knife and expose the bad joint by making a shallow cut in the surface of the panel about 1/2 inch square. Take the magnifying glass and look closely to ensure the cut surrounds the bad spot. Carefully peel the covering off in small layers. Don't get in a hurry or the covering will come off in chunks and possibly break a good cell. Once the cell edge or foil has been exposed, use the knife edge to scrape the last of the covering away from the edge of the foil. Now you must prepare the bad joint for repair. Take a pencil eraser or small piece of sandpaper and lightly buff the area on both sides of the break. If the foil has lifted from the cell, buff the small silver edge of the cell with the eraser. You are now ready to repair the bad joint. You make repairs by forming a solder bridge over the break. Before you proceed be aware that the solder and panel covering, both produce toxic fumes when they are heated. Ventilate your work area. This is a common hazard in all electronic repair and serves as a warning to those who may not have been told about it in shop class. Now you can shape a small piece of copper wire into a U shape and pre-tin it with solder. Pretinning goes a long way in reducing the time the iron spends in contact with the cell. High temperatures can destroy a cell. Also remember that the backing may also not tolerate high heat. Apply a small amount of solder to the tip of your iron. Just apply enough to form a bead that will not drip with the iron held vertically, with the tip down. Place the U-shaped piece of wire on the area to be bridged with a pair of tweezers and apply the iron. Just as soon as you see solder flowing, remove the iron. Once the solder cools examine the bridge with the magniying glass. If the solder did not bridge the gap apply another small bead of solder. Do not hold the iron on the work area any longer than it takes to flow the solder. Wait for the area to cool completely before applying the iron a second time. You can now test the repair with the voltmeter as the panel is exposed to the sun or bright light. If the cell repair is working you can proceed to the next step.

Once the repaired area has cooled completely, seal it with fingernail polish or Crazy glue. Just a light coat will do. When this has dried, apply the silicon RTV to fill in the hole in the panel covering. Bead the RTV just above the covering and once it starts to firm up, smooth off even with the top of the panel. The fingernail polish was first applied to prevent corrosion of the conductor by the mild acid the RTV excretes. You now should have a panel that will give you good service and usable power. Δ

Trusses—low-cost marvels to roof over most large spaces

By Martin Harris

When you strip away all the frills, building construction is nothing more than enclosing a volume of space to create a micro-climate for human activity. You can call it architecture if you like, thus enlisting some notions of aesthetic superiority, but that doesn't change the basic function. You can fudge the issue by arguing that some buildings are very nearly solid (the Pyramids, for example) and have no internal space, or you can argue that monumental gates and colonnades which create no micro-climate are architecture; and maybe they are. But then, since there's no sharp line between black and white, you could argue that those two colors don't exist either.

A better way to roof

I mention all this because this column is about something the construction industry (or architecture, if you prefer) has not been able to do very often over the last 10,000 years—come up with a new and better way of roofing over a space. It took thousands of years for builders to move from throwing tree-trunks over two walls to arches and domes. It took thousands more before steel and concrete were used to create, in effect, bigger and better tree-trunks. Only in the last few hundred years has the industry come up with the roof truss (a collection of little pieces so assembled as to span a large space) and only in the last score of years have trusses become available to the mass market at extraordinarily low cost. It's all a little remarkable, from an historic point of view, but it's now so commonplace that we take it for granted.

Wood roof trusses to span anywhere from 30 to 60 feet (and even more, with specialized designs) can now be bought from lumber yards at prices between $1 and $2 per lineal foot. That's pretty good, considering that old-style 30-foot roof beams are hard to come by these days and, if available, cost more than one can afford and weigh more than one can lift.

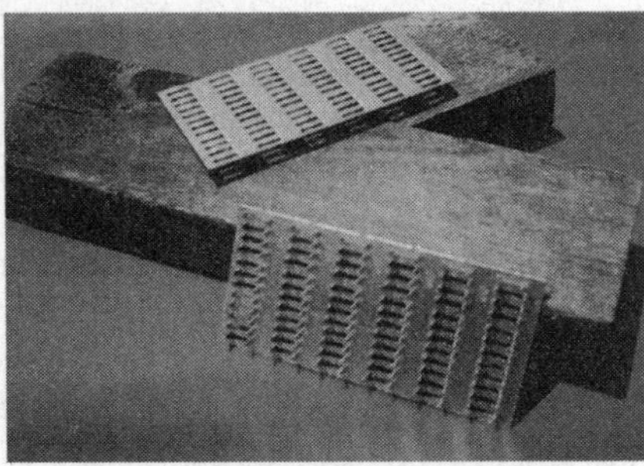

Figure 1. The critical element of modern wood truss construction is the joint connector. Here we see how a typical connector is placed to span the connection between two pieces of the truss frame. In the foreground, a second connector is placed to show how the teeth are stamped out of the base metal.

Widely used

These wood-engineering marvels are so cost-effective that they've pretty well claimed the market for roofing of low-cost housing, agricultural structures, and commercial/industrial buildings where fire resistance isn't a building code requirement. Maybe wood trusses aren't used in every new structure in one of those categories, but they are definitely considered. If they're not used, it's only because other considerations outweigh cost-effectiveness—considerations like aesthetics, fire codes, unusually short spans and the like.

And that's my point in this article. Wood trusses may be the engineering innovation that comes along only once in every few thousand years, but they still have their drawbacks and cautions. Here's a brief review about what's good, and what's not so good, about wood trusses.

Extraordinarily strong

Let's start with a brief description of what the modern light-weight wood truss is. It comes in a variety of overall shapes—pitched or flat roof designs, sloped or flat internal ceiling profiles. It can span between supporting walls or cantilever out beyond them. It's made, almost always, of ordinary softwood 2x4's and 2x6's, held together at the joints with a variety of wood and/or metal fasteners. It's very delicate when not in its intended upright position, and can easily be ruined by clumsy field-erection practices. The critical nature of the joints is such that they're almost never assembled on site, but rather in a manufacturing plant and then trucked to their final destination. They're surprisingly light-weight, fragile in appearance, but engineered with such sophistication that they're extraordinarily strong once erected.

In this respect, you might say that they're a product of the computer age. Yes, engineers have known how to calculate the design stresses for a hundred years or so, and larger building

Figure 2. This photo of a connector in place shows how its multiple teeth firmly grip both pieces of the truss frame.

Figure 3. Here's a site-built truss. The joints are made up with short wood scabs and nails. Is it properly engineered? Probably not. Will it hold up? Probably yes, until there's a major snowstorm.

projects have used custom truss designs for several hundred years, going back to when enormous wood frame trusses were intuitively designed by skilled master-builders. Both England and New England countrysides are filled with examples. But custom engineering is expensive—too expensive for most budget-driven residential or light commercial construction. The computer changed all that.

Computer designed

Today, in almost all parts of the country, one can go to a local lumberyard with a building design on the back of an envelope, watch the technician keyboard all the critical dimensions—spans, snow loads, roof pitch, and so on into the software formula—and, a few seconds later, watch the printer spit out a complete roof truss design with every piece of lumber identified as to size, every joint identified as to strength, and a complete cost estimate to boot.

If you can't choose between two alternate designs, ask the computer to do both. It's usually free. The lumberyard or truss-assembly plant provides this service in the expectation of selling trusses that wouldn't be sold if the potential buyer had to go out and buy expensive engineering services for their design.

If the readily-available computer design program is the key to the recent remarkable success of the wood truss industry, that's only part of the story. It's the part most visible to the typical truss buyer (a do-it-yourself homeowner or a building contractor, for example) but there's another part that's almost as important and not so visible. That's the behind-the-scenes engineering and testing which has gone into joint fastener design.

Saves wood & money

Wood trusses are an economic success precisely because they're tightly engineered to get every last bit of strength out of each wood component, thus keeping wood quantities down, overall weight down, and price down. Success in this end of the engineering task creates a problem at the other end—fastening the pieces together. The tension and compression loads at the end of each stick are far more than can be handled with a few nails or bolts. Special fasteners had to be invented.

Figure 4. This set of trusses was salvaged from a demolished building and re-used. Unfortunately, they don't fit the new, narrower, building. The double plate girder at the top of the wall picks up the roof load, not at the truss corner joint, but where there's only the bottom chord to transfer the load. If the owner's lucky, he'll get away with this error.

After experimenting with plywood gusset plates and various combinations of glue and nails or screws, the industry turned to a new invention—a metal plate punch-stamped so as to create hundreds of little mini-nails.

Using a hydraulic press, a truss-builder simply assembles the wood components in a jig, places the right-size fastener over the joint between several pieces, and brings down a hydraulic press to force the tiny steel fingers into the several pieces of wood.

Using this system, a truss-builder meets the joint strength requirement. An equivalent number of nails or bolts would reduce the wood to toothpicks.

. . . but it's not all roses

Now let's look at possible drawbacks to the light-weight wood truss system, starting with this same fastener system, because the fastener system is also, if you wish, a drawback.

Because these multi-prong fasteners must be pressed into the wood truss components using heavy hydraulic equipment, truss manufacturing can't very well be an on-site activity. A builder's only other choice is to bring heavy-duty presses to the site or to adopt some other, potentially more labor-intensive and maybe less reliable joint system, such as plywood gussets, construction adhesive, and bolts.

Transportation

The need for factory manufacture raises the next drawback. Once assembled, these trusses are big. Sometimes, in fact, they're too big to truck. Take, for example, a 30-foot truss with an 8:12 double roof pitch. Assembled, this truss will be 10 feet from base to ridge. That's too wide to lay flat on a flat-bed trailer and too high to stand up on anything other than a lowboy.

These dimensions, in turn, explain why truss haulers use special trailers in which trusses are placed ridge down, their points very nearly scraping the ground. Some trusses are too big to use even this approach successfully. In such cases manufacturers build a flat-top truss and furnish a small triangle cap-truss with it, to be assembled on site.

Figure 5. This truss (from Figure 4) is held onto the building frame by only four nails (two show in this photo). Not enough! Hurricane clips should be used.

Blocks attic space

This idea, making each truss out of several components, brings us, in a way, to the next drawback—conventional truss design creates a large volume of unusable attic space. Instead of the traditional rafter-frame, clear-span attic, trusses (spaced, usually, two feet on center) create a jungle-gym of wood framing of no possible utility.

This isn't a particularly difficult problem. If the potential second floor under-the-roof space is big enough to be useable, it's big enough to be framed with sets of three trusses—a right-angle on the left, a right angle, mirror-image, on the right, and a cap truss which bridges the two and thus creates a useable space. If there's a price for this, it's design rather than monetary—the need to support the right-angle sides of the two "base" trusses with a column system from the floor below.

Using a couple of extra internal columns has an advantage with respect to another drawback of truss construction. With long spans and heavy roof snow loads, it's easy for the structural loads thus created at the bearing points of the truss (the two outside ends, usually) to exceed the allowable crushing strength of the wood fibers in the supporting framing. If there are no internal columns, the designer needs to provide for bearing blocks or steel plates to help distribute the loads which the long trusses concentrate.

This isn't exactly rocket science engineering, but it is essential, and it's surprising how many truss-type buildings go up without the designers worrying about this feature of the design. (It's the same as pole-barn builders who unwittingly allow the load per pole to exceed the bearing capacity of the subsoil it sits in.)

Not good looking?

With this brief list, we run out of real drawbacks to wood truss construction and can continue only by listing drawbacks which are aesthetic or imaginary rather than engineering or financial.

First among these is the somewhat valid argument that wood trusses are not real good-looking. That's true. Because they're so tightly engineered, wood trusses have a spindly, almost flimsy appearance. If, when you ask your builder to use trusses, you expect

Figure 6. The owner tried to strengthen this truss joint with more nails. He succeeded only in damaging it further.

something out of an English manor hall, you're going to be unpleasantly surprised. You'll see, not heavy timber and massive metal joint connections, but skinny pieces of dimensional lumber with stamped metal plates here and there.

Figure 7. Modern trusses are too spindly to look good if left exposed.

Appearance solutions

Not to worry, however. If exposed overhead trusses are your design wish, you can get that image by simply bunching two or more of the spindly standard types together, perhaps covering them with wood trim to add bulk and hide their true nature.

Combining two results in a heavier double truss every four feet (the usual spacing being two feet). You'll have to forget $^5/_8$"plywood roof decking and go instead to the $1^1/_8$" product to safely span the four-foot gap you've created. If you bunch three or four trusses together, the spacing rises to six or eight feet, and you'll have to use cross-purlins to help the plywood deck stay up. That's OK. It's more structure overhead to admire.

Fire safe

If aesthetic inadequacy is one charge levelled at conventional wood trusses, at least it's somewhat true. Without foundation of any sort is the other charge—that these trusses are more vulnerable to fire than steel. Not so.

These light-weight trusses need not be made of wood. They can be made of light-gauge steel framing, of the sort increasingly used in housing construction and available in sizes that

Figure 8. Old-timers, in contrast, built their trusses out of massive hand-hewn timbers. This Vermont example is 150 years old.

duplicate the usual studs and joists of traditional carpentry. And, of course, steel is far stronger than wood: the elements of the truss can be lighter and the joints more easily assembled. But such light steel is far from fire-proof; it will soften and collapse because of heat long before wood will ignite and burn enough to lose a comparable amount of strength. That's why such steel-framed buildings aren't considered fire-proof. They're called non-combustible, and to achieve some degree of fire-resistance that a building code might require, they have to be covered with protective insulation. So much for the fire-safety mythology surrounding steel construction.

But steel has an advantage that recommends it to do-it-yourself builders. Because the basic material is so much stronger than wood, joints are far easier to execute. In fact, trusses can be fabricated under engineering control, the pieces properly sized and punched for connectors, dismantled, shipped as a compact bundle, and re-assembled by the owner using little more than erector set tools. That's not something you can do with wood trusses, and it makes a lot of difference in terms of product usefulness.

All these options make the basic light-weight truss concept one that's hard for builders to ignore. Depending on your preferences, you can go for low-cost utility, final appearance, factory or on-site fabrication, custom exterior slopes and interior cross-member arrangement. That ought to be enough to recommend it to even the choosiest of commercial or do-it-yourself builders. Δ

A BHM Writer's Profile

Kristin Rogers

Kristin Rogers lives in her backwoods home where she cooks, gardens, writes, and generally domesticates. When she's not cooking, Rogers can usually be found at the local farmer's market or selling her wares at the "Gourmet Gardener" outlet.

Rogers has written several articles for *Backwoods Home Magazine* on a variety of topics, including her struggles with Child Protective Services. She also writes a gourmet gardening column for a local newspaper.

Planning to make a living in the country

By Martin Harris

It's Friday afternoon in Boston. We're at the Northern Artery, gateway to rural New England, watching thousands of urban workers flee the city for the weekend at their up-country farmsteads.

Fifty-two times a year, the same frantic scene plays out at cities across America. This country may be 98% urban, but not out of pure choice. Poll after poll shows that, given their druthers and a solution to the economic problem, most Americans would rather be small-towners or rural dwellers. Some recent books on the subject, Beyond the Suburbs by John Hedbers is one, marshall statistics to show that increasing numbers of us are succeeding at doing just that.

A new option

My grandfather never had that privilege. He was a mill-worker in a time when just providing the basics of life took almost all of his disposable income. He never dreamed of a day when wealth, transport systems, and work options would be such that "the weekend exodus" would be commonplace. We take for granted, now, that urbanites can humanize their workaday life by means of a weekend respite a little closer to nature.

More than aesthetics is at stake. To this middle-class component of our society, the base in the country provides economic support as well. The economic benefit is mostly home-grown food, but also a range of goods and services from safe schools to fuelwood, from furnishings to wholesome associations. It's a wedge to solving the economic problem as well, not only through avoided costs—food, fuel, a lower housing investment—but through direct revenues such as crafts, part-time farming produce, services to neighbors.

Many Americans are taking the next logical step. As Hedbers' book illustrates and as readers of *Backwoods Home* already know, it a logical progression from the inner suburbs of pre-WWII America to the outer suburbs of the '50's and '60's, then to the long-commute exurbs of the '70's and '80's, finally to the truly rural (beyond-the-suburbs) settlement pattern emerging today. It's gotten little publicity, but in huge numbers Americans are moving to the country.

No help wanted

It's gotten no government support, either. Unlike earlier phases of the escape from the cities, made possible by such government programs as mortgage insurance and highway-building, today's escapees are almost anti-government. With high-tech communications, their own skills, and a few acres, they want to be free of government regulations and corporate hierarchies, physically lethal neighborhoods and intellectually lethal schools. It's no accident that those who choose to live beyond the suburbs frequently choose to be self-employed, to home-school their children, to keep an old pick-up truck in their driveway, and not to object when their neighbor does the same.

Back to the future

Actually, this almost unreported demographic movement is in the mainstream of American history. Only relatively recently did full-time commercial farming become a dominant rural activity, its demands excluding all non-farm or even part-time activities. For most of our history, in contrast, our Jeffersonian ideal was the part-time farmer/artisan, with one foot in town, economically and philosophically speaking, and the other in the country. It's taken a while, but we seem to be returning to that lost ideal.

Non-farm income needed

If you're like most of us, you'll need income from both urban and rural sources to create your rural economic foundation. Traditional rural occupations such as farming, ranching, and logging are barely profitable for people who are multi-generational experts. Don't think that you as an urban escapee can make a living off the land better than the folks you came to settle amongst. Don't burn that urban bridge until you're sure you won't need it.

Maybe you can, as an individual entrepreneur, sell your urban skill to small-town or rural clients. Maybe, with a little re-training, you can acquire a related urban skill of value to your neighbors. Maybe, with a little luck, you can find a new niche in offering a non-farm product or service to your community or region. For starters, think of those services you, as a newcomer, need; and recognize that in most of rural America there are now lots of newcomers.

I say non-farm because, in the country, just about everyone's a farmer or a part-time farmer. It may be part of the newcomer's idealized life-style, but it's also the basis of the old-timers' survival system. Understandably, therefore, it's difficult to produce income from an activity that people were already doing for themselves even before you arrived.

A BHM Writer's Profile

Lorne S. Inglehart

Lorne S. Inglehart spent his childhood in Bannockburn, Ontario, where his father owned and operated a lumber camp and mill. Later he moved to Texas, where he worked as an electrician. None of his poems were published during his lifetime. "A Fish Story" appeared in *Backwoods Home Magazine* Jan/Feb 1993. Mostly, he was a teller of stories. One of his favorites was "The Cremation of Sam McGee" by Robert W. Service. He died in 1978 leaving a hole in my heart.

—Jo Mason (his daughter)

Possibilities

Don't expect to earn a living from commercial agriculture. Don't even get into commercial agriculture without talking to real farmers first. You're probably fantasizing from images and not from realities.

Do consider "niche" agriculture (the selling of specialized, relatively high-value products to a limited market). Well done, your enterprise will at least cover its own costs. Skillfully done, it may earn a profit in a real, bookkeeping sense.

Don't think that you can live outside the money economy by raising your own food and cutting your own firewood. There are still taxes and health insurance, car registrations and clothing purchases.

Do consider reducing your dependence on the money economy. Realize that the food you grow and sell to yourself is the most profitable agriculture you'll undertake, replacing after-tax earnings you'd otherwise use to put inferior products on your family's table.

Don't count on significant income from conventional part-time farming, either. Unless you have friends back in town, unusual neighbors who don't garden, adjacent farmers who don't hay, and so on, you'll find that your crops are ready just when everyone else's are.

Do try to differentiate your part-time farming from the pack. With a greenhouse you can have crops for market when others don't. With organic gardening you can reach the health-conscious consumer. With some crops you can become identified as a particular producer of a particular product, not just another anonymous source for some standard commodity.

Don't count on significant income from leasing your land to real farmers. While there's demand for rental cropland in some areas, there's also the inexorable economics of commercial farming. Renters can't afford much more than your own per-acre expense of ownership, and most likely aren't going to be able to lime and fertilize land they don't own unless they have a long-term agreement. If your land's been rented out before, it may already have been pretty well mined out of nutrients, and will command less because of its lowered productivity.

Do consider very carefully field crops as a cash crop. There is the oats and oat-straw market for the horsey set; there is hay for unlanded livestock raisers and short-landed farmers; there is corn for the beef and dairy producers; there's a seed-crop demand for everything from triticale to trefoil. Be sure you have a market before you invest your money in equipment and your time in the field.

Don't overlook pick-your-own in everything from strawberries to Christmas trees, but gauge your local competition very carefully before you plunge.

Don't forget to look beyond farming, full-time or part-time, for the supplementary income you'll need. If it was easy to earn money in agriculture, America wouldn't be losing its farmers so fast.

Do consider barter and other non-cash exchanges with your neighbors for goods and services. We can't legally advise you to join the underground economy, but you get the idea.

Don't over-invest in one option. Keep options open, stay flexible, and be quick to adapt to changing markets and demands.

Do advertise—not in the grating, commercial, sense, but in a low key. Let your neighbors know what you have to offer. Join networks. Put your logo on the door of your pick-up. Cultivate word-of-mouth—it will bring in 90% of your jobs. Forget that awful urban practice of leaving unhappy customers behind because there were plenty more to choose from. In the country, good word spreads fast, and the bad word spreads even faster.

Be introspective. Think about what you're doing and search for improvement. When you're perfect, then sit back and relax.

Be a brain-picker. Get ideas and suggestions whenever and wherever you can.

Sources to contact

For agriculture, see what local growers are doing, both in livestock and produce. Try local farmers' markets. Try local small-town and nearby city buyers' co-operatives. If you're aggressive, try local grocery stores and restaurants. You might even want to try the government—county Extension Agents, the USDA Office for Small-Scale Agriculture, Room 635, Hamilton Building, Washington, DC, 20250. Try the State agricultural office. Keep in mind that it was New Hampshire's Steve Taylor who coined the phrase "niche agriculture." Try your area organic farming association. Try forward contracting anything from beef to eggs with your former urban neighbors.

For home industry, join a local home-industry network, if there is one. Some even publish and distribute membership directories to all area households. All sorts of desk jobs, even workbench jobs and kitchen jobs, can be a home industry. Be imaginative, find a need, and meet it.

For employment, talk to local entrepreneurs who may need some part-time help. Talk to State government. They're frequently looking for people to service a given region. You may end up as a fire-safety inspector or a jobs counsellor, working out of your home to service the local area. Talk to your local community college or private schools. They're always looking for good instructors. Probably it won't pay to talk to your local public schools. They guard the gates with all sorts of teacher-certification requirements. Even some more distant company, if your skills are rare enough, may take you on as a remote employee via computer and modem.

For entrepreneurship, the same basic rule prevails. Identify a need or a market niche. Tool up and meet it. Don't chase every new whim—folks who got radon-detection franchises are now a little sorry. But be alert to real needs. It would be nice to have a mini-backhoe or dozer in a community where no one else has those tools. Get yourself qualified as a kitchen design consultant or a desktop publisher. Get yourself certified as an electrician or a wetlands expert, as an on-site sewage disposal design technician or a property appraiser.

You can do it

Can you make a living in the country? Yes. It almost surely won't be conventional farming, but it will most probably be some mix of niche agriculture and a non-farm "urban" occupation. You may not make as much per hour as you did at Trans-Global Amalgamated Widget, but you won't be dumped the year before retirement, you'll get to keep more of what you earn, and you'll get to talk back to your boss—you. Thomas Jefferson will be proud of you. Δ

A BHM Writer's Profile

Country living is probably the biggest influence in Darlene Campbell's life. She recalls helping to raise calves and rabbits with her father, and as a youngster wanted to become a veterinarian. She began writing in elementary school, where she had a serial published in the school newspaper. An early marriage and two tours in Japan put veterinary medicine out of the picture, but her desire to write continued.

Her homesteading career began in the desert foothills of Arizona, where she lived with her husband and children without utilities. A generator, gas lights, and gas refrigerators provided the comforts of life. Water was hauled in a tanker and gravity-fed to the house. She raised goats, pigs, rabbits, calves, chickens, turkeys, horses, and Samoyed dogs.

In 1979, she moved with her family to eastern Oklahoma, where she grew a garden large enough to can 300 quarts of vegetables a season, raised rabbits, and learned to tan hides. She helped her husband develop their farm into a certified tree farm by clearing brush and thinning overgrown stands of pine and cedar.

She devoted more time to her writing and got a job with the local newspaper as the features editor. She was associate editor for *Country Christian Magazine*. She has written many articles and has sold two books to a publisher. Today Darlene writes about raising animals and cooking, and she publishes a newsletter, *The Christian Homesteader*, from her home. She has eight children, fourteen grandchildren, and two great-grandchildren.

Just for kids — a backwoods kitchen garden

By Lucy Shober

In pioneer days, many families kept a "kitchen garden." Right outside the back door, they grew their own herbs, salad greens and other vegetables for use at meal times.

Did you ever stop to think about your own kitchen garden? Right on the shelves of your cupboard are enough ingredients to create a botanical spectacle that will keep your family green till spring! Take this magazine to the kitchen with you right now and peruse the shelves for some planting material. Got any potatoes? An onion or two? How about the dry bean department? Now raid the refrigerator; some carrots and a turnip or two will round out the supply list.

With these kitchen ingredients, you can keep your family supplied with fresh greens all winter long. Just borrow a sunny window and follow the directions below. Happy gardening!

Fresh onion greens

First you will need a glass that tapers inward toward the bottom. (see picture) Take an onion that will fit half way down into the glass and place it root side down into the glass.

Notice the point in the glass where the root sits, and fill it with water to that point. Don't let the water cover the whole onion, or it will rot! (Everyone in the family will be mad at you for the smell that will happen.) Soon your onion will produce its long graceful root system. At the top of the bulb a green sprout should appear. Now it's time to change the water in your glass, and to continue to change it about every three days. When the onion greens grow to be about six inches long, you may begin to snip them off to use as a salad topping. One onion might produce several stalks, so if you "plant" several onions, then you will have a long lasting supply of fresh produce—even in December!

Start a potato garden

This is a great project to take along to school. First you have to raid the pantry. Find the most wrinkled looking spud in the sack. It should also have nice long sprouts growing out of it. (The kind of tater that looks like mom must have bought it the day you were born!) The reason that you want a wrinkled potato, is that the flesh of the spud is the food for the baby plant. If the sprouts have started growing, the potato skin will wrinkle as its insides are being digested by the new

plant being born. Now scrounge around for a tall sided bucket or can, punch holes into the bottom, and fill it with about five inches of dirt. Lay the potato into the soil and cover it about two inches deep. Treat it as you would any houseplant, only whenever you see the leaves peeping through the dirt, cover them with a little more soil. Do this until you've reached the top of the can, then just water the plant and keep it in a sunny window. The lush green leaves will be a delight, but when you get tired of tending them, just pour the whole pot out—but keep your "eyes" open! What happened to that wrinkled old spud? Invite your best friend over for supper that night, because there is nothing better than fresh picked potatoes! (Perhaps a pinch of onion greens on top would be nice.)

Greenbeangreens?

You might have to visit a health food store for this project, but it's well worth the trip. Find some mung or adzuki beans, and cover the bottom of a jar with them. Rinse them daily with water, but don't let them sit in it. In about a week, you will have a miniature jungle of tangled sprouted beans for salads and sandwiches—even potato toppings! (You can add all sorts of flavor to these greens, try sprouting raw hulled sunflower or radish seeds for a peppery taste. For a nutty flavor add some buckwheat or even clover seed. Just be sure that your seed hasn't been treated with pesticides and is a food grade product. Yum!

Add zip to salads

Most everyone has had a carrot top garden at one time or another, but did you ever try chopping up those frilly greens to perk up a salad? How about turnip green tops for an earthy zest? Now quit wrinkling your nose! They are really a treat in mid-winter, especially if you grow them yourself! Slice the tops from some carrots and put them in a saucer of water green side up. For the turnips, poke the plump roots with three toothpicks and sit them (pointed side down) onto the rim of a water filled glass. As the greens of these plants become frilly and curly, snip them into your salad bowl.

If you enjoy your kitchen garden, then experiment with the spice shelf too. Lots of spices are simply tasty seeds that might "grow on you" if given a chance. Good luck! Δ

Hairy the Fireplace Potatapillar

You could use everything grown in your kitchen garden to create a lovable monster. Hairy sizzles and hisses as he bakes in his nest of hot coals at the bottom of your fireplace. When he's cooked, he is the tastiest varmint that ever graced a plate! Cut out Hairy's recipe card and trace its shape onto several pieces of paper. Cut these out, then copy or paste any other fun recipes on to them to start your own recipe collection.

Hairy Potatapillar

Take one large potato and place it on an eight by eight inch piece of thick aluminum foil. Slice the potato almost all the way to the bottom at half inch intervals along its whole length. Into each slit slip a chunk of butter and a slice or two of carrot. (You could use the bottoms of the ones from your kitchen garden.) Throw a few extra slices along the top of the potato. Now fold the foil tightly around the potato, and put it into the hot coals of your fireplace (of course you need adult help for this!) After about thirty minutes turn the potato over. When the other side has cooked for twenty or thirty minutes, have your adult check for doneness by poking the tater with a fork. If it is soft inside, it's done. Carefully unwrap Hairy (who's not hairy yet!) and remove several of the carrots from his top. Now take your sprouts and give hairy his top knot. Take the toothpicks and first stab a carrot, then slip the onion leaf over the pick. Poke these into Hairy's front end for antennae and eyes. Put Hairy into a bed of fresh turnip greens for his lunch, and then you lunch on him!

Apples Galore

By Anne Westbrook Dominick

Apples. Everyone has favorites. I have two. One is the Granny Smith which I'm told won't grow to ripening in southern New Hampshire where I live; still, I have a couple in for the try. My other is the Baldwin. It ripens here but, unfortunately, bears only every other year. But no matter, there are many, many apples to be grown (or bought if the right market is hit at the right time) and enjoyed.

Cortlands, McIntoshes, Gravensteins, Northern Spies, Winesaps, Liberties, R.I. Greenings, Pippins, Jonathans, Pound Sweets, and a myraid of Deliciouses are just a smidgen of the varieties available.

What a person uses in the following recipes is really a matter of individual taste. When I mention a kind of apple it's only because either the person who gave me the recipe designated that variety or it's a little personal tradition that when I have that apple I make that dish. Enough said and on with some eatings.

Apples and pork go together, no question about that. The following recipe was given to me by Fred Zinn, the head chef at Hinsdayle Greyhound Park where the restaurant boasts gourmet status far beyond the track.

Pork Normandy

Ingredients:

- 8 thin slices of pork tenderloin
- a bit of flour
- a bit of butter
- 2 teaspoons minced shallots
- 1 cup sliced mushrooms
- 1 Granny Smith apple, peeled, cored, and sliced
- 3 to 4 ounces of applejack brandy
- 6 ounces heavy cream

Preparation:

Lightly coat the pork with the flour and saute at medium high heat in melted butter until golden brown. Add the shallots, mushrooms and apple and saute briefly. Add the brandy, which may or may not flambe. (Be careful: step back away from the pan as you pour in the brandy. Whether or not it flambes depends on many things; if it does all that happens is it burns off the alcohol more quickly.) Simmer until the brandy is reduced by about half—three to five minutes. Stir in the cream and cook until it reaches the desired thickness. Serve from the pan when done. Serves four.

Apples are traditional with ducks and geese as well as pork and one sure-fire way to bring them together is in stuffings. There are about as many stuffings as there are cooks. The following is the one I always start with and add extras when the mood or supply hits me.

Apple stuffing

Ingredients:

- ½ cup minced onions
- 2 cups apples cored and diced (not peeled)
- 4 cups lightly packed soft bread crumbs
- salt and pepper to taste
- 2 teaspoons poultry seasoning
- 1 tablespoon lemon juice
- 1 or 2 tablespoons sugar if the apples are very tart
- 2 tablespoons melted butter or margarine
- ¼ cup apple juice

Preparation:

In a bowl mix all ingredients. This is enough to stuff a duck or capon or pork shoulder. Cut in half to stuff two Cornish game hens, standard chicken, or four pork chops; double it for a turkey.

Apples really can dress up any meat. The above recipe called for lemon juice. So does the next one and quite a few of the others. That's because lemon juice on sliced apples prevents them from browning. In the following, any apple can be used, but I happen to prefer an apple that has a distinct flavor and is a bit on the sweet side. Ham's own dominating flavor needs a softening counter taste to make the mix interesting.

Apple ham salad

Ingredients:

4 McIntosh or Liberty apples, cored and diced (not peeled)
1 tablespoon lemon juice
2 cups diced cooked ham
2/3 cup sliced celery
½ cup crumbled blue cheese
¼ cup vegetable oil
2 tablespoons vinegar

Preparation:

In a bowl mix the first five ingredients. Thoroughly mix the oil and vinegar and add to apple ham mix. Serves four.

It's hard to think about apple salads and not think of Waldorf Salad. My mother made it frequently and we all loved it.

Waldorf salad

Ingredients:

2 cups apples, cored and diced (not peeled)
1 tablespoon lemon juice
1 tablespoon sugar
salt to taste
1 cup sliced celery
½ cup diced walnuts
½ cup raisins
½ cup mayonnaise

Preparation:

In a bowl mix the apples and lemon juice. Add all the remaining ingredients. Serves 4.

Just as apples can enhance meats, they do the same for most vegetables. A salad I make all winter follows. Colors are fun to play with in this one. Sometimes cabbage and apples can both be red, other times green, and yet other times the colors can be mixed.

Apple slaw

Ingredients:

4 cups shredded cabbage
2 large apples, cored and diced (not peeled)
1 small onion, minced
2 tablespoons lemon juice
½ cup yogurt or sour cream
¼ cup mayonnaise
1 tablespoon sugar

Preparation:

In a bowl combine the first four ingredients. Mix the last three ingredients until well mixed and add to the salad. Serves six.

The apples and vegetable combinations don't need to be in salads. Some are mighty good hot side-dishes like this one.

Apples and sweet potatoes

Ingredients:

3 apples, peeled, cored and sliced
1 tablespoon lemon juice
1½ pounds sweet potatoes, peeled and sliced
¼ cup apple juice, cider or vinegar
1 tablespoon melted butter or margarine

Preparation:

Mix apples and lemon juice. In a baking dish place a layer of sweet potatoes then a layer of apples. Continue until apples and sweet potatoes are finished. Pour in the apple liquid and dribble melted shortening over the top. Cover casserole and bake in a 350° oven for one hour. Uncover and bake another 15 minutes. Serves four to six.

Every fall on harvest night, the night I'm so worried about frost that I bring in the winter squash, I make the following. It can be a meal by itself.

Apple stuffed winter squash

Ingredients:

2 acorn or medium sized butternut squashes
1 tablespoon butter or margarine
3 cups apples peeled, cored and diced
½ cup onion, diced
2 cups cottage cheese
¾ cup grated cheddar cheese
¼ cup lemon juice
¼ teaspoon cinnamon

Preparation:

Cut squash in half, remove the seeds and bake cut side down in a 350° oven until just tender, about 30 minutes. Melt butter or margarine in frying pan and saute apples and onion until the onion is transparent. In a bowl, mix the apples and onion with the last four ingredients. Fill squash cavities with the apple mix, return to baking pan and cover with foil. Bake another 20 minutes in a 350° oven. Serves four.

I grew up in the apple orchard section of New York State and never had apple dumplings until my sister moved to Pennsylvania and learned it there. I fell in love with them the first time Emily Baker made them for me. They're now a harvest time treat, although they're really just as good made with apples in storage.

Apple dumpling

Ingredients:

1 pie crust (see apple pie recipe below)
6 apples, peeled, cored, and quartered
cinnamon
sugar
6 tablespoons butter
milk
½ cup brown sugar (optional)
½ cup butter (optional)

Preparation:

Roll out pie crust and cut into six squares big enough to encase the apples. Sprinkle apples with sugar and cinnamon. On each square put an apple's quarters back together, top each with a tablespoon of butter, and bring up corners of dough to enclose the apple. Seal edges with a little milk and pinch together. Lower into boiling water, cover tightly, and cook 15 minutes. The dumplings can be steamed instead for 30 minutes. Or for variety can be baked in 350° oven until dough is browned, about 45 minutes. For a rich treat, cream brown sugar and butter and dab on hot dumplings when served.

Of course apple pie is the standard by which all other apple desserts are rated.

Apple pie

Ingredients for pie crust:

Pie crust:
1½ cups flour
½ teaspoon salt
½ cup shortening at room temperature
3 tablespoons water

Preparation:

Sift flour and salt into a bowl. Cut in shortening with a fork or pastry blender until the mix is like coarse grain. Mix in water one tablespoon at a time—it may need less or more—until the dough holds together. Form dough into two balls to be rolled into bottom and top crusts. (Handle the dough as little as possible to ensure a tender flaky crust.)

Ingredients for apple mix:

6 to 8 apples, peeled, cored, and sliced
½ to ⅔ cup sugar, depending on tartness of apple and taste
2 tablespoons flour or 1 tablespoon cornstarch
¾ teaspoon cinnamon
¼ teaspoon nutmeg
1 tablespoon butter
1 tablespoon lemon juice

Preparation:

In a bowl, mix the first five ingredients and place in the lower pie crust. Dot with butter and sprinkle with lemon juice. Cover with the upper pie crust, seal the top and bottom around the edge, and slit the top in a few places to release steam. Bake in 450° oven for 10 minutes. Reduce temperature to 350° and bake 45 minutes more. Serve hot or cold.

Called apple butter, it is really a lot more like jelly—but not overbearingly sweet as many are. It's mighty good on a warm biscuit in the middle of winter.

Apple butter

Ingredients:

5 pounds apples, stems removed and quartered
2 cups cider or cider vinegar
brown sugar
2 teaspoons cinnamon
½ teaspoon allspice
½ teaspoon ground cloves
½ teaspoon nutmeg

Preparation:

Put apples and cider or cider vinegar in pan and cook slowly until apples are soft. Put apples through food mill or sieve. Measure the pulp and add ½ to ⅔ cup sugar, depending on taste, for each cup. Add spices and cook over low heat, stirring constantly until the mixture sheets from a spoon or until a small quantity dropped on a plate does not form a liquid rim around the edge. Ladle into hot sterilized jars and seal immediately. Makes about 3 pints. Δ

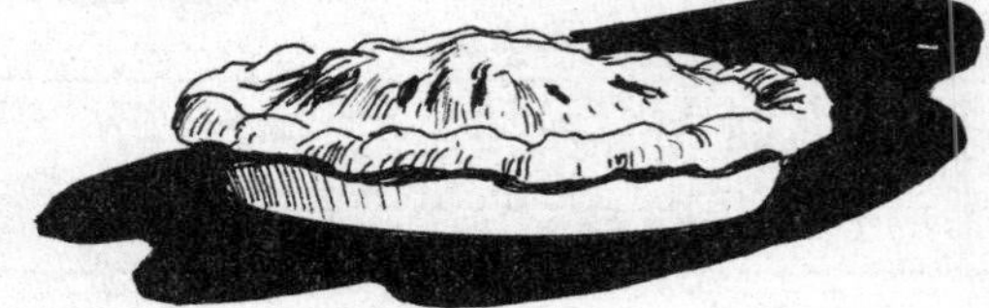

Nuclear superstition

By Petr Beckmann

(This article will make informative reading for people interested in the ongoing debate in this magazine about food irradiation. For background you may want to read Russ Davis' article, "The sensible way to store and use food," in Issue No. 17, since that article started the debate. Relevant letters were printed in Issue No. 19 (page 81), Issue No. 20 (page 82), and Issue No. 21 (page 83). —Editor)

Several tens of thousands of years ago, man conquered fire and subjugated it to his needs.

Do you know why this was such an epoch-making event? Not because of the heat in itself, nor because of any space heating. The northern latitudes with their cruel winters were uninhabitable without fire. Before fire was tamed, man lived in Mesopotamia, Africa, China, Central America, and other tropical and semi-tropical places; what he did not need was more heat.

No, the taming of fire had a very different significance: it made man the only animal able to jump out of its original place in the food chain. Insects eat plants, and small birds eat insects, and birds of prey eat small birds.

Man gathered berries, but only of a limited range. They had to be digestible, they had to be non-poisonous, they had to be soft enough to chew, void of thorns and void of parasites, or he died before the wolves and bears ate him.

Fire changed all that. It softened inedible food, it killed its parasites, and enormously widened the range of food available to man. (It also enabled him to move to regions previously prohibited by severe winters.)

About 10,000 years ago, the second great food revolution took place: the agricultural revolution. No longer at the mercy of nature's charity, man learned to grow his own food and to husband his own animals.

But this food was subject to spoilage. To this day in the Third World about one third of the harvest falls victim to rodents, insects, rot, mold, and other forms of spoilage.

In the advanced countries they learned how to preserve food, sort of. First, they "salted it away," which made it, well, very salty. Even before the advent of refrigerators, people knew that food lasts longer in the cold, and they would break up the ice during the spring melt and transport it to caves where it lasted through the summer. Electric refrigeration, when it came, was imperfect, took up space and consumed much energy. To ship fruit and vegetables in refrigerator railroad trucks from California and Florida to the rest of the country was a triumph, but an imperfect one: tomatoes are shipped before they are quite ripe, left to "ripen" during the trip and at the store. But if you grow your own tomatoes to full ripeness, you know the difference. As for canning, I don't have to tell you that food out of a can is not the same as fresh food.

Chemical preservation has its drawbacks, too. Nitrates used in sausages, for example, are carcinogens, not terribly dangerous ones (for it is the dose that makes the poison), but still formally carcinogens. More important, chemical preservatives are ineffective against dangerous parasites such as the salmonella bacterium in chicken, the trichinella worm in pork, and several others.

Virtually all types of food spoilage, rot, mold, fermentation, etc., are due to microorganisms. So is food poisoning, including the most common, salmonellosis (70%), and the most dreaded, botulism.

Some 30 years ago a most wonderful way of killing these microbes without affecting the food was developed: irradiation. A strong dose of ionizing radiation (very similar to X-rays) will kill the microbes without significantly affecting the surroundings in which they live. At present, the most common application is not food irradiation, but sterilization of disposable medical equipment. More than half of it, including devices permanently inserted in a patient's body, is sterilized this way.

The irradiated target cannot possibly become radioactive, at least not more than to begin with, for all foods and most other objects are slightly radioactive anyway. There is a very good physical reason why irradiation by gamma rays cannot induce radioactivity in the target. I will not bore you with that reason; instead, I will just ask whether you can imagine that physicians would allow devices to bc inserted in bleeding wounds or other parts of the bodies of their patients if they were significantly radioactive.

What irradiation does to food is no less than wondrous. Irradiated strawberries will last for more than two weeks at 38° F without molding; potatoes will not sprout for weeks even if not refrigerated; fruit like peaches and mangoes can be harvested only after it has fully ripened, and only then is it shipped without danger of spoilage; and endless other applications. In general, the interval during which food stays unspoiled is prolonged from days to weeks, sometimes without refrigeration. Virtually all advanced countries have approved and are using food irradiation, though they approve and regulate each food group separately.

But perhaps even more important, food irradiation protects you from disease. A significant fraction of raw chicken is infested with salmonella bacteria, and a significant fraction of raw pork is infested with microscopic trichinella worms (up to 30% in both cases, as random samples have shown). It is left to you to kill them by the high temperatures of frying, cooking, roasting etc., all the way through the meat.

What if you don't succeed? Here is the answer: 33 million Americans a year become ill due to microbial contamination of their food. Some 4,000 (mainly very young and very old) die from severe salmonellosis. Trichinosis is a rare disease, and "only" some 100 Americans die from it every year, though the number is rising, mainly due to the recent popularity of underdone "pink pork." But irradiated poultry and pork are salmonella-free and trichinella-free even when raw.

Unfortunately, the salmonella bacterium and the trichinella worm have powerful friends: organizations such as Food & Water, Inc., and other well-heeled groups who hate technology and want to de-industrialize America. They work with lies and, much worse, with half-truths, better denoted as three-quarter-lies.

An example of an outright (and fantastic) lie is the claim that the purpose of food irradiation is to let the nuclear industry get rid of its wastes. In fact, practically all irradiation is now performed by cobalt 60, which is specially made for the purpose in Canada, whence it is imported to U.S. irradiation plants.

Now for some half-truths, or rather three-quarter lies by which the Luddites try to dupe you.

They make the ominous claim that the radioactive doses to which foods are exposed are lethal. Darn right they are. So is the heat in a baker's oven lethal. What does that have to do with the wholesomeness of bread after it has been baked in it?

They claim that chemical changes take place in foods during irradiation, and some of them might be dangerous. Yes, some very slight chemical changes do take place, in particular, a very small amount of so-called radiolytes appear in some foods. What they don't tell you is that these same radiolytes are present in non-irradiated foods, where they are produced by conventional processing such as cooking. Not a single substance absent from other foods has ever been detected in irradiated food

We cannot know, they direly warn, whether one day food irradia- tion will not reveal hidden hazards after all. But neither can we know this for cooking, frying, baking, canning, knitting or playing bridge, for the simple reason that it is impossible to prove a negative.

However, food irradiation has been approved not only by the developed countries' special agencies and the World Health Organization, but by the world's most conservative and infuriatingly cautious health watcher, the U.S. Food and Drug Administration (FDA). It has only permitted the irradiation of poultry in 1992, though among the many tests was one, completed in 1985, in which 600,000 lbs. of irradiated chicken meat was fed to several generations of test mice, hamsters, rats, rabbits, and dogs. The FDA is so overly—indeed, irresponsibly—careful that it literally lets Americans die for lack of drugs that have been approved for years in Europe, but the FDA is still testing them. If the FDA has approved food irradiation (of wheat, wheat flour, potatoes, fresh fruit and vegetables, spices, pork, and poultry, with further groups to be approved), I don't think you need be overly worried over this point.

Whom should you believe, me or the Food & Water Friends of Salmonella?

Neither.

Truth is not found by choosing whom to parrot; it is found by comparing statements to all available facts. You cannot irradiate food yourself, but you can go to the library and read both sides of the issue and search for the holes that one side conceals and ignores. I am not worried that you will miss them; and you will have found the truth, not parroted its shadowy imitation.

Try Food Irradiation, Academic Press, New York, 1986; or send $3 for Irradiated Foods, American Council on Science and Health, 1995 Broadway, 18th fl., New York, NY 10023; look for more in the subject catalog, and ask the librarian to help you.

There is, however, one point that is more sinister than any physical, chemical or medical considerations, and it is one that you can test yourself immediately.

All irradiated food in the U.S. is labeled as such by the "radura," an international symbol identifying it. As an American you can buy it if you want to, and you don't have to if you don't. It is not an election where the majority decides for everybody, including the dissident minority, because there can bc only one U.S. president and only one winning answer to a referendum. In contrast, buying irradiated food is not only your personal decision, but it does not affect anyone but you or your family. Suppose the various Knights of Salmonella were right in all their dire warnings, why would they seek to influence a decision that does not affect them?

Because they are after political power. After political power of the kind that has drenched this century in blood: the coercive power that knows only two variants of activity: whatever is not forbidden is compulsory.

"Thou shalt eat what I eat" is the present battle cry of the superstition mongers; and more coercion, more uniformity, more totalitarianism will follow.

Don't let yourself be duped.

Stand up for truth and reject the totalitarian superstition mongers.

Protect the health of your children and your own freedom.

(Petr Beckmann writes for Access to Energy, Box 2298, Boulder, CO 80306. A 12-issues- per-year subscription is $25.) Δ

PREPARING FOR WINTER

November/December 1993
No. 24
$3.50 U.S.
$4.50 Canada

Backwoods Home magazine

... a practical journal of self reliance!

The First Thanksgiving

Drying Food
Wind Power
Cabin Fever
Muffin Magic

Note from the publisher

Dave Duffy

Survey results

Our survey results from last issue have been tabulated, and they show that *BHM* readers are intelligent, interesting, dynamic, wholesome, and all around swell people. Christopher Maxwell has a detailed account on page 8.

3 for 2 offer a big hit

Our 3 for 2 offer that began last issue and will run through December 31 of this year is a major success. Basically the offer revolves around three items: a one-year subscription to the magazine, the Best of the First Two Years book, and The Third Year book. Buy two of these items and we'll give you the third free. Use any combination you like. E.G.: buy two subscriptions and get one of the books free, or buy two books and get another book free, or buy two subscriptions and get a third free. We'll mail the items to whoever you designate, and we'll enclose a gift card if you tell us to. The back cover of this issue has the details, and you can use the order form on page 98. The minimum amount you must enclose is $36.90, which will cover the cost of the three items and the postage. Canadians or other foreign, of course, must enclose more for postage.

It is no heavy handed sales pitch when I emphasize to you that this is a very good offer. These books sell like crazy anyway, but we figured we could get a ton of them into the hands of people who could profit from them if we gave one of them away. And that's what is happening.

One of the books or a subscription would make a humdinger of a Christmas or Chanukah gift. It's a one-time shot you have, because on December 31 the offer will end.

Radio show

We're definitely on line to do a radio show over WWCR, a shortwave station broadcasting around the world. Our slot – Saturday night about 10:30 p.m. Central time – will broadcast mainly to North America. By the time you read this we should be on the air. Tune your shortwave dial to 7.435 mhz. It'll be a half hour show to begin with called *"Backwoods Home Magazine's* Self Reliance Show," or something like that. If we can't do it right we'll discontinue it; otherwise we'll quickly expand to an hour.

Fourth Vita-Mix winner

Marvin D. Cook of Talkeetna, Alaska is our fourth Vita-Mix winner. He was selected in a random drawing from among our paid subscribers. We'll pick two more winners, one for each of the next two issues.

Log home industry spoiled

Those of you who worry that we are selling out to the advertisers might notice that no log home manufacturers advertise in *BHM* any more. Our log home special issue (Issue No. 22) keeps generating hate mail from the log home industry. A newspaper article reported that we "slammed" log homes. Fans of log homes write insulting letters about Martin Harris, questioning his capability as an architect.

The funny thing is, we didn't say log homes aren't good houses. We had several articles where people who live in log homes expressed their satisfaction and pleasure with their homes, some articles about what to look for in materials, kits, and accessories, and an article about how to solve the problems in log construction, which has its good points and its drawbacks like every other form of construction. In short, the type of information our readers expect from *BHM*.

That wasn't enough for the manufacturers of log homes. Anything less than unrestrained, gushing praise of log homes is considered an insult to them. They want every article to say, "Log homes are wonderful, log homes are beautiful, log homes are absolutely perfect in every way."

We aren't unfamiliar with advertisers who want favorable coverage of their product, but we got more demands for favorable articles from log home companies than we have had in four years of printing *BHM*. Some of them just don't understand that we work for the readers, not for the advertisers.

We still don't have anything against log homes. If you like them, that's reason enough to buy or build one. They look great, and if designed and built right they can be among the most durable and low maintenance wood structures made. But if hiding their few inherent problems is the only way we can get log home advertisers, we'll just have to live without them. Δ

Dave Duffy

My View

Flushing toilets with other people's money

It's the season of the spendy politician, and it seems that everyone in government, from the federal level on down to the town level, is turning to tax increases as a way to solve funding problems in recession-ridden economies. It's a solution that has always been favored over frugal spending by politicians, but it's a solution that is almost always wrong.

Tax schemes never get presented for what they are, namely a way to increase the influence of government over our lives. Instead they are portrayed as investments in the future – investments in education, infrastructure, jobs, or whatever it takes to convince you to fork over your dough and give up some of your personal liberty to a bureaucrat. When the "investment" angle doesn't work, politicians usually try and convince the bulk of the voters that "they" won't be the ones to pay for or suffer from the tax.

All the devious strategies to convince you to pay more taxes can be dissected into their various strategical elements, so as a tax payer you may find it enlightening, possibly alarming, to see how it all works. To dissect a tax scheme designed to dupe you, you'll probably have to go no further than your own hometown.

We found ours in our hometown – Ashland, Oregon, a beautiful city of about 17,000 that is dependent, in part, on the tourists who flock here to see its excellent eight-month-long Shakespearean Theatre. Here's how our local politicians pulled off their latest tax scheme:

It started earlier this year when the city council decided that it was necessary to improve the city's sewer system. A tax scheme always starts with a necessary need. Council members decided that the tax scheme to be presented to the citizens should be simple and painless, so they opted to add a 1% meals tax at local restaurants, putting the burden of the new tax, they assured voters, on the shoulders of tourists and people who can afford to eat out (the rich?).

So they put the tax measure on the ballot in a special city election. The tax, of course, had a not-so-well publicized provision that permitted council members, if their future wisdom so dictated, to raise it as high as 5%.

The tax was the main business of a special election, and the public debate for and against it was fairly furious, with all city councilors but one extolling its virtues. The lone dissenter, the astute Pat Acklin, observed "I don't see why guests in our community should subsidize our toilet flushing."

Despite the debate, as in all special elections only a fraction of the voters turned out so only a fraction of the citizenry got to pass a tax (55% to 45%) on everybody else. The restaurant owners who would be forced to collect the tax howled of course, but there were too few of them so they were ignored.

So all went well for the politicians, as it usually does in these special elections "designed" to do something "necessary and good" for the community. But then something unexpected happened: Soon after the tax was passed, and nearly two months before it was to take effect, the city council voted to raise the 1% meals tax to its maximum of 5%.

But the usual good timing of the politician was way off this time. This decision caught their constituencies by surprise. In fact, when the sleepy citizens of Ashland read their newspapers the morning after the council raised the tax, many concluded that they had been duped. And as if in one voice, the voters roared, "That's not what we voted for."

The city council's arrogance not only caused residents to support a meals tax recall measure that will go on yet another election ballot in November, but it put the entire meals tax scheme under the public microscope. People wanted to know what happened. Well here, in a nutshell, is a dissection of the Ashland City Council meals tax into its various and devious strategies. See if it bears any resemblance to a tax scheme targeted for you.

First, the city council presented a benefit to the city's residents that they said residents wouldn't have to pay for. That should have been a tip-off. A "something for nothing" promise should make all consumers run like hell, but it is a ploy used regularly by politicians at all levels of government.

Second, the city council singled out a segment of their own community – restaurant owners – that was too small a group to resist a tax forced on them. "Divide and rule," said Machiavelli, and politicians do it on a regular basis.

Third, the city council made the tax small enough (1%) to be palatable by disguising the real size of the tax (5%) in a clause that could be executed later. Craftier politicians would have waited a year before increasing the tax.

Fourth, the council presented the tax in a special election. There are so many special elections in small communities that residents get weary of going to them, so the supporters of whatever is up for a vote – in this case a tax – have a better chance to march out their vote. It's simply a method of diluting the vote to your own advantage. Kid stuff, right?

The Ashland City Council did everything according to the politician's slick little unpublished book, except they got too antsy and arrogant and accidentally blew their cover.

In November, Ashland voters have a chance to repeal the meals tax and find another way to finance the flushing of their toilets. I'm sure the tourists who already contribute mightily to the local economy will be grateful. So will their neighbors, the restaurant owners.

Ashland voters' victimization by its own elected officials should be a lesson to us all, because what happened in Ashland is what is happening all over America today – politicians are convincing more and more voters to force taxes on other people to pay for government services only a few have decided are necessary. Experience teaches us that more taxes translates into nothing other than more government, and by gosh haven't we learned yet that more government is not the solution, but the cause of most of our problems.

The people of Ashland have a smelly mess on their hands, but it isn't in their toilets. Three cheers for a community that can admit it made a mistake and head right back to the ballot box to correct it. More of us should wake up to the smell that awoke the residents of Ashland. Δ

Dave Duffy

Drying food—a low cost, easy way to preserve your harvest

By Carla Emery

Sun drying is the oldest type of food preservation. Nowadays it is the least common form. Too bad, because drying is a cheap, easy way to preserve, and everybody loves the results.

You can dry fruits, vegetables, meats, fish, herbs, berries, edible flowers, nuts, and eggs. You can make jerked meats, vegetable chips (corn, potato, zucchini...), and much more.

Food drying is something you can do year round. Most of it of course happens during harvest, but you can also dehydrate leftover food of every sort (remove and discard all fat) and then save it to toss into some later stew, soup, casserole, or munch for a snack. You can dry such odd things as peas, sliced carrots, even leftover spaghetti casserole!

You can also dry gleanings from your root cellar storage that you've salvaged, such as half a fruit or vegetable when the other half was spoiled and went to the animals or compost. Low-wattage dehydrators work well on electricity from alternative power sources and are still cheaper than canning. Dried foods require less space and weigh less than foods preserved in any other manner.

Dried foods are preserved because of their very low moisture content, so if in doubt, it's better to get them too dry rather than leave them too moist. The moisture content of a well-dried food varies with the food, as little as 5% for leafy vegetables, or up to 25 % for acid fruits.

Most microscopic beasties won't grow in a low-moisture environment. The beasties aren't dead, however, just waiting. Research on drying and dehydrators is going forward at a marvelous speed, so your drying results can be better all the time. Recent problems with canning lids, shortages of jars, and threats to public power have really impressed on me the importance of knowing how and being equipped to dry.

Friends who fed me their home-dried foods eliminated my last shred of prejudice against dried vegetables. They were delicious!

Small, thin, leafy herbs are the easiest foods to dry. Apples, apricots, cherries, and coconut are the easiest fruits. Easy vegetables are: mature kidney, mongo, pinto, red, black, and soy beans; green lentils; chili peppers; parsley; celery tops; mature sugar, cow, chick, pigeon, or other peas; sweet corn; sweet potatoes; and onions.

Drying info and supplies

Get the latest Extension bulletins on home drying, probably free or at least cheap. Dry It-You'll Like It by Gen MacManiman, (Dry It!, P.O. Box 546, Fall City, WA 98024) $6.95, is a fun drying book, the first of them and still a good one! Gen, now 77 and still going strong, offers her book, her personal line of Living Foods Dehydrators (also the first on the dryer market and constantly improving), plans to build your own dryer, and a basic catalog (free) of home drying supplies.

From Gen's catalog you can order heat-fused polypropylene tray screening that is non-stick, absolutely food-safe, and easy to clean. You can get dryer thermometers, an electric food grinder specially adapted to powder dried herbs and vegetables for making your own instant soups and teas (powdered dried vegetables and meats are also nutritious added to pet food or baked goods). She also sells guar gum, a natural, excellent thickener for fruit leathers. Her growbox attachment turns the dryer into a little hothouse for germinating seeds or sprouts. She offers teflon sheeting, a permanent, non-stick, wipe-clean, base for drying fruit leathers on.

Other good books on drying: Home Food Dehydration, the Hows, Whats, and Whys by Emma Wheeler, 1974, 160 pages, attempts to put all the pertinent facts about drying under one cover. (Wheeler Enterprises, 7855 S. 114th, Seattle, WA 98178.) Home Food Dehydrating: Economical "Do-It-Yourself" Methods for Preserving, Storing and Cooking is a 151-page book that is mostly recipes using dried foods—also a good and useful thing. (Horizon Publishers, P.O. Box 490, 55 East 300 South, Bountiful, UT 84010.)

Pre-drying treatments

Dips for fruits: Fruits are not blanched. But some people believe that the larger, lighter ones may be improved by dipping in ascorbic acid, salt water, fruit juice, or honey solution before drying. The fruit dips are basically for apples, pears, apricots, peaches, and such light-colored fruits that turn brown if exposed to air, an oxidation reaction. Mere change of color would be no big deal, but when oxidation happens it is also damaging flavor and, truly significant, destroying some of the Vitamins C and A. Most dark-colored fruits like figs, prunes, grapes, don't oxidize. For the ones that do, here are harmless (as compared to sulfuring) ways to prevent or minimize it.

Salt water dip: To keep fruits from darkening, you can slice or chop them directly into a gallon of water that has 6 T. flaked pickling salt in it. Soak no more than 5 minutes so it doesn't get mushy with water content or too salty tasting.

Ascorbic acid dip: "Ascorbic acid" is a form of Vitamin C. To make it, crush 5 one-gram Vitamin C tablets, or add 1 or 2 T. ascorbic acid crystals or powder, to 1 quart lukewarm water. Slice or chop your fruit right into this solution. Remove the fruit from its soaking before it gets soggy. Drain and dry.

Commercial fruit preservative: This is a powdered mixture of L-scorbate, sugar, and maybe also citric acid. Just follow directions on package.

Blanching: A hot water "dip" for vegetables. Vegetables usually are blanched, but they don't have to be. Blanching is accomplished by cutting up and steaming or boiling the food briefly before it is dried, same as with vegetables to be frozen. The reasons for blanching are: 1) to reduce the risk of spoiling of low-acid vegetables; 2) to halt enzyme action, especially the enzyme that causes first ripening, then over-ripening; 3) to tenderize them. However, drying slows down the enzyme action anyway. Those who research in this field say that all vegetables will retain better flavor, color, and possibly also nutrition, if they are blanched before drying, except for chili peppers, onions, celery, and garlic, which should not be blanched. But some home dryers disagree and don't blanch. Farmers' Bulletin 841, put out by the USDA in 1917, agrees: "Blanching of vegetables is considered desirable by some housekeepers, but it is not strictly essential to successful drying."

To steam blanch: You need a heavy pot, or double boiler, that has a tight-fitting lid, plus a wire basket that can be suspended over about 2" of hard-boiling water. The chopped or sliced vegetable in the wire basket shouldn't be more than 2 or 2 1/2 inches deep. The reason you don't want to put too much food in is so the steam flow will stay strong enough for all the food to blanch properly.

Put it in over the boiling water. Put the lid on tight. If you don't have a steamer, a sieve hanging in the pan over the boiling water will do, or a bag with the food in it suspended over the edge of the pan.

The important thing is to keep the food out of the boiling water below so that you are actually steaming it and not boiling it. Keep a lid on up above so your steam isn't getting away. Leave it there for the number of minutes suggested for steam blanching. Or just estimate: leave them in there until they are heated clear through and wilted, or until it looks translucent almost clear to the center when cut, tender but not completely cooked.

To boiling-water blanch: Start out with the kettle, but with lots more water in it. Put the food in the wire basket, but in this case you dunk the basket right down until the vegetable is all covered by the boiling water. Start counting as soon as the water starts boiling again and leave it in there for the recommended amount of time. You can use the same water over and over.

After blanching: Then pull out, drain, chill by plunging into ice water, or under cold running water, and drain again. Proceed to dry.

To sulfur or not: The "sulfur" used for this purpose isn't usually pure sulfur. It's one or another preservative compound containing sulfur that prevents darkening of light-colored fruits and repels insects. I don't give a hoot or a howl what color things are, dark skins are just as good as light ones, and vice versa. I think that whatever insects would consider inedible probably wouldn't be healthy for my kids either. I hate using chemicals unnecessarily, and unsulfured tastes much better to me and digests easier.

Drying sulfur fumes are injurious. If you sulfur, you must do your sulfuring outside and avoid breathing the fumes! But I'm not even going to tell you how to do it. That 1917 Farmers' Bulletin doesn't say one word in its 29 pages of small print about sulfur. The people who wrote it had never heard of the practice and they were drying tons of food every year.

Gerald Lehman, supplier of food dryers to the Amish gets the last word here: "There is no need for chemicals or additives. Dried and properly stored dried foods will last as much as five years. Simply slice, dry, place in jar, and store in cool, dark area."

Detailed step-by-step drying instructions

1. Gather your vegetables in the garden. Harvest at the peak of flavor, better while slightly immature than overripe, unless you're making leather.

You can make fruit leather out of overripe fruits, but you're better off to raise chickens and pigs on the overripe vegetables. Get started on the drying as soon after picking the harvest as possible. For sun dried foods, start early in the morning. Then you've got all that first day to get them started drying. Start your drying early in the morning of a day that promises to be dry and hot.

2. Wash off the dirt if there is any. Scrub if necessary. Dry off.

3. Do the necessary shelling, peeling, slicing, or what not. Vegetables to be dried are generally first cut up very thin unless they are already small like peas. Slice about 1/4" thick, a little thicker for peaches, tomatoes, and zucchini. An important rule of drying is that smaller pieces give you faster drying and better color and taste. If you slice peaches rather than merely halve and pit them, it takes more time at the start, but it saves time and struggle later on. Same goes for your other foods, especially vegetables.

Because vegetables are low in acid and spoil easier, they need to be cut thinner than fruits to dry quickly enough before any microscopic beasties can get going.

On the other hand, you've got a point of diminishing return on the thin slicing. Carrots, zucchini, pumpkin, sweet potatoes, squash, and turnips thinly sliced and dried turn into wonderful snack chips, good plain, good with a dip. But if you slice them too thin, some foods like tomatoes and zucchini tend to stick to the tray. (Unless you're using Gen's wonderful non-stick liners.) But then again, almost everything sticks to some degree or other, and that cures itself as they continue drying.

4. The next step is blanching. For vegetables only, especially if the vegetables are old, or have been gathered too long, or were grown under very dry conditions.

5. Now you spread your vegetables or fruit on the drying trays, one layer only in thickness. Except for leafy stuff like parsley or herbs which can be loosely mounded a couple inches deep.

Don't dry very moist foods together with almost-dry ones. Dry strong-flavored (or odored) foods by themselves. Set each fruit separately (not touching) with air space between it and the next one. When drying look-alike herbs and fruit leathers, label them before drying.

6. Now set the trays out in the sun or in your attic or in your solar or oven or electric drying situation. Dry at a low temperature for better flavor and color, safer storage, and no risk of burning.

The drying temperature must be high enough that the food will dry before it spoils, but low enough that the food doesn't cook or get hard on the outside and be damp inside. Within those limits, the faster a food dries, the better its final quality will be.

7. Turn the fruit often enough to keep it from sticking. Turn big-hunk kinds of food two or three times a day at least to speed drying and prevent sticking. Stir food that is spread in small pieces. Using a dehydrator, move most-nearly-dry foods to the bottom trays and put new and moist ones into the top. As foods shrink, you can consolidate to save tray space.

8. Fairly dry food may last a month or two. For longer storage, it needs to be completely dry. Vegetables should be dried until hard, so hard they are brittle and will shatter when struck by a hammer, or dried slices break when bent. Fruits are dry enough when between leathery and brittle. Some fruits such as figs, cherries, raisins, and dates, never stop being sticky.

Sun drying

You can dry either by sunshine, in an oven, or in a dryer ("dehydrator"). I prefer sunshine drying over oven drying. Taste is good, no expense, and there's no risk of burning or scorching. Sun drying is the basic commercial method too. Most apricots, raisins, figs, peaches, etc., your grocery store dried fruits, were sun dried.

Climate for sun drying: Your climate matters a lot. I live in a region where when fruit is in season, the days are very dry and very hot. Hot days when the sun shines brightly all day long are perfect for sun drying. So outdoor drying is easy here in northern Idaho and in the dry mid-West and Southwest. It's harder in the rainy, humid coastal Northwest.

Bugs: If you are drying early in the season before the flies and wasps are about, you can simply put the food out on trays. Sun drying works best if the wasps aren't around yet.

They eat meat and fruit especially. Fruit set out to dry not only attracts hoardes of them, which is dangerous for the children, but they actually will eat it up themselves. Cherries and apricots usually come before the wasps, so I can just lay them out plain with at most a porous cloth over the top. They'll go ahead and dry underneath it. Once the bugs are about, you must dry under a cheesecloth or nylon net, using something to raise it so that there's no chance of it blowing onto the food, especially into a sticky leather. Or else put the food outside in a screened bug-proof setup.

Flies are the other possible problem. A fly now can mean a maggot later in some types of food, especially meats. That's the real advantage of drying inside the house like in a sunny window spot, or up in your attic which is probably warm, dry, and bug free. Or in the rear window of your car with the windows rolled down only about 1/2 inch.

You can make a screened-in sun dryer by starting with something wooden on four legs with a vaguely boxlike structure. Insects are the biggest threat to purely open-air drying. Or else dry indoors in the oven or in a dehydrator.

Secrets of sun drying

1. Don't dry outdoors where there is traffic pollution because of possible lead contamination of your food.
2. Don't ever lay food to dry directly on galvanized screen. It contains zinc and cadmium and will contaminate food.
3. Fruits can be dried nicely at 85° F., or higher, but a temperature of 100° F. or more is best for drying vegetables.
4. Always dry in full sun in a place where the air is moving as freely as possible.
5. Begin your drying with the trays covered with cheesecloth or some gauzy cloth that is propped up to keep it from touching the fruit in order to protect it from insects.
6. Fruits can get dry enough to store in a couple days. Vegetables may need as long as 3 or 4 days. It usually takes about 3 times as long to sun dry as to accomplish it in a dehydrator or oven.
7. Researchers have discovered that if you keep the drying process continuous by using an artificial drying system during the night, your food dries much faster and there is better quality, less loss of nutrition and less risk of mold.
8. At the end of each day, turn your drying pieces and take your trays inside the house for the night to avoid dew. Set them out again the next sunny morning until the drying is done.
9. If insect eggs may have been laid on your food, "pasteurize" before storing.

Drying in an oven or dehydrator

If you have an oven, you have a drier. Actually, if you even have a very hot, dry area such as in your attic, your car's rear window, around your heater or cook stove, you have a good drying environment. But oven drying, unlike sun drying, means you have to be on hand and keep an eye on what's going on. Using a dehydrator is more like sun drying in that it's usually foolproof and you can walk away and forget about it and it will do fine without you.

Temperature: The biggest problem with oven drying is that it often is hard to get a steady enough heat at a low enough temperature. The ideal drying temperature is 95° F. to 120° F. From 130° up to 150° F. is manageable, but not desirable. Over 150° F. is potentially disastrous.

Judging Temperature: Some ovens don't have a thermometer. If you don't have an oven thermometer, you can buy a portable one and put it in there, toward the rear of your top tray is best. If you can't get an oven thermometer, you can judge temperature by feel. The food should feel cooler than the air in the oven. If it feels warmer to you, you either need less heat or the oven door should be open wider.

Air circulation: This is also a problem in the oven if you have a tight-fitting door. You want the air around the food to absorb moisture from it, and then carry it away. So prop the oven door open at least a half inch. Gas ovens need to be open at least eight inches or more. Leave an oven door open at least four to eight inches. It helps to put a fan at one side of the open door to drive the air through the oven. Occasionally change the fan placement from one side of the oven door to the other while drying.

Food placement: Don't overload trays, and don't make your trays solid wall to wall or the air can't circulate properly. The food nearest the heat will scorch and that farthest from it won't dry. Every couple hours or so swap tray positions around in the oven and stir small pieces of food on the tray itself to get it more evenly distributed and get places where wetness is hiding exposed to the heat. Turn over large chunks.

Done? Oven drying is much quicker than attic, on-a-string, or outside drying. Vegetables may be done in as little as 5 to 12 hours, fruits in 6 hours or so.

Homemade drying trays and outdoor dryer: You can make portable things to dry food on by making square (more or less) frames of soft lumber. Across the top staple or thumbtack a single thickness of curtain netting or some other strong but very porous cloth or Gen's plastic screening, but not a metal screen since most metal screens contain elements that will badly contaminate your food.

It will resemble a window screen with a wooden frame. If you make your frame at least a couple inches smaller than the inside of your oven, you can also use these trays for oven drying.

If you have a problem with the cloth sagging reinforce it underneath with string stretched from side to side. These screens are then best set up on posts or something outside so that air circulates through the mesh and all around your fruit.

Inside the house, you can arrange a stack with 3 or 4 inches between each tray over the rear of your wood cook stove or heater and dry food that way too.

Homemade dehydrator: There are plans for making an electrical dehydator in Dry It, You'll Like It, and in Gen's catalog. Or you can get a set by writing Bulletin Mailing Service, Industrial Building, Oregon State University, Corvallis, OR 97331-4202, and asking for Extension Circular #855, "How to Build a Portable Electric Food Dehydrator."

Ready-made dehydrators: The most adaptable and best dryer on the market is probably Gen's Living Foods Dehydrator, available from 3023-362nd SE, Fall City, WA 98024, (206) 222-5587.

There are also solar models that use a curved collector panel so there's no need to move the unit. Dryers of a previous generation were designed to sit on a woodburning stove. You might still be able to find an antique one, or a modern one made on the oldtime principle.

And there are many, many more options. Have fun looking over the possibilities and deciding which one is best for your family!

Fruit leathers

Another way to dry fruit, or certain vegetables, is to leather them. Leathers are lightweight, high in nutrition, and they store and pack easily for hikes and camping. They are a good way to make use of overripe fruits, and are good healthful "candy" for the kids.

Apricots and peaches make the nicest leathers, but you can make good ones out of pears, plums, rhubarb, unseeded berries, and many other foods or combinations of foods.

Leather from somewhat overripe fruit: All the rule books say to start with only the best produce when preserving, but fruit leather is a blessed exception to that. If fruit is too ripe or bruised but short of rotten you can still make wonderful leather of it. In fact, slightly overripe fruit actually makes a sweeter, better-tasting leather! You just wash it, cut out the worst, mash, and dry. Bananas, even almost-brown, make fine fruit leather.

Steps to "leather" making

1. For any fruit, basically you just rinse it off, grind or force it through a sieve, mash it with a potato masher, or put it through a food mill or blender. Peels left on make for a disagreeably grainy leather, especially pear peelings. Take pits and seeds out at whatever stage is appropriate. Too many seeds left in can really spoil a leather.

You can store the mashed fruit in the freezer until you can get around to making leather of it, and it will be all right. Even if it has started a wine-type fermentation, it will still make good fruit leather!

2. To make vegetables (squash, sweet potato, pumpkin...) into leather, you have to precook and then sweeten and/or spice them to taste. You may like your fruit leathers better also if you add 1 or 2 T. of a sweetener per batch, and 1 t. lemon juice to light-colored fruits.

You can vary sweetening and spices as you please, but you don't need to sweeten as much as you might think because as the leather dries and gets more concentrated it gets sweeter, and also as it dries there is a chemical change that causes creation of more natural sugar.

3. It needs to have the consistency of a smooth puree, and be thin enough to pour. Add more fruit juice (any fruit juice will be great) or water if thinning is needed. Apple and pumpkin tend to need thinning.

But too much water makes a puree that's too thin; thin puree tends to make a leather that sticks to the drying surface. Grape and berry purees tend to be too thin.

If the problem to start with is a puree that's too thin you can thicken it by 1) combining with a thicker sort of fruit puree; or 2) slowly cooking it down over low heat to evaporate some of that water out before you start drying; or 3) adding a thickener.

There are lots of possible thickeners out there: guar gum (1 t. guar gum per 1 c. juice and let rest 10 minutes before you proceed); or psyllium seed husks (1 T. per 1 c. juice and let soak 5 minutes before proceeding); or slippery elm (2 T. per 1 c. juice and let soak 5 minutes), or wheat or oat bran, or chia or flax seeds.

4. If you're making leather of the light fruits (apple, apricot, peach, or pear) heat puree to almost boiling (about 180° F.) before drying and that will retard the browning.

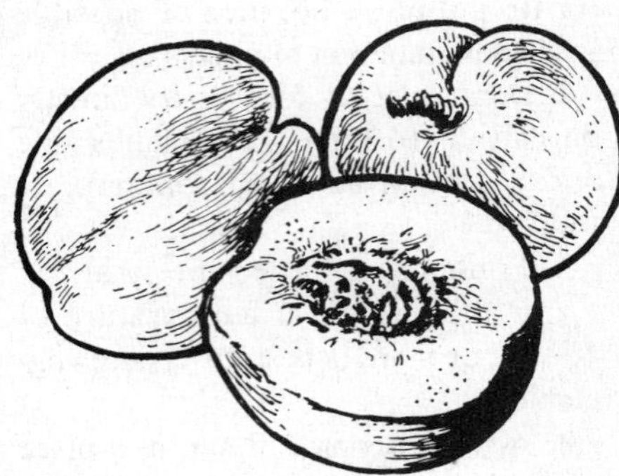

5. Line a drying rack or cookie tray with food-safe plastic. Don't dry leather on wax paper or foil. The leather will hopelessly stick to them. Low-pectin fruits naturally stick more than high-pectin fruits. Combine with apple if you want to raise the pectin amount.

If you're expecting a sticking problem, you can lightly coat the drying surface with a non-stick vegetable spray or vegetable oil to solve that.

If your plastic is flimsy stuff and likely to blow into the leather, tape or clothespin the loose edges to each side of the pan.

A 12" x 17" cookie sheet will be just right for about 2 cups of puree. For larger quantities, one system is to cover the top of an outdoor table with plastic wrap fastened at the sides and ends with tape.

Pour your puree onto that. To ward off bugs, you can make a cheesecloth tent over it.

6. Pour your puree in and get it spread an equal depth by carefully tilt-

ing the tray one way and then another. The thinner your layer is, the quicker and easier it will dry. I recommend 1/8" to 1/4". Get it too thick and you'll have trouble with it spoiling, or you'll just plain get tired of having it around before it finally dries. If you get it thicker in the center than at the edges you'll end up with leather that's brittle around the edges while still sticky in the middle.

7. You can dry by sun, oven, or dehydrator. Even home economists say that sun drying makes the best fruit leathers! They taste better and keep longer.

When oven drying, try not to get the heat above 130° F, definitely not over 140° F.! Oven drying with insufficient air circulation or too high heat tends to make for a brittle leather. High heat also runs the risk of scorching the fruit, or even of melting the plastic! It takes longer to oven-dry fruit leather than plain fruit, but your leather could be done within 6 hours. In a dehydrator, dry at 120° F. Dry for 6 to 8 hours. Rotate pan or shelves often. Pull it off its backing. Dry with the down side up for about an equal time, and then you're done.

Drying time in the sunshine depends on how hot it is and how humid. As fast as 8 hours is possible.

8. Fruit leathers that are still slightly sticky to the touch, but peel readily from the plastic are dried enough if they'll be eaten within a month or so, or frozen. They're nicer for finger food, but will store only up to 3 months or so at room temperature, not indefinitely (a year or more) like they will if dried until no longer sticky.

Leather that is completely dried is mold-proof but tends to crack, crumble, and not roll. Pear, pineapple, and rhubarb leathers just naturally get more brittle during drying and storage than other kinds.

9. When your fruit leather is dry, cut it in strips about 1 1/4" x 2", or into squares. If you made strips, roll each one up tightly layered in waxed paper or plastic wrap. Wrap with plastic or paper on the outside. Or store in flat sheets with something between them.

Enclose that in a tightly-covered moisture and bug-proof container. Or you can just bag them up in plastic and store in the freezer. If the leather is not adequately protected from light, air, warmth, and moisture during storage, it will tend to darken and deteriorate.

10. To serve, you can cook up like dried fruit if you like, but the children enjoy snacking on hand-held chunks so much that's generally the way mine goes. Children love them as much as if they were candy. Another option is to dissolve them in water and use as a pie filling, or serve as a dessert topping over a pudding or ice cream, or stir in to flavor yogurt.

Applesauce leather combos: Mix applesauce with berries, or any strong-flavored fruit, or any scarce fruit to stretch it.

Crisp, fruit wafers: Add 1/2 c. wheat bran per 1 c. thin fruit puree. Mix well, and proceed immediately as if to make a fruit leather. What you'll get is a delicious snack wafer. You can use oat bran the same way (especially good with tropical fruit juices), only it needs to soak for several hours before drying.

Fruit leather "candy": Sprinkle a breadboard with powdered sugar and work the leather strips on it, patting and rolling until about 1/8" thick and powdered.

Leather-juice combo: The essence of this method is that you steam or precook your pitted fruit. Then pour the panful into a sieve. What stays in the sieve gets made into fruit leather by the above recipes. What runs through (without a struggle) gets made into juice.

The more juice you get off, the quicker what's left will dry. This is really a great way to make your fruit juice without struggle and without waste!

Fruit paste candy: Another use for your fruit pulp. The pulp of two or more kinds of fruit can be combined, too, or you could start from scratch with fresh or canned fruit. Just put the pulp through a fine strainer. Then measure it. For each pint of pulp, add 1 1/3 c. sugar. Cook, stirring constantly, until thick and clear. Then turn out on an oiled platter. Let dry until a good tough film is formed on the top. Then turn it out onto a plastic screen to finish drying. Dry until it loses its stickiness. The sooner you can get it dried, the better. I recommend open air and sunshine for the job.

Storing dried food

The "conditioning" option: Toss your dried food loosely into an open-topped container for about a week. Stir 2 or 3 times a day. Keep it covered with a screen or porous cloth fastened around the rim with a rubber band or string to keep out bugs.

The purpose is to allow any excess moisture from some pieces to be absorbed by the drier ones. Then, if you wish, you can repack more tightly.

The pasteurization option: Some dryers heat their dried foods up once after they're done drying and before storing to "pasteurize" them. Other home dryers consider this step unnecessary and never do it. It's basically a final line of defense against bug problems. To pasteurize: heat the dried food in a 175 F. oven for 15 minutes, or in a 160 F. oven for 30 minutes before storing. Or else put in your freezer for 48 hours.

To prevent sticking: Before bagging up sticky dried fruits, you can reduce sticking by shaking them in a bag of dusting material.

Gen McManiman suggests dusting bananas with powdered oats, apples with cinnamon, pears with nutmeg, tomato slices with garlic powder or chili mix, and pumpkin pie leathers with pumpkin pie spice.

1. Store in small batches because any small still-moist piece can cause

the whole container's contents to mold.

2. If you live in a moist climate, put the dried food inside the jar, and screw the lid on tightly as soon as you've finished drying, so it can't accumulate moisture again.

3. The lid does not have to be a perfect-sealing canning style lid. Save your money. On the other hand, it's nice if the container is moisture-proof, bug-proof, and dust-proof. But the reality is that you can use almost anything for a while, and we do: even a paper bag, a recycled mayonnaise jar and lid, or a plastic box with a tight-fitting lid.

4. Most folks store in glass jars or clear plastic bags so they can easily check and see just what's going on in there. Or you can store in paper.

5. In a humid climate, if your plastic or paper bags aren't air tight, you could put them inside a larger glass or metal container and put a tight lid onto that.

That outer glass or metal will also protect against insects or rodents. Dried food should never be stored in direct contact with metal! (Line them with plastic or paper.)

6. Label jars and packages with the name of the food and when you dried it.

An easy system is to just put a strip of masking tape on the container and write on that. It doesn't hurt dried food to freeze and thaw.

7. Store out of direct light and in a dry, cool room. You can keep food dark enough by storing inside a cardboard box or under a sheet of black plastic.

8. Check once or twice a week for the first several weeks, occasionally after that. If you see moisture beads inside the jar, the food should be dried some more. Mold is the result of food that's too moist when stored or that is packaged so openly in such a humid environment that moisture is absorbed.

9. Dried food should stay in prime condition for at least 6 months and may last up to five years, but there will be slow but steady deterioration in the meantime.

10. If the bugs get into your dried food, you can salvage it by removing them, and then roasting the dried food at 300° F. for 30 minutes. Then re-package and store again in containers that don't allow air circulation, or insect passage. It should be all right.

But check again after a few weeks. If it shows signs of bugs, give it yet another heat treatment. Bugs are not poisonous, just visually unappealing.

Using dried food

Cooking dried fruit: Less sugar is needed for dried than for fresh fruit, probably none. That's because the drying process changes the starch in the fruit to sugar. The dryness and the sugar content were the forces that combined to preserve it. A little lemon juice though usually improves the flavor. Soak before cooking, 6 hours or more.

About soaking dried food: You can eat it straight, or "rehydrate" (or "refresh") it by soaking or cooking in water, broth, or fruit juice.

The warmer the water is, the quicker the food will soak it up. Don't add sugar or salt to rehydrating fluid because they both hold back water absorption.

Basic stewed dried fruit: Pour 1 c. boiling water over 1 c. dried fruit. Add 1/4 t. cinnamon, 1/4 t. nutmeg, and a pinch of ginger. Let set until it softens to your taste. Tastes good sweetened with honey. Or mixed with yogurt.

Fruit granola: Chop dried fruit up into small chunks. Half raisins and half other fruit such as apples, apricots, or peaches is good. For every two cups chopped dried fruit, add 7 cups rolled grain (all one kind or a combo such as half oats and half wheat). Optional, peanuts, sunflower seeds, or other nuts and seeds. Stir together until well mixed.

Dried fruit jam: Use dried fruit in any combination that suits you. Add extra sweetener if you like. 1/2 c. dried apricots with 1/4 c. dates, for example, is good. Make this in a blender and moisten with a fruit juice to spreadability. One cup pineapple juice does it in that apricot-date combo. It helps to soak the dried fruit overnight in the juice before the blending happens. You can use this dried fruit jam like a syrup on pancakes and waffles too.

Using Dried Vegetables: Add them to stews, soups, or sauces. Or make a basic soup mix by powdering them in a blender. Add herbs or spices and package for quick soup. Combine with dried milk for an instant cream soup mix.

Dried vegetable slices and dip: Slices of dried carrot, cucumber, eggplant, and tomato are good with a dip.

Instant Spaghetti Sauce: To a basic tomato puree, add dried onion, dried green pepper, dried basil, and oregano.

Vegetable powder: You can grind any thoroughly dried vegetables in a blender or in Gen's special powdering machine. Store in tightly sealed, small packages. To use, just add to boiling water. You can create your own formulas for instant soups, or extra nutrition and flavoring for casseroles or stews.

(This article is excerpted from Carla Emery's <u>Old Fashioned Recipe Book: an Encyclopedia of Country Living</u>, which can be ordered directly from her. To order send $25 plus $3.50 postage to Carla Emery, Box 209, Kendrik, ID 83537, for a 3-hole punch style book, complete with three metal rings for the holes. These are homemade, handmade books, printed and assembled with love from Carla.) Δ

> Discontent is the want of self-reliance: it is infirmity of will.
> —Ralph Waldo Emerson

Gathering low cost firewood

By John R. Horton

Fireplaces and wood stoves are more efficient with each new decade. Heatilators, inserts, blowers, and a host of heating bells and whistles have rekindled the desirability of wood heat. Today, the key for enjoyment of that wood heat is in discovering many hot firewood resources that balance best with the checkbook.

Department of Energy figures reveal that the average cost of delivered cordwood nearly doubled in the last 10 years. By contrast, in that same period, the cost of utilities in most of the nation stabilized. The stark difference in cost between firewood and utilities combined to create the greatest decline of wood heating in history.

Further statistics released this year by California-based Hearth Products Association (HPA) show that while many homes have wood heat devices, less than 15% are heated by wood as the main energy source. The HPA stresses that a prime reason for the decline is the spiraling cost of firewood. The nationwide average of $125 per cord can dampen fireplace spirits.

Many folks enjoy the aesthetics of a toasty fireplace or woodstove. But given the significant disparity between the costs of firewood and utilities, more folks now figure that they benefit financially by turning up the thermostat. For those who desire wood heating in spite of the cost, firewood cost-cutting tactics exist to provide both money in the pocket and a glowing hearth.

Following are five practical ways to acquire a regular supply of quality cordwood and kindling at low or, in some cases, no cost. Many of these tips can be put into practice no farther away than your community's back yard.

Free firewood from the Forest Service

Forest Service firewood permits are available to state residents. For most states, the average for such permits is $10 a cord, usually with limits of between five and ten cords a year per household.

Even better, many ranger districts offer free permits, usually for two to five cords a year. The downside is that the permittee must collect, split, haul and stack the wood. The type and amount of wood, though, can be well worth the labor.

My own free wood-hauling permit allowed a harvest of two cords of downed, easily accessible, old-growth fir. Leftover logging rounds and limbs, it was all superb firewood, easily splittable, and would have cost as much as $150 per cord from many firewood suppliers. For the combined $45 cost of a rental chain saw and newly-purchased splitting maul, I saved as much as $250, gas included. It was a month's worth of exercise that also paid off in the fireplace.

Those two cords lasted three months. Consumed during the coldest part of winter on the Oregon coast, the savings in utilities was $180. That savings, plus free firewood, is household budget mathematics that equals dollars and sense.

Road clearing and utility cutting

Another free resource is the stacks of wood often left for gleaning by road commission and utilities department tree-clearing crews. Frequently required to clear highway and power-line easements, their pains can be a fireplace gain. The wood can be of any variety, so the discriminating harvester is best off biding his or her time. On the other hand, get it while the getting is good, or someone else will.

At the edge of a turnout on a major highway near my home, I recently collected a full cord of firebox-length alder, the result of efforts by a road crew. If not for an alert neighbor, my total could have been two cords. While not the best firewood, alder runs about $100 a cord in my area. That savings is $100 more in my pocket.

Private tree trimmers

Private tree trimmers, like roadside cutting crews, are sometimes eager for someone to haul their cuttings away. Some even pay a fee for such service. A well-timed proposal can reap a nice haul of free fuel, depending on the situation and the tree trimmer. More than one tree trimmer also sells cordwood at reduced prices.

One tree cutter who advertises on shopping center bulletin boards is happy to hear from those in need of firewood.

"I don't make a living with firewood," says Dale Russell, of Lake Cutting Service in Seal Rock, Oregon. "But, firewood for sale earns vacation money."

Russell recommends that customers follow his lead and place ads in newspapers or on bulletin boards. He also touts the effectiveness of staking a well-placed "Firewood Needed" sign by the road, including phone number and type of wood sought.

Russell adds that he and most tree trimmers usually are not "professional" firewood haulers. Consequently, tree trimmers are often open to negotiating price. He asserts that deal-seeking customers who ask him, "Will you take less?" usually receive a five-to-ten dollar discount on full cords.

Consumer tips

While the easiest, but most expensive, method of obtaining fuel is by way of the firewood delivery person, a few easy-to-follow steps may reduce costs and potential hassles.

Consider the options: Many firewood dealers advertise on bulletin boards, as well as in the yellow pages. After copying several phone numbers, compare costs.

Reputable wood haulers recommend that new clients ask whether the amount of wood promised is an actual cord (by measurement, a cord is a tight stack of wood four feet wide by eight feet long by four feet high). Another reasonable query concerns seasoning. Dry wood catches fire easier than unseasoned. If it's important to burn the wood now, check out how dry it is.

Estimates from the Oregon Department of Energy reveal that dry wood has a moisture range of 20%, as compared to 60% in unseasoned wood. The difference in ranges relates directly to BTU output. Nearly one-half of total energy is consumed by wet wood in a steaming process. So obtaining seasoned wood, and keeping it dry, goes a long way toward big savings and conservation of time, effort, and a valuable resource: trees.

One veteran firewood hauler agrees that establishing wood dryness is important, and says it is easy to spot.

"I don't care what kind of wood it is," asserts wood-hauler Socorro Acevez, "the wetter it is the more pitch you'll have in your chimney. A crusty layer of pitch and soot can catch fire," he says, "so I never burn any wood that is not dry."

According to Acevez, dry, split firewood tends to be lighter than wet wood, both in color and weight. Also, seasoned wood tends to have off-color bands, or striations. For example, Acevez says that fir is well-seasoned when he can see clusters of inch-wide, burgundy-colored bands on cross sections of split chunks. That's what he prefers to burn, and what he reserves for special customers.

Acevez recommends that customers specify in advance the kind of wood they want. With split wood often preferred over limb wood, he cautions that customers make sure beforehand what they bargain for. Length, too, is a factor. Stove wood is usually shorter than pieces burned in full-length fireplaces.

Also, Acevez says that tight-grained oak and medium-grained fir burn hot and long, compared to softer alder and spruce. Alder and spruce may be cheaper, per cord, but usually put out half the BTUs of oak and fir. He confides that a client's real money's worth lies in the species they order.

If in doubt, and the delivery person lives fairly close, eyeball the particular stack in question. After all, you may even want to haul it yourself, possibly at a substantial savings of some 10 to 25 percent.

Whether hauling wood by oneself or having it delivered, Acevez advises that many problems can be resolved early by defining exact terms. He says that nearly all of his deals made by telephone are consummated exactly as negotiated. With some haulers, though, misunderstandings can happen.

Not long ago, I called a hauler for price comparisons on delivered firewood. Agreeing to provide a cord of old-growth fir from a commercial harvester, the delivery person quoted $80. The deal nearly failed, though, when another person called back to confirm a higher price. The delivery man telephoned not long after and cleaned up the untidy error.

One victory won, I neglected to negotiate delivery and stacking into the price. The delivery was made as scheduled, but I had to laboriously stack the wood myself. Late stacking negotiations broke down due to an early haggling oversight.

Obtaining kindling is another important factor in the wood box equation. Sometimes, small limb wood and gleanings can be had from commercial trimmers and firewood deliverers. More resources are lumber stores, lumber mills, and construction sites.

Frequently, these places are happy to give their excess scrap away. Well-placed phone calls or visits can result in old pallets, scrap two-by-fours, or bundles of limb wood.

It's best to burn clean, dry wood. Firewood that is unseasoned, or dried wood stacked in a damp environment, dramatically reduces firebox efficiency, and leads to more frequent maintenance problems.

Most of these ideas can be adapted to any locale. For example, many urbanites reside less than an hour from rural harvesting possibilities, and tree trimmers and forest service offices can provide a wealth of firewood information. Operating a fireplace or woodstove can be cheap, though not easy, even if you don't own your own woodlot. Δ

Protect your home and family from fire

By Larry D. Weber

Are you prepared to handle a fire emergency in your home? If you are like most Americans, the answer is probably no. Each year in the United States, there are twenty times more deaths caused by fire than by floods, tornadoes, hurricanes and earthquakes combined! Home fires can occur anywhere and at anytime and to anybody — young, old, rich or poor. No one is impervious to the hazards of fire.

According to statistics complied by the National Fire Data Center for the Federal Emergency Management Agency (FEMA), seventy-five percent of all Americans who die in fires die in home fires. The same statistics also show the destruction of over 700,000 homes and more than two billion dollars in property damages per year.

It is possible that many people who die from fires in their homes do so because they gave little thought to fire safety awareness. This article is intended as an essential guide so that you may increase your own fire safety awareness.

There are numerous ways in which a fire can start in your home. Matches, cigarettes and cigarette lighters that are carelessly tossed aside, or left where young children could find them, have been a major source of fires in the home. Here are a few lifesaving household tips:

- Always keep matches in a metal container. After use, break them in half before disposal.
- Store all used cleaning rags and polishing cloths in a closed metal container.
- Store all paints, paint thinners and removers, varnishes and cleaning fluids, etc. in their original, tightly closed containers.
- Check all storage areas (including your attic, basement, garage, etc.) for whatever might be a fire hazard, and properly discard those items.

Smoke detectors

One of the best lifesavers is the home smoke detector. National organizations such as the National Fire Protection Association (NFPA) and the United States Fire Administration (USFA) strongly advise that every home should have smoke detectors on every level, including the basement.

Since smoke detectors first appeared on the market, the nation's home fire death rate has dropped significantly.

The results of a study on home fires completed by FEMA indicate the following:

• Your chances of dying in a home fire are reduced by up to 50% if smoke detectors are properly installed and maintained.

• In about 40% of all home fires studied, smoke detectors provided the first warning of a fire.

A smoke detector is an early warning system that sounds an alarm when something is burning. Smoke detectors, unlike fire extinguishers and sprinkler devices, do not put out fires.

There are two basic kinds of smoke detectors on the market today. One incorporates ionization while the other works on the photoelectric cell principal. Both provide adequate warning. Briefly, the detector that works on the ionization principle utilizes a tiny amount of radioactive material (americium 241) to ionize the air in a small chamber. When smoke passes through the ionized chamber, an electric current is interrupted and sets off the alarm. By contrast, the photoelectric type of smoke detector usually contains a small electric bulb in a chamber. When smoke passes in front of it, the light is dispersed, causing a photoelectric cell to trigger the alarm.

When purchasing smoke detectors for your home, make sure that they carry the seal of a creditable testing laboratory and always follow the manufacturer's installation, operating, and maintenance instructions.

In addition to smoke detectors, residential sprinkling systems are available for your home. The sprinkler systems will spray water automatically in the area of the fire, before the fire can spread. Sprinkler systems are much more expensive to install than smoke detectors, costing up to $3.50 per square foot, depending on the age of your home.

Fire extinguishers

Every home should have fire extinguishers for key areas, such as the kitchen, garage, or workshop. Fire extinguishers are storage cylinders that contain water or chemicals and are designed to extinguish small fires.

Each fire extinguisher is labeled according to the type of fire it is to be used on. If you used an extinguisher with the wrong chemical agent against certain types of fires, you could cause the fire to spread or you could seriously injure yourself. Fire extinguishers are labeled A, B, C, D, ABC or BC. The most popular ones for the home are the ABC and BC types. Following is a summary of the correct applications for each type of extinguisher:

• Type A: Contains chemicals to put out fires in paper, wood, cloth, rubber and many types of plastic.

• Type B: Contains chemicals to put out fires in oil, gasoline, paint, lacquer, solvent, cooking grease and other flammable liquids.

• Type C: Contains chemicals to put out electrical fires in wiring, fuse boxes and other electrical components.

• Type D: Contains chemicals to put out fires caused by combustible metals such as sodium or magnesium.

• Type ABC: Is a multipurpose dry chemical extinguisher to put out most home fires.

• Type BC: Is a multipurpose dry chemical extinguisher to put out home kitchen fires.

All members of the household should know where all fire extinguishers are located and should be instructed on how to properly use them before a real fire emergency exists.

But remember, fire extinguishers are of little or no use in fighting a fire if not fully charged and in operating condition!

Have an escape plan

Every year, approximately two-thirds of the people who die as a result of a fire in their homes had not properly developed their own fire escape plan. Carefully formulating your escape plan does not have to be a difficult task, but your life and the lives of your loved ones may depend on how well you do this job.

First, make a step-by-step, room-by-room, inspection of your home. Make sure there are two ways out of every room. One exit will be your regular entrance or door, for instance, while the other will probably be a window to the outside. Double check the exits that you have designat-

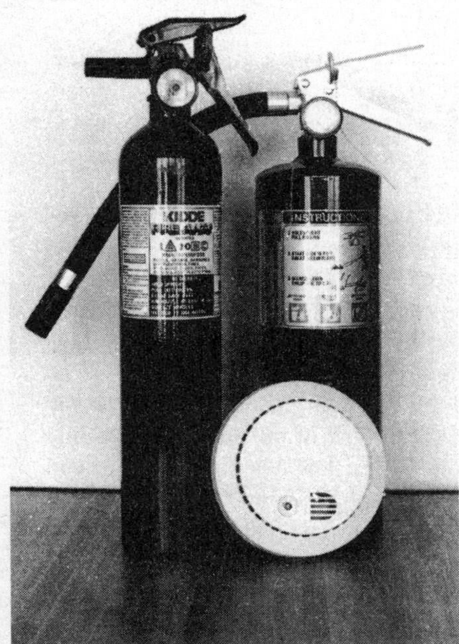

All members of the household should know where all fire extinguishers are and know how to properly use them.

ed to be sure that windows and doors open and close properly. Do not use locks that require keys to open the door from the inside. Next to each emergency window or door exit on a second or higher floor where you are unable to safely reach the ground, a deck, balcony or garage roof, etc., you should have a safety ladder or rope ladder that is "UL Listed" (indicating approval by Underwriters Laboratories, Inc.).

One person should be made responsible for calling the local fire department. All emergency telephone numbers should be posted by each telephone in your home. Decide who will be responsible for helping young children and elderly occupants out of the house, and establish a meeting point outside in a well-lighted area so you can take a head count after exiting.

There are no set rules for escaping a fire. Every household should conduct a fire rehearsal or drill several times each year. Your escape plan must be properly prepared and tested to be effective. Show your escape plan to your local fire department. They may be able to offer additional ideas to help improve your plan.

Escaping

Even though you have taken steps to fireproof your home, fires can still break out. There are a few simple rules to follow if your home is on fire.

Do not open any door without first checking to see if the door is hot. You can do this by using the palm of your hand against the door. If it is really warm, or if you notice smoke entering your room from underneath the door, **do not** open the door! Take an alternative escape route immediately. Remember to keep low and crawl beneath any smoke. This allows for safer breathing and better visibility.

Never go back inside a burning house! Uncountable numbers of lives have been lost because people have re-entered their burning homes. Just one deep breath of hot smoke or toxic fumes can be fatal. Inform firefighters if someone is still in the burning house and where he or she can be found.

Most of us have no idea what it is like to be in a real fire. We may feel that being injured by fire only happens

In about 40% of all home fires, smoke detectors give the first warning.

to someone else, but all of us are vulnerable. Statistics tell us that the number of injuries and deaths from fires increases each year. The amount of attention that you pay to fire safety could be the key to your survival! Δ

A BHM Writer's Profile

Russ Davis, known variously to his friends as either "Doc" or "Grizz," has published seven books, including two outdoor cook books. Number eight is in the works. He has also authored numerous articles for *BHM* and other outdoor, gun, and police magazines.

Until recently, when he moved to the high plateau country of rural southwest Wyoming, he was a therapist in private practice in Iowa, where he was also an Iowa Law Enforcement Academy-certified instructor. A founding member of the International Law Enforcement Training Group, Davis specializes in teaching hostage negotiators and in training SWAT teams, using techniques he developed and which have been adopted throughout the United States and in a number of friendly foreign countries.

Davis is an avid cook who describes himself as "a writing fool," and enjoys his role as a "plain ole country counselor." He has a Ph.D. in counseling psychology and has travelled extensively, including living 11 years in Europe, primarily Germany.

Winter protection and planting of fruit trees

By Martin Waterman

Universities and research stations are turning out better quality, disease resistant, and hardier fruit trees than our parents or grandparents could ever imagine. One thing that has not changed is the protection that most fruit trees need to properly survive our winters so that they can continue producing for years to come.

The first lines of defense are of a preventive nature. They are the proper selection of variety and site. These two considerations are probably the most important in protecting your fruit trees from the ravages of winter.

Variety selection involves choosing a fruit tree with sufficient hardiness to survive winters at your location. Too many times trees are doomed to perish because they are too tender for a particular area.

Plant hardiness

Plant hardiness is expressed by the United States Department of Agriculture by using a numbered system. This information is contained on the new USDA Plant Hardiness Zone Map. This map divides North America (including Mexico) into 10 climactic zones. The map cannot be totally definitive since it covers so much ground and deals with historic information, but even so, many nursery and seed companies have adopted the map and its zones in rating their own stock. In their catalogs they will usually state the best zone for each variety.

When using this information, a general rule of thumb is that it is better to err on the conservative side. For instance, if you live in Zone 6, you would be better off growing the cherry tree suited to Zone 5 than growing the one that does well in Zone 6 or 7. Another consideration that should be part of your planning is that there are microclimates or areas within a zone that have special conditions that can help you grow plants that would normally not be suited for your zone.

A young plum tree with a plastic tree guard to prevent damage from mice and rabbits during the winter.

For instance, southern slopes with longer sun exposure, sites near large bodies of water that retain heat, and even sites in cities may be warmer than can be plotted on the hardiness map. This is the reason some gardeners have been successful at pushing the geographic limits of certain varieties and being able to grow them where they would normally never grow. The plant hardiness zone map is available at libraries and is contained in most seed and nursery catalogs.

If you want a copy of the giant USDA Plant Hardiness Zone Map (S/N 001-000-04550-4), you can get one by sending $6.50 to the Superintendent of Documents, Government Printing Office, Washington, D.C., 24020. You may want to call the information desk at (202) 783-3238 to order or better yet to ask for any of the many subject bibliographies that tell you the information that is available from the USDA that may be applicable to your plans. Much of this information is free, and remember that these services are supported by your tax dollars.

Mulching

Mulching is an important practice because it protects in two ways. In the years in which there is little or no snowfall, mulching acts like a blanket to keep the roots warm enough to prevent root injury. With many of the species of fruit trees, the parts below the soil are more tender and prone to winter damage than the parts that are above the soil. Therefore, mulching also acts to prevent damage during the freeze and thaw cycles by making their effect less severe. This is of particular interest to those who live in climates that can be highly variable with great fluctuations in winter temperatures.

There are also advantages to mulching that carry on into summer. Mulching has the ability to suppress weed growth and to hold moisture, thus making weeding and watering duties less time consuming.

There are many kinds of mulches that can be used but the organic ones are probably the best and the least expensive. Sawdust, bark and hay are probably the most popular and easiest to obtain. I prefer a three to four inch bed of a mixture of sawdust and bark that I get from a nearby sawmill. I spread this around the trunk outwards about four feet to where the root zone ends on my young trees. One slight disadvantage to using this mixture is that as it decomposes it uses nitrogen. This is easily corrected by adding fertilizer, which should be done anyway. When using hay as a mulch, one has to be careful not to introduce hay seed or else you will be doing more weeding than you expected.

Protect from wildlife

Wildlife is another potential source of winter damage. Mice and rabbits love to eat the bark of fruit trees, with young trees being their favorites. Mice can easily girdle a tree by eating around the bark of the trunk, thus killing the tree. The best defense against mice and rabbits is tree guards. These usually consist of plastic or wire mesh wrapped around the lower trunk of the tree.

Asphalted paper can be used as well. Whatever covering you use, be careful to wrap as far down as the root level. It also helps to surround the trunk area with some stones since meadow mice love to work below the surface of the snow.

In the case of deep snowfall areas where the lower branches can be reached by mice or rabbits, a repellent can be painted or sprayed on. As far as mice protection is concerned, I use tree guards as extra protection. I am very fortunate when it comes to mice protection since the neighbor's abundant cats are very successful at keeping mice from doing any damage.

If mice become a big problem, you may have to use mouse bait. This can be put in small sections of ceramic or plastic pipe placed throughout the garden or orchard to keep the bait dry and to entice the curious mice.

Deer can be a much greater problem than mice, especially in winters with above average snowfall when the hungry deer are attracted to easily accessible food. Many deer repellents work, but the best one seems to be a commercial electric fence.

Some fruit growers have been successful at hanging bars of soap throughout the orchard. It is thought that the smell reminds deer of hunters. Almost everything has been tried, from human hair gathered from the local barber to dumping human urine around the orchard. If you have substantial damage by deer, a fence is about the only sure deterrent.

Sunscald

In late winter the sun can also cause damage to the trunks of some trees. This is known as winter sunscald or southwest injury. It is caused when the temperatures begin to warm above the freezing mark and the temperature difference in the bark can be 4° between the north and the south side of the tree.

This freezing and thawing kills the bark on the south side of the tree where the sap has began to run. A cover of white latex paint on the trunk can be used where trees are prone to this type of winter injury. (Incidently, by looking for southwest injury you can help orientate yourself if you are lost.) This injury rarely occurs in a wooded area since these trees are shaded to some extent. In clearings and landscaped properties that have the freeze/thaw cycles, the trees with the damage are easily identified.

George Colpitts (he's 80, loves fruit) standing by a 3 year old Montmorency sour cherry tree. Note the sawdust bark mulch mixture for root protection.

Fertilizer

Do not overfertilize your fruit trees, particularly after the end of July. This will produce excessive new growth and use too much of the energy that the tree needs to overwinter properly. In addition, this new growth will not have the proper time to prepare for winter, which can lead to winter damage. Remember, in the wild there is no one to fertilize and care for fruit trees, and growing them to produce maximum fruit annually will take some research to understand the physiology and perks of the trees that you choose.

Get to know your tree's requirements and shortcomings and remember: an ounce of prevention can be equal to bushels of plums, apples or whatever you decide to grow.

Winter planting of fruit trees

I have always been a strong proponent of planting fruit trees in the winter or at least in late autumn. I have planted cherries, pears, apples, plums and dozens of other varieties in this manner and have never lost a tree or shrub.

The nursery industry is geared toward spring planting which, in my opinion, is one of the worst times to plant a fruit tree. Firstly, the dormant tree does not have time to repair and grow new roots before the hot days of spring and summer arrive. Therefore, you have a tree that you have to constantly water and that may still undergo great stress and even die.

By planting the same tree the previous autumn or winter many things happen differently. Even though the tree may appear dormant and devoid of foliage, the roots will probably not be fully dormant. Therefore, the tree will be growing new roots until the ground freezes hard. In the early spring, the tree's roots will begin to grow again and the tree will be prepared for the coming season. I have found that by planting in the autumn or early winter a difference can be made by having the tree begin to fruit one or two years earlier than a spring-planted fruit tree.

Probably the biggest advantage of winter planting is price. I have found that towards the end of summer most nurseries will discount their fruit trees as much as 50% so that they do not have to carry them over the winter and go to the trouble of planting them in a field and digging them up in the spring. This is particularly true of department stores that just want to get rid of their nursery stock.

Most consumers are leary about buying trees this time of year since spring planting has been ingrained in our system because that is the way it has always been done. Besides, if you are buying fruit trees from a chain department store with a seasonal garden center, the person who is trying to sell you a fruit tree will probably be back to selling goldfish when the garden center closes for the season.

Therefore, do your homework. Pick up some gardening magazines and send for free catalogs. Ask the local folks to find out which varieties grow best in the area. Visit local area nurseries that grow and propagate their own trees. These trees will already be tested for the local areas. And finally, get a good book on preserving. If you do your homework correctly, you'll need it. Δ

They Disappear

It's been a long time
Since I'd been to the city
And I was surprised to see them
There on the streets,
In their haggard clothes . . .
their empty faces . . .
begging money if they catch your eye.
They're everywhere.
Where were they before?
Where were they when I lived here?
Days pass.
I walk the streets as I go about my business
And, gradually,
They disappear.

John Earl Silveira
Ojai, California

A BHM Writer's Profile

Since 1970, when Marjorie Burris and her husband bought their 40-acre homestead in the central Arizona mountains, necessity has forced them to learn self sufficiency. They use native plants for medicine, cure their own meat, and maintain and repair all their equipment.

Burris grew up in southern Illinois, but has lived most of her adult life in the west. She is a registered nurse, specializing in operating room nursing. Her greatest pleasure has been watching her three boys grow up in the backwoods. Now they bring their own children to the homestead to pass along backwoods values and skills.

Burris began writing after she retired from nursing. Her articles and stories have appeared in *Backwoods Home Magazine* and other publications.

Ostriches and emus — backwoods bonanza or feathered pyramid?

By Vern Modeland

Picture it. You're settled in on your dream backwoods homestead. Life's necessities are coming under control—after considerable budget strain. Then, along comes this friend with a story about how people are making bunches of thousands of dollars of income on five acres and less. Raising birds. Big birds.

"Raise ratites," he or she tells you with the pride of tossing out a new word. "It's gonna be the meat of the future."

Ratites include Asian and African ostriches, their less-aggressive Australian cousins, the emus, and South American rheas. Ostrich and emu meat measures lower in fat, cholesterol and calories than poultry. It is also very high in protein content, and it has a taste and appearance that is akin to beef. Proponents say ostrich and emu meat has barely tapped its potential among health-conscious consumers. It's already gained some measure of acceptance in Europe and Japan.

McOstrich-burgers? Emu foo yung?

Your typical mature ostrich or emu can dress out to 100 or more pounds of meat that is said to sell for up to $20 a pound at retail. And there are those fine big feathers. And that fancy hide. Both have recognized markets.

Ostrich and emu feathers fetch as much as $70 to $80 a pound for use in decorating wearing apparel and in making high quality feather dusters. A mature bird can support 16 pounds of plucking per year.

Ostrich and emu leather glamorizes belts, hats, boots, purses, wallets and briefcases. The tanned hide from a single ostrich can net its producer as much as $462.

Emu oil is developing a market of its own for applications in skin care and cosmetics. Various health claims also are being explored for the unsaturated, non-toxic and penetrating emollient. The carcass of a 14-month old emu can yield more than a gallon of it. Outback Secrets, Inc. (6918 LBJ Freeway, #105, Dallas TX 75240), will sell you a two ounce bottle of emu oil to use on your skin for $25.

"Rub some on your hands and by the time you reach that door (about six feet away), they'll feel dry," says Susan Thompson, an Arkansas emu raiser.

Count your pennies

Industry sources throw around numbers like $30,000 as the potential gross income possible from a single ratite in a year. That includes egg production. And these big birds will thrive in any climate where cattle do, proponents say.

Dave Snyder, who lives near Clayton, Oklahoma, compares his interest in the birds to what he knows about cattle. He figures it takes 100 or so acres to support 100 head of beef in Oklahoma. "You can raise 100 ostriches or emus on just two to five acres," Snyder says.

Unlike its larger cousin, the ostrich, a mature emu can easily be handled.

Susan Thompson and John Paul Swearengin have 14 birds on about an acre of otherwise fallow oak-shaded hillside south of War Eagle Creek in Arkansas. Susan became interested in ratite raising when she attended a presentation about a year ago as a part of an investment planning series put on by her employer. "I want to quit this job and have more time for my son and my hobbies," she says. "I think I'll be able to in another year."

After the presentation by the Arkansas Emu Association, Susan and

J.P. scraped together $9000 to buy a pair of breeding-age emus.

"We've made $8000 of it back and have watched those birds appreciate four times in value," Susan says, nodding toward the pens close to the back door of their house. She figures their $9000 investment will be worth $60,000 in a year at the present rate of growth in the emu market.

Birds in the 'hood

Ratite raising appears to be expanding most rapidly up through the middle of the United States, out from Texas, where organized activity seems to have begun. It's well into Louisiana and Oklahoma, north to Iowa, and east as far as Tennessee and Kentucky.

One sizeable supplier is in the southwest corner of Indiana. Gene Pfeiffer's Southwind Ostrich Ranch, near Mt. Vernon, employs 16 people and has a population of 425 birds. Southwind ships eggs guaranteed to be fertile, for $1500 each, to customers in all parts of the United States and to Canada, according to its treasurer, Mark Aiton.

Ostrich and emu chicks command prices as high as $4000 to $9000 each. Mature birds range in price between $25,000 and $60,000. Southwind will supply breeder birds at $65,000 to $70,000 a pair.

One source estimates there may be as many as 50,000 adult ostriches in the U.S. today on some 3,500 ranches and farms. If a mass market can be developed, the same source says that at least three to five times that number of adult birds will be necessary to support a viable meat-supplying industry.

It's hard to get a handle on just how big the industry is or how fast it's growing, Susan Thompson observes. A lot of people she knows don't answer surveys. "They don't want the IRS to know," she says.

Such pricey birds have hatched their own insurance specialists who write coverage for mortality, accidents, and even for transportation of the long-necked, spindly-legged dummies. Thompson and Swearengin insured their emus for a rate equal to 12 percent of their purchase price. However, as insurers and breeders gain experience, premiums should go down, Thompson says.

There is an American Ostrich Breeders Association. This national support group has seen its membership grow from around 500 in 1989 to more than 2700 today. And some 3000 emu proponents are banded together as the American Emu Association, which also started in 1989. That organization has tripled its size in a year, with 13 percent of the 3000 members joining in just 45 days this spring. Ratite associations have regional and state affiliates and also sponsor regular conventions and seminars. They are producing monthly journals and other literature, as well as video tapes, to inform the uninformed and support the involved.

A big "If"

Creation of a major consumer market for ostrich steaks or emu meat loaf is a very formidable task, and organization and funding for it appears to be little more than sizzle at present. The action now is in breeding, then hatching and selling, the chicks. And it

Flightless but fast of foot, emus are curious, playful, friendly—and expensive.

Swearengin shows off newly-arrived ratite incubator. It has 120 egg capacity.

takes big money to play. Startup costs can easily be as much as $100,000 to get three adult birds, insurance, and a special incubator and hatcher, to build pens and sheds, to stock feed and to pay for veterinary services.

The Small Business Administration (SBA) has been approached to make at least one loan, to a ratite breeder in Tennessee. That application is still under evaluation, says an SBA spokesperson in Nashville.

Extension and credit services caution that there is considerable risk if you're thinking of sinking the family's savings into hatching and raising these comical big birds. Lee Kline, a longtime Iowa farm broadcaster, goes a step further. He fears that all the attention that ostriches and emus are getting might just amount to a "feathered pyramid."

"It boils down to the fact no markets have developed," says Bob Penquite of the University of Arkansas' Small Business Development branch office at Harrison. "As a breeder, I'd aim for a two year payoff—nothing long term," Penquite recommends to anyone who might be considering startup.

Thompson and Swearengin found the most financial cooperation at two small local banks. Gary Bunch is president of Madison Bank and Trust, founded in 1911 in one of the dozen wooden buildings that define the town square in Kingston, Ark. (population less than 200). Bunch says he made their loan based on collateral and the added security of a co-signer more than on any future he sees for investment in ratites.

Lots to learn

Being a successful ratite breeder has a demanding learning curve, emphasizes Anthony Pescatore of the Department of Animal Sciences, University of Kentucky, Lexington. The university is in the process of surveying all Kentucky counties to learn more about the growth of ostrich and emu raising in the Bluegrass State. Pescatore says that their survey had, in its early stages, identified 40 ratite-raisers, all of whom had less than four years experience.

"On your own, you'll make mistakes," Pescatore warns. "It's hard to get these birds to survive the first three months."

Pescatore suggests that internship might be the best way for a newcomer to really learn about ostriches or emus without making costly and disappointing mistakes. He recommends finding a breeder who will allow you to work alongside him or her for a time in order to gain hands-on experience before investing in your own birds.

Dave Snyder in Oklahoma started out with ostrich eggs that he got from a breeder in Texas.

"They didn't do well," Snyder admits. In fact, most of his eggs didn't hatch. He suspects they might have been allowed to get too cold before he got them home last winter.

Careful handling and special incubators are essential. Even then, sources say, expect only a percentage of eggs to hatch into the 10-inch tall chicks. The highest fertility figure given was 60 percent.

Still, even infertile ratite eggs can be marketed. The avocado-colored emu eggs and cantaloupe-sized ostrich shells fetch as much as $35 each from craftsfolk with an urge to carve and decorate them. A happy, healthy ratite

Yearling emus exhibit a fondness for fresh grapes.

will lay 20 to 50 eggs a year over a productive span of more than two decades, industry sources claim.

The main advantage that slightly smaller (five-foot tall) emus have over their eight- to nine-foot tall, 300-pound relatives seems to be their temperament. Ostriches do not take lightly to the gathering up of their eggs, say the experienced, and they are both agile and painfully accurate with the two toes on the ends of their long legs, which are built to propel the bird 30 to 45 miles an hour in 12-foot strides.

Emus, on the other hand, tend to be shy. "They're a step above turkeys in intelligence," adds Susan Thompson. Her 14 emus take about a half hour a day to feed, water and check, says Thompson, and they provide entertainment with their antics, especially when hand-fed grapes or cooled with a sprinkler hose on a hot summer day.

That's quite a coop

Five-foot or higher fences of barbless wire are required to keep adult ratites down on the farm. Pens 40 feet by 60 feet will hold six to ten young emus or one pair of adults. Pens twice that size are in order for ostriches. One association publication also recommends adding a perimeter fence as an additional security measure, in case birds should escape from their pens. Building fenced passageways to aid in moving the birds from pen to pen is also suggested.

Three-sided shelters, each holding a feed bin and a supply of fresh water, complete the recommended facilities.

Foragers in the wild, these big birds thrive in captivity on a diet very high in protein. Commercial ratite ration is alfalfa-based and is not cheap—35 cents a day per chick and 85 cents a day per adult bird, according to one report.

Thompson and Swearengin find they are spending about twice as much per pound for ratite feed as what JP's mother spends on cattle feed for her 400 acre spread.

Garden hose spray is a treat for adult emu.

Another consideration in planning any migration into the exotic bird business is the threat of theft that such expensive curiosities poses. Ostriches and emus have attracted fans from the criminal element, too. To counter ratite rustling, there is tattooing, DNA testing, and one inexpensive but high-tech solution. A $7 micro-chip passive electronic device can be implanted shortly after birth to make each bird uniquely identifiable by a ten digit code for the rest of its life.

High stakes

The short of it appears to be that raising ratites can undoubtedly be an exciting and interesting, though risky, investment that, at present, is based more on future potential than on any current certainty.

Ostrich and emu fanciers and suppliers eagerly say, "Just wait!" The people who loan money say that that might be a very good idea.

Ostrich and Emu Information Sources

• American Ostrich Breeders Association, 3840 Hulen St., Suite 210, Ft. Worth, TX 76107. Phone (817) 731-8597. Founded in 1989 to share knowledge and further development of markets, research and resources. Has state and regional chapters, publications and conventions. Basic membership $100.

• American Emu Association, P.O. Box 8174, Dallas, TX 75205. Phone (214) 528-2359. They, too, have organized regional and state affiliates, publications and a schedule of regional and national meetings and seminars.

• The Center for Appropriate Technology Transfer for Rural Areas, ATTRA, has a packet of information for anyone thinking about becoming a ratite raiser. It is available free. Write ATTRA at Box 3657, Fayetteville, AR, 72702, or call 1-800-346-9140.

• The Small Business Administration and state university extension services also are gathering good information on the ratite industry. See your local phone book.

Publications

• Emu Today & Tomorrow. P.O. Box 7, Nardin, OK, 74646-0007. Phone (405) 628-2933. Monthly magazine. Subscription price: $15 per year.

• The Ostrich News. P.O. Box 860, 502 "C" Street, Cache, OK 73527-0860. Phone (405) 429-3765. Monthly magazine at $48 per year. Also publishes annuals and a directory. Δ

Small engine maintenance for women

By Michelle Richards

How many small engines do you have on your homestead? I counted mine the other day and came up with eight. These engines help me live a simple life out in the boonies. They do jobs for me that make my life easier and save me lots of energy, which is very important as I am disabled and over the hill in age.

These tools make it possible to continue to live the lifestyle I have chosen. Seven of the eight engines are five horsepower, or under, and pump water, blow snow, generate electricity, till the garden, cut brush, cut firewood, and propel a small boat.

All these engines must run, and do the jobs they were designed to do, or my survival is in question. For those of you who also have small engines around the homestead, who rely on them as I do, this article is written to help you keep them maintained and to help you diagnose a problem if it does occur. There's nothing more frustrating to me than to be out fishing and the engine won't start or going to the woodlot only to find the chainsaw starts, but runs roughly or sputters and dies. Instead of getting your chores done, you end up driving into town to your local repair shop.

Today's small engines are rugged little critters, and I've found that because of that fact, most people neglect them. Where they change the oil religiously in their automobile, they don't on their lawnmower. They take their car in for a tuneup, but don't remember the tiller. This neglect is the main reason their engines fail, or do not run for their rated life expectancy. Recently a friend brought me her tiller and asked me to look it over to see if it could be repaired. My diagnosis? It was a disaster. Why did it fail? It failed because the air cleaner had never been changed. This five hp Tecumseh engine literally ground its innards to death because of dirt that got into the combustion chamber. On top of that, the oil in the crankcase had never been changed. Just topped off when it was low. The oil lost its ability to lubricate, and was full of grit particles and dirt. That's death to engines.

Two types of engines

I asked her why the engine was allowed to get in this condition and she replied that her husband was in charge of engines and she had no working knowledge other than using the tiller in her garden. I gave her some small tips on maintenance procedures and showed her the engine and why it failed. She apparently went home and advised her husband that a $3 filter and a dollar in oil on a regular basis would have saved their $750 tiller from the junkyard. About two weeks later I saw her in the grocery store and she proudly told me the chainsaw wouldn't start the week before, and she fixed it herself.

So ladies, you can learn a camshaft from a crankshaft, and how to maintain your engines. It is not beyond your comprehension. So this is especially written for you.

Small engines are of two types. Two stroke or four stroke. At this point, the only reason this is important to you is the lubrication methods are different. The two stroke requires you mix the oil with the gas. The four stroke is like your auto engine. There is a separate compartment for the oil and a separate fuel tank.

To identify them, two stroke engines are generally used on chainsaws, weedwhackers, and other tools that are used at many angles. Chainsaws are a great example of this. Think about all the various angles in which a chain saw is required to run when cutting down a tree. Upside down or 90 degree angles aren't uncommon. So having the oil mixed with the gas keeps the engine lubricated no matter how it's tilted or angled.

Four stroke engines are usually found on tools such as lawnmowers which stay horizontal most of the time they are in service. Thus the oil stays in the bottom of the crankcase where slingers or other mechanical parts distribute the oil to the areas of the engine that require it. Another easy way to know is, generally, two stroke engines are on tools you must lift and carry, i.e., chainsaws and weedwhackers. They have many fewer parts than a four stroke engine so they are lighter. Four stroke engines are on tillers and most lawnmowers.

The oil is not only a lubricator, it also helps with heat transfer. Small engines run very hot and are generally air cooled, so it's imperative the oil is mixed in the proper proportions in the gasoline (two stroke engines), or kept clean and up to the required level in the crankcase.

Engine cooling vital

Inadequate cooling is the second most prevalent reason for engine failure. First, keep the engine clean. It's a simple procedure. After using the engine in the garden or mowing the lawn, let it idle under no load for a few minutes to let it cool down for a while before you turn it off. This is very important. As I said before, these critters run very hot, especially if they've just tilled heavy soil or cut high grass. Letting them cool down to normal operating temperatures before turning them off will allow the metals to cool down slowly. It will add many hours to the life expectancy of your engine.

After turning it off, let it cool and then clean all the dirt, twigs, and grass off the cooling fins and the engine block. These engines "cool themselves" by radiating heat into the surrounding air. If they're covered with matted grass clippings, dirt and oil, they can't cool.

Second, never remove the engine shrouds. They aren't put there for looks. They are designed to channel air around your engine to help it cool. I can't tell you how many people take these sheet metal shrouds off the engine because grass clippings get caught in them, and think they are helping their engine to cool.

Think of the system on your small engine like the air conditioning ducts or heat ducts from your furnace or air conditioning system. The ducts provide passageways to move hot or cold air where it's needed. The engine has the same kind of system. The flywheel acts as a fan and forces air into the shrouded area around the engine, thus carrying off the heat as the cooler air races by. By removing the shroud or not repairing dents to it, you are defeating the cooling system.

Fuel mix

Now let's get to fuel and fuel mix. As we learned earlier, the two stroke requires you mix oil with the gas. This really can be confusing, especially if you have three or four engines that require different ratios in the mix. You will find the ratio mix in your manual that came with the engine, or many times it's printed right on the gas/oil tank cap.

There are two firm rules on this. Use only two stroke engine oil in two stroke engines. Do not use car engine oil like SAE 10W-30W, or the like. Two stroke engines burn oil and are designed to do this, and require the proper oil in the gasoline. Mix the gasoline and oil thoroughly, and I mean thoroughly. One great method is to take your gas and oil can to the gas station and make the mix right there at the pump. Fill the gas can about 1/3 full and then add the proper amount of oil, then fill the container. The gasoline pumping quite rapidly out of the nozzle mixes the oil and gas together quite well. Later when you go to fill your tiller or generator, shake the gas can vigorously before filling the tank.

The oil must be in very small particles and suspended evenly in the mix, so the engine gets lubricated evenly. If the oil is not mixed thoroughly, the engine starves for lubrication, and the spark plug gets big "globs" of oil stuck on it so it can't fire. You'll spend wasted time taking out the plug, cleaning and drying it to keep your engine running.

Gasoline is also important. Head for your manual for types of gasoline and octane rating your engine requires. Some older engines require leaded gasoline. Most of the newer engines run on leaded or unleaded.

Once gasoline is on hand, use it. Don't buy 10 gallons of gasoline and use five gallons per year to mow your lawn for two years. Gasoline allowed to sit gets stale and gummy. This gummy stuff sticks especially to carburetor parts and air passages which eventually will restrict air flow, thus changing the air-gasoline mixture that's required for good engine operation. This simple precaution will save you a lot of downtime and lots of money. A replacement carburetor or a carburetor rebuild will cost you $25 to $50. Using gasoline within 30 days, as you can see, is very cost effective.

Benefits of simple care

This article has been very simplistic in nature and gives you very basic information on small engines. If followed, it will save you lots of downtime and lots of expense. On one hand, I appreciate people who don't maintain their equipment, as it is a means of income to me. But on the other hand, I hate waste. As an ad for oil filters says on TV: "You can pay me now, or you can pay me later." You can do simple maintenance like cooling slowly, changing oil, proper fuel mixing, changing air filters, all for little or no cost.

Why pay me, or another technician, lots of money for a valve job, carburetor rebuild, or engine overhaul that's needed because of neglect? Today's small engines are rated for approximately 1000 hours of life expectancy before complete rebuilding or replacement is necessary. That doesn't sound like a lot, does it? But figure how you use your lawnmower. Two hours a week for a six-month season would be about average, or 48 hours a year. At this rate your engine could last 20 years.

Simple home maintenance coupled with a couple of trips to a small engine technician for tune-ups and inspection over that 20-year life can save you lots of money and your engine will roar to life and do its job consistently.

If you have no manual for your engine, either go to a small engine sales shop and request one or write the engine manufacturer directly. If you have an old engine, when writing the manufacturer, tell them the information that's on the engine specification plate. If you can find no plate, tell the manufacturer what machinery the engine powers and the approximate age. This will help them get an appropriate manual to you. Δ

Preparing for snow-ins

By Dynah Geissal

If you live in an area where there is a possibility of getting snowed in, you'll need to plan ahead for such an event. A good goal is to have enough food, water, and fuel for light and heat for two weeks.

You will need at least one gallon of water per person per day. You can obtain water for cooking or washing from snow, if necessary. However, it takes a lot of snow to produce even a little bit of water.

Be sure to have plenty of candles and holders on hand, and be sure you know where they are. When the power goes out, you don't want to be scurrying around trying to remember where you stored them. Though you can always fashion holders out of something, don't wait until you need them. Store a couple of good flashlights and fresh batteries too. You may prefer kerosene lamps. Buy a gallon of fresh kerosene, or at least test what you have on hand to make sure it's still good. It can get sludgy after sitting a long while. Check your wicks and trim them. Replace them, if necessary, and fill the lamps with fuel. If you have woodstoves you'll be fine for heat and cooking, as long as your wood supply is adequate.

Now it's time to think about food. What you need, of course, depends on how self-sufficient you are. For the purpose of this article, we'll assume most everything needs to be purchased. The main things to consider are nutrition and what your family likes to eat. It doesn't do much good to have nutritious, easy-to-store food if no one wants to eat it.

Start with breakfast. You will need a cereal of some sort. Granola is perfect if you make it yourself (store-bought can be heavy in fat and sugar). It contains fruit, as well as nuts and seeds for protein. If your family prefers something else, such as rolled oats or whole wheat berries, store up on that instead. In this case, you'll need to add fruit, which can be canned or dried. Remember that canned fruit takes up a lot of room, though. If you buy canned fruit, try to get it in natural juice instead of syrup. Canned or powdered juice should also be stored, but be sure it's real juice. Add some sort of protein food such as nuts or seeds. You'll need to store enough powdered milk for cereal and for drinking at each meal. Some powdered milks are more palatable than others, so try them out ahead of time. Adding a bit of vanilla is helpful to the taste.

Sandwiches are easy for lunch. You'll need enough whole wheat flour to keep your family supplied with bread. In addition to flour you'll need oil, honey, yeast and salt. If you haven't made bread before, learn how ahead of time. Peanut butter can be a little boring day after day. But it's nutritious and filling, so stock up on plenty. You'll also need fruit and milk, as you did for breakfast, and you'll need a vegetable as well. If you have a root cellar, store up on fresh carrots. Without a cellar, you'll have to resort to canned or dried ones. Here again, canned food takes up a lot of space, but it is easier to prepare. You will need dried vegetables to put into cooked dishes, such as rice or soup, so make sure you have enough.

Beans are a natural for dinner; they're filling and full of protein. They need to be accompanied by a grain, which could be in the form of tortillas or cornbread or rice, or whatever else you prefer. You will also need an animal product, which could include milk. Beans can be pretty dull unless you spice them up with herbs and dried vegetables, such as tomatoes or onion. Add fruit to this meal, and try to get in as many vegetables as you can. Mix and match these foods any way that appeals to you. Here's a list to get you started. Consider the amounts to be minimums.

Cereal-1/2 cup per person per day (pppd).
Fruit -1 1/2 cup pppd.
Powdered milk -1 1/3 cups pppd.
Nuts or seeds -1/2 cup pppd.
Peanut butter -1/4 cup pppd.
Vegetables -1 cup pppd.
Beans - 1/2 cup pppd.
Rice, cornmeal -1/2 cup pppd.
Whole wheat flour - enough for 4 slices of bread pppd.
Honey - enough for bread and cereal and/or sandwiches.
Salt - for bread.
Oil - for bread, cooking.

Jerky is nice to have, but very expensive. If you buy it, try to get it naturally made.

It will become easier to supplement this admittedly very basic diet as you move toward self-sufficiency. A hen will give you an egg for breakfast, and a goat will give you a gallon of milk. You'll learn to make your own jerky (goat jerky is wonderful). And a pig will give you ham, bacon and sausage that doesn't need refrigeration if you choose to make it the old fashioned way.

If medicine is necessary for any family members, it should be next on your list of supplies. Don't store medicine for long periods, though, and rotate the supplies. Every rural home should have first aid supplies. Make sure yours is well stocked.

A family can use a lot of toilet paper in two weeks, so make sure you have enough on hand.

That should do it for basic supplies for people, but don't forget any animals that are in your care. Also add any special things that your particular family would not want to do without.

I hope this gives you a start in preparedness for snow-ins, or for any other emergency. Δ

Cabin fever

By Dynah Geissal

If winters are long where you live you need to plan ahead in order to avoid the dreaded cabin fever. Make it a year round effort. If you're like most homesteaders there's never enough time in any season except winter. So start keeping a list right now. Whenever you wish you had time to do something, put it on the list. Some of these items will be chores that never seem to get done. But others should be fun and some could be educational.

Have you always wanted to learn about the Middle East? Make it a project for the winter.

Have you wanted to learn to draw or to play a musical instrument? Put that on the list. Do you promise yourself every year that this winter you're going to ice skate on your creek in the light of a full moon? Do it this year—but for now, put it on your list. Look on your calender and find out the dates when it would be possible and make a notation.

You get the idea. Pretty soon ideas will be pouring out! Chores work the same way. If you need to clean out that kitchen cabinet but never seem to have the time, write it down and one winter day just do it. Not as fun as some of the other items but you'll feel good when it's done.

Another suggestion: Turn off the TV! While TV purportedly entertains and therefore could help to dispel cabin fever, in reality it works the other way. People sit glassy-eyed and dull. They feel spaced out and bored but are mesmerized by the action they are watching. Read a book instead. Or play a game or start a new project. These things will feel good while you're doing them as well as after.

The next recommendation is physical as well as mental. Get outside every day. And I don't mean just to do chores. On even the coldest day you can dress warmly and get out for an hour or two. Take a walk through the pasture or the woods. Get out your cross country skiis or snowshoes. Make it a habit and it will become one of the best parts of your day. You'll experience things you otherwise wouldn't and will come back invigorated.

If there are kids in your family, just elaborate on the above. Get some books of things to do with kids. We had several, but there was one that the kids especially liked. When winter days dragged we opened the book. Even the ones that didn't sound so great turned out to be fun, such as having a picnic on the living room floor. It sounds kind of dumb, but it became something they looked forward to every winter. Or how about a winter barbecue with a bonfire and blankets to keep everyone warm?

And here again: Turn off the TV! Young minds and bodies need to be used, not entertained. Whatever they do on their own is more valuable than just watching. Make going to the library a regular part of your trip to town. Be sure to have plenty of art supplies, simple musical instruments and toys that let children be creative. Some of these include as many wooden blocks as you can stand to have around, Lego, Tinkertoys, Lincoln Logs, and boxes of various shapes and sizes. Toys like these provide endless pleasure and don't become boring because they can be used in innumerable ways.

Let the children help with the cooking now and then or even do some of their own under your supervision. Include them in your chores when you can. And once again, get them outside every day for a couple of hours at least. If the weather is especially fierce, dress them warmly and head up to the barn loft for stories or games. We also had an outbuilding set up for the kids. No heat. But they were out of the weather, yet could still be as rambunctious as they wanted. They were able to let off steam in the most inclement weather. There was a radio and ping pong for the older kids and Tonka trucks, balls and other outdoor types of toys for the younger kids.

I hope this gives you some ideas. With a little thought and planning, winter can become your favorite time of the year. It can be the time you value most because it's the period of least demands from the farm. It is a season to play, to learn and to enjoy life. Δ

Fall pumpkins and squash

By Sandy McPherson Carrubba

One year our children's Halloween pumpkin rotted. My husband smashed it into the garden plot. At that time, our garden was composed of clay with a small amount of topsoil.

The pumpkin was covered with soil and the entire plot was topped with a layer of leaves. In the spring, I began my struggle with the hard, impacted soil. To my amazement, tiny plants were showing. My husband remembered he had composted the pumpkin in that spot.

We were shocked that the seeds survived and sprouted. Masses of them came up. When I called our county extension office, I was told the tiny plants couldn't be moved.

Carefully, I dug around them in the early morning. What did I have to lose? The plants had a shallow root structure and several leaves. I replanted four young pumpkin plants. Then, I watered them and hoped for the best.

Our garden plot wasn't very big yet, so I moved the pumpkins to the back of small space near the fence. When the vines wanted more room that summer, they climbed the fence.

By August we had green pumpkins that ripened before September.

The following year, we tried putting table scraps and butternut squash seeds directly into the garden spot where we wanted the squash to grow the following year. That squash vine yielded 22 fruit.

When we have grown butternut squash and pumpkins this way, they seem stronger, better-yielding plants. The decaying material feeds and strengthens the new plant. Putting in seeds alone or too early hasn't worked for us.

Compost material, egg shells, potato skins, table scraps, or manure, makes the difference. We mark the spot now, so we don't have to guess what we might have the following spring. Disturbing the spot by rototilling seems to make them come up faster.

We have learned through trial and error. At times, lots of errors. We learned not to plant a vine where one grew the previous year. The squash vine borer winters underground. If plants become infested, put a pin into the vine where you find "sawdust." Then, step on the invader. Go up as far as the stem is hollow to get all the borers.

Never keep a plant for composting that was infested with the borer. You may have missed some and they'll spoil your new crop.

Don't pick squash or pumpkins until fully ripe, unless the temperature threatens to plummet below 32°F. They are susceptible to frost damage.

Don't store fruit on cement floor in the garage or basement. Place them on a board in a cool, dry place.

Don't expose the fruit, once picked, to sunlight or they will split open. They keep for months, otherwise.

Don't be skimpy with organic material. The more you use, the better the yield. Mulch with grass clippings to keep roots warm in the cooler weather and moist in dry conditions.

Don't keep a plant that develops yellow blotches on its leaves. That indicates mosaic virus which strikes during wet years. The plant should be destroyed.

Cucurbits don't always need a large cleared area. Just give their roots good soil, enriched with compost.

Squash and pumpkins do not require full sun. The vines grow easily and well. They will grow over grass, fences, or whatever is in their way. We've found vines going up our apple trees.

Their large green leaves and attractive yellow flowers offer color in your garden. Male blossoms are delicious to eat and can be harvested in early morning. It's fascinating to watch the fruit develop. During the winter, squash and pumpkin cookies and cakes bring memories of summer and delight to the palate.

We've planted pumpkins and butternut squash in the fall and enjoyed them all year round. Δ

Wind power from the past

By Larry Elliott

For over six weeks I'd traveled hundreds of miles over dusty, rutted roads that sometimes seemed to go on forever. Wheat fields, cattle, an occasional horse, and perhaps a mailbox standing as a lonely sentinel pointing directions to another lonely ranch road, were the only things to break the monotony. If I was real lucky, I'd see an old pickup truck coming in the opposite direction with the driver giving a cautious wave and nod to this unknown traveler.

The landscape in eastern Montana is flat from horizon to horizon and only rarely studded with, perhaps, a wind blown tree or dusty little town. It was this very condition that brought this western Pennsylvania young man so many miles in search of the elusive "wind charger." There were few areas of the country in the 1930s and 1940s that had more use for, or numbers of, these marvels of "modern" technology.

For many years they gave isolated farmers and ranchers a source of electric power beyond the grid. Forty years later, they are silent rusting relics of the days before the Rural Electrification Administration (REA). Before the government decided to string wires for endless miles, only to serve perhaps one or two lonely ranches, wind chargers kept many a light burning even before some city dwellers could boast as much.

The energy crunch of the 1970s sent quite a few people out in search of these iron workhorses of the past in hopes of finding one that hadn't been sent to the scrapper to help build a liberty ship or tank during World War II. Occasionally, with luck and a lot of searching, one could be found that, with some new parts and a fresh coat of paint, could once again harvest all those watts blowing by us each day.

I was no different in my desire to discover a Jacobs (which, by the way, was the Cadillac of its day) or even a Wincharger, (the Model T equivalent). But I also wanted to learn a little something of the people who originally had lived with these units and discover just what could be operated from them and how much living on one differed from, say, living on city power. These people were true alternative energy pioneers out of necessity rather than ideology. I felt their opinions would be valuable.

Marcellus Jacobs stands on tower holding his 3-kilowatt wind electric plant in this vintage 1940s portrait.

I kept somewhat of a diary of my travels and made a point of sitting down and talking with anyone who had owned a "charger," had lived with one, or perhaps had been a dealer. I managed to meet several people whose recollections became memorable to me, but one in particular was a man who really helped open a window to the past. His name was Bill Bowden and, even in his seventies, he still looked the part of a grizzled, wind blown rancher.

What made his experiences of extra value was his participation in an early wind electric study by a certain midwest college whose name he couldn't recall. It seems that during the 1930s several colleges and even the government, showed a real interest in finding out just how much maintenance was required on these commercial wind generators, what their monthly and yearly electric production amounted to, and whether some models actually performed at all better than the rest.

The area of Montana Bill called home was a pretty isolated rural area in the 1930s and for the most part still is. There was no TV, and radio was still an infant industry, so any information or sales advice on wind generators had to come from farm magazines or newspapers.

Sometimes a local hardware store or farm equipment dealer would take on a dealership and set up displays at the local county fair. It was at a county fair that Bill first got a look at the latest in windcharger equipment. During the 1930s and 1940s over 15 manufacturers of windchargers competed fiercely for the highly specialized market that these overworked "gridless" farmers represented. There were names like Parris-Dunn, Wincharger, WinPower, Wind King, and Air Electric, just to name a few.

Wincharger corporation had a line of chargers displayed that ranged from small 6 volt 80 watt plants, used to keep a radio battery charged, to units up to 110 volts at 1500 watts. Zenith radio corporation even gave these 6 volt chargers free with the purchase of a radio. My, how times have changed!

The company displaying equipment that really caught Bill's eye, though, was the Jacobs Wind Electric Company. They had only one model of generator, a 32 volt 1500 watt unit of massive proportions and rugged design. It dwarfed all others at the fair. The generator was displayed on the

This is part of an ad from a 1930s handbill that shows the many uses that wind power could be put to.

back of a Ford pickup, and Bill said the company sales manager, Marcellus Jacobs himself, promoted the virtues and benefits of his generator with a lot of flair and enthusiasm.

Unlike some windcharger manufacturers, the Jacobs company sold a complete line of appliances and accessories to go along with the 32-volt current these units produced. Radios, freezers, toasters, blenders, refrigerators, power tools and many other items were on open display to help entice the often overworked farmers or their wives into buying these labor saving devices.

Of particular interest to Bill and his wife was a massive freezer that could keep food frozen for better than seven days, even if the power went off. This especially appealed to his wife, who looked after the feeding of their six kids. Unlike many farmers in the 1930s, Bill felt fortunate to have an above average income from his wheat farming. This allowed him to buy the expensive Jacobs with all the accessories. To get a feel for the expense Bill had to absorb, consider that a new Hudson cost a little over $750. A new Dodge or Ford pickup was just a little over $600. A complete Jacobs system without the accessories was over $1000. Most windchargers today are cheap by comparison.

Bill told me that the day the Jacobs system was delivered and set up it had an impact on the family's daily duties and activities as significant as a new baby. No longer did they have to pump water by hand for laundry or dishes. The wash board became a rarely-used relic.

Fibber Magee and Molly, Amos and Andy, and President Roosevelt soon became familiar voices as the family sat beside the big new 32 volt radio. No longer would it die in the middle of a funny line or important message, as the old radio did, simply because the old dry cell battery decided to give up the ghost.

I guess you could say that life became easier for Bill and his family though still not easy. I don't think life on a Montana ranch in the 1930s could ever be described as easy.

Before long Bill added many more labor saving devices to the system. He said he had at least 40 mazda bulbs (a brand name of bulb now long gone and replaced by a Japanese car) of 25 to 100 watts. For his wife, a washing machine, iron, vacuum, heating pad, corn popper and toaster. For Bill, a sickle bar grinder and flood light for the barnyard.

He even managed to run a 5 cubic foot refrigerator. This was a real treat. Remember, in the 1930s on a ranch as isolated as his, even an ice box would have been a luxury. As strange as it may seem in this age of instant everything and pleasure on demand, Bill's wife found she was as popular as Santa Claus with local kids who could eat homemade strawberry ice cream in July because of this wind powered reefer. Can you imagine the pleasure a hard working field hand must have felt as ice cold lemonade cut through the dust of a summer day?

The college mentioned earlier loaned Bill several watt-hour meters that let him tabulate the amount of power his Jacobs produced on a monthly or yearly basis. By his recollections 170 kwh were produced in October of 1937 or '38. He remembered the month because of a prank a kid from a neighboring ranch tried to pull on him.

Seems the boy climbed the tower wrapped in a white sheet with the intention of howling like a ghost to scare Bill's kids. As it turned out the boy got the sheet all wrapped around the tower and couldn't climb down. He cried until Bill helped him get untangled. Bill says the boy's father gave him a good "whooping" that he remembers to this day.

In the months of July and August, Bill claimed the production fell off quite a bit. He said he still produced over 70 kwh on average and never ran short of power. Remember that back then the REA figured 100 kwh was more than sufficient to supply all the electrical needs most farmers would have. Compare that to the average 1000 to 1500 kwh thought to be only average in most homes today. Most farms and ranches use far more than this.

During World War II, gas rationing was started in order to supply adequate fuel for the war effort. Bill said that a rancher such as himself got special allotments of fuels because wheat farmers, and farmers in general, were considered critical industries. His Jacobs helped to reduce the amount of fuel he would have needed to run a gas generator.

This reduction was considered so important that windcharger manufacturers were also given special allotments of copper, brass and steel by the government, to help in production of more windchargers. For many windcharger manufacturers the war was a boom time, since farmers and ranchers had more money to spend and the windchargers used an energy source that couldn't be rationed.

Bill used his Jacobs for over 18 years before the REA came in around 1954. He said that having the REA bring in electricity gave him the added benefit of a phone, since the REA also brought in phone lines, but the Jacobs was a more reliable supplier of electricity, especially in winter when lines were down quite often. Seems the REA demanded that he take his Jacobs down before they would hook him up.

In 18 years of use Bill said maintenance was not a problem. A yearly grease job and repainting of props every five or six years could keep it up and running. Bill said he had three sets of batteries over the years and had bought the last set only three years before selling his system. He sold his generator and all that went with it for $200 to a rancher who wouldn't get electricity from the REA for another ten years.

When asked if he felt a farmer could depend on wind-generated electricity, he emphatically stated,"Yes. Using all of our equipment as freely as desired, we never had been without sufficient power."

It's now 1993 and only seven short years to a new century. The technology of those years long ago is needed more now than ever if we are to meet the twenty first century head on. If old Bill is still with us, he is well into his eighties and, and even though he probably doesn't think of himself as an environmentalist, I'm sure he would approve of what is now being done on wind farms or new homesteads still beyond the grid.

President Lincoln once called wind "the least tapped force in nature." Bill tapped it many years ago, and it seems there will still be enough to last until another author writes about another Bill in another era.

(Larry Elliott is owner/operator of Solar Tech of Bend, Oregon. For more information, call 1-503-388-2053.) Δ

A BHM Writer's Profile

Larry Elliott is a 44-year-old inventor/tinkerer/business owner living on 40 acres of central Oregon high desert. For over 20 years, he has been active in designing, using, and selling equipment for securing energy independence. He has been writing for *Backwoods Home Magazine* about independent energy topics since 1993.

Elliott has incorporated solar electric, wind generators, and energy conservation on his present homestead, as well as his previous farm in western Pennsylvania in the 1970's. The backwoods and rural living have always been a part of Elliott's everyday life. His present business, Solar Tech, is growing steadily and keeps him quite busy.

Wind power in the present

By Mick Sagrillo

You're about to make the big decision: Should a wind generator be in your future? You've analyzed your resources, both environmental and monetary, and weighed the pros and cons of having a wind generator. The only question left is: Which system should you choose?

I can't answer that question for you. However, I can give you the tools to help you make that big decision. Those tools include detailed information, specifications, and power curves for a number of wind systems, all presented in one format.

Background

This article will review all of the commercially available wind systems that are sold in the United States by bona fide manufacturers. An explanation is in order.

In the late '70s and early '80s, the federal and state governments offered tax rebates and incentives to folks who bought renewable energy systems, including wind generators. The objective of the program was to help a fledgling renewable energy (RE) industry get off the ground, while weaning the United States from foreign energy supplies by growing more of our own. While the intentions of the tax incentive program were good, the results for the wind industry were nearly devastating. (Similar results occurred with the other renewables, but this article will be restricted to wind electric systems.)

Scores of companies opened shop and began building wind electric equipment. Virtually all of these companies failed. Customers, however, were left with wind generators that didn't work, plus a bad taste in their mouths for RE.

The vantage point

Lake Michigan Wind & Sun, of which I am owner, is in the business of rebuilding and making parts for dozens of different models of wind generators that were manufactured by now-defunct companies. We do a lot of reverse engineering. That is, we try to figure out where system design flaws are so that we can correct them. By making the necessary upgrades, customers can turn a poorly designed wind generator into a usable piece of equipment.

Because of the services we perform, we have a unique perspective as to where the wind energy marketplace is. We have no allegiance to any one manufacturer. We are in business primarily because all but a handful of wind generator manufacturers failed to build reliable equipment. As we found out a decade ago, anyone can make a wind generator. But making one that will work for years is another matter entirely.

So when I say "bona fide manufacturers," I am not trying to slight anyone. I do, however, want to inform readers as to who the successful manufacturers are. I have tried to fairly represent their products in relation to all others reviewed. They are the survivors, because they have learned how to manufacture reliable products that withstand the test of time.

Two more points before we start. First, this article does not include either the Survivor or Soma wind generators. Neither machine is commercially available in the United States at this time.

Second, a word on failures is in order. You may know someone who has, or had, one of the wind generators reviewed here that has suffered a failure of some sort, maybe even a catastrophic failure. Don't prejudge all wind generators based on a few isolated instances. Sure, there have been failures, even with the best of wind systems. Paul Gipe, of the American Wind Energy Association, reminds us to look only as far as the automotive industry for a comparison. The auto industry is a multi-billion dollar industry spanning over nine decades. Yet they still don't always get it right, as evidenced by the numerous annual recalls of their products.

What you should be interested in is trends, not the occasional failure. Problems with wind generators usually occur early in the system's life. All wind generator manufacturers have experienced some failures, as have all other RE equipment manufacturers. Numerous reports of problems with a particular manufacturer should raise a red flag in your mind. However, as stated earlier, those systems have not been included in this article.

I have extensive experience with all of the systems reviewed here, with the exception of the Rutland Windchargers. This machine is a newcomer to the U.S. (We recently installed a test machine at our shop. An article on our Rutland Windcharger test will appear in a later issue.) However, Marlec, the manufacturer, has sold more than 20,000 of these units worldwide. They obviously have a proven design.

The envelope, please

The following table summarizes all of the various features that you should seriously consider when shopping for your wind system. Explanations for the column headings follow. All of the specs have been provided by the manufacturers.

Wind generator comparison table

			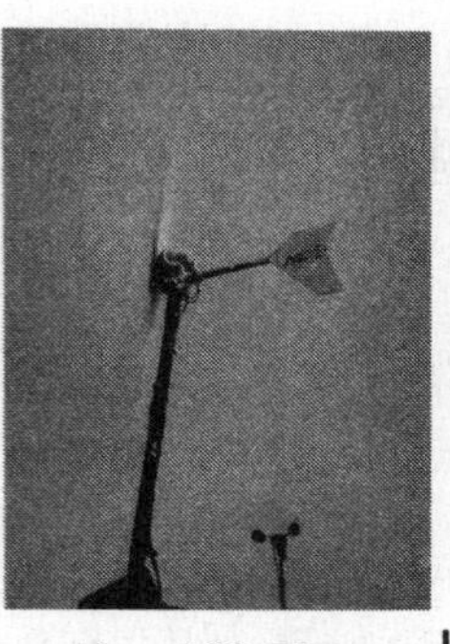		
Model	Furlmatic 910	Windseeker	Neo 600 Plus	Whisper 600	Whisper 1000
Manufacturer	Marlec Engineering	Southwest Windpower	Wind Baron Corp.	World Power Technologies	World Power Technologies
Rated Output in Watts	150	500-12V 600-24V	600	600	1000
Rated Wind Speed	36 mph	30 mph	24 mph	25 mph	25 mph
Rated rpm	900 rpm	2000 rpm	1500 rpm	1100 rpm	935 rpm
Cut-in Wind Speed	4 mph	5 mph	4 - 5 mph	7 mph	7 mph
Rotor Diameter	3 feet	5 feet	6 feet	7 feet	9 feet
Number of Blades	6	2	2	2	2
Blade Material	Glass reinforced nylon	Sitka Spruce or Basswood	Basswood	Basswood	Basswood
Airfoil	True	True	True	True	True
Lateral Thrust	100 pounds	100 pounds	127 pounds	150 pounds	250 pounds
Governor System	Side-facing	Tilt-up	Tilt-back	Tilt-up	Tilt-up
Gov. Wind Speed	37 mph	35 mph		27 mph	27 mph
Shut-down Mechanism	none	none	Dynamic Brake	Dynamic Brake	Dynamic Brake
Tower Top Weight	38 pounds	20 pounds	20 pounds	40 pounds	55 pounds
Marine Option Aval?	No	Yes	Yes / Industrial	Available soon	Available soon
Generator Type	PM Alternator	PM Alternator	PM 3 phase Alternator	PM 3 phase Alternator	PM 3 phase Alternator
Tower Top Cost	$820	$875-$925	$925 w Regulatr	$990	$1,500
Cost per Watt	$5.47	$1.75-$1.55	$1.63 w Regultr	$1.65	$1.50
Battery Systems	12V & 24V	12V to 180V	12/24,36,48,180	12V to 240V	12V to 240V
Utility Intertie Aval?	No	No	No	No	Yes
Resistance Heating?	No	No	Yes	Yes	Yes
Water Pumping?	with batteries	DC	AC/DC	AC	AC
Est.Mo.kWh @10mph	15 kWh (14%)	60 kWh (17%)	77 kWh (17%)	70 kWh (16%)	120 kWh (16%)
Est.Mo.kWh @12mph	22 kWh (20%)	90 kWh (25%)	114 kWh (25%)	110 kWh (25%)	190 kWh (26%)
Warranty	1 year	1 year	2 years	2 years	2 years
Time in Business	15 years	8 years	15 years	4 (15) years	4 (15) years
Routine Maintenance	None Recommended	None Recommended	Visual Inspection	Visual Inspection	Visual Inspection
Notes	US Import Duties	Built-in Regulator	5',3-Blade Comp Prop for Marine	Includes Rectifier Box	Includes Rectifier Box

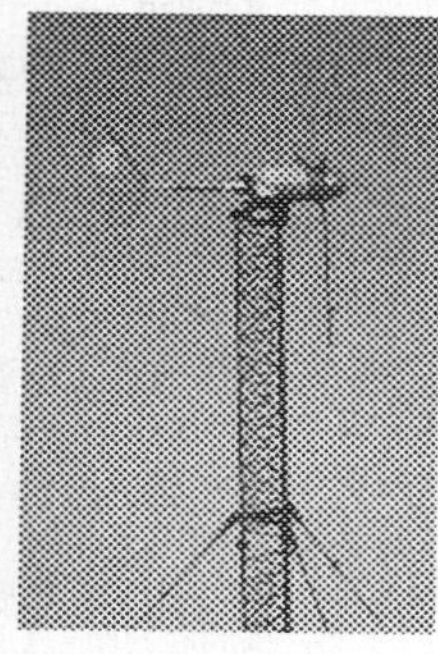

BWC 1500	Jacobs Short Case	Jacobs Long Case	Whisper 3000	BWC Excel	Jacobs 23-10
Bergey Windpower	Lake Michigan Wind & Sun	Lake Michigan Wind & Sun	World Power Technologies	Bergey Windpower	Wind Turbine Industries
1500	1800-24V 2400- 32V to 48V	2400-24V 3000-32V to 48V 4000-200V UTI	3000	10,000	10,000
28 mph	18 mph	25 mph	25 mph	27 mph	25 mph
500 rpm	225 rpm	275 rpm	625 rpm	350 rpm	200 rpm
8 mph	6 mph	6 mph	7 mph	7 rpm	8 mph
10 feet	14 feet	14 feet	14.8 feet	23 feet	23 feet
3	3	3	2	3	3
Fiberglas	Sitka Spruce	Sitka Spruce	Basswood	Fiberglas	Sitka Spruce
Single-surface	True	True	True	Single-surface	True
375 pounds	750 pounds	800 pounds	700 pounds	2000 pounds	1500 pounds
Side-facing	Blade-activated	Blade-activated	Tilt-up	Side-facing	Blade-activated & Side-facing
30 mph	18 mph	23.5 mph	27 mph	33 mph	25 mph
Folding Tail & Dynamic Brake	Folding Tail	Folding Tail	Dynamic Brake	Folding Tail & Dynamic Brake	Mechanical Brake
168 pounds	450 pounds	550 pounds	130 pounds	1020 pounds	1400 pounds
Yes	Yes	Yes	Available soon	Yes	Standard
PM 3 phase Alternator	DC Generator	DC Generator	PM 3 phase Alternator	PM 3 phase Alternator	Brushless 3 ph. Alternator
$3395-$3595	$4,600	$5,200	$3,200	$15,995-$17,995	$13,100
$2.26-$2.40	$1.92	$1.73-$1.30	$1.07	$1.60-$1.80	$1.31
12V to 120V	12V to 120V	12V to120V	12V to 240V	48V or 120V	120V
No	Yes	Yes	Yes	Yes	Yes
Possible	Yes	Yes	Yes	Possible	Yes
AC	DC	DC	AC	AC	AC
125 kWh (12%)	250 kWh (18%)	340 kWh (16%)	320 kWh (15%)	925 kWh (13%)	850 kWh (12%)
220 kWh (20%)	440 kWh (30%)	520 kWh (24%)	520 kWh (24%)	1425 kWh (20%)	1250 kWh (18%)
3 years	1 year	1 year	2 years	3 years	1 year
15 years	12 years	12 years	4 (15) years	15 years	6 years
Visual Inspection	Visual 2X & Grease	Visual 2X & Grease	Visual Inspection	Visual Inspection	Grease & Oil Change
			Includes Rectifier Box		Gear box (not direct drive)

Manufacturer and model: The various models are listed in order of increasing output to help with comparisons. Manufacturers' (or their major distributors') addresses and phone numbers appear at the end of the article. All of the wind generators presented are new equipment with the exception of the remanufactured Jacobs Wind Electric generators. Even though the old Jacobs has not been made for 40 years, it is still considered by many to be state-of-the-art technology. They have been "remanufactured" (that is, rebuilt with all new components and put back onto the streets with a warranty) by various companies for at least two decades. The Jacobs wind generator is the yardstick by which many judge today's wind equipment.

Rated output: In general, this refers to the maximum power output of the system. Any wind generator may peak at a higher power output than the rated output. This is because the faster you spin a wind generator, the more it will produce, until it overproduces to the point that it burns out. Manufacturers rate their generators safely below the point of self-destruction.

Rated wind speed: This is the wind speed at which the wind generator reaches its rated output. You will notice that there is no standard rated wind speed, although most companies rate their systems somewhere around 25 to 28 mph.

With regard to rated wind speed, note that not all wind generators are created equal, even if they have comparable rated outputs. In the past, some manufacturers have abused the concept of rated output by fudging the rated wind speed. For example, a wind generator that reaches its rated power at 50 mph is obviously not the same animal as one which hits that same rated output at 25 mph. How often do you see 50 mph winds?

Rated rpm: This refers to the alternator or generator rpm at which rated output occurs. Generally, the smaller the rotor, the faster the blades spin. Rpm will have an effect on the amount of noise that the wind generator produces. We'll consider noise later.

Cut-in wind speed: This is the wind speed at which the wind generator begins producing power. For all practical purposes, there is no usable power in the wind below 7 mph, even though the blades may be spinning. This holds true unless you greatly oversize the rotor to allow it to capture power in low wind speeds. But then you open up all sorts of worm cans when trying to control generator output at higher wind speeds.

Rotor diameter: This is the "fuel collecting" part of the wind generator. The bigger the rotor diameter, the larger the collecting area and therefore, the greater the wind system's output, or the lower its rated wind speed.

Number of blades: This refers to the number of blades in the rotor. This is primarily a design consideration for the manufacturer. The greater the number of blades, the more torque the rotor can produce. A certain amount of torque is necessary to get the rotor spinning from a stopped position. However, torque is inversely related to rotor conversion efficiency. When you are trying to generate electricity competitively with the power company, efficiency is of prime concern.

The fewer the number of blades in the rotor, the more efficient the rotor becomes. One blade is the ideal, but poses some dynamic balance problems. Two-blade or three-blade rotors are seen most often. The question arises, why use three blades if two are more efficient? Time for a digression.

"Yaw" is a term that refers to a wind generator which is pivoting on its bearings around the tower top to follow the continually changing direction of the wind. Two bladed rotors pose a problem as the wind generator yaws. A two-bladed rotor actually sets up a chatter as it yaws, which causes a strain on all of the mechanical components. Chattering occurs during yawing because of the continuous changing of the position of the blades in the plane of rotation. When the blades are in the vertical position (that is, at right angles to the tower, or parallel to the ground) they pose maximum resistance (or inertia) to any yawing motion. The result is a rhythmic starting and stopping of the yaw twice per revolution of the rotor. This starting and stopping of the yaw is what is seen as blade chatter.

Three-bladed rotors eliminate the chattering problem because there is never enough inertia from the one blade in the horizontal position to set up a blade chatter in the first place. The horizontal blade is more than counterbalanced by the other two blades working somewhere off on their own. Well balanced three-bladed rotors operate very smoothly with no noticeable vibration or chatter.

World Power Technologies has come up with a unique solution to the two-blade problem on their Whisper wind generators. The blades are mounted on a spring plate. The spring plate flexes to absorb some of the yawing vibration and therefore helps mitigate the yawing chatter on the Whisper wind generators.

Blade material: This refers to what the blade is constructed of. Within the last decade, blade material has fallen into one of two categories: wood or extruded fiberglass. While more expensive for materials and labor, wood is still considered by many as the material of choice for blades. Blades do a lot of flexing. That's what trees did as a side job for most of their lives.

There is no question that Sitka spruce is the "primo" material for wood blades. Sitka has one of the highest strength-to-weight ratios of any materials ever used by blade makers, as well as airplane and boat builders. Done properly, however, extruded fiberglass also makes an excellent blade material. Bergey holds the secrets with extruded fiberglass.

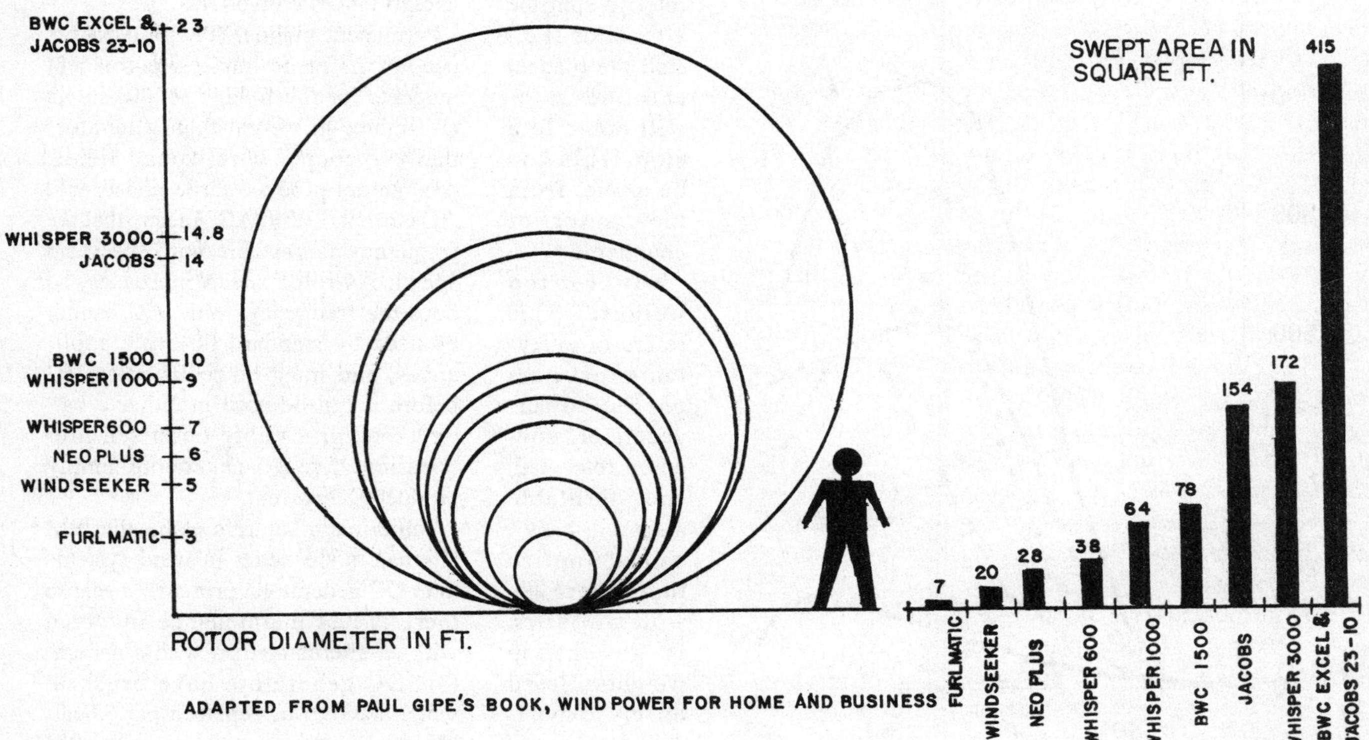

Airfoil: This refers to the airfoil of the blade. Two types of airfoils are used by wind generator manufacturers; true airfoils and single-surface airfoils.

The cross section of a true airfoil blade would look much like an airplane wing; that is, curved on one side and more or less flat on the opposite side. Single-surface airfoils have matching curves on both sides. They are easily formed by the extrusion process.

The differences between the airfoils occur in three areas: performance, noise, and manufacturing cost. True airfoils are quieter and perform better than single-surface airfoils. But single surface airfoils are cheaper to manufacture than the more complex, true airfoils.

Lateral thrust: Lateral thrust at the tower top is mainly a design consideration for tower manufacturers. Lateral thrust is a function of swept area of the rotor, the resistance the tower presents to the wind, and wind speed. The greater the lateral thrust, the stronger (and therefore, more expensive) the tower must be and the larger the concrete footings must be.

Governor system: This refers to the manner in which the wind generator protects itself from high winds and rotor overspeed situations. Governing is necessary for two reasons; to protect the generator itself from overproducing and burning out, and to protect the entire system from flying apart in high winds.

The governing devices used on all of these wind generators fall into two general categories; those that reduce the area of the rotor facing the wind and those that change the blade pitch.

Changing the swept area of the rotor is accomplished by either tilting the rotor up and out of the wind (Neo and Whispers) or by side-facing the rotor out of the wind by moving it around the tower (Rutland and Bergeys). In either case, the rotor is offset either above or to the side of a pivot point. Wind pressure on the rotor causes it to pivot out of the wind. These governing mechanisms are almost a foolproof method of controlling rotor speed. They do come with a cost though. Once the rotor governs by tilting up or side facing, it produces little power.

Blade-activated governors work by pitching the blades out of their ideal alignment to the wind. The greater the rotor speed, the greater the degree of pitch. Having more moving parts than either the tilt-up or side-facing mechanisms, they are considerably more complicated governing devices. However, they offer much better power curves, as we will see later.

Governing wind speed: This is the wind velocity at which the governing mechanism is fully operational.

Shut-down mechanism: This refers to the manner in which the rotor can be stopped and the generator shut down. This is desirable for maintenance or repairs, or whenever else you do not want the rotor to be turning.

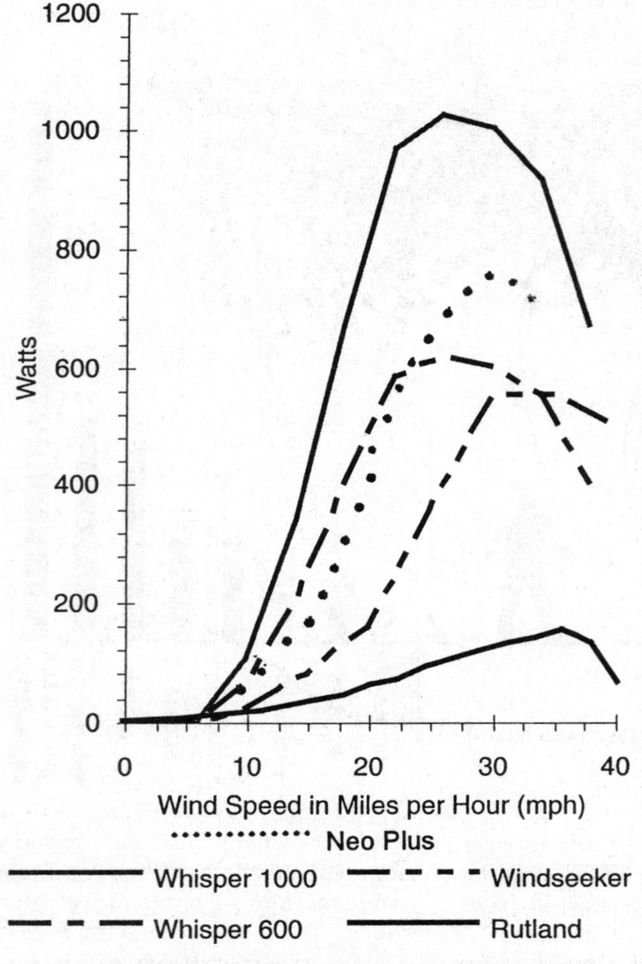

Above: Power curves for small wind generators.

The most common system used is to fold the tail (all of these systems have tails) so that it is parallel to the blades. This takes the rotor out of the wind, and it will cease to rotate. Folding the tail involves either cranking or uncranking a cable which will furl or unfurl the tail, depending on the system. The cable winch is at the base of the tower, meaning you must go out to the tower to accomplish the shutdown. Wind Turbine Industries uses the winch to activate a mechanical brake which slows the rotor to a stop on the 10kw Jakes.

Dynamic braking is unique to permanent magnet alternators. Dynamic braking works as follows: if you short out the three phases of a permanent magnet alternator, it will overpower the ability of the rotor to spin the alternator (i.e., stall the blades) and the rotor will come to a stop. This can be done from the comfort of your home.

Tower top weight: This refers to everything that goes on the tower: generator, governor, rotor, tail, and turntable assembly. You'll notice that there is wide variation in tower top weights. Based on my experience I side with the "school of heavy metal," manufacturers who believe that beefiness of components is directly related to the longevity of equipment life. Marine option indicates whether the unit is suitable for use in a marine climate (within one mile of an ocean or on an island) or if this option is available for an additional price.

Generator type: This describes the electrical generator that is used in the system. Three types are used: permanent magnet alternators, DC generators, or brushless alternators. A little about the pros and cons of each is in order. But first, another digression.

Electrical generating devices work by having a wire (or series of wires) pass through a magnetic field. The movement of the wire through the magnetic field causes a current to flow through that wire. It's the flowing current that we are after for our batteries and grid intertie inverters.

Permanent magnet (PM) alternators use, as the name implies, permanent magnets for the field. PM alternators are lighter in weight than generators that use copper wire-wound fields. Alternators produce three phase wild AC current. "Wild AC" means that the frequency is variable with the wind speed. As rotor speed increases, so does the frequency. Wild AC cannot be used by standard 60-cycle appliances, and must be rectified to DC before it can be used in either a battery bank or a utility tie-in synchronous inverter. DC generators simply produce DC current.

Some manufacturers claim that PM alternators are better in wind systems than DC generators, primarily because there is less maintenance involved with an alternator than with a generator. DC generators have brushes, which have to be replaced periodically, maybe every six years or so. PM alternators do not have brushes. (From my perspective, replacing brushes twice a decade can hardly be construed as a maintenance problem.)

The real advantage of permanent magnets to a manufacturer is that the magnets are cheap. Compared to the cost of the copper wire needed in a wound field, permanent magnets are a bargain. Cheaper materials means that a manufacturer can be more competitive in pricing his product.

The advantages to a system owner of PM alternators are two. First, you can take advantage of dynamic braking, described earlier. Second, three-phase AC current can be transmitted through wires more efficiently than DC current, meaning that you can keep your wire costs down.

However, there is a disadvantage to a PM alternator when compared to a generator with a wound field. Because the magnets in a PM alternator are permanent, the amount of magnetism they exude, or their flux density, is fixed at the magnet's maximum amount. The amount of flux density in a wire-wound field magnet, however, is proportional to the amount of current that it draws and, somewhat, to the amount of voltage present. (I'm going to simplify this greatly, so all you electrical engineers out there, please don't drop your teeth!) In other words, the higher the voltage present in a wire-wound field, the more current the field will draw, and, therefore, the stronger the magnet will be. However, as the rotor speeds up, the flux density of the field increases accordingly.

The nice thing about this arrangement is that the magnets in a wire-wound field generator put very little magnetic drag on the spinning armature when little wind is blowing. But there's plenty of magnetic drag available when the wind is cranking, and the generator is peaking. The power curve of a DC wire-wound field generator nicely follows the power available at increasing wind speeds (the cube law). That's just the way you want it. PM alternators, on the other hand, always have maximum magnetic drag on the current-generating stator. This means that performance is at its peak at only one spot, really, on the entire power curve. All other points on the power curve are a compromise, especially at the low wind speed end of the curve, the part of the curve where the wind system spends most of its life.

In order to overcome this problem, manufacturers using PM alternators have to design more torque into their blades just to get the rotor spinning in low winds. But remember, torque is inversely related to efficiency. So while PM alternators are simpler (no brushes) and cheaper to build than DC generators, the simplicity comes at a price.

To be fair, DC generators come at a price, too. They are more expensive than PM alternators.

Brushless alternators offer the best of both worlds. The fields are wire-wound rather than permanent magnets, but there are no brushes to replace. Their power curve is similar to a DC generator. On the down side, brushless are considerably more complicated, and therefore more expensive to replace, than either DC generators or PM alternators.

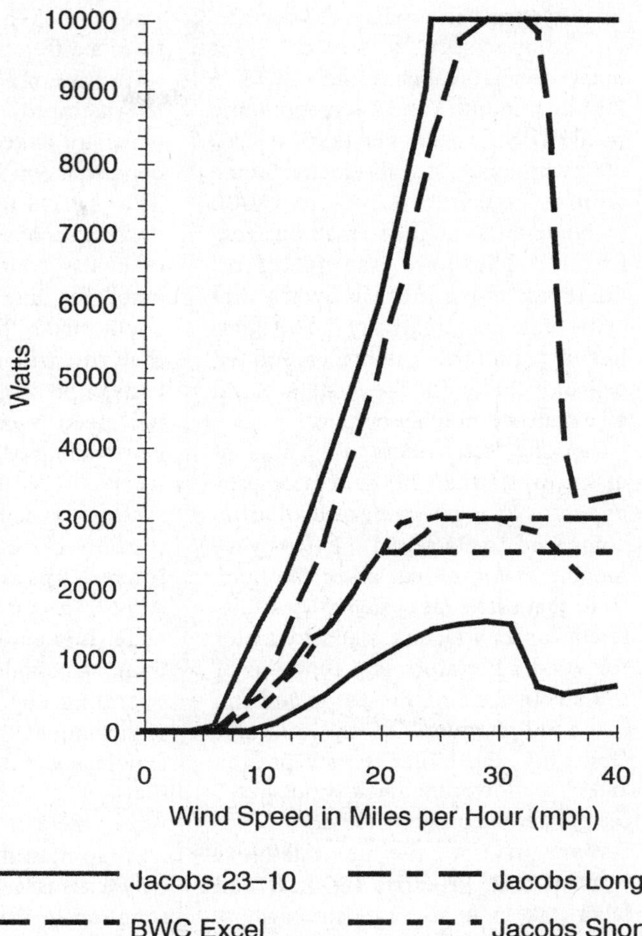

Above: Power curves for large wind generators.

Tower top cost: This is the cost of the complete wind-generating device. In most cases, it does not include the cost of any controls, except where noted in the "special notes." This is because different end uses require different types of controllers, and some end uses don't require any controller.

Cost per watt: This refers to the tower top cost divided by the rated output in watts. This figure is included so that you can make direct comparisons with the cost of PV panels.

Available systems refers to what use the wind generator can be put to. Different end uses will utilize different control systems, which are not interchangeable.

Battery systems: This is self explanatory. The voltages available for the battery systems are listed.

UTI systems: This refers to utility tie-in systems—that is, using the utility grid as your storage.

Resistance heating: This means that the wind system is used for space heating. These controls are the simplest and least expensive end-use option.

Water pumping: This means that a control package is available to pump water with an electrical pump run off of the wind generator directly. No batteries. This category designates whether an AC or DC pump is used. Because of the wide variety of controllers available, prices have not been included. Contact the manufacturer with specific needs and for price quotes.

Estimated monthly output at sites with average wind speeds of 10 mph and 12 mph: These are included so that you have some idea as to what a wind system will produce at your site. For comparisons, a very efficient home or small cabin would use 75 to 200 kwh/month. The "average home in the U.S." (whatever that is) uses 600kwh/month. An all-electric home would consume 1200 to 2000 kwh/month, as might a small business or farm. These are manufacturers' numbers, not mine. Be aware that "your mileage might vary." The number in parentheses is the calculated capacity factor for the system based on estimated monthly output.

Capacity factor refers to the amount of kilowatts that the generator produces over a given period of time compared to its potential if it were running at full output all of the time. Note that different systems boast different capacity factors. Capacity factor for wind generators is a function of the swept area of the rotor and the rated wind speed of the system. Generally, the larger the swept area and/or the lower the rated wind speed, the greater the capacity factor.

Warranty: All the manufacturers warrant their products for parts and labor (that is, in house repairs) against defects in materials or workmanship. This means that you must return the defective part to the factory for evaluation and repair or replacement at the discretion of the factory. Standard practice is that you will pay shipping both ways, just as with any other consumer good. Warranties do not cover improper installation, neglect, use of unauthorized components, abuse, or "acts of god" (this is why you have homeowners insurance). Manufacturer liability is for the defective part only, and does not include incidental or consequential damages.

Time in business: This is included so that you can see that these manufacturers are not fly-by-nighters. All of these folks have established businesses and have done extensive business in, as well as outside of, the U.S.

Footnote: Whisper wind generators have been available for only four years. Prior to that, the company was known as Whirlwind and manufactured a different line of wind systems.

Routine maintenance: This refers to what needs to be done to the wind generator to keep it in prime operating condition for a long life. How long? That's hard to say. I recently took down a Jacobs that had seen 60 years of nearly continuous duty. Properly cared for, any one of these systems could match that. This doesn't mean that you will never have to replace parts or do some major repairs. Blades will need repainting and probably a new leading edge eventually. Bearings wear out and need replacing. Some systems, as noted, need annual greasings or oil changes. Bolts might loosen up and need tightening. Adjustments might be needed here or there. It is unrealistic to expect something as complex as a wind generator operating continuously in the harsh environment that it lives in to work flawlessly with no maintenance. If that's your belief, then don't buy a wind generator.

Some manufacturers recommend only a visual inspection as their maintenance. Bergey Windpower Company, for example, suggests that after you install one of their units, once a year you need to go out to the base of the tower and look up to see if it is still running. That's it for another year. There is no question that Bergey builds the most maintenance-free wind generators available in the industry. However, I am a little more conservative than they are. Many of the catastrophic failures that I have seen over the years with various systems were due to something as seemingly inconsequential as a bolt loosening up. I believe that the prudent wind generator owner should thoroughly inspect his/her system twice a year at a minimum; once on a nice fall day before winter hits and again on a warm spring day before thunderstorm season. As they say, prevention is the best cure. Preventive maintenance becomes more important as your investment in the system increases.

Most of the great strides in reduced maintenance have come, not from new designs, but from new materials. The designs for today's wind generators have been around for a long time. For example, the side-facing governing mechanism was patented in 1898 and used on waterpumpers. The tilt-up style of governing was patented in 1931. And the blade-activated governor was patented in 1951. However, such things as graphite impregnated nylon used in some bushings or the alaphatic resin tapes that are used for leading edge protection were just being developed ten years ago. Continuous upgrading by incorporating modern materials in wind system components has helped greatly in the maintenance arena. The manufacturer who cuts corners by using cheap materials is the one who is courting trouble with his customers.

Power curves

The power curves for all of the wind systems reviewed have been put together so that you can more easily compare one system to another. The curves compare the power output of the various systems as a function of wind speed. However, be aware that this is still an "apples and oranges" comparison. To use the PV analogy, it is better to compare all panels of a given wattage than to put all panels made on the same chart. The problem with wind generators is that there are not that many models available to choose from. Because some equipment outputs are close though, some reasonable comparisons can be made.

Noise

Questions often arise about how much noise a particular wind generator makes. For the most part, a well designed wind generator is relatively quiet. By the time the wind generator is cranking enough to cause some noise, trees are rustling and buildings are rattling as well.

Noise from a wind generator can come from two sources; mechanical noise and blade noise. Mechanical noise would emanate from something such as a gearbox. Most of the systems reviewed are direct drive, meaning the blade is coupled directly to the generating device. Only the 10kw Jacobs utilizes a gearbox.

Blade noise can be caused by two things; rpm and/or the airfoil. Rpm should be obvious. The faster something spins, the more noise it is likely to make. The shape of the airfoil can also have an effect on the amount of noise the blades make. As a rule, true airfoils are quieter than single-surface airfoils.

Installation

The installation of a wind generator on a tower can be accomplished with either the use of gin pole or a crane. A gin pole is sort of a boom that is mounted on top of your tower. Using cables and rigging, either the entire wind generator or its component parts are hoisted to the top of the tower, where they are installed. This is relatively easy to do with the smaller systems. However, only an experienced crew should attempt this with something as large as a 10kw system. These wind generators are probably better installed with the help of a crane.

An alternative is to install a tilt-up tower. Tilt-up towers tilt down to ground level, where the wind generator can be easily installed and serviced. Tilt-up towers are generally more expensive than either freestanding or guyed towers.

My choice?

"So, Mick, what do you recommend?" is the most frequently asked question that I get. The answer: "It all depends on your situation."

I can honestly say that, properly speced out and installed, any one of these machines will do a fine job of producing electricity for you for many years. They all have their own personalities and idiosyncrasies, just like the cars we drive. And, just like the cars we drive, they come in a variety of shapes and prices. Finally, just like the cars we choose, they will all get us from point A to point B. However, not all cars, nor all wind generators, are created equal. Quality comes at a price.

Hopefully, you now have before you all the tools you need to make an educated choice. But make sure that you digest the facts and figures in light of your needs and pocketbook for a while, so that you may choose well.

The manufacturers

The manufacturers for the systems reviewed can be contacted for prices or more information. Or you can contact your favorite wind generator dealer.

Bergey Windpower Company, 2001 Priestly Ave., Norman, OK 73069, Phone 405-364-4212, Fax 405-364-2078. Manufactures the BWC 1500 and the BWC Excel.

Lake Michigan Wind & Sun, E3971 Bluebird Rd., Forestville, WI 54213, Phone 414-837-2267, Fax 414-837-7523. Remanufactures the Jacobs "short case" and Jacobs "long case."

Southwest Windpower, 1855 Kiabab Lane #5, Flagstaff, AZ 86001, Phone 602-779-9463, Fax 602-779-1485. Manufactures the Windseeker.

Trillium Windmills, Inc., R.R. #2, Orillia, Ontario, Canada L3V 6H2, Phone 705-326-6513, Fax 705-325-9104. North American distributor for the Rutland Windchargers (which are manufactured by Marlec Engineering Co., Ltd., of England).

Wind Baron Corporation, 3920 E. Huntington Dr., Flagstaff, AZ 86004, Phone 602-526-6400, Fax 602-526-5498. Manufactures the NEO PLUS.

Wind Turbine Industries, Corp., 16801 Industrial Circle S.E., Prior Lake, MN 55372, Phone 612-447-6064, Fax 612-447-6050. Manufactures the Jacobs 23-10.

World Power Technologies, 19 Lake Avenue North, Duluth, MN 55802, Phone 218-722-1492, Fax 218-722-0791. Manufactures the Whisper 600, Whisper 1000, and Whisper 3000.

A BHM Writer's Profile

James E. Robertson says, "I was lucky enough to catch wind of *BHM* in the beginning. I enjoy the magazine very much, mainly because it presents a forum where people exchange knowledge and ideas.

"One day, a friend of mine who I had taught the basics of string craft and who always borrowed my *BHM*, suggested that I write down the directions and send them to *BHM*. I had never done anything like this before, but as you can see [p. 82] I took my friend's advice and gave it a shot. Glad I did too!

"For not only was it a good feeling seeing my work in print, I also received responses from people, either with questions or wanting a piece of string art already made. The best was to come when a very nice lady from Ohio responded and we found that we shared many of the same interests. We became pen pals and have been corresponding ever since."

AMERICANA

Thanksgiving — a celebration of freedom and harvest

By John Silveira

"What are you writing about this issue?" I heard a voice ask.

I glanced up from the menu and was surprised to see Dave Duffy's poker playing pal, O. E. MacDougal, sliding into the seat on the other side of the booth.

"Can we talk about something else?" I asked. It was my way of saying I don't have the slightest idea.

The waitress approached and placed a cup of coffee in front of Mac. He thanked her, then turned back to me.

"How'd you find me here?" I asked.

"Coincidence. I was just coming down here for breakfast and I saw your car out front. By the way, did Dave mention I'm going up to Oregon to go fishing with him and Butch?"

Dave, of course, is Dave Duffy, the fellow who publishes this magazine. Butch is Richard Blunt, the fellow whose food column is often included in the magazine. I don't know where he got the nickname Butch and as near as I can tell, no one but his best friends call him that.

Dave, Mac, and Butch have been friends for years and Mac is fast becoming a good friend of mine.

"Fishing? Oregon?" I had visions of sitting in a rowboat or fishing from a wooden pier on one of those lakes. "Sounds like fun."

"Do you want to go?"

"I don't think I can afford it."

"Ride up with me. You can stay with Dave's family when we get there. You'll be fed. You won't even need a car."

"Maybe I'll call and ask him," I said.

"He told me to invite you."

"Really?"

He nodded.

"When is it?"

"Butch is flying in October 9th. I'll be leaving here either the 7th or the 8th."

I could see myself drifting lazily across some secluded lake in Oregon.

The waitress reappeared. She poured more coffee for Mac without asking.

"More coffee, sir?" she asked me, the coffee pot cocked and ready to pour.

"Please," I said.

"Call me when you're ready to order," she said to me. "Your order's coming up, Mac."

"Thanks, Hon," he said.

She smiled and walked away, touching him lightly on the shoulder as she passed him. I've never gone anywhere in this county with Mac that he does not know at least one person and it's usually a woman holding a coffee pot.

"Well, what are you going to write about this issue?" he asked again.

"I really don't know."

"How about fishing?"

I shook my head. "Duffy wants something timely and topical."

"What's coming up?"

"My lunch if I have to write about Christmas or Thanksgiving."

"Is that what he wants? You to write about one or the other?"

I nodded.

"I would think they'd be interesting to write about."

"What's so interesting about stuffing yourself with turkey or the misery of Christmas shopping?"

"You don't like Christmas shopping?"

I shook my head.

"It can be fun."

I cringed.

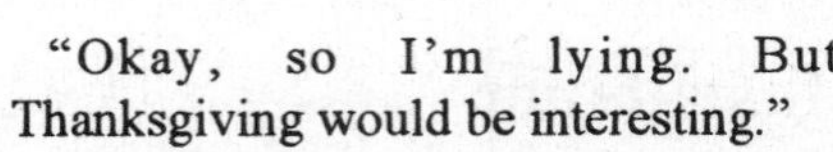

"Okay, so I'm lying. But Thanksgiving would be interesting."

"What's so interesting about Thanksgiving?"

"Did you know it's the oldest American holiday? And though thanksgivings are celebrated around the world, and date back into prehistory, the American celebration is unique."

"Prehistory? There were thanksgivings before the Pilgrims?"

He nodded.

The waitress brought a plate with some funny looking flat cakes on it and placed it in front of him along with two little bowls.

"What are those?" I asked.

"Potato pancakes," he said.

"I didn't even hear you order them."

"Oh, they just know. I always get them when I come in here."

I picked up my menu again. "I didn't see them on the menu."

"They're not. The cook makes them special for me. Ever have them?"

I stared at his pancakes and shook my head.

"Do you want to try some?"

I hemmed and hawed. They smelled good. "Okay," I said.

He gestured to the waitress and she went back to the kitchen.

"What were we talking about?" I asked.

"You asked about thanksgivings before the Pilgrims."

"Oh, yeah."

He started eating his pancakes.

An ancient holiday

"Thanksgiving celebrations aren't recent inventions and they were probably celebrated by prehistoric men and even today there are thanksgivings celebrated in other cultures."

"No kidding. When did the first thanksgiving take place?"

"No one's sure. But we can draw some conclusions. For instance, there's lots of speculation as to what's behind the ancient paintings that have been discovered in caves in Europe. Some of those paintings are over 30,000 years old. And, though no one really knows why they were painted or what the artists intended to convey and maybe we never will, there's good reason to suspect some of them may have been part of thanksgiving celebrations.

"There are also biblical references to thanksgivings. Cain's first offerings of fruits and Abel's offerings of the firstborn of the flocks, recounted in Genesis, are thanksgiving celebrations.

"The Feast of the Tabernacles, celebrated in October by the Jews, is an ancient thanksgiving festival that followed the harvest and lasted seven days.

"Later, in the Middle Ages, the English celebrated with a festival called Harvest Home in which villagers met the last wagon load of grain as it was brought back to the barn. They decorated it with ribbons and flowers and they danced around it. This was followed by a thanksgiving festival.

"And later yet, when the first English settlers arrived on the east coast of this continent, they discovered the Indians there had a four day celebration called the Green Corn Dance. It followed the harvest and it was a thanksgiving festival."

"What's that stuff in the bowls you're putting on them?" I asked, referring to his pancakes.

"One's sour cream. The other's apple sauce. Most people like one or the other on them. I like both."

"Hmm," I said. "So thanksgivings are some sort of harvest festival."

"Usually," he said, "but not always. The Greeks celebrated thanksgivings to commemorate military victories, sporting victories, safe trips, and even some personage's surviving an illness. And, of course, they celebrated successful harvests, too. The Greek city-states, whose main form of entertainment was to wage war with each other, often suspended their wars just to celebrate these thanksgiving harvest celebrations."

I'll bet not one person in a hundred can tell you what the Mayflower Compact was and why it's so important. We think freedom and democracy started with the Revolutionary War, the Constitution and the Bill of Rights. But it all started on a ship anchored off the Massachusetts coast.

"That's kind of odd."

"What's that?"

"A thanksgiving celebration for a military victory."

"Not really. In 1863, there were two thanksgiving proclamations issued by Lincoln. The first was to commemorate the Union victory at Gettysburg. The second was to establish the Thanksgiving Day we now celebrate."

"Do you mind if I make notes?" I asked.

"Go ahead."

He took another bite of his pancakes and my stomach started to audibly growl when the waitress brought my potato pancakes.

"I figured I'd bring you sour cream and apple sauce, just like Mac's," she said.

I thanked her and put a little of each on a corner of one of the pancakes then cut off a piece with my fork. "Hmm. These are pretty good, Mac."

He nodded.

"You said it's the oldest American holiday?"

"That's right. When Europeans first settled the new world, Christmas was not celebrated as a holiday. But, as long ago as 1578, English settlers in Newfoundland were setting aside part of a day for prayer and thanksgiving and in 1621, a year after the Pilgrims arrived in Plymouth, Governor Bradford proclaimed a day of prayer, rejoicing, and festivities."

"That's the Thanksgiving we celebrate now, isn't it?"

He nodded.

"What made them want to have a celebration?"

"What do you know about the Pilgrims?"

"Not much," I said. "They landed at Plymouth Rock. They wore funny clothes. They ate turkey."

"You're a true representative sample of the American education system," he said.

"So, what's the big deal about them?"

Pilgrims fled religious persecution

"You have to know who they were, first. The Pilgrims who landed at Plymouth Rock were fleeing religious persecution and, although they themselves would later prove to be very intolerant, they brought with them the seeds of freedom and democracy that our country was founded upon."

"So, you're saying, when we celebrate our Thanksgiving, we celebrate...well..."

"Go ahead, use the word—freedom. You shouldn't be embarrassed when you say it. It's not a dangerous word."

"Okay," I said.

"Let me give you a little background on them. I won't bore you with how the Pilgrims fled from England to Holland to escape religious persecution, or why they left Holland to go to the new world where there were hills of gold, rivers of silver, bumper harvests and the Indians worshipped the white man."

"Are you kidding?"

"No. This continent's always gotten good P.R."

"How many of them were there?"

"You mean, how many were on the Mayflower?"

"Yeah."

"Not counting the ship's crew, there were 102 men, women, and children as well as dogs, cats, birds..."

"Birds? Like chickens?"

"No, like pet birds."

"Why pet birds?"

"The Pilgrims were human, too. If you were moving, you'd bring those two cats of your's with you."

"Okay. Did they bring farm animals, too?"

"Some."

"Mac, can I ask you something personal?"

"Sure."

"Did you once teach history or something?"

"No."

"Hmm. By the way, these potato pancakes are really good."

"I know, you said that."

Pencil poised, I asked, "Did all 102 survive the trip?"

"No, one of the Pilgrims died on the way over, but another was born en route so 102 left and 102 reached their destination."

"Well, it sounded like a pretty good trip then."

"Actually, it was a horrible trip. There were storms, there were weevils in the flour, the ship stunk like an outhouse, the quarters were cramped, and the crew was belligerent and cruel to them. In fact, after running into several storms, the crew wanted to turn back. But their attitude toward the Pilgrims radically changed when, one day, one of the sailors who had been especially cruel suddenly dropped dead for no apparent reason and the sailors, a superstitious lot, saw it as an omen or a warning from God. After that, there were still storms, there were still weevils, the ship was still cramped and still stunk, but the crew was a lot nicer to them."

"How long did the trip take?"

"Nine and a half weeks."

"Why did they choose to go to Massachusetts?"

"They didn't. They were supposed to go to Virginia."

"What happened?"

"They missed."

"But Virginia and Massachusetts aren't even that close together. How'd they miss it by so much?"

"The vagaries of sailing and navigation in those times."

I wrote it down. "Did landing in Massachusetts cause any problems?"

"Sure it did. They not only landed further north, in a climate harsher than the one they had intended, their charter, the legal document that granted them 80,000 acres of land in Virginia, was no good in this strange land. The charter was their legal right to be in the new world. It provided them land and it was going to provide them with their governing body. Now they had no land, no rights, no government."

"So, what happened?"

The Mayflower Compact

"Well, it's what happened that makes the Pilgrims so important in American history. They drafted a document that would govern themselves and they elected a governor, a man named John Carver. The document they drew up was known as the Mayflower Compact. The Mayflower Compact was the first time, in the new world, that a body of free men drew up a set of laws to govern themselves. It was also the first time a governor was elected democratically. Colonial governors had always been appointed by the king and served at his pleasure. The Pilgrims elected one and he was one of their own.

"Nowadays, the significance of this is lost on Americans. I'll bet not one person in a hundred can tell you what the Mayflower Compact was and why it's so important. We think freedom and democracy started with the Revolutionary War, the Constitution, and the Bill of Rights. But it all started on a ship anchored off the Massachusetts coast. I've always wondered if the Pilgrims themselves were aware of the significance of their act or if they were as much unaware of the historical impact their act would have as most Americans today are oblivious to what they did."

"And it is in part the signing of the Mayflower Compact that we celebrate at Thanksgiving?" I suggested somewhat hopefully.

"That's right."

"Hmm," I said and made a few more notes. "So, how did that first Thanksgiving come about?"

"To understand what Thanksgiving meant to them, you've got to understand how rough their lives were. They first sighted land in November 1620 after nine and a half weeks at sea, and they first set foot on land out on Cape Cod in what is now Provincetown. What they found there was unsuitable for establishing a colony so they got back aboard ship and continued to explore the coast.

"Finally, they found a protected cove and landed again. There they established a settlement and called it Plymouth Colony, after the town of

Plymouth, England, from where they had set sail.

"They built a common house that was a small cabin about 20 feet square. Most of the Pilgrims lived in this while others lived in small dugouts they dug in the ground and covered with sod."

"Didn't they live in log cabins?"

"No. Once they established their colony, they tried to build typical English cottages with the thatch roof, but they didn't weather well in the new world and they often caught fire. It was the Swedes, who had come from a harsher climate to settle in Delaware, who introduced the log cabin, which many people consider an American invention. And though it later became an American icon, the original Pilgrims never saw one."

He had already finished his potato pancakes and he caught the waitress's eye.

A fatal winter

"In December, things went from bad to worse for the Pilgrims. The wife of William Bradford, the man who was to be elected governor of the colony and would be reelected 30 times, had already fallen overboard and drowned in November.

"In December, other settlers started dying. In less than ninety days, half of them were dead of scurvy or pneumonia.

"They always buried their dead after nightfall and hid the graves from the Indians. They feared them and didn't want them to know how weak the settlement was becoming."

"By March, 48 were dead including the baby born at sea. Of the 54 who survived, 21 were under the age of 16."

"I guess the ship went back too soon," I said.

"What do you mean?"

"Well, they were trapped. If the ship had stuck around, they could have gotten away."

"Actually, the Mayflower was still anchored off the coast. It was waiting for better weather to return to England. And, in April, when it set sail, not a one of the settlers went with her. They were going to stick it out in the new world."

"No kidding."

When the waitress got there, Mac asked for another order of the pancakes.

"Make that two," I said.

"By the time the ship left," Mac continued, "the Pilgrims still had not made contact with the Indians. They often saw them but every time they tried to approach them, the Indians ran away. So, you can imagine their surprise when, one day, an Indian strode into the Pilgrims's settlement and started to speak to them in English. He told them his name was Samoset and he had learned English from English fishermen his own tribe had had contact with along the coast of Maine."

"What English fishermen?" I asked.

"The English had been fishing off the North American coast for almost a century by this time. They just hadn't established many colonies."

"Oh."

Squanto

"He told the Pilgrims that the local Indians were friendly. Then he introduced them to the local chief, Massasoit. Then, as a final surprise, he told them that living among Massasoit's people was another Indian, a man named Squanto, who also spoke English.

"Squanto should be another American icon. His life is one of those adventures that should have been made into a Hollywood movie. When he was younger, he had been taken to England by a ship captain, and there he learned to speak English. After he was brought back and had returned to his village, another ship's captain kidnapped him, along with several other Indians, and sold them as slaves in Spain.

"Eventually, he was owned by Spanish friars and, though they treated him kindly, he finally escaped from them and returned to England. There he found a friendly sea captain who brought him back to the new world. But this time, when he walked into his village, he discovered that everyone who had lived in the village had died of some sickness. For awhile, he wandered through the wilderness until he went to live with Massasoit's tribe."

"He must have developed a serious dislike for the white man."

"On the contrary. He not only helped the Pilgrims, he spent the rest of his life living among them. Without his help, we don't know if the Plymouth colony could have survived. He taught them the skills they needed to live. He showed them how to grow Indian corn and other vegetables. He taught them how and where to hunt, and how to fish."

"What's there to hunting and fishing?"

"None of the Pilgrims knew how to hunt. They made so much noise, fumbling around in the woods, they scared game away. And among the things they neglected to bring from Europe were fishing nets and hooks.

"With Squanto's help, crops were bountiful, game on the table was plentiful, and if there were any problems at all it was that the Massasoit's tribe became so friendly they were always there and always eating, faster than the Pilgrims could store it. Finally, they had to ask Massasoit to tell his people to stay away. Only then were the Pilgrims able to lay in their harvest for their second winter.

The first pilgrim Thanksgiving

"The harvest proved to be so bountiful, the Pilgrim's decided to hold a Thanksgiving feast. And because their success had depended on the help they got from the Indians, they sent Squanto to the camp of Massasoit and invited him and his people to join in the celebration. But when Massasoit showed up, the Pilgrims were surprised to see he brought with him ninety braves."

"That meant that there were more Indians at the first Thanksgiving than there where Pilgrims."

"That's right."

The waitress returned with the second order.

"How'd they feed 'em all?" I asked.

"They sent out for pizza."

He took a sip of his coffee. "Actually, the Indians contributed to the celebration. They went into the forest and killed five deer and they supplied Indian pudding, some of the vegetables, and who knows what else. There are no accurate records of what they brought or what else was served."

"What's Indian pudding?" I asked.

"It's a concoction of cornbread and molasses. I don't know who eats it anymore. But you can still find it in New England."

"Isn't Thanksgiving the last Thursday in November?"

"No, it's the fourth Thursday. Every once in awhile there are five Thursdays in November."

"So, is that when the first Thanksgiving was held?"

"I don't think so. No one actually knows when it was held. But it's likely that it was actually celebrated in October."

I looked at him for an explanation.

"That's when the last of harvest would have come in. Not much is growing in New England after that."

"How did the Indians react to the white man's holiday?"

"Well I said before, they had their own harvest festival, the Green Corn dance, which they were celebrating long before the first white man ever set foot in the new world. And because the Green Corn Dance lasted four days, on the evening of the first day of the Pilgrim's Thanksgiving, the Indians didn't go home. They didn't go home the second day, either. On the third day, they finally went home, but 90 Indians ate more food than the Pilgrims had expected and it cut into their winter stores."

"I can imagine. What did they eat at that first Thanksgiving?"

"Oh, they ate fish including eel, lobster, clams, and oysters; they had native vegetables Squanto had shown them how to grow, including Indian corn, pumpkin, peas, beans; they had native wild plums and berries including strawberries, gooseberries, and cherries which the Indians had taught them to preserve by drying. They also made wine. And, of course, they had wild turkey, venison, wild duck, and goose."

"No football games," I said.

"No, but the Pilgrims marched around with their muskets, blew horns, played games, and shot their muskets. And the Indians played games and demonstrated their prowess with their bows and arrows."

"Did they have a Thanksgiving the following year?"

"No. The harvest in 1622 was too poor. But in July of 1623 they had another Thanksgiving."

"In July?"

"Yes. It was to celebrate the end of a drought that had threatened to destroy their crops. In fact, after the drought broke, the fall harvest was so good that they had another Thanksgiving feast after the harvest."

"Did they invite the Indians to that one?"

"Sure they did and this time Massasoit brought 120 of his people but they also brought plenty of food with them."

"Were Thanksgivings held regularly after that?"

"No, but the idea of a Thanksgiving celebration was catching on even though no one had yet thought to make it an official annual event. In fact, since there was no set day, as the event spread from one locale to another, it was held at different times depending on the local harvest.

"However, as more territory was added to Colonial America, it started to become, more and more, just a New England holiday.

"Then, in 1789, President George Washington issued a proclamation declaring a national day of Thanksgiving to be observed on November 26, 1789. By this time, a lot of people identified Thanksgiving with the Puritans, so they saw it as a Puritan religious holiday. But Washington suggested all religious denominations should celebrate it. It was a smart move on his part. More people were open to it. Still, the first nationwide Thanksgiving celebration met with resistance."

"Why?"

"Because it was proposed by the new federal government. The states felt such proclamations were the right of the states and looked on the federal proclamation as an attempt by federal authorities to meddle in the affairs of the states."

"Really?"

"Uh huh. Remember, we had so recently become Americans that most were not used to the idea of being Americans; we were still Virginians, or New Yorkers, or Pennsylvanians, or whatever.

"And resistance didn't end there. When Jefferson became President, he considered Thanksgiving a pagan ritual. And even those who disagreed with him and wanted a national Thanksgiving celebration couldn't agree on when it should be held."

"What were the grounds for disagreement?"

"Many felt it should coincide with the harvest. But the further south you go in the United States, the longer the growing season is and the later the harvest is.

"In spite of all this, with each passing year, more and more people started feeling 'American,' and pioneers moving west to find their own promised land were reenacting the travels of the Pilgrims, and there was an urge to take this Thanksgiving festival with them."

"So, they did," I said presumptively.

"They sure did."

"You said Washington designated it should be on November 26, 1789? What day of the week was that? It didn't happen to be..."

"That's right. It was the fourth Thursday in November."

"I guess I'd have expected you to know that."

The waitress came back with separate checks but Mac grabbed them both and put them on the table with some cash.

"However, it was still not an annual holiday until 1863 when Lincoln proclaimed it a national holiday."

"So," I said making more notes, "we can thank Abraham Lincoln for the modern Thanksgiving holiday."

Sarah J. Hale

"I wouldn't," he replied. "Thanks should be given to Sarah J. Hale."

"Who's Sarah J. Hale? Is that HALE?"

He nodded. "She was the editor of a magazine called Godey's Lady's Book, published in Boston. She made establishing Thanksgiving as a national holiday a crusade. She wrote editorials and sent letters to anyone and everyone she thought could help her cause. This included whatever President was in office. By the time of the Civil War she was corresponding with President Lincoln and at her urging, he finally issued a proclamation establishing a national day of Thanksgiving to be celebrated on the last Thursday in November. The tradition was continued by President Andrew Johnson and the Presidents who followed him. But, people being people, these proclamations were resisted by some who saw the celebration as a religious holiday and felt that churches, not the government, should proclaim the holiday."

The fourth Thursday

"You said Lincoln called for Thanksgiving on the last Thursday."

"He did, and that's how it was celebrated until 1939 when President Franklin Roosevelt, under pressure from store owners, proclaimed that Thanksgiving would be celebrated on the next to last Thursday in November. But the change was not well received and by 1941, Congress made the fourth Thursday the official Thanksgiving Day."

"Why would anyone care which Thursday Thanksgiving is celebrated on?"

"Traditionally, the biggest shopping period in the United States occurs between Thanksgiving and Christmas. In fact, the Friday after Thanksgiving is the biggest shopping day of the year in the United States. Remember, in the 1930's the Great Depression was still in full swing and many shop owners thought it would stimulate business if they could add a week to the shopping period that fell between the two holidays. Roosevelt agreed with them.

"But a lot of other people didn't. Many families ignored Roosevelt's change and celebrated what they considered to be the now traditional Thanksgiving. Then, like I said, Congress stepped in and set the date we're now familiar with."

The waitress took the check and brought the change. Mac is a pretty good tipper.

"Well, how about that fishing trip?" he asked as we left the restaurant.

"I'll call Dave," I said.

"Good. By the way, what are you writing about for the issue after this one?"

I shrugged.

"You'll think of something," he said. Δ

A BHM Writer's Profile

The family of the Rev. Dr. J.D. Hooker lives back off a gravel road, in rural Dekalb County, Indiana. They raise hogs and wolf/German shepherd hybrids, a unique and highly competent type of working dog. He and his wife of 22 years have four daughters and a grand-daughter.

For us, says Hooker, the backwoods type lifestyle is the perfect way to live and raise a family. He admits that they do have decades of experience in living independently, but says, it's only because so many years have passed while we've been busy enjoying our way of life.

Design and build a barn

By Don Fallick

Of the many considerations involved in planning a barn, two of the most important, and most often neglected by novices, are animal control and manure handling. If you design your barn right, your animals will go just where you want them to, with very little effort on your part. Do it "wrong" and you'll be fighting your livestock several times every day. This can range from inconvenient with goats to hilarious with chickens. With cattle and horses, which are bigger than you, it can be downright dangerous.

Livestock handling

If you are going to keep several kinds of stock in the same barn, it is not necessary to design a special room for each species. The same room that serves as a lambing pen in the spring can be used for raising goat kids or foals. The important feature of a properly designed barn is that every room opens onto a common hall with doors or gates big enough to completely block the hall when opened outward. This makes it easy to separate species, by driving the whole herd down the hall and simply opening and closing gates to make each critter go where it's supposed to.

You can separate animals by species, even separate kids and calves from their mothers, without having to drag them or entice them with grains or "treats." It's simple. Suppose you have a horse, a cow, and a few goats. The dominant animal, usually the horse, will go into the barn first, followed, perhaps, by the goats and the cow. You open the door to the horse stall, so it blocks the hall, and beyond it, you open the gate to the goat pen. Then you open the main barn door at the end of the hall, and all the animals enter in order. Close the barn door before the cow enters. The horse will go right into his stall. Close the horse stall door, and the goats have nowhere else to go but into their pen. Then you can open the cow pen gate, and the main barn door and drive the cow right into her stall.

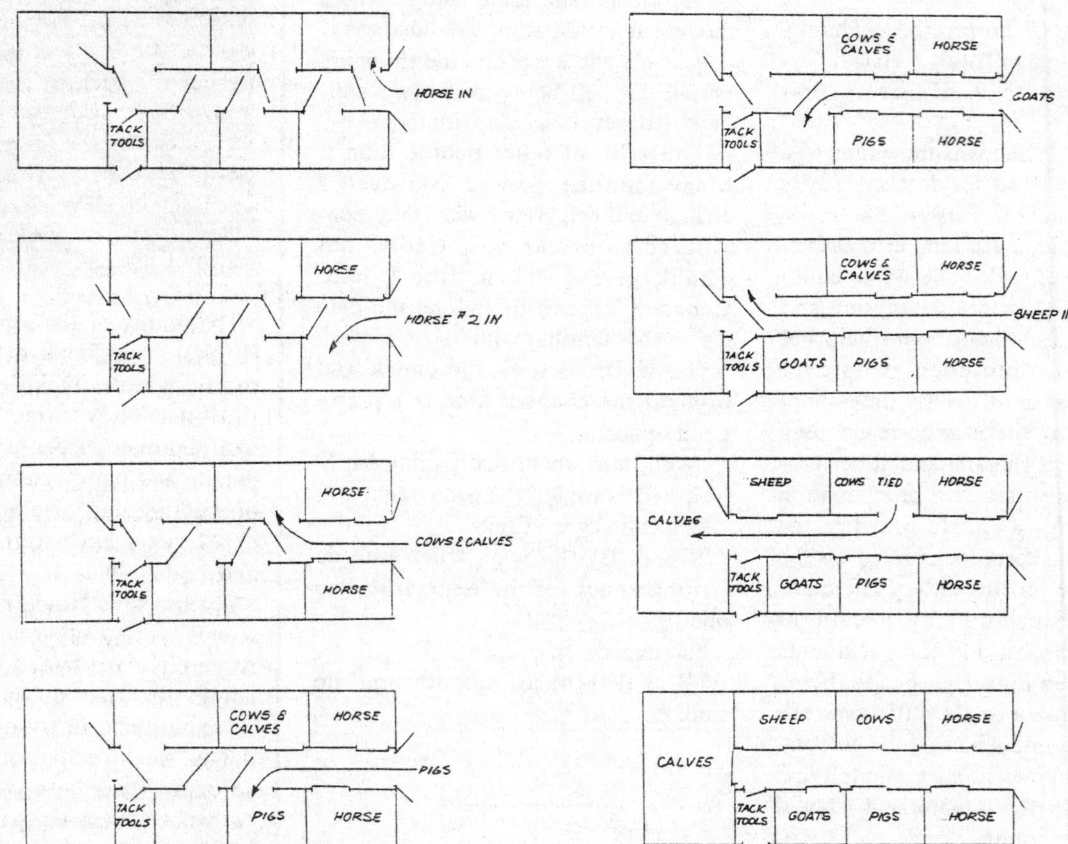

The same principle applies when building a milk parlor for goats. To eliminate the hassle of trying to get only one goat at a time into the parlor, you build it with two doors: one for the goats to enter the parlor by and another for them to leave by. These work best if they are goat sized, in which case you'll need another, larger door for you. The entrance door opens in, while the exit door opens out, and both lock from the inside. With a setup like this it's easy to train the goats to come into the parlor one at a time, and leave after they've been milked, especially if you feed grain while milking, and "free choice" hay afterward. The principle remains the same: allow the animal nowhere to go but where you want it to go, and you won't have to convince it every time.

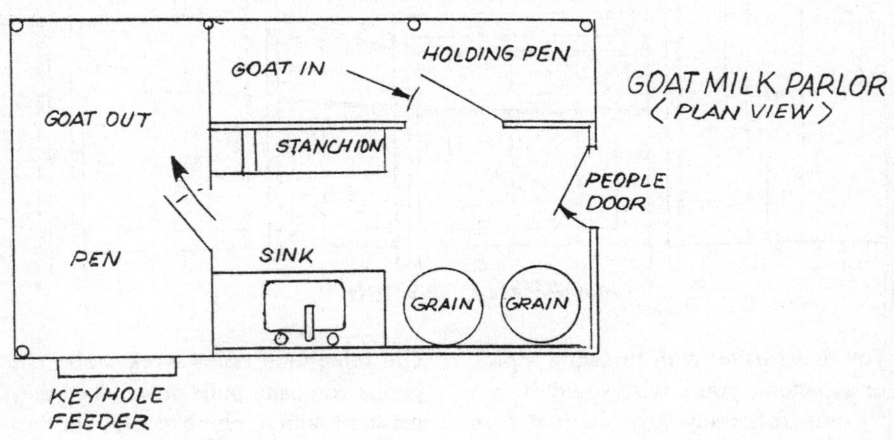

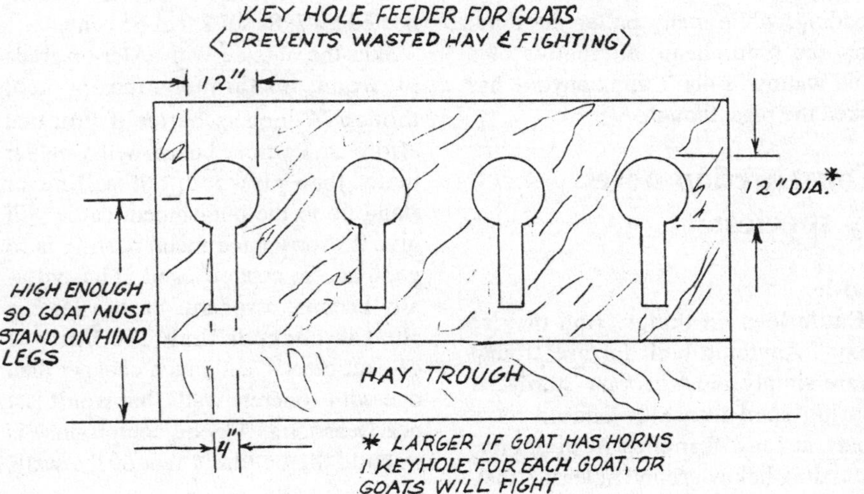

Feed and manure handling

After handling of the stock themselves, the most important aspect of a barn to the animal keeper is ease of handling feed and manure. In the Midwest, most barns are built with an earthen ramp leading up to the haymow, usually in the center of the barn. This makes it easy to back a truck up to the haymow and unload hay and other feeds, which can be pitched down to the animals on the lower story as needed. Often, feeders are arranged so grain can also be fed directly from the hay mow. Similar patterns of barns can be found all over the country.

Handling of manure is a far more complex issue. It depends to a large extent on the species of livestock, as well as the method of manure handling and its eventual disposition. Cattle produce copious amounts of manure, which is sloppy and must be shoveled, hosed or scraped away frequently. Horses produce drier manure, but equally large amounts of urine which must also be dealt with (though the bedding itself only needs to be changed once each day). Goats and sheep produce small amounts of very dry manure, which can be left to accumulate for a long time, if they have sufficient clean bedding to sleep on. Pigs are very clean animals, and will not drop manure in their bed area, if there is room for them to walk 12 feet away from it upon arising.

Truthfully, most livestock need little protection from the elements, except for the wind and direct sunlight. They will need more feed in cold weather, though. In many parts of the country, including the mountains of Colorado and the upper Midwest, it's quite common for cattle to sleep in three-sided, concrete floored "loafing sheds," and only enter a barn to be milked. The manure is scraped out by a tractor with a blade on the front or back, and pushed into piles to compost, or loaded directly into manure spreaders. In the milk parlor, the cow stalls are arranged so any manure or urine released during milking can easily be hosed into a manure channel, and then out of the barn. I have even seen horses kept in loafing sheds quite successfully. Sheep are rarely kept in anything more substantial, except around lambing season. Goats and pigs need more protection, though in warmer climates goats too can sleep in a loafing shed.

Replacing bedding for even one horse every day can quickly become a real chore, if the barn is not arranged to make this easy. One way to fix this is to install a door from the stable directly to the yard, so the bedding can be forked out of the stable and out of the barn in one operation.

Stables should *not* have concrete

floors, even though this would make manure handling much easier. Impervious concrete keeps the urine trapped in the bedding, and can cause hoof problems even if the bedding is changed daily.

One solution to this problem is to use sand for the floor. The sand soaks up the urine in the top inch or so, which can be shoveled out and replaced as needed, like cat litter. Eventually, it all needs to be removed and replaced, though, and this can be a very big job.

A more traditional solution is to make floors of wood, three or four inches thick. This allows for raking as well as shoveling of the bedding, which is placed on top of the wooden floor. The problem with wooden floors is that they, too, eventually need to be replaced, which can be quite expensive.

The cheapest solution, and the least satisfactory, from the standpoint of hygiene, is bedding directly on an earthen floor. The earth gets compacted by the horse walking on it, and becomes as hard as concrete. It turns to mud where the horse has scraped away bedding material, which horses all do. It catches pitchfork tines and shovels nearly as much as wood, and needs to be removed periodically like sand, but must be broken up with a pick before it can be shoveled out. It makes for very heavy compost, which can be a real pain if you are handling manure without benefit of a tractor. But it's literally dirt cheap, and horses like it. Whichever method you decide to use, plan your barn so the flooring is easy to replace, and level with the rest of the barn.

It's tempting to make a goat barn no taller than goat height, to conserve materials and heat in winter. This is false economy. You will eventually need to get into the barn to remove composted manure. Goat manure, with a little bedding thrown in, composts into an extremely dry, tough layer of felt-like substance that must be cut before it can be shoveled. If you don't have room to swing a pick or a mattock, you'll wish you did!

BARN WITH CENTRAL AISLE

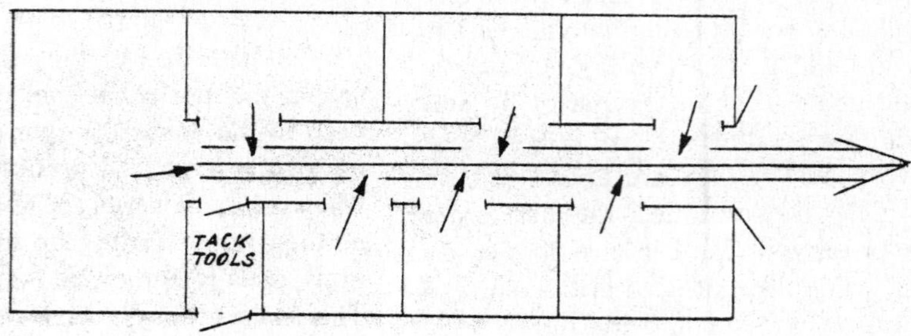

MANURE PITCHED INTO AISLE & SCRAPED OUT WITH TRACTOR OR CARRIED OUT WITH GARDEN CART

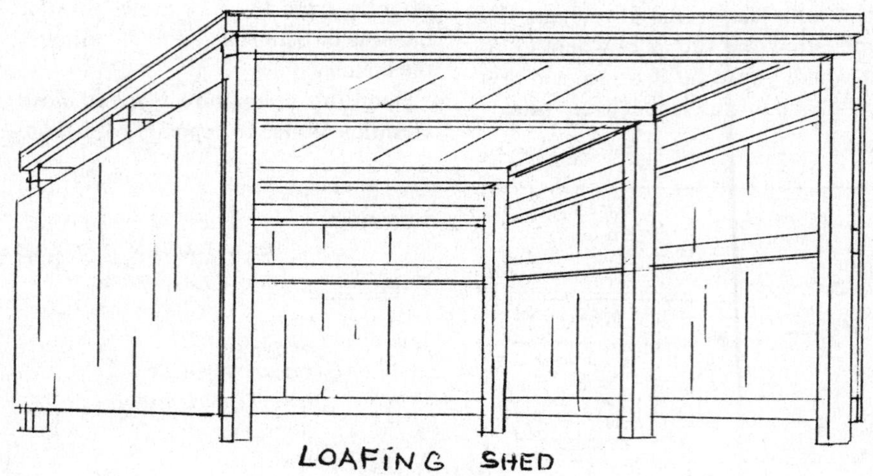

LOAFING SHED

Some folks say pigs do just fine when raised on a clean concrete floor. Others go for straw or even sawdust bedding, while many prefer the time-honored (and cheap) alternative of a mud wallow. I don't think anyone has asked the pigs, though.

Construction notes by species:

Cattle:

Cattle lean on things. And they're heavy. Anything built for use around cattle simply must be very sturdy. A loafing shed for cattle should have posts at least 8 inches in diameter, extending below ground at least 3 feet. Old telephone poles work well. The phone company pulls poles when they get too tough to climb safely, but they may still be sound from a structural point of view. The posts can be connected by 2x8s set 2 feet on center.

Skin the outside with exterior grade plywood, no thinner than 5/8 inch, though ¾ inch is better if you can afford it. Particle board will weather better than plywood, but will never stand up to the punishment cattle will give it. Corrugated metal roofing is so good and so cost efficient, it has virtually become standard. Such a loafing shed is cheaper than one built of cement blocks, and much cheaper than one with concrete walls, but won't last nearly as long. A good compromise is to build the bottom 4 feet of the walls of reinforced concrete or reinforced cement blocks. Then build the top of the walls of wood.

A milk parlor for cattle should be built similar to a barn, but remember that cleanliness is also a very important consideration in a milk parlor. For this reason, I personally favor walls of concrete, at least at the bottom. If you do use cement block, painting them will make them much easier to clean. To fasten the frame tops of the walls to the concrete or cement blocks, set L-bolts in the top of the concrete or fill the cement blocks with sand where the L-bolts will be set, except for the top course. Then fill with cement and set the L-bolts in every third block. The L-bolts will be used to bolt down the bottom plate of the frame portion of the wall.

A slick way to position the L-bolts exactly is to drill the bottom plate first and install the L-bolts in it loosely, then use it to position the bolts in the wet cement. After the cement is dry, the bottom plate can be removed and the wall framed, installed, and bolted down.

Horses:

Horses present special problems for the barn builder. They're as big and heavy as cattle, they kick things, and they frequently "crib," or chew on wood. Any horse barn or stall simply must be built with lumber no smaller than 2x8s, as high as the horse can kick. All boards used as dividers should be screwed to their posts, not because utensils won't hold (they will), but to make it easier to remove and replace the pieces of the old boards, after the horse breaks them. Stall walls should be planned with large, long span horizontal boards, to minimize the number of nails and screws, for two reasons:

1. Horses will crib around the nails, and may hurt their tongues, lips and teeth.

2. Long boards are more flexible, and therefore more durable around horses, than short boards.

Some people who have never kept horses might think it would be cheaper to run horizontal stringers at the top and bottom of the wall, and maybe even in the center, then screw vertical boards to the stringers. This is false economy, because it places the bottoms of the vertical boards where they are subject to rotting from the wet bedding. And you dare not use pressure treated lumber in a stall, where the horse may be inclined to crib on it. It also places the center stringer right where the horse who is inclined to crib can best reach it.

Pigs:

In point of fact, pigs need to be protected from the heat and wind, and, to a lesser extent, from the cold. Their subcutaneous fat does protect them from cold temperatures, especially if they are housed in a cabin small enough to trap their body heat. Exact sizes vary with the breed of pig. A proper pig cabin should be large enough for the pig to turn around in, however. "A-frame" huts are quite common where pigs are kept outdoors. In an indoor barn, the pigs will still need a small enough sleeping area to keep comfortable.

Since pigs do not perspire, their only method of cooling off is the pig wallow. Pigs do not actually prefer mud and will seek cool water to wallow in during hot seasons if given the chance. But you must give them someplace to cool off, for their health. If your pigs are housed outdoors, in a hut, this is no problem, but if your sty is inside a large barn, some provision must be made for a hog wallow. If you don't have running water to the barn, at least in summer, you'll find yourself hauling an awful lot of water to the pigs.

Goats:

Goats get along fine in the cold (except at kidding time), as long as their barns aren't drafty. But they are quite intelligent, and can be difficult to keep in. Besides being able to jump unbelievably high, goats have prehensile tongues, and can unlock most standard latches, even including spring hook latches.

I once rigged such a latch so the hook was inside a coffee can which made it difficult for me to let myself out of the pen when I was working inside it. After I got it finished, I tested it by going inside, unlocking the latch and letting myself out. The goats watched in fascination. Then I went

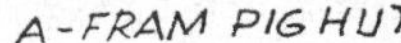

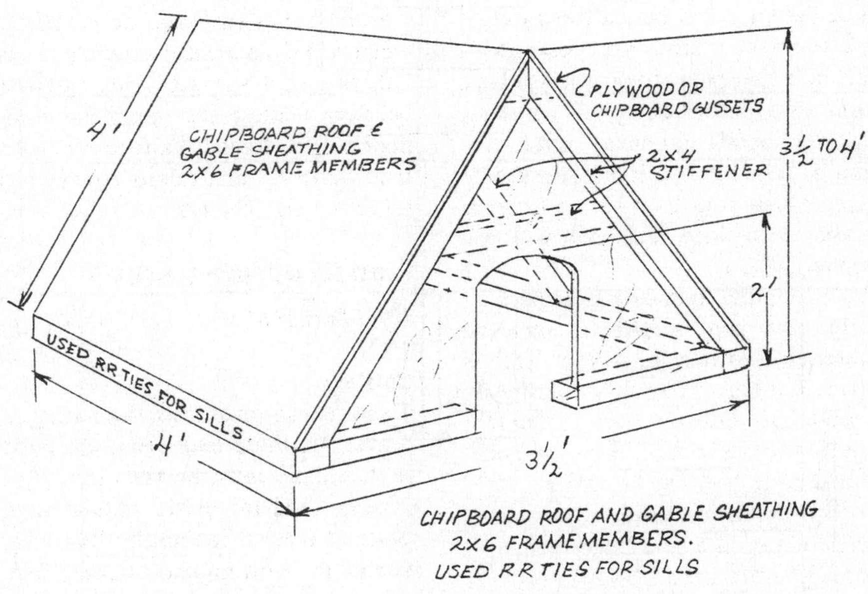

out, locked the hook, shook it to make sure it was latched—and got less than three paces from the gate before a goat nudged me. That's how quick they figured out how to unlock it!

Goats also love to push on anything handy, so goat barn walls must be sturdy. It helps if you can contrive to have the wall boards nailed onto the walls from the inside of the barn, not the outside. One way to do this is to frame two opposite walls and side them from the inside, then scab studs to the corners and frame the other two walls.

Goats in the wild do not live in caves, so they'll never be comfortable in a barn that has no windows, and you'll want light to see by when examining kids or milking. This can be a problem, as goats, and especially kids, jump around so much, there is real danger of them breaking the glass unless it is protected with expanded metal mesh, if you can get it, or 2-inch mesh welded wire fence (not woven wire, it's not strong enough).

Sheep:

Unless you live in a polar region, sheep don't really need a barn. A loafing shed to keep off the sun in the summer and the wind the rest of the year works fine. Some folks like to bring their sheep into a pen in a great barn during lambing time. With the advent of electric sheep clippers, it has also become common to see sheep brought to the barn for shearing.

Siting

It should go without saying that where you build your barn is at least as important as how you build it. Unless you do everything with tractors, you'll find it most convenient to place your compost pile downhill from the barn, even if this means you'll have to carry it uphill to the garden. Composted manure is much lighter than fresh, wet, manure.

More important, the barn must be situated where it will benefit from good drainage, and where it will be easy to bring water and power to it. I know people who've been milking cows for 30 years in a barn with neither electricity nor running water. It can be done, and done well. But if you do it, there will be times when you will really wish for good, strong light, or plenty of running water. Δ

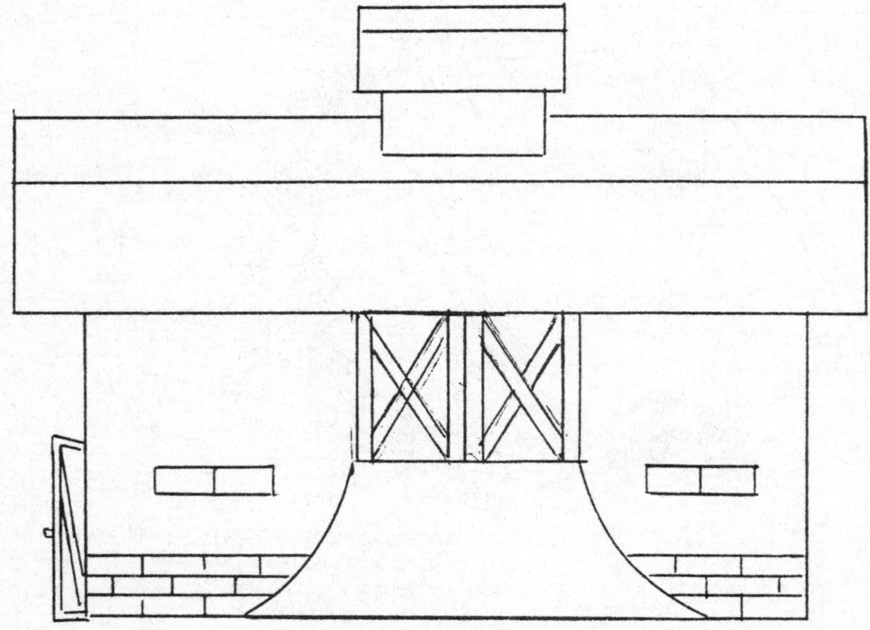

Just for kids — some good clean fun!

By Lucy Shober

When a chill hits the air and the first cool winds of winter begin blowing, there's no better place to be than in a hot bubbly bathtub. The soapy steam wafts away your troubles and gently coaxes your bones into a lazy stupor.

You could stack up a pile of good books beside your tub, but they might go unread as you slip into that dreamy world. Sometimes it's fun to pamper yourself and balance a bowl of fancy snacks on the ledge and a cold drink in the soap dish. It's likely, though, that the chocolate-covered pretzel crumbs floating in the bath water could affect your mood!

Perhaps the next time that you sneak away for an hour in the tub, you could just sit and think . . . just think. When you get all of your private thinking done, try mulling over some of these steamy facts. Read on, and if you get into a stew from too much thinking, then have a good time practicing some bathtub science with the facts you have learned.

Question: Have you ever wondered why you even have to use soap? How does it get you any cleaner than plain water?

Fact: Soap is made of tiny molecules. One end of the molecule is attracted to water, and the other end to oil. When you swish yourself around in soapy water, the oily dirt gets stuck to one end of the molecule, and the bath water hooks onto the other end. This leaves you sweet and lovely.

Question: Why does your hair feel so scummy when you wash it with a bar of soap? Shouldn't it pull the dirt away from your hair as well as your skin?

Fact: Soap molecules attach to little particles of calcium and other salts in your bath water, and makes them heavier than the water. They then fall to the bottom or sides of the tub (bathtub ring!) or latch on to your hair. Shampoos and detergents were invented to deal with this problem.

Question: Why does a soap bubble float and then fall?

Fact: When you blow a bubble, the hot air from your lungs rises. As it cools, the bubble in which it is wrapped will sink. Hot air balloons are a huge example of this scientific trick at work.

Question: Who in the world invented soap?

Fact: We don't have any names, but when archaeologists uncovered the ancient city of Pompeii (the one that was covered in volcanic ash about 2000 years ago), they found a soap factory! The bars of soap were pretty much like the ones you use today. Before soaps were invented, though, people washed themselves in olive oil...a prospect that you probably don't even want to think about...gakk! If you know someone with a wildflower garden, ask them to grow a plant called Bouncing Bet. This is also called Soapwort because you can wash your hands with the foamy lather made when its stems are swished in water.

Question: What makes a bubble?

Fact: All of the molecules on the water surface lock on to each other. This is called surface tension. If you blow air into the water, the molecules still want to hold on to each other, so they form a little fence around the air...a bubble! Add soap, and the fence becomes more elastic. The molecules

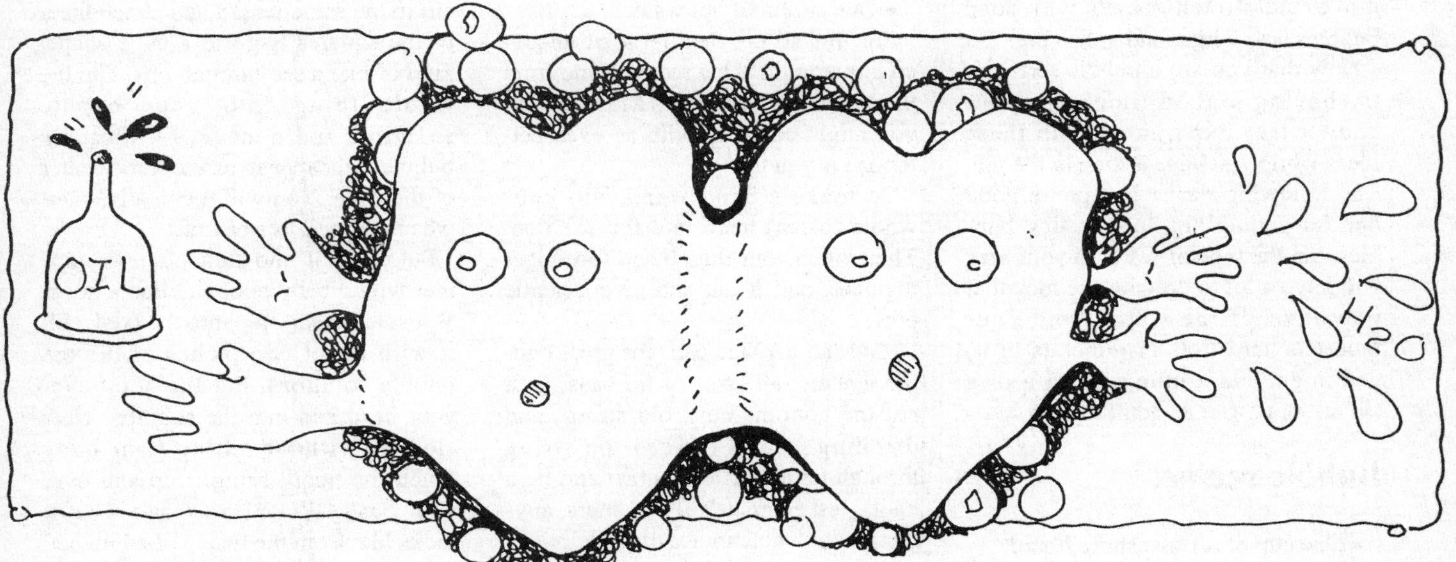

Soap molecules have one oil-loving and one water-loving end.

Raid the garbage can for great bubble makers.

have more play in them and they can move and stretch. That's why soap bubbles last longer and get so big.

Now that you are a bubble scientist, try having a good time with your knowledge. Experiment with these ideas while you have a soak in the tub. The following recipe is a pretty good one for getting big, long-lasting bubbles, but the type of water in your area will have a lot to do with the luck that you have. If the water from your faucet is hard (lots of minerals in it) you might add a little soda to it or a tad of borax. Get an adult to help.

Bubble recipe:

- One cup of dishwashing liquid.
- Two tablespoons of Glycerin. (This is a byproduct of soap making; you can get some at the drug store.)
- One gallon of hot water.

Stir this all up, then let it sit uncovered overnight. This recipe came from the Louisiana Children's Museum, but you might come up with an even better one if you try.

To make a hand wand, dip your whole (clean) hand into the solution. Then touch your thumb and forefinger together, pull it out and give a gentle puff.

Raid the garbage can for great bubble makers: all sizes of tin cans, (just cut the bottoms out), old strings and drinking straws (thread the string through both ends of a straw and tie a knot), last summer's fly swatters, anything with a hole in it will work.

Make a square bubble by using a thin wire frame. Electric fence wire works great. First make two squares the same size. Then take four wires cut to the same length and attach them to the squares to form a cube shape, kind of like a see-through box. Dip the whole thing into your bubble solution, and a magic little square bubble will appear in the very center of the cube. You will feel really smart when you pull this one off!

Put yourself into a bubble next summer with a baby pool and hoola hoop. With clean feet, step into the pool (fill it with about two inches of diluted bubble solution). Put the hoop over your head and into the solution. Now slowly, without letting your body touch the hoop, bring it up and over your head. WOW! So that's what it looks like from the inside of a bubble!

Have fun on your next bath day and make up some new experiments. Δ

Muffin magic

By Jennifer Stein Barker

Muffins are a very versatile food. They are quick and easy to prepare. Warm muffins make a great breakfast, cool ones go perfectly in sack lunches, and all make a great snack any time! Good muffins are fluffy and crisp, full of goodies, and well-browned. The tops are evenly rounded with a pebbly surface.

To achieve an even texture, overmixing must be avoided. Stir the liquid ingredients into the dry ingredients just enough to moisten all the flour, leaving the batter a little lumpy. Spoon into the prepared muffin tins with as little further mixing as possible. The leavening ingredient (soda and/or baking powder) will have started working as soon as the liquid comes into contact with it, and overmixing will knock the batter down. The oven temperature must be correct too, for muffins to have a good texture, shape, and crust.

You will notice there is no added salt in any of these recipes. Salt is mostly a matter of taste, and it will help a tiny bit in keeping them fresher longer. If you wish, you may add 1/4 - 1/2 tsp. natural salt to the recipes.

Apple oat-bran muffins

Makes 10 muffins:

- 3/4 cup oat bran
- 1 cup whole wheat pastry flour
- 1/2 tsp. soda
- 1/2 tsp. baking powder
- 1 tsp. cinnamon
- 1/2 tsp. ginger
- 1 egg, beaten
- 1 Tbsp. oil
- 3/4 cup buttermilk
- 1/4 cup maple syrup
- 3/4 cup apples, peeled and finely chopped
- 1/4 cup raisins
- 1/4 cup chopped walnuts

Preheat the oven to 400 degrees, and oil a muffin tin or line it with baking cups.

In a large bowl, stir together the oat bran, flour, soda, baking powder, cinnamon, and ginger.

In a separate bowl, whisk together the egg, oil, buttermilk, and maple syrup.

Stir into the dry ingredients with the apple, raisins, and walnuts, mixing just enough to moisten.

Spoon batter into muffin tins, and bake 20 to 25 minutes, or until muffins test done.

Peach-almond muffins

Makes 1 dozen muffins:

- 1 cup chopped dried peaches
- 1/2 cup rolled oats
- 1 egg
- 1/4 cup oil
- 1/4 cup honey
- 3/4 cup water
- 1/2 cup chopped almonds
- 1/2 tsp. almond extract
- 2 cups whole wheat pastry flour
- 1/3 cup milk powder
- 2 tsp. baking powder
- 1/4 tsp. baking soda
- 1/4 tsp. cinnamon

In a medium bowl, soak the chopped peaches for 30 minutes in 2/3 cup hot tap water. Add the oats, and soak 5 minutes more.

Preheat the oven to 400 degrees. Prepare muffin tins by oiling them or lining them with muffin papers.

Into the soaked peaches, whisk the egg, oil, honey, 3/4 cup water, chopped almonds, and almond extract.

In a separate bowl, stir together the flour, milk powder, baking powder, soda, and cinnamon until very well mixed.

Stir the dry mixture into the wet mixture all at once, stirring just until all ingredients are thoroughly moistened. Do not overmix.

Divide the batter evenly between the muffin tins, and bake for 20 minutes or until muffins are golden and test done.

Cornmeal muffins with peaches

In the middle of winter, open a can of juice-packed peaches for a taste of summer.

Makes 1 dozen muffins:

- 1 cup whole wheat pastry flour
- 3/4 cup yellow cornmeal
- 1 Tbsp. baking powder
- 2 eggs
- 1 Tbsp. honey
- 1/4 cup canola oil
- 1/2 cup peach slices, cut into 1/2" chunks
- 1 cup juice (from can) or milk

Heat the oven to 425 degrees, and oil a muffin tin or line it with baking cups (these muffins have a tendency to stick to the pan).

In a medium bowl, stir together the flour, cornmeal, and baking powder until thoroughly blended.

In a smaller bowl, lightly beat the eggs and then stir in the honey, oil, peaches, and juice or milk.

Add the liquids to the dry ingredients all at once, stirring until everything is just barely moistened.

Spoon the batter into the prepared muffin tin. Bake for 15 minutes or until the muffins test done. Serve warm.

Sourdough date-nut muffins

Makes 1 dozen muffins:

- 1 3/4 cups whole wheat pastry flour
- 2 tsp. baking powder
- 1 cup chopped dates
- 1/2 cup chopped walnuts
- 1 egg, beaten
- 1/4 cup oil
- 3 Tbsp. honey
- 1/2 cup sourdough starter
- 3/4 cup milk

Preheat the oven to 400 degrees and oil a muffin tin or line it with baking cups.

Sift together the flour and baking powder. Add the dates and nuts, and toss to coat. Set aside.

In a medium bowl, stir together the egg, oil, honey, sourdough starter, and milk.

Add the dry mixture to the wet, and stir just enough to thoroughly moisten all ingredients.

Divide evenly among the muffin tins. Bake for 20 to 25 minutes, or until the muffins test done.

Blueberry poppy-seed muffins

Makes 1 dozen muffins:

- 1/4 cup poppy seeds
- 1 cup milk
- 2 cups whole wheat pastry flour
- 3 tsp. baking powder
- 1/2 tsp. grated nutmeg
- 1/2 tsp. grated lemon peel
- 1 egg, beaten
- 1/4 cup oil
- 3 Tbsp. honey
- 1 cup fresh or frozen blueberries

Soak the poppy seeds in the milk for 30 minutes. Preheat the oven to 400 degrees, and oil a muffin tin or line it with baking cups.

In a medium bowl, stir together the flour, baking powder, nutmeg, and lemon peel. Set aside.

Add the egg, oil, and honey to the poppy seed mixture, and stir well.

Add the flour mixture, and stir just until all ingredients are moistened. Then fold the blueberries in carefully, just until evenly distributed.

Spoon the mixture into the prepared muffin tins, and bake for 20 to 25 minutes, or until the muffins test done. Δ

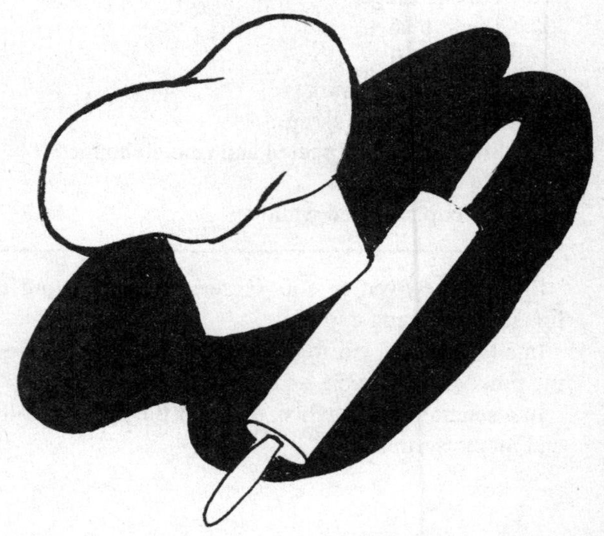

Getting sugar from trees

By Craig Russell

Money doesn't grow on trees but sugar and syrup do; or at least the sweet saps they can be made from grow in some trees. With some work, this might convert to money and will surely provide quality edibles for the would-be self-sufficient.

Nearly everyone is familiar with the sugar maple and the syrup and sugar that is made from it. Fewer know that all maples have sweet edible saps and any that reach sufficient size can be tapped for these products. Seemingly only a few wild food enthusiasts and old timers are aware that sycamores, birches, walnuts and hickories fall into the same category. While all of these trees were exploited by the Indians and the early settlers who learned sugaring from them, many dropped from general use as cheaper sources of sugar became available.

Admittedly, sycamore saps have rather low sugar concentrations and most people find the finished products inferior to those of maple. Ewell Gibbons, the wild foods expert, considered Sycamore syrup similar to low grade black strap molasses. The boiling sap gives off a maple scent and I would compare the end result to an inferior maple product. I suspect that the problem may be with our primitive means of production. The sugar content is very low in sycamore sap; and by the time it has been boiled down to syrup, there has probably been some scorching. Modern evaporators might well produce a better tasting product.

Most birches fall into the same or lower categories but the sweet birches (yellow and black birch) have saps with a fairly high sugar concentration that can be boiled down to a delicious syrup much like sorghum molasses with just a hint of wintergreen. The sweet birches share an essential oil with the wintergreen plant. Today commercial wintergreen flavoring is usually artificial, but natural wintergreen oil or flavoring is generally distilled from the sweet birches, usually black birch, which has the stronger wintergreen flavor, not from the wintergreen plant itself. The wintergreen essence is very volatile and some add twigs to the boiling sap to insure the retention of this characteristic birch flavor. Other than the maple products, this is the best known sweet from trees and one of the best.

While hickories and walnuts are probably the least remembered sugar trees, they didn't fall from favor because they produce inferior products. Old timers I have known who made mixed or nut sugars reported that in a wet or normal year, tapping walnuts or hickories had no noticeable effect on nut yields; but doing so in a dry year, could reduce the nut crop. So I suspect that cheap cane sugar and the desire to preserve the nut crops are the factors that led to a decline in tapping nut trees. All members of the walnut and hickory clans reportedly produce good sweets, even those that produce inferior nuts. If shagbark and pignut hickories are typical (by member of this group), hickory sugars and syrups are not very distinctive—-good sweets but just not very distinctive.

The black walnut and butternut or white walnut make earthy distinctive syrups and sugars that find favor with most of those who try them. However, not many have tried them. Having a "new" product, no matter how good, does not insure economic success, unless you can market it. So I don't believe that I would rush into commercial nut sugar production in a big way. But it could still have a place on a homestead or in a nut business. One thing that I think we should all remember is that sweets from trees are very old products and that emphasizing this, say with an old fashion sugaring, would not only introduce the "new" products, it could get a lot of attention for nuts and any other related products someone wanted to market.

Other sugar trees are tapped the like maples and sugaring on a large scale has to be hard work. It takes 30-50 gallons of sap, depending on the year, the type and the tree (Sycamores & Birches take even more) to produce one gallon of syrup. A gallon of syrup makes about eight pounds of sugar. So if it reaches a commercial scale, a modern sugar house with large evaporators is probably the way to go. Even tours of this would attract the public's attention but wouldn't replace a special event where they could see you do it the old way.

Specialty products would be another way of introducing syrups or sugars from trees and getting premium prices for them. For instance, I like all nut pies—Black Walnut most of all. When Black Walnut pies are made with black walnut syrup, they are worth killing for. Nut fudges and maple walnut divinities are other possibilities. However, if you are looking for self reliance, not a business or a sideline income, a range top or even an open fire can be pressed into service to produce all the syrup and sugar a family can use.

While in some areas you could produce a variety of syrups and sugars, many oldtimers tapped any or all sugar trees at hand and found the end result was sweet. Some people find Black Walnut or even Butternut syrups strong at first, so blending those with hickories or maples might actually widen their acceptance. All Juglans and Carya species are good sugar trees. This includes the Persian or English Walnut. Strangely, sugar trees were never exploited in the old world despite their potentially productive relatives in Eurasia.

While any maple large enough to tap will produce sugar, sugar maple, the closely related black maple and the Norway maple saps usually have the highest sugar content; but boxelder (ash leafed maple), red maple and plane tree are close behind. For some reason many old-timers considered the silver maple a poor producer; but, in my limited experience, it seemed as good as any other. Maple sap is usually about 2.5% sugar. Nut saps are slightly lower and sweet birches contain only about half as much sugar. However, the sugar content and even the amount of sap produced can vary widely from tree to tree even within the same species and even with the same tree from year to year. Maples with sugar sap content of 5% or even higher are not uncommon. The highest recorded sugar content was about 9%. But a good nut tree will out produce a poor maple; just as a good silver maple will out produce a poor box elder, black maple or Norway maple. Birches tend to make up for their low sugar content by producing the most copious sap flow of any sugar tree I've ever tried.

Today some of the very best sugar trees are among the least used. The sugar maple, the black maple, the southern sugar maple (also known as Florida maple and hamock maple) and the boxelders are all known in some areas simply as sugar trees. The first two and the last are the trees most commonly used in commercial maple syrup production today. The southern sugar maple was an important sugar source to the Indians and in colonial and pioneer times but today is hardly tapped at all. The same could be said of most of the nut trees.

When they reach sufficient size to tap, small maples like striped and mountain also can produce good syrup. The small western and imported maples, such as vine, rocky mountain, English field, full moon, amur and Japanese, would probably serve as well.

A medium sized western maple, the big tooth or cayon maple, is a close relative, perhaps a race, of the sugar maple. Yet, I don't know if it is currently used for sugar at all.

The big leaf maple is also under utilized. Some years ago I talked to a fellow who had helped make syrup from these trees in Oregon; but I don't know of any large scale production and I do know people in that area who get maple syrup from the east.

The point is there are many areas outside of the northeastern US and central and eastern Canada that can provide sweets from trees.

The taps for collecting sap are known as spiles. If your local hardware store doesn't have or cannot get metal ones which come in several styles, they can often be ordered from farm catalogs or publications aimed at back to the landers. If this doesn't work out or you just want to do it yourself, cut some large elderberry canes into four inch sections, sharpen one end and cut a notch on the top side near the other end, remove the pith with an iron rod and you are ready to sugar. Although it is a little harder to work, small branches of staghorn sumac and its close relatives can be used in the same way. Homemade spiles generally do require larger, deeper holes than their commercial counterparts. Now, with a bit

A BHM Writer's Profile

Michelle Richards

Michelle Richards describes herself as a "45-year-old woman, disabled, gun dealer, small engine technician." She built her own solar-powered, wood heated home in the wilds of northern Minnesota over the last seven years, and is still building. Says she: "It never ends."

This hunter and gun enthusiast also likes "wasting hours over a fishing pole" on the beautiful northern lakes. Of all the articles she has written for *Backwoods Home Magazine*, Richards' personal favorite is "Social conditioning, women, & self defense."

sized to your spiles, drill a hole slanted slightly upward into your tree. The depth of the holes range from one to three inches, depending on thickness of the bark and the size of the spiles. Tap the spile snugly into the hole, taking care not to seal off sap ducts you have just opened. Then hang your buckets and start collecting sap. Ice cream buckets or any similarly sized container will do. Some even use five gallon buckets.

Taps on the sunny side of the tree are most productive. The average tree a foot or so in diameter can take two spiles. Go up from there. Very large trees can take numerous spiles. Each should be a foot or more from its neighbors. If you want just a few gallons for an experiment or a small batch of syrup for a special treat, this can be collected by clipping the end off of a low branch, sticking a plastic milk jug over the wound and tying the jug firmly in place. Anyone who has ever licked the late winter icicles that form on broken birch or maple branches will get the idea.

The tedious part is boiling it down. It takes forever and when it starts to reach the proper consistency, it can quickly boil over if not watched closely. Old-timers would keep it quiet with a dab of butter. Margarine seems to work as well. But don't let it get too hot. If the thickening sap starts to stick to the sides, your products may have a scorched flavor that will detract from your enjoyment if not their food value.

Sugaring is best done on warm sunny days following cold frosty nights, while things are thawing but before the leaves appear. In Pennsylvania, the season usually runs from late January until early April with the maples reaching peak production first, followed by the nut trees and then the birches.

Syrup reaches the proper consistency at 7° above boiling water, sugar is done at 22° above boiling water. For your area, note the temperature at which it starts to boil and add the appropriate number of degrees to know when it is done. Syrup can be decanted into clean glass jars or jugs. It should be cooled somewhat before putting it in most plastics. Sugar may be poured into greased bread pans or similar containers to cool or into small molds to make maple candies like we see in the stores.

Remember, don't overcook the syrup or burn the sugar.

Birch and maple saps are not only the raw material for syrup, they are traditional spring tonics. It stands to reason that at a time when fresh foods were not available in the winter, these raw saps were important sources of nutrients. Unlike many tonics which you have to grin and bare, these saps are usually consumed with relish. Even though the sugar is so dilute in most saps that it can't be detected. I often drink most of my initial production.

Other traditional spring tonics like birch, sassafras and spice bush teas were considered best when brewed in sugar saps. At the right time of year, any "sugar tree" saps can be a practical source of pure drinking water.

Although they have some distinguishing characteristics and are usually listed as separate species, many botanists consider the sugar, black and Florida (southern sugar) maples as races or varieties of a single species. Intermediate specimens are common and the sugar maple and southern sugar maple clearly integrate in Virginia.

Some experts even consider the small but ornamental chalk maple which is widespread but not very common in the south as no more than a variety of the previous group.

The big tooth or canyon maple is another close relative of the sugar maple and is considered by some to be simply a western race of that tree.

The roots of human culture were founded in early man's ability to utilize what nature provided. While we have come a long way, we seem to neglect much of our heritage. Those of us who remember the old ways not only assure our self-reliance, we help to preserve the culture in ways that an opera or a play never could. Before I get too mushy, I should admit at least some of my interest in "sugar trees" is based on a weakness for sweets. But, I do like to keep the record straight. It bothers me when I talk to someone who calls a Florida maple, a sugar tree and doesn't know you can tap it.

When I was growing up, I was asked to identify the source of some syrup on several occasions and never got beyond birch or maple. I always suspected that those who claimed to be able to detect a difference at the species level had an ability based on prior knowledge. When I read Stalking the Wild Asparagus in the late sixties, I was relieved to learn that Ewell Gibbons had made pure syrups from sugar maple, red maple, silver maple, Norway maple, plane tree maple and boxelder and that a panel of tasters was unable to detect any differences between the various products. Years later when I picked up a Peterson Guide to Edible Wild Plants, I was even more relieved to see that they listed sugar as well as syrup as among the foods obtainable from sweet birches. Because even though I've eaten mixed sugars that contained some birch, I've had some heated arguments with old timers and other wild food enthusiasts who insisted that you could not make birch sugar, only syrup. In retrospect, this idea may have originated from the fact that birch sugar would lack all traces of the characteristic (birch) wintergreen flavor or simply from the fact that it takes so much sap to make syrup. Who would want to reduce it even more? While I've yet to make pure birch sugar, it is one of those things I intend to do. Not that I believe we should do things simply because we can. I recommend sweets from "sugar trees" because they are some of the best edibles available and being self-reliant deserves some rewards. Δ

Thermal mass has its place, but R value is the more efficient

By Martin Harris

A recent letter to *Backwoods Home* asked why the construction industry focuses on R values in measuring the insulating performance of building materials. In the writer's opinion, M values deserve equal consideration. He's right, of course.

R & M definitions

R values (R stands for "resistance," meaning resistance to heat transfer through a given material) get more attention because they're the new kid on the block, historically speaking. But for most of the long history of this industry, people who wanted to heat or cool their building used M values (M stands for "mass," meaning the ability of a given amount of a construction material to store heat) because materials with high R values hadn't yet been invented.

New England, with its winter cold and summer heat, happened to be settled by an inventive bunch of ex-Europeans at a time when technology was exploding. With a standard of living that rose fairly steadily through the 18th and 19th centuries, it's no accident that folks here were experimenting with metal stoves and brick insulation in the walls of their wood-frame buildings, with spring-fed milk coolers and sawdust in the walls of their ice-storage sheds, with air-over-ice cooling systems and earth-set barns, and with creating Yankee innovations that caught on nationwide.

By the 20th century, though, the fountainhead of heat-control innovation had moved elsewhere. Neither fiberglass nor mineral wool, electric storage heat (using bricks for M value), nor super-insulated housing (based on super-high R-values) were invented here. What New Englanders did was pioneer the transition from M value to R value in energy management, and it shows up today in the way early 19th century farmhouses were insulated with brick, while only a few decades later builders shifted to sawdust or newspaper, even bunched hay or seaweed.

The same experimentation was taking place in Europe over the same time period, as builders there also came to realize that "empty" air is a better insulating material than "solid" masonry. Ideas like punching dozens of little core holes in brick, or "popcorning" little pellets of clay for use as a pour-type insulating material, came from Prussia and Lithuania, former members of the economically innovative Hanseatic League, and by the 18th century these same communities were quietly innovating in construction techniques as well.

Technological innovations

Such devices don't work too well, however, and were rapidly supplanted when researchers in England and America invented mineral wool and then fiberglass, and even more recently a variety of tongue-twister foam-type chemicals of extraordinary heat-transfer resisting capabilities.

These inventions were, in fact, so extraordinarily effective, low in cost and high in R value, that people pretty much forgot about M value. Erecting buildings with high mass, thick walls, vaulted ceilings, and so on, was becoming an obsolete, high-cost practice anyway, as lighter framing and panelization techniques were devised, so it's not surprising that, except for a few researchers (and an occasional *Backwoods Home* reader), most people don't even know that the M value concept ever existed.

That's too bad, because it has a real place in construction, and in fact is still used.

Historical examples:

When New Englanders built their classic Cape center-chimney farmhouses two centuries ago, they made the chimneys massive (often nine-feet square at the base) so that the huge mass of masonry would act as a heat sink, absorbing heat from the fireplaces when wood was being burned, re-radiating heat back into the rooms when the fires went out.

Even earlier, Anasazi Indians in the Southwest were doing the same thing. They sized their stone or mud-brick walls and roofs precisely enough to absorb intensive daytime solar heat gain (keeping the interiors cool) and to radiate that stored heat during the chill desert nights (keeping the interiors warm). Walls too thin or thick wouldn't match their mass to the daily solar cycle, and these folks understood that.

Today, innovative builders use rock storage or water storage (both are favorites as high-mass, low-cost, heat-storage materials) to capture daytime heat for nighttime use in greenhouses or residences.

The Trombe wall hit a brief peak of popularity 20 years ago during the first Arab oil crisis: it uses a wall of water or masonry just inside a large window to capture solar energy in a building for subsequent re-use. Operable vents at floor and ceiling allow the occupant, after sundown, to set up a natural airflow withdrawing energy from the high-M wall to keep the building comfortable; during the day the vents remain closed and the wall soaks up the sun's rays. Sophisticated designs include curtains which open during daylight and are closed to prevent heat loss through the window at night.

A hundred years ago, American farmers borrowed a Pennsylvania Dutch barn design concept—the cow stable—as a walk-out basement for dairy management systems that were cool in summer and warm (or at least warmer) in winter. Yes, these designs have ventilation problems, and have since been abandoned, but they use the annual cycle of solar heat stored in the ground just as the later Trombe wall uses the diurnal cycle of solar heat stored in water or masonry. Connecticut settlers used the same principles in their housing even before the Revolution, and today earth-set and earth-sheltered housing is making a real comeback (see *Backwoods Home* Issue #9 on this subject).

These examples illustrate how high-M-value construction materials work: they're very good at absorbing and releasing heat (the opposite of high-R-value materials). If you have periodic sources of excess heat—a fireplace fire, daily sunshine, or annual temperature changes—construction based on high-M-value materials can temporarily store the excess energy for later release.

But not much later: high-M-value materials will give up heat energy as rapidly as they absorb it. If it takes a week to heat up the mass of a farmhouse fireplace, it will likewise take a week for all that heat to go back out into the surrounding rooms. If it takes a day for an Anasazi pueblo to warm up, it will cool down overnight. If it takes half a year for the sun to heat the ground on three sides of your earth-set house, you can draw on that heat for the other half.

Using M with R

If you want to store heat for a longer time than its natural cycle in a high-M container, you'll have to encapsulate it in a high-R material: only materials high in R-value will store heat for long periods of time, which they do by preventing heat transfer to the adjacent environment.

If you don't have periodic sources of excess or free heat, high-M materials will store the energy from whatever you choose to buy and burn and will keep you warm for a while after the fire goes out; but they'll radiate as much to the outside world as to your inside room, and so they are not as efficient performers as they might appear to be.

Given the way the M system works, it's understandable that the heavier materials—water and stone, traditionally—are the best storage media. Lead and the other heavy metals would be even better, but then they're also a lot more expensive. Materials low in mass (almost the same as weight, but technically not quite) are also low in M value: you can't store much heat in a batt of fiberglass.

Logs not so hot

Materials in the mass mid-range, logs for example, aren't particularly good at storing heat, although the log-home industry claims that virtue for them. Logs are better than plywood; but then, if you piled on plywood 8 inches thick, you'd have the same value as an 8-inch log wall. An 8-inch log wall isn't as good, M-wise, as an 8-inch solid masonry wall because it doesn't weigh as much.

And you need a lot of M to equal a little R. It would take about 8 feet of solid concrete to equal the R-value of a typical 2x4 stud wall infilled with fiberglass insulation.

The ground rules

Does it pay, then, to design with M-values in mind? Absolutely. But the ground rules should be observed.

Build your building into the ground to capture free solar heat. Don't think that it's economical to buy heat; put it in the ground under your floor slab, and later withdraw it (unless, of course, you insulate around your heat sink and can buy fuel somewhere at some off-season low price).

Build a Trombe wall to capture daytime solar gain for nighttime use. We'll describe the design in a future article.

Store excess or free heat in water or stone but be careful that you don't spend more on the elaborate valves, pipes, controls, and gadgets of so-called "active" solar than the same investment, if put into insulation or even into the bank at interest, could have gained for you. Unless your primary goal is impressing the neighbors (not unknown, in some parts of the country) spending a thousand on solar panels to capture a ten-spot-worth of annual energy makes sense only when the interest rate on money is less than 1%.

Log construction is not a particularly high-M design option. If you want high-M, you'll have to go to masonry or concrete. If you want high M inside your log cabin, do it with a central chimney. An end-wall chimney will radiate heat to the out-of-doors almost as quickly as you pour it in by operating your fireplace. That's why the old-timers in New England put their chimneys in the centers of their houses, while down in the Carolinas the chimneys are end-wall or even semi-detached from the basic structure.

Dollar for dollar, you'll save more energy by going for high R rather than high M. Exception: you have a supply of nice flat stones and free labor.

If you're going for cooling, you'll accomplish it at lower cost with roofs or shading overhangs than with mass. It's particularly difficult, structurally, to put enough mass overhead to retard a really substantial solar heat problem. That's why, incidentally, earth-set housing is most economically accomplished when the roof is framed and insulated rather than concrete-slabbed and dirt-covered.

Non-monetary values

All of the above explains why I'd focus my search for energy-efficiency in construction in R-value, and I'd use M-value as a sort of supporting player. But that's just my opinion: it's based on a dollar-for-dollar kind of analysis, and doesn't take into account the non-monetary values involved in construction. That's why people in northern and eastern Europe—most of them only a generation or two away from rural village life in wood houses of frame or log design—now consider such construction to be second-rate, impermanent, and somewhat lower class. They would rather freeze—genteelly—during the long northern winters in new concrete or brick buildings.

And that's why Americans, most of whom have discretionary income levels that eastern Europeans can only dream about, likewise base our housing design choices on factors other than the economics of building insulation.

That's as it should be: if you total up all the cash-purchase requirements in the annual family budget, the incremental cost of heat needed because of selecting a less-than-perfect structural insulating system is pretty marginal. And, where firewood or coal come from some backyard source, that cost is even lower.

All of which suggests that it's okay for each of us to select the building design we like without obsessing over insulation levels. After all, if we want to save some serious money, we can do it easier and better by bartering goods and services with neighbors than by avoiding log or stone construction because it isn't quite as energy-efficient as other techniques.

(Martin Harris is a Vermont architect, co-founder of the *New England Builder*, and author of numerous home-building articles.)
Δ

A BHM Writer's Profile

Jo Mason is a free- lance writer who lives near College Station, Texas. She writes on a variety of subjects, including food/cooking, Texana, profiles, and astrology. Her work has appeared in many national publications, besides *Backwoods Home Magazine.*

Venison recipes

By Richard Blunt

While sitting at my desk working with some venison recipes for this issue, it occurred to me that over the years I have been taking this wonderful meat for granted. Because of my career in the food industry, I have had easy access to venison as well as bear, buffalo, elk, and even rattlesnake. When I decide to include venison as a menu selection, I simply call my supplier and order the desired cuts. Most good deer hunters, of course, just go to their freezers and select the pieces that suit their needs.

My selection is raised on a game farm in New Zealand. I order it and think no more about it. The venison in the hunter's freezer may have come out of the back forty and is part of the continued enjoyment and satisfaction experienced from a successful hunt. But most folks in this country do not have either of these options for obvious reasons—they're not food industry pros and they don't hunt. And that leaves more venison for me. I kind of like that.

During the time when self-sufficiency had real meaning and hunting was more necessity than sport, meats like venison, bear, moose, and wild boar were common on the family dinner table. These meats became so popular they became standard items in markets and restaurants throughout the country. In the late nineteenth century, hunting limits were imposed in an effort to preserve these animals in the wild. Today, venison is considered a real delicacy. Even finding a cookbook that treats it with respect can be difficult.

With this in mind, those fortunate enough to have it available have an opportunity to treat themselves to some good food. Having meat from a clean fast kill that has been properly butchered, chilled, and hung, a hunter can gain the reputation of being a fine cook as well as a good shot. All you need now is a good selection of herbs and spices in your kitchen and the world of gourmet venison dishes is at your fingertips.

Venison is best to eat when the animal is between the ages of one and three. As the animal ages beyond this, the meat becomes tough and should be marinated to achieve best results. Also, venison is a very lean meat and in many recipes it requires larding (adding fat) during cooking to make the meat moist and tender. If you can, arrange for a professional meat cutter to butcher your deer, especially if you want boneless roast and steaks. Watch and ask plenty of questions, and the next time, maybe you can do it for yourself. Ask him to show you how to estimate the animal's age. Butchering fees vary. My boss and her husband exchange the hide in return for the butchering.

I am going to share three recipes with you. Each will deal with a specific characteristic of the meat. The first is a sausage recipe, the second uses a marinade, and the last omits the use of a marinade and keeps the use of herbs and spices to a minimum to allow you to experience the "true" taste of venison. This way, when you begin creating your own recipes, you will know how the natural taste of the meat contributes to the taste of the finished product. Remember, the younger the animal, the better the meat will taste.

The following sausage recipe demonstrates how versatile venison is and how well its flavor blends with other meats and spices. If you want further details about sausage making, refer to my column in the July/Aug 1993 issue (#22).

Venison Sausage

Ingredients:

6 lbs venison, cut into 1" strips
2 lbs pork shoulder or butt cut into 1" strips
½ lb fatty bacon cut into 1" strips
1 ½ tsp salt
2 tsp coriander
½ tsp mustard seed
½ tsp basil leaf
½ tsp garlic powder
2 Tbsp *freshly* ground black pepper
1 Tbsp light or dark brown sugar
½ tsp dried thyme

Preparation:

1. After cutting the venison, pork, and bacon, put it back in the refrigerator for a couple of hours. This will chill it to the proper temperature and make it easier to grind.
2. When the meat is chilled, put it through the grinder using the coarse screen, then put it through again using the fine screen.
3. In a large mixing bowl, thoroughly combine the ground meat, the spice mixture, and the salt.
4. To check the flavor, saute a little of the mixture until it is cooked, then taste it and adjust the seasoning if necessary.
5. Cover the sausage and refrigerate it overnight to allow the flavors to penetrate the meat.
6. The next day I stuff it into casings and smoke it. This is the only sausage I make in which I use a sausage casing. If I am not going to smoke it, I poach the sausage in hot water

until it floats. Once cooled, it can be pan fried or broiled (or if you like, it can still be smoked after boiling). I, for one, always smoke mine. If you use a water smoker, add some good beer or ale to the water pan for added flavor.

The next recipe incorporates a marinade that will help tenderize the meat from an older animal and also improve the flavor.

Roast Leg of Venison

Ingredients:

1 leg of venison (about 6 lbs)
Strips of bacon (enough to cover the leg)
Freshly ground black pepper and salt for rubbing

Marinade

Ingredients:

2 carrots (diced)
2 onions (diced)
2 stalks of celery (diced)
2 cloves of garlic (finely diced)
1 tsp dried basil leaf
1 tsp dried thyme leaf
½ tsp cayenne pepper
4 whole cloves
2 Tbsp Dijon mustard
4 cups dry red wine
½ cup vinegar
½ cup peanut oil

Preparation:

1. Season the leg by rubbing it with salt and *freshly* ground pepper.
2. Place the diced vegetables in a large stainless steel or glass bowl and place the leg on top of them.
3. Mix the herbs and spices with the Dijon mustard, red wine, vinegar, and peanut oil. Add this to the bowl. Cover and marinate in the refrigerator for two days, turning occasionally (four to six hours).
4. When marinating is complete, remove the leg and dry it with paper towels. Place the meat on a rack in a suitable roasting pan and cover it with the strips of bacon. Save the remaining marinade to make the sauce.
5. Place the meat in a preheated 400° oven for fifteen minutes, then reduce the oven temperature to 275°. Let it roast, basting frequently with the pan juice. The meat will take about 1¼ hours to reach an internal temperature of 125° (this is if you like your meat rare). If you prefer your meat cooked until it is medium, continue to roast it until the internal temperature reaches 135° to 140°. This will take about another half hour. If you don't own a meat thermometer, I suggest that you get one; it is the only way I will roast meat.

Set the meat aside on a warm platter for at least fifteen minutes before cutting.

Sauce

Ingredients:

2 cups of good beef stock
1 cup reserved marinade
¼ cup sherry
3 Tbsp butter or margarine (soft)
3 Tbsp flour

Preparation:

1. Combine the beef stock, marinade, and sherry. Pour this mixture into the roasting pan and mix it with any remaining juices in the pan and use this to rinse the pan. Then pour this mixture into a sauce pan and bring it to a simmer. Continue to simmer until the liquid is reduced to about two cups. Remove from the heat and allow the oil to rise to the surface as the liquid cools and remove as much of it as you can with a ladle or a large spoon.
2. Combine the butter with the flour and mix it until it is well blended. Now return the sauce to the heat and bring it to a simmer again. As it is simmering, add the butter-flour mixture, about one Tbsp at a time, while stirring. Continue until the sauce reaches the desired thickness (about like a thin gravy) and continue to simmer it for about ten more minutes. This continued simmering cooks the flour and gives the sauce a smooth and nonchalky taste. Do not allow the sauce to burn or stick to the bottom of the pot.

The next and last recipe is for those lucky enough to get a young deer. Remember, three years or younger. Ask your butcher to help you to determine the age if you're not sure. If you really like venison, this recipe is even good for older animals.

Char Broiled Venison Steaks

3 steaks cut to 3/4" thickness (about 2 lbs. of meat)

Basting Sauce

Ingredients:

1 large clove of garlic
1 Tbsp Dijon mustard
1/2 tsp black pepper (freshly ground)
1/2 tsp thyme leaves
1/4 cup butter
2 tsp soy sauce
1/4 tsp savory leaves

Preparation:

1. Place the butter in a pan over a very low heat to melt it. Squeeze the garlic through a garlic press into the melting butter and add the remaining ingredients. Stir and remove from the heat immediately. Do not cook.

2. Brush the steaks with the sauce and allow them to sit for one half hour.

3. Broil over hot coals until they're cooked the way you like them, rare or medium.

Here is an option. After brushing some sauce on the steaks, return the remaining sauce to a low heat and add 3 Tbsp of currant jelly. Stir this until the jelly melts. Just before the steaks are removed from the grill, brush this sauce on both sides, then serve immediately.

You know, it's been so much fun writing this month's column, in the future, I will address other kinds of game including rattlesnake. Δ

More venison sausages

By Bill Palmroth

Although venison can be used successfully in making many types of sausage, I strongly recommend that venison fat not be used in the sausage. It gives the sausage an off-flavor, does not keep well, and is tallowy when eaten cold. Pork fat is best for ground processed meats because it adds flavor and juice to the meat, keeps well, and is not tallowy when cold. The amount of fat you add to your sausage can vary with taste.

Basic ground meat mix

Ingredients:

5 lbs. lean venison
1 lb. pork back fat
2-4 Tbsp. salt

Preparation:

Grind the meat and fat thoroughly, mix in salt, and add one of the seasoning recipes that follow. Keep mixture cold.

The following seasoning recipes are for the above quantities of meat. These are just a few suggested seasoning combinations, and spices may be modified to suit your personal taste. Add seasonings to the basic meat mix and knead like bread until thoroughly mixed. Keep cold at all times.

Salami seasoning

2 Tbsp. sugar
1 Tbsp. cayenne pepper
1 tsp. ground cloves
1 Tbsp. fine-ground pepper
2 tsp. garlic powder
3/4 cup dry milk (mix to a thin paste)

Sausage seasoning

2 Tbsp. sugar
1 tsp. cayenne pepper
1 1/2 Tbsp. ground chili powder
1 Tbsp. garlic powder
1 1/2 tsp. ground celery seed
3/4 cup dry milk (mix to a thin paste)

Weiner seasoning

1 1/2 tsp. ground white pepper
1 1/4 tsp. ground coriander
1 1/2 tsp. mustard powder

Pepperoni seasoning

2 Tbsp. sugar
1 tsp. ground cumin
1 1/4 tsp. leaf oregano
1 tsp. thyme
1 Tbsp. cracked pepper
1 Tbsp. fine ground pepper
3 Tbsp. chili powder
1 tsp. whole anise
3/4 cup dry milk (mix to thin paste)

There are several methods you can use to stuff and cook your meat mixes. You may either purchase casings or use cans to shape the sausage. Dried casing may be ordered from almost any butcher. They come in both large and small sizes. If you use casings, you will need to make them pliable by soaking in a solution of one pint warm water, one Tbsp. of vinegar, and one tsp. salt for three hours. Rinse casings thoroughly before stuffing, then cook using one of the following methods:

Oven method of cooking:

Place filled cans or stuffed casings on rack in baking pan and bake at 325 degrees for 1 1/4 hours. Cool, package and store.

Smokehouse method of cooking:

Hang in portable smoker—do not allow sausages to touch each other. Smoke at 160 degrees for about eight hours. Test for doneness (internal temperature should be 165 degrees). Remove from smoker, refrigerate or wrap and freeze.

Personally, I prefer the smoking method over the oven method, because smoke cooking tends to develop more delicate and tantalizing flavors in the sausage. Keep in mind, however, that the flavor of the finished product is governed entirely by the type of wood used for creating the smoke. Dry hardwoods, such as hickory, maple and alder, are necessary for creating the smoke if a palatable flavor is to be developed. This kind of homemade sausage contains no preservatives, so it cannot be treated like store-bought products. It must be frozen if it is to be kept for an extended period of time. It should keep for up to six months in the freezer if sufficiently wrapped.

If you have never tasted deer or elk meat sausage, there is a pleasant surprise in store for you. Δ

A BHM Writer's Profile

Martin S. Harris, Jr. holds a Master of Fine arts in Architecture and Urban Planning from Princeton University. He is a registered architect, serves in many public service capacities, and is a freelance writer.

Martin has written articles on a range of building issues for *Backwoods Home* over a period of four years.

A BHM Staffer Profile

As *Backwoods Home Magazine's* graphics consultant, Bill Mikalson is responsible for turning Don Childers' original art into striking magazine covers. Mikalson admits that his covers are not as good as the originals. Their purpose is not just to look pretty, but also to attract the attention of prosective readers. As many new readers can attest, they work.

Born in 1950 in a small Wisconsin town, William Allen Mikalson grew up in a printing family. At the age of 12, he began his career sweeping up in his parents' printing plant. By the age of 18, his experience included all areas of the industry. He has college degrees in Industrial Technology and Communications, and is an experienced writer and photographer.

Mikalson has managed several printing plants but found he preferred working as an industry consultant. He currently lives and works on a boat in the Caribbean Sea.